The FOURTH EDITION
Adolescent
Experience

The Adolescent Experience

FOURTH EDITION

Thomas P. Gullotta

Child and Family Agency of Southeast Connecticut, New London, Connecticut and Eastern Connecticut State University, Willimantic, Connecticut

Gerald R. Adams

University of Guelph, Ontario, Canada

Carol A. Markstrom

West Virginia University, Morgantown, West Virginia

Academic Press

San Diego   London   Boston   New York   Sydney   Tokyo   Toronto

Academic Press
A Harcourt Science and Technology Company
525 B Street, Suite 1900, San Diego, California 92101-4495, USA
http://www.apnet.com

Academic Press
24-28 Oval Road, London NW1 7DX, UK
http://www.hbuk.co.uk/ap/

Library of Congress Catalog Card Number: 99-63849

International Standard Book Number: 0-12-305560-1 (text)
International Standard Book Number: 0-12-305561-X (test questions)

PRINTED IN THE UNITED STATES OF AMERICA
99   00   01   02   03   04   EB   9   8   7   6   5   4   3   2   1

To Bernie, who gave me the gift of humility.
Your Dad

CONTENTS

CHAPTER **2**   **Theories and Research Methods**

PART **TWO**   **Patterns of Adolescent Development**

CHAPTER **3**   **Intellectual and Cognitive Development**

CHAPTER **4** **Identity Development and Self-Concept**

CHAPTER **5** **Gender Differences and Sex-Role Development**

CHAPTER **6** **Physical Growth and Sexual Development**

PART THREE Influences on Adolescent Development

CHAPTER **9** Education

PART **FOUR** **Dealing with Issues of Concern: Prevention and Treatment**

CHAPTER **10** **Helping Adolescents: Intervention and Prevention**

CHAPTER **11**   **Adolescent Sexuality: Issues for Concern**

CHAPTER **14**   **Eating Disorders**

CHAPTER **15**   **Depression and Suicide in Adolescence**

PART FIVE   Parting Thoughts

CHAPTER 16   Of Time and Soothsaying

For most readers, this will be the first time they have opened this book. Yet it has been in print for more than 15 years across three editions. As I reflect on the latest 3-year journey to bring this volume to print, it was a difficult trek that recalls the passage Dickens used to open *A Tale of Two Cities*. Remember the line, "It was the best of times and the worst of times."

How so? Well, first understand that the creation of a scholarly work is ideally a collaborative venture in which the vision of the authors is sharpened through an editorial process involving independent scholarly reviews and publisher copy-editing. Over three editions, 60 plus reviewers, and three copyeditors, this book had grown to encyclopedic proportions. Earlier drafts of this fourth edition reflected a potbellied tome written by committee. Our vision, our voice, and our need to speak directly to the reader had been gradually lost over the years in attempts to homogenize material to satisfy conflicting reviewer viewpoints. To regain that vision, that voice, that reader intimacy we so desired took five rewrites and 3 years. It took moving to a new publishing company, and it took reasserting that this book belonged to the authors—not faceless contradictory reviewers.

Those reviewers who did not want the contributions of sociology and history recognized in our understanding of the adolescent experience will be disappointed. Those reviewers who sought to diminish the practical applied focus of this volume will also be disappointed. And that one reviewer who sought to have references to literature removed and did not realize that *Lolita* was a novel will be especially displeased.

It has been said that we have written a book that is as much a handbook of the adolescent experience suitable for a professional audience as it is for a textbook. We hope that assessment is true. We hope that the reader will not relegate this book to some cardboard carton for attic storage but will wear it out over the years, for that is truly our intention.

The authors have worked with young people for many years. Each of us has expressed our regard for this life stage in different ways. Carol has been interested in the development of young people's spirituality. Gerald has focused his research interests on identity development. For myself, directing as I do a large mental health counseling agency for young people and their families, I have been concerned with developing practical approaches to reducing violent behavior among our youth. This interest has resulted in several co-edited books and in several research and demonstration projects. I share this information with the reader because the recent tragedies involving youth killing other youth should not be surprising to any one who cared to pay any attention to the society around us.

To quickly illustrate this point, we have known for years and discussed in this textbook across three editions that the line between the suicidal act and homicide is ever so thin. The intense anger that we believe is connected with the suicide, if expressed outward, is just as deadly. Now reflect on the past decade and a half. The individual act of suicide—this intense anger expressed inward—became associated, thanks to media exposure, with the killing of an estranged loved one followed by the destruction of the self. These first role models generalized in short time to the workplace killing, where again, a troubled, deeply depressed, and angry individual expressed those emotions in a grand and bloody finale certain to monopolize the media's attention. Is it then really so surprising that alienated youth equally angry, equally depressed, equally wanting to make a statement copy the behavior? Certainly, other factors contribute to this tragic situation, and as you read this book, they will reveal themselves to you.

But if there is a single point this book wants to drive home, it is that young people need to belong, they need to be valued, and they need to be able to make a meaningful contribution to society. If the reader takes away only this one statement and works to make this come true for the young people around them, then we will have succeeded in our purpose.

To help give this point meaning, we have taken a broad view of adolescence. We have drawn from many disciplines knowledge that those who wish to work with youth can use. We have provided theoretical structures supported by history and research that can be used to build new interventions in the coming years. We hope we have done this in a conversational tone that uses images from films, music, and—yes—literature to deepen those understandings. Whether we have been successful in our efforts, you, the reader, will decide.

Before I close this brief introduction, I would like to express our deep gratitude to Dr. George Zimmar and Rebecca Orbegoso at Academic Press for supporting us in this effort and to C. Debra Laughton, who urged us, during the worst of times, not to let this voice be silenced. Finally, my gratitude to my colleagues for their work on this volume and who have allowed me to dedicate this fourth edition to my son, who challenges my understanding of adolescence every day.

Thomas P. Gullotta
Gerald R. Adams
Carol A. Markstrom

ONE

Welcome to the Study of Adolescence

Welcome to the Study of Adolescence

WELL HELLO THERE. If you are like most students we know, you're opening this book for the first time the night before the semester begins. We suspect that you have questions not only about the course but about this book. While we can't tell you what chapters your instructor will assign for reading or what assessments will be used to determine your semester grade, we can share with you the lines of scholarship that were linked to create our view of the adolescent experience.

It is one of our intentions in this chapter to introduce you to the four principle themes that appear throughout the book. Once we've done that we'll explore with you the many different meanings that have been applied to the word "adolescence." The first theme is that *all knowledge is rooted in the past*. From those roots emerge new shoots of inquiry leading scholars, like yourself, in fresh directions exploring, refining, and at times rejecting previously held beliefs. The second theme is that *development occurs in context and context determines development*. That is, the physical and socioemotional growth of young people is directly affected by forces like heredity, and the influences of family, peers, and community; not to mention gender, race, and ethnicity. The third theme celebrates *the racial and ethnic complexity of North America*. We believe the residents of Canada and the United States are unique. Just look around you. Despite ethnic and racial tensions, we seem able to pull from the diverse cultures sharing this continent the foods, dress, language, and even mannerisms from one culture and to refashion them into something universally American. Now, don't confuse this with the concept of a "melting pot." It is not. Rather, consider it to be a complex stew, chock full of ingredients sharing a common base (democracy and personal freedom as just two examples) that permits each ingredient to retain its distinctive flavor. The fourth principle theme is that *you can create change leading to a healthier life for yourself and others*. This book, through three previous editions and now in its fourth, has called on students to care for themselves and others in ways that encourage health-promoting behavior. Thus, in the final section of this book, we share with you ways in which you can analyze problem situations so that you can design applied interventions to improve your health and that of others. So with that as our agenda, let's begin this semester's journey with a closer look at each one of these themes and then struggle to define the word "adolescence."

A HISTORICAL OVERVIEW OF ADOLESCENCE

History is more than the study of a progression of events along a time continuum seemingly punctuated by major wars. It is the study of humanity—of its accomplishments, its failures, its conflicts, and, most important, its construction of social reality. This last dimension of history offers a valuable perspective on the dynamics of all human behavior. The way in which members of a society perceive a social or historical event is shaped by many forces influenced by the time in which they live, so that one generation's social reality may be completely different from that of another. While this book incorporates historical elements from other cultures, readers should recognize that it relies on European and North American views of childhood and adolescence for two reasons. The first is the wealth of European and North American social historical information available. The second is the influence this dominant group has exercised in North America over the centuries.

Because each new generation has its own concept of social reality, it should come as no surprise that views of childhood and adolescence have changed over the centuries. One way we can observe this changing view of childhood is through art. For example, in his masterpiece *Centuries of Childhood*, Phillippe Aries (1962) writes that childhood was not used as a theme in medieval art until the 12th century. But when children did appear, they were portrayed as miniature adults with none of the qualities that make young children obviously different from adults. It was not until the 17th century that children were commonly depicted as children, and painters used them as the central focus in family portraits.

Medieval society had little concept of children as being uniquely different from adults. As soon as children were able to function without the care of an adult, they became adults themselves. Indeed, Aries's (1962) review of medieval language, crafts, and games suggests that during this time period the word "child" was synonymous with our understanding today of the words "lad" or "son."

The general consensus among social historians is that parents only recently have begun to be supportive of their children. From antiquity until approximately the 13th century A.D., parents frequently resolved their economic and personal difficulties with their children by abandoning them to a monastery, nunnery, or relegating them to servitude in another house. For yet another 4 centuries, parents often dealt with their children in very rigid ways. (See Box 1-1 for an example of that rigidity, which would be considered by most as cruelty today.) Children were viewed as physical objects to be molded like soft wax or clay into shape through strict and often harsh training (de Mause, 1974; Shorter, 1975; Hufton, 1995).

During the 17th and 18th centuries, however, children began to be viewed in more empathic and nurturing ways by their parents. As raising children became less a process of conquering their spirits and more a process of training and socializing, these years gradually emerged in the minds of scholars as a distinctive period of growth. However, it would take until the late 19th century for adolescence to

BOX **1-1**   **Thomas Dick's Advice on Child Rearing**

In a widely read book on "moral instruction" published in 1847, Thomas Dick wrote:

> From the age of ten or twelve months, and earlier if possible, every parent ought to commence the establishment of authority over his children. . . this authority is to be acquired—not by passionately chiding and beating children at an early age—but by accustoming them to perceive *that our will must always prevail over theirs*, and in no instance allowing them to gain an ascendancy, or to counteract a command when it has once been given. . . for example, if a child shows a desire to have anything in his hand that he sees, or has anything in his hand with which he is delighted, let the parent take it from him; and when he does so, let no consideration whatever make him restore it at that time. Then, at a considerable interval, perhaps a whole day is little enough, let the same thing be repeated.
>
> Such experiments, if properly conducted, would gradually produce in children habits of obedience; but they require to be managed with judgement and prudence, and gradually extended from one thing to another, till absolute submission is produced; care, however, being taken that the child be not unnecessarily contradicted or irritated. The Rev. Mr. Cecil in some of his writings, relates an experiment of this kind which he tried on his own daughter, a little girl of about three or four years old. She was standing one day before a fire amusing herself with a string of beads, with which she appeared to be highly delighted. Her father approached her and said, "What is this you are playing with, my little dear?" "My beads, papa." "Show me these beads, my dear." She at once handed them to her father, who immediately threw them into the fire. "Now," said he, "let them remain there." She immediately began to cry. "You must not cry, my dear, but be quite contented." She then sat down on the floor and amused herself with some other toys.[1] About two or three days after this he purchased another string of beads much more valuable and brilliant, which he immediately presented to her. She was much delighted with the appearance of the new set of beads. "Now," said her father, "I make a present of these to you because you were a good girl and gave me your beads when I asked for them." She felt, in this case, that obedience and submission to her parent were attended with happy effects, and would be disposed in future conduct to rely on his wisdom and affect (Dick, 1847, pp. 46–47).

[1] We suspect she was fashioning a voodoo doll of dear old dad—and was waiting for *it* to go into the fire.

Children provided a cheap and necessary source of labor in the early days of North America.

produce new intellectual growth from the earlier writings of the philosophers Aristotle and Rousseau. The ancient Greek philosopher Aristotle wrote of a youthful character type with an unstable personality who was easily given to passionate behavior (Kett, 1977). Nearly 2000 years later, Rousseau (1762/1966) called the years from 12 to 15 "the age of reason." Taking a different view from that of Aristotle, Rousseau saw these years as a time of life characterized by boundless energy, strength, curiosity, and rational functioning. As you will see in Chapter 2, elements of these scholars observations are incorporated into many of the theories explaining young people's actions.

Adolescence as a Social Invention

Although the recognition of adolescence evolved over thousands of years, as a social reality it is quite recent. While some authorities prefer to speak of the "discovery of adolescence" (Musgrove, 1964), most adolescence historians see it as a social invention driven by several major socioeconomic movements in North America (Kett, 1977; Palladino, 1996).

Among these momentous social events were technological and economic changes that increased industrialization in North America and encouraged migration from the farm to the city. In this shift young people became less of an economic asset and more of a liability. How so? Well, on the farm children and adolescents were needed to help tend the livestock and harvest the crops. During the early years of industrialization, young people were important as a source of cheap labor performing simple repetitive chores in mills. But with advancing technology (for example, McCormick's reaper) and the arrival of millions of European immigrants (remember Ellis Island), young people were no longer needed in the labor pool and by 1914 every U.S. state save one had passed child labor laws. These laws were followed by statutes limiting the hours older youth might work each week. In later years, these regulations would be joined by compulsory education legislation and special legal protections for juveniles, which viewed their delinquent behavior very differently from the criminal acts of adults.

From the Popularization of the Concept to the Development of a Science

As sociohistorical factors extended childhood at the turn of this century, increased attention was given to adolescence. Popular lectures, articles, and books encouraged societal recognition of this increasingly special stage of life. One of the most influential figures in this movement was the President of Clark University, G. Stanley Hall. Through his writings, Hall encouraged mothers to observe and record the course of their children's growth and development. In these efforts, he popularized the concept of adolescence and urged parents to recognize the importance of the adolescent years in the total development of the person.

Drawing heavily upon Charles Darwin's writings, Hall expanded the increasingly popular biological (eugenics) perspective to include developmental features.[2] His monumental two-volume work *Adolescence: Its Psychology, and Its Relations to Physiology, Anthropology, Sociology, Sex, Crime, Religion, and Education* appeared in 1904 and for the next 25 years dominated thinking about adolescence.

While many of Hall's beliefs have fallen into disfavor, they served to kindle interest in adolescence as a crucial period of physical, intellectual, and social change among educators and other professionals at the turn of the century. For example, working with adolescents took on special meaning through Hall's proposal that society could be changed by educating adolescents to become something better than the previous generation. According to Hall, providing appropriate experiences leading to prosocial behaviors created the potential for the internalization of character traits that were genetically transmissible to offspring.

Clearly, Hall's work had a strong biological focus. His "social reality" was strongly influenced by Darwin's (1859) *Origin of the Species* and the growing popularity of the eugenics movement. From his work, other scholars representing different belief systems began to conceptualize this life stage from their social reality. In Chapter 2 we will examine more closely specific adolescent theorists in three of these belief systems. For now, however, let's take a general look at those belief systems. We can classify them as psychological, sociological, and genetic theories.

Psychological Theories

Psychological explanations of behavior involve an understanding of the internal drives and motivations that influence behavior. Three often-used explanations for adolescent behavior are psychoanalytic theory, psychosocial theory, and social learning theory.

Psychoanalytic theory believes early childhood experiences leave a lasting imprint on the individual's personality. Behavior occurring in adolescence is traced, in this model, back to earlier childhood experiences and unresolved issues related to that period. In Chapter 2, we'll review the psychosexual stages and the contributions Sigmund Freud and his daughter Anna have made to the study of adolescence.

Psychosocial theory acknowledges the internal processes in early childhood that influence psychological traits like self-esteem, locus-of-control, and cognition, but includes the relationship of adolescents to their social environment. This perspective is broader than psychoanalytic theory in that it acknowledges the influence of other individuals, groups, and systems like schools, church, and work on the development of the individual. In the next chapter, the work of Erik Erikson will be used to illustrate this perspective.

---

[2]This was the heydey of the eugenics movement which sought human improvement by genetic control. Using this perspective, individuals were wrongly sterilized. Others were admitted without due process for life to state hospitals for the insane and feebleminded. And in the 1930s and 1940s millions of so-called "misfits" were murdered in Nazi Germany.

Social learning theory understands development across the life span to be the cumulative effect of countless learning experiences that are integrated to form a personality. This has been enriched in recent years by an appreciation of the role expectations and meaning has for those learning experiences. We'll use the work of Albert Bandura to illustrate this special case of social-learning theory called cognitive behaviorism.

Sociological Theories

Sociological theories examine the relationship of adolescents to their social environment. These explanations are less concerned with factors like motivation and internal psychological traits like self-esteem and are more concerned with how other individuals, groups, and institutions relate to the adolescent. For example, is the adolescent highly valued in society or is the adolescent less valued? Is adolescence a universal experience across societies or is it unique to time and place? The writings of Kingsley Davis and Margaret Mead will help answer these questions in the next chapter.

Behavioral Genetics

Behavioral genetics refers to the belief that virtually all behavior is rooted in our genes. As you know, genes are composed of DNA, the building blocks of life. A seemingly countless number of these building blocks combine to form chromosomes. Every human has 23 pairs of chromosomes. With the creation of each new human life, the embryo inherits half of its genetic material (chromosomes) from its mother and half from its father. Alone or in combination with a multitude of environmental factors, personality and behavior are thought to evolve. In Chapter 2, we'll review the evidence supporting this view of behavior.

From history to the evolution of different understandings of the adolescent experience, this first theme repeats itself throughout this book. We'll remind you of this point as we examine subjects where social opinion and corresponding social reality has changed over time. This point leads us to the next theme of this text—developmental contextualism.

DEVELOPMENTAL CONTEXTUALISM

One way to understand a term like "developmental contextualism" is to examine its components. For example, to scholars of human relations, development refers to the growth and evolution of a human being over time. From a developmentalist's perspective, time (called the life cycle) begins with birth and proceeds in a series of sequential steps to infancy, early childhood, middle childhood, early adolescence and adolescence to eventual old age and death. Notice we used the word sequential. Developmentalists believe that this passage through life is physically, intellectually, socially, emotionally, and in all other aspects *consecutive* and has accompanying requirements. For example, to conceive a child has as a minimum requirement the capacity to produce an egg and a sperm. Depending on a person's point in the life

Within Urie Bronfenbrenner's ecological model, parents represent a vitally important microsystem.

cycle, (s)he may be too young to produce the egg or sperm or too old. In others words, and to paraphrase a religious text, there is a time for every purpose and a purpose for every time.

The second word in this phrase is "contextualism." The suffix -*ism* means a fundamental principle. So what is this fundamental principal? "Contextual" means the biological, intrapersonal (within the person), interpersonal (between persons), societal, and cultural soup that saturates every aspect of a person's development. Notice we used the word "soup" in this definition. Consider that word. For a moment, imagine on the stove a large kettle filled with broth and vegetables slowly cooking. Each ingredient in that kettle has a unique identity and yet in the process of becoming soup those ingredients undergo a transformation. They change color, taste, and texture as the result of that cooking process. Change the cooking process by, say, roasting those ingredients and the outcome is different. Add other ingredients and the outcome changes yet again. From this cooking lesson we derive the second principle of this book that *development occurs in context and context determines development* (Adams, Montemayor, & Gullotta, 1996 a,b). This last statement, as we will see, owes much to Urie Bronfenbrenner's (1989) work on ecological theory.

Rather than imaging the world of the individual as a bowl of soup, Bronfenbrenner (1989) envisioned it as a series of nested, interdependent outward-expanding levels that range from very close or immediate influences, such as mother–child interactions, to more distant influences, such as those that are cultural (see Fig. 1-1). The relationship between these levels and the perceived significance of their importance to the individual through experience and activities are the essential features of ecological theory.

FIGURE 1-1

A schematic of ecological
theory.

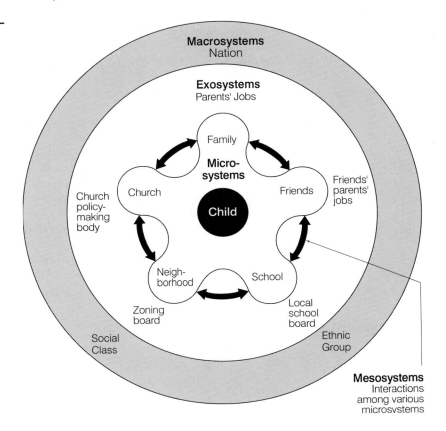

Bronfenbrenner (1989) refers to the innermost level involving face-to-face daily interactions in settings such as the home, school, and peer group as a *microsystem*. At the next level, several microsystems like parents, teachers, and peers act simultaneously to create a *mesosystem*. It is their simultaneous actions on the individual in this mesosystem that produce responses called behaviors. An example would be the implication for an adolescent based on a school meeting between the building principal and their parents regarding the teenager's classroom behavior. Two microsystems (school principal and parents) connect to interact with the child concerning behavior. The *exosystem* is the next level beyond a mesosystem. It can be envisioned as the community which surrounds the individual. Unlike persons in frequent contact with the individual directly effecting behavioral responses, the exosystem exercises a more subtle, but nevertheless profound, impact on the individual. For example, a decision to close a high school and relocate students elsewhere or to redistrict a school system can have a huge impact on friendship networks and a student's academic identity. These are not parental, teacher, or peer decisions, but broader community decisions. Those decisions occur in the exosystem. The next level of Bronfenbrenner's model is the *macrosystem*. It is the general cultural values and other social conditions that constitute the meaning of the word "society" for that person. Some elements of the macrosystem include social class; residence (urban versus rural); labor factors (the status of national economy); and ethnic, racial, and religious membership. The final level of Bronfenbrenner's model includes a dimension of time called the *chronosystem*. In ecological theory it is the general patterning of environmental events and social conditions that reflect societal transitions; it is the sociohistorical conditions of one's lifetime. Each generation experiences its own unique historical events and cultural transition that affect human behavior and development.

The ecological position can be seen as a person-in-context perspective. It recognizes the importance of viewing the adolescent as being rooted in layers of social environments. These range from the intimate microsystem (mother–adolescent) to the furthest removed macrosystem (the effects of the national unemployment rate on the availability of summer employment for young people).

In this section we acknowledged race, ethnicity, and religious membership as macrosystem influences on the development of the adolescent. In the next section we take a closer look at this third theme.

NORTH AMERICA'S MULTICULTURALISM

The third theme this book celebrates is *the racial and ethnic complexity of North America*. From the peoples who are believed to have crossed the Bering land bridge tens of thousands of years ago to first settle North America to the Europeans, Africans, Asians, and Arabians who followed millenniums later, this land has transformed all. As we noted earlier, this transformation did not result in the "melting pot" American.[3] No, whether living in Canada or in the United States, individuals who trace their ancestry to China, Italy, or any other part of the world maintain aspects of that cultural heritage in their life. We may see this demonstrated in the way in which they interpret daily events (a reported injury to an arrested individual may cause some to believe the person was a victim of police brutality), behave toward authority (in some cultures teachers are very highly regarded), or express preferences in food (many Mexican-Americans favor hotly spiced foods) or drink (alcohol is frowned upon in Islamic cultures) or in a myriad of other ways. Nor are we so naive as to be ignorant of the tensions that these heterogeneous origins create. Where there are differences of view, the potential for disagreement exists. Where people do not look alike, when they call God by different names, or when they place within-group prosperity over communal prosperity, anger and violence may result, particularly among the young. Still, we believe there is something unique about North America. That uniqueness, of incorporating aspects of other cultures into mainstream American life, offers us

---

[3] When we use the word "American" in this book, we are referring to individuals residing in Canada and the United States.

hope that Canada and the United States will avoid the seemingly current world trend of reestablishing nationalistic territorial boundaries.

In this text and in every chapter we discuss the strengths that *diverse* cultures bring to the rearing of their youth.[4] We believe that only when you examine individual behavior and personal development in the broader context of other cultures will you understand them. We also believe that such analysis will bring you closer to self-understanding and effective perspective-taking with all adolescents. If you expect to become an educator, counselor, youth worker, or parent, this understanding will be useful as you work to help young people grow into a healthy adulthood, which incidentally brings us to the fourth theme of this book.

A PREVENTIVE/EARLY INTERVENTION FOCUS

The authors of this book really believe you matter in this world. We also believe that you desire information that you can use to help yourself and others. Because we hold these beliefs, our fourth theme focuses on providing you with comprehensive information on several issues of concern comparable to the knowledge contained in books that two of the authors edit for social scientists.[5] Further, we believe that many of the dysfunctional behaviors explored in the last section of this textbook like delinquency, drug abuse, and suicide can be either prevented or minimized. Because we hold that belief, we examine these behaviors from a perspective that will encourage you to consider what actions might be taken to either prevent the behavior from occurring or that might reduce its intensity. Even behaviors that suggest a strong genetic component like persistent depression, we believe and research supports, can benefit significantly from these approaches (Munoz, 1997).

To achieve the objective of this final theme, we'll share with you a paradigm called primary prevention. Primary prevention seeks to promote health, to avoid ill health when possible, or to reduce the severity of ill health if it is unavoidable (Albee & Gullotta, 1997). In this last section, we'll also discuss, when appropriate, counseling, educational, and pharmacological interventions that have been shown to help young people who are behaving dysfunctionally. Most importantly, we provide you with an outline that can be used for either prevention or intervention

[4]We will use the word "diverse" in this text to represent young people whose origin cannot be traced to European ancestry. We prefer this term to "minority" which increasingly is construed as a prejudicial word. Further, we use the words "White" to indicate European ancestry, Black to indicate African ancestry, Asian to indicate Pacific ancestry, and Latino to indicate South American ancestry. On occasion, the word Hispanic will be used when U.S. Census data are cited. Hispanic is a U.S. Bureau of Census created term. In the choice of the word Black rather than African-American, colleagues from the West Indies and other locales point out that the word African-American is not inclusive and suggested the continued use of Black in this edition.

[5]Gerald Adams and Thomas Gullotta, along with Raymond Montemayor, edit a professional book series entitled *Advances in Adolescent Development*.

purposes. We would urge you to use its framework to construct approaches for health promotion and intervention for each of the problem areas discussed in Chapters 11–14.

Four reccurring themes (the importance of history, development occurs in context, the multicultural richness of North America, and applying knowledge to improve health) will guide you in your understanding of adolescence. But wait; as we asked earlier, what does adolescence mean?

WHAT IS ADOLESCENCE?

In this chapter we have said that understandings of childhood and adolescence are evolving and that adolescence was invented by society because it was becoming increasingly difficult to incorporate young people as workers into those societies (Ben-Amos, 1995). There is even reason to believe that G7 nations, the most technologically developed nations in the world, are encouraging a lengthening extension of adolescence sometimes called "youth" (Keniston, 1975). Consider, for a moment, the value of a high school diploma in nations like Japan, Germany, Canada, and the United States. Is it not the belief that a college diploma is essential? And is it not the growing belief that even a college degree is inadequate and that further postgraduate study is important? For many "youth," this extended schooling experience continues a financial dependence of varying degrees on parents, impedes meaningful employment, and delays marriage (Cote and Allahar, 1994). Those three elements (financial independence, gainful employment, and marriage) are features many life span theorists associate with adulthood. Notice how this varying conception (by the way, that's an example of historical social reality) can have a profound effect on how scholars define adolescence as they struggle to develop the means to determine when this life stage begins and ends. Let's look at five approaches to solving this dilemma.

A Physiological Definition

A physiological definition is a commonly used measuring stick to define the adolescent period (Douvan & Gold, 1966; Jones, 1949). In this definition, adolescence begins when the reproductive organs and secondary sex characteristics (body hair, breasts) begin to change in late childhood. Adulthood is achieved with the full maturation of the reproductive system. Given that testicle growth is predictive of pubic hair and skeletal changes in boys, it is assumed that the beginning and end of male adolescence are related to sexual development. Similarly, consistent production of fertile eggs and regularity of the menstrual cycle signal the end of adolescence for girls (Douvan & Gold, 1966).

While seemingly a clear and straightforward definition, it is difficult to determine if adolescence actually begins with hormonal changes that occur at least 2 to 3 years before major body changes are visible or whether it begins when secondary sex characteristics emerge. Likewise, fertility is an unclear and unseen element for

Some scientists believe that adolescence concludes with the full development of formal abstract thinking.

determining the end of adolescence. Consider also that while a boy at 14 or a girl at 12 may have completed biological growth and be fertile, might they also be so immature emotionally and socially that it is in their best interest and society's not to recognize them as adults? Apparently, society believes so and has enacted laws establishing among other things minimum ages at which marriage or consensual sexual relations may occur.

A Cognitive Definition

Others have suggested a reasoning-based, cognitive definition of adolescence. Acquiring the ability to reason enables a youth to use symbols, abstractions, and complex problem-solving strategies in thinking. From this perspective, children come to develop thinking processes that are independent of concrete and observable objects in the immediate environment to include abstract thoughts and metacognition (thinking about thinking; for example, "I wonder what I was thinking about when I did that?"). These young people are thought to be changing fundamentally and leaving childhood for adolescence. Although this approach is logical (with due respects to the ever-rational Spock of "Star Trek" fame) and has been supported by many specialists in adolescence (for example, Ausubel & Ausubel, 1966; Elkind, 1967), measuring this cognitive transition is not easy. Experience with youth suggests that this cognitive process is ever so gradual. Thus, at what point in this reasoning transition would we recognize the child as an adolescent? If one is to be considered an adolescent, is abstract thinking necessary in understanding both academic or social ideas and interpersonal relationships? Likewise, what is the end of adolescence? Is it the ability to use abstract thinking and logical reasoning in all physical and social realms of life? If so, are one-third of North American adults who do not use abstract and logical thinking processes mired in perpetual childhood? Since cognitive development doesn't occur all at once, but happens gradually in a complex manner, a cognitive definition of adolescence is limited in its ability to set out the beginning and ending of adolescence.

A Sociological Definition

The sociological definition of adolescence uses very different standards for defining adolescence. Mixing its criteria, it defines the onset of sexual maturity as the start of adolescence while using social criteria to determine its end. For example, Hans Sebald (1968) has argued that adolescence ends when young people have established behaviors consistent with the demands of their social world and when society recognizes their entry into adulthood. Sometimes this entry is through a formal rite of passage, an event with considerable societal support and ceremony (Blumenkrantz & Gavazzi, 1993). LaVoie (1973) has argued, however, that coping abilities and societal recognition may not occur at the same time. The adolescent may attain one without the other. For example, consider the multitude of passages that exist for youth in North American society. Typically, youth can acquire a driver's license at one age, leave school at another, and enroll in the armed forces, purchase alcoholic beverages, enter into legally binding contracts, or get married at still other ages. Which one or several of these passage rites would you consider the marker for adulthood?

Clearly, the sociological approach has ambiguities. Given time and circumstances, the end of adolescence and the beginning of adulthood may be nearly impossible to define. For example, during times of war 18-year-old youth eligible for service in the armed forces are typically extended rights of adulthood like drinking alcoholic beverages that are lost in times of peace. Does violent conflict and the risk of death spur entry into adulthood? If it does, should we consider those youth who carry guns and use them in our communities adults and entitled to the privileges therein? And if violent conflict is not an adult marker, what subjective rationale does determine adulthood?

Chronological and Eclectic Definitions

Some professionals have dealt with the problem of defining adolescence by using a simple chronological distinction (C. E. Ramsey, 1967) or an eclectic definition of adolescence incorporating markers from a variety of perspectives (McCandless, 1970). Once again, however, both of these strategies have noticeable limitations. The chronological definition of the second decade of life as adolescence is just too simple. It has little flexibility and may create false assumptions about the beginning and end of this period. For example, a sexually undeveloped (prepubescent) 10-year-old is best viewed as a child and not as an adolescent, while a 22-year-old who is living at home, going to school, and fully dependent on parents for emotional and financial support may best be considered a late adolescent.

The eclectic approach, which maintains that multiple definitional perspectives should be combined, creates problems of measurement and inconsistency. If one uses physiological, sociological, and psychological indexes, does a person have to measure up to all three to be considered as entering or leaving adolescence? What a mess this would create in being "carded" to get into an event!

If you feel about ready to scream, we don't blame you. You have every right to feel frustrated—so are the specialists. Any of these definitions can be justified, but the point is that each poses unique problems. If your first response is, "I don't care," think again. Realize that the definition you choose will have tremendous implications for social policy, and social policy (macrosystem that it is) impacts everyone. Your choice of a definition will embrace some youth while excluding others. For example, in many medical insurance policies in the United States, dependent children are covered after age 18 only if they continue their education. Otherwise, they are considered independent and are given adult status. So, if you're 19 and not in school and in need of health care, your access to that care will be dependent on possessing an individual health care policy in contrast to those 19-year-old college students who find themselves listed on their parent's policies as dependents. See how definitions can matter! Of the imperfect definitions that exist, the learner's permit definition has gained favor in recent years among many adolescent scholars.

A Learner's Permit Definition

The learner's permit definition contends that adolescence is best understood as a period of transition that differs in length for each individual. It is best viewed as a growing-up process that includes making decisions and making mistakes. However, the context is such that the mistakes will ideally result in minor negative outcomes, ones that young people can recover from without lasting negative consequences. Adolescence is thus a gradual phasing into adulthood, in which youth are given increasing responsibilities with each new granted freedom. Zimring (1982) calls this view a learner's permit theory of adolescence: "The adolescent must be protected from the full burden of adult responsibilities, but pushed along by degrees toward the moral and legal accountability that we consider appropriate to adulthood" (1982, p. 96). Thus, adolescence is a period of experimentation, of practice in making decisions, of making mistakes and discovering one's errors, and of gradually assuming new freedoms while building toward adult responsibilities.

In legal parlance it is common to talk about the *age of majority*. In simple terms this means a period when one's freedoms and responsibilities are equivalent to those of adults. In the phasing process of a learner's permit theory of adolescence, several forms of age of majority might be appropriate. At 16 years of age, for example, we may say to adolescents that they have proven their competence to

Adolescence is a gradual phase into adulthood.

drive by passing a driver's test. They are free to be licensed and drive but are also expected to obey all driving laws and to assume responsibility for their actions on the road. Another age of majority may be 17 or 18, when youths decide whether to continue their formal schooling. At 20 or 21, youths arrive at a societally prescribed drinking age of majority. They can drink alcohol within legal restrictions, can become intoxicated if they desire, but are held responsible for their actions while drunk.

In the learner's permit theory, adolescence emerges when the young person is given freedoms not afforded a child. In junior high schools, for example, students can commonly select a small portion of their academic curriculum, have initial opportunities to take part in school government, and have expanding choices of extracurricular activities. This process broadens with each new educational phase in high school, college, or vocational training. However, each new phase of freedom brings increasing responsibilities. Adolescence ends when a youth has acquired the age of majority for legal, economic, work, school, and moral responsibilities. Thus, each youth ends adolescence at a different point in life.

While we don't have an ideal solution to the problems surrounding a definition of adolescence, we understand it to be a social invention that changes according to economic, political, or technological conditions. In North American society, the definition currently seems to coincide with the phases of education provided for adolescents. Early adolescence is that time spent in middle school or junior high school. Middle adolescence is the high school years. Late adolescence is that period provided for in college, technical school training, apprenticeships, or entry-level military service. And to this we add youth (or young adulthood). This is an extended time of education for advanced training, during which young adults remain economically dependent on the family or other institutions to provide financial support.

SOME FINAL REFLECTIONS

Okay, we've made it clear that three themes appear throughout this book (the importance of history, development in context, and multiculturalism). The fourth theme, concerned with promoting health and early intervention to reduce the severity of problem behaviors, appears in the final section and in earlier chapters, where appropriate. There are some other points of which you should be aware.

1. This book is interdisciplinary. It emerges from a belief that no discipline owns adolescence. Each discipline we reviewed added immeasurably to our understanding of this life period. You should know that the authors of this book hold degrees in english, education, social work, sociology, psychology, human development, and family relations. (And you think you've been in school a long time!) We used all of those studies and others, like nursing, adolescent medicine, sociology, and history, to bring you a comprehensive overview of the adolescent experience.

2. This book presents a balanced view of the adolescent experience as understood by several disciplines. Still, this book is not value free. No book can be. Clearly, our principle themes reveal we subscribe to certain understandings. To say otherwise would be to misrepresent our intentions. The difference between this and other books is that you'll know when we're expressing a belief. Now, having said this, please, don't ever be afraid to take issue with us in class. Remember the concept of social reality; it's important to push the envelope of knowledge forward to improve our collective understanding of young people. So, just do it!

3. One last note before you begin your journey of adolescence life. This book treats you as the adult readers you are. When appropriate, we have used popular culture and literature to bring this material to life. (Yes, all those stories you should have read in high school or freshman literature will now return to haunt you.) Occasionally, in difficult conceptual passages you'll find examples of our off-beat dark humor. We hope you can laugh a little with us. It relieves stress and improves concentration.

Well, that's the first chapter. Wasn't so bad now—was it? It's time to put this book aside and rest those eyes. Perhaps have a cup coffee or a Coke, a bagel or a bag of chips. Come to think of it, as we're interested in promoting health, forget that last suggestion. Have an apple instead. Anyway, we're glad you are taking

B O X **1-2**   **Signing On to The Adolescent Experience List-Serv**

To sign on to the *Adolescent Experience* list-serv follow these steps exactly. (1) Send an e-mail message to <majordomo@cfapress.org>, (2) in the subject area type <list>, (3) in the message area type <subscribe>, press the space bar to insert a space, and then type <adolescence>, (4) press the "send" button to transmit your e-mail message. During the academic year, we check our messages daily and enjoy the opportunity to interact with students across North America. (PS: Remember not to type the brackets < >. Just type the letters appearing between the brackets < >.)

this course and look forward to exploring this life stage with you. Incidentally, if you would like to sign on to a list-serv with other students across North America to discuss topics in this book with the authors just follow the directions listed in Box 1-2.

MAJOR POINTS TO REMEMBER

1. There are four principle themes to this book. They are: (1) all knowledge is rooted in the past; (2) development occurs in context and context determines development; (3) North America has a rich racial and ethnic complexity; and (4) you can create change leading to a healthier life for yourself and others.
2. History enables us to observe how social reality changes with time, place, and communal beliefs.
3. Developmental contextualism is rooted in ecological theory, which sees the interrelateness of all behavior.
4. While multiculturalism can contribute to misunderstandings and conflict, it can also strengthen a culture that is resilient enough to incorporate aspects of those cultures into its own.
5. Primary prevention offers a way to promote health and reduce the severity of many dysfunctional behaviors.
6. There are five principle definitions of adolescence. They are: (1) physiological, (2) cognitive, (3) sociological, (4) chronological/eclectic, and (5) the learner's permit theory.

Theories and Research Methods

IT IS A warm summer night. The air hangs heavy on those still awake. Fireflies draw ephemeral lines in the darkness. The year is 1915. Sitting in his kitchen, Albert Einstein pushes back his chair, stands, and stretches. He has just put the finishing touches on his theory of gravity. But instead of smiling, he is disturbed. He mumbles to himself, "This must be wrong." Einstein has predicted that the world exists in an expanding universe. Such a thought is pure nonsense. Since the time of Aristotle, the idea that the heavens are stationary has been accepted as truth by all. And so Einstein reworks his theory to correspond with accepted knowledge. For 12 years his original version lies untouched, until the astronomer Edwin Hubble shakes the world with his observation that the universe is expanding. Einstein had been right after all (Lightman, 1983).

Einstein was the victim of *social reality*. Remember that term from the first chapter? Social reality means simply that an idea may be defined as true by a group of people whether it is true or not. History is filled with similar mistakes made by greater and lesser figures alike. This fact illustrates well a uniquely paradoxical human situation. Humans have a great need to understand, to fashion models of how things work, and to comprehend why they work the way they do. These understandings lead to explanations that are called *theories*. Theories seek to predict how something might respond in a given circumstance. For a theory to be useful, it must be applicable over many varying circumstances. It must show how something works or operates; how certain events or conditions can predict certain outcomes.

And yet, despite all this theoretical inquisitiveness, humans have a steady track record of narrow-mindedness rooted in their construction of truth. For example, consider Galileo's experiences with the Inquisition. His scientific curiosity led him to the observation that the earth was not the center of the universe, that the earth revolved around the sun. Galileo's proclamation was greeted with scorn and disapproval, and eventually he was tried by the church as a heretic and banished.

Or what about Joseph Langley's fall from grace? His heresy, which eventually led to his dismissal from the Smithsonian Institution, and his professional disgrace was to imagine that someday humans might travel in heavier-than-air flying machines powered by the newly developed internal combustion engine. His correspondence with an English colleague put these fantastic ideas in print. That colleague was H. G. Welles (Pauwels & Bergier, 1988).

Albert Einstein's willingness to subscribe to social reality altered his theory of gravity.

Einstein and Galileo's experiences illustrate the one certain truth contained in this chapter—that truth is to hold no explanation sacred. Theory, like truth, evolves. Its shape changes as curious human beings question and explore further how the world behaves. Remember also that these new explanations are always grounded in the defined reality of the time and, therefore, are subject to further revision as current understandings change (Gullotta, 1996).

To illustrate, contrast your early childhood classroom learning experiences of the discoverer Columbus with more recent memories of the 500th anniversary of his arrival to American shores. Unlike those early childhood lessons, this anniversary was tempered by discussions and demonstrations that not all people were joyous about this event. Native American Indians reminded us that the genocide of native populations was one prominent outcome of the arrival of Western Europeans. From their perspective, Columbus was far less a saint and much more a sinner. His adventures led to disease, death, exploitation, and the loss of culture by the native populations that preceded his arrival. As this example illustrates, different groups are very likely to hold different understandings of events leading to different social realities. This can occur on as large a scale as historical events, such as Columbus landing in the New World, or on as small a scale as parent–adolescent disputes.

This chapter has two purposes. First, we examine several explanations of the adolescent years. With a few exceptions, it is from these core theoretical explanations that nearly all other writings about adolescent behavior have emerged. These theories are the original ideas that have been built upon to help us to describe, explain, and predict adolescent behavior.

The second purpose of this chapter is to explore basic principles of scientific inquiry. For example, to determine whether a theory is practical and reliable, social scientists test it through the use of research hypotheses. If the theory has predictive power then these informed guesses or hypotheses should be correct. Obviously, the more often a theory correctly predicts behavior the more useful that theory becomes in designing programs and developing public policy. Therefore, we briefly examine how research studies are designed. How is information gathered for research studies? And we explore some of the relationships that exist between theory and research.

THEORIES OF ADOLESCENT BEHAVIOR AND DEVELOPMENT

Psychoanalytic Theory

The first theoretical perspective on adolescence was introduced to North American audiences in the early 1900s when Sigmund Freud addressed the faculty at Clark University. This address was given at the invitation of G. Stanley Hall, who, as we noted in the first chapter, was one of the major figures to popularize the study of adolescence. As an aside, the police were in attendance the day Sigmund

Freud spoke waiting to arrest him for obscenity should he start to discuss sex. He wisely avoided the topic. Still, from that speaking engagement psychoanalytic thought caught fire in Canada and the United States. And while its major tenets never were strongly supported by empirical evidence, it dominated understandings of adolescent behavior well into the 1970s (Sulloway, 1983).

Psychoanalytic theory (Freud, 1959) consists of the recognition of two powerful forces in direct opposition—inherent instinctual (sexual and aggressive) needs and the need to live in a social group. According to this perspective, humans are individualistic and selfish, but still in need of social living. Hence, Sigmund Freud thought people are in constant conflict. On the one hand, they want to maximize their instinctual gratification—the *id*. On the other, they must learn to do so in socially sanctioned ways to avoid punishment as a social being. To avoid punishment a personality mechanism evolves early in the child's life that is referred to as the *ego*. The ego is the executive of personality. It distributes and governs the involvement of psychic activities in the internal and external world. The ego activities are involved with perceptions, discrimination, recognition, and experience relevant to the satisfaction of instinctual demands. The ego has the ability to test reality—that is, to manipulate actions in the external world to determine whether they are effective in reaching a goal. The ego's major function is to attempt to satisfy the demands of the id (instinctual drives) from the external world while observing the dictates of the third component of personality, the superego.

The *superego* is the judge of all behavior. It is our internalized moral code. It develops through differentiation of part of the ego's function into an internal regulation system. Through experience with parents, the child is thought to assimilate what he or she perceives to be the parental standard of good and bad. It has two parts. The *ego-ideal* comprises the child's perceptions of the parents' view of what is right and wrong. The *conscience*, which is the antithesis of the ego-ideal, punishes behavior that is unacceptable by eliciting feelings of inferiority and guilt.

In essence what we have is an "id" that wants what it wants when it wants it. An "ego" that seeks to satisfy the "id," but yet wants to avoid punishment, and a "superego" that judges the intended action and, depending on the strength of its voice, can restrain the instinctual urges of sex and aggression.

Through a series of life stages the child gradually comes to internalize standards through socialization experiences with family members and the anxiety associated with balancing individual needs and societal sanctions is dealt with through the development of *defense mechanisms*. A defense mechanism can be thought of as a means by which personality deals with painful experiences, internal conflicts, personal inadequacies, and the associated anxiety.

Beginning in childhood, during the *oral stage*, the instinctual needs are satisfied through autoerotic stimulation of the mouth. Through accepting and rejecting what is edible and inedible the child learns defense mechanisms associated with introjection (swallowing up and making part of oneself others' behaviors, etc.) and denial (refusal to recognize something). Likewise, by being cared for by an

To paraphrase Mae West, "Is that a cigar you're holding or are you just happy to see me?" If the humor is lost on you, go to Chapter 10, page 285, for an explanation.

effective parent the child learns identification processes. In the toddler years, or the *anal stage*, the focus is on voiding and withholding feces. The child learns to retain his feces as a form of a hostile reaction and to eliminate as a sign of giving or loving. The defense mechanism that fully matures in the anal stage is denial. The next stage is know as the *phallic stage*. Based on the classic legend of Oedipus, Freud believed that children develop a hidden desire to possess the opposite-sex parent. However, they are threatened by the appearance that, for boys, the father and, for girls, the mother will stop them from accomplishing this goal. The fear of being punished by the same-sex parent creates anxiety that leads to the defense mechanism of repression. That is, forcing the sexual incestuous fantasy or desire into the unconscious. In late childhood, or the *latency period*, the conflict between sexual fantasies of the opposite-sex parent and social sanctions are repressed. This frees up energy to expand new interests, activities, and achievements that involve school, community, and peer groups. Therefore, by early adolescence the child is capable of partial sublimation of instincts through socially acceptable channels. For example, aggressive and sexual instinctual urges can be channeled into creative arts, music, or drama. Adolescence, however, brings new and forceful implications in coping with sexual instincts.

To summarize, the child progresses through four stages. Across this developmental pathway certain issues must be resolved that result in the formation of defense mechanisms that will be used for life. Unlike other theories that see the individual evolving across the lifespan, this theory sees psychic growth essentially completed in the final stage of adolescence. The rest of life is a revisiting of these earlier stages.

Anna Freud (1958), Sigmund's daughter, refers to adolescence as a period of internal disharmony. She maintains that with the onset of adolescence the intrapsychic equilibrium between instinctual demands and ego mechanisms is temporarily disrupted, resulting in a period of storm and stress. New and strong sexual urges emerge during the adolescent years. The personality consolidation of the latency youth is threatened by a new genital or sexual orientation that revives the pregential urges that have been controlled through the ego defense of repression. You know, that old Oedipal fantasy thing. *Repression* is a defense mechanism guarding against instinctual forces through hiding from one's consciousness certain unthinkable fantasies such as incestuous urges toward Mom or Dad. The anxiety accompanying pregential urges and the Oedipal striving renews the use of old defense mechanisms. Engaged in psychological combat, the demanding id (instinctual needs) is constantly confronting the ego, therein creating the image of the adolescent as continuously undergoing vacillations in ego functioning and emotional tone. Overly sensitive to the words and actions of other people, the adolescent is thought to be coping with the establishment of defense mechanisms, which are viewed as legitimate and normal attempts at restoring intrapsychic peace and ending the unconscious Oedipal war.

According to Anna Freud, several major problems and appropriate defense mechanisms are characteristic of the period of adolescence. First, the ego attempts

Erikson's life stage model continues to influence the thinking of adolescent researchers.

to displace the conflict associated with the reemergence of an Oedipal relationship with the parent. She argues that in a defensive attempt to mitigate the anxiety associated with the regressive urge to return to this early attachment to the parent, the adolescent withdraws love from the parent and extends feelings of love toward a parent substitute (*displacement*). This process often leads the adolescent to treat the parent with a callous indifference while expending much time and energy on the parent substitute. Reflect for a moment on your adolescent years. Do you recall a time when you transferred your admiration, respect, and caring to another adult perhaps a teacher, neighbor, or youth leader? Anna Freud would use this perspective to explain that behavior.

Another solution to this same problem is a defensive reversal of affect. When the adolescent reacts with just the opposite affect experienced with the parent during childhood, the youth is responding with a defense mechanism called *reaction formation*. This negative reaction toward the displacement of love from a parent to a significant other does not diminish the regressive urges characteristics of adolescence. Rather, it further heightens the anxiety accompanying this urge and increases defensive behaviors of denial, uncooperativeness, and hostility. Still other adolescents resolve this same issue by withdrawing into themselves. Unfortunately, this reaction merely inflates the ego process and one's sense of self-importance. The resolution gives rise to increased narcissism (self-love) and the corresponding fantasies of omnipotence (all-powerfulness).

The last reaction to pregenital urges associated with infantile sexual instincts focuses upon the pathological defense mechanism known as regression. Through regressive behavior the adolescent returns to earlier coping mechanisms where the internalization of the "primary identification" figure (parent) is capable of reducing anxiety. The adolescent incorporates and acts out the perceived qualities of the parent that soothed the early infantile sexual needs.

While much of psychoanalytic theory remains unsupported by research, certain aspects, such as the use of defense mechanisms, remain in usage. Further, any student that ignored psychoanalytic theory would have a large "intellectual cultural and historical gap" in their understanding of the evolution of the field of adolescent psychology and development.

Psychosocial Theory

The psychosocial perspective of adolescence examines the relationship between the psychological adjustment of growing up and the social conditions that foster or hinder it. Stress and crisis are important psychological elements in this growth process as are stages of development and turning points. Resolutions in growth can be either positive or negative, and the resolution at one turning point has implications for later turning points.

Erik H. Erikson is the eminent example of this perspective. He views adolescence not as a period of personality consolidation but as an important stage of life that functions as a transition between important issues and events in the life

TABLE **2-1**   Erikson's Eight Major Dilemmas and Their Approximate Life Stage

Crisis point	Stage in life
Basic trust versus mistrust	Infancy
Autonomy versus shame and doubt	Toddlerhood
Initiative versus guilt	Childhood
Industry versus inferiority	Early Adolescences
Identity versus role confusion	Adolescence
Intimacy versus isolation	Youth
Generativity versus stagnation	Adulthood
Integrity versus despair	Old age

course. According to Erikson (1954), with the personal resolution of each new life crisis, the personality incorporates a new quality into the ego-identity or global personality. Therefore, a healthy personality is acquired through the resolution of a series of life crises called *dilemmas*. With each new resolution there is a corresponding personal recognition of a meaningful accomplishment and a growing sense of personal achievement.

Erikson identified eight major dilemmas that are universally experienced over the life course (see Table 2-1). In the first crisis the child establishes a sense of *basic trust* through social and physical care by an effective caregiver. In the second crisis, the child explores the world and is given secure psychological space to find a sense of *autonomy*. In the third crisis, the child is supported in his or her initiative to master new learning tasks and develops a *sense of initiative*. The first three crises are primarily issues of childhood. In early adolescence, the child is encouraged to strive toward competence, mastery, and achievement and to develop a *sense of industry*. This is followed by the fifth normative crisis of answering "who am I" and "what can I be?" To answer these questions, previous and present identifications are combined into a meaningful sense of *identity*. In late adolescence or young adulthood the search for *intimacy* is to be found in mutual sharing and trust. For many, this leads to a growing need for partnership, affiliation, and ultimately marriage or family. Middle and late adulthood crises focus on *generativity* (caring for others) and *integrity* (accepting what has been).

In Erikson's psychosocial perspective, adolescence and youth are associated with the development of industry, identity, and intimacy. Although the family establishes the basic foundation for positive development, the broader social and cultural environments also influence development. Erikson believes that in the course of our lives we experience several important dilemmas that can be resolved in either a positive or a negative fashion. Positive resolution is necessary to ensure a fully functioning, capable, and mature individual. Learning that one is competent and capable of industry, locating an identity in a social world with meaningful interpersonal connections, and developing intimate involvement with another are some of the essential ingredients of a successful adolescence, youth, and adulthood.

Social Learning Theory

While social learning theory does not attempt to provide a comprehensive explanation of the adolescent experience, it does provide important learning principles that can be used to understand adolescent behavior. From learning theories that contend that all behavior can be explained by a stimulus and response, to those that consider reinforcement, to those that incorporate cognition, we have chosen one model to examine.

Foremost among the modern social learning theorists is Albert Bandura (1977). He has proposed that the cognitive processes that mediate behavioral change, like those in adolescence, are influenced by prompting or modifying the *self-efficacy* or experience leading to the mastery of skills or tasks. Think of self-efficacy as "I can do that and it's important to me that I do it well." While helping others to experience effective performance creates within oneself a sense of being capable, Bandura has demonstrated that increased "efficacy expectations" enhance the probability that the desired behavior will occur.

Four social mechanisms increase expectations of personal mastery. First, when an adolescent sees others perform successfully or when self-instruction leads to a successful outcome, behavioral change is encouraged. Second, when young people observe a role model, whether real, such as a sports figure, or imaginary, such as a film or book character, this example can heighten teenagers expectations of gaining self-efficacy or capability. Further, encouragement, suggestions, exhortations, and interpretation of success can help self-efficacy expectations. Finally, fear-provoking thoughts about perceived inability or ineptitude can create such strong emotional states that only through observing others cope with similar problems will an adolescent see how to handle these dysfunctional fears.

Observational learning, such as watching others behave and observing how they are rewarded or punished, has very powerful effects upon children and adolescents. Bandura (1969) notes that: (1) an adolescent can acquire new ways of behaving, (2) observations of others can increase or decrease behavioral inhibitions, and (3) viewing others behavior can serve as the impetus for engaging in the same behavior. Thus, modeling can produce new behaviors by providing cues, inhibiting or disinhibiting behavioral tendencies, or facilitating previously learned behaviors.

Many adolescent behaviors can be explained from these three simple primary effects. For example, social interactions between youth or adults can encourage new behaviors through observational learning. Just observe the youth around you and notice how similar clothes, language, hairstyles, and mannerisms are worn or displayed within a circle of friends. Consider your own adolescence. Was there an adult, rock star, or other person whose mannerisms you copied? By watching others, the adolescent learns many kinds of social behaviors.

Sociological Theory

The perspective of sociology on adolescence focuses on general cultural factors that influence behavior. The influences of norms on behavior, mores, cultural expectations, social rituals, group pressures, or technological influences are the key to understanding adolescence. Kingsley Davis (1940) has provided the classic illustration of this perspective in his treatise on parent–youth conflict.

The essence of Davis' argument is that because modern society changes very rapidly, each new generation is reared in a social milieu different from that of the previous generation. Since each generation's experience of its own cultural and historical content guides its actions and provides the basis for meaning, parents find it difficult to provide direction to the new generation, and conflict is inevitable. According to Davis (1940),

> Since the parent is supposed to socialize the child, he tends to apply the erstwhile but now inappropriate content (of his own). He makes this mistake, and cannot remedy it, because, due to the logic of personality growth, his basic orientation was formed by the experiences of his own childhood. He cannot modernize his point of view, because he is the product of those experiences . . . . To change the basic conceptions by which he has learned to judge the rightness and reality of all specific situations would be to render subsequent experience meaningless, to make an empty caricature of what had been his life" (p. 525).

This conflict may, according to Davis, also be for other reasons. As adolescents are arriving at their peak physical abilities and are filled with tremendous energy, their parents are beginning to lose energy and are trying to find ways to conserve what energy they have left. So society limits competition between adolescents and their parents to reduce or limit competitive feelings of jealousy. But in the process this diminishes a wide variety of opportunities for adolescents with their parents and other adults. Davis argues the result is heightened frustration in many adolescents and that this results in increased conflict between adolescents and their parents.

Another important source of conflict is that adolescents dream of utopian ideals, where life can be fair and just to all people. But parents have become pragmatists through life experiences and the usual conservatism that comes with age makes them appear to be at odds with their offspring. As one might guess, this natural dichotomy over social reality provides the ground for conflicting communications between the generations.

The last major source of conflict is that many parents find it hard to let their children achieve a smooth emancipation from the family. In North American society there are few institutionalized steps to guide this ticklish process. Thus, ambiguity rules the situation often creating conditions for conflict over the relinquishment of parental authority.

Observations such as these may have influenced Margaret Mead's (1970) thoughts on culture and social change. Mead suggests there are three general cultural types. In the first cultural type called *postfigurative*, parents and grandparents

Margaret Mead's anthropological research encouraged North Americans to appreciate the diversity of the adolescent experience.

serve as the guide for cultural stability and continuity by expressing that their general way of life is unchanging. In postfigurative cultures, group membership and identity are generally predetermined and ascribed at birth. That is, you are and do what you are told to be and do. In postfigurative cultures, children grow up to live according to their adult peers and family members expectations.

In a *cofigurative* culture the natural order is generational differences. Mead would consider Kingsley Davis' understanding as cofigurative. That is, each new generation is expected to be different from the other and with little to offer the other. Thus, each new generation acquires the values, norms, and mores from peers and not from parents.

The third cultural type is called *prefigurative* and may be on the cultural horizon if Mead's speculations are correct. In a prefigurative culture adults learn from and emulate the new authority of youth. The interesting question this raises is how we should interpret current modern adult lifestyles. Are adults who emulate adolescent dress, hair styles, and entertainment interests foreshadowing this new culture? Or are they hanging on to an ever-fading memory of their own past youth with bodies stretching even spandex to unimaginable proportions? Maybe reengineering those aging behavioral genes for eternal youth is the answer. In fact, the influence of genes on behavior is examined next.

Genes and Behavior

What are genes? *Genes* are composed of long strings of DNA (deoxyribose nucleic acid), the chemical building block of all living matter. How do genes work? Each gene contains a set of instructions that permit the replication of one kind of protein molecule. Proteins exist in thousands of variations. Amazingly, each protein has a specific function. Once correctly assembled and working harmoniously, these proteins result in life.

Some genes are called *structural genes*. A structural gene generally ignores the environment and performs its specific function of producing proteins or enzymes. A second gene, which *is* sensitive to the environment, is called a *regulator gene*. The activity of these genes can be widely influenced by a variety of factors including exposure to heat, heavy metals like lead, or viruses.

To understand how genes operate it might be useful to imagine each gene as a food recipe that enables signaling molecules to copy ingredients and then use step-by-step processes to assemble and create new material. A flawed recipe, that is, flawed DNA, missing some vital information or providing misinformation is believed by some to explain dysfunctional behavior.

The question is whether this flaw is solely genetic, genetic and environmental, or only the result of environmental factors. *Selectionists* like Michael Gazzaniga (1992) believe that all behavior is hardwired; that is, genetic. As he writes:

> For the selectionist, the absolute truth is that all we do in life is discover what is already built into our brains. While the environment may shape the way in which any given organism develops, it shapes it only as far as preexisting capacities in that

organism allow. Thus, the environment selects from the built-in options; it does not modify them (Gazzaniga, 1992, p. 3).

Representative of the interplay between environment and genes is Robert Plomin (1994). *Instructionists* favor a dialogue between nature and nurture. For example, some human characteristics like height are highly inheritable; 90% of your height can be attributed to the genes you received from your parents. But other characteristics or behaviors do not have this effect size. As Plomin states:

> [Genetic research] provides the strongest available evidence for the importance of environmental influence. That is, twin and adoption studies usually find more than half the variance in behavioral development cannot be accounted for by genetic factors. For example, if identical twins are 40% concordant for schizophrenia, as recent studies suggest, no genetic explanation can account for the 60% discordance between these pairs of genetically identical individuals (Plomin, 1994, p. 28).

The *environmental* position that behavior is the result of parenting, community, and societal factors is represented by George Albee. In his writings he notes that the limitation of genetic approaches is that the vast majority of life's problems are not disorders that can be traced to some gene. That is, the sadness resulting from the loss of a parent or seeing ones parents divorce is not the result of flawed genes, but environmental factors. The problem with genetic explanations is that they ignore the devastation wreaked upon the helpless "by blows of fate, [and] by the damaging forces of a racist, sexist, ageist society" (Albee, 1980, p. 76; see also Albee, 1985a,b, 1996; Albee & Gullotta, 1997).

For the authors of this book, we acknowledge the fluctuating importance genes exercise on behavior. However, we are and urge others to be cautious. For example, published reports linking reading disabilities to genes on chromosome 15, schizophrenia to chromosome 5, and (as we reported in the last edition of this book) manic depression to chromosome 11 have not proven true.

This is not to say that an interaction between personality, environment, and heredity is not possible. Indeed, we believe that heredity is a very strong contributing factor in major emotional illnesses like the affective disorders and schizophrenia.[1] However—and this is the point—it is not the *only* contributing factor. The environment matters. Even in that circumstance where, if ever it was found that genetic factors were to account for 100% of a particular behavior, the environment will largely determine the ability of the individual to function in society. That is, the ability of parents and others to be loving and supportive and the access the young person has to special education, supportive therapy, and pharmacological treatments will determine the young person's ability to succeed.

---

[1] When the term affective disorder is used, it refers to profound excitement (mania), depression, or swings between mania and depression (bipolar). The term schizophrenia refers to behaviors characterized by withdrawal from reality with accompanying mood, behavioral, or intellectual thought disturbances.

Each of us is special in our own way.

INDIVIDUALITY AND RELATEDNESS

Across all of these theories there is a recognition of the individual and the relationships within which the person emerges. For example, Kingsley Davis sees adolescents as growing up in an environment of naturally occurring conflict between parents and youth. This conflict leads to independence in its positive form and hostile communication in its undesirable form. For the Freuds, conflict is a necessary feature in resolving childhood dependency on parents and to reconcile unconscious sexual fantasies and desires so that young people can move forward to find suitable sexual partners outside the family. For Erik Erikson, the young person faces a series of psychological and social crisis points where the family, school, and peer group provide challenges and expectations to change and grow. Likewise, these institutions also provide the necessary positive encouragement when one has made acceptable choices. In Albert Bandura's model of social-learning theory, social interactions regarding the ability to influence one's own life or self-efficacy, role modeling, rewards/punishment, and inhibitions/disinhibitions determine the behavior of young people.

In each of these theories there are individual aspects of the person that represent uniqueness, specialness, and personal psychological mechanisms. Further, each of the theories provide a form of relatedness and communion with others that either encourages or impedes healthy development. In these and the other theories discussed in this book we demonstrate, time and time again, that development occurs in context and context influences development.

Before we extend our discussion into how these different explanations of human behavior might be tested, we think it would be useful to take a moment and ask you to reconsider the material just discussed. Ask yourself these questions: Which theory sees all behavior emerging from the instinctual drives of sex and aggression? Which theory believes role modeling to be a major shaping influence of behavior? Which theory sees life as a series of developmental challenges shaping personality at each stop along the way? How does sociological theory differ from psychological theory? Finally, what is the difference between a selectionist and an instructionist? As you answer these questions, is one explanation emerging as a better explanation for adolescent behavior than others? If so, then notice how through the rest of this book you interpret events through the lenses of that theory. Or are you taking elements of each theory and constructing your own view of the adolescence experience? If so, then notice the usefulness of your personal theory of adolescence as you read the book. In either case, a theory is only as useful as its predictive power. To test a theory involves research, and as this book is filled with information from research studies, it would be useful to briefly review how those studies are conducted.

RESEARCH METHODS AND THE SCIENTIFIC PROCESS

Four Principles of Social Science

Assuming you accept the position that all behavior has a reason and, if given identical circumstances, behaviors will recur, then trying to understand that process makes sense. By observing humans behave in different ways, researchers can gain an understanding as to what factors either encourage or hamper healthy growth. There are four basic assumptions that drive most social science research.

Social Regularity

The first assumption is that all human behavior is *lawful*. That is, when all things are equal, people will behave in the same ways under the same social conditions. Thus, behavior can be studied. To draw a simple example from physics, if one drops an apple, it will fall to the ground. It will not fall up or sideways, but always down. Just as objects obey the laws of physics, human behavior is thought to obey laws based on genetic and environmental conditions. This process of scientific inquiry assumes that human behavior has social regularity and that repeated experimentation will result in replicable findings if the experiments are performed under the same conditions.

Cause-and-Effect versus Association

Next, social regularity exists in two forms. First, it appears in the form of a *simple association*. That is, when two behaviors repeatedly occur together, but neither has been shown to cause the other, social regularity happens in the form of an association or correlation. For example, one commonly reported correlation is that poverty is associated with juvenile delinquency. Now, to be a poor youth does not mean being delinquent, but delinquent behavior is disproportionately reported among the poor. Typically, correlations reflect the occurrence of two behaviors because of some unknown third factor. In this example, delinquency may be associated with poverty because of the higher police scrutiny that impoverished neighborhoods receive compared to middle-income neighborhoods. More police may mean there is more opportunity to be observed and arrested.

The second form of social regularity is *cause-and-effect*. That is, what is the actual cause of a behavior? What factor must precede the occurrence of a behavior? In social learning terms, what is the stimulus that temporally precedes the response? In causality the cause-and-effect is based on the assumption that the cause must precede the effect. For example, to prove that a causal relationship exists between delinquency and poverty, we would have to show that poverty *always* comes before a delinquent act. We should note that for ethical reasons not much of social science research is cause-and-effect.

Operationalization

Key to the scientific process is the belief that all behaviors and social processes can be clearly defined or operationalized. *Operationalization* refers to a clear and concise definition of (1) the research variable, (2) its basic elements, and (3) its measurability. To test predictions about behavior, the researcher must define each research variable by using clear and concise definitions in a way that allows accurate measurement.

In this process, the researcher begins by creating a *hypothesis*. A hypothesis is a statement about the relationship between two or more variables in the form of either a correlation or cause-and-effect. The next step is *experimentation* in which the researcher studies the effect of an independent variable on a dependent variable. Typically, *the independent variable* takes the form of an experimental stimulus. Many times it consists in a contrast between a treatment group and a control group; in this case the stimulus is the treatment. Other times it involves comparing two levels of the experimental stimulus treatment (for example, low peer support versus high peer support). The *dependent variable* is the behavior that is thought to change or occur because of the effects of the independent variable.

Reliability and Validity

Finally, the scientific process requires that both the independent and the dependent variables be measured with acceptable levels of reliability and validity. *Reliability* is the trustworthiness of the measures used to assess the levels of the variables. For instance, peer support of close friends might be assessed by a questionnaire that the friends complete. If answers tend to be very similar when the questionnaire is completed on different occasions, the questionnaire is said to have high reliability, but if their answers differ greatly from one time to the next even though other conditions remain the same, we say the measure has low reliability.

Validity concerns whether a measure actually measures what it is supposed to. Two kinds of validity must be considered, internal and external. If our questionnaire turned out not to measure peer support of close friends, it would have low internal validity. External validity means that the measure applies or generalizes to the whole population we are interested in.

Internal and external validity are characteristics of whole research studies as well as of measures of variables. They are achieved by designing studies carefully. The internal validity of a study assures us that the independent variable, rather than some unknown third variable, called a *confounding* variable, causes the effect. External validity tells us what we learn from an experiment can be generalized to a larger population. It is obtained by using random samples of known populations groups.

In summary, scientific inquiry is built on the belief of social regularity, which results in consistent correlation or cause-and-effect relations. To test for these, the researcher must operationalize the hypothesized relations through the use of independent and dependent variables. To do so, one must measure the variables with concern for the reliability and validity of the measurement.

Theories as Frames of Reference

Good research uses theories like the ones discussed in this chapter as a frame of reference. How does a theory provide a frame of reference for researchers? First, a theory defines meaningful behaviors. That is, the social processes that predict those behaviors and the central concerns of study. Next, a theory provides direction for how "truth" should be sought by telling us what research methods should be used to seek social facts to support the theoretical predictions. Thus, a theory provides the criteria for establishing evidence that either support or refute hypotheses. Finally, a theory suggests the appropriate data-collection techniques for testing hypotheses that emerge from the research problem.

Research Methods for Studying Adolescence

But how do researchers test their theories of how adolescents behave, and how do they assess their interventions to help young people grow into healthy and productive young adults? To avoid the problems associated with casual observation, such as observer bias and the tendency to generalize too readily from a small number of observations, researchers turn to the scientific process and its basic research methods. Thus, adolescence researchers gather data systematically and, if possible, assess them experimentally. The four most common general strategies are examined next.

Questionnaires and Interviews

The most common method of collecting data about adolescents is through surveys or interviews. Typically, a survey questionnaire is a series of prearranged questions

The successful research interviewer is socially skilled.

to which a person responds. Questions can be either "open-ended" or "closed-ended." Open-ended questions ask subjects to answer in their own words; for example, "Please share how you feel after you have had an argument with a close friend?" The open-ended question has the advantages of allowing free expression and encouraging the respondent to provide breadth and depth in a response. The primary disadvantages are that unless motivation to respond is high, the response rate may be low or the questionnaire may be only partly completed.

In contrast, the closed-ended questionnaire consists of a "stem" followed by two or more choices such as "yes/no" or "true/ false" or a range of choices such as "agree/disagree/no opinion." The major advantages of the closed-ended format are: (1) it is easy to complete, (2) it can be finished quickly, (3) it is specific, (4) it can provide a common choice for all to consider, and (5) it is easier to score, code, and tabulate than the open-ended survey. The primary disadvantage is that the respondent may respond without carefully contemplating each alternative.

In contrast to the questionnaire, the interview brings the researcher and the subject face-to-face. The interviewer becomes an important part of the research process. This person needs to be warm and friendly, socially skilled, accurate, and sensitive in asking questions and must avoid giving cues that influence the respondents answers called experimenter bias. As in the survey, interview questions may be open- or closed-ended. Depending on the degree to which the adolescent can respond freely and at will on the topic under examination, these open- or closed-ended discussions are called unstructured, semi-structured, or structured interviews.

The advantages of interviewing are the opportunity to discuss the purpose of the study with the respondent, the opportunity to establish rapport and trust, the opportunity to probe and clarify, and a higher probability of obtaining sensitive and personal information. One notable limitation is the varying length and responsiveness by each research subject (Adams & Schvaneveldt, 1985).

Observation

Interviews and questionnaires provide self-reported information about behavior, but what adolescents say they do isn't necessarily what they actually do. In the study of many behaviors, particularly more public or common behaviors, observational studies may provide the most direct objective information. Indeed, many valuable insights have come from such direct observations. One need only turn to such works as Margaret Mead's (1928) *Coming of Age in Samoa*, Masters and Johnson's (1966) *Human Sexual Response*, or Leon Dash's (1996) *Rosa Lee: A Mother and Her Family in Urban America.*

When observation is possible, it is almost always preferred. If the behavior the researcher wishes to study is likely to occur in public places, or if semi-controlled conditions can be developed to observe the natural occurrence of the behavior, then observation can and should be used. Four types of observations have been used in the study of adolescence—participant, naturalistic, field, and laboratory observations.

Participant observation   One of the earliest forms of observational data collection, participant observation research, evolved from ethnography. Researchers using this strategy enter the social world of their subjects, live with them, listen to them, and ask questions, seeking the dynamics underlying human behavior, group relations, norms, and more. The observers either announce their intent openly or infiltrate a group much as a spy would. Generally, an open statement of research intent is preferred. However, the study of deviant or socially undesirable behaviors often makes it impossible to openly state a research intent because the subjects would not then display the behavior.

Participant-observers develop an intimate and intense relationship with their subjects. Adams and Schvaneveldt (1985) describe the major phases of such research: (1) a surface encounter in which initial contacts are made, (2) the development of rapport, (3) an acceptance of meaningful roles and interpersonal exchange and (4) a phase of trust and sharing. Each of these four phases is difficult to obtain and demanding of both time and involvement.

Loyd Humphreys' (1970) classic study of homosexual behaviors that included youth and adults is an excellent example of the participant-observer method. Humphreys used participant observation to study impersonal sexual exchanges between late adolescents/young adults and middle-aged men in public rest rooms. In so doing he was able to provide a sensitive description of the psychodynamics of sexual behavior between unacquainted men. We recommend reading this work to appreciate the complexity of participant observation research and to consider the serious ethical issues involved with such investigations. For example, Humphrey (1970) participated in the sexual behavior that occurred. Was his participation necessary to gather the information needed for this study is a question we'd like you to consider.

Naturalistic observation   Another technique of observation study is naturalistic observation. The researcher, avoiding any tampering with the normal environment, observes the subjects' particular behaviors. This technique differs from participant observation in that the researcher follows a detailed observational rating form. Behaviors are counted, their durations are timed, and the time between events or behaviors is measured. Generally, formal hypotheses are constructed and observations are used to confirm or reject the proposed relation between an event and a behavior.

For example, one could use naturalistic observation to study relationship patterns between police and youth living on the street. It might be hypothesized that newly assigned police officers would have more authoritarian exchanges with these youth than officers who knew them better. It might also be hypothesized that in exchange for information police who knew these youth ignored certain deviant acts. Through observing interactions between street youth and police over several weeks, one could test these assumptions.

Field observation   The observer/researcher may at times need to manipulate subjects' environments in a field setting to test a hypothesis. For example, the research may change aspects of the physical setting to create differing psychological effects. Two settings might be created to provide differences in physical distance between two adolescent friendship pairs. The observer would record the type of communication that occurred in the distant and close sitting environments. It might be hypothesized, for example, that close environments would generate more disclosure of personal information, while distant environments would result in more joking behavior.

Laboratory observation   In the laboratory observation study, different conditions are created in a controlled setting for behavior to be observed and measured. Study participants are then brought to the lab and observed in this controlled environment. One frequent use of the laboratory setting is to study adolescent–

FIGURE 2-1

Basic experimental design.

Pretest------ **Experimental Manipulation**-----**Post-test**

Random
Assignment

Pretest------ **Control Group**------------------**Post-test**

parent exchanges for particular behaviors. An ongoing study in the lab of one of the authors illustrates this technique. Adolescents and their parents are invited to participate in this study. If after learning about the intention of the study and its requirements they agree then they sit down in a comfortable room equipped with recording devices and are asked to complete the task. In this instance, the task is to take 20 minutes and plan a 2-week vacation together. Money is not the issue. Time is the only limiting factor. Discussion ensues. Once finished the family is thanked, debriefed, and dismissed. The discussion is transcribed. Then each meaningful "thought unit" is distinguished and coded against a system that is trying to understand how family members engage in communications that assist or hamper a sense of being special, unique, and independent and a sense of belonging and of being connected and united. The communication patterns are then used to predict individual differences in adolescents' levels of identity formation, self-esteem, and empathetic or perspective-taking abilities.

Observational data collection is limited by ethical constraints. In particular, the home has been considered a refuge from outside observation. Further, many behaviors within the family are so infrequent that it is far too expensive to use observational research. Nonetheless, many of the findings, principles, and conclusions offered in this book are based on research studies derived from observation.

Experimentation

A less frequently used technique in the study of adolescence is *experimentation*. The basic experimental design involves a direct comparison of an experimental group and a control group. Although there are several variations, the basic strategy is as follows (see Fig. 2-1).

Subjects are randomly placed in either the experimental or control group. Each group is given a pretest on the behavior of interest. Then the experimental group is given the research treatment and the control group receives either passive attention or no attention at all. After the experimental manipulation, both groups are given another assessment called a posttest. The logic is that if the experimental treatment actually causes a change in behavior, then the experimental group's posttest scores should exceed both its pretest scores and the control group's posttest scores.

A study of loneliness and its relation to social communication skills illustrates the use of experimentation. One of the authors of this book is currently testing the hypothesis that if lonely adolescents are given help in improving their social skills, they will develop an expanded social network and report less loneliness. He has identified a group of lonely college-age students. Half are randomly selected for a social skills training program and the other half are left on their own. Being "left on your own" is called standard treatment. It means that the intervention is not made available to those participants. However, there is no restriction prohibiting individuals in standard treatment from independently choosing activities that might ease their loneliness, such as joining a club or engaging in other activities. Each subject is pretested on reported social relations and loneliness. At the end of the training period, both groups are retested. If improving socials skills affected social relations, the experimental group should report increased social networks and decreased loneliness, while the control group should report no change. In this instance, preliminary data suggest the hypothesis and expectations are to be confirmed.

The main strength of experimentation is its ability to test for cause-and-effect relations. Its major weaknesses are that it is expensive and that finding volunteer participants is sometimes difficult.

Evaluation

The use of research methods to assess a program is called evaluation. By using interviews, questionnaires, observations, and experimentation, program effectiveness and management can be improved. Further, program evaluation can be used to justify support for prevention and intervention efforts, while negative evaluations can be used to improve efforts or to redirect funding to more fruitful endeavors.

Social scientists design evaluation methods to determine whether program goals are being reached. They commonly use three types of evaluation. Some programs hire an evaluator to engage in continuous evaluation in which both the outcome and impact of the program are assessed to determine its success. Sometimes, when a quick decision is required, a one-time evaluation can provide the necessary assessment, as in judging cost effectiveness or management practices. Finally, policy research helps identify, through the evaluation process, new program directions. Policy research is usually undertaken to advise a legislature or funding source of need.

There is no single method used in evaluation. Any method can be adapted to evaluation research. However, three general conditions are needed if any method is to be effective: (1) the program structure, operation, and management style must be known; (2) the specific goals and proposed effects of the program must be clear; and (3) the link of the program structure and operation to goals and effects must be stated. Unless these three conditions are met, it is unlikely that any connection between the program and its outcome can be correctly evaluated.

Developmental Research Design

All research takes place within a specific design. We observed in Fig. 2-1 the basic design for the experimental research strategy. This is the strongest technique for studying cause-and-effect relationships. However, many kinds of research questions do not lend themselves to experimental designs. In these instances, social scientists typically will use one of three other techniques—case history, cross-sectional, or longitudinal research designs.

Case history design   From examining a select group of individuals and gathering relevant information about them, researchers at times can gain special insight and understanding into their behavior, lifestyle, and other aspects of their lives. This information is usually gathered in several ways, including clinical or other records, interviews, and observations. For example, many years ago the first author of this text used a case history approach to gain insight into why young people run away from home. At that time, runaways were considered deviant youth, and their parents were seen as playing little, if any, role in precipitating the event. In the process of reviewing histories from a runaway program and interviewing street youth, he discovered that many of these young people had been thrown out of their homes and that their families played a very significant role. Interestingly, this unexpected finding, when reported at two professional meetings, seriously conflicted with the social reality of that day and he was booed at these professional meetings! If there was an upside to this event, it resulted in his first meeting with the second author of this book with whom he has collaborated for 20 years.

Cross-sectional design   It is often assumed that there are major differences in behavior between early, middle, and late adolescents. To study whether these differences exist a researcher will collect data at the *same* time from 13-, 16-, and 19-year-olds (representing early, middle, and late adolescence). What is held constant in a cross-sectional study is the time the data is collected. The variable that differs is the age of the adolescent. The researcher then examines if there are differences between the 13-, 16-, and 19-year-olds on the various measures that were used. These measures might test knowledge, maturity, identity development, or sexual experience. Any significant age differences are thought to reflect developmental differences that exist between the three age groups. Cross-sectional studies are a useful shortcut in the study of adolescent development. However, when time and finances permit, the preferred technique is the longitudinal research design.

Longitudinal design   The longitudinal design also controls for time but in a different way. It tracks the same group over time. To illustrate, let's say that in 1980 a group of 5-year-old children are identified for some study purpose. This group is then followed and retested every 5 years until they reach the age of 20, using the same measures. Thus, measurements were taken in 1985 when the children were 10 years old, in 1990 when they were 15, and lastly in 1995 when they reached 20. The measures taken are then compared over time. Each child, now a young adult, has a score for each year and hence is her or his own comparison. Any difference between the age groups is based on developmental changes within the children who have been studied over the 15 years of their lives. This is a very powerful design (see Box 2-1).

BOX 2-1   Evaluating Research Reports

While it's easy to get lost in the complexity of a research study, here are several questions to ask yourself as you read a study to determine the quality of the work:

1. Is there a theoretical basis for the study? Good studies clearly state the theory or theories that are directing the line of research.
2. Are the hypotheses plainly stated and consistent with the theory?
3. Do the researchers provide information on the reliability and validity of their measures?

4. Is the sample representative of a larger population? Were subjects acquired through random selection from a population? Or were the subjects used only because they were available? Remember that as the sample becomes more limited, the generalizabilty of the study narrows.
5. Are the conclusions consistent with the evidence provided in the report?
6. Do the researchers discuss the limitations of their study?

Ethics in Adolescent Research

We've reviewed the basic principles of conducting research, but we would be remiss if we did not discuss the importance of ethical research. Many important issues in adolescence will appropriately remain unaddressed because of ethical concerns. Adolescent researchers work under guidelines that morally constrain their conduct and minimize psychological and physical risks for study participants. Subjects must be assured of confidentiality and the freedom to withdraw at any point if they wish to and to know the purpose of the study.

These ethical guidelines are a necessary and important part of research. They assure honesty and integrity in the research process. The constraints on the researcher are far outweighed by the assurance of an open, fair, and safe experience for research participants.

SUMMARY

Let's take a broad look at what we've learned in this chapter. First, theories are assumptions about human behavior. They are rooted in the historical time in which they are developed and are subject to social reality. To be useful a theory needs to be able to have predictive power. Next, we examined several examples of theories that have been offered to explain human behavior. We noted that we can trace the lineage of most of the other explanations in this book to this handful of theories. We then examined the various ways in which research is undertaken.

One final note: in writing and revising this textbook over nearly 20 years we have read literally thousands of published studies that describe, analyze, and explain adolescent behavior. These studies provide the social facts that we used to draw our conclusions. To gain a deeper appreciation of this process, we would urge you to visit your college or university library and "walk the stacks." Visit the current periodical shelves and examine any of the following publications: *Journal of Adolescent Research, Journal of Early Adolescence, Youth & Society, Journal of Adolescence, Journal of Adolescent Health Care, Journal of Youth and Adolescence, Child Development, Developmental Psychology,* and *Journal of Research on Adolescence.* Notice in these journals the research that appears and the steps the researchers took to assure its integrity.

MAJOR POINTS TO REMEMBER

1. Theories are assumptions about human behavior. A good theory has strong predictive power and is applicable in many situations.
2. Psychoanalytic theory focuses on psychosexual and emotional stages of growth and the corresponding emergence of defense mechanisms.
3. Psychosocial theory examines the interface between crisis and stress, the resolution of turning points in development, and the sociocultural conditions that facilitate growth and development.
4. Psychological theory examines the basic psychological processes that determine changes in behavior.
5. Sociological theory is concerned with cultural norms, mores, expectations, rituals, and technology and how these social institutional features influence behaviors by individuals and groups.
6. Behavioral genetic theory is divided into one school that believes all human behavior is genetic and a second school that believes environment is an influencing factor.
7. Social science is based on assumptions that human behavior is lawful and regular, that cause-and-effect relations can be established, that all theoretical notions can be operationalized, and that reliability and validity are the underpinnings of good science.
8. Theory provides a useful frame of reference, important research variables, major research questions, and useful research methods.
9. Questionnaires, interviews, observations, experimentation, and evaluation research techniques are used to understand adolescent behavior and development. Each method has its own strengths and limitations.
10. Good research follows a code of ethics that protects the psychological and physical health of the participant.

TWO

Patterns of
Adolescent
Development

Intellectual and Cognitive Development

WE LIVE DURING a time of amazing discoveries. Science is providing us with new insights in how life forms and magnificent visions of the universe. We can see the smallest of chromosome fragments and details of giant black holes at the center of the Milky Way galaxy. The many mysteries of human behavior are also unfolding. In this chapter we explore one such mystery—the nature of human intelligence. We share clues regarding intelligence and how scholars believe adolescents understand, explain, and ultimately use knowledge.

For example, recent news releases suggest that scientists have discovered that with the right balance of nutrients infants will experience significant brain cell growth—far in excess of what anyone had thought was previously possible. A well-fed and nourished infant appears able to grow tens of thousands of new neural connections every day. And the upper limit of how many neurons an infant can grow is as yet unknown. But one thing is certain, neural development makes a contribution to a young child's chances for becoming an intelligent human being.

But before we close this discussion, consider the position of David Perkins (1995), who states that much of intelligence is "learnable." That is, the neural theory of intelligence is only partially correct. Perkins maintains that experience and stimulation are vitally important, as they feed the brain's neurons. Further, reflectiveness (the ability to cope and adapt) is important because it provides us with a way to think about our thinking (metacognition) and to search for different strategies for using our minds productively. Perkins contends that we need a theory of intelligence that recognizes neural, experiential, and reflective dimensions. He goes on to say that these three features of intelligence intensify the impact of each other and can even compensate for one another when there are limitations.

Our reading of Perkins (1995) provocative book *Outsmarting IQ* suggests to us that the *neural dimension* of intelligence determines which special talents individuals will possess. The *experiential dimension* gives us the knowledge of day-to-day experience that allows us to develop expertise in specific domains or situations. That is, no one has expertise in everything, but rather knowledge in specific areas gained through experience. And finally, the *reflective dimension* of intelligence supports our ability to cope and adapt to novelty. Reflectiveness provides a self-awareness of thought that allows us to break away from old ways of thinking to explore new ways.

But we're getting ahead of ourselves. To appreciate young people's behavior, it is important to understand how they understand the world around them. Thus, in this chapter we examine intelligence and cognitive development and its evolution during adolescence, and we present several ways in which adolescent intellectual development is studied. Let's begin with the meaning of intelligence.

THE MEANING OF INTELLIGENCE

While social scientists do not agree on a single definition of intelligence, it is generally thought to be the underlying potential to function successfully and comprehend the realities of the world around us. Intelligence includes (1) the ability to deal with and comprehend abstractions; (2) the ability to acquire new knowledge or learn from experience; and (3) the ability to solve perceptual, mental, or social problems in new or unfamiliar situations.

There are several ways to conceptualize and study intelligence. Early researchers like Charles Spearman and H. H. Goddard believed that intelligence was a single-dimensional faculty, which they called the "g" factor. On the other hand, J. P. Guilford (1967) believed intelligence consisted of more than 120 abilities. Each of these abilities he saw as different viewpoints with practical implications, more than as fixed "truths" about the nature of intelligence (Brody, 1992).

At present, three research perspectives dominate this field of study (Keating, 1990; Sternberg & Wagner, 1994). Let's briefly look at each.

A Measurement Perspective

The *psychometric viewpoint* is the first of these understandings. Psychometric refers to tests that measure psychological aptitudes (also called potentials).

One of Gardner's forms of intelligence is musical/rhythmic.

Psychometrically based assessments include responding to informational questions, solving puzzles, examining geometric figures, and defining words. If you have ever taken a group or individual intelligence test, it was psychometrically oriented. Often these tests of intelligence result in a score, called the Intelligence Quotient (or IQ) that is used to estimate intelligence. Some tests provide a single score to represent a single large dimension of intelligence. Other tests give multiple intelligence scores for different aspects of intelligence like verbal reasoning or mathematical abilities. This second group of tests sees intelligence as a complex multidimensional concept (Fogarty, 1998).

Whether intelligence is a single or more complex concept continues to be hotly debated with the multiple-dimensional viewpoint gaining popularity in recent years. For example, Howard Gardner's (1983, 1995) theory of multiple intelligences contends that each of us has several forms of intelligence in varying amounts. Gardner proposes the following seven types of intelligence: (1) verbal, (2) mathematical, (3) spatial, (4) kinesthetic (movement), (5) musical, (6) self-reflective, and (7) interpersonal.[1] He argues that when we use a standard test to measure intelligence, we need to recognize that we may be only measuring a few forms of intelligence like book smarts and not others like the use of color, form, and shape (art smarts) (see Table 3-1).

Using findings from studies of brain-damaged patients, idiot-savants, and other "exceptional" individuals, Gardner concludes that we possess neurological modules in our brains that are specialized for linguistic, musical, logical-mathematical, and five other information-processing purposes. How one develops these neurological features of the brain is based, Gardner contends, on social experience and opportunity.

In contrast to Spearman, Goddard, and Binet, who championed psychometric tests, Gardner is skeptical of relying upon single tests to determine intellectual ability. He suggests our individual intelligence is largely context-bound to our social realities and experience. Indeed, he proposes that particular forms of intelligence are likely to be found by individuals who work in certain occupational fields. Why? Because each field encourages a specific kind of intelligence. In short, repeated practice develops a particular intelligence. For example, linguistic intelligence is found with writers, announcers, and actors. Musical intelligence resides with musicians and music critics. Spatial intelligence is a gift bestowed to painters, sculptors, and architects. Logical-mathematical intelligence is the domain of mathematicians and scientists, while body-kinesthetic intelligence is possessed by athletes and dancers. However, caution is in order. Gardner is not saying that the rest of us lack these intelligences but that some of us are more gifted in certain areas than others.

Robert Sternberg (1988) agrees with Gardner that there are multiple aspects of intelligence and offers three general forms—componential, experiential, and contextual intelligence. *Componential* intelligence focuses on our abilities to think

---

[1]In recent years Gardner (1995) has discussed an eighth form of intelligence. The *naturalist* is particular adept at identifying flora and fauna.

T A B L E 3-1 **The Basic Tools of Multiple Intelligence**[a]

Verbal/linguistic
  Reading
  Vocabulary
  Formal speech
  Journal diary keeping
  Creative writing
  Poetry
  Verbal debate
  Impromptu speaking
  Humor/jokes
  Storytelling

Body/kinesthetic
  Folk/creative dance
  Role playing
  Physical gestures
  Drama
  Martial arts
  Body language
  Physical exercise
  Mime
  Inventing
  Sports games

Musical/rhythmic
  Rhythmic patterns
  Vocal sounds/tones
  Music composition/creation
  Percussion vibrations
  Humming
  Environmental sounds
  Instrumental sounds
  Singing
  Tonal patterns
  Music performances

Logical/mathematical
  Abstract symbols/formulas
  Outlining
  Graphic organizers
  Number sequences
  Calculation
  Deciphering codes
  Forcing relationship
  Syllogisms
  Problem solving
  Pattern games

Interpersonal
  Giving feedback
  Intuiting others' feelings
  Cooperative learning strategies
  Person-to-person communication
  Empathy practices
  Division of labor
  Collaboration skills
  Receiving feedback
  Sensing others' motives
  Group projects

Visual/spatial
  Visualization
  Active imagination
  Color schemes
  Patterns/designs
  Painting
  Drawing
  Mind-mapping
  Pretending
  Sculpture
  Visual pictures

Intrapersonal
  Meditation methods
  Metacognition techniques
  Thinking strategies
  Emotional processing
  "Know thyself" procedures
  Mindfulness practices
  Focusing/concentration skills
  Higer-order reasoning
  Complex guided imagery
  "Centering" practices

[a] As Suggested by *In Seven Ways of Knowing* (David Lazear, 1991, p. 172).

through the gathering, storing, and processing of information. *Experiential* intelligence deals with the ability to gain insight and to be creative, while *contextual* intelligence is concerned with applying knowledge and thinking to practical solutions.

To illustrate, imagine a classroom filled with young people. In this classroom we have some youth who are very good at solving difficult mathematical problems (componential intelligence). Other students will be better at solving problems through creative solutions (experiential intelligence) or by applying the mathematical principle to a real-life problem (contextual intelligence). Understandably, these differences can make it difficult to teach large groups of adolescents (Sternberg, Torff, & Grigorenko, 1998). For this reason, some Canadian and U.S. school systems are experimenting with magnet schools where the educational curriculum focuses on a specific form of intelligence like arts and the theatre, science and mathematics, or history and literature. In these educational programs, students (with their parent's permission) chose the magnet school best suited for their learning needs.

To summarize, intelligence can be measured using tests. These tests assess general knowledge, problem solving skills, and how much a person knows about his culture. Some tests provide a single estimate or IQ score of general intelligence, while others give estimates of several forms of intelligence. Although the psychometric perspective is widely used to measure intelligence, it has faults. It can identify components of intelligence but says little or nothing about the cause of those components. Psychometric tests allow us to identify brighter students within a group, but it doesn't help us to explain how intelligence grows or how we might foster it for a young person. Assuming that people have "learnable" intelligence (Perkins, 1995), the psychometric perspective has clear limitations, and other models must be considered (see Box 3-1).

Cognitive Stage Development

Another way to consider intelligence is to examine the intellectual processes that change as young people grow older. This view is known as the cognitive development perspective. In this model not only is the solution to the problem important but also the mental process used to arrive at the correct answer (Ceci, 1990).

Jean Piaget is recognized universally for his foundational work in this area. By studying his children, Piaget described a set of fixed sequential stages where each advancement is qualitatively distinct from the next. His work showed how infants (sensorimotor), young children (preoperational), school-age children (concrete), and adolescents (formal operations) have very distinctive features in the way they think.

For example, in infancy the child focuses on the discovery of relationships that exist between bodily sensations and motor behavior. With maturity, and during early childhood, this evolves into the use of symbols to represent the internalization of external objects. This is most evident in the use of language. During the school ages, growth in thinking involves the development of logical or rational thinking and its mastery. Finally, starting in early adolescence, young people begin to

BOX **3-1**   Massive IQ Gains in Just a Single Generation!

Imagine going into a supermarket and reading this headline on the cover of that authoritative publication, the *National Enquirer*. What's more, imagine later in a college library finding a similar title appearing in one of the most prestigious journals of the American Psychological Association. Actually, it's not as unimaginable as you might think. In a review article, one author compared numerous data sets from Canada, New Zealand, the Netherlands, the United States, France, Norway, and Great Britain to find increases in IQ ranging from 5 to 25 points in a single generation. Many of these gains were traced to substantial environmental influences (Flynn, 1987). Among other interesting findings in this paper was a hint as to why U.S. students may not be scoring well on SAT tests.

To begin, depending on the intelligence measured, a person's IQ can increase as the result of learning more information or as the result of developing better problem-solving skills. In examining the data, Flynn (1987) found that U.S. IQ gains in recent decades were due primarily to an increase in information gain and not problem-solving ability.

For example, from 1963 to 1981, comparisons on the Wechsler Adult Intelligence Scale tests (WAIS) showed an overall IQ gain of 3.33 points, while SAT verbal tests showed a decline of 4.32 IQ points. By examining the tests, we learn that the WAIS measures elementary academic skills, whereas the SAT determines higher-level skills like problem solving. Thus, while U.S. students have made gains in lower-level academic skills, its students have not developed more advanced skills associated with complex problem-solving.

How might one resolve this problem? Several steps to address this deficit can be taken. To improve advanced problem-solving skills, teachers can encourage students to write critically and to read challenging books. What's a challenging book? It's one that has not been dumbed-down to a 4th grade reading level like most of todays high school and college textbooks! Further, programs like "Odyssey of the Mind," which develop abstract group problem-solving skills should be encouraged. To some, this means a return to basics. We disagree. What this means is less of a preoccupation with teaching toward test regurgitation and more instruction on problem solving and learning how to learn.

develop the ability to engage in abstract and hypothetical thinking. These stages emerge with the biological development of the child and his/her interaction with the environment. As the child's biological readiness emerges, and the demands of the environment require more complexity, the two interact to create a disequilibrium that pushes the child forward into new ways of adapting, perceiving, and dealing with the environment. As you read, you'll see that elements of this stage are found in the study of ego development, social perspective taking stages, moral development, and other forms of social cognition discussed throughout this textbook (for example, see Chapter 4 on identity development).

The strength of the cognitive development model is its stage-based roots. It recognizes neurological and experiential features of intelligence. It identifies reflective components of intelligence but doesn't describe their role for each stage. This model is age linked and is useful in helping educators create age-appropriate educational experiences for young people. For example, from the cognitive developmental perspective, children cannot be accelerated beyond the natural maturing path. Thus, to expect preoperational youths to solve problems that require formal operational abilities is educationally wrong.

Information Processing

A third way of studying intelligence is based on information processing and its basic components. Not concerned with developmental stages, these scholars study mental-processing speed and capacity, attention and memory, and other cognitive processes. For example, scientists are studying how and why speed in responding is important, what elements a person attends to and remembers, and what series of strategies a person uses in solving a problem.

Some scientists liken the function of the mind to that of a set of subprograms in a computer's software. From this perspective, individuals arrange thoughts by selecting information that is of interest, encoding the information, storing and retrieving this information, and drawing decisions about similar or different types of information to solve problems. The function, then, of thinking is for effective and efficient problem-solving of tasks using a kind of "library" of the mind.

Among others, Keating (1990) suggests that information-processing abilities during adolescence include selective attention, short- and long-term memory, the speed of information retrieval and processing, and organizational strategies that are used to store and use information. To this list, one can also add the importance of the ability to think about thinking (meta-cognition). This reflective ability heightens self-consciousness and can lead to improvements in meta-cognitive abilities. Imagine for a moment how amazing it really is that humans can think about thinking about thinking! Have you ever considered that we could be sharing the same thoughts right now? Downright amazing isn't it!

A strength of information-processing models of intelligence is that they support the neural and reflective dimensions that Perkins suggests are essential for learnable intelligence. Thus, the basic neurology provides the hardware and the processing of the information for reflective intelligence. Nevertheless, few information-processing models incorporate the experiential side of how knowledge is acquired through socialization experiences (Ceci, 1990).

Summary

As we've seen, models of intelligence vary from the simple one-dimensional perspective to the complex multidimensional perspectives. At the present time, the most widely accepted model of intelligence is a multidimensional perspective that suggests multiple forms of intelligence. Intelligence can be measured through tests that have strong psychometric or other measurement characteristics. Some scholars have examined the cognitive processes of intelligence. Other scientists have explored qualitative types or stages that emerge with maturation and experience. And still others have focused on how information is obtained, stored, retrieved, and utilized. Regardless of the perspective, all models are interested in how individuals become more effective and efficient problem-solvers who can adapt to the changing needs and demands of life.

DEVELOPMENTAL PATTERNS IN GENERAL INTELLECTUAL GROWTH

General Patterns

Over the years several research analyses of intellectual development during childhood and adolescence have been published (Demetriou & Efklides, 1994; Sternberg & Wagner, 1994; Perkins, 1995). Of these, one study by McCall, Appelbaum, and Hogarty (1973) remains the seminal investigation. These researchers compared mean IQ scores over a 15-year age span and confirmed that in any group of youths different patterns of intellectual growth before and during adolescence existed. Examining longitudinal data, these investigators identified five such common patterns of growth. These patterns are depicted in Fig. 3-1. Cluster 1 shows a relatively stable pattern in IQ change and reflects the most common pattern. Clusters 2 and 3 show decreases in childhood, but in adolescence Cluster 3 increases and Cluster 2 decreases. In contrast, Clusters 4 and 5 show sharp increases during childhood with corresponding decreases in IQ gains during adolescence. Thus, the relationship between IQ scores in childhood and adolescence is (1) a pattern of stability, (2) an increase followed by a decrease, or (3) a decrease followed by an increase. From this we would observe, Who says people don't change? Intelligence is neither fixed nor stable. Rather, it appears sometimes to expand and at other times to shrink!

These investigators report that between the ages of 3 and 17 a child's IQ score can vary by 28.5 points (with the range of confidence being plus or minus 5, meaning that a score of 100 is the same as − 5 (or 95) and +5 (or 105). They also found that one in every three children's scores increased by 30 points (8 times the range of confidence). Further, one in seven children's scores increased by as much as 40 points (close to 7 times the confidence range). Not surprisingly, high IQ

FIGURE 3-1

Changes in mean IQ over age for five IQ clusters. (From "Developmental Changes in Mental Performance" by R. B. McCall, M. J. Appelbaum, and P. S. Hogarty, Monographs of the Society for Research in Child Development, 1973, 38, Whole Series No. 150.).

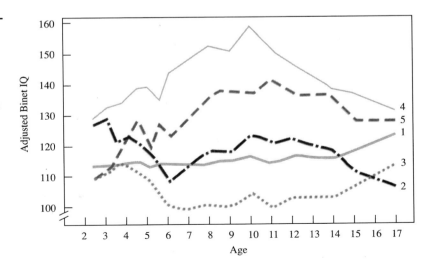

children in early childhood were the most likely to show substantial increases in IQ scores, while low IQ children were the least likely. We want you to note that this study, published in the early 1970s, confirms the recent meta-analysis published in *Nature* that seriously challenged historic understandings on the influence of genes on IQ (Devlin, Daniels, & Roeder, 1997).[2] Examining 212 earlier studies, Devlin and his associates (1997) used sophisticated statistical methods to conclude that in contrast to previous beliefs that genes accounted for up to 80% of intellectual ability the percentage was less than 50%. Clearly, as McCall et al. and Devlin have found, intelligence is not a fixed but a highly variable psychological factor influenced by *both* genetic and environmental forces.

Sociocultural Distinctions

As we just noted, sociocultural factors influence intelligence. Young people who increase in intelligence come from homes in which their parents stimulated and encouraged intellectual thought and tasks. Youths with declining intellectual ability come from families in which intellectual stimulation is absent. Often, these families are trapped in poverty. In the McCall et al. study, males tended to increase in intelligence more than girls. Females who exhibited masculine sex-role attitudes tended to increase in intelligence more than their associates who displayed more traditional feminine sex roles.

As we review reports on children's intellectual growth, we conclude that a child raised in an environment where there is encouragement to read and given the opportunity to discuss what is read grows in intelligence. Young people who are taught math skills and practice those skills gain in intelligence. Youth who are intellectually challenged apply that learning in novel ways to problems and increase in intelligence. In short, novel continual stimulation of a young person's intellect will foster intelligence while the absence of such stimulation will surely deaden any individual.

Personality Differences

It appears that several personality characteristics are associated with a higher IQ (McCall et al., 1973). For preschool children, independent and competitive behaviors are predictive of intellectual gains. For elementary school-aged children, independence, competitiveness, initiative, and problem-solving behaviors predict increases in IQ scores. For adolescents, behaviors like interpersonal distance, coldness, and introversion suggest gains in IQ.

Perkins (1995) has identified four "defaults" in human thinking that limit intellectual growth. These defaults are autonomic behaviors that reduce intellectual growth. He labels them hasty, narrow, fuzzy, and sprawling thinking. Each behavior

[2]In several chapters we'll use the word meta-analysis to establish a significant point. So what's a meta-analysis? It's a statistical method of handling many studies concerned with same topic (in this case IQ) that enables a researcher to systematically count and evaluate previous findings. From this statistical review the researcher can draw conclusions such as that the influence of genes on IQ has been overrated. A pretty powerful statement if you think about it.

has a personality type associated with it. For example, *hasty* thinking is impulsive. It results in mindless behavior where actions occur before serious thought happens. On the other hand, *narrow* thinking concerns a fixed, dogmatic inflexibility that confines thoughts and decreases creative or imaginative thinking. *Fuzzy* thinking involves the failure to identify or differentiate the important points of a concept. It is associated with problems of clarity, precision, or clear distinction-making. Finally, *sprawling* thinking is mental wandering in a disorganized and unstructured manner.

While some thought processes stimulate intellectual growth, others like impulsiveness, dogmatism, haziness, and jumbled thinking limit that growth. Intelligence can be fettered by personality and thought processes that check the development of experiential and reflective aspects of intelligence.

Summary

Adolescence is marked by important changes in intellectual development. For some young people, it is a period of rapid positive change. For others, it is a period of intellectual stability. For still others, a decline occurs. Regardless of the outcome, for all adolescents, the developmental trend in intellectual change is tied to a host of biological and environmental factors. These include sex-role orientation, income, and the level of stimulation present for the child. While inheriting a specific genetic potential is important, one cannot underestimate the importance of environmental conditions. Interacting in very complex ways, these environmental influences have significant effects on intellectual growth.

STAGES IN COGNITIVE DEVELOPMENT

Mechanisms of Change

Piaget developed his theory of cognitive development, in part, by observing his children.

As we noted earlier, the cognitive development perspective stresses sequential changes in how youths come to know and understand the world around them. One strength of this perspective is its use of theoretical assumptions about how youths develop new abilities to understand their physical and social world. According to the cognitive development perspective, the study of intelligence is the study of thinking. The founder of this perspective is Jean Piaget, who, working with Barbara Inhelder, wrote the seminal book *The Growth of Logical Thinking* (1958), which quite literally began an educational movement.

Inhelder and Piaget (1958) propose that cognition (thought) plays two essential roles. First, cognition is composed of *organizing units* that structure meaning and relations. Second, cognition allows the individual *to adapt* to environmental change. The adaptation mechanisms include a balance between assimilation and accommodation processes. The *assimilation* of information involves the mental altering of information to agree with an existing thought or belief (called a cognitive structure). For example, an adolescent attending a meeting at which abortion issues are debated could use parts of the debate to support an existing (already held) view on abortion. The opposite adaptive process is called *accommodation*. In this instance, a learning experience leads to a shift in an existing understanding. For example, as a result of the previously mentioned debate, the adolescent might come to view the issue of abortion from a different perspective and change his/her thoughts about the subject. In that change resulting from new information an accommodation has occurred. Obviously, accommodation is a primary way in which people learn within Piaget's model.

According to Inhelder and Piaget, adaptation to one's environment involves an *equilibrium* (balance) between assimilation and accommodation. At times it is clearly adaptive to modify one's thoughts; at other times it is appropriate to seek out information that confirms an existing perspective. It is only when one system dominates the other that limited adaptiveness in cognitive growth and functioning occurs. Thus, assimilation, accommodation, and equilibrium are the basic mechanisms of cognitive development in Piaget's stage conception of development.

The cognitive development perspective assumes that cognition is changed through an interaction between maturational or biological mechanisms and environmental experiences as the individual grows older. Further, it assumes that a series of major sequential changes occur in how an individual understands the world and that at varying stages in childhood and adolescence different kinds of mental representations and logical operations are used for processing information and understanding the world.

Mental Processes during Infancy and Childhood

In infancy, the child gains knowledge of its world through experimentation with what can and cannot occur. During this period of life, action equals knowledge. By touching, mouthing, and moving objects the infant develops internal nervous system representations of its actions on the world. These organized patterns of functioning are called *schemes*. When an infant engages in behaviors like the sucking reflex, grasping, and picking up and shaking items like a rattle or dropping a toy and observing where it falls, that child is organizing patterns of functioning (schemes) that are the hallmark of the *sensorimotor* stage.

This first developmental stage provides the child with mental representations that gradually evolve to become symbolic thought. With time, the infant begins to comprehend cause-and-effect or causality. By pretending and through trial-and-error, the child establishes the foundation for identification and imitation. From simple actions like dropping objects or driving imaginary cars this process develops.

Piaget's next stage occurs in the preschool years and is called *preoperational*. Preoperational children increase their use of symbolic thinking and become less dependent on sensorimotor activity to understand the world around them. Through the association between language and thought, the preoperational child uses the mental symbol of words to represent something that is not physically present to them. Learning about the world is accelerated because specific step-by-step actions of the sensorimotor stage are replaced by mental images and their mental manipulations. Linguistically, children can now imagine possibilities. However, given the child's age, this form of thinking is limited. The preschool child restricts his/her concentration to a single aspect of the object and ignores other features. This single limited view is called *centration*. Because centration focuses on the obvious (usually visual) elements of the object, it leads to inaccuracy in thought, for, as we know, appearance is not everything. That is, there are unobservable (internal or psychological) features and symbolic signs that objects or actions have that make it misleading to "judge a book by it's cover"—to use an old cliche.

A major hallmark of the preschool child's thinking process during the preoperational stage is *egocentrism*, meaning that the child does not take into account the different physical perspective or the emotional viewpoint of others. This leads to a failure to recognize that his or her actions trigger others' reactions. Fortunately for both children and society, with experience, young people gradually achieve a primitive level of reasoning (intuitive thought) and gain the notion of functionality where actions, events, and outcomes are seen as being related.

It is during middle childhood and early adolescence (approximately 7 to 12 years) that children acquire the ability to be organized and use logical mental processes. These *concrete operations* enable youths to use logic to solve problems such as the container question. This famous dilemma poses this question: When the same amount of liquid is poured from a tall skinny container into a short fat one, is the amount of liquid poured the same? Because the early adolescent has gained the ability to apply the principle of conservation of size (an understanding of volume, weight, etc.) this young person can correctly answer the question. The concrete operational child is no longer solely influenced by appearance. These youth can now apply multiple perspectives to a situation that allows them to decenter.

While decentering children are less egocentric and are capable of new forms of logical applications, these young people generally remain tied to mental applications of concrete and physical reality. This begins to change as young people leave childhood and enter adolescence.

Mental Processes in Adolescence

The very strength of concrete logical operations is also its limitation. A child at the concrete-operations stage finds it difficult to intellectually compete with older children. These youths are not able to solve problems involving hypothetical settings and have difficulty reasoning through completely verbal or highly complex information. Only in adolescence, with the gradual emergence of the stage of *formal operations*, is the young person likely to engage successfully in such complex thought. While concrete thought is limited to solutions of tangible problems, the stage of formal-operations enables adolescents to engage in combinational thought. That is, to solve verbal and hypothetical problems and to understand proportionality.

It is in this stage that the young person begins to see that combinations of facts can be used to produce specific results. For example, if presented with five jars containing colorless liquids and told that combining three of the liquids will produce a specific color, a young child is likely to combine all five, whereas a slightly older (elementary school-age) child would generally proceed by combining pairs and probably stop after exploring paired combinations. Not until adolescence is a youth likely to try all possible combinations and to keep trying until the right combination turns up. Thus, combinatorial reasoning, or the ability to generate all possible combinations of a given set of elements, is one feature of primary formal operations.

Another difficult task for the concrete-operations child involves the isolation of separate effects for several variables in a verbal task. However, with the development of formal operational thought, the adolescent is increasingly able to combine and separate the order of information in verbal form. For example, until they reach 12 or 13 years of age, most young people are unable to solve the following problem: "Edith is fairer than Susan; Edith is darker than Lilly; who is the darkest of the three?" (Wadsworth, 1971, p. 104). Can you solve this task or are you having trouble coming up with the answer! You can see by this example that to solve this task one must combine, order, and compare information. This requires very organized formal logic.[3]

The ability to recognize a hypothetical problem is another important element of formal operations. It permits the adolescent to search for a valid solution regardless of the initial hypothesis. To illustrate, if a logical argument began with "Suppose that snow is black," a child in the concrete-operations stage could not answer because snow is white. Because snow is white and that's all there is to it, the child would be unable to continue with problem. However, an adolescent could overlook this information—"Ah yes, black snow"—and focus on the logical conclusion by extracting the structure of the argument from its contents.

Understanding proportionality through reciprocity enables adolescents to generate solutions to highly complex problems. For example, even though very young children can use a balance beam or fulcrum, such as the seesaw at the playground, they have considerable difficulty in understanding the concept of proportionality and balance. Concrete-operations children can generally take a small weight and, through trial-and-error, place it closer to or farther from a fulcrum to balance a heavier weight on the other side. But they are unable to combine the information of weight and length to deal with proportions until after the formal-operations state has emerged.

Clearly, these new capacities (formal operations) in the thinking process create the potential for important changes during adolescence. To Piaget the emergence of an abstract system of propositional thinking, where principles of logic could be applied to both concrete things and abstract ideas, drive the changes that occur in adolescence. This propositional thinking allows the individual to consider alternatives of reality and to even think about reality itself—which leads us to the profound observation that Einstein must have been a formal operator.

In writing about cognitive development, Keating (1980) associates the five following outcomes with the development of formal operations during adolescence.

---

[3]By the way, the answer is Susan.

1. In contrast to childhood thinking, with its sensible here-and-now emphasis, adolescent thinking is associated with the world of possibilities. With an ever-increasing ability to use abstractions, the adolescent can distinguish both the real and the concrete from the abstract or the possible. Both the observable world and the world of possibility become interesting problems.

2. Through the ability to test hypotheses, scientific reasoning emerges. Hypothetical reasoning enables the adolescent to recognize the notion of falsification. That is, hypotheses can be generated and then eliminated as unsupportable, no matter how possible. Indeed, the adolescent spends time attempting to identify the impossible—a fascinating task in itself.

3. The adolescent can now think about the future by planning and exploring the possibilities of causation.

4. Thinking about thoughts (metacognition) is now possible. The adolescent becomes aware of cognitive activities and the mechanisms that make the cognitive process efficient or inefficient and spends time considering the internal cognitive regulation of how and what one thinks. Thus, introspection (or self-examination) becomes an integral part of every-day life.

5. The sophistication of formal operations opens the door to new topics—and an expansion of thought. Horizons broaden, not the least of which include religion, justice, morality, and identity.

The ability to appreciate the relationship between reality and possibility, combinatorial reasoning, proportionality, and hypothetical deduction were originally proposed as structural aspects of thinking that emerge with formal reasoning on all tasks. However, this new ability is not the same for all youths. Michael D. Berzonsky (1978) has proposed a branch model for the establishment of formal operations. As Fig. 3-2 shows, the application of formal operations in this model is both content specific and based on esthetic and personal knowledge. *Esthetic* knowledge comes from exposure to music, literature, and the arts, while *personal*

FIGURE 3-2

The branch model of cognitive development. (From "Formal Reasoning in Adolescence: An Alternative View" by M. D. Berzonsky, *Adolescence,* 1978, 13, 279–290.).

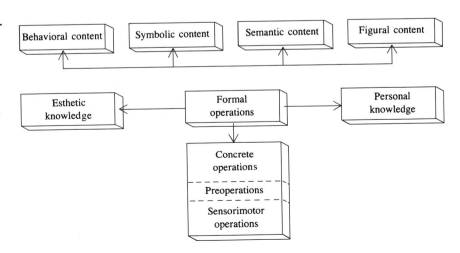

knowledge comes from interpersonal relations and concrete experiences. Further, the ability to use formal operations is not only relative to particular learning experiences but also to behavioral, symbolic, semantic, or figural content. *Behavioral* content involves nonverbal behaviors (for example, attitudes, motives, or intentions); *symbolic* content includes written symbols; *semantic* content involves ideas and meaning; and *figural* content involves visual representations of concrete objects.

The Berzonsky branch model suggests that formal operations emerges in a slower more gradual manner than originally proposed by Piaget. Thus, while younger adolescents may be able to use formal operations in one subject, they may not be able to in others. With increased age and more experience with schooling, personal relationships, and life in general, older youths are more likely to apply (transfer) formal operations to increasingly wider areas of their lives. But if David Perkins, Howard Gardner, and Robert Sternberg are correct, then all of us may only be adept at using formal operations in one or two areas of intelligence. If this is true, then the implication is that in many—could it be most?—areas of our lives we only use concrete operations.

Formal Operations and Egocentrism

While the emergence of new logical-reasoning operations during childhood and adolescence offer opportunities for deeper understanding, any emerging mental system can have negative side effects. With the development of formal operations, one negative side effect is the growth of egocentrism. For example, during childhood the individual is attuned to concrete objects or experiences and so is

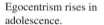

Egocentrism rises in adolescence.

perceptually (visually) bound to his or her immediate environment. Thus, childhood egocentrism consists of an inability to differentiate between mental constructions and perceptual information. For school-age children, the information rather than the mental process determines the product. Challenging their position on something leads the school-age child to change the information to fit their assumptions but does not lead to a changed position. Fortunately, through experiences in which children learn that there is information that conflicts with their hypothesis, they come to understand the arbitrary nature of mental activities and mental constructions and gradually learn to differentiate them from perceptual reality.

With the gradual development of formal operations, adolescents can conceptualize their own thoughts from those of other people. They can also construct contrary-to-fact propositions and reason about them. Recognizing the implications of these developments, Elkind (1967) proposed a corresponding theory of egocentrism. According to his account of how egocentrism emerges:

> Formal operational thought not only enables the adolescent to conceptualize his thought, it also permits him to conceptualize the thought of other people. It is this capacity to take account of other people's thought, however, which is the crux of adolescent egocentrism. This egocentrism emerges because, while the adolescent can now recognize the thoughts of others, he fails to differentiate between the objects toward which the thoughts of others are directed and those which are the focus of his own concern (p. 1029).

In failing to make this differentiation, the adolescent falsely believes that other people are as engrossed with his or her thoughts and behavior as the adolescent is. Drawing from his clinical experiences, Elkind (1967) believes that adolescent egocentrism is demonstrated in preoccupation with and self-consciousness about physical appearance and interpersonal behavior. In particular, Elkind thinks that young people are inclined to anticipate the reactions of others in social situations and to assume that others are as admiring or as critical of them as they are of themselves. Thus, adolescents construct what Elkind calls an imaginary audience, an illusion thought by adolescents to be operative in all social settings. It is this imaginary audience that heightens self-consciousness (see Table 3-2).

Although adolescents fail to distinguish their concerns from those of others, they tend to overdifferentiate their own feelings. Because they see themselves as very important to the imaginary audience, they regard themselves and their feelings as being unique and special. They feel that no one can ever know how intensely they feel. This feeling of uniqueness and intensity, which Elkind labels the personal fable, can create thoughts such as a belief in one's own immortality, the ability to influence animals, or, in the case of one of the authors, that he was a character in a soap opera with all those around him playing roles. Now wasn't that the plot of the film "The Truman Show"?

With age, adolescent egocentrism gradually disappears. Through social and intellectual experiences, adolescents come to differentiate between self-preoccupations and the interests of others and to realize that others are concerned about

T A B L E **3-2**   **Items Measuring Personal Fable, Imaginary Audience, and Self-Focus in Adolescent Egocentrism**

(Enright, Shukla, & Lapsley, 1980) *Adolescent egocentrism/sociocentrism scale*	*(Elkind & Bowen, 1979)* *Imaginary-audience scale*

Personal fable
   Coming to accept that no one will ever really
     understand me.
 	
Imaginary audience
   When walking in late to a group meeting, trying not to
     distract everyone's attention.
Self-focus
   Thinking about my own feelings.
	Imaginary audience (abiding self)
	   When someone watches me work. . .
	     I get very nervous.
	     I don't mind at all.
	     I get a little nervous.
	
	Imaginery audience (transient self)
	   You are sitting in class and have discovered that your
	     jeans have a small but noticeable split along the
	     side seam. Your teacher has offered extra credit to
	     anyone who can write the correct answer to a
	     question on the blackboard. Would you
	   • Go to the blackboard as though nothing had
	     happened?
	   • Go to the blackboard and try to hide the split?
	   • Remain seated?

Source: R. D. Enright, D. G. Shukla, & D. K. Lapsley, "Adolescent Egocentrism-Sociocentrism and Self-Consciousness," *Journal of Youth and Adolescence.* 1980, *9*, pp. 101–116; and D. Elkind & R. Bowen. "Imaginary Audience Behavior in Children and Adolescents," *Developmental Psychology.* 1979, *15*, pp. 38–44.

different (but sometimes related) thoughts, issues, and behaviors. Thus, adolescents gradually merge the feelings of others into their own thoughts and feelings and recognize their own limitations.

INTELLIGENCE AND SOCIAL INFORMATION PROCESSING

As the study of intelligence evolves, the individual is being seen as more active in the learning process (Sternberg & Powell, 1983). Recall that early intelligence theories assumed a general "g" factor in intelligence and associated higher mental abilities with attention, memory, and comprehension. But this initial research focused more on the content, or the informational component, of intelligence—what Perkins (1994) would call the knowledge of expertise. As new scholars addressed this question, individuals like David Wechsler (1955) recognized that intelligence consisted of multiple factors of which he identified two (verbal and performance). The first, the *verbal component* of intelligence focuses on factors like information, comprehension, arithmetic, vocabulary, similarities, and digit span, while the second, *performance component*, is concerned with picture completion, picture arrangement, coding, mazes, and other skills that have to do with visual and spatial representations.

Still other scholars concentrated on the complexity of intelligence. To illustrate, consider J. P. Guilford (1967), who developed an intricate model of intelligence proposing no less than 120 mental abilities. This proposal is based on five operations, four contents, and six products ($5 \times 4 \times 6 = 120$ mental abilities).

In Guilford's theory, *operations* (not unlike those referred to in cognitive stage theory) are cognitive processes such as awareness, discovery, integration, and differentiation. These operations include aspects of memory, the generation of many ideas (divergent production), arriving at a single most suitable conclusion or response (convergent production), and evaluation as a process. *Contents* of intelligence include visual or spatial representation and symbolic content such as that found in letters or words. The *products* of intelligence include such components of information as units, classes, relations, systems, transformations, and implications. Thus, a given young person's form of intelligence may center primarily on select aspects of operations, content, and products. Given this, the challenge to educators is to find the form of intelligence that any given youth has and maximize it, while helping the child to nurture other, less-well-developed forms.

Although early work recognized the content of information processing, the intermediate steps of Guilford's work on operations helped advance an information-processing model of cognition. In this model, the adolescent is viewed as an active, information-seeking person who engages in complex thinking. Indeed, a new breed of researchers has moved toward studying both information and the way in which it is processed to become useful to a person. For example, Robert Sternberg (1977) has put forth the concept of *componential analysis*. Components are elementary processes by which people make internal representations of external objects or ideas and perform mental manipulations.

Sternberg identifies five forms of information-processing components. *Metacomponents* are complex decision-making and problem-solving processes. *Performance components* are the actual internal manipulation processes. *Acquisition components* involve learning new information that can be stored in short-term memory or transferred to long-term memory. *Retention components* involve a librarylike mechanism with an organizational capacity to retrieve information. And *transfer components* are processes that generalize information from one task or problem to another. Each of these components is an essential mechanism to understanding intelligence.

Sternberg and Powell (1983) contend that from an information-processing view of intellectual development there are several types of intellect. Processes need a knowledge base on which to operate; therefore, we can examine both the amount of knowledge acquired and the processes that work on specific knowledge bases. We can study memory capacity and why it increases, up to a point, with age. We can consider the techniques that people use in information-processing tasks. We can explore how internal representations of knowledge or information occur, how they are separated or integrated, and how they change. We can look at lags in processing time and difficulties in processing information that delay understanding. And finally, we can examine the role of the integration of information-processing activities by ego mechanisms. Sternberg and Powell contend that the core of intelligence lies in the way a person allocates and adapts mental processes and resources to any given task.

Regarding adolescence, we know that control strategies involving metacomponents mature between childhood and adolescence. More effective use of instructional rules and guidelines and more efficient task performance emerge during adolescence. Information processing becomes broader with age: greater arrays of information are used, and there is more combinational thinking and better encoding of information. Adolescents have greater sophistication in comprehension than children because of their ability to look at connections; that is, the interrelationships existing between all things. As a section-closing aside, the subject of connections was wonderfully addressed by James Burke in the PBS series "Connections." Frequently replayed on cable television channels like "The Learning Channel" and "The Discovery Channel," we encourage you to be intellectually stimulated and entertained by Mr. Burke.

INTELLECTUAL DIFFERENCES AND DIVERSE YOUTHS

Several attempts have been made to explain the cognitive and intellectual differences that appear between different racial/ethnic groups. In this section we examine three that are used frequently. They are cultural deprivation/cultural difference, social class/sociocultural variation, and ethnoneurology/brain function theories. It should be noted that each of these perspectives contains an important contextual element that is consistent with the general nature of developmental contextualism. That is, human development is shaped partly by the social, economic, political, and cultural settings in which people live. Furthermore, this influences the nature of the social context in which people interact. Therefore, human behavior can be linked with an institutional context and result in productive social living. However, it can also be in discord in which case the individual and his or her behavior is not productive.

Cultural Deprivation/Cultural Difference Hypotheses

A frequently used hypothesis to explain poor academic achievement among diverse youths living in inner cities, cultural deprivation suggests that inadequate socialization within a culture of poverty explains poor school performance. Thus, low-income and failing diverse youths are thought to live in an inadequate social environment. Critics contend this perspective is overly focused on identification to a mainstream White culture and ignores the integrity of diverse ethnic cultural groups. As a result of these observations, the cultural deprivation perspective has been replaced by a cultural difference hypothesis.

The cultural difference hypothesis maintains that diverse youths belong to rich alternative and highly adequate cultures that are characterized by unique language, communication styles, and cognitive and motivational processes (Banks, 1988). From this perspective, it is considered unfortunate that these cultural differences are not encouraged by the schools that Native Americans, Mexican Americans, and other diverse youths attend. This lack of attention to diversity hampers the learning of these youths.

To illustrate, Cohen (1969) identified two distinct learning styles among U.S. children. In the *analytic style* the individual prefers to work independently, is competitive and task oriented, and is not highly responsive to the immediate social environment. In contrast, the individual with a *relational style* is more sensitive to others, is focused on common goals, and is cooperative in his or her work style. (These distinctions are similar to concepts of individuality and connectedness as dimensions of identity formation, which are discussed in the next chapter.)

Anthropological research reveals that family and friendship groups that perform shared or group functions socialize in a relational learning style. More formal, hierarchical, or individualized task performance groups socialize in an analytic style of learning. Reviewing the literature, Banks (1988) suggests that Mexican-American and Black students are more likely to score higher on relational learning styles while Whites score higher on analytic styles. (Banks also reports that boys tend to be more analytic and girls more relational.)

Social Class Hypothesis

Other social scientists (particularly sociologists) have asserted that the difference within ethnic groups is as great as the variation that occurs between groups. While all ethnic groups like Italian Americans, Mexican Americans, or French Canadians share certain general beliefs and values, there are whopping differences within each group. Some of these differences can be explained by socioeconomic factors like education and income. For example, Wilson (1978) argued that social class exerts a substantial influence on ethnic behavior. What this means is that socioeconomic status (SES) more than race or ethnicity determines values, attitudes, and behaviors.

In his literature review Banks (1988) responds to the social class hypothesis by acknowledging the importance of social class in several aspects of cognitive and academic performance, but notes that despite these influences, ethnicity continued to exert strong effects. As Banks points out, middle-income diverse families maintain contact with extended family members and friends less successful than themselves. Is this so surprising? Consider your own ethnic heritage. Does your family still enjoy special foods, celebrate certain holidays, or recognize specific moments in history unique to your ethnic or racial group? What Banks is saying is that while SES matters, heritage matters as much or more.

Ethnoneurology/Brain Function Hypothesis

Some educators mistakenly assume that all children arrive to be educated with the same general cognitive abilities. Too often the teachers at these schools assume that an analytic teaching style is appropriate for all youths. Sometimes, it is appropriate but at other times an analytic teaching is not appropriate. For example, Gardner (1995) believes that in order to successfully teach, instructors must encourage the multiple intelligences that youths possess by presenting information in a variety of ways and by having a sincere and truer interest in the youths than in the subject matter.[4]

TenHouten (1989) offered a refinement of the cultural differences perspective by combining information on dual-brain theory (cerebral lateralization) and ethnocultural perspectives. Dual-brain theory states that the brain is divided into two hemispheres (halves or sides). The left hemisphere is thought to control language, verbal knowledge, and verbal usage. The right hemisphere, which also makes some contributions to language, is most important for spatial orientation and exploration, visual memory, and esthetic comprehension and production. If the left hemisphere is damaged one can observe problems in reading, writing, arithmetic, and other academic-related skill problems. In contrast, if the right hemisphere is injured one might see problems with peer relationships, hand–eye coordination, geometry, spatial orientation, and other personal relationships.

TenHouten (1989) hypothesized that individual hemisphericity, or the tendency to be left brain versus right brain dominated (or the reverse) is influenced by sociocultural factors. For example, he notes that membership in a nonmodern, archaic, aboriginal cultural—emphasizing spatial skills like gathering, hunting, and path-finding—would encourage a reliance on, and relatively high performance in, RH-dependent (right hemisphere) gestalt-synthetic thought. On the other hand, belonging to a modern, industrial, and technological society—in which elaborated linguistic skills are instilled by a mass educational system—could contribute to reliance on, and relatively high performance in, LH-dependent (left hemisphere) logical-analytic thought.

He went on to review numerous studies to test his assumptions by comparing aboriginal and White Australian school-aged children and their parents. Through the use of complex brain function tests for skills such as performance hemisphericity, hemispheric activation, hemispheric preference, and lateral flexibility, he concluded that context-based sociocultural experiences combined with different brain functions result in significant differences in cognitive styles between aboriginal and nonaboriginal children.

Findings like these suggest that economic, political, and cultural factors can contribute to a cognitive orientation, or mode of thought, which results in children's tending toward a particular hemispheric brain-orientation learning style. Some people will be socialized in a culture that encourages the left hemispheric logical-analytic learning style. Others will be reared in a culture that encourages the use of right-hemispheric relational learning styles. (Note: neither form of

---

[4]Incidentally, this is one reason why we use literature, film, and song. If you can relate to the reading assignment through an illustration we've used then a greater understanding of the reading material should occur. By the way, you could help us. If in a reading assignment you think of a film, book, or song that makes the point, please use the list-serv described in Box 1-2 in Chapter 1 and share it with us. We want and need to learn from you too.

learning is better, just different.) The former will learn best in an individualized learning environment that focuses on thinking, abstractions, and considering tasks independently. The latter will learn best in cooperative, role-modeled, observer environments that allow for hands-on manipulation and visual-spatial examination of learning tasks.

Summary

Environmental (contextual) factors can be readily identified to account for differences between ethnic groups in cognitive performance and educational attainment. Sociocultural variations in cognitive and motivational styles have been documented. Ethnic differences may be due to cultural characteristics and influenced by social class or socioeconomic factors. Some evidence suggests that ethnoneurological differences influence cognitive learning styles and may encourage one form of hemispheric learning over another. We believe, with Gardner (1995), that educational outcomes can be determined for diverse children by the degree to which teachers recognize natural and explainable differences in cognitive styles and structure their teaching to accommodate these differences.

A CRITICAL HABIT OF MIND

It could be argued that the authors of this book should be less fixed on a concern over intelligence as the major focus of cognitive ability and more on critical thinking. Don't worry—we believe that critical thinking should be expected of all youths regardless of intelligence.

The ability to relate well to others is a factor in both academic and career success.

Let's draw on the work of Daniel Keating to understand what a critical habit of mind should be. Keating and Sasse (1996) contend that critical thinking has three broad domains: conceptual flexibility, reflective thinking, and cognitive self-regulation. The first, *conceptual flexibility*, involves the creation of links between ideas and the application of a particular concept to novel content. Types of conceptual flexibility are seen in divergent thinking, analogical thinking, and applying algorithms. *Reflective thinking* is at the core of critical thought and involves making qualifying conclusions about the value of ideas. Where conceptual flexibility is essential for generating new ideas, reflective thinking is necessary to determine the right or wrong and the usefulness or unusefulness of ideas. Reflective thinking involves formal reasoning, deductive logic, and scientific thinking. The final aspect of an adequate critical habit of mind is *cognitive self-regulation*. This involves the selection and organization of cognitive activities (sometimes called executive function) needed to effectively and efficiently problem-solve. Cognitive self-regulation encompasses inquiry, information gathering, questioning, and comprehension.

SOCIAL INTELLIGENCE: BEYOND ACADEMIC IQ?

Academic IQ is a good (but not a foolproof) predictor of academic success. We suspect you know intelligent young people who don't do well in school and less intelligent youth who do very well academically. The common belief is that people who are intelligent will be more adaptive to life's problems. This belief ignores the reality that youths need to be adaptive beyond the classroom. In fact, most individuals spend only a small portion of their life as students. (As a second aside, this contrasts with the authors, who have spent between them a total of 54 years in formal education... and we still have trouble getting things right! Go figure that one!) So, like Howard Gardener's concept of interpersonal intelligence or Robert Sternberg's description of different forms of brightness, several scholars have tried to measure social intelligence. That is, the form of intelligence that predicts success and adaptability in social settings.

For example, Epstein and Meier (1989) developed a measure of competence in constructive thinking. This measure was designed to assess the effectiveness of a person's ability to control his or her emotional life and to cope with the problems of daily living. Epstein and Meier administered this questionnaire to undergraduates and assessed their success in social activities that are common to late adolescents. They correlated academic IQ with the Constructive Thinking Inventory and found a modest correlation. However, academic IQ didn't correlate with success in daily life. Rather, their version of social intelligence predicted such success. Now, the correlations were relatively small ($rs = .20$ to $.39$), but the findings suggest that social intelligence might be measured through constructive thinking and that social intelligence might predict more than academic intelligence success in daily social activities.[5] While Nathan Brody (1992) has raised challenges to these findings, he doesn't dispute that social intelligence may be a legitimate form of IQ.

Ford and Tisak (1983; see also Brown & Anthony, 1990) have also tested social and academic intelligence among high school students. In their study social intelligence was measured by behavior in an interview situation. Academic intelligence was obtained from a group test of IQ. The two kinds of intelligence were correlated at about $r = .20$. Again, a modest association was observed. However, in this study, both academic and social intelligence correlated (range $r = .23$ and .47) with social competence in the interview setting. While the social intelligence scores were slightly better at predicting social competence, academic intelligence was also predictive of social behaviors in the interview.

We suspect that separating academic from social intelligence will never be easy. And it may be that both forms of intelligence predict social success, as both measure adaptation to life. Epstein and Meier (1989) did find evidence to suggest that social intelligence is predictive of social adaptability. But as Ford and Tisak (1983) report, its power to predict may not be substantially beyond that of academic intelligence. Still, we subscribe to Perkins (1994) view that skill in social knowledge, when coupled with reflective thinking and problem solving abilities, leads to a more socially competent individual. Taking this perspective helps us to understand how bright students may do poorly in social settings. And how sometimes less academically inclined students can do well in social situations. Clearly, for some youth, there are dramatic differences in their social and intellectual abilities. Yet, some of these very same youths can compensate at times for these deficits. We think this happens for those adolescents who have strong reflective components to their level of intelligence. These youths are able to see that when one strategy for managing their social or academic life fails they can turn to another to cope and adapt. Of course, that's a guess, as proof for it awaits your thesis or dissertation.

CONCLUSION

This and the two chapters that follow contain difficult information. They discuss topics and concepts that you have not likely read before. Don't rush through this material. Spread your reading over a few nights and take notes. The simple process of jotting down information improves recall.

OK, here's a quick test for the primary themes of this book. Did you see how history repeats itself in studies that challenged solely genetic explanations for intelligence decades ago? Did you see how time, place, circumstance, and culture can strongly influence intelligence? That's developmental contextualism, my friend. Did you see how respecting another culture could influence teaching styles that

---

[5] What's a correlation? It's the degree of agreement between two conditions or variables. Remember that just because factors may relate does not mean they establish causality. To refresh your memory on this issue, you may want to revisit Chapter 2.

could influence how a young person learns? If you answered "yes" to these three questions, well done.

MAJOR POINTS TO REMEMBER

1. A definition of intelligence includes the ability to understand both the physical and the social worlds.
2. In the psychometric assessment of intelligence, mental age and chronological age are compared on the performance of intellectual tasks. In the cognitive development perspective, intelligence is assessed on the basis of whether specific cognitive abilities (such as seriation, verbal deduction, proportionality, and so forth) are used in the solution of a problem.
3. Data from both psychometric and cognitive development studies confirm that important changes in intellectual ability occur during adolescence.
4. In general, intelligence is not totally fixed at birth (or inherited). Rather, certain factors in personality, family relations, and schooling can influence intellectual growth. However, the influence of each factor on IQ gain or loss appears to be limited.
5. Intelligence can be understood from an information-processing perspective. Operational strategies of processing can be examined to study how knowledge is gained and used.
6. Sequential developmental stages can be found for ways of knowing. For both men and women there is an evolution from being passive to active learners.
7. A critical habit of mind can be acquired where individuals are encouraged to be analytic and thoughtful. Schools are thought to be generally inattentive to the development of this form of cognitive development.
8. Social intelligence focuses on the ability to understand social living. Some evidence suggests that social intelligence predicts social skills. However, academic intelligence holds a similar predictive association with social living. But social intelligence appears to be somewhat stronger in such predictions.

Identity
Development
and Self-Concept

SOME YOUNG PEOPLE appear to get through adolescence in a smooth and unruffled fashion. Others experience occasional ups and downs. Still others confront adolescence head-on. This last group of young people appears hostile, belligerent, and sometimes belittling to those around them. The authors of this book can remember belonging to all three groups during our adolescence. We took long, lonely walks in which fantasy and introspection were intertwined in a "head trip" about self-perceptions and thoughts about the future. An onlooker would have had little doubt that we were deep in thought, lost to the world around us, and absorbed in ourselves. As is often the case, adolescence was both intensely demanding and frustrating. There were no no clear immediate answers, and there were far too many questions that needed to be answered.

While this struggle toward self-understanding, satisfaction, and membership extends across the lifespan, it is during adolescence that issues of self-worth, confidence, and feelings about capability are most keenly felt. We believe these issues intensify as young people transition from elementary school to secondary school, from parent to peer group, and from a child to a person capable of reproduction. Take a moment and think back to your own adolescence. Do you recall feeling insecure about moving to junior high school? Did you question your ability to make friends or be successful in high school? Did you begin to wonder and worry about what the future might hold for you? These concerns represent part of the struggle of answering the question Who am I? In this chapter we examine several aspects of identity development and how self-concept relates to identity development. As much of this material is probably new to you, we encourage you to read this chapter over 2 days, highlighting or underlining important points as you read.

IDENTITY DEVELOPMENT

To help us answer questions such as What do I want to become? and Who do I want to be? (which are at the heart of the struggle to establish an identity) we draw upon the writings of one of North America's greatest authors, Mark Twain. Therefore, permit us to introduce you to a favorite literary friend of ours, Huckleberry Finn. His journey with the escaped slave Jim down the Mississippi river can be interpreted in many ways. For our purposes, we'll use Huckleberry as a young lad struggling to define himself in relationship to the society in which

The fictional character, Huck Finn, well illustrates Erikson's passage from child to adult.

E.W.Kemble
-1884-

he lives. Pause for a moment. Create a mental picture of Clemens' (1884/1962) notorious, barefoot, pipe-smoking, unruly lad at the beginning of *The Adventures of Huckleberry Finn*. Remember that Miss Watson has taken Huck into her home; he has started sleeping in a bed rather than sleeping with the hogs; and he is even going to school. That is, until his drunken brutal father reappears and drags Huck off to live in a cabin on a small river island. With Huck in mind, let's begin our discussion of identity.

No discussion of identity can begin without acknowledging that Erik Erikson (1968) laid the foundation for research on adolescent identity development with the publication of his book *Identity: Youth and Crisis*. In that book Erikson saw adolescence as a major junction in life in which young people focus intense energy on issues like self-definition and self-esteem. Through a combination of factors associated with physical development, occupational and social choices, and expectations by parents and peers, Erikson maintained that young people are engaged in a period of "identity crisis." In an accommodation (or ego integration) process, the adolescent draws on resolutions from earlier life crises and experiences to resolve the search for a sense of personal direction (See also Cote, 1996; Grotevant, 1992.). What does this mean? Well, from the first of Erikson's eight stages, the successful resolution of basic trust vs mistrust will result in *hope*, leading to confidence and optimism about the future. Achieving autonomy (stage two) provides the individual with a *sense of will and self-control*. In Erikson's third stage, the struggle is between initiative and guilt. Initiative gives *purpose and the strength to pursue goals*. The industrious youth (stage four) acquires a sense of *competence and knowledge* that will enable her or him to demonstrate that ability. In adolescence (identity achievement vs role confusion), these earlier crises are interwoven into addressing the new crisis of *fidelity*. That is, coming to grips with being true, genuine, and faithful to yourself and others. If successful in handling these crises, then the young person can commit to friendships and intimate relationships and to political, religious, and other belief systems (Erikson, 1965, 1968; Markstrom, Sabino, Turner, & Berman, 1997).

Thus, the question of Who am I? is addressed during the adolescent years in the relationship not only to the self but to others as well. Think back now to Huckleberry; his search for a sense of personal direction was initially motivated by a desire to escape a drunken father whose beatings had become too frequent. This decision to escape begins his journey of self-discovery. That journey will pit the beliefs of his childhood and cultural training against a higher order of values. The choices Huckleberry will make during that journey will define him as a person.

The Meaning of Identity

To further delve into the meaning of identity, it is a complex psychological state that provides a sense of direction, commitment, and trust in a personal ideal or self-image. A sense of identity integrates sex-role identification, beliefs and ideology, accepted group norms and standards, and self-conception. Ego identity is a complex role image that summarizes one's past, gives meaning to the present, and directs behavior in the future. It includes a sense of self-direction, individual fidelity, and basic internalized values. As a psychological construct, identity formation evolves over time. Beginning in childhood, we learn about ourselves, our family, work, leisure, religion, and politics. Each of these aspects of everyday life becomes a part of who we are and who we will become (Baumeister, 1986).

While identity is a gradual developmental process, it is during adolescence that identity becomes conscious and strong due to several factors (Adams & Marshall, 1996; Kroger, 1989). Foremost among these are the physiological changes that accompany the maturation of the body. New and erotic sensations accompany changes in the endocrine system, leading to an awareness of sexuality (Blos, 1962). These bodily changes require the adolescent to cope with a new sense of self-consciousness and sexual impulses that have not been experienced before. It is also during adolescence that adults expect more responsible behavior from adolescents urging them to channel their strengths and abilities into higher forms of competition, achievement, and competence. With this new body awareness and a growing sense of social maturity, adolescents begin to think about their role in society. They become concerned with how others might view their behavior and begin to wonder about how an assumed role or newly acquired skills might meet future needs.

By creating institutions like schools, most technologically advanced societies have acknowledged the need for a period of sheltered growth for adolescents (Cote, 1996). To ease the transformation from childhood, adolescents are placed in educational and social environments that permit a limited degree of experimentation. Erikson (1959) calls this time period a *psychosocial moratorium*:

> The period can be viewed as a psychosocial moratorium during which the individual through free role experimentation may find a niche in some section of his society, a niche which is firmly defined and yet seems to be uniquely made for him. In finding it the young adult gains an assured sense of inner continuity and social sameness which will bridge what he was as a child and what he is about to become, and will reconcile his conception of himself and his community's recognition of him (p. 110).

According to Erikson, adolescents with a strong sense of ego identity see themselves as distinct individuals and have a consistent self-image. In the search for identity, the adolescent experiments with many roles, shifting back and forth in an attempt to find the "real me." This shifting role play is both a conscious and an unconscious ego identity struggle.

Identity Crisis

From Erikson's perspective, identity consists of several interrelated elements (Bourne, 1978a). It can be viewed as a *developmental outcome* of early childhood experiences, as a summary of *adaptive accomplishments*, and as a *structural configuration* of personality. But most of all, identity can be thought of as a *dynamic process* of testing, selecting, and integrating self-images and personal ideologies. To arrive at a wholesome and integrated sense of identity during adolescence, Erikson maintains that one must experience a "crisis."

The *concept of crisis* is often misunderstood. Both Erikson (1968) and Allport (1964) have attempted to describe what is meant by crisis in normal development. According to Allport:

> a crisis...is a situation of emotional and mental stress requiring significant alterations of outlook within a short period of time. These alterations of outlook frequently involve changes in the structure of personality. The resulting changes may be progressive in the life or they may be regressive. By definition, a person in crisis cannot stand still...He must either separate himself further from childhood and move toward adulthood, or else move backward to earlier levels of adjustment (p. 235).

Erikson describes this experience as a feeling of suspended animation with preceding events irrelevant to what is to come. The young person faces a multitude of decisions on vocational choice and training, marriage, and ideology and becomes increasingly uneasy, anxious, and compelled to resolve the tension. For our friend Huckleberry this moment is faced when he struggles with the decision to turn the runaway slave Jim over to bounty hunters:

In the search for an identity, young people often challenge authority.

Why, me...I warn't to blame, because I didn't run Jim off from his rightful owner; but it warn't no use, conscience up and says, every time, "But you knowed he was running for his freedom...What had poor Miss Watson done to you, that you could see her [slave] go off right under your eyes and never say one single word..., I got to feeling so mean and so miserable [for breaking the social mores supporting slavery that] I most wished I was dead..., [Huck leaves the raft with the intention of turning Jim in when he is confronted on the river by two men searching for runaway slaves. They ask:] Is your man white or black? [At that moment, Huck cannot find the words to betray Jim and chooses instead to protect him by lying. Afterwards, he reflects on his actions:] They went off, and I got aboard the raft, feeling bad and low, because I knowed very well I had done wrong.... Then I thought a minute, and says to myself, hold on—s'pose you'd a done right and give Jim up; would you felt better than what you do now? No, says I, I'd feel bad.... (Clemens, 1884/1962, pp. 123, 127–128).

For most adolescents, as with Huck, coping with this tension results in an altered personality. From this point in the novel forward Huck will dedicate himself to keeping Jim from being captured. A decision that puts him into direct conflict with the values and standards of the society in which he lives. After struggling with his moral dilemma, Huck chooses for himself friendship and loyalty to Jim over society's conventions. Huck goes through a self-transformation and internalizes new values based on freedom, rights, and autonomy. However, for some adolescents a challenge such as this becomes too great. Erikson argues that these youths may meet the challenge with regressive behavior or apathy and a kind of "paralysis of will." Like Huck, at first, stuck in the mud of social convention, these youths fall into apathy and never question the rightness of convention. Unlike Huck, apathetic youth remain frozen in their will to make decisions, take sides, or reconsider what rings true for them.

A state of crisis, with its corresponding search for answers, creates the force behind identity development. The best possible outcome occurs when youths search for self- definitions and integrate these self-made images into their personality makeup. However, some young people are unable to meet these challenges and regress into a state of role confusion (Erikson, 1959). The overall portrait of a *role-confused* youth is a disturbing one. This adolescent is unable to arrive at a psychosocial self-definition and finds all decision-making to be threatening and conflictual. Failure to make decisions creates an ever-growing sense of isolation. These symptoms are accompanied by related feelings of shame, lack of pride, alienation, and perceptions of being manipulated by others. The total estrangement of role confusion is reflected in Erikson's (1968) example of Biff's remark in Arthur Miller's (1949) *Death of a Salesman*: "I just can't take hold, Mom, I can't take hold of some kind of life" (p. 131). Or for those students who watch the weekend films on cable music channels, this estrangement is found in John Travolta's character in "Saturday Night Fever."

Other adolescents resolve their identity crisis through even less desirable means. Erikson (1959) describes these adolescents as individuals with a *negative identity*. These youth find commitment in undesirable identifications with criminal, delinquent, or antisocial groups; cliques, or antiheroes. Parents of adolescents who develop negative identities are thought to be overly concerned with social status and to prefer facades of social prominence over true involvement and meaningful relationships. Erikson refers to these parents as overpowering and inescapable. These parents appear to love their children in undesirable ways and to complain about their relationships with their spouses. Such parents demand that their children give meaning to their existence while treating them as possessions that must be jealously guarded lest they be stolen away by others.

Identity Status: Four Levels of Identity Formation

Over the years several frameworks measuring the evolving ego identity have been devised (Boyd & Koskela, 1970; Bosma, 1992; Marcia, 1966; Matteson, 1977; Rasmussen, 1964; Simmons, 1970). Of these, one has emerged more useful than others (Marcia, Waterman, Matteson, Archer, & Orlofsky, 1993). Using an interview technique, James Marcia (1966) identified crisis and commitment as major variables leading to a state of identity. According to Marcia, "crisis" refers to the adolescent's *period of engagement* in choosing among meaningful alternatives and "commitment refers to the degree of *personal investment* the individual exhibits" (1966, p. 551). Thus, a state of crisis is a period of searching for answers, while a commitment is a meaningful choice that guides behavior. In

TABLE **4-1**   Marcia's Four Identity Statuses

Status	Past or present crisis	Commitment
Diffusion	No	No
Foreclosure	No	Yes
Moratorium	Yes	No
Identity achievement	Yes	Yes

Source: Adapted from J. Marcia, "Development and Validation of Ego-Identity Status," *Journal of Personality and Psychology,* 1966, *3*, pp. 551–558.

Marcia's interview technique, individuals were questioned about their *experience with searching* (crisis) and their *commitment* on occupational, political, religious, and ideological issues.

Using reported states of involvement with crisis and commitment, Marcia (1966) described four *types of identity status*: diffusion, foreclosure, moratorium, and identity achievement. These statuses provide a summary label for individuals in different levels of identity formation. Table 4-1 lists these four statuses and shows their relationships to reported crisis and commitment. Erikson (1968) portrayed identity achievement and identity diffusion as polar opposites in identity formation. According to Marcia (1966), an *identity-diffused* youths is one who is likely to report having neither experienced a sense of needing to search for personal answers nor made any strong commitment to a given perspective in life. As Marcia states, "he is either uninterested in ideological matters or takes a smorgasbord approach in which one outlook seems as good to him as another and he is not averse to sampling from all" (p. 552).

At the other extreme is the *identity-achieved* youth. These youths not only report a period of struggle and exploration about occupational, political, and religious matters but bring this struggle to a meaningful closure through decisions on each. Their commitments are strong and well defined. Their pathways are vividly marked. Although identity-achieved youths can be convinced to change their minds, it takes a great deal of effort and thought before they are willing to change commitments.

In between these two extremes are foreclosed and moratorium adolescents. The *foreclosed* adolescent shares with the identity-achieved youth a sense of commitment, but the quality of this commitment and the manner in which it is derived vary tremendously. The foreclosed youths does not experience struggle or a state of crisis. Instead, these young people assume a commitment handed to them by others—most often their parents. Such adolescents are capable of expressing a commitment but cannot describe how they acquired it or they state that what is good enough for their parents is good enough for them.

TABLE **4-2**   **Sample Items from The Objective Measure of Ego-Identity Status**

Status	Item
Diffusion	I haven't chosen the occupation I really want to get into, but I am working toward becoming a "____" until something better comes along.
	When it comes to religion, I just haven't found any that I am really into myself.
Foreclosure	I guess I'am pretty much like my folks when it comes to politics. I follow what they do in terms of voting and such.
	I've never really questioned my religion. If it's right for my parents, it must be right for me.
Moratorium	I just can't decide how capable I am as a person and what job's I'll be right for.
	There are so many different political parties and ideals. I can't decide which to follow until I figure it all out.
Identity-achievement	A person's faith is unique to each individual. I've considered and reconsidered it myself and know what I can believe.
	It took me a while to figure it out, but now I really know what I want for a career.

Moratorium adolescents are searching for answers to many personal questions. In their search for personal commitment and meaning, they appear to be struggling with unresolved questions and offer to the world a bewildered appearance like the adolescent protagonists in the television series "The Wonder Years" or "Clarissa Explains It All."

An alternative to Marcia's (1966) interview technique is to study identity formation through the use of written questionnaires (Adams, Shea, & Fitch, 1979; Bennion & Adams, 1986; Grotevant & Adams, 1984). To illustrate this approach consult Table 4-2 in which we list a few questionnaire items to illustrate Marcia's four identity status categories.

For the rest of this chapter, we'll use Marcia's (1966) framework to provide a description of the psychological and social behaviors associated with each identity status, to examine the functions of identity, and to explore whether a person is fixed in a given identity status or is capable of changing from one category to another. Finally, we'll discuss the influence of the family on identity formation.

Psychological Characteristics and Social Behavior of the Four Identity Statuses

Diffusion

Logan (1978) suggests that identity-diffused adolescents use several psychological defenses to control the anxiety that stems from an undefined identity. Some adolescents temporarily escape the anxiety of meaninglessness by engaging in intense, immediate experiences that heighten their senses and provide them with an immediate, "right now" sensation. Thus, wild behavior at parties, drug usage, fast driving, or other actions momentarily ward off the anxiety associated with identity

The identity-diffused youth is prone to fads in an often futile attempt to escape their sense of alienation.

confusion. Other adolescents move from one peer group to another, establishing a temporary sense of belonging by peer association. Still others engage in fad behavior, such as extreme body piercing, multiple tattoos, outlandish dress and hairstyles, and other forms of extreme behavior. Thus, a *life of meaninglessness* is transformed into a *commitment to fads*.

Feelings of inferiority, alienation, and ambivalence are often reported by identity-diffused adolescents (Donovan, 1975a,b). These youths report poor physical, moral, ethical, personal, and social self-concepts (LaVoie, 1976), while maintaining a high need for dependence on others to structure their lives (Schenkel, 1975). Diffused youths are also likely to exhibit stereotyping thoughts and behaviors (Streitmatter & Pate, 1989). These findings are noteworthy because a healthy and clear identity depends on a sense of independence in making choices, which allows an individual to sort out, analyze, and structure their own environment. Further, for diffused youths, a less developed or clearly differentiated sense of self is observed on constructs such as moral reasoning (Halt, 1979), developmental themes of early childhood (Orlofsky & Frank, 1986), sex-role orientation and resolution of earlier childhood psychosocial crises (Prager, 1983; Selva & Dusek, 1984), cognitive development (Leadbeater & Dionne, 1981; Protinsky & Wilkerson, 1986), stages of ego development (Ginsburg & Orlofsky, 1981), locus of control (Abraham, 1983), and perceptions of the future (Rappaport,

Enrich, & Wilson, 1985). Simply put, diffused youths cannot identify the parts of a whole, and so they confuse their own sense of self with that of others. Think of a double-exposed negative in which people are blurred together, and you have a sense of the confusion these youths experience.

Other studies indicate that in meeting and relating to people, role-confused (identity-diffused) youths are tense and anxious. They display guilt and insecurity, suspicion, and jealousy in interpersonal contexts (Kahn, Zimmerman, Csikszentmihali, & Getzels, 1985; Vandenplas-Holper & Campos, 1990). For a moment, consider how hard it would be to present yourself to others if you have no idea of who you are. This uncertainty about the self would make anyone feel anxious and insecure. If identity-diffused young people don't know who they are, how can they share themselves with others?

Diffused adolescents appear unable to focus their attention in complex social interactions. Because their social environment is blurred they have the need to exercise considerable control over their environment. Thus, it should not be surprising that they view their social environment as very demanding of their energy and attention—similar to the individual with poor eyesight who squints and strains to unsuccessfully decipher writing on a blackboard (Adams, Ryan, Hoffman, Dobson, & Nielsen, 1985; Read, Adams, & Dobson, 1984). Collectively, these and other studies suggest that diffused adolescents are less mature than expected in their cognitive complexity and emotional and general individual development (Slugoski, Marcia, & Koopman, 1984; Streitmatter, 1989).

Further, Berzonsky (1992) describes diffused adolescents as avoidant oriented. That is, they avoid making decisions for as long as possible. Other studies of social behaviors indicate that diffused youths may be less cooperative in social interactions (Slugoski et al., 1984), more manipulative and deceptive (Read et al., 1984), more readily influenced by peer pressure (Adams et al., 1985), and more likely to engage in socially deviant behavior (Jones, 1992). In studies of interpersonal attraction, diffused subjects prefer others who also do not hold personal commitments (Goldman, Rosenzweig, & Lutter, 1980). Given this, consider how easily a group of teenagers with little, if any, sense of what they stand for or value and who are readily influenced by peer pressure to engage in socially unacceptable ways could get into serious trouble quickly. All it would take is one foolish youth pressuring others to do something that isn't right to start a tragic chain of events.

Overall, identity-diffused adolescents offer an image of a bleak inner life, barren of loving people (Donovan, 1975a,b). Studies suggest these adolescents cope with stress through social withdrawal, manipulation, and conformity. Further, diffused adolescents are the least likely of the four identity-status groups to have immediate or long-term intimate relationships with friends or lovers of either sex (Craig-Bray, Adams, & Dobson, 1988; Fitch & Adams, 1983; Hodgson & Fischer, 1979; Kacerguis & Adams, 1980; Kahn et al., 1985; Marcia, 1976; Orlofsky, 1978; Tesch & Whitbourne, 1982; Whitbourne & Tesch, 1985). Clearly, identity-diffused (or role-confused) youths are desperately in need of help.

Foreclosure

While identity-diffused adolescents are prone to impulsive acts (Waterman & Waterman, 1974), foreclosed youths are quite the opposite (Donovan, 1975a, 1975b). Generally speaking, foreclosed adolescents pursue quiet, orderly, and industrious lives. Interestingly, they tend to endorse authoritarian values, such as obedience, strong leadership, and respect for authority (Marcia, 1966), while maintaining a strong parent-instilled goal orientation.

Berzonsky (1992) refers to foreclosed adolescents as normative oriented. That is, these adolescents conform to the expectations of significant others like parents and teachers. Although many foreclosed adolescents appear to have lower levels of complexity in understanding themselves, a surprising number parallel the more advanced self-complexity levels of moratorium and identity-achieved youths (Adams & Shea, 1979). However, their self-understanding draws its strength from others supporting them. When the support of others is withdrawn, foreclosed youth become easily lost and confused, needing to turn to someone like a political or religious leader or something like a value system to provide them with new structure and meaning.

Evidence indicates that foreclosed adolescents have a strong need for social approval (Orlofsky, Marcia, & Lesser, 1973) and maintain very dependent relationships with significant others (Matteson, 1977; Orlofsky et al., 1973). One might think of these youths as enmeshed in a web of relationships without which they couldn't stand confidently. It should be noted that Kroger (1995) makes a distinction between adolescents who are in a "firm" foreclosure status (no indication that they would change) and those in a "developmental" foreclosure status (openness to change). It appears that higher nurturance seeking (caretaker enmeshment) and more frequent occurrences of early memory themes of security seeking are linked to firm foreclosures.

In two investigations of the relationship between identity status and interpersonal style, foreclosure was observed most often in loving and affectionate homes. Although warm and gratifying, parental behavior appeared to stifle autonomous growth for these adolescents. These young people remained cautious and dependent on others. They were hard-working, talkative, and constructive, but were unlikely to offer either creative leadership or direction (Donovan, 1975a,b).

Other studies show that foreclosed adolescents are less likely to establish solidarity in group contexts or to express their emotional tension (Slugoski et al., 1984). Drawing upon our own work, we have observed that foreclosed late adolescents have relatively constricted personalities, with less competitive striving and fewer analytic thinking capabilities than their peers (Adams et al., 1985; Read et al., 1984). When these findings are placed in the context that firmly foreclosed youth are extremely rigid in their commitments (Rappaport et al., 1985) and immature in their social behavior styles, one can see them as frozen in their developmental progression, rigid in their overcompliance, and generally unadaptive. However,

The moratorium youth is actively searching for answers to their identity.

as Kroger (1995) cautions, this last description is best applied to firm and not developmental foreclosed adolescents. Developmental foreclosed adolescents are likely, in time, to show some of these characteristics, but have the capacity to move beyond this form of rigidity and overcompliance.

Moratorium

Of the four identity statuses, moratorium youths are the most anxious of the four identity-status groups (Marcia, 1980). These young people are actively searching, looking, exploring, and seeking answers for their identity. The tension of the "hunt" leaves these youths understandably with anxiety. However, they maintain a stable sense of self-esteem, similar to that of identity-achieved youths (Marcia, 1980), while functioning at reasonably high levels of moral reasoning and cognitive complexity (Adams & Shea, 1979; Podd, 1972). They appear to be highly self-directive (Waterman, Beubel & Waterman, 1970) and yet are open to exploring alternative values (Munro & Adams, 1977b). On the whole, these youths lack well-defined goals and values, are highly explorative, and, given their self-consciousness, are able to describe their feelings clearly and deeply (Donovan, 1975a,b). Our own work indicates that moratorium adolescents are comfortable thinking about themselves and their ideas and see themselves as able to deal with demanding interpersonal environments (Read et al., 1984; Adams et al., 1985).

Overall, moratorium youths are introspective and explorative, actively monitoring their own thoughts, perceptions, and goals. Berzonsky (1992) describes them as information-oriented, where decisions are based on a wide and relevant body of information.

Identity-moratorium adolescents are highly active and social (Donovan, 1975 a,b). Their daily activities are less restricted than youth in the other statuses. They appear emotionally responsive and capable of expressing feelings of affection toward others (Donovan, 1975a,b). Thus, they are capable of forming intimate relationships (Fitch & Adams, 1981; Orlofsky et al., 1973). They use socially mature persuasion behaviors with their peers (Slugoski et al., 1984; Read et al., 1984) and, in contrast to their diffused peers, are less likely to be influenced by undesirable peer pressure (Adams et al., 1985). In general, moratorium adolescents, while searching for personal commitments, appear comfortable with others and are socially adept and effective.

Earlier we noted type differences in foreclosed identity status, so we ask, Are all moratorium experiences similar? Baumeister and his colleagues (1985) believe that there are actually two kinds of identity crisis. The first crisis, the *identity conflict*, is the product of multiple aspects of the self and incompatible commitments that need reconciliation. The conflict results from an inconsistency between a person's goals or values. In contrast, the second type of crisis, the *identity deficit*, is characterized by an inadequately defined self that lacks commitments, goals, or values from which to base decisions, actions, or choices. According to Baumeister and his associates, motivation crises arise when a person lacking guiding commitments struggles to make such commitments. They speculate that an identity conflict (the first crisis) results from situational demands that call for reconciliation. An identity deficit (the second crisis) is more likely to be produced by factors associated with the normal development of a maturing organism.

Both emotional states and corresponding behaviors are thought to accompany the two kinds of crises. Adolescents experiencing an identity deficit are seen as engaging in an ongoing personal struggle. They are likely to experience feelings of vagueness, preoccupation with unresolved questions, anxiety, feelings of confusion, and self-consciousness associated with rumination, and occasional bewilderment. These underlying subjective experiences fuel an emotional conflict between the desire to obtain commitment and the reluctance to give up future possibilities.

The hallmark subjective experience of identity conflict is the feeling of being in an impossible situation in which one cannot act without betraying oneself or loyalty to another. Feelings of guilt and difficulty in maintaining dignity are common. The subjective experience of being torn between incompatible commitments does not call for new commitments. Rather, too many commitments are present, and resolution requires either the compromise of existing commitments or letting go of incompatible ones.

In this light reconsider Huckleberry's dilemma. As a pre-Civil war southerner, Huckleberry's social and religious upbringing taught him to view the slave Jim as property. Yet, Huck sees Jim not as goods but as a caring and loving friend.

Therein lies the conflict. The commitment to a friend clashes with his commitment to the norms of society. As we know, Huck resolves this personal crisis by letting go of conventional teachings and establishing for himself a new set of social rules that places his friendship with Jim above all else.

How are identity crises resolved? Baumeister and his colleagues (1985) suggest that the resolution of an identity deficit is a two-step process. The first step involves values and the second addresses instrumental issues. The resolution of the first aspect of identity requires *rumination about values and beliefs*. It requires that the individual examine abstract and vaguely defined constructs, define them, and establish a set of consistent values. Instrumental resolution involves *translating the abstract values into goals* and the corresponding ways of fulfilling them. So when Huck decides to renounce southern society's values toward Blacks and to reject religious teachings about stealing property and replace them with a personal code of conduct that places friendship above both, he has engaged in instrumental resolution. In contrast, an identity conflict requires resolving which critical value will be assumed over another or which behavior will be acceptable over another. This may require only a single step.

Identity Achievement

Identity-achieved youths have the most complex, highly adaptive personality profile of the four identity-status groups. These adolescents have the highest levels of cognitive complexity (Adams & Shea, 1979), moral-reasoning abilities (Podd, 1972; Rowe & Marcia, 1980), self-esteem (Adams, Shea, & Fitch, 1979; Bruer, 1973), and reflective (or analytic) cognitive style (Berzonsky, 1992; Leadbeater & Dionne, 1981; Protinsky & Wilkerson, 1986; Waterman & Waterman, 1974). Other evidence suggests that identity-achieved adolescents are future oriented and

Identity-achieved youth are comfortable with themselves.

are capable of recognizing things to come in their futures (Freilino & Hummel, 1985; Protter, 1973; Rappaport et al., 1985). This is important because they see more about the world, plan more for what is to come, and prepare more thoroughly for what is needed to become successful.

In concept-attainment tasks, like those associated with school experiences, identity-achieved youths are capable of outperforming other identity-status groups (Marcia, 1966). In school they often obtain higher grades (Cross & Allen, 1970) and report greater satisfaction with their schooling experiences (Waterman & Waterman, 1970). When placed in high-conformity, stressful situations, identity-achieved youths are less inclined to conform (Toder & Marcia, 1973). Further, when they do conform, they do so for the sake of achievement (Adams et al., 1985). In general, these youths live orderly, active (Donovan, 1975a), and self-directed lives (Donovan, 1975b).

The personality and social profiles of identity-achieved adolescents suggest a harmony between individuation and social needs for relatedness (Orlofsky & Frank, 1986). Studies suggest that these adolescents show strong positive characteristics reflecting self-confidence, security, social adeptness, psychological complexity, and emotional maturity (Adams et al., 1985; Ginsburg & Orlofsky, 1981; Josselson, 1982; Kahn et al., 1985; Kroger, 1985; Prager, 1982; Rappaport et al., 1985; Selva & Dusek, 1984; Slugoski et al., 1984).

According to Waterman (1984, 1992) complexity in the level of individualism is associated with social adeptness, social intimacy, and social relatedness. For example, social-behavioral studies show that identity-achieved adolescents are not likely to conform to peer pressure except when it is needed to be successful (Adams et al., 1985). They are likely to use highly effective social-interaction and social-influence behaviors in working with and dealing with others (Read et al., 1984; Slugoski et al., 1984). And identity-achieved youth are the most likely of the four identity-status groups to have made deep commitments to same-sex friends and to have established strong heterosexual relationships (Craig-Bray et al., 1988; Fitch & Adams, 1981; Kacerguis & Adams, 1980; Kahn et al., 1985; Whitbourne & Tesch, 1985). As such, we suspect that youths with highly differentiated and complex personalities have more to give to others in their relationships and may have more coping skills in relating to others (for a comparison of identity statuses for women see Box 4-1).

The Functions of Identity

A primary assumption underlying this discussion of identity formation is that personality serves several functions for behavior (Baumeister & Muraven, 1996). We believe that, as the central core of personality, identity does the following: First, it provides the *structure for understanding* who we are and answers the question Who am I? To quote the great psychologist William James, "It is the organized me." Second, it is the mechanism, or the ego structure, that *provides*

BOX **4-1**   **A Study of Differences among Women's Identities**

Ruthellen Josselon (1987) has provided a descriptive portrait of identity development between adolescence and adulthood for a group of women studied first in college and again in middle adulthood. Arguing that no one had looked seriously at how identity is organized for women, she focused her clinical interviews on this select population. Drawing on the hypothesis that career, achievement, and independence are issues of individuality that organize males' identity and that relatedness, connectedness, union, and caring are focal to females' identity, Josselson analyzed the nature of the four identity statuses for women.

Identity-diffusion women appear to fail to internalize important lessons from relationships and social experience. They have poor integration abilities and thus reject little as unacceptable. Hence everything and anything is possibly part of the self. Fragmentation of the self is externalized in the form of interest in helping others. Lacking organizing principles in the self—a reflection of low ego development—these women seek external authority figures to guide their behavior.

Foreclosed women focus much of their attention on family closeness and harmony. They spend considerable energy reproducing the warming lovingness of their childhood with their own family. They have a strong sense of duty, mortality, and values. They are hardworking, responsible, and able in their careers. Although not insightful, they are effective. However, foreclosed women reflect in their words and deeds concerns for security and safety reflective of early stages of psychosocial development.

Moratorium women, as a group, struggle to untangle their familiar ties and attempt to resolve their guilt for not having lived out family expectations and desires. As a group they need and seek relationships to help them build new identifications. Many use these identifications to move on into an identity-achievement status. Those who remain in moratorium seem to be caught in conflict and are unable to transcend it. Moratorium women need supportive others to help them arrive at self-definitions and differentiation of self. As a whole, moratorium women are insightful, self-reflective, and sensitive people.

Identity-achievement women are distinguished as a group in their independence. They strive to have an effect on their world. They recognize a need to find themselves and their own pathway to self-definition. In contrast to other statuses they have a considerable capacity to tolerate guilt. In their relationships they find men who are ego supports. That is, they form relationships with men who help them become less dependent on their parents and who are supportive of their accomplishments. In total, identity-achievement women balance work, relationships, and personal interests. They are confident, flexible, and successful—at work, in relationships, and at play.

Josselson concludes that women's identity is to a great extent a matter of whom they know and the relational connections they develop. Much of their identity is *anchored* in relationships with friends, mates, children, and partners. Indeed, women find themselves in the web of relatedness.

meaning and direction through the construction of reality. Third, identity enables the adolescent to make *choices based on alternatives*, thereby providing a sense of personal control or free will. Fourth, identity functions to provide an *integration* between values, beliefs, and commitments. Finally, identity enables adolescents to *realize their potential*. That is, it provides a personal sense of future goals.

Together, these basic functions allow for a core identity that gives meaning, direction, goals, and commitment to life. These aspects of identity push an individual to strive for consistency. They influence behaviors, social relationships, and social interdependence. Let's look next at identity development across adolescence.

Identity Statuses as Developmental Stages

In his earliest writings, Marcia described identity statuses as groupings reflecting individual differences at a single point in time between adolescents. Later, he wrote that identity statuses should not be seen as static but as fluid and developmental (Marcia, 1976). Several cross-sectional and longitudinal research studies have tested this last point (Marcia, 1976; Meilman, 1979; Waterman et al., 1974; Waterman & Goldman, 1976). The data from these studies clearly indicated change over time in identity status.

A careful review of the research literature on identity development during early adolescence has revealed that identity statuses could be detected in young people as early as the sixth grade (Archer & Waterman, 1983). Further, these reviewed studies showed that as grade level or age increased, the number of identity-achieved and moratorium youths grew, while the number of foreclosed and diffused youths decreased. A second similar comprehensive review of identity development drew similar conclusions (Waterman, 1982). Finally, few consistent sex differences have been observed in patterns of identity development (Archer, 1989).

These reviews support a position that identity formation is a central element in the adolescent experience. Still, as Erikson (1968) has stated it is at best " . . . a process of increasing differentiation" (p. 23)—that is, a gradual process of evolution from simple role confusion to a highly complex and committed role structure. Considerable scholarly work remains to identify the events that are associated with this transforming process (see Kroger & Green, 1996).

Importance of Ethnic Identity Formation

Clearly, forming an identity is a critical task for adolescents and is influenced by many sources. Identity formation is no less complex for the ethnically diverse adolescent and, in fact, is sometimes more complicated. In addition to establishing identity in a variety of ideological and interpersonal domains, ethnically diverse youth also face the task of forming an ethnic identity. Indeed, ethnicity is ever present in the diverse adolescent's personality and psychosocial development. Ideally, diverse adolescents acquire knowledge of their cultural practices and values in the context of a larger accepting society, and an integration of the two occurs. However, and not surprisingly, conflicting values between cultures often complicate the task of identity formation—especially when negative biases and stereotypes are projected onto diverse youth by the majority culture. Typical developmental progress common to all adolescents, like gains in knowledge, desires to belong to a peer group, and increased self-consciousness, make ethnically diverse youth vulnerable to rejection and criticism (Markstrom-Adams & Spencer, 1994).

Social scientists like Cross (1971) and Jackson (1975) have developed ethnically diverse models of identity formation. From this work, Atkinson, Morten, and Sue (1993) developed a five-stage *minority identity development* (MID) model. This model focuses on attitudes of minority individuals toward: (1) themselves,

(2) others within their group, (3) members of other minority groups, and (4) the majority group. Depending on favorable or unfavorable attitudes toward these various groups, five identity outcomes are possible. It should be noted that while these outcomes are called stages they do not represent development stages in the sense of being hierarchical and sequential.

Conformity identifies the first stage. It distinguishes those who hold unfavorable attitudes toward themselves, toward others of their group, and toward those of other minority groups. These young people maintain a favorable attitude toward the majority group that is shown by the high value they place on the majority group's norms and mores.

The next stage of the MID model is *dissonance*. This stage is marked by discomfort over the rejection of one's self, one's ethnic group, and other minority groups. Further, individuals are uncomfortable with their (previous) unquestioning endorsement of the majority group. While acquiring information that challenges (previously held) attitudes in the conformity stage, it is common for diverse youth to experience cultural confusion.

Some diverse youth assume stage three of the MID model, *resistance and immersion*. In this stage individuals appreciate themselves and others of their group. They feel some commonality with other minority groups, while displaying behaviors of own-group superiority. Their attitude toward the majority group is unfavorable, and these youths are highly concerned with oppression that is directed toward their group.

It is during the fourth stage, *introspection*, that the minority individual experiences discomfort over the rigidly held attitudes of the resistance-and-immersion stage just described. Questions concerning one's basis for self-appreciation and with one's unequivocal appreciation of the group occur. Further, discomfort is felt over the (earlier) ethnocentrism shown in judging other minority groups and the unfavorable attitudes expressed toward the majority group.

Atkinson et al. (1993) contend that the most desirable stage of the MID model is the fifth, *synergetic articulation and awareness*. In this case, favorable attitudes are held toward the self, toward one's group, and toward other minority groups and a selective appreciation is advanced toward the dominant group.

Similarities have been found between the minority identity development model and some of the identity statuses identified by James Marcia (1966). Phinney (1989) and Markstrom-Adams and Spencer (1994) link identity foreclosure to the conformity and the resistance-and-immersion stages of the MID model. Both of these MID stages are characterized by unquestioning allegiance to either the majority group (conformity) or to the minority group (resistance and immersion). Foreclosure, conformity, resistance, and immersion share high commitment to some identity and a lack of exploration in respect to other identity outcomes.

Identity moratorium can be linked to the dissonance and the introspection stages of the MID model. These stages share a degree of discomfort and questioning concerning one's current state in the identity-formation process. Also, earlier foreclosed commitments are called into question.

One identity status that does not have a parallel in the minority identity development model is diffusion. Diffusion in ethnic identity is similar to the acculturation attitude of alienation/marginalization. Individuals characterized by alienation/marginalization are not concerned with identity issues, are not in identity crisis or conflict, and are not identified with either their own group or the majority group. Phinney (1995) describes these individuals as (1) poorly identifying as a group member, (2) having little involvement in ethnic behaviors, (3) negatively evaluating the ethnic group, (4) preferring the majority group, (5) having little interest or knowledge about the ethnic group, and (6) having little commitment or sense of belonging to the ethnic group.

Regarding what experts consider the healthiest form of identity for diverse youths, parallels can be drawn between identity achievement, the synergetic articulation and awareness stage in the MID model, and integration/biculturalism as an attitude toward acculturation. Common to all is the belief that forming an ethnic identity requires careful, thoughtful consideration of identity issues. Internal examination and the process of challenging less mature forms of identity has occurred. The young person has an understanding of one's self in respect to his or her ethnic group, other minority groups, and the majority group. A firm commitment to an ethnic identity is obtained through this exploration process. Synergetic articulation and integration/biculturalism more specifically address the content of ethnic identity. The ideal form of an ethnic identity is proposed to be one that is rooted in the ethnic culture of the individual, while incorporating useful and helpful aspects of the majority culture into one's sense of self. Phinney (1995) understands ethnic identity as a continuum ranging from low to high. Research findings support this in that self-perceptions that are representative of the integrated/bicultural orientation have been associated with more positive feelings toward the self among ethnic-minority adolescents (Phinney, 1992; Phinney & Chavira, 1992; Phinney et al., 1992).

Family Contributions to Identity Formation

Several reviews offer strong evidence for the importance of the family in identity development (Grotevant, 1983; Marcia, 1980; Matteson, 1977; Baumeister & Muraven, 1996). A synopsis of these reviews indicates that different parental factors are associated with each identity status. For example, diffused adolescents appear to come from rejecting and detached families. In these families, the father is often absent due to either separation or divorce. The fathers who are at home are not very encouraging of the adolescent and are negative toward the adolescent.

Foreclosed youths seem to come from child-centered families in which the parents demonstrate intrusive and child-possessive behaviors. The parents of foreclosed adolescents appear highly encouraging and supportive, with one or both parents assuming a dominant leadership role in the home. Family members express very low levels of emotion and appear to show little encouragement of individual differences. There is evidence of strong pressures to conform to family values and beliefs.

Studies suggest that moratorium youths, particularly males, struggle to separate themselves from their mothers. The homes of these youths are generally active. Autonomy and self-expression appear to be encouraged, as are individual differences in expression and behavior.

Finally, identity-achieved youths view their parents in positive but occasionally ambivalent terms. These youths seem to come from homes with high praise, minimal parental control, and secure attachments (Kroger & Haslett, 1988). One investigation suggests that identity-achieved males, in particular, are as likely to come from homes with fathers absent as from homes with fathers present (Crossman, Shea, & Adams, 1980). Indeed, a slightly higher proportion of identity-achieved males may come from single-parent homes in which the mothers provide important early experiences for their sons' occupational-identity development.

Three of our studies have examined adolescents' and parents' perceptions of family relationships among the four types of identity statuses (Adams, 1985; Adams & Jones, 1983; Campbell, Adams, & Dobson, 1984). As Fig. 4-1 indicates, the data corroborate the conclusions drawn from previous reviews. Diffused youths experience rejection and low levels of affection. Foreclosed adolescents have affectionate and possible emotionally enmeshed family lives.break Moratorium and identity-achieved youths come from homes that are affectionate and encouraging

Foreclosed adolescents have affectionate and possibly emotionally enmeshed family lives.

FIGURE 4-1

A summary of family correlates associated with individual differences in identity formation during middle and late adolescence. (*Source:* Conclusions drawn from G. R. Adams, "Family Correlates of Female Adolescents' Ego-Identity Development." *Journal of Adolescence*, 1985, *8*, pp. 69–82; E. Campbell, G. R. Adams and W. R. Dobson "Familial Correlates of Identity Formation in Late Adolescence: A study of the Predictive Utility of Connectedness and Individuality in Family Relations," *Journal of Youth and Adolescence*, 1984, *13*, pp. 509–525; and G. R. Adams & R. M. Jones, "Female Adolescence Identity Development." *Developmental Psychology*, 1983. *19*, pp. 249–256.)

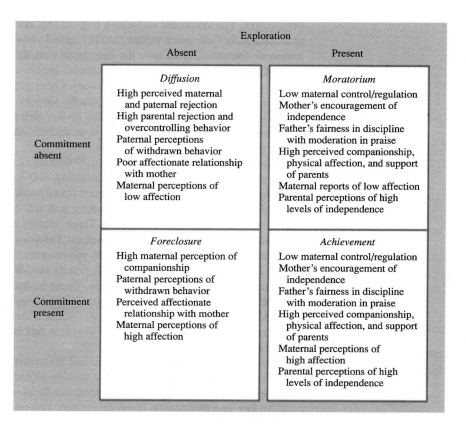

and provide strong independence training. Finally, Adams and Montemayor (1988) have completed several longitudinal studies showing that a warm home life that allows for a moderate degree of disagreement creates an environment for psychological growth in individuation (see Adams, Dyk, & Bennion, 1987; Bosma & Gerrits, 1985).

Normality versus Pathology in Identity

From the beginning, Erikson was interested in abnormal development in identity formation. In his early work he focused on acute identity diffusion. Even though Erikson has written on this issue, surprisingly little research has been completed on the distinctions between normality and pathology in identity. From a psychiatric perspective, identity diffusion involves a marked tendency to manifest contradictory character traits (arrogance versus timidity, greed versus self-denial, and the like); temporal discontinuity in how the individual sees the past, present, or future; a lack of authenticity; feelings of emptiness; gender- or sex-role diffusion; and possibly problems with a sense of ethnicity (Akhtar,1984). Some psychiatric classifications can result in such diverse categories as psychotic identity distur- bances, multiple-personality disorders, or adolescent identity crises. Still other professionals suggest that a narcissistic personality disorder is an appropriate def- inition for identity diffusion (Adams & Markstrom, 1987).

The nomenclature of the American Psychiatric Association indicates that identity-diffused adolescents are excessively self-focused and self-conscious. Adams, Abraham, and Markstrom (1989) conducted research to determine whether excessive self-focusing and self-consciousness were evident among identity- diffused adolescents. Three studies were completed to investigate the self-focusing and self-conscious behaviors of diffused, foreclosed, moratorium, and identity- achieved adolescents. Consistently, evidence was found linking identity-diffusion with overly self-focused behavior, self-consciousness, and extreme self-awareness. Hopefully, these pilot investigations will encourage research interest in the char- acteristics of acute identity disorders, as far too little attention has been given to this important research question.

Conclusion

We began this chapter with a discussion of one of America's most famous liter- ary characters, Huckleberry Finn. Mark Twain created a fictional character whose life was changed by the compassion shown to him by others, adventure, difficult personal choices, and, ultimately, society's affirmation of his worth. Huckleberry evolved from the role confusion common to dysfunctional families, through a psy- chosocial moratorium and adventurous river journey, to making personal decisions and future choices. Fundamental to this transformation was Huck's acceptance of differences between himself and others, which became a consolidating force in his emerging achieved identity.

Many of us take the same general steps toward a stable sense of identity after experimentation, deliberation, and consolidation on roles, values, and beliefs. As young people enter adulthood, most have settled on foreclosure, moratorium, and identity achievement. Some, however, remain in a state of diffusion. The first group of youths are likely to find a productive and supportive niche in society. The latter (identity-diffused) are less likely to find adulthood a comfortable and productive place. And, unfortunately, many of the identity-diffused youths we have known ended up experiencing many of the social problems we examine later in this book.

SELF-CONCEPT

There are strong links between self-concept and identity formation. Erikson (1968) has suggested that the very basis of identity rests on the need to maintain a healthy sense of self-esteem. Individuals, through basic self-love needs, strive to define themselves in socially approved and acceptable ways. Only when the social system either refutes or fails to accept the value system of a teenager's sense of identity does the adolescent engage in self-devaluation. From our clinical and research experiences, we believe that a healthy identity provides the basis for a sense of personal competence, a positive self-concept, and a strong sense of personal worth. But let's turn to the individual who is recognized as the most prominent scholar to investigate self-concept in adolescence—that is, the late Morris Rosenberg, sociologist, author, and youth advocate.

Rosenberg described the major characteristics of a positive self-concept and then, drawing on several large-scale longitudinal studies of adolescents, established the association between self-concept and psychological well-being (Rosenberg & Kaplan, 1982; Rosenberg, 1979, 1982). While others have expanded on these associations, no one has yet done a better job at integrating the linkages. Thus, in this final section we focus exclusively on his seminal work.

Rosenberg believed that a good self-concept included a high self-esteem, feelings of "mattering," stability in self-concept, low vulnerability, a sense of personal control, low levels of public anxiety, and what he referred to as a "harmonious plane coordination" (Rosenberg, 1985). Drawing on the Youth in Transition Study, a sample of 2213 tenth-grade boys; the New York State Study, which included 1678 boys and girls who were juniors and seniors in 10 high schools; and the Baltimore City Study, involving 1155 students who were 12 years of age or older, Rosenberg assessed the degree to which each of the proposed aspects of a good self-concept was predictive of psychological well-being. Let's examine his conclusions.

Self-Esteem

Self-esteem is recognized as a powerful motivational force. It is thought to be based on a human need to be valued or to hold a positive self-evaluation. It does not mean feelings of superiority, feelings of perfection, or feelings of competence or efficacy. It refers, instead, to a sense of self-acceptance, a personal liking for one's self, and respect for oneself.

Rosenberg reports data suggesting a moderate association between low self-esteem and dysphoric (unhealthy) measures of psychological well-being. Dysphoria refers to hostility, embitterment, disenchantment, or other negative emotional states. Its opposite, euphoria, refers to positive emotional states and a sense of psychological comfort. In the three studies under consideration, low self-esteem was observed to be associated with a greater likelihood of depression, lower levels of happiness, more negative emotional states, greater anxiety, irritability, aggressiveness, impulsivity, and alienation. In contrast, high self-esteem was associated with a sense of command over one's life, willingness to take moderate risks, candidness, and feelings of life satisfaction. As Gecas (1982) has reported, adolescents with high self-esteem are likely to be both happier and more effective human beings. And to this we add that happy and effective human beings are more likely to strive to find a positive place for themselves in their schools, homes, work, and community settings (Gullotta, 1997).

Mattering

In contrast to self-esteem, the concept of mattering has been given little attention. It refers to the degree to which a person feels that he or she counts or makes a difference. Rosenberg (1985) identifies two types. *Societal mattering* involves feelings of making a difference in the broader sociopolitical events of society. *Interpersonal mattering* refers to whether one has an impact on specific significant others. Rosenberg argues that the essential ingredient of interpersonal mattering is feeling that one is the object of another person's attention or notice. Some obvious corollaries of mattering include feeling missed if absent, being of concern to others, feelings of being someone else's ego extension, and feeling that others depend on one. To us, this is the glue of social bonding, belonging, and being needed.

It is often observed that adolescents who perceive that they matter very little to others are highly depressed, unhappy, and report a wide variety of other negative emotional states. Furthermore, they are prone to considerable tension and general anxiety. Likewise, they express feelings of hostility, bitterness, and alienation. Such adolescents see themselves as unimportant, unnoticed, peripheral, and irrelevant to others. In Rosenberg's terms, they are dysphoric.

Stability of Self-Concept

A stable self-concept provides a consistent frame of reference from which to act. It promotes certainty and decisiveness. Rosenberg (1985) notes that there is considerable reason to conclude that a shifting (or volatile) self-concept creates a doubt about the self that is likely to be associated with dysphoria.

Findings from the longitudinal studies suggest that instability is associated more with general anxiety than with depression. Perhaps a better conclusion is that instability creates a volatile self-concept (Markus & Kunda, 1986) that is associated with uneasiness, uncertainty, and psychological discomfort. Early adolescents, in particular, may be at substantial risk when body changes are most pronounced and self-concept is least stable.

Locus-of-Control

Locus-of-control refers to whether people believe that outcomes are caused by their personal actions. Rosenberg (1985) states that locus-of-control increases steadily during adolescence. Further, a low sense of locus-of-control is associated with anxiety, impulsivity, irritability, resentment, alienation, depressive states, and low self-esteem. Thus, lower states of internalized personal control result in dysphoric outcomes in psychological well-being.

Scarr, Weinberg, and Levine (1986) elaborate on the connection between locus-of-control and self-esteem. Many studies demonstrate that youth who do well in school attribute their academic success to their ability. Failure is attributed to a lack of effort. In general, these adolescents assume they will succeed if they try harder.

As such, these youths have an internal locus-of-control where they believe they are in control of what happens to them. Unfortunately, other students believe that failure is due to factors other than themselves. They believe in external forces influencing their success or failure. This is an external locus-of-control. Adolescents with an internal locus-of-control tend to hold higher self-esteem while youths with an external locus-of-control control hold lower self-esteem (Henderson & Dweck, 1990).

Vulnerability

Self-concept also includes an individual's degree of sensitivity to criticism. Hypersensitivity, touchiness, and the like are characteristics of a vulnerable adolescent. As Rosenberg (1985) commented, "the hypersensitive person might be described as one with a 'psychological sunburn'; the most delicate touch generates the most acute anguish" (p. 228). As such, a vulnerable adolescent is most sensitive when his or her self-esteem is threatened. Derogation, criticism, scorn, or belittlement can become perilous experiences for the hypersensitive adolescent. But internal threats can also be critical. Inappropriate conduct, lack of self-control, reckless remarks toward others, or poor judgment can cause shame, remorse, or guilt. These negative emotional states can result in equally powerful internal threats to one's self-esteem and corresponding vulnerability.

Evidence (Rosenberg, 1985) demonstrates that highly sensitive or vulnerable adolescents are easily influenced by threats to their self-esteem. The outcome is depression and anxiety. Further, younger adolescents appear to be somewhat more vulnerable than older adolescents, with girls about twice as vulnerable as boys.

Self-Consciousness

Self-consciousness is expressed in two general forms. One form involves *public anxiety* in social contexts. Another form involves *preoccupation with the self*. In Rosenberg's (1985) review, he found that adolescents who were highly preoccupied with themselves were more likely to be anxious or depressed. Similar conclusions were observed for public anxiety too. Once again, early adolescents are most likely to be vulnerable to higher states of self-consciousness (Hauck, Martens, & Wetzel, 1986).

Plane Coordination

Self-concept is an enormously complex psychological phenomenon, with many planes or levels. We could speak of the plane of reality, the plane of possibility, the plane of self- representation, and so forth. Rosenberg (1985) maintained that the management of the various planes is a central issue in understanding self-concept. For the healthy adolescent, he proposed, there should be a harmony between what the adolescent really is as a person in the eyes of others, how accurately the adolescent sees his or her own characteristics, and the consistency with which the self is presented to others. A false front or facade, with the presenting self highly discrepant from the experienced self, is thought to be unhealthy.

Conclusion

Self-concept is a complex psychological construct, reflecting the essential ingredients of individuality within society. It includes conscious and unconscious components. Furthermore, it has strong implications for motivation, self-esteem, and psychological well-being. High self-esteem, a sense of mattering, low vulnerability, high belief in personal control, reasonable stability, modest self-consciousness, and good harmony between the presented and the extant self are thought to be the most healthy for an adolescent's psychological well-being. Further, adolescents are most at risk for dysphoric mental-health problems during early adolescence, which is associated with problems of self-concept and psychological well-being.

SUMMARY

Exhausted? You should be if you read straight through this chapter. Unfamiliar concepts in any field are difficult to grasp the first time. That's why we encouraged you to spread your reading over 2 nights. Don't be concerned if all the technical terms seem like Greek. Try to associate a character—literary or otherwise—to each status and you'll find that your recall will improve. In keeping with the major themes of this book, did you see how maturity and life events can influence identity? That's developmental contextualism. We used Huck Finn, but we could have chosen hundreds of lesser-known adolescent literary and film characters to map the journey to identity. It is one of the principle themes in the coming-of-age novels and films that crowd book and video store shelves. Given our interest in the development of ethnically and racially diverse youths, did you see and appreciate the increased complexity of being a minority in a majority culture? Finally, Mark Twain ,writing about Huck in the 1880's, helped us point out, yet again, that all the subjects discussed in this book are not unique to this time. Looking at the past can sometimes help us avoid falling into old patterns of behavior that didn't work then and will not now. Take a well-deserved break and remember that a quick way to review chapter material is to read the major points that follow.

MAJOR POINTS TO REMEMBER

1. Psychological well-being includes aspects of self-confidence, perceived ability to perform well, self-efficacy, psychological comfort, and feeling good about oneself. Aspects of self-development that are correlated with

psychological well-being include self-esteem, mattering, stability, locus-of-control, vulnerability, self-consciousness, and plane coordination.

2. Identity formation is a dynamic process of structuring elements of personality that summarize individual accomplishments.

3. An identity crisis is a period of intense exploration and searching for acceptable commitments.

4. Four labels for the stages in identity formation are diffusion, foreclosure, moratorium, and identity achievement.

5. Over the course of the high school and college years, both male and female adolescents are inclined to progress from diffusion to more advanced identity statuses.

6. An advanced identity status has been shown to be a possible correlate but not a cause of intimacy development.

7. The formation of an ethnic identity is a complex task for diverse adolescents. The healthiest ethnic identity is thought to be one that is achieved and indicative of a bicultural/integrated orientation.

8. Each of the four identity statuses is associated with specific family-relations styles. Diffused youths appear to come primarily from detached families, while foreclosed adolescents come from extremely warm, overly indulgent, child-centered families. Moratorium youths appear to come from warm but highly independent families. Finally, identity-achievement adolescents come from highly interactive families in which the parents use minimal control and high praise.

Gender Differences and Sex-Role Development

WE BELIEVE ALONG with other educators that it's helpful for students to hold certain mental images or impressions as they begin reading about a new subject. Hopefully, as the student then reads, discusses, and intellectually manipulates the material still newer images and deeper understandings will emerge. Sounds very Piagetian, doesn't it?

As we begin to discuss gender differences and sex-role development, consider for a moment Fay Wray's role as the ape-desired femme fatale in the 1930s movie *King Kong* and Sylvester Stallone or Steven Segal in most any of their films.[1] These actors portrayed men and women in archetypal sex roles. Fay screamed and fainted whenever King Kong appeared and acted coy and desirable at other times around the film's male hero. Sylvester or Steven, on the other hand, displayed little emotion and even fewer words through most of their films as they confronted and dispatched evil in a most sober physical and often mechanical fashion. The message these films sent was that women were emotionally laden (archetypal feminine behavior) while men were rational beyond feelings (archetypal masculine behavior). Now contrast those messages with the images of Sigourney Weaver in the *Alien* film series, Carrie Fisher in the *Star Wars* film series, Dustin Hoffman in *Tootsie* or *Kramer vs Kramer*, and Robin Williams in *Mrs. Doubtfire*. These films suggest a more complex emotional and intellectual capacity for both men and women and that is what this chapter is about.

Before we proceed further, let's define three terms that appear often in this chapter. The first is feminine. *Feminine* refers to behaviors that historically have been associated with females. These are typically described using words like dependent, compliant, and emotional. *Masculine* refers to behaviors that historically have been associated with males, typically described using words like aggressive, tough, and daring. The final term is androgynous. *Androgynous* behavior is a blending of both masculine and feminine behaviors. For example, the male poet who races motorcycles, or the female basketball player who paints.

Incidentally, is one sex-role style more preferable than another? In her book, *The Lenses of Gender*, the noted psychologist Sandra Bem (1993) states there is no one correct gender style for males or females. Indeed, adult attempts to force children and adolescents into rigid roles are both unnecessary and constricting. Bem believes and we concur that the world is big enough to accommodate the multitude of gender roles that exist. In short, what is necessary is an increase in toleration.

[1] The concluding line to *King Kong* was, "T'was Beauty that killed the beast."

Fay Wray's character in *King Kong* depicts archetypal feminine behavior.

Toleration in this sense is synonymous with egalitarianism. *Egalitarianism* implies the opportunity for the equal sharing of roles and behaviors. If they choose, boys and girls can select to do both "male" and "female" things. From this perspective, choice is based on interest, not gender. Further, it is assumed that a balance will occur between couples in their behaviors and accepted roles.

In the pages that follow, we examine evidence that society is liberalizing its views about sex roles, and we examine the costs and benefits adolescents might expect as they grow toward adulthood. In so doing, we examine issues about gender differences and sex-role development.

What are gender differences? *Gender differences* focus on whether biological or genetic distinctions exist between boys and girls beyond their obvious physical differences. *Sex-role development* is concerned with the degree to which males and females internalize traditional societal characteristics thought to be associated with being female or male (Money, 1994). Let's begin our discussion by returning to the concept of egalitarianism and ask the question: Is there a movement toward role sharing?

THE MOVEMENT TOWARD ROLE SHARING

We suspect that egalitarianism is on the increase in North America. One way to determine if this suspicion is correct would be to examine census data for changes.

Looking at the past, for nearly all women, their identity was rooted in marriage and work in the home. Their duty was to be a homemaker and wife. The workday of this "traditional" woman would be spent cooking, cleaning, ironing, caring for young children, and preparing the home for the husband's arrival. While each of these activities is essential to the successful functioning of a home, the absence of paid wages at a time when the value of money grew considerably (1910–1918) gave their hard work a lower prestige value than men's paid work. If sex-role equity has indeed improved then neither men nor women should find themselves confined to these expectations.

In general, the evidence points to the broadening of women's and men's roles in today's society. To illustrate, since the Second World War, women and men have increasingly delayed the age at which they marry. Compared to first marriages that occurred in the 1940s where both partners were in their teens, today's females marry at age 24 and males at age 26 (Census Bureau, 1996, Chart 149, page 105). Delaying marriage enables men and women to pursue wider work and educational opportunities as shown again by the following census data. In 1960, 42% of women over the age of 25 had completed high school as compared to 82% who achieved this goal in 1995. Equally impressive gains were made in completing college. In 1960, 6% completed college. By 1995, this had grown to 20%. Similar gains were made by men—39% compared to 82% for high school completion and 10% compared to 26% for college completion, respectively, by year (Census Bureau, 1996, Chart 242, p. 159).

Similar observations for women can be made regarding employment status. While men have been expected all along to earn a wage, thus resulting in their labor force participation over the decades hovering around 80%, women's rates show a significant increase. The most dramatic growth has been for married women. Moving beyond single-digit percentage rates at the turn of the century, by 1960 28% of married women worked. This figure more than doubled over the next three decades such that by 1995 70% of married women were employed outside the home (Census Bureau, 1996, Chart 626, p. 400). This new ability to earn an income coupled with higher educational achievements gave women the potential for more decision-making power in their relationships with males (Gullotta, Adams, & Alexander, 1986). Whether that decision-making opportunity is exercised is another matter. For example, in one recent study where young people were asked to share plans about their future, more females than males spoke about marriage and having children at an earlier age. Further, female adolescents discussed futures that were more family focused than did their male counterparts (Green & Wheatley, 1992).

In addition to interviews, researchers can employ survey techniques to determine whether changes in societal expectations are occurring. For example, using longitudinal data, Thornton, Alwin, and Camburn (1983) reported a trend toward egalitarian sex-role concepts among females during the 1970s and the 1980s. In their sample, the endorsement of egalitarian behaviors correlated with being younger, having more education, and having spent more time in the labor force. Interestingly, behaviors like higher church attendance and a fundamentalist religious identification promoted the continuation of traditional sex-role attitudes. Findings also suggested that mothers' sex-role attitudes were important in shaping the attitudes of their children. Egalitarian mothers were more likely to have egalitarian children.

In summary, data suggest that society is inching toward egalitarianism. However, as Bem (1993) and the studies discussed demonstrate, this is not universal. While laws have been passed to make the workplace more equitable, while gains in educational achievement have been made, and while some groups express egalitarian attitudes, these behaviors coexist with equally strong traditional attitudes.

CONCEPTUALIZING GENDER DIFFERENCES

Recalling that gender differences focus on whether biological or genetic distinctions exist beyond physical distinctions between females and males, some social scientists argue these differences are inevitable because of biological destiny. Others contend that these differences have provided excuses to discriminate against females. Still others maintain that no meaningful or real differences actually exist. Let's examine the arguments for biological or genetic distinctions.

At the simplest level, we could state that genes rule. While biologists studying animal life commonly use the chromosomal distinctions that determine whether one is female or male to explain differences between the sexes in courtship, aggression, parenting, and other behaviors, one can question how useful this approach may be in studying human behavior (Montemayor, 1990).

A second perspective is *sociobiology*. This conceptualization, sometimes called human ethology, contends that genetically based evolutionary factors predict the differences between the sexes and even races. Ethologists support such assumptions through genetic studies with both animals and human beings. One position that human ethologists maintain is that basic genetic differences are predictive of control behaviors that occur within social groups, which result in hierarchical status differences. Thus, some individuals have a higher social status because of a genetically determined higher level of dominance behaviors. Studies with birds and with mammals are cited to support this position (E. O. Wilson, 1975). To date, the most notable ethological work with adolescents has been undertaken by Savin-Williams (1979).

While it may appear that the basic conceptualizations of geneticists and ethologists are the same, they are not. The genetic hypothesis assumes that chromosomal differences cause basic physiological, biochemical, or neurological differences that result in behavior. The ethological perspective recognizes that biological/genetic differences exist. But to that understanding it adds evolutionary development. Over time, differences evolve. Finally, it presumes a biosocial connection. That is, differences emerge in social status that influence behaviors like mate selection and aggression.

It has been argued that in our primitive past, dominance in the form of threat and appeasement assured access to food and sex.[2] However, Savin-Williams (1979) believes that the need for dominance and the prestige attached to it are more directly linked with the need to maintain self-esteem, self-respect, and self-worth. If you accept this position then differences between the sexes are due to biological bases that result in different types of control behavior for each sex. Ethologists suggest that males achieve social control and status through physical and aggressive behaviors, while females use interpersonal or social influence behaviors. If this hypothesis is correct, then it is very understandable why males are encouraged by society to focus on assertive actions like those seen in the movies "Die Hard" and "Terminator." In contrast, then, females are encouraged to focus on appearance, attraction, and social power. Like Scarlet O'Hara in the film "Gone With the Wind," a female will use her charm and beauty to try to achieve her ends.

For students who would like to explore this area of scholarship further we recommend a recent study by Anderson, Crawford, Nadeau, and Lindberg (1992) on the socioecology of ideals of female body shape. Using a cross-cultural comparison, these scholars explored the implications of food supply, climate, social dominance of women, and the value of women's work and the consequences of adolescent sexuality on girls to understand patterns in attitudes toward female fatness versus thinness and sex roles. The complexity of the ethological viewpoint is clearly detailed, and the journal article makes for very provocative reading.

Let's now examine several consistent findings regarding gender differences (Schlegel & Barry, 1991; Shapiro, 1990). While some of these differences may be due to the situational factors in which they are observed (Maccoby, 1990), others clearly are not.

Physiological differences. Animal studies, most often with rhesus monkeys, show that the male hormone testosterone produces different reactions in males than in females to the interest and care of infants.

Aggression. Consistent findings show that boys engage in more fantasy about fights and mock-fighting behavior than girls. Nevertheless, gender differences regarding aggressive behavior are not found consistently in areas like verbal communication or in competition.

Nonverbal skills. Females are more adept at discerning other people's emotions than are males.

Verbal skills or ability. While evidence suggests this trend is declining, females show better language skills and reading comprehension than males. This begins about pubescence but gradually fades as adolescents mature into adults.

Visual–spatial tasks. While differences are not observed in childhood, boys become better able than girls to identify seeable figures inside ambiguous patterns of dots or lines in adolescence. This distinction between the sexes continues into adulthood.

To these, three other central differences warrant discussion.

---

[2]There are many scholars and practitioners who would contend that date rape, wife-beating, and other forms of male dominance over women are an extension of this primitive past (Garske, 1996).

Aggression

Regardless of age, several major reviews of research on aggression have concluded that males are more physically aggressive than females (Eron, Walder, & Lefkowitz, 1971; Johnson, 1972; Maccoby & Jacklin, 1974; Reiss & Roth, 1993; Shaprio, 1990). While caution is in order, as females have been shown to be more aggressive in some family conflict situations (Lips & Colwill, 1978), the general assumption that males are more aggressive than females still holds.

A number of explanations have been advanced for this commonly replicated finding. Some have argued for an evolutionary explanation to explain the difference. That is, males became stronger, larger, and more aggressive than females to assure the survival of the group. Though a novel thought, it is difficult to defend with data. A more popular current line of thinking to explain sex differences in aggressive behavior is based on physiology. In this instance, some scholars suggest that aggression is associated with the male Y-chromosome. However, the findings in support of this argument are very mixed, as you'll discover in Chapter 13 on delinquency. A variation on this theory is that the Y-chromosome may be associated with a readiness to learn aggressive behavior, while the female X-chromosome may have an inhibitory effect that minimizes aggressive learning. Still another argument is that the male hormone androgen, produced in the testes, is responsible for aggressiveness. Indeed, a common approach to controlling the aggressive behavior of male animals is to castrate them—ouch!

Regardless of which, if any, hypothesis emerges as the explanation for sex differences in aggression, we believe that solely physiological explanations will prove eventually fruitless. Progress in understanding aggressive behavior will occur when models incorporate environmental factors that are compatible with the concept that human development happens in a rich environmental setting. By the way, that's developmental contextualism!

Influenceability

While males are thought to be more aggressive, women are commonly seen as more influenceable. In other words, in conformity or persuasion situations women are believed to be more readily swayed by another's position. In fact, a review of 61 persuasion studies, 64 conformity studies involving group pressure, and 23 conformity studies not involving group pressure showed that across ages women are consistently more readily influenced by social pressure than are men (Eagly & Carli, 1981: see also Eagly, 1987). We are not surprised with such a reported finding for adolescent women, given that our studies comparing adolescent boys and girls on empathic abilities and tendencies have consistently shown females to be significantly more empathic (Adams, 1981b; Adams, Schvaneveldt, & Jenson, 1979). Demonstrating strong empathic tendencies, females appear to experience an emotional attachment to or identification with another person that enhances their tendency to be influenced by that person (see also Camarena, Sarigioani, & Petersen, 1990). This judgment is bolstered by evidence indicating that females report a need to feel emotionally attached to another person before they feel they can share things about themselves. Conversely, for males, self-disclosure apparently comes before the development of emotional attachment (Adams & Shea, 1981).

Capacity for Friendship and Intimate Relations

Although both sexes develop friendships across the life cycle, there is good evidence that females are more interested and capable of developing and maintaining intimate relations than males (Brenenson & Benarroch, 1998). Judith Fischer (1981) has reviewed numerous studies of adolescents that support this finding. Her review indicates that girls have friendships of greater depth and intimacy than do boys in self-disclosure patterns, show greater depth in the topics disclosed to others, use friends for greater support and sharing, and establish more committed and mature intimate relations than do males in late adolescence. Fischer also reports data supporting the idea that females develop skills in relating to others earlier than do males. Other findings indicate that interpersonal competence is related to friendship intimacy during adolescence and that friendship intimacy is predictive of adjustment. It should be noted that these last findings are observed for middle but not early adolescents (Buhrmester, 1990).

The gender differences discussed in this section have been found repeatedly in studies between male and females across the life span. We believe these differences are based on biological and psychological mechanisms. While these differences may well be gender specific, they are heavily influenced by complex social factors (Jackson, Hodge, & Ingram, 1994) (see Box 5-1).

THEORIES OF SEX-ROLE DEVELOPMENT

To this point we have focused on gender differences. However, many of the differences between males and females are based on their acceptance of what they and society judge to be appropriate sex-typed behavior. This process of identifying and accepting specific sex-typed behavior based on societal standards results in a sex-role identity. Let's examine the theories most frequently used to explain sex-role development and then look at the personality, behavioral, and family-life correlates of sex roles.

Social Learning Theories

Within the field of psychology one of the most popular explanations for sex-role development is social learning theory. The basic premise is that boys learn "boy" things and girls learn "girl" things through society's encouragement of them to engage in sex-appropriate behavior. A combination of reinforcement and

BOX **5-1**   An Explanation for Gender Differences

The prominent developmental psychologist Eleanor Maccoby (1990) has provided a compelling account for why boys and girls differ in their gender relationships. Focusing on the common observation that children prefer same-sex playmates, she offers an explanation for children's interest in same-sex playmates and their avoidance of the opposite sex.

Maccoby suggests that the rough-and-tumble play of boys and their focus on competition and control are objectionable to most girls. Furthermore, because girls find it difficult to influence boys behavior, they try to avoid interacting with boys.

She goes on to state that two distinct cultures emerge during the course of growing up. The male culture (all-male groups) practices behaviors like interrupting others, commanding or threatening, bragging, oppositional behavior, and heckling. In contrast, the female culture (all-female groups) exhibit behaviors such as expressing agreement, pausing for a speaker, taking turns in speaking, and acknowledging another's point of view.

Maccoby suggests that the male culture has primarily an egoistic function, while the female culture has a socially binding function.

As boys and girls mature into men and women the two cultures are increasingly likely to interact. What happens? Often the cultures clash. To quote Maccoby (1990):

> People of both sexes are faced with a relatively unfamiliar situation to which they must adapt. Young women are less likely to receive the reciprocal agreement, opportunities to talk, and so on that they have learned to expect when interacting with female partners. Men have been accustomed to counter dominance and competitive reactions to their own power assertions, and they now find themselves with partners who agree with them and otherwise offer enabling responses. (P. 517)

Guess which group finds it hardest to adjust? Maccoby suggests that in heterosexual relationships women will find it harder to adapt than men. Do you agree?

punishment is used to encourage gender-appropriate conduct. Most social learning theorists contend that children and adolescents observe role models engaging in gender-appropriate behavior. These youths are reinforced for their imitation of such behavior, whereas they are punished for engaging in opposite gender conduct and activities. Underlying this theoretical perspective is the belief that one can then change an adolescent's sex-role behavior by changing role models or modifying reinforcements. Furthermore, because each culture role-models different images or messages, differences in sex-role behavior are accounted for by the nature of the roles being modeled.

This straightforward social learning perspective is clearly behaviorist. In the extreme form the behaviorist perspective focuses on stimuli and responses while ignoring any mediating variables, such as temperament or cognitive capacity. However, a cognitive social learning camp has emerged that recognizes that mental processes play an important role in sex-role development. In particular, it is assumed that as children or adolescents experience the consequences of their actions, they form expectancies about the likely consequences of future behaviors. Therefore, as expectancies emerge through reinforced or punished actions, they come to guide behavior.

Cognitive Development Theories

In contrast to social learning theories, cognitive development theories focus on the youths's concepts about masculinity, femininity, and gender-appropriate conduct. Thought is given importance over actual behavior. In these theories the ways in which children organize their thoughts about sex roles are viewed as organizing schemata (thought processes) that guide them in selecting information from their environment and actively organizing it. From a developmental perspective the schema concerning sex-role behaviors and attitudes changes as children mature, with both innate development and environmental (or experiential) learning recognized as important influences on how youths think about sex typing.

Several cognitive development theories have evolved to describe sex-role development. For example, Kohlberg (1969) believes that the basis for sex typing is children's cognitive organization of their world. He sees children as developing a gender identity early in life which provides them with the basic self-categorization of what it means to be a boy or a girl. This gender-identity schema serves the role of selecting and organizing information about what is gender appropriate. As the schema becomes stable or constant in a child's mind, it increasingly dominates how social information that the child observes is organized.

Kohlberg's point is that children have relatively innate views about gender identity. Once identity solidifies, it functions to select and organize information. Although societal factors influence the child's standards, the child's own thinking processes are more powerful in determining attitudes, preferences, or values about sex roles (see Box 5-2).

A second cognitive development model to explain sex-role development has been proposed by J. H. Block (1973). Using stages of ego development, she draws on concepts of agency and communion in describing sex-role development. *Agency* refers to the tendency to be individualistic or self-assertive. *Communion* refers to interpersonal harmony, altruism, cooperativeness, and group consensus. In Block's developmental framework, young children are individualistic and self-assertive (agency) and then move toward conformity with roles that are sex appropriate. In latter years, when they are capable of introspection and self-consciousness, the female and male are able to integrate aspects of masculinity or femininity into their sex type. As Huston (1983) writes, in an analysis of Block's theory, the content of sex roles is determined by the child's cultural and social experience, although maturational variables provide the structure for how children think about sex-typed content.

In all cognitive development theories, young people move from oversimplified, underdeveloped, or disorganized states of sex-role perceptions into a more stable pattern of conformity to gender-specific societal standards, with a final movement to greater selection, choice, and integration of both masculine and feminine characteristics later in life. In recent years cognitive development theory has been advanced with the application of information processing concepts.

BOX **5-2** **Sex Differences in the Development of Moral Judgement**

The way in which women and men make moral judgements about proper and improper behavior is another way in which theorists like Gilligan (1982), Kohlberg (1969), and Miller (1976) believe the sexes are different. From Lawrence Kohlberg's (1969) perspective, moral reasoning evolves with increasing age in youths. While his levels should not be rigidly applied, as young people can at different ages be at different levels of moral development, there is with age and higher intellect forward movement across his three levels and six subtypes. Those levels are:

Level One: Preconventional Morality
Within this level and other levels are two types of motivational behavior. The first is a punishment-and-obedience orientation. That is, compliant behavior occurs to avoid punishment by others. The second more-advanced type of motivational behavior is hedonistically driven. That is, compliant behavior occurs to gain rewards or positive reinforcement.

Level Two: Conventional Morality
The third type of behavior is motivated by wanting to avoid the disapproval of others. The fourth more-advanced type shows concern for maintaining justice, law, and order.

Level Three: Postconventional Morality
The fifth type of motivation is an effort to realize the respect of the community. The sixth and highest form of motivation is to act on internal individual principles of right and wrong behavior.

Kohlberg's sample for developing this theoretical model was boys. When girls were presented with the 10 moral dilemmas that required them to either obey authority figures even though the act would be harmful to others or to take another action, they scored lower than their male counterparts. Where boys averaged at Level 2, Type 4 (law and order), girls attained Level 2, Type 1 ("I want to comply so you will not disapprove of me"). Are girls morally less complex than boys? A colleague of Kohlberg's, Carol Gilligan (1977, 1982), and others (Miller, 1976, Miller & Stiver, 1997) believe otherwise. They write that the healthy psychological growth of women is rooted in their empathic use of growth-promoting relationships. In Carol Gilligan's work, she envisions a different moral pathway for women. Like Kohlberg her model consists of three levels but without subtypes. Those levels are:

Level One: Preconventional Morality
At level one, the female is concerned for her safety and survival.

Level Two: Conventional Morality
At the second level the female is concerned with being responsible and caring for others.

Level Three: Postconventional Morality
At the third and highest level, women develop a universal understanding and concern for others in which they become active decision-makers.

What do you think? Are women and men fundamentally different in the way in which they resolve moral dilemmas?

Information-processing models, like those proposed by Bem (1981) or Martin and Halverson (1981), hold that schemata consist of expectations that guide and organize an individual's perceptions. The sex-role schema serves as an anticipatory thinking structure that compels the young person to seek information that is consistent with currently held sex-typing attitudes. Information that is inconsistent with the current schema is ignored, transformed, or reorganized. Within this model, the sex-role schema is believed to be stable and not easily subject to change. This view of sex-role development sees individuals as active in the construction of their perceptual realities.

Psychoanalytic Theory

Combining emotional features with social cognition, Sigmund Freud offered one of the earliest theories of sex-role development. He wrongly believed that the foundation of sex-role development began with a child's sexual interest in the opposite sex parent. According to psychoanalytic theory, a boy sexually desires his mother and envies his father for the father's possession of her time and attention. Thus, the father is the target of the boy's hostility, and the mother is the target of his sexual impulses and interest. Recognizing, however, that his impulses must go unfulfilled and aware that an expression of those feelings could result in the loss of either or both parents' love, the boy represses his impulses. As a defense against the threat of these sexual and hostile impulses, the child engages in an identification process. Through this process, the child is thought both to internalize the moral standards of the more threatening parent and to transform his or her personality through socialization (see Fig. 5-1).

While many practitioners continue to use psychoanalytic theory to explain sex-typed identity, very little empirical evidence can be found to support it (Damon, 1983). Indeed, the evidence suggests that once a child has developed a stable gender identity, he or she will spontaneously seek out and develop sex-appropriate values and standards. Furthermore, because youths perceive what is similar to them as good, they will likely identify with the same-sex parent as a model. This identification process is completed when the youth develops a strong

FIGURE 5-1

Three theoretical models explaining sex-role development

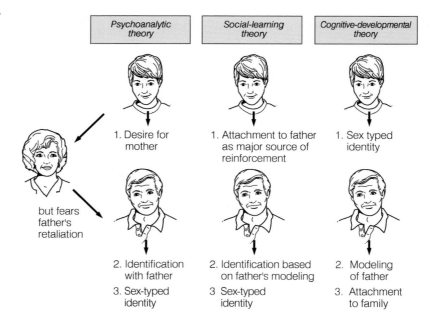

and lasting emotional attachment to the same-sex parent. This attachment encourages conformity to that parent's standards and role-modeled behaviors.

CORRELATES OF SEX ROLES

In 1974, Sandra Bem (1974, 1993) provided the seminal analysis of sex-role development identifying four basic sex types. Using this information, she compared four groups. Looking at Fig. 5-2, the reader can see that a *feminine* person is high on femininity but low on masculinity. Think of Fay Wray in *King Kong*. A *masculine* person is high on masculinity and low on femininity. Think of Stallone in *Rambo*. But two additional sex types can also be identified. An *undifferentiated* person can be low on both femininity and masculinity. Think of the androids in the *Aliens* film series. A person high on both masculinity and femininity is referred to as *androgynous*. Think of Sigourney Weaver in *Aliens*. (see Box 5-3).

In recent years, as old views of masculine and feminine sex types were challenged, new and broader definitions of sex typing emerged (see Table 5-1). These new views hold that caring, a feminine characteristic, or leadership, a masculine characteristic, are desirable traits irrespective of gender. Both characteristics and others enable females and males to display a wider and, in our opinion, richer range of behaviors. In contrast to the past when psychologists believed that masculinity for males and femininity for females were the preferred, if not the ideal, forms of sex typing, the prevalent attitude today is that both sexes can internalize instrumental and expressive characteristics and competencies. Contemporary theory proposes that the internalization of the socially desirable attributes associated with masculinity—independence, self confidence, and activity—and those associated with femininity—nurturing, helping, and kindness—in the form of androgyny, results in a healthy and adaptive sex-role concept for young people (Bem, 1993). What, then, does the research literature indicate regarding this assumption? We'll examine this question next.

FIGURE 5-2

Bem's categorization of four sex types. (From "The Measurement of Psychological Androgyny," by S. L. Bem, *Journal of Consulting and Clinical Psychology*, 1974, *42*, 155–162. Copyright 1974 by the American Psychological Association. Reprinted by permission.)

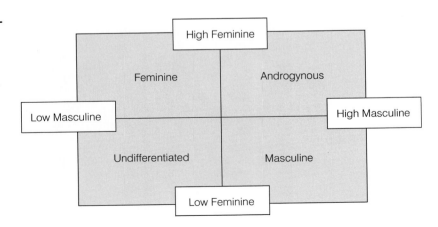

BOX **5-3** A Biological Connection with Sex Roles

The natural production of the male steroid known as testosterone in the testes and in females' ovaries and adrenal glands has been shown to be associated with a masculinizing effect resulting in increased body hair, muscular structure, and sex drive. Animal researchers have found that it is associated with aggressiveness, particularly for males. Baucom, Besch, and Callahan (1985) have tested the association between testosterone concentrations and sex roles. Measuring the testosterone concentration of saliva samples provided by females, they computed a correlation between the measurement and assessments of masculinity and femininity. These investigators observed that undifferentiated females had higher levels of testosterone than did feminine sex-typed women. Further, women with higher levels of masculinity (androgynous and masculine sex typing) had higher testosterone levels than did feminine sex-typed

peers. Likewise, self-reported data indicated that females with higher testosterone concentrations perceived themselves as self-directed, resourceful, action-oriented persons. In comparison, lower testosterone concentration was associated with self-perceived conventionality, well-socialized and caring/nurturing attitudes, and moodiness.

Studies such as these suggest a biological link between hormones and psychological mechanisms such as sex roles. Furthermore, these findings provide important information supporting an ethological view of relationships between biological and psychological processes. If these investigators had studied prepubescent, pubescent, and menopausal women, what association between hormone production and sex roles might we expect to observe? Can you think of other critical tests of the biological/psychological connection's influence on sex roles and related social behaviors or constructs?

Sigourney Weaver's character in *Aliens* depicts the feminine and masculine integration found in the androgynous personality.

T A B L E   **5-1**   Masculine and Feminine Characteristics

Masculine	Feminine
Aggressive	Dependent
Competitive	Compliant
Logical	Emotional
Rough	Gentle
Loud	Quiet
Objective	Subjective
Uncaring	Caring
Blunt	Tactful
World oriented	Home oriented

Source: Derived from I. K. Braverman, D. M. Brarerman, F. E. Clarkson, P. S. Rosenkrantz, & S. R. Vogel, "Sex Role Stereotypes and Clinical Judgments of Mental Health," *Journal of Consulting and Clinical Psychology,* 1970, *34,* pp. 1–7; E. Maccoby and C. N. Jacklin, *The Psychology of Sex Differences.* Stanford, Calif.: Stanford University Press, Copyright © 1974; and S. Weitz, *Sex Roles,* New York: Oxford University Press. Copyright © 1977.

SEX ROLES AND PERSONALITY

A search of the research literature provides support for the belief that undifferentiated adolescents have the least desirable personality profiles and that masculine, feminine, and androgynous adolescents have more socially desirable personalities. While clear distinctions between masculine, feminine, and androgynous behavior favoring one over another cannot be made, there are hints that androgyny may have advantages over masculine and feminine sex types.

For example, K. Wells (1980) assessed the adjustment of high school students based on sex-role development. In this study androgynous youths, particularly males, reported better social adjustment than other youths. Other research suggests that highly feminine females are significantly inhibited in their individuality, achievement, and expression of autonomy (Block, Von der Lippe, & Block, 1973), with highly masculine males being more prone to high anxiety (Hartford, Willis, & Deabler, 1967). Behavioral research has found that more feminine individuals (both boys and girls) are less prone to loneliness (Wheeler, Reis, & Nezlek, 1983). With feminine individuals being more interpersonally focused, this last finding should not be surprising.

Clinical investigations of sex typing have also provided evidence of the personality correlates of sex roles. For example, Shaw (1982) finds that androgynous people see potentially disruptive life events as less stressful than other sex types. In a mixed finding, Frank, McLaughlin, and Crusco (1984) offer evidence that when dysphoric states of stress (reflected by somatization, obsessiveness, sensitivity, depression, anxiety, fears, and hostility) were assessed, masculine women reported relatively low and feminine men relatively high degrees of distress. Thus, masculinity may be an enhancing factor for women, while femininity may be a harmful factor for males. Overall, however, a number of investigations reveal that undifferentiated adolescents are least likely to report socially desirable characteristics on self-concept and identity development measures (Schiedel & Marcia, 1985; Selva & Dusek, 1984; Ziegler, Dusek, & Carter, 1984). And androgynous youths consistently show the highest or most advanced development of identity, self-esteem, and self-concept (Lamke, 1982; Lamke & Abraham, 1984; Mullis & McKinley, 1989). Further, the more positive outcomes for androgynous youths appear to be associated with desirable or positive resolutions of earlier life crises associated with the formation of trust, autonomy, industry, and identity (Ziegler & Dusek, 1985).

Supporting the general observation made at the beginning of this chapter that masculine, feminine, or androgynous sex types are comparable, there are indications that androgynous youths may have a slight advantage. Those findings suggest that androgynous adolescents are more adaptive, flexible, and socially adept than their masculine or feminine peers.

ETHNICITY AND THE MASCULINE SEX-ROLE ORIENTATION

The term *macho* is taken from the Spanish word "machismo" and means the "essence or soul of masculinity." It represents "a system of ideas forming a world view that chauvinistically exalts male dominance by assuming masculinity, virility, and physicality to be the ideal essence of real men who are adversarial warriors competing for scare resources in a dangerous world" (Mosher & Tomkins, 1987, pp. 64–65). Machismo is linked with a patriarchal ideology, and both terms are commonly associated with Mexican-American, Puerto Rican, and other Latino males (Torres, 1998). Nonetheless, some evidence exists that these concepts may be gradually decreasing among Mexican-American families (Ramirez, 1989). More importantly, however, is that machismo is not limited to Latino males but is found among men of different ethnic backgrounds (Casas, Wagenheim, Banchero, & Mendoza-Romero, 1995).

Although machismo can be found in different ethnic groups, it expresses itself differently. For example, Harris (1992) states that masculinity among Black males is expressed in a self-limiting sense of demonstrated emotions. Because of historical influences like slavery, Black males have learned to conceal their emotions from others by demonstrating aloof expressions, detached behaviors, fearlessness, and expressionlessness. Such concealment is adaptive because it is seen by others as power, strength, courage, and pride which serve to insulate Black men from discriminatory and prejudicial practices. These behaviors also indirectly produce feelings of empowerment and elicit respect from others for the Black male (Harris, 1992). However, these self-limiting emotions (or "attitude") are also maladaptive and dysfunctional for Black males. Harris (1992) notes that exaggerated behavior such as fearlessness and detachment are conducive to the same-sex friendships that are observed in gangs. As the masculinity demonstrated in gang activity is not tolerated by the larger society, these young men find even greater societal rejection and encourage police attention.

Higher masculinity also was observed in Black and White young men's attitudes about gender roles (Blee & Tickamyer, 1995). While rigid gender-role attitudes existed with both groups, they displayed certain differences. For example, White adolescents were more conservative than Black youths on attitudes about women working. Otherwise, they were more liberal in respect to gender roles. Interestingly, both groups became more favorable toward women working as the age of the sample increased. From this last finding, we might speculate that rigid sex role attitudes diminish with age.

The appearance of machismo attitudes across North American ethnic groups underscores the importance of this issue for Canadian and U.S. youths. Indeed, Casas et al. (1995) contend that the highly masculine male is at risk in respect to feelings, thoughts, and behaviors. For example, Pleck, Sonenstein, and Ku (1994) found a clear association between a masculine ideology and problematic male adolescent behaviors. Regardless of race or ethnic group, problem behaviors associated with high masculinity were school suspensions, substance use, police involvement, unprotected sexual activity, and forcing sex on another.

The process by which male children learn machismo begins in the home and is encouraged by the male peer group in adolescence. Mosher and Tomkins (1987) state that a macho approach toward life is supported by the following:

1. Beginning in infancy and continuing over the course of childhood, parents socialize male children into becoming "real men." This is achieved partially by not responding to the male child's cries of distress until it is expressed as anger.

2. The expression of fear in boys is discouraged by parents. For example, boys are forced to stay in a feared situation until habituation reduces the fear. Ideally, in response to perceived threat and danger, fear will be replaced by excitement.

3. Parents exhibit disgust when fear is displayed. Eventually, the boy will feel self-disgust and self-contempt in response to his fear. A "real-boy" learns to confront fear and distress with anger and aggressive behavior.

4. The boy feels pride in his ability to repress fear and distress. Subsequently, he feels disgust and contempt for those who cannot do the same.

5. Due to the socialization practices of parents, a hostile-dominant interpersonal style prevails in the male offspring. Anger, pride, excitement, and other forms of superior masculinity are used to control others considered weaker, inferior, and submissive.

6. The boy discovers that a strategy involving surprise heightens his own feelings of excitement, as well as inducing fear in others and gaining control over them.

7. The macho male is suspicious of relaxed enjoyment and engages in continual excitement-seeking. Joy only comes from victory.

From Mosher and Tomkins (1987) perspective, machismo is rooted firmly in childhood experiences. Significant during adolescence is the reinforcement of these behaviors by the peer group. Judgments of the adolescent boy's transition into manhood are made by the male peer group in the fight, danger, and callous sex scenes. The *fight* scene refers to the youths's battle to gain admission to the male peer group. Acceptance and friendship are rewards for teens who demonstrate courage and toughness. The *danger* scene is evidenced by the need to engage in reckless behavior and to take on the challenge of "the dare." Engaging in sexual intercourse as a means to prove one's masculinity and subsequently to boast of such exploits in the male peer group is necessary to pass the *callous sex* scene.

Machismo demands a high price from the males who adhere to its tenets. Any feeling that hints of weakness and vulnerability is denied and dismissed. Honest emotions are suppressed and replaced by anger and feelings of power and superiority over others. Even positive feelings are repressed since they can only derived from experiences of success, victory, and dominance. Self-awareness is limited because the self is defined only according to traits that support the superior notions of masculinity. Relationships lack true mutuality and reciprocity; thus, the development of intimacy is hindered.

If, as Mosher and Tomkins (1987) suggest, the roots of machismo are laid in childhood by parents and perpetuated in adolescence by the male peer group, how might machismo youths desiring change be helped? Casas et al. (1995) and Torres (1998) note that even admitting the need for help is regarded as a humiliating experience for these youths. Therapy requires the disclosure of personal feelings and perceived shortcomings, which are likely to heighten feelings of vulnerability among these youths. These youths have been led to believe that therapy is a "female experience" that is needed by weak individuals who cannot cope and problem-solve for themselves.

Thus, the youth worker must be sensitive to the male's feelings of vulnerability and offer assurances that admitting the need for help is a sign of strength. Interventions that have been found to be useful with these men are educational in nature such as workshops, seminars, and classes rather than individual counseling (Casas et al., 1995). Since a highly masculine sex-role orientation is characterized by repressing emotions, these men need to be taught how to identify and express emotions. By aiding men to understand, accept, and express their feelings appropriately, more than the emotional self is given care. It has been found that men who subscribe to machismo deny illness. In denying illness, they delay treatment for physical ailments that could be life-threatening (Casas et al., 1995).

THE INFLUENCE OF SOCIETY ON SEX ROLES

What is the influence of society on sex roles? In one early investigation J. H. Block (1973) argued that society encouraged a more androgynous sex-role identity for males as they aged but reinforced females to maintain a feminine orientation.

While some data (Mills, 1981) support Block's findings, other data from life-span samples suggest otherwise. For example, Spence and Helmreich (1979) compared masculinity and femininity scores for male and female high school students, college students, parents of elementary school children, and parents of college students. In contrast to Block's assertion, with advancing age, male masculinity responses increased, while females showed no developmental pattern. Similarly, at all ages females were more supportive of egalitarian (role-sharing) roles for men and women than were males. Conversely, Hyde and Phillis (1979) compared the scores of subjects ages 13 to 85 on an androgyny measure. These researchers reported that the percentage (frequency) of androgynous identities was lower for males ages 13 to 40 but increased for older males. Females showed just the opposite trend; more androgynous females were found in the younger group. Recent replication studies find both genders becoming more feminine with age (Hyde, Krajnik, & Skuldt-Niederberger, 1991). Collectively, these studies suggest that maturational or environmental influences can change one's sex-role orientation.

Indeed, the results of a very creative study by Abrahams, Feldman, and Nash (1978) suggest that we identify with the sex-role orientation that best fits our current life situation. These researchers suspected that when individuals who were living together, married without children, married and expecting a child, or married with children were compared, major differences in sex-role preference would occur. The general logic was that the first two life situations would heighten androgynous (role-sharing) tendencies but that in the last two situations a greater division of labor would occur. The male would see himself as having to emphasize his career and financial responsibilities, and the female would emphasize child care and domestic activities. The results of the study supported this hypothesis.

Thus, major life experiences may reinforce masculine or feminine identities. Males and females can be expected to express sex-role identities that are best suited for social adjustment to their present life situation. For very young adolescents, this is likely to mean a very masculine orientation for boys and a feminine one for girls. To illustrate, when 7-, 10-, and 14-year-old youths were compared on dominance and nurturance measures, a developmental trend toward increased attribution of dominance to males and nurturance to females was found with age (Rothbaum, 1977). Other evidence points to older adolescence (high school) as the time period of highest stereotypical sex-role behavior (Urberg, 1979). With maturation during the college years, new life events appear to move many adolescents toward more egalitarian and/or androgynous preferences. Not surprisingly, given earlier discussions in this chapter this pattern of sex role behavior fluctuates given life circumstances (Bem, 1993) (see Box 5-3).

In a comprehensive review of the literature, Hill and Lynch (1989) offer evidence that an increase in gender-differential socialization accounts for increases in adolescent boys' identification with masculine characteristics and girls' identification with feminine characteristics. According to these authors, widening gender differences emerge during adolescence in self-consciousness, achievement, self-concept and self-esteem, friendships and intimacy, activity levels, and aggression. As boys

BOX **5-4** **Are the Youth Cultures of Canadian Adolescents Different for Males and Females?**

The term "youth culture" includes the social context, structure, dynamics, and content of social interactions between adolescents and signifies the every-day experiences of youths (van Roosmalen & Krahn, 1996). Most youth culture research has occurred in the public domain, which critics contend is biased in favor of males. Both traditional and feminist social scientists maintain that a distinction is needed between public- and private-sphere youth culture. Is this distinction evident among Canadian youth? If it is evident, what activities mark the public sphere and which ones the private? Using data from Canadian high school seniors, van Roosmalen and Krahn (1996) attempted to answer these questions. The activities of male and female seniors were assessed according to the domains of the home; the social sphere; the working environment; involvement in sports, clubs, and hobbies, and in the social sphere of the street.

A Home-Based Culture of Youth

Males and females indicated that they spend time hanging around doing nothing. Females were more likely to state that they "hang around," while males indicated they "hang out." At any rate, hanging around can occur at home, at a friend's house, in the neighborhood, at the mall, and other locations. Females were more likely to hang around at their house or a friend's house, which supports the concept of a home-based culture for females. In contrast, males were more likely to hang out at locations other than home (e.g., the mall or a park).

The home-based culture can also be examined in respect to television viewing. Although males and females were low to moderate in the amount of time they watched television, males watched more television than females. Females were more likely to pair doing something while hanging around or watching television. van Roosmalen and Krahn (1996) contend these finding support finding that home is more of a realm of work for females, but more of a location for leisure among males.

Social Youth Culture

Dating, cruising the streets, and time spent with family and friends were examined in respect to the social youths culture. Dating was one of the few youth culture pursuits that boys had a lower rate of participation. Girls reported dating more frequently than boys, and reported spending more time preparing for dates. Given the gender discrepancy in respect to dating, it may be that young men and young women define dating differently.

Boys were more likely to report spending time cruising the streets. Girls were more likely to report spending time at the mall or visiting and talking with friends. These finding are indicative of traditional gender role socialization in which males are oriented toward autonomy and women toward interpersonal connectedness (van Roosmalen and Krahn, 1996).

A Culture of Work Employment

Over half of the adolescents, approximately equal numbers of males and females, reported working on a part-time basis. In respect to work, then, there appeared to not be separate cultures for males and females. However, boys did work more hours per week than girls and took home higher earnings. More females than males worked in clerical and cashier-type work, and more males than females worked as laborers. Females more so than males were involved in nonpaid work, most notably, household work.

Participatory Youth Culture

Overall, 72.8% of adolescents reported involvement in sports or exercise, and 60.6% reported participation in clubs. It was found that boys were more likely to participate in sports and to belong to clubs. There also were gender differences in the kinds of sporting activities in which males and females were engaged. Boys were more likely to be involved in team sports than were females, and females were more likely to be involved in unorganized individual sports. The gender difference in orientation toward competitive sports is consistent with traditional sex-role socialization of boys being encouraged toward more-competitive and aggressive activities. The activities of women frequently reflected more passive, reflective pursuits (e.g., taking pictures or practicing an instrument).

More boys than girls also were involved in hobbies. Girls did engage in hobbies, but they were quite different than those of the boys. The hobbies of both genders were reflective of traditional sex roles. Boys were more involved with computers or working on their cars, while the most common hobby of females was sewing.

A Street-Based Culture of Youth

This domain was assessed according to alcohol and drug use. Drinking alcohol was common among both genders, but was more frequent among males. As well, both males and females tended to do their drinking in a party situation. Drug use was lower than alcohol use, and males more so than females reported using drugs.

Conclusions

The authors conclude from these findings that it is not appropriate to define a home-based youth culture exclusively for girls and a street-based youth culture for only boys. Adolescent girls and boys did engage in the same activities, but at different rates of participation. Gender-role socialization may account for some of the variation in respect to rates of participation. Nonetheless, although many of the activities of young women do center around the home, they are increasing there involvement in other spheres such as the work environment. From these findings it does not appear that young men are highly involved in a youth culture that surrounds the home, such as, meeting with friends at home or hanging out at home. Nonetheless, both young men and women are involved in the various social realms outside of the home, and large numbers of both sexes are involved in the youth culture surrounding alcohol use.

Do the findings of this study sound familiar? Have your experiences been similar or different?

and girls experience growth spurts, they become anxious and self-conscious about their appearance. In turn, they draw on stereotypical perceptions and behaviors to provide them with a sense of security. This behavior seems particularly evident for girls. For boys, puberty is often associated with greater adult tolerance for independence and more likely punishment for displays of emotion (Galambos, Almeida, & Petersen, 1990).

In a recent study on the family context of gender intensification in early adolescence, Crouter, Manke, and McHale (1995) examined the possibility that gender-differential socialization might occur in families in which parents maintained a traditional division of labor with more egalitarian households. In comparing these two family ecologies, the role of an opposite-sex sibling became apparent. The most striking results, in a complex set of findings, were that adolescents exhibited an increasingly sex-typed pattern of involvement in household duties from one year to the next when the parents divided chores along traditional lines and when there was a younger sibling of the opposite-sex in the household. The implication of this study is that gender intensification during adolescence may be linked to the traditionality of the parents and the presence of an opposite-sex sibling that pushes an adolescent son to become more involved with the father and an adolescent daughter to become more involved with the mother.

CONCLUSION

Some time ago, Joseph Pleck (1983) suggested that the concept of androgyny, worthwhile as it is, should be replaced by gender-role transcendence. That is, society should view an individual's competence based on ability and performance not on gender. Supporting this view, Sandra Bem (1993) states that gender polarization serves to drive people apart rather than to bring them together. While some would argue that these ideas are going against our evolutionary path, anatomical destiny, or some universal force, the goal of egalitarianism and its ultimate thought of transcendence beyond gender-role specificity appeals to us as a worthy pursuit. We would like to believe that people have evolved to a point where individuals, regardless of gender, can use their talents. This should seem all the more important in a society where democratic ideals of freedom and individuality provide the basic foundation for so many ideals, principles, and rights.

As you reflect on the material you've just read, how does it feel? Do you agree that from a historical standpoint changes have occurred in how men and women relate to each other? Is this job related or have other factors interceded? From the standpoint of developmental contextualism, do you see gender differences and sex roles emerging from a single viewpoint or from a variety of viewpoints? Finally, where pride can insulate diverse youths from harm, did you see where that same pride can create difficulties for young people? Before you close your book for the night, take a moment to consider these questions and your mental responses to them. You'll be surprised at how this simple exercise will increase your recall of material later.

MAJOR POINTS TO REMEMBER

1. Societal practices encourage a strong differentiation between boys and girls. However, contemporary society is changing in its attitudes.
2. Some have argued that society is becoming increasingly liberalized. However, research evidence suggests that attitudes about men's and women's roles are changing only gradually.
3. Sex differences involve differences in behavior thought to be based on a highly complex interaction between biochemistry, genetic differences, and socialization processes. Sex-role identity involves the internalization or adoption of behaviors thought appropriate for masculine, feminine, or androgynous behavior.
4. Most adolescents identify with or prefer either a masculine or a feminine sex role identity. A mixture of the two qualities is relatively rare in adolescence proper but begins to emerge during late adolescence, especially in boys.
5. Androgynous boys and girls seem to be somewhat better socially adjusted and have a greater capacity for forming friendships.

6. Machismo is a heightened form of masculinity found among males from a variety of ethnic backgrounds. High masculinity is associated with a variety of adolescent behavioral problems such as suspension from school, use of drugs, police arrests, and sexual activity.

7. The process of identifying and accepting specific sex-typed behavior based on societal standards of maleness and femaleness results in a sex-role identity. Social learning theories focusing on reinforcement, punishment, and identification of role models were early frameworks for understanding sex-role identity. More contemporary cognitive development theories focus on thought processes, organizational schemata, maturational factors, and organismic variables to explain sex-role development and behaviors.

8. Survey and interview data suggest a gradual movement in society toward an egalitarian, role-sharing view of family roles and living. Analyses of shifts in motives and values in need for achievement, need for affiliation, and related social constructs indicate that as females are making gains in need for achievement, men are responding with increased interest in need for power.

Physical Growth and Sexual Development

FOR A MOMENT, think back to the 6th grade. Do you recall being interested in the opposite sex? Now, compare those memories with these notes exchanged by two 6th-grade girls at the close of the school year:

Hi Nicole,

Did any of your boyfriends ever give you a hickey? They aren't bad. I told you about mine. I cried it was bad. I put ice on it. I could have died. It feels pretty good, but you got to get it in a spot where nobody will know it's there, Ray, the one I went out with, asked me if I wanted a hickey, and I said OK but put it somewhere where you can't see it. He said he puts them on the back of your neck under your hair. Well, got to go, bye again.
Michelle

9:12 Monday

When I was with Rachel, she didn't say anything about you or Julie. I think she doesn't know if she can trust me. Oh well, either way, it'll get back to you. Wow! Can you believe tomorrow's our last day of school? ROWDY TIME. Julie says she got a funny feeling this is going to be a *wild* summer. I hope so. But you still got to introduce me to Mike! He's cute, I hope you think so. If my mother isn't home, do you want to celebrate school being out? Try and get some booze. You said you drank. I hate the taste but I drink the crap anyway, Kevin drinks too. Maybe he'll get some stuff too. Well, got to go now. Write back please.
Michelle

This early adolescent correspondence shows the power of peer influence, budding sexuality, experimentation with adult roles, and the parent's continued role as moral guide. When we read this correspondence, it recalls for us, as we hope it does for you, a time of attempting to understand the changes in our bodies and learn what certain terms meant—words like "hickey," "french kiss," or "petting"—and wondering at age 12 whether we did it or it was done to us. In remembering these and other experiences, we laughed so as not to cry, for these were serious issues—of body size and appearance, of intimacy and relationships, and, importantly, issues of sexuality.

Today, as we approach the close of one millennium to enter another, these issues are ever-so-real for young people. Adolescence is filled with concerns about growth, physical appearance, relationships, intimacy, and a growing interest with sexuality. These concerns have two origins. The first is the biological process that transforms children into individuals capable of creating life. The second is the developmental–contextual process surrounding young people that seeks to discourage them from the use of their reproductive functions. In this chapter, we examine several aspects of adolescent physical development and then explore several of the issues that today's young people confront as their sexuality emerges.

PHYSICAL AND BIOLOGICAL ASPECTS OF PUBERTY

Have you ever given any thought to the word "puberty"? We mean its *meaning*. If you look it up in a dictionary, you'll find it is derived from the Latin *puber* meaning "adult." Most dictionaries define it as the period of life in which one passes from childhood to maturity. That's interesting, isn't it? It would seem the Romans and the wordsmiths have skipped over adolescence—a time by today's understanding of ever-so-gradual maturity. Puberty doesn't just happen. It is a complex physiological process that begins in childhood and slowly unfolds to the point of highly visible changes most often appearing during the teenage years (Warren, 1983). Puberty has three markers. The first is a spurt in physical growth. Young people add both height and weight to their frames during this time. Next is the maturation and regulation of body hormonal activity. The fits and starts of hormonal releases associated with early adolescence reach their highest levels of activity in middle adolescence to begin a gradual decline over the rest of the life span. The third marker of puberty is the appearance of hair in the area of the genitals, under the arms, and on the face. For females, the breast begins to develop, and for males, the testes descend. Collectively, these changes are referred to as the appearance of secondary sex characteristics.

THE HORMONAL BASIS OF PUBERTY

"It must be the hormones!" is one of those statements of frustration that parents are apt to make when an adolescent rockets off to new worlds or crashes mightily to the ground. There is considerable truth in this observation. The onset of puberty is essentially regulated by endocrine glands like the pituitary, thyroid, and adrenals, which secrete chemicals called hormones into the bloodstream or through the lymphatic system.[1] These hormones interact with existing cells to create biological changes in the organism.

One of the endocrine glands, the *pituitary*, is referred to as the "master gland" for puberty. A small oval-shaped organ attached to the base of the brain, its chemical secretions control the other endocrine glands influencing growth, metabolism, and other aspects of development.[2] In turn, the pituitary is controlled by the *hypothalamus*. While the pituitary gland controls the general level of endocrine

---

[1] The lymphatic system is an interconnected system of spaces between tissues and organs by which a watery liquid called lymph circulates. Lymph carries hormones, removes bacteria, and undertakes several other vital functions.

[2] Gland is derived from the Latin word "glans" meaning "acorn."

production, it is the hypothalamus that instructs the pituitary gland on the optimum level of hormone secretion. Think of it as a kind of a command central-to-dispatcher relationship.

Once instructed by the hypothalamus, the pituitary gland secretes hormones known as gonadotropins, which activate the testes, the ovaries, and parts of the endocrine system called the *gonads*, which are responsible for the production of eggs and sperm.[3]

As the hypothalamus disengages its inhibitory mechanism, it becomes increasingly less sensitive to gonadal hormones. Thus, the amount of sex hormones secreted increases, and the child gradually moves toward physical and sexual maturity. Interestingly, pubertal hormonal maturation occurs about a year before changes in the body and its sex organs are visible (Daniel, 1983; Higham, 1980).

There is evidence to suggest that the hypothalamus, the pituitary gland, and the gonads working in combination conceivably could trigger pubertal change even before birth, but this does not occur due to an *inhibitory effect* of the hypothalamus until certain physical conditions are met (Higham, 1980). Some authorities believe that when a critical weight is reached, certain metabolic rates cause the hypothalamus to shut off this inhibitory mechanism. Evidence suggests that a weight of 48 kilograms (105.6 pounds) is needed before menarche can occur (Frisch & Revelle, 1971). Other evidence suggests that menarche will not occur until total body weight includes approximately 17% fat (Frisch, 1983) (see Box 6-1).

BODY DEVELOPMENT

The most eye-catching physical changes during adolescence occur when boys grow taller than their mothers and girls begin to develop breasts and wider hips. These changes are striking and invariably bring comments by friends and family. Generally, girls are about 11 years old when this growth spurt begins, and boys are about 13 years old (Brooks-Gunn & Petersen, 1983). In both sexes the growth spurt is primarily associated with the lengthening of the upper body. Still, the legs reach their peak growth before the upper body, which happens to account for the leggy look of early adolescents (Petersen & Taylor, 1980).

As muscle tissues grow during this growth spurt, body fat decreases. Bodies look thinner, leaner, and taller. Generally, boys develop not only larger muscles than girls but also markedly different physical characteristics associated with musculature. For example, males develop more strength in relation to muscle size, larger hearts, higher systolic blood pressure, and a higher capacity for carrying oxygen in the blood than females (Petersen & Taylor, 1980). With this developing

---

[3]In females, the gonadotropin follide stimulating hormone (FSH) stimulates the growth of the ovarian follicles (these contain maturing eggs) and the gonadotropin leutenizing hormone (LH) induces ovulation. Both hormones interact to stimulate estrogen secretion from the ovaries. In males, FSH stimulates the growth of the tubules in the testes and affects spermatogenesis (production of sperm) and LH stimulates the production of the hormone testosterone.

B O X **6-1**   **Puberty in the Year 2250**

Imagine a toddler displaying all the features of puberty— a three year old girl with fully developed breasts or a boy just slightly older with a deep male voice. That is what we will see by the year 2050, if the age at which puberty arrives keeps getting younger at its current pace (Peterson, 1979a, p. 45).

Is Anne Peterson (1979) correct in her assessment? Evidence suggests that in Norway during the 1840s the average age for menarche was 17. Today, it is 13. In the United States, where children appear to mature up to a year earlier than children in European countries, the age has declined from 14.2 to 12.5 from the turn of this century to the present. Indeed, J.M. Tanner (1962, 1975), acknowledged to be the world's authority on adolescent physical development, has reported findings that the age

of menarche has declined an average of 4 months in each decade over the past century. Two centuries ago a pregnant 13-year-old was unimaginable. Today, it is possible, though rare, for an 10-year-old to give birth.

Why is this occurring? Three possibilities have been offered. First, the overall health of the population has improved. Thus, illness and disease, which stunted development in the past, have been conquered. Second, our diets are much richer in vitamins, minerals, and other healthy elements (not to mention fat and sugar). Thus, the opportunity to reach that ideal weight or percentage of body fat arrives at an earlier age. Last, it's the Greenhouse effect! The suggestion here is that warm weather stimulates early maturation. It works for plants doesn't it? What are your thoughts?

body, this young fellow will give his father serious competition in sports and other physical competition. Dad can no longer assume he will win in physical contests because of superior strength or speed.[4]

As noted earlier, there is also a major change in the width of the shoulders and hips for boys and girls. Before puberty boys' and girls' body builds are fairly similar. With puberty, boys' shoulders broaden more than girl's, while girls' hips widen more than boys (Faust, 1977).

Although changes in height and breadth are important, society gives greater notice to the maturation of the reproductive system during this period (Logan, Calder, & Cohen, 1980). This maturation occurs in several stages. These stages are: (1) the initiation of puberty, which occurs approximately 6 months earlier in girls than in boys; (2) the development of secondary sex characteristics, which takes approximately 4 years; and (3) menarche, which occurs approximately 2 years after the onset of pubertal change (Marshall & Tanner, 1969, 1970). It should be noted that for each youth the timing and duration of these changes can vary enormously (Slap, Khalid, Paikoff, Brooks-Gunn, & Warren, 1994).

Other markers of puberty also vary between the sexes (Angold & Worthman, 1993). For example, genital hair appears about 2 years earlier for females than it

---

[4]Remember in Chapter 2 our discussion of Kingsley Davis and the factors that served to separate youth from parents? One of these factors was the youth's growing strength to the parents declining strength. That tenet of Davis' theory has a physiological basis.

As adolescents grow older, satisfaction with one's body generally increases.

does for males. Interestingly, however, is that the time between pubic hair appearance and breast development in females is greater than the time between pubic hair appearance and genital development in males. The reason for this is due to endocrinological differences between the sexes in hormonal production (Petersen & Taylor, 1980).

The Psychological Impact of Body Development

Simply put, puberty is a powerful shaper of adolescent self-image. Whether influenced by hormones (Susman et al., 1987) or societal messages that define for all of us the body ideal, adolescents confront reality each morning as they stare directly into the bathroom mirror. On several aspects of puberty, researchers report the following findings:

1. The appearance of body hair has little psychological impact on adolescents. This is probably because hair growth is less associated with symbolic messages of sexual and reproductive meaning in our culture (Brooks-Gunn, 1986).

2. Overweight adolescents, whether male or female, generally have a poor self-esteem, a poor self-image, and are self-conscious about their appearance. In contrast, underweight females are most satisfied with their appearance (Blyth et al., 1980; Tobin-Richards, Boxer, & Petersen, 1983).

3. As adolescents grow older, satisfaction with ones body generally increases. Nevertheless, pubertal changes do contribute to stress and possible depressive and aggressive behavior associated with body image (Paikoff, Brooks-Gunn & Warren, 1991).

4. And finally, young adolescent girls often have a difficult time acknowledging feelings about their changing bodies (Petersen, 1979).

It is this last finding that we will explore more fully. In a review of the psychological significance of puberty for girls, Jean Brooks-Gunn (1986) notes that menarche portends increasing social maturity, perceived and real peer prestige, self-esteem, heightened self-awareness of one's body, and increased self-consciousness (see also Koff, Rierdan, & Jacobson, 1981; Simmons, Blyth, & McKinney, 1983).

However, menarche is also associated with a mixture of positive and negative emotions. In one study, Brooks-Gunn reported about 20% having positive emotions about menarche, 20% reported negative emotions, 20% had mixed emotions, and the rest had neutral emotions (Ruble & Brooks-Gunn, 1982). Likewise, it appears that early-maturing girls who are unprepared for menarche report more negative experiences and emotions than do on-time or prepared peers. To test this assumption, two researchers compared premenarcheal and postmenarcheal 6th-grade girls on a commonly used depression scale. Their results confirmed the assumption that very early menarche is associated with higher levels of depression (Rierdan & Koff, 1991). Interestingly, these researchers did not observe signs of depression in young women whose menarche experience began in the 7th grade assumedly when the menarche is a normative experience.

Another puberty issue for girls is breast development. Once again, Jean Brooks-Gunn (1986) reports that breast growth is associated generally with higher reported adjustment, more positive body image, and more positive peer relations. However, there are also negative experiences. Early-developing girls report considerable teasing about their breast growth, with most of it coming from mothers, fathers, and female peers (Brooks-Gunn, Newman, Holderness, & Warren, 1994). The most common psychological reactions by girls to teasing are embarrassment and anger.

Clearly, weight and other physical features have a direct bearing on adolescents' perceptions of themselves. Of most interest in this section, though, was the repeated finding that young females who matured before their peers suffered most. We suspect that it is the separation experience from their same-sex peers combined with the added attention their appearance brings from others that is responsible for their discomfort. Next, we'll look closer at how body development affects relationships with family and peers.

The Social Impact of Body Development

How does body development affect adolescents' relations with family members and peers? Studies suggest the following:

1. Boys midway through puberty are more assertive and disruptive with their families than either prepubertal or late pubertal boys (Steinberg & Hill, 1978).

2. During puberty, boys become more assertive with their mothers. Generally speaking, mothers respond to this assertiveness with equal assertion or with anger to their sons' behavior. This pattern of mother–son interaction draws father into taking a more assertive stance toward the son, with the outcome typically being less assertiveness by the son toward the mother. Over time tensions decrease, and the family interaction pattern again assumes a relatively stable state (Steinberg, 1979). We should recognize that while stability has returned each family member has likely learned a new lesson. That is, the son is growing up and is to be recognized as an increasingly mature person (Bulcroft, 1991).

3. Like their male counterparts, relationships between girls and their mothers become more stressful with the onset of menses. However, it appears mother–daughter conflict decreases to premenarcheal levels about a year after the onset of menses (Brooks-Gunn et al., 1994; Hill, Holmbeck, Marlow, Green, & Lynch, 1985a,b; Steinberg & Hill, 1978).

Recall how the sociologist Kingsley Davis in Chapter 2 saw tension between parent and child as an inevitable outgrowth of physical maturation. The child matures into prime sexual prowess while the parent declines into old age. This is one explanation for the tension between parent and child. Or using Sigmund Freud, you could take a position that the tension between parent and child establishes an incest barrier between the two. Thus, instinctive (sexual) urges are repressed. Or using a genetic position, you could attribute this tension to the less-than-regulated spurts of hormones that make living with an adolescent challenging. For ourselves, we favor a social learning explanation that sees tensions highest between adolescents and those most likely to be responsible for their daily care. Learned patterns of behavior and authority undergo profound transformation as sons, daughters, and parents strive to learn new behaviors that encourage adolescents' autonomy and social maturation.

Finally, an important investigation suggests that the onset of puberty can play a significant role in early dating patterns. This study examined the effects of school structure, onset of puberty, and dating experiences on self-esteem. Although the onset of puberty had little effect on girls' self-esteem in this study, early-maturing girls who had begun dating had very low self-esteem. Further, if they attended a junior high school rather than a K–8 school, their self-esteem was even lower. In keeping with earlier observations, it appears that girls who begin to mature early and who face new social circumstances are likely to experience higher levels of social/emotional stress than their on-time peers (Simmons, Blyth, Van Cleave, & Bush, 1979). Additional evidence from a second study found that earlier-maturing girls who were naturally heavier and stouter than their peers were considerably less satisfied with their body image (Blyth, Simmons, & Zakin, 1985). Therefore, although maturing early may give these girls a more adult appearance, in relation to their peers, they are heavier. Given the cultural ideal of thinness (Brumberg, 1997; Faust, 1983), these girls are likely to view their early growth as less than ideal.

SOCIOCULTURAL ASPECTS OF PUBERTY

In an ever-widening circle of contextual influences, we have moved from personal aspects of physical development to family and peers to the broader influences of culture on development. These broader ecological influences can be seen in several ways. In this section we examine three. First, how society helps young people prepare for puberty. Next, what body images are portrayed by society? And third, what relationship exists between sex-role and development for adolescent females?

Preparation for Bodily Change

The transformation from child to a sexual being capable of reproduction has been celebrated in literature, song, and film. From *Lolita* (Nabokov, 1958) and songs like Bob Seger's "Night Moves" to films like the *Summer of '42*, adults are keenly aware of the early adolescent's new capacities but are, nevertheless, very uneasy with this development.

To illustrate, in one investigation of the preparation for and reactions to first menses in several cultures, Logan (1980) reported that most information for premenarcheal girls came either from informal conversations with female friends or from mothers. In this study 68% of the respondents said that their mothers were their primary source of information. Individuals who were informed of the occurrence of menarche included mother (87%), sister (16%), female friend (13%), another female relative (12%), and teacher (4%). Like the teacher, the father was rarely informed (3%).

In a more recent study, Brooks-Gunn and her associates (1994) offer evidence that fathers are uncomfortable or are seen by their daughters as uncomfortable dealing with this issue. One can suspect that the mother usually tells the father that their daughter "has become a woman," but the father is unlikely to be directly involved in heralding the event. The reactions of these individuals to the adolescents differed, ranging from advice on how to use a sanitary napkin (42%) to variations on "It's not much fun, but you'll get used to it" (13%) and "Be careful not to let others know" (2%). The most common reactions reported by girls themselves reflect fright and emotional upset. Still, it should be noted that many girls showed no particular reaction one way or another.

The literature on boys' is not much different. For example, one study reported that 90% of the sampled males indicated that they had received no formal information about nocturnal emissions. Further, what little information they received from peers was inadequate. For those boys with the natural curiosity and initiative to find information, reading materials were the only answer (Shipman, 1968). Still, in some ways, this is an improvement over the past.

As readers will soon learn, prior to the 1940s masturbation was viewed as a sinful wasting disease that sapped physical and emotional energy from those who practiced it. For example, in the 21st edition of *Sexual Disorders in Men and Women* Robinson (1939) devoted 12 chapters to this "disorder." For Stekel (1967),

Research shows that beauty has its advantages in our society.

a psychoanalyst writing in the latter half of the 19th century, masturbation was responsible for suicidal ideation.

While an unsuccessful search of the adolescent research literature would suggest that this is an ignored area, the personal experience of the first author with his teenage son would suggest otherwise. Excellent opportunities to fully discuss these issues were available not only through an ecumenical church program but also through the 7th-grade human development class offered at school. These are not unique experiences as many communities across North America offer similar programs. Hopefully, evaluations of these efforts will appear shortly in the literature.

Images of the Body

Beauty is in the eye of the media. And that eye holds beauty to the strictest standards emphasizing lean, muscular, shapely bodies and blemish-free faces. These standards are reflections of a broader cultural ideal that can be traced to the early Greeks. But rather than in marble sculptures in which women achieved goddess dimensions and men appeared in the form of Adonis, today's ideals are readily seen in advertisements, billboard pictures, and magazine covers. Imperfections, hidden by the ideal representations chiseled in stone, are clear in the camera lens that captures them.

No wonder Joan Brumberg (1997) contends that thinness and perfection are the core of feminine beauty as portrayed by the advertising media. But do adolescents and adults internalize these sociocultural messages? Sharlene Hesse-Biber (1996) offers qualitative evidence that females see facial attractiveness, body height, and body parts such as legs as central factors in the judgment of appearance; men, who historically have been less concerned about appearance, are expressing increased worry about their weight and fitness. Clearly, certain idealized standards of facial beauty exist (Brumberg, 1997; Cunningham, 1986; Keating, 1985). Likewise, physical attractiveness functions as a mediator of the impact of pubertal change for girls (Zakin, Blyth, & Simmons, 1984).

Society also communicates to youngsters the importance of appropriate dress (Brumberg, 1997; Solomon, 1986). Adolescent's concerns about their clothing can be seen through the findings of numerous research reports. For example, the wearing of used clothing is often viewed as embarrassing to adolescents (Hinton & Margerum, 1984). Still, trends come and go and in the late 1990s the retro-1960s and -1970s and the grunge looks are fashionable in Canada and the United States.[5] Brand names are extremely important (Lennon, 1986), and peer popularity and status are correlated with clothing conformity (L. L. Davis, 1984).

[5]This extends also to music and television shows. Thanks to "VH1," the "Disney Channel," "Nick at Night," and scores of other cable channels we find our students quite current on the songs, films, and television shows from the 1950s onward. We are amazed to hear Generation X students make statements like, "Oh, I used to watch "Lassie" weekdays at 6 A.M. on Nickelodeon. By the way, bet you didn't know that Timmy's mom repeated that role in 'Lost in Space'." It only goes to show that what is old is new again.

Clearly, cultural messages are that thinness, attractiveness, and dress matter. One measure of that impact is a growing body of literature indicating that extremes in physical appearance have a major influence on social relations, perceptions, personality development, and social behavior (Brumberg, 1997; Adams, 1977a,b, 1980).

To illustrate, beginning with initial interactions with strangers, most of us are easily swayed in our assumptions about another's behavior and characteristics by physical appearance. Individuals who are judged to be attractive are generally thought of in positive terms. We suspect attractive individuals to be warm, friendly, successful, independent, and intelligent, while unattractive persons are viewed in unbecoming and undesirable terms.

Studies suggest that the effects of physical appearance on social behavior do not stop with perceptions. Rather, we are inclined to be more solicitous, helpful, and cooperative with attractive than with unattractive persons. According to the biblical forecast, the meek shall inherit the earth, but the research literature suggests that beautiful individuals will share in that inheritance (Eagly, Ashmore, Makhijani, & Lorgo, 1991).

It would be nice if the influence of physical appearance stopped there—that while all this attention is nice, attractive individuals profit little from it. But, that is not the case. For example, attractive individuals, when contrasted with unattractive peers, have been shown to be better adjusted socially (Lerner & Lerner, 1977), to maintain higher perceptions of social effectiveness (Kleck, 1975), and to have more healthy personality attributes (Adams, 1977a). The social behavior of these individuals is also more effective. Facially attractive males and females appear to be more effective in resisting peer pressures (Adams, 1977b) and to maintain a more resistant and assertive style in the face of undesirable social circumstances (Jackson & Huston, 1975), while being able to influence others (Chaiken, 1979; Dion & Stein, 1978; Goldman & Lewis, 1977).

Why do we behave this way? Two explanations have been offered. First, we all hold certain impressions of how other people should look. When that expectation is challenged, there is a tendency to become anxious. To reduce this anxiety, we either stare or end our contact with that person as soon as possible. Now, over time and with repeated exposures, we will be less inclined to experience arousal and anxiety, but our first reaction to novel and unexpected physical appearance is generally either staring or avoidance. Of course, staring makes any person feel self-conscious, while abrupt departure makes any person feel unwanted. This is especially true for adolescents who are self-conscious by nature.

The second explanation is rooted in the self-fulling prophecy. One classic study provides an understanding into how this works (Snyder, Tanke, & Berscheid, 1977). The researchers had male students conduct a telephone conversation with either an attractive or an unattractive female. Each female research subject was randomly assigned to either the unattractive or attractive condition. This process resulted in average physical appearance for the research subjects in both conditions. Further, the female subjects were not aware that the males had been told that they were to have a conversation with either a very attractive or a very unattractive female.

The conversations were tape-recorded and scored on a variety of measures that assessed interpersonal effectiveness.

In keeping with a self-fulfilling prophecy, women in the "perceived" attractive condition became very adept in their phone conversation, while the women in the "perceived" unattractive condition became socially ineffective. This investigation suggests that when others view us as attractive, they may subtly encourage us to become more animated, confident, and adept in our social behavior. However, when we are viewed as unattractive, we are likely to be treated in ways that lead us to behave unsuccessfully. To some degree, we are what others expect us to be.

Gender-Related Role Expectations

One of the most influential adolescent researchers of the past 25 years, John Hill has asserted that society pushes pubescent females to hold traditional views of femininity. Hill and Lynch (1983) note that protective behaviors such as chaperoning, increased parental vigilance, and the lessening of permissiveness rise as girls become adolescents.

Evidence indicates that girls develop specialized interests related to academic achievement, become less self-assured, show heightened interest in interpersonal relationships, and are less self-confident but more self-conscious during early adolescence. Focusing on more expressive and feminine interests and behaviors, female adolescents are thought to be increasingly channeled to recognize their role as bearers of children. Thus, the onset of puberty brings forth yet another complicating cultural reality for girls to deal with, particularly if it is seen as interfering with the adolescent's own interests and aspirations.

Summary

So far in this chapter we've examined the physical processes that transform a child into an adolescent capable of sexual reproduction. From a contextual viewpoint, we've explored the different meanings puberty has for the individual, for those around the individual, and for the larger society. The second part of this chapter examines how the young person puts biology into practice.

ADOLESCENT SEXUALITY: TWO PERSPECTIVES

There are two common perspectives of adolescent sexuality. The first understands young people as responding to instinctual, biologically driven sexual impulses. The second position understands adolescent sexuality as socially shaped and learned behavior.

Supporters of the first view argue that the same hormones that trigger puberty are also responsible for their sexual behavior. For example, several studies measuring male testosterone levels suggest that as the level of testosterone increases, so does male sexual activity (see Miller & Fox, 1987). Even though Sigmund Freud (1933, 1953) was not a biologist, his theory of human behavior certainly contained biological premises. In his view, unconscious innate drives move the young person toward genital sexuality. Indeed, were it not for the superego, the id in all of us would operate unrestrained. To illustrate, imagine all human behavior mirroring that found in those forgettable teenage exploitation films released at Spring break that depict young men and women dressed in little or nothing acting out instinctual mating rituals and you have the essence of Freud's perspective.

Proponents of the second position view sexual behavior as more socially learned than biologically driven. According to social-control theory, society communicates its behavioral expectations through parents, the arts, the media, and other sources (Hirschi, 1969). These communications are then imitated by young people. For example, several researchers have used social-control theory to explain the finding that daughters living in single-parent families in which the parent is dating are often more sexually active than are daughters from two-parent families (see Miller & Fox, 1987). The implication is that the daughters in these families are modeling the behavior of their parent (Thorton & Camburn, 1987).

Emotional Closeness in Adolescence

The need for closeness, a sense of emotional feeling for another, and the ability to share feelings honestly are some of the attributes of intimacy. As young people approach adolescence, their gradual drift away from their parents encourages them to seek peers with whom to share their innermost thoughts. This desire to share must be balanced against possible exploitation. Nevertheless, young people risk hurt feelings and rejection in order to form close relationships and romantic involvements that blossom sometimes only briefly. Mitchell (1976) understands intimacy to be "interwoven with the impulse for sexual expression" (pp. 442–443). He suggests that strong emotions for an individual, when coupled with physical

The need for closeness gives rise to intimacy.

contact, lead many young people to conclude that they are "in love"—a phrase that many adults tend to reject with such disparaging remarks as "Why, it's only puppy love" or "It's only a summer crush." Such remarks Mitchell judges to be unfair value judgments of the sincerity and depth of the emotional feelings young people can have for each other even if the relationship is brief.

Notice, we are not using the word love here. Why? Because love is more than momentary intimacy. One of the most widely accepted models for explaining love is offered by Sternberg (1988). His global theory of love contains three components. The first part is *intimacy*. As noted earlier, intimacy involves the giving and receiving of emotional support. It involves honest communication between the intimates. It includes the sharing of emotions, mutual understanding, and valuing. But importantly, this intimacy extends over time. This intimacy involves the blending of two separate and individual identities into a shared couple identity.

The second part is concerned with *passion*. Sternberg includes in this concept not only physical sexual desire but emotional needs as well. For example, most of us have experienced at one time or another the physical excitement that caressing a sexually attractive individual can bring. This biological experience as Masters, Johnson, and Kolodny (1994, p. 53) phrase it is, "relatively straight-forward and predictable." But passion can also involve affective needs. Where some people may be physiologically aroused, others may be aroused by having emotional needs met. In this instance, it is not the physical beauty of the other person but other factors like financial security, emotional stability, humor, intelligence, or status the other individual offers that evokes passion.

The third element in this global theory of love encompasses *decision and commitment*. The decision is whether one person loves another. The commitment is a willingness to invest in and maintain that love over time.

Given this theory of love, are young people able to love? Assuming you accept Erikson's developmental stages for sociopsychological growth across the life span, love (as Sternberg defines it) is not possible during adolescence. This is because genuine intimacy is not possible. Adolescence is a time for discovering, modeling, and reshaping the self. Once and only after that has been achieved does Erikson believe that intimacy (the formation of a couple identity) can occur.

If the need for emotional closeness becomes coupled with physical sexual drives, as it does in adolescence, a conflict must inevitably arise between earlier parental and societal teachings about the standards for sexual intimacy (touching, caressing, fondling, body contact) and the young person's desire for that contact. The *traditional standard* forbids sexual intimacy (intercourse) until marriage. A variation of the traditional standard, the *double standard*, demands virginity from females but permits males to have sexual experiences with women. Thus, it is not unusual or surprising to find studies reporting that a reason young women gave for stopping short of intercourse was morals (see, for example, Langer, Zimmerman, & Katz, 1995).

Reiss's (1967) classic work first documented a shift in moral and sexual standards to a new position that condoned physical intimacy outside of marriage. He observed a gradual movement away from traditional standards of approving sexual intimacy only with marriage or the promise of marriage to a new set of standards based on the degree of affection existing between two partners. To the abstinence standard and the double standard Reiss added *permissiveness with affection* and *permissiveness without affection* as two new standards of male/female sexual intimacy. The emergence of these standards, wherein a couple decides to pursue a sexual relationship with or without emotional commitments, indicates an increasing regard for the quality of the relationship, whether based on affection or mutual physical desires.

While powerful, affection and physical desire are not the only forces motivating sexual behavior. The sexual behavior of adolescents is affected by their memberships in countless institutions. Their behavior is shaped not only by their own needs but also by their upbringing. For example, several studies show that the higher the degree of religiosity, the greater the chances that premarital sexual activity will not occur (Brewster, Cooksey, Guilkey, & Rindfuss, 1998; Langer, Zimmerman, & Katz, 1995; Murstein & Mercy, 1994).

For adolescents, moral issues are more likely to arise when they perceive the world as no longer having absolute answers. Facing issues of conformity, double-standards, and independence, the adolescent must also face sexuality as another growth dilemma. The issue becomes how a young person balances moral teachings against the natural desire to engage in sexual activity. Almost always, the young person disobeys the moral rule and experiences guilt as s(he) learns that moral beliefs do not always agree with personal desires. The resolution of this situation occurs during adolescence. It is a natural process of examination, trial and error, and introspection leading to maturity.

Learning the Language

In some respects we have progressed a bit too fast, moving from the need for being close all the way to sexual relations. In between are numerous staging points, from learning about sex to dating rituals to actual sexual behavior. We examine these aspects of the adolescent sexual experience in the rest of this chapter.

To begin, where do adolescents go for information about their sexuality? Ansuini and her associates suggest that young people learn about human sexuality from individuals other than their parents (Ansuini, Fiddler-Woite, & Woite, 1996). In examining their sample of 700 males and females ranging in ages from 9 to 50, these researchers divided the data into five age groupings (9-to-19, 20-to-29, 30-to-39, 40-to-49, and over 50). For young people under the age of 19, they reported that siblings were the primary source of sexuality information (36%), followed by other (25%), teacher (15%), parent (14%), and adult relative (10%). Interestingly, in the 20-to-29 and 30-to-39 age groups, teachers were more often cited as the source of information than youths under 19 (34, 26, and 15%, respectively). For the over-30 age groups, the primary source of information was other (friends and the media). This recent study continues a general pattern of behavior documented in earlier studies that parents are not the source of information about human sexuality. Friends, siblings, and the media are the sexual educators of youths (Dickinson, 1978; McNamara, King, & Green, 1979; Nadelson, Notman, & Gillon, 1980; Thornburg, 1981).

Of further interest is students' expressed desire for their parents to be the source of sex information (Handelsman, Cabral, & Weisfeld, 1987). Scholars report that adolescents want to be able to talk about sex with their parents (Gullotta, Adams, & Montemayor, 1993). They speculate that parental inhibitions may forestall such open communications and may encourage young people to consult their peers. More interesting still are the mixed findings regarding parent's influence on the sexual behavior of their adolescents. In two recent studies positive parent–adolescent communications had no direct influence on young people's sexual behavior (Miller, Norton, Fan, & Christopher, 1998; Taris & Semin, 1997). In the third study measuring the impact of African-American fathers on adolescent behavior, fathers did exert a delaying effect if they disapproved of premarital sexual relations. For the sample of 750 inner-city youths between the ages of 14 and 17, this influence was felt even if their father was not living with them. What mattered was that he was involved in their lives.

Given that parents are not frequently consulted on such issues and that the peer group may not be able to provide the most accurate information, where might one go? We might suggest the library or the community bookstore, with a sigh of relief, that since our adolescence the books on human sexuality have been moved out of the closed stacks and onto the open bookshelves. From a few volumes, bookstores now have row upon row of books devoted to sexuality. Fully illustrated "how to" manuals abound as do videos. But are there materials that do more than offer young people a physiological bedroom rush? Are there materials that will provide them the information they seek or will they avoid politically sensitive topics like homosexuality, abortion, and the enjoyment of sex as many earlier books have done?

In revising this textbook, we had the opportunity to examine many books published for young people on human sexuality. Although some have the failings of their predecessors, the majority are written from the perspective that no subject area is forbidden. That is, the natural inquisitiveness young people have should be dealt with openly.

For example, Fenwick and Walker (1994) in *How Sex Works* offer this straightforward prose about oral sex:

> Oral sex means stimulating a partner's genitals with the lips and tongue. Couples may use oral sex as part of foreplay, or may continue to orgasm as an alternative to intercourse . . . Like all sexual contact, oral sex is more pleasant if the genitals are clean. Oral sex avoids the risks of pregnancy, but a genital infection or cold sores near the mouth can be transmitted during oral sex; there is also a risk of contracting HIV (Fenwick & Walker, 1994, p. 51).

For those who may be squeamish about their children, brothers, or sisters reading about oral sex, may we remind you that nearly every R-rated film containing a steamy sex scene on cable television begins or ends with someone's head in someone else's underwear. Better to read, understand, and make an informed and intelligent decision about human sexual behavior than to experiment in ignorance.[6]

---

[6]Don't assume this last statement is an edorsement of adolescent sexual activity. It is not. We would prefer it if young people would abstain from sexual activity until they are emotionally and intellectually prepared to accept the responsibility for their behavior.

DATING

When a boy and a girl plan to meet alone or in a group at some place at some time, a date has been arranged. Confront young adolescents with this information and most will blush, stammer, and protest that it is just "the gang" getting together. To the critics who comment that young people are dating too soon in our society, Kett (1977) offers evidence that young Americans courted in the earliest colonial times. Nor can one escape the fact that the early colonists practiced a "dating" behavior made necessary by the distance and adverse weather called *bundling*, in which males and females visited in one another's beds separated by only a wooden board. As Rothman (1987, p. 46) shares, the late 1700s was "a low point in premarital sexual restraint." She believes bundling was partly responsible for the early arrival of children in nearly one-third of the new colonial marriages of that time. Seems the planks had holes!

Dating Behavior

In North America, dating appears to follow a five stage pattern (Dunphy, 1963). Early adolescence is marked by small, unisex groups with three to nine members. These boy groups and girl groups in Stage 1 "hang around" separately and engage in some activities but mostly talk. As these unisex groups grow older, they increasingly make contact with and talk to one another (Stage 2). In Stage 3 the unisex groupings begin to break down, with the leaders of each group forming heterosexual relationships, but it is not until Stage 4 that the groups fully integrate. In Stage 5 the groups begin to disintegrate and the couple emerges as the dominant relationship form.

As young people grow older and their interest in the opposite sex increases, in Dunphy's model the leaders of the unisex groupings are the first to create heterosexual relationships. Though we may like to think that charm and honesty are the attributes most sought after in a dating partner, they are not. As noted earlier in this chapter, physical appearance emerges as the dominating influence.

Dating Expectations

Given that by age 16, over 85% of adolescents report having their first date, what expectations are generated when two persons agree to a date (Thornton, 1990)? It appears that clothing, physical touch, reputation, and the location of the date provide strong cues for males. This is not necessarily the case with young women. For example, research suggests that young men view young women's tight jeans, low-cut blouses, or shorts as indications of desired sexual activity. But most young women attach no such sexual connotations to their dress. Rather, they view their clothing as an attempt at being fashionable.

To illustrate, consider this recent study in which researchers sought to understand how clothing influenced adolescents' perceptions of date rape (Cassidy & Hurrell, 1995). Their sample of 352 high school students was presented with a vignette in which an acquaintance couple attend a school event in his car. The sequence of events is couple conversation, his attempts to kiss and touch her, her request that he stop, his refusal, and ensuing sexual intercourse. One-third of the student sample received the vignette with a picture of the female provocatively dressed, one-third saw the female dressed conservatively, and one third did not receive a picture. The influence of the provocatively dressed picture on student attitudes was significant. Thirty-seven percent of the sample that had the provocatively dressed picture reported they felt the female was responsible for the male's behavior as compared to 4%, who had the conservatively dressed picture, and to 6%, who had no picture. Clearly, dress mattered in this study.

It would appear that the desire to be fashionable places young women at risk for assault. The same is true for touch. Males perceived being tickled and having their hair stroked by a dating partner as an encouragement to make sexual advances. Females did not share the same perception (Zellman, Johnson, Giarruse, & Goodchilds, 1979).

On issues such as your date's reputation and the location of the date, there was agreement between the sexes. For both sexes having a reputation as being sexually active was likely to create expectations of sexual activity on a date. Likewise, males and females agreed that going to a young man's home when his mother and father weren't home clearly implied the expectation of sexual activity (Miller, Christopherson, & King, 1993; Zellman et al., 1979).

The location of a date, the clothes a girl wears, and other behavior, like tickling, are behavioral cues for boys *but* not necessarily for girls.

B O X **6-2** Courtship Violence

Consider the words "romance," "courtship," and "love." What images do these words convey to you? Are they images of two lovers walking hand in hand, of kindness and gentleness, of caring and concern? Or are your images of a couple pushing, grabbing, shoving, slapping, kicking, biting, and hitting each other? Most of us have assumed that courtship violence is a rare event. It is not. Physical violence occurs in 9% to 57% of high school dating experiences (Avery-Leaf, Cascardi, & O'Leary, 1994). Further, it has been estimated that 15 to 25% of women will be raped during their lifetime. Nearly 59% of these individuals will know their attacker (Rickel & Hendren, 1993).

In a recent study of risk factors for date rape among adolescent women the authors identified three contributing variables (Vicary, Klingaman, & Harkness, 1995). The first is early female physical maturation. Early maturation brings the attention of males—many of whom are much older than the female. Inexperienced in Mead's rules of the road, the young woman is decidedly disadvantaged to the point of being exploited in negotiating this dating relationship with older males. The next factor is poor self-esteem, which, again, can place a vulnerable individual in undesirable situations. The final factor is miscommunication. As noted in the dating expectations section of this book, males and females interpret behavior differently. Many innocent female actions are seen as sexual advances by males. These incorrect interpretations can lead to tragedy.

Other findings suggest that many of the patterns of abuse evident in other forms of family violence also appear to be present in courtship violence. For example, it appears that the abuser and the abused often share the belief that the violent act was spontaneous, not premeditated. Violence does not necessarily end the relationship—many relationships continue. Studies suggest that males use violence to exercise power and control over a dating partner. Men who use these tactics tend to have fathers who behaved in a similar way (Christopher, Madura, & Weaver, 1998; Ronfeldt, Kimerling, & Arias, 1998). Disturbingly, many male attackers see their victim as "deserving" the assault (Rickel & Hendren, 1993). This "deserving" is fixed in jealousy (Riggs, O'Leary, & Breslin, 1990; Cano, Avery-Leaf, Cascardi, & O'Leary, 1998). A look or a warming friendship that cools a current relationship can easily excite hostile feelings rooted in fears of loss that lead to harming another. Other findings reveal that a history of victimization is predictive of courtship aggression (Gwartney-Gibbs, Stockard, & Bohmer, 1987) and, strange as it might seem, couple violence may stimulate greater couple commitment (Billingham, 1987). Finally, evidence suggests that individuals in violent relationships view themselves as "handicapped"—that is, as having "fewer alternative partners than those who broke up" their violent courtship (Cate, Henton, Koval, Christopher, & Loyd, 1982, p. 88).

These findings should generate concern. It appears that male and female young people are at considerable risk for misunderstandings with regard to sexual activity on a date. Such misunderstandings can lead to tragic situations (see Box 6-2).

As intimacy grows in the dating relationship, the desire to express feelings physically increases. Through questioning more than 300 college students, Knox and Wilson (1981) found that the two sexes substantially agreed on the length of time a relationship needs to exist before kissing is considered appropriate. The majority of both sexes find kissing to be permissible on the first date, with near-universal agreement that it may occur on the second date. This level of agreement quickly descends into disagreement between the sexes when other sexual behaviors (particularly intercourse) are considered, with males believing these sexual behaviors to be appropriate sooner than females.

In another study of behavioral expectations in the dating process, Australian adolescent expectations also changed as the relationship continued, with males and females increasingly becoming sexually liberal (McCabe & Collins, 1984). For instance, "necking" was practiced by 47% of couples after the first date, 82% after several dates, and 88% when young people were going steady. Regarding the behavior of mutual masturbation, 18% of couples engaged in the behavior after the first date, 45% after several dates, and 64% who were going steady.

These findings lend support to the claim that a gradual change in behavior from a traditional sexual orientation to permissiveness with affection has occurred (see Box 6-3). In the next section we examine the evidence for this position and recent observations that young people in our society are in the midst of a return to more conservative (traditional) sexual relationships.

BOX **6-3** **Still a Virgin at 16**

Jim came into the office asking if I could see him for a few minutes. He appeared terribly upset as he accepted my offer to sit down. When I asked this 16-year-old what was wrong, he shook his head and said in a low, serious voice, "I think I'm queer."

When I asked him what he meant by "queer," he related to me an incident that had occurred over the weekend. A girl in his class had asked him out for a date. He had accepted the invitation and suggested that they catch a movie. After the film, she wanted to take a drive to a local park. At the park, Jim related, she suggested they go for a walk. At this point in his story, Jim began to shake his head again. Letting out a slow sigh, he mumbled, "I must be queer. You see, when we were walking, she began to tickle me, and I kinda returned the tickling. Well, that went on for a while and then she kissed me."

"That's nice," I said.

"No, you don't understand," Jim said. "She really kissed me. Hey, but that wasn't all. Here she is making out like there's no tomorrow when she puts my hand under her skirt and she's not wearing anything! I didn't know what to do. I stood there dumbfounded, not believing what was going on. So I asked her to stop, and I told her that I liked her a lot but that I wasn't ready yet. I said I just wanted to be her friend right now."

"What was her response to that?" I asked.

Jim said she appeared a little embarrassed but agreed. The rest of the evening was uneventful. They returned to the car, hamburgers were eaten at a local eatery, and a good-night kiss was exchanged. Later that same evening Jim began to question his "manliness." By Monday morning he had convinced himself that he was a homosexual.

I reassured Jim that he was not a homosexual on the basis of that incident. I helped him see that his upbringing in a deeply religious family and his own sincere beliefs about the emotional feelings one needs to have for a person before permitting sexual intimacy to occur would have made it wrong for him to continue. As we talked, it was evident that Jim was seeking reassurance that he had behaved properly within his own value system as opposed to being "one of the boys." Jim left an hour or so later believing that maintaining his values had been the proper thing to do.

Do you think that young people are being pressured into sexual activity at an earlier age? Should a counselor have shown greater concern over Jim's refusal to become sexually intimate?

CONTEMPORARY SEXUAL BEHAVIOR

In her book *Male and Female* (1949), Margaret Mead described dating behavior in the United States as a highly elaborate game in which young people are confronted with balancing their sexual needs against society's prohibition of sexual intercourse. Mead found the resolution of this dilemma to be in petting:

> The curious adjustment that American culture has made to this anomalous situation is petting, a variety of sexual practices that will not result in pregnancy. Technical virginity has become . . . less important, but the prohibition of extra-marital pregnancy remains. Petting is the answer to the dilemma. But petting has emotional effects of its own. It requires a very special sort of adjustment in both male and female. The first rule of petting is the need for keeping control of just how far the physical behavior is to go; one sweeping impulse . . . and the game is lost . . . The controls on this dangerous game . . . are placed in the hands of the girl. The boy is expected to ask for as much as possible, the girl to yield as little as possible (p. 290).

In an investigation by Robinson and associates (1991), examining 20 years of the sexual revolution, it has been observed that continuing liberalization in sexual attitudes are observed for both men and women, with the largest shift for women. However, fewer women now endorse promiscuity, with greater disapproval of promiscuous females than males.

Certainly, we are confronted with a barrage of messages implying that chastity is an ancient relic of former generations. For example, it has been estimated that young people viewed nearly 14,000 sexual acts during the 1987–1988 television season. Of these, a miserly 165 focused on sexually transmitted disease, pregnancy, or birth control (Palladino, 1996). One might imagine that adolescent sexual behavior is one area for which there exists a well-documented base of empirical knowledge (see Box 6-4). Frankly, nothing could be further from

---

BOX 6-4 You Would If You Loved Me!

Mead (1949) wrote of the girl in the adolescent relationship as being in the driver's seat in determining how sexually advanced a relationship becomes. This is unquestionably a difficult seat to be in, as the male attempts to use every ploy imaginable to convince the girl to "surrender." It may be that this situation is changing, and then again it may not be. Regardless, we would like you to make a list of the various lines you have either heard or used in your dating career. Here are some examples.

- Let's make tonight really special.
- Where do those cute freckles go?
- I promise I won't hurt you.
- I want to make you feel like a woman (man).
- When's your mother coming home?

What might your responses be to these lines and those on your own list? Do you agree with Mead that the girl is still the brake in adolescent sexual relationships?

the truth. In fact, it is rather shocking to find that the entire area of research on adolescent sexuality is fraught with methodological problems. In this section we examine several sexual behaviors—masturbation, kissing and petting, and intercourse—in light of the extremely small and dated body of available research.

Masturbation

Masturbation has been thought to result in insanity, blindness, pimples, infections, and weakening of the brain and, most frightening of all, it tends to cause that dread disease in which the penis drops off (see Fig. 6-1). Although we may be amused at these myths of yesteryear, painful consequences awaited the young lad (masturbation was viewed as primarily a male disorder called spermatorrhea) caught by his parents in the act of "self-abuse," as this passage from the 1887 edition of *The Practical Home Physician* indicates:

> As for the treatment of masturbation no rules can be given. The habit must of course be stopped as soon as possible.... In some cases it may be absolutely necessary to employ mechanical means for preventing the practice in individuals who are too young to summon the moral strength necessary to overcome the habit. If any such mechanical means must be used, the most effectual is probably the application of a small Spanish fly-blister plaster to the parts in such a way as to keep them constantly so tender that the child is restrained by pain from meddling with them (Lyman, Fenger, Jones, & Belfield, 1877).

Or consider these encouraging words found in *Confidential Chats with Boys* by

FIGURE 6.1

The imagined results of masturbation, circa 1895. Pictures such as these regarding the crippling effects of masturbation appeared regularly in 19th-century medical books. (Source: Pierce, R. V. (1985) *The People's Common Sense Medical Advisor*. Buffalo, NY: World's Dispensary Printing Office.)

The Testicle in
a healthy condition.

A Testicle
wasted by Masturbation.

Shoulders touching and hand holding are likely the first sexual contact one has with another.

Dr. William Lee Howard[7] (1911):

> Of course there are many diseases which are not due to wasting of life's energy or vicious habits, but more than one-half of the degeneracy and insanity in our land *is* due to these awful mistakes. Neither the lion, eagle, nor the rose, has wasted or poisoned the vital fluid or dust by bad habits, or lost their power by ruinous indulgence . . . Every day I hear the cry: "Oh! Doctor Howard, if I only had known these things when I was a youth! What a different man I would be today!" I have had men tell me that they would willingly have cut an arm off for such knowledge as you boys are getting, and consider the fee cheap at that (Howard, 1911, pp. 53–55).

The passage of time fortunately has persuaded most parents and adolescents to keep the use of their hands and view masturbation for what it is—a normal, natural sexual behavior. The level of male self-reported masturbation has remained relatively unchanged over the past 40 years. Several studies suggest that 80% of all males have masturbated by age 14 (Kinsey, Pomeroy, & Martin, 1948; Ramsey,

[7]Dr. Howard—a regular Masters and Johnson and Dr. Ruth rolled into one—is also the author of *Plain Facts on Sex Hygiene, Sex Problems Solved*, and *Confidential Chats with Girls*. Imagine the information to be found on those pages. The first author of this book, Tom Gullotta, is a collector of this type of historical misinformation. He would be most interested in acquiring copies of these "great" works. You can contact Tom through The Adolescent Experience list-serv described in the first chapter in Box 1-2.

1943; Sorensen, 1973). By the age of 18, the percentage increases to more than 90% (Kinsey et al., 1948).

For females, change in masturbation practices has been noted in the research literature. Kinsey, Pomeroy, Martin, and Gebhard reported in 1953 that by age 15, some 20% of the females in their study had masturbated and that the percentage had increased to a third by age 19. These figures may be gradually changing, however; according to Dupold and Young's (1979) review of the literature, female acceptance of masturbation seems to be growing. Indeed, a more recent study by M. D. Newcomb (1984) of 115 sexually active women with a mean age of 25 revealed that the average age of first masturbation was just under 14 years and that young adults reported masturbating approximately seven times a month.

From Kissing to Petting

Although masturbation is probably the first sexual experience in many adolescents' lives, kissing is, with the possible exception of hand holding or slow dancing, the first sexual contact with a person of the opposite sex. The touching of lips opens new possibilities in the dating relationship. The tongue can now be used to tickle the ear lobe, or it can be used in a French kiss, in which the tongue is thrust into the mouth of the partner in what many consider a symbolic act of intercourse. Mead's (1949) historical rules of dating diplomacy, if we applied them here, would set the French kiss as the second way station (the first being the kiss itself). Should a girl accept or return a French kiss, the male is permitted to become increasingly sexually aroused. Should a girl keep her teeth firmly clenched, the male is given the clear indication that she does not seek further intimacy.

This further intimacy is considered petting. There are several definitions of light and heavy petting. Some consider *light petting* to be activity outside a partner's clothes (squeezing of a female's breasts through her garments or the gentle rubbing of the genitals against a partner's leg) and *heavy petting* to be the direct caressing and touching of a partner's body. Others define light petting as activity restricted to above the waist (which may or may not involve direct body contact) and heavy petting to be activity below the waist involving genital contact short of intercourse. Examining data from Smith and Udry's (1985) and Dupold and Young's (1979) works reveals that no remarkable changes have occurred in the reported frequency of petting behaviors during the past 30 years. Studies seem to show that about 60% of the adolescent population by age 15 has been involved in light petting and about 30% in heavy petting. Where changes have occurred in the past three decades have been in the under-15 group. It seems that both males and females are starting to pet earlier than their parents did.

Sexual Intercourse

Although much has been written over the past 20 years about suspected adolescent sexual behavior in the United States, our knowledge remains very limited.

Recent attempts to support extensive surveys to better understand adolescent sexuality were neither supported nor funded by the United States federal government. Therefore, even though we suspect changes are occurring, current data to confirm those suspicions not only remain elusive but also generate more questions than answers.

We suspect that young people are more open in discussing sexual issues, particularly about discussing AIDS. But this does not generalize to sexually active youth taking additional precautions (St. Lawrence, Brasfield, Jefferson, Allyene, & Shirley, 1994; Murstein & Mercy, 1994). We believe that permissiveness with affection, regardless of marital intention, has become the sexual standard. Thus, female sexual intercourse rates by age 19 should approach those of males. From small nonnormative studies, we suspect that today's youth are no more sexually liberal than their parents were when they were young.[8] Indeed, there is some evidence to suggest that today's college female students may be not only less sexually active but more cautious in selecting their sexual partners than previous college populations (Murstein & Mercy, 1994). From the scant data that is available, let us see if we can discern change in adolescent coital behavior since Kinsey and his colleagues (1948, 1953) published their findings.

Adolescent Female Coital Behavior

As Table 6-1 indicates, the studies published in the 1970s containing data on sexual intercourse for adolescents (ages 13 to 19) show a growth in the incidence of coitus. Kinsey and associates (1953) reported that 2% of females between the ages of 13 and 15 had engaged in sexual intercourse with a male. Several studies in the 1970s all show marked increases in the number of adolescent females admitting to coitus, with Sorensen's (1973) 30% considerably higher by at least 10% than other estimates.

By later adolescence (16 to 19 years of age), the incidence of coitus for females in Kinsey's (1953) data was 18%. This percentage also grew in the 1970s, with Sorensen's (1973) 57% considerably higher again by at least 19% than other estimates. Now compare these figures with data reported by Hayes (1987) and Thornton (1990). For 13- to 15-year-olds, coital behavior approximates 1970s studies other than Sorensen's. Certainly, these lower figures provide no ringing confirmation of increased early adolescent female promiscuity in the 1980s. For 16- to 19-year-olds, Hayes's (1987) 58% and Thornton's (1990) 54% more closely approximate Sorensen's 57% estimate for female coital activity. The Forrest and Singh (1990) data reporting on American women's sexual behavior between 1982 and 1988 stand as an exception to this collection of data. They report that 74% of American women have had sexual intercourse by age 19. There is evidence to support the Forrest and Singh study.

This supporting study is of 246 students attending a small highly select coeducational eastern college. It finds that 76% of the female sample reported not being

---

[8]Today's undergraduate student likely has a parent who attended high school in the 1960s and college in the mid-1960s to mid-1970s.

TABLE **6-1**   Incidence of Coitus in Early and Later Adolescence (in %)

Studies	Females		Males	
	13 to 16	16 to 19	13 to 16	16 to 19
Kinsey, Pomeroy, & Martin (1948)	—	—	10	42
Kinsey, Pomeroy, Martin, & Gebhard (1948)	2	18	—	—
Vener, Stewart, & Hager (1972)	10	25	24	34
Sorensen (1973)	30	57	44	72
Vener & Stewart (1974)	17	33	33	36
Miller & Simon (1974)	7	22	9	21
Jessor & Jessor (1975)	—	38	—	27
Hayes (1987)	5	58	17	78
Thornton (1990)	9	54	22	64
Forrest & Singh (1990)	—	74	—	—
Sonenstein, Pleck, & Ku (1991)	—	—	21	79

virgins (Murstein & Mercy, 1994). For this group, 15% had experienced coital behavior by age 15. This figure is less than Sorenson's (30%) and approximates Vener and Stewart's (17%). The level of sexual activity by age 19 is slightly more than that reported by Forrest and Singh (1990).

Adolescent Male Coital Behavior

For young adolescent males between the ages of 13 and 15, Kinsey and colleagues (1948) found that 10% had experienced coitus. With one exception, studies in the 1970s saw this percentage double, triple, or, in the studies of Sorensen (1973), more than quadruple (44%).

For adolescent males between the ages of 16 and 19, Kinsey and his associates (1948) reported 42% had experienced sexual intercourse. Interestingly, with the exception of Sorensen's data showing 72%, all the other 1970s studies report figures actually lower than Kinsey's—21% (Miller & Simon, 1974); 27% (Jessor & Jessor, 1975), and 34 and 36% (Vener & Stewart, 1974; Vener, Stewart, & Hager, 1972).

Now compare these figures again with data reported by Hayes (1987) and Thorton (1990). For 13- to 15-year-old males, reported coital behavior is less than reports from three other 1970s studies. The Sonenstein, Pleck, and Ku (1991) data

Early dating increases the likelihood of coital activity by middle adolescence.

is similar to reported rates of early adolescent sexual activity in the 1970s. Popular perceptions of excessive early adolescent male sexual behavior do not appear to be confirmed by these data. For 16- to 19-year-olds, Hayes's (1987) 78%, Sonenstein, Pleck, and Ku (1991) 79%, and Thorton's (1990) 64% approximate Sorensen's 72% estimate taken in 1973 for male coital activity.

Again, the Murstein and Mercy (1994) findings offer supporting evidence. For this small sample of elite college males, 16% had experienced coital behavior by age 15. This figure is less than Sorenson's (44%) and all other studies reported in Table 6-1 save two (Kinsey et al., 1948; Miller and Simon, 1974). However, by age 19 the level of sexual activity is 91% and exceeds all the cited studies in Table 6-1.

Before we draw conclusions from these reports, we should consider situational factors that also influence coital activity. For example, studies report that as socioeconomic status declines, sexual activity increases. Black youth become sexually active earlier than White youth. Young people living in single-parent households report a higher incidence of coital activity, while adolescents who attend church, do well in school, and are in academic rather than vocational tracks reported lower activity (Billy, Rodgers, & Udry, 1984; Coleman, Ganong, & Ellis, 1985; Costa, Jessor, Donovan, & Fortenberry, 1995; Day, 1992; Jessor, Costa, Jessor, & Donovan, 1983; Langer, Zimmerman, & Katz, 1995; Miller, Christensen, & Olsen, 1987; Miller & Heaton, 1991; Miller & Moore, 1990; Miller, McCoy, & Olson, 1986; Miller, McCoy, Olson, & Wallace, 1986; Newcomb, Huba, & Bentler, 1986; Thornton & Camburn, 1989). Our review of these studies lead us to these conclusions:

• Early dating experiences increase the likelihood of coital activity by middle adolescence.

- Parental expectations of high academic performance and consistent religious participation discourage coital activity.
- A positive family–youth relationship has little influence on coital activity. However, Taris and Semin (1997) report that for African-Americans, father's disapproval of early sexual activity and his involvement with his children discouraged adolescent sexual behavior. And Fisher (1989) reports that greater sexual communication between adolescents and their parents may actually be associated with greater sexual activity for daughters.
- For White females, the presence of a stepfather is associated with earlier coital activity.
- Discipline, if too permissive or overly strict, encourages coital activity.
- Drug and alcohol usage is associated with earlier coital activity.
- For females, fear of AIDS discourages coital behavior.

As we review these findings, the following cautions need to be heeded as it is very likely that each study suffers from at least one of the following problems:

- Many studies lose sizable portions of their original sample to parental objections.
- Today's young people, in an attempt to fit themselves into societal expectations for their behavior, may overreport their sexual activity, whereas earlier generations may have attempted to minimize their experiences.
- Although virginity and sexual intercourse may be clearly understandable terms to researchers, these words may have entirely different meanings for adolescents and, as recent events suggest, for adults, too.
- Small nonnormative samples offer limited insight into national behavioral trends.

With these limitations accounted for, has a sexual revolution occurred? We suspect that over the past 2 decades a gradual shift toward permissiveness with affection has become the standard and not a free-love stampede. Indeed, as concern about the HIV retrovirus continues to grow in the United States and Canada, we suspect that within certain subgroups of the adolescent population sexual activity may be actually declining.

Ethnic Differences in Sex Behavior

As noted earlier, there are differences between ethnic adolescent groups in the frequency, rate, and timing of sexual intercourse. These differences would matter for little if it were not for the consequences of teenage sexual intercourse. Issues of pregnancy, health, education, and even life-threatening illnesses are part of the larger issues associated with present-day sexual behavior (Brooks-Gunn & Furstenberg, 1991).

Some studies find that Black youths are more likely to be sexually active than White teenagers, while Mexican-American youths are less likely to be sexually active than either of the other groups. For instance, among 10th-grade adolescents,

Langer, Zimmerman, and Katz (1995) found that Latino and White youths were more likely to be virgins than Black youths.

Feelings about oneself after first intercourse were also examined in this study. Of the virgins who thought they would feel good about themselves after their first intercourse, they were more likely to be male, Black, to not value their virginity, and were more open to peer influence in decision-making. Gender differences also were examined in the perceived ability to say "no" to unwanted sexual activity in this study. In this regard, females (61%) were more likely to answer that they could say no to unwanted sex than males (32%) (Zimmerman, Sprecher, Langer, & Holloway, 1995).

In an attempt to explain the higher incidence of Black premarital sexual intercourse, Furstenberg and his associates offer several explanations (Furstenberg, Morgan, Moore, & Peterson, 1987). The first is a genetic (hormonal) explanation. It states that the earlier onset of menarche among Black females increases the possibility of sexual intercourse. A second sociological perspective focuses on the disadvantaged socioeconomic position of Blacks. It reasons that economic and social advancement is limited for low-income Black youths. Facing poorer lifetime economic prospects, the decision to become a parent is less costly than it would be for youths with higher lifetime expectations. If the first explanation is true, then early menarche, regardless of ethnicity, should be a stronger predictor of sexual behavior than ethnicity. If the second perspective is correct, then comparable socioeconomic conditions should reduce ethnic or racial differences in sexual behavior.

Furstenberg et al. (1987) also suggest that other factors like different sexual norms, greater tolerance about early childbearing, poorer school performance, and poorer supervision in single-parent households due to limited economic, energy, or supporting resources may be more influential than ethnicity or hormones in predicting teenage sexual behavior.

Testing these assumptions in a national sample of 15- to 16-year-old White and Black teenagers, these researchers observed that several ecological factors accounted for the differences between Black and White teenagers in sexual behavior. Some evidence suggested that socioeconomic factors, as measured by the mother's education, partially accounted for the difference. However, other evidence suggested that peer group influences were an even stronger factor (Furstenberg et al., 1987). Findings like these have inspired other investigators to use the Furstenberg model to test possible adolescent ethnic or racial group differences with socioeconomic factors.

For example, when Aneshensel, Fielder, and Becerra (1989) compared the sexual behavior of White and Mexican-American adolescent youths controlling for socioeconomic factors, they observed that the minority status hypothesis remained supported despite some SES effects. This suggested that social, attitudinal, or behavioral factors unique to being Latino were responsible for the lower rate of sexual activity. The authors noted these factors might be religion, values regarding abortion, and the mother's education and availability.

In a second study, Wyatt (1990) completed a large survey study of Black and White Los Angeles youths. Controlling for socioeconomic factors, she found few ethnic-related differences. She observed:

> the occurrence of adolescent sexual behavior hasn't changed, but the age of onset has. We have begun to refine the contributors to early onset and have found that ethnicity as a variable is less significant than SES, the presence and consistency of parents in the home, women's sexual abuse histories, and the age of onset of sexual behaviors that precede intercourse. These findings also highlight the value of educating children about the advantages of delaying coitus and offering them a realistic appraisal of the consequences of sexual activity. Adolescents are not likely to refrain from sex, but the more their decision making is based on their own desire for sex, the more likely they may be to accept the responsibility that comes with being sexually active" (p. 202).

From these studies we conclude that differences between ethnic groups are due to several factors. Those factors are: cultural values, attitudes, and norms in combination with economic, political, and social conditions. In our opinion, these conditions better explain differences in sexual behavior among racial groups than biological or genetic factors.

Homosexuality

According to Savin-Williams and Rodriguez (1993) heterosexism so dominates the visibility of sexual behavior in most textbooks on adolescent psychology that homosexuality in its various forms—lesbian, bisexual, gay—remains invisible. However, a 1986–1987 representative sample of approximately 35,000 junior and senior high school students reveals that 1% of the sample admits to at least one homosexual encounter, while far more youth report homosexual fantasies (2.6%) and homosexual attractions (4.5%).

Researchers indicate that at an early age lesbians, bisexuals, and gays perceive themselves as being "different." This feeling of difference comes from a lack of sexual interest in persons of the opposite sex or an attraction to both sexes. In time, denial of interest gives way to feelings of sexual attraction to the same or both sexes. Often, this awareness is accompanied by guilt and self-condemnation. Many homosexual youths defend against these feelings by "passing" as heterosexual (Grossman, 1997; Savin-Williams, 1998; Savin-Williams and Rodriguez, 1993).

A repeated claim about homosexuality is that it is a chosen lifestyle. That is, homosexuals could become "straight" if only they chose to do so. However, as we discussed in Chapter 2, the study of the influence of genetics on human behavior remains in its infancy. Still, it is not unreasonable to assume that genetic or biochemical differences in the human body may expose an individual to a greater probability of developing certain behaviors, such as homosexuality, in a complex and as-yet not-understood interaction with environmental factors.

For example, LeVay (1991) speculates that male homosexuality may be tied to the genes responsible for prenatal brain development—in particular, those genes that provide instructions to the hypothalamus. His work reveals that certain hypothalamus cell groupings differ between homosexual and heterosexual men. He speculates that this difference influences sexual preference.

From examining a small sample of brothers, Hamer (cited in Marshall, 1995) believes that the "gay factor" is inherited from the mother. In this research sample the tip of the X-chromosome differs between straight and gay males. It should be noted that attempts to replicate this finding have not proven successful to date.

Recently, Holden (1998, p.1639) reports in *Science* that high prenatal exposure to the male sex hormone androgen may generate a "partial masculinization" of a woman's brain structures contributing to a lesbian sexual orientation.

Twin studies by Bailey and Pillard (cited in Holden, 1992, 1995) give a broad range, from 30 to 70%, to the possible influence of genetics on homosexual behavior. This expansive range suggests the crudeness of the science of the field. Further, it underscores a principle theme of this book that nearly always multiple factors including biology interact to shape behavior.

Several authors argue that adolescents and adults who identify themselves as bisexual, lesbian, or gay experience major stressors in the management of their sexual orientation. They are at particular risk for serious bouts of depression and for suicidal behavior. Widespread stigmatization due to negative attitudes, harassment, and even interpersonal violence directed at the homosexual community reinforces the self-derogation, so commonly seen among gay adolescents (D'Augelli, 1993; Grossman, 1997; Hershberger, Pilkington, & D'Augelli, 1997).

Scholars concerned with this population suggest that schools need to have safe settings such as university dorms that reduce harassment and victimization. Institutions need to be intolerant of harassment and victimization of homosexuals. Supporting organizations, focusing on the needs of lesbian, gay, and bisexual youths, should be developed. Further, just as feminists argue for increased visibility of the achievements of women in the educational curriculum, so too should material on homosexuality, homophobia, and related issues be included in educational curriculum materials (D'Augelli, 1993; Grossman, 1997; Philips, McMillen, Sparks, & Ueberle, 1995).

Implications

What are some of the implications that one might draw from this overview? First, there are enough threads of evidence to suggest that young people are moving toward a standard of permissiveness with affection. Second, this gradual shift is more accelerated for women than for men. Whether, as some argue, the Pill has provided the impetus for change (a position we do not readily support) or whether it has been a by-product of the women's movement, today's adolescent females are beginning to approach parity with adolescent males in a number of sexual behaviors by age 19.

Should we be alarmed by this revelation? We believe that there is no cause for alarm over the desire young people have for one another. It is very hard, in fact, to imagine sexual intimacy as not being one of the most satisfying and enjoyable experiences of life so long as both partners are willing and well-informed participants.

The changes that need to occur are not with our young people but with the handling of the entire issue of sexuality by adults. It is in adults' fear and their inability to discuss sexual issues with young people that they commit perhaps the greatest error of all. This error is immersing young people in ignorance, so that experimentation and peer advice replace sound knowledge.

Knowledge in this area is equated with sex education. Opponents of sex education contend that by informing young people about themselves and their bodies, sex education contributes to increased sexual activity. Yet, a review by Anne Grunseit and her associates (1997) found little evidence to support this claim. Indeed, of the 47 experimental studies reviewed, 25 neither increased nor decreased sexual activity. Seventeen studies used interventions that either delayed the onset of sexual activity or reduced rates of unsafe/unwise sexual activities as compared to a control group. Only 3 appeared to increase sexual activity (Grunseit, Kippax, Aggleton, Baldo, & Slutkin, 1997). Further, in a meta-analysis of the effectiveness of adolescent pregnancy prevention programs, the authors report that these efforts did not overall increase sexual activity among youths but did increase the use of birth control among sexually active youths, correspondingly reducing pregnancy rates (Franklin, Grant, Corcoran, Miller, & Bultman, 1997). Other reviews by Blau and Gullotta (1993) and Berne and Berne (1995) lend further support to these findings. They report:

- Studies of "Just Say No to Sex" efforts are not successful. But when combined with human sexuality education programs, these programs have been able to somewhat delay the onset of sexual activity.
- Contraception rarely occurs before sexual intimacy. It is only after the relationship has developed that discussions regarding contraceptives typically occur. Thus, demonstrations of contraceptive devices are highly unlikely to stimulate spurious sexual activity.
- Interestingly while sexual activity has increased, the rate per 1000 of adolescent pregnancies has decreased, suggesting education works.[9]

If you draw the same conclusion that we do, that adolescent sexual intimacy is reasonably probable, then the provision of honest, unprejudiced information is essential. Indeed, with the threat of AIDS growing, knowledge is essential. The issue is not preventing sexual activity but ensuring that people can decide for themselves whether they are emotionally ready and willing and medically protected to engage in such activity.

SUMMARY

We've covered a lot of material in this chapter. First we saw that while puberty is a biological process it is influenced by numerous social and environmental factors occurring at many levels. Historically, we learned that adolescent sexual behavior is not unique to this generation. In fact, rates of sexual behavior appear not to be strikingly different from those of your parents' generation (and remember the colonial practice of "bundling"!). We observed several differences between racial

---

[9]Education in the sense we use it here includes all sources of information (media, classroom, parents, etc.).

and ethnic groups. And finally you read that the authors of this book recommend providing youths with the knowledge necessary to enable them to make informed decisions about their lives not because they endorse premature sexual activity but because ignorance is deadly.

MAJOR POINTS TO REMEMBER

1. Understanding the basic endocrinological changes associated with puberty requires an understanding of how the hypothalamus, the pituitary gland, and the gonads work together.
2. To understand the full complexity of physical growth and development, one must appreciate the biological, psychological, and sociocultural aspects of individual development.
3. Changes in body development are generally visible by the 13th birthday. They reach their peak spurt some 2 years earlier in girls than in boys.
4. The psychological consequences of physical development may be more dramatic for those adolescents who begin maturing early, are obese, or start dating early.
5. Parents are likely to make major changes in the manner in which they interact with their adolescents during the onset of puberty.
6. Closeness involves the need for a sense of emotional feeling for another and the ability to share feelings. The need for closeness is balanced against parental and societal teachings about the standard for sexual intimacy.
7. It is not believed that adolescents can achieve intimacy.
8. There are essentially four standards of sexual intimacy: the traditional standard, the double standard, permissiveness with affection, and permissiveness without affection.
9. The overwhelming majority of adolescents learns about their sexual being from experimentation and from peers.
10. Dating originates as the result of a gradual process beginning with small unisex groups and ending in couples.
11. Mead suggests that Americans play an elaborate dating game in which females are expected to be solely responsible for how far the relationship goes.
12. Although male masturbation rates remain relatively unchanged, there is evidence that female masturbation rates are increasing.
13. Petting appears to be on the increase, with most adolescents reporting involvement in light petting by age 15.
14. Despite rumors of a sexual revolution, there is conflicting information that one has occurred. Early sexual activity appears relatively unchanged over the years. By age 19, it appears that female sexual behavior is approaching male sexual behavior.

15. The relations between ethnic group membership and sexual behavior are complex and involve economic, social, historical, racial, political, and educational factors.
16. Homosexual behavior may have a partial genetic origin. Regardless of its origin, many homosexual youth experience a very difficult time in adolescence.
17. Although it is true that sex education increases interest in sex, it does not follow that sex education encourages premarital sexual activity.

THREE

Influences of Adolescent Development

The Family

MOST YOUNG PEOPLE are blessed with warm, understanding, nurturing mothers and fathers. Looking back now at those years, we find it hard to understand why we were so reluctant for our friends to see us with our families. One wonders why we felt self-conscious (dressed in ragged, twice-patched jeans) when we were caught in family activities by our friends. The same tolerance and patience they showed toward us, we find today's generation of parents demonstrating as their children color their lips black, shave their heads, and decorate their bodies with rings in every imaginable, or is that unimaginable, spot.

Despite gloom-and-doom writings suggesting the demise of the family, most U.S. families report satisfaction with family life and family members (National Commission on Children, 1991). We believe that the family is an enduring institution whose purpose remains unaltered from the past. Further, scholars suggest that its functions can be carried out by widely varying family structures and that there is no single ideal family form (Demo, 1992; Gullotta, Adams, & Alexander, 1986).

In this chapter we examine the family and how it affects and is affected by the adolescent. Let's begin this discussion with a general portrait of family relations and interactions among adolescents.

A PORTRAIT OF FAMILY RELATIONS

If one is to believe Hollywood scriptwriters, adolescence is marked by a high degree of family conflict. These disputes have often been depicted as a generation gap. But, other than in television soaps and teenage-rebellion movies, there is little empirical evidence to support a belief that a major generation gap exists between parents and young people (Lerner, 1993).

For example, two studies examining family life found young people to be generally satisfied with the quality of family life and in strong agreement with their parents on a number of issues. The first study by the National Commission on Children (1991) surveyed 1700 households with children between the ages of 10 and 17. When asked, Who cares about them?, 94% reported their mother cared; 82% felt their father cared; 43% felt their grandparents cared; 33% felt a teacher cared; and 15% felt a minister, priest, or rabbi cared for them. To the question, "Do you have an "excellent" relationship with your children?", 78%

Most young people report feelling that their parents care for them.

of intact families with "happy" marriages said yes. Fifty-four percent of intact families with "unhappy" marriages said yes. Stepfamilies in "happy" marriages said yes 54% of the time. This decreased to 33% if the remarriage was "unhappy." Sixty-four percent of the one-parent households responded yes. In general, these findings indicate adolescents perceive having several caring family and community members and, in turn, parents view themselves as having good relationships with their children.

In the second study the overwhelming majority of high school seniors in 1990 indicated agreement with their parents on topics such as what to do with your life (71%), how to dress (62%), the value of an education (86%), roles for women (71%), racial issues (64%), and religion (69%). In this study the greatest disagreement occurred with the topics of how to spend money (59% disagreed), dating behaviors (53% disagreed), and, interestingly, politics (52% disagreed). Of particular interest is the fact that these reported agreement/disagreement levels have remained virtually unchanged since 1975 (Institute for Social Research, 1992). This study and others like it (Galambos, 1992) confirm the belief that family values and views are carried over from childhood and adolescence into adulthood. Or, as one bit of folk wisdom goes, "You grow up to be what your parents are." Frightening isn't it!

Other evidence further confirms these points. For example, in a telephone study, 31 male and 33 female 10th-graders were questioned on three random occasions to determine the level of conflict between parent and child. Of 192 contacts, 68 were marked by parent/child conflict (Montemayor, 1981). Although one argument occurred (on average) every 3 days, this level of disagreement does not by any standards paint a picture of high parent–adolescent conflict (also see, Larson,

Richards, Moneta, Holmbeck, & Duckett, 1996). Further, many of these conflicts were, at best, minor skirmishes, not major warfare.

Understandably, when the quality of family life does deteriorate the conflict between adolescents and their parents increases (Whittaker & Bry, 1991). Interestingly, most disagreement between adolescents and their parents are not resolved. Studies suggest that fewer than 20% reach a compromise or negotiated settlement. The most common approach toward not solving a problem is to let the issue fade away. Problem-solving decreases as adolescents grow older and if they are males (Smetana, Yau, & Hanson, 1991).

Finally, Montemayor and Hanson (1985) questioned the commonly held belief that arguments between adolescents and their parents most often involve independence issues. Their study of 64 young people and their families suggests that it is interpersonal issues rather than independence issues which cause disagreements.

Recall from the second chapter that Kingsley Davis believed that disagreements were inevitable between the generations and that it was healthy and natural to have some distancing between parents and their adolescents. In *Crossing Paths: How Your Child's Adolescence Triggers Your Own Crisis*, Laurence and Wendy Steinberg (1994) unwittingly offer a modern day version of Kingsley Davis' hypothesis. They confirmed that while life with adolescents wasn't filled with constant conflict, it did trigger a parental crisis for 40% of their sample. In that study, some parents felt abandoned as their children turned to peers. Others felt jealous about the fun their offspring appeared to be having. Still others expressed feelings that their careers had peaked, their strength diminished, and their life's opportunities declined while their children seemed to have everything ahead of them. Add to this that as the adolescent began the emotional distancing that often accompanied disagreements, the parent experienced it as a loss or even a source of regret. Therefore, the adolescent's distancing triggered, for some parents, a state of depression and remorse, and in this depressed state, the parental marriage suffered.

Too often we think of only parents and their effect on the adolescent. Clearly, the adolescent can have a powerful influence on the well-being of the parent. Indeed, we are amazed at how adults with children between the ages of 12 and 21 age. That's right, get old! For reasons that surely can't be due to age alone, parent's life insurance rates jump, grey hairs sprout where hair can still be found, and sagging waistlines increasingly hang over belts whose owners refuse to concede the obvious. Why, this has the makings of a sequel to Bram Stoker's *Dracula* with the transferring of the life force but more on that later. Now that we know parents and their adolescent offspring are not constantly at each other's throats (pun intended), let's look at the evidence on their frequency of communication. Urie Bronfenbrenner (1970, 1974) has long argued that parents are increasingly spending less time with their offspring, thus permitting others to influence children's development.

In particular, Bronfenbrenner argues that the peer group has come to replace the family as a prime influence in adolescence. For example, one group of researchers reported that part-time work decreased the time adolescents spent with their families but had no effect on the time spent with peers (Greenberger, Steinberg,

As young people grow older, the peer group grows in importance.

Vaux & McAuliffe, 1980). In another study, observational data drawn from parks, fast-food outlets, schools, and the like showed that adolescents spent most of their time with friends, not parents. There were, however, some interesting gender variations. For instance, from age 13 to age 16, sons interacted with parents more than daughters did. Between the ages of 16 and 19, daughters outdistanced sons in time spent with parents (Montemayor & Van Komen, 1980). We conclude from this last study that both sexes are highly peer-oriented and that males and females at different times in adolescence are influenced to a different extent by their parents (Collins & Russell, 1991; Montemayor & Flannery, 1991; Paikoff & Brooks-Gunn, 1991).

Data from the National Commission on Children (1991) further underscore these observations. Eighty-one percent of the parents interviewed did not feel they spent enough time with their children. When queried about their involvement with their 14- to 17- year-old children, 34% had played a game with their adolescent in the past week; 75% had spoken with the adolescent's teacher in the last year; 64% had attended a PTA meeting; 43% had helped with homework; 49% had gone on a class trip; and 40% were involved with a youth group. Compared to other age groups, youths over the age of 14 spent less time with their parents than did younger children. When young people were asked with what frequency did their parents miss important events, 58% of mothers and 43% of fathers almost never missed an event.

Given that adolescent males and females interact differently with their parents, what is the nature of that interaction? Youniss and Smoller (1985) observed that the adolescents in their study, while pursuing independence from their family, nevertheless sought the family's continued emotional support and guidance. Another particularly interesting finding involved adolescents' views of their parents. It appeared that parents played very specific roles. Fathers were viewed as the enforcer of family and societal values. Mothers were seen as supportive and as using reason rather than discipline. Although fathers were described by young people in this study as trying to be helpful, they were perceived, especially by daughters, as distant and impersonal. This supports the observation that adolescents more often seek advice from their mothers than their fathers (Greene & Grimsley, 1990).

In a recent summary of general trends on parent–adolescent relations, Montemayor (1994) indicates that "well-functioning adolescents have warm relations with their parents who exert age-appropriate control over them . . . [and that] adolescents in these families are likely to identify with the goals and values of their parents" (p. 2). Similar findings have been reported for British (Shucksmith, Hendry, & Glendinning, 1995) and Italian (Marta, 1997) youth. Further, Montemayor suggests that the onset of puberty, sexual development, and passage from middle schools or junior high school into high school present new environmental contexts in which adolescents' psychological development unfolds and within which relationships with mothers and fathers are transformed. He concludes that the adolescent's psychological development is neither dramatic nor abrupt but a gradual evolution.

Some Basic Family Functions

We understand the generation gap to be no more than a hairline crack. Certainly, there is disagreement but not universal and rampant conflict between young and old. Unquestionably, the peer group is a powerful influence, but one should not dismiss the influence of home life on the adolescent. Young people may not want their families on stage as they parade with their peers through malls, but most want and need their parents in the wings to support their fledgling attempts at adult roles.

Although the frequency of interaction with parents declines during adolescence, we believe parental influence remains high. Indeed, the early theoretical work of Ausubel and Sullivan (1970) suggests that parents, in their benevolent love for their offspring, actually encourage movement away from the family and toward greater peer involvement. In the early years of a child's life, immaturity leads to dependence. This dependency on parental approval creates a manageable and obedient child, but one who is overly identified with the parent. However, as the child is allowed to experience other sources of gratification (such as peers), the child comes to recognize that the parent is incapable of being all things at all times. Thus, peer interaction allows the youth to develop a sense of independence. In this way the power of the peer group to provide other sources of information and gratification reduces parental authority.

One approach for understanding adolescent development and behavior within families can be found in family systems theory. As with other theories, this one has special terms like "elements" and "boundaries" that have specific meanings. For example, an *element* is a unit within a system—in this case the members of a family. Another term is boundaries. *Boundaries* define a system by establishing what elements belong to it. Boundaries can be either open or closed. A family with *open boundaries* would have much interaction with the outside world—friends, clubs, organizations. A *closed boundary* implies the family keeps to itself, with a minimal amount of outside interaction (Gullotta, 1996). Boundaries define the parameters of the family, clarify role expectations and role performance, and contribute to the stability of relationships between family members. Further, hierarchies exist within these boundaries. In this example about families, parents, particularly a two-parent family, would hold the most power (Leigh, 1986).

Given the intimate relationships existing between family members, members in this system are susceptible to causality and the associated effects. What's that? Well, it means that when one family member experiences an event, all family members are affected, even if the event occurred outside of the family boundary. To illustrate, if an adolescent is failing in school, the family is likely to be informed by the school. Once informed, the parents may take actions like curtailing television viewing or paying for a tutor to help the student improve her/his grades. These actions impact not only mom, dad, and the student but other brothers and sisters as well. For example, these actions might limit their TV viewing too and reduce the finances otherwise available to the family. One final note, even with the constant changes that occur around families, all families (systems) strive to maintain balance and engage in behavior toward that end (Lamanna & Riedmann, 1991).

A special case of family systems theory can be found in David Olson's circumplex model. By measuring behaviors like cohesion (warmth, closeness) and adaptability (flexibility), families can be placed into one of 16 family system categories. For all families, cohesion, adaptability, and communication are vital functions that the family provides across the life span (Olson, Russell, & Sprenkle, 1980).

The first of these, *cohesion*, establishes the conditions for identification and fosters closeness. In the next instance, *adaptability*, the family provides an example of how family power can change, of how role relationships can develop, and how relationship rules can be formed. Adolescents who experience rigid (low adaptability) family behavior are likely to internalize a rigid interaction style. For readers of Charles Dickens an example of rigid family upbringing can be found with Estella, the adopted daughter of Miss Haversham in *Great Expectations*, who saw her role in life to punish men. On the other hand, too much adaptability can create a chaotic style. Thus, a reasonable balance is most appropriate for this function. A similar conclusion can be drawn on cohesion. Too much closeness like that found between Amanda Wingfield and Laura Wingfield, the mother and crippled daughter, in Tennessee Williams' brilliant play *The Glass Menagerie* entangles the adolescent in his or her family, while not enough creates a sense of detachment

FIGURE 7-1

A conceptual relationship
between dimensions of
cohesion and adaptability in
parenting styles.

	Warm and loving	*Hostile and cold*
Controlling and restrictive	Overprotective or indulgent	Dictatorial and antagonistic
Permissive and understanding	Democratic and cooperative	Indifferent and detached

among family members. Finally, the family provides a network of *communication* experiences in which the individual learns to speak, listen, interact, and negotiate with others.

To summarize, there is no other social group that allows the adolescent to experience and experiment with feelings, interaction styles, or communication skills so freely as the family. Adolescents with too much or too little experience in each of the three basic family functions are likely to be placed at a disadvantage in their intellectual and social development. Next, we'll examine parental discipline styles.

Parental Discipline Styles

Drawing upon the work of Earl Schaefer (1959), Wesley Becker (1964) conceived the four parental behavioral patterns depicted in Fig. 7-1. As you consider the matrix, realize that a warm but controlling parent who restricts the behavior of the child will be either overprotective or indulgent in their parenting style. Conversely, a cold or unemotional parent who controls the child through restrictive parenting practices will be dictatorial and antagonistic. Should a parent be undemanding and permissive with the child but highly nurturing, the parenting style will be democratic and cooperative. Finally, if a parent is cold or hostile and also permissive, the parenting style will be one of indifference and detachment.

Becker links these parenting styles to certain outcomes. For example, in a warm and controlling family environment, a child is likely to become a polite, neat, dependent adolescent. In a hostile but controlling environment, a child is likely to grow up withdrawn, neurotic, and quarrelsome. A warm and permissive family environment is thought to create an active, highly social person who is very independent. But a hostile and permissive environment is associated with a noncompliant and aggressive adolescent.

With this information as background, let's consider how families can either facilitate or retard the development of its offspring.

Parental Communication and Healthy Personality Development

There is growing evidence that a family systems' tolerance for (a) relationship intimacy (connectedness) and (b) differing viewpoints and expressions are

A cold or hostile parenting style leads to indifference and detachment.

major contributing factors to social adjustment and healthy personality formation (e.g., Anderson & Sabatelli, 1992; Gavazzi & Sabatelli, 1990; Cooper & Grotevant, 1987; Grotevant & Cooper, 1985). Early work by Bowen (1976; 1978) proposed that the degree to which the family encourages separate and unique viewpoints and behaviors encourage healthy personality development in regard to self-differentiation. Self-differentiated individuals are believed to be more capable of establishing a balance between the self (individuality) and the social connections and relationships (relatedness) that are supportive of the self. Numerous studies have shown that communication patterns in families strongly influence identity development and social adjustment (Bartle & Sabatelli, 1989; 1995; Cooper & Grotevant, 1987; Cooper, Grotevant, & Condon, 1983; Grotevant & Cooper, 1985).

Not surprisingly, there appears to be gender differences in family communication patterns to sons and daughters. These differences are traceable to traditional sex role attitudes wherein males are encouraged to be autonomous and females to be connected. This parental behavior, skewing the direction of identity formation, may result in youth practicing stereotyped sex roles (Bartle & Rosen, 1994).

In our own research, the second author is currently recording communication behaviors that either aid or inhibit individuality and connectedness. With this baseline of conversation behaviors, he expects to be able to help parents and adolescents develop effective and healthy communication patterns. Facilitating individuality involves a respect for others that enhances a feeling of uniqueness and specialness. Communication behaviors that involve clarifying, valuing, and promoting are facilitating behaviors. Constraining behaviors of individuality include expressions of self-absorption, assuming intention, and being judgmental. Facilitating social connections or relatedness involves sensitivity and respect for others and enhances a sense of belonging. Communication behaviors that involve agreeing, prompting, and cooperating are facilitating behaviors. Behaviors that discount and devalue (constrain) connectedness include rejection, intolerance, and disagreement.

In general, he has found that higher family scores on the facilitation of individuality and social connectedness relate to a more advanced identity status. Recall that in Chapter 4 on identity and self-concept you read that a more advanced identity status is associated with many healthy personal and social characteristics. Thus, encouraging positive communication behaviors should support healthy individual development.

Parenting and Antisocial Adolescent Behaviors

In her seminal research, Diana Baumrind (1978) states that one of the major functions of the family is to encourage social competence in its offspring. The family promotes this behavior three ways with the first being *connection*. That is, helping the adolescent relate to others without denying self-realization in a warm, positive, and stable manner. The second is *regulation*. This refers to the family's establishment of rules and providing the youth with supervision such that the adolescent comes to obey reasonable laws while confronting injustice. The final one is *autonomy* and involves the family's promoting the self-worth and positive identity of the young person (Adams, Marshall, Ketsetzis, Brusch, & Keating, 1996; Barber, 1997). The failure to develop social competence in these areas is a major reason for adolescent alienation.

Baumrind's (1978) research, supported by other studies, suggests that an *authoritative* discipline style which combines supportive parenting with reasonable and firm control that recognizes children's individual interests, is very helpful toward shaping social competence (Hines, 1997; Shucksmith et al., 1995). In contrast, an *authoritarian* parenting style that treats children as inferiors and fails to encourage them to express their own opinions discourages the development of social competency. Several investigations exploring antisocial behaviors during adolescence support Baumrind's conclusion. Overcontrolling and restrictive interactions between parent and child have been associated with suicide (Blau, 1996; Kerfoot, 1980), drug abuse (Palmer & Liddle, 1996), and male aggression (Bandura, 1960; Seydlitz & Jenkins, 1998). Not surprisingly, a hostile relationship between parents is related to problem youth behavior (Buehler, Krishnakumar, Stone, Anthony, Pemberton, Gerard, & Barber, 1998). Despite these findings, a word of caution is in order; to conclude that parenting alone caused these behaviors would be both unfair and untrue. Numerous other factors including poverty, heredity, social conditions, and the child's personal temperament may also play roles in the formation of antisocial behaviors (Ge, Conger, Cadoret, Neiderhiser, Yates, Troughton, & Stewart, 1996; Stice & Gonzales, 1998). In the next section we continue with our discussion on the importance of connection, regulation, and autonomy in regards to development (see Box 7-1).

BOX **7-1**   Preserving Families

It was a late fall afternoon. Fog clung to the ground. Skies were overcast, and a wet chill cut through Sharon's clothing. A 12-year-old junior high school student, she hurried home from a friend's house. She had promised her mother and stepfather that she would be home for dinner. Nearing home, she heard the radio blaring from the kitchen and knew instinctively that her mother and stepfather had been using drugs. She dreaded their behavior when they were drinking or snorting coke. Rude suggestive remarks and boisterous laughter about her sexual development had become commonplace. On this particular evening, in the presence of her mother, Sharon was forcibly disrobed and raped by her stepfather. Sharon eventually fled the house and reported the assault to friends whose parents contacted the police.

Two years later the court trial against her mother and stepfather was concluded. Sharon's stepfather was sentenced to 7 years for his sexual assault. Her mother was given probation with orders to continue in an outpatient drug treatment program. She was further ordered to work with the intervening agency in an attempt to reunite her with Sharon, now 14, and in frequent trouble in the community.

This reunification effort is part of a recent nationwide movement called intensive family preservation. The three most common forms of this clinical intervention are (1) efforts to maintain the family unit or at least part of that unit after a young person has been determined to be at imminent risk of removal from it by local protective service authorities; (2) efforts to reunify a family that has been separated for abuse, neglect, or for reasons of imprisonment; and (3) efforts to stabilize a family unit and improve their level of functioning after reunification has occurred. The development of intensive family preservation services is an admission that even severely dysfunctional families are often times less damaging to young people than institutional care or independent living. This admission has resulted in the significant investment of

resources in Canada and the United States to assist family members in developing the necessary skills to more successfully live together (Blau, Whewell, Gullotta, & Bloom, 1994; Eyberse, Maffuid, & Blau, 1996).

In Sharon's situation a foster home, outpatient counseling, and self-help services had not comforted the hurt she had so wrongly endured. In the past year she had become increasingly defiant and sexually active. This is a pattern of behavior not unusual for young people victimized by family members. As Garnefski and Arends (1998) report from their Netherlands sample, the sexually abused young person experiences a significant psychological trauma that often results in acting-out behaviors and the development of mental health problems, especially suicidal feelings. The judge in this court case, recognizing this all-too-familiar pattern, took the unusual action of attempting to reunite child with her repentant mother. The reunification effort brought a master's-level mental health clinician into the family's home for up to 20 hours a week. This clinician is supported by other professional staff such that the family has access to help in their home 24 hours a day, 365 days a year, if necessary.

Fourteen months have passed since the reunification effort began. They have been trying months. Sharon has left home overnight on several occasions. Living together for both mother and daughter remains tense, and tears of anger and hurt flow freely. Yet, unlike so many other young people with similar stories, Sharon has not disappeared to the street and to a short life of addiction. Sharon has not been bounced from one foster home to another. Sharon does not find herself in a correctional school or living independently at government expense in some cheap motel. Some may take issue with these seemingly modest achievements. For those individuals, we suggest a walk along the streets of New Orleans, Los Angeles, Toronto, Seattle, or a dozen other cities at 2:30 A.M. to observe the Sharons of this world living in misery.

Self-Regulation and Family Relationships

After many years of interviewing families, we have concluded that what parents want most for their children is for them to establish an internalized sense of direction (identity), social responsibility (morality), and independence (autonomy). With a very few exceptions, adolescents want these things too. As we noted in the previous section, these behaviors can be either advanced or hindered by the family's behavior.

Collins, Gleason, and Sesma (1997) have discussed three broad themes in the development of behavioral self-regulation. First, rather than understanding self-regulation to be a trait, they see this competence as emerging from a parent–adolescent relationship that encourages individuation (expressing autonomous viewpoints, being oneself) and connectedness (feeling love and bonding to family). They support this position by noting Baumrind's (1991) work where authoritative parent–child relationships (which are marked by parental expectations of mature behavior, warmth and encouragement, mutuality and shared communication, and training in social responsibility) are predictive of greater maturity and social responsibility. Further, they note that neglectful parenting (associated with few expectations, low involvement, unresponsiveness, and parent-centered attitudes) are associated with antisocial behaviors and lower levels of achievement and maturity. It would seem that authoritative parenting encourages adolescent social responsibility, caring, and supportive interpersonal behaviors that promote the internalization of self-regulation. Whereas the self-absorption and lower responsibility found with neglectful parents discourage the development of internalization.

Second, rather than understand family behavior to be a reaction to adolescent behavior (Hartup, 1983), Collins and associates (1997) argue that the influence flows in both directions. Shared decision-making, discussions about controversy, and mutual clarifications are important if effective parenting is to occur. Adolescent internalization and self-regulation become a joint process of establishing and accepting standards of conduct, with parents encouraging compliant behavior but remaining open to discussion about the nature and meaning of these standards. Again, Baumrind's (1991) evidence supports the effectiveness of authoritative parenting.

Third, self-regulation can no longer be viewed as a process of adolescent internalization that is influenced solely by the family or the peer group. Rather, we must think of "relations among relationships" (Collins et al., 1997, p. 88). Both family and peer relationships influence the adolescent's behavioral regulation. To make this point, Collins et al. (1997) look to the work of others (Brown, Mounts, Lamborn, & Steinberg, 1993; Durbin, Darling, Steinberg, & Brown, 1993) to make the following argument. Particular parenting styles are linked to certain behaviors and predispositions. These behaviors then guide adolescents into particular peer groups. After all, recall that in an earlier chapter we observed that like-minded people tend to be attracted toward each other. Once with those peers, group norms reinforce behaviors. In this way, family relationships support specific personality characteristics. In turn, these characteristics encourage young people to become members of particular peer groups. Completing the feedback loop, the peer group reinforces the original socializing behaviors that were acquired from the family.

In summary, this line of scholarship suggests we should think of the development of behavioral regulation as a relational process. That is, the family encourages and negotiates certain behaviors with the adolescent which the peer group later reinforces.

Implications of Basic Family Functions for Intervention with Families

A democratic, warm, interacting, and partially restricting family structure is probably best for healthy adolescent development (Kandel, 1990). This authoritative parenting style offers the adolescent moderate cohesion, high flexibility and adaptiveness, and encourages social interaction and communication between family members. More often than not, adolescents in trouble live in families that do not practice these behaviors. When these young people get into trouble and helping services are offered that are not family focused, it is highly unlikely those services will prove effective. For this reason, we urge educators and other helping professionals to build social-intervention programs that recognize the family as a major influence on adolescent behavior. Further, we hope that future interventionists will build elements into their programs that examine the adolescent's family-support system and attempts to remedy weaknesses. In particular, we urge that these efforts emphasize the three basic family functions of cohesion, adaptiveness, and communication. Although there are other important variables, these three are central to the positive functioning of a family.

A warm, interacting, and partially restricting family structure is conducive for healthy adolescent development.

FAMILY CHANGES

Life was so much simpler in the old days. There was Mom, Dad, the dog, the cat, and two, three, or maybe four children. The grandparents lived in the same town, and the family's ancestors were buried there too. Mom stayed at home. Dad always said that's where a married woman belonged. She sewed, cleaned, cooked, and cared for the children before settling back in the evening to read *Life's* feature story about Clark Gable's latest movie. Divorces were unheard of among the good people, and it was only the widowed who remarried. If this portrait of times past were only true then this chapter might have expressed concern about the changes that are shaping North American families today. Women have left the kitchen for the workplace and are beginning to achieve long-deserved job equity in the marketplace. Marriages made today stand an almost equal chance of being broken tomorrow. Remarriages bringing young people from past families together in new families are common. Let's examine several of these changes and understand how contemporary families and their children have adapted to them.

Mothers in the Work Force

When one considers that the early farms were self-sufficient units, the issue of women in the workforce as a recent family change becomes essentially a question of semantics. On the farm, women tended the family garden, cared for livestock, nursed children, made clothing, and preformed hundreds of other tasks. She was doctor, teacher, lover, soldier, and mother (Vanek, 1980). As the agrarian economy turned industrial and the home was no longer the center of production, the woman's role changed from producer to carer for children and home while males traveled to work in the factories. Certain industries were female dominated, but the women in these positions like shoe manufacturing or dress-making were generally single rather than married. Thus, it is not surprising to see that the official percentage of married women in the United States' work force was 4% in 1890 and less than 15% in 1940. With the advent of World War II, the number of working married women climbed, and it reached nearly 30% in 1956, 42% in 1974, 59% in 1980, and well in excess of 70% in the 1990s (Gullotta et al., 1986; U.S. Census Bureau, 1997, Chart 632 p. 404). With that growth has evolved a new understanding of a mother's employment in relationship to her children and husband.

The early post-war social-scientific literature on mothers in the work force portrayed the children as victims. According to Bossard (1954), working mothers were physically exhausted and thus neglected the supervision and training of their children. As a result, the children felt lonely and neglected and took advantage of the lack of maternal control by behaving in an antisocial manner. Bossard and other early researchers (Glueck & Glueck, 1957) recognized that in many families the mother had to work for economic reasons. Nevertheless, the early research in this area reflected a decidedly dim view of maternal employment, particularly those who worked either part-time or for the enjoyment that work brought.

However, as the number of women in the labor force continued to grow in the 1960s and as additional data were collected, a decidedly different perspective emerged on the effects of working mothers on their adolescents. Evidence appeared that the working mother was not a destructive influence on son, daughter, or marriage (Douvan, 1963).

Today, studies collecting data on such variables as achievement, childrearing practices, adolescent personality adjustment, and adolescents' attitudes toward working mothers show advantages in social and emotional growth result for young girls whose mothers work (Haveman, Wolfe, & Spauling, 1991). Boys neither benefit from nor are harmed socially or emotionally by their mothers' working. These studies find that work is generally a satisfying experience for mothers, that adolescents do not experience high stress resulting from such work situations, and that the family system is adaptable (Armistead, Wierson, & Forehand, 1990; Bird & Kemerait, 1990; Gottfried & Gottfried, 1988; Hillman & Sawilowsky, 1991; Paulson, Koman, & Hill, 1990; Orthner, 1990). And although mother's employment may only equal 25% to 33% of father's income, it is responsible for keeping many families out of poverty, creating savings, and purchasing the family home (Hanson & Ooms, 1991).

Data from the National Commission on Children (1991) suggest that even though working mothers may feel uneasy about how much time they spend with their children, the children do not share these same feelings. When asked if they have "the right amount of time" with their family, 66% of not-employed women said yes; 60% of women working less than 34 hours per week said yes; 29% of women working between 35 and 40 hours per week said yes; and 22% of women working more than 41 hours per week said yes. Interestingly, their children, regardless of mother's working situation, felt that time and attention received was adequate for at least 80% of the sample. Overall, to use an often-stated cliche, it appears it is not the quantity but the quality of time spent with the child that affects the mother/child relationship.

Fathers in the Home

If the world were to end today and the only records of our civilization that survived for future study were the family television shows of the 1950s, what a unique picture they would offer of American family life. Regardless of the show, future archaeologists would observe fathers at home and involved with their families. How confused these scientists would be if they uncovered a university library, for no amount of searching in the literature on the father's role in the family would turn up anything to support what they saw and heard on film.

It is only recently that society has held the view that fathers have an important role in the caring and nurturing of their children. As recent as 1960, dad's responsibility to the family was to put food on the table, clothes on the family members' backs, and the roof over their heads. All other responsibilities (save perhaps mowing the lawn and external house maintenance) fell to the wife. This primitive division of labor could be defended when the father was in the fields and the mother was filling several roles in the home; but as mothers have found themselves in the work force in unprecedented numbers, this division of labor no longer makes sense.

In a classic paper on the subject, Pleck (1979) offered three different views on a role system that finds husbands spending significantly less time on housework and child care then their employed wives. The first, *the traditional perspective*, suggests that the father's role is financial support, not housework or parenting. The second, *the exploitation perspective*, contends that men use housekeeping and parenting responsibilities against women to keep them in servitude. The third, *the changing-roles perspective*, suggests that an evolutionary process is occurring. "Reflecting a transitional problem of adjustment" (p. 485), women's roles have changed much faster than have men's roles.

Two decades have passed since Pleck published his observations. Have husbands changed their behavior? Results are not encouraging. For example, while Demo (1992) reports that men are helping more around the house, women still carry at least twice the workload (Coltrane & Ishii-Kuntz, 1992). In another study on child-caring behavior, fathers spent only an average of 21 minutes per week with their children and most of this time was spent with sons (Crouter & Crowley, 1990). This behavior changes if mother and father work different shifts. When this occurs, father's time with his children increases significantly (Brayfield, 1995). The quality of the marriage also appears to have an effect on time involvement. As the quality of the marriage deteriorates so, too, does time with children (Harris & Morgan, 1991). Somewhat more encouragingly, in a study of 91 Canadian families, fathers were found to be more accepting of their adolescent children as family time increased (Almeida & Galambos, 1991).

From the National Commission on Children (1991), we can draw two inferences. First, 82% of the youths sampled felt that their father really cared for them. Second, 43% reported their fathers almost never missed an important event in their lives. Nevertheless, it appears that even though 72% of women between the ages of 25 and 54 are in the labor force significant role changes have not occurred. Child care has been purchased or sought from relatives. Household cleaning chores continue to be performed by mother or outside help. The preparation of meals if not performed by mother is accomplished by visits to fast-food restaurants. These expenses sap 46% of her wage earnings (Hanson & Ooms, 1991).

Collectively, these findings present less than encouraging evidence as to father's involvement in family life. And yet, a gradual change may be under way with fathers acting in a more equitable fashion (Doherty, Kouneski, & Erickson, 1998). This behavioral change might be discerned if longitudinal data were available. Thus, researchers will study with great interest family leave data that will be generated in the coming years. With the 1993 passage of the Family and Medical Leave Act, workers in firms with 50 or more employees may request up to 12 weeks of unpaid leave a year for purposes such as the birth of a child, adoption, and the care of a sick family member (Landers, 1993). Once analyzed, will this

It is not uncommon for young people to experience distress after a parent's divorce.

data demonstrate greater involvement of fathers in the family? Some answers to this questions should be available early in the next century.

Divorce

The entry of women into the work force . . . has its own effects on divorce rates. A positive by-product of women's economic independence is that a woman who can earn a decent living herself does not have to remain in an impossible marriage because of money alone. . . . Moreover, wives' employment subtly alters relationships of power and submission within marriage. A wife's new independence can strengthen the husband–wife relationship, but increased equality also can produce new stresses or cause old stresses and resentments to surface. Women who are less submissive by and large will put up with less and expect more. One consequence may be the realization that a marriage has not lived up to the high hopes of husband or wife and a decision to end it, particularly when cultural attitudes toward divorce make it far less socially shameful than it once was (Keniston, 1977, pp. 21–22).

Although this passage indicates that divorce has freed both men and women from the shackles of marriages that do not work, the question of the feelings of the "by- products"—the children—is another matter.

In one of the earliest studies of the reactions of adolescents to their parents' divorce, Reinhard (1977) found surprisingly few negative feelings. The majority of the sample, even though unhappy with the divorce, did not view their parents' decision as senseless or immature but as the correct action. Adolescents in this study saw themselves as assuming more responsibility in the family as a result of the divorce but did not view this responsibility negatively, nor did they express anger or a sense of loss of love. They also did not try to conceal the divorce from peers. Significantly, peers seemed to respond in an accepting fashion, and social relationships were enhanced as a result. Finally, these young people did not report any antisocial behavior, leading one generally to conclude that the divorce of their parents was not a particularly earth-shaking experience.

Since the publication of this study, countless other studies have appeared—many with contradicting findings. There are several reasons for these mixed results. One reason is the ages of the youths at which data are collected vary enormously from study to study. Next, the point of time youths are interviewed and the length of time between the announcement of parental separation, the announcement of the divorce, and the time since divorce differ from study to study. Finally, other factors like family income after the divorce, custody arrangements, and biological parental postdivorce relationships are often not accounted for adequately (Amato & Keith, 1991a,b; Hines, 1997; Tasker & Richards, 1994). With these concerns in mind, what trends can be discerned?

With a few notable exceptions, Reinhard's (1977) general findings reappear in the current literature. Even the exceptions that exist suggesting, for example, that self-concept and academic performance suffer (Cornwell, Eggebeen, & Mesch, 1996), that drug use and antisocial behavior is higher (Neher & Short, 1998) or that girls living with their mothers in a single-parent family are at-risk for a teen pregnancy (Cornwell et al., 1996) must be treated cautiously, for there are confounding variables (like parental emotional illness and alcoholism) that make it extremely difficult to attribute acting-out behavior to single-parent homes. These methodological problems are most noticeable with the clinical studies on divorce and children by Wallerstein (Wallerstein, 1989; Wallerstein & Blakeslee, 1989), which suggest that adolescents are at high risk for emotional distress following a family divorce. This distress may become apparent years after the event occurred. Wallerstein describes it as a sleeper effect in which the child having experienced divorce has, when a young adult, difficulties committing to an intimate relationship. Or young people, seemingly role-diffused, appear unable to establish life goals for themselves (Wallerstein, 1989; Wallerstein & Blakeslee, 1989).

There are research data to support the clinical observations of Judith Wallerstein. For example, adolescent males are reported to have greater difficulties if living with his now-single mother. Both adolescent sexes are at increased risk for depression. When questioned, older adolescents express negative attitudes about marriage (Amato & Keith, 1991; Hines, 1997; Tasker & Richards, 1994). Representative of the extensive literature in this area, one group of researchers using a national sample report that older male and female adolescents living with their opposite-sex parent are more likely to dropout of school (Lee, Burkam, Zimiles, & Ladewski (1994).

And yet as Hetherington and Furstenberg (1989) appropriately caution, the Wallerstein clinical sample had a large number of families which had been dysfunctional for years before the divorce occurred. Inability to control for these sample effects may have skewed her findings toward higher levels of dysfunctional behavior in their offspring.

Support for this observation can be found in a recent study of divorce and parent–child relationships that found difficulties in the relationship existing prior to the divorce. The authors conclude that a poor marriage increases the likelihood of difficulties after divorce (Amato & Booth, 1996). Indeed, several studies conclude that chronic marital conflict is more harmful to young people than divorce (Hines, 1997). In other studies on a variety of measures such as locus of control and ego identity (Crossman, Shea, & Adams, 1980) and androgynous sex-role orientation (Kurdek & Siesky, 1980a), young people do not differ significantly from their peers in intact homes.

Adjusting to Parental Divorce?

While the Wallerstein data will remain controversial, we believe her clinical judgement is astute and insightful. Wallerstein (1983) believes that young people must resolve six tasks in order to get on with their own lives in a healthy fashion. The first task is to *acknowledge the marital rupture*. Ideally, after an initial regression, young people will come to grips with this fact by the end of the first year. The second task is to *disengage from parental conflict* and to resolve for themselves that they cannot save their parents or replace a divorced spouse (Sessa & Steinberg, 1991).

The next task is the *resolution of loss*. In a divorce all young people feel hurt and rejected, some more than others. Young people can carry these feelings for years. Moderating this sense of loss is the ability to share this loss. The ability to reach out to friends for social support is important in accepting a divorce. Equally important is the way the parents approach the divorce. Warm, loving relationships maintained by both parents with their offspring after a divorce facilitate adjustment (Hines, 1997), but continued parental battles and anger increase adolescent stress and dysfunctional behavior (Forehand, McCombs, Long, Brody, & Fauber, 1988; Hines, 1997).

The fourth task is the *resolution of anger and self-blame*. Wallerstein (1983) believes that young people do not accept the concept of no-fault divorce. They hold one or both parents or themselves responsible. Their anger, until resolved, may be expressed internally in withdrawal or depression or externally in acting-out behavior in the family, at school, or in the larger community. The fifth task involves *accepting the permanence of the divorce*, giving up dreams that the divorced couple will reunite. The last task to be accomplished is *achieving realistic hope regarding relationships*. Young people need to come, in the end, to believe they are capable of establishing meaningful relationships and not be obsessed with fears over their ability to love and care for another.

When young people do not succeed in handling these tasks, intrapersonal or interpersonal difficulties are sure to arise. Thus, studies reporting academic difficulties (Cornwell et al., 1996; Pong, 1997;), that drug use is higher (Fleweling & Bauman, 1990; Needle, Su, & Doherty, 1990) that sexual experiences are earlier (Flewelling & Bauman, 1990), and that emotional problems are higher (Hines, 1997) should not be surprising. Nor should it be surprising that many of these same studies describe lonely, needy, and vulnerable young people who fear disappointment in love, express lower life-attainment expectations, and feel powerless (DeVall, Stoneman, & Brody, 1986; Parish, 1987; Wallerstein, 1985, 1987, 1989).

Examining the issue of expected disappointment in love relationships, one group of Canadian researchers questioned a group of college students to understand if there was a relationship between young persons' attachment to others and their parents' divorce. These social scientists found that when the parental divorce was the result of "overt anger," issues involving the children, or an extramarital affair than the student was more likely to be skeptical about developing a lasting relationship with another person (Walker & Ehrenberg, 1998).

Is it possible to cope and adapt after parents divorce? From the literature reviews cited earlier, evidence is clear that many young people can manage this life event (Amato & Keith, 1991; Hines, 1997). To illustrate, in one study 4 years after the parents' divorce the sample of upper-middle-class young people evidenced little self-blame or hope for parental reconciliation. These young people, the authors wrote, had a high level of interpersonal reasoning and an internal locus of control and were older than children cited in other studies who were less able to cope. Furthermore, because the divorce had not occurred recently, the authors believe, these young people were able to place this event in perspective (Kurdek, Blisk, and Siesky, 1981).

The role of the biological father in divorced families is not clear. Some studies identify him as playing an important role (Asmussen & Larson, 1991). For example, one series of studies supports father's emotional value in the family by showing that young people from divorced families have lower levels of self-esteem than do young people from nondivorced homes (Parish & Taylor, 1979; Young & Parish, 1977). Other scholars find his presence less important than his continued adequate financial support (Furstenberg, Allison, & Morgan, 1987; Morrison & Cherlin, 1995). In this last regard, the Census Bureau (1991) reports that 4 months after a father leaves a household income for that household drops 37%.

In interpreting the results of these studies, we would agree with others that divorce does not always leave serious psychological scars on young people (Cherlin, Furstenberg, Chase-Lansdale, Kiernan, Robins, Morrison, & Teitler, 1991; Santrock, 1987). Although it is true that 40% of young people living in the United States and Canada will live sometime in a divorced household and even though it is also true that these households experience considerable pain, it is also true that in many instances this emotional suffering was present long before a divorce occurred (Cherlin et al., 1991; Long, Forehand, Fauber, & Brody, 1987).

It is not divorce per se that is solely responsible for this hurt. Divorce is the culmination rather than the instigation of pain for many of these young people. Further, in our clinical work we have found that although the divorce process is extremely stressful for adolescents, long-term disability seldom occurs.

Finally, the reports of more marital dissatisfaction by adult children of divorced parents may result from a more realistic and honest appraisal of the marriage contract. The higher levels of separation or divorce in this group may represent fewer inhibitions about ending an unsuccessful marriage, which in its unhappiness and conflict may do more psychological damage to children than a divorce.

Implications

There is no question that adolescents experience considerable stress in their parents' divorce process, but this stress does not have to create lasting emotional damage. In the studies we have reviewed, those young people, who were able to muster the necessary emotional supports around them to make it through the upheavals in the family's life, escaped the problems of others unable to do so. How then might we help young people going through this stressful life event?

The role of the community should be to extend that necessary emotional support. This support can be as informal as lending an ear in a friendly way or it can be the formation of self-help groups through community mental health centers or churches. For those young people who want counseling, the counseling should focus on helping them establish an identity separate from their families.' Family therapy (with both parents present) should focus on avoiding the use of the children as chess pieces in the divorce process. The parents should be helped to:

- Work on resolving their conflicts or at least not inflict them on the children.
- Work on developing or maintaining a caring, supportive relationship with their children.
- Develop or take advantage of whatever social support systems are available.

School personnel can help young people realize that they are not responsible for the divorce and that the adolescent cannot heal the break. The staff can also help them realize that the feelings of loneliness and anxiety accompanying a divorce are not permanent, that single-parent families can be emotionally nurturing, and that young people cannot expect happiness but must work at having a satisfying life. These efforts will not eliminate the hurt, but they can provide the incentive to seek the emotional supports necessary to cope with it.

Remarriage

Over the years that it takes most people to marry; to acquire a house, a dog, and a car; and to have children, they have time to adapt to change. Yet consider the newly remarried family with children. In some ways it is analogous to a frozen dinner. Preparation time is minimal—just marry and combine. The potential for things going haywire in this "instant family" is high (Fine & Kurdek, 1992; Hines, 1997; Lee et al., 1994).

And yet our understanding of remarried life is that it can be successful. Many stresses must be handled and readjustments made, but stepparents and stepchildren can succeed if the new family resolves four somewhat amorphous issues.

The first issue is the *entry of a new stepparent into a family*. Several writers have discussed the difficulty many stepparents have in entering a family in which the position of mother or father has been "frozen" and filled by the child(ren) (Amato & Keith, 1991; Visher & Visher, 1983). Freezing happens when the single parent turns to children between marriages for emotional support, love, and even guidance. Reordering this structure is a delicate and often painful process, during which offspring feel rejected by their natural parent.

Roles and boundaries are unclear in newly formed stepfamilies (Hines, 1997). Some authors have gone so far as to say that "organizational disturbance in step-families is inevitable" (Fast & Cain, 1966, p. 485); others have commented that stepfamilies are "forever scrambling to maintain some semblance of equilibrium" (Visher & Visher, 1978, p. 255). This search for order is the second issue that new families must resolve. It occurs partly because society has not been able to re-spond quickly enough to the new variations found within stepfamilies. Historically, a stepparent was a new individual in a household who replaced a dead parent, not a living one. In replacing a living parent, a stepparent becomes an "added" parent (Gullotta et al., 1986). Furthermore, the replaced parent rarely disappears. Thus, the new stepparent not only is initially frozen out of a role but also has the additional burden of wondering what that role should be. The authors of this book believe that time, understanding, and tolerance often will resolve this issue. A stepparent's role is not ascribed but achieved, and that role can vary from family to family. For example, in some families the stepfather may take the role of the biological father or, as Fine and Kurdek (1992) observe, adopt an adjunctive parenting style in which he monitors behavior rather than discipline behavior. These researchers find the adjunctive parenting style was used successfully by stepfathers.

The ability to thaw a family's structure to permit a stepparent to play a role is advanced or retarded by the immediate and long-term *reactions of offspring* to the remarriage. Young people in a remarriage face some difficult new life circum-stances. Not only have they been separated from one natural parent, but they have obtained a surrogate parent, possibly new half-brothers and half-sisters, and other assorted kinfolk. The potential for conflict is certainly present.

Accordingly, it is not surprising that some studies show that remarriage has negative effects on young people. More mental health problems, especially de-pression, are reported for young people in remarried homes (Hines, 1997; Lee et al., 1994). Academic difficulties are evident (Lee et al., 1994). For early adoles-cents it may be that a young person's poor adjustment to remarriage results from wishes that the biological parents would remarry, guilt over imagining that he/she caused the divorce, or, understandably, the failure to resolve the loss.

Finally, some studies find that adolescent girls in remarried households with stepfathers have a more difficult time than boys. For example, they are more likely to drop out of school when living with a stepfather than with a stepmother (Lee et al., 1994). In families with stepfathers, they appear to become sexually active earlier (Cornwell et al., 1996). Kalter (1977) offers the possible explanation that much of this acting-out behavior is due to a "lack of incest barrier between stepfather and daughter" (p. 47). Goldstein (1974) suggests that much of the hostility between adolescent girls and stepfathers may be an attempt to "protect the participants from their sexual impulses" (p. 438). Impulses that may result in the sexual assault of the adolescent by the stepparent. On the other hand, it may be these daughters are having difficulty in accepting their mothers as sexually active beings.

We believe there is a lowered incest barrier. These feelings are complicated by the stepfamily's struggle for cohesiveness at the same time the adolescent is trying to separate from the family. One author suggests that the resolution of this situation rests, to a great extent, with the natural mother's ability to "maintain the incest taboo" (that is, to ensure that the relationship does not acquire incestuous overtones). If she is successful in establishing the taboo, she relieves her daughter and her new husband of the need to maintain a mask of "pseudo-hostility" (Goldstein, 1974).

But not all the writings about young people living in stepfamilies are filled with warnings. Several studies have observed that stepfamilies can be successful. For example, adolescent males appear to do less well living in a single-parent female-headed household than with a stepfather (Tasker & Richards, 1994). This is true particularly when the stepfather is warm, supportive, and uses an authoritative parenting style (Hines, 1997). Challenging the understanding that girls do less well with stepfathers, another study finds that both girls and boys had higher self-esteem and fewer social problems in families with stepfathers than families with stepmothers (Fine & Kurdek, 1992). Finally, MacDonald and DeMaris (1995) using a nationally representative sample of Black and White families with children find that marital conflict is not higher in remarried families. Further, the experiences of Black youths are no different than are the experiences of White youths (Fine, McKenry, Donnelly, & Voydanoff, 1992). These last statements remind us of an observation Nye (1957) once made that young people's behaviors are affected less by the form of their family than by the degree of happiness found there.

We would like to emphasize this last point. There is nothing sacred about any family form. Young people wither just as quickly in unhappy and unnourishing nuclear families as in unhappy and unnourishing divorced or remarried families. We will admit that young people prosper more readily in a nuclear family untouched by severe marital turmoil. However, it is not the single-parent or remarried family structure that impedes maturation. Rather, it is the turmoil found in the original nuclear family that contributes to developmental delays—delays that can be reversed in a new family form.

Parenting Issues

The final issue that the stepfamily must resolve is parenting. Children's fairy tales are filled with stories of the cruelty that stepparents (stepmothers in particular) show to their stepchildren. For example, who among us has not felt anger toward Hansel and Gretel's, Snow White's, or Cinderella's wicked stepmother? Stepfathers have escaped this stigmatization, although it has been suggested that the giant in "Jack and the Beanstalk" symbolizes a stepfather (Visher & Visher, 1978).

One reason stepmothers have fared so poorly in the research literature is that they are so intimately connected to children. Stepparenting is no easy task, particularly when the children are adolescents. One group of scholars have found that

The extended family is a source of strong support for many families.

young people's adjustment to stepfamily life is related to the degree of consistency and parental agreement that exists in the new family (Fine, Donnelly, & Voydanoff, 1991). Not surprisingly, adolescents have the greatest difficulty in accepting discipline from a stepparent. Because stepmothers are more likely than stepfathers to have close contact with the children in the new family, a stepmother faces more disciplinary issues, and problems inevitably arise involving her authority to discipline her husband's children (Fine & Kurdek, 1992). From our experience, we believe that a stepparent should not try to step into the role of natural parent too quickly. We believe that it may be better in the beginning for the stepparent to attempt friendships with their new stepchildren rather than parent relationships.

Permitting a young person the time to mourn enables the stepparent to move from friend, perhaps, to parent with a smaller chance of rejection. Drawing upon the parenting research literature, when parents are cooperating with each other in a consistent fashion, it reduces the chance that stepmothers (or stepfathers) will be viewed as witches (or evil giants) and will increase the probability that the French term for stepmother, belle-mere (beautiful mother), will be applied (Barber, 1992; Wagner, Cohen, & Brook, 1996).

DIVERSE FAMILIES AND THEIR ADOLESCENTS

Social Support among Ethnic and Racially Diverse Families

For many diverse people the extended family is its strongest source of social and parenting support (Taylor, 1996). For example, in some American Indian tribes this extended parental network is found in the extension of the title "mother" to one's mothers' sisters and the term "father" is given to one's fathers' brothers (Burgess, 1980). In these extended families, grandparents are active in the parenting process, and young people seek their grandparents on a frequent basis (Lum, 1996). American Indian children are regarded as important members of the family, and fulfilling their emotional and physical needs are an important part of family life (Burgess, 1980). For many American Indian tribes the concept of extended family reaches beyond blood and marriage ties to include the community. The Lakota Sioux use the term *tiospaye* to describe this understanding. In the tiospaye, individual needs and responsibilities becomes matters of the extended family and community. For example, LaFromboise and Low (1989) write that when problems are experienced by American Indian adolescents, the community and extended kin take steps to restore the adolescent's connections within the group.

Like the American Indians, cooperative parenting is common with many Black families. For hundreds of years, the extended Black family has offered significant aid in childrearing and the socialization of offspring (Lum, 1996; Taylor, 1986). For example, in Taylor's (1986) study of social support in Black families, older adolescents and young adults reported receiving significant support from family members. Similarly, Berg-Cross, Kidd, and Carr (1990) reported that when stress levels rose in families with adolescents, communication and solidarity increased among family members. In another study, social scientists had Black Americans report a serious problem and then list who they would approach for help. An overwhelming majority (82.5%) would seek help from family members (Taylor, Hardison, & Chatters, 1996).

In an important paper, Jarrett (1995) discusses those factors that enable Black adolescents to be "socially mobile." The phrase "socially mobile" refers to youths who make it despite incredible obstacles like severely depressed neighborhoods and grinding poverty. "Making it" means graduating from high school and avoiding teen pregnancy or involvement with the police. What helped these young people to make it? Jarrett (1995) identified five family characteristics which she labels "community-bridging" because they link successful young people to helping opportunities and institutions in the community. They are:

A *supportive adult network* is the first characteristic and refers to the parents' connections with kinship networks. Through strong social bonds, young people receive support from many adults. For example, parents living in a dangerous neighborhood may ask relatives residing in a safer neighborhood to care for their son or daughter. In this example, extended family members enable the young person to obtain resources that otherwise would not be available.

The second characteristic, *restricted family–community relations*, describes parental actions that establish physical or symbolic barriers that protect the adolescent from those in the community who could physically, socially, or emotionally harm the young person. Our earlier example of moving the youth to live in another neighborhood illustrates this parental action.

The next characteristic of families with socially mobile youth is *stringent parental monitoring strategies*. The time, location, and friendships of adolescents are closely monitored by parents and friends to protect the adolescent from environmental risks. To illustrate, within many families young men and women are not permitted to be on the streets after dark without an adult. The hope is that these youths will not be exposed to situations that could have a tragic ending. When an adult is not available, a younger sibling might accompany the adolescent. In this instance, the thinking is that the older youth would not knowingly endanger the younger child.

   Strategic alliances with supportive institutions and organizations is the fourth characteristic. Here, churches and schools are the key institutions that families turn to for positive social activities and support (see Box 7-2). For many Black families, the Church and its teachings provide the moral structure necessary to enable them

---

BOX **7-2** **Adolescents Living in Rural Communities**

The U.S. Bureau of the Census (1989) defines "rural" as communities with less than 2500 people. With images of malls and theatres nearby, it is difficult for most of us to recognize that many Canadian and U.S. adolescents live in rural areas. Less surprising is that these youths are frequently overlooked in research efforts. Therefore, in contrast to their urban counterparts, little is known about rural adolescents (Jessor, 1993). What we do know is that services for these youths are lacking (Cutrona, Halvorson & Russell, 1996).

   The following details several of the problems that face rural families and youths.

1. Adolescent problems like the use of drugs, delinquency, and school violence typically associated with urban areas are growing concerns in rural settings.

2. Other problems like dropping-out of school, unemployment, poor housing, poverty, and substance abuse are found in many rural areas. Regarding employment opportunities, rural areas are typically dependent on industries that have declined in recent years (e.g., agriculture, textile mills, etc.) (Cutrona et al., 1996). It is a myth that rural poverty is easier to bear than urban poverty because families can raise their own foods. The fact is few rural families raise their own food or live on farms (Dyk, 1993). Often, the cost of transporting goods to rural areas and the lack of store competition often results in higher prices than found in urban areas.

3. Geographical isolation and limited funding often limits access to services like counseling, child care, and shelters for battered women and children (see Dyk,

1993). Cutrona et al. (1996) note that providing counseling services in rural areas is complicated by (a) communication and travel barriers, (b) the fact that many mental health counselors prefer to work in urban areas, and (c) limited financial and insurance resources for families to pay for care.

4. Rural social isolation results in fewer opportunities for social interaction with peers and others. Opportunities for social support are diminished as well. Loneliness is a frequent outcome of social isolation and contributes to conditions like depression. Higher rates of suicide among rural adolescents lend support these observations (Cutrona et al., 1996).

5. Ethnically and racially diverse adolescents are at particular risk in rural areas because they frequently are in the minority. In many cases, there is limited access to appropriate cultural-socialization experiences and to adult role models who can help build ethnic group pride and ethnic identity.

6. A common dilemma for rural youths is whether to stay in one's community after graduation from high school. For example, Photiadis (1985) reports that rural Appalachian youths frequently feel trapped between their parents' expectations, the lack of jobs in the their communities, and uncertainties about future employment.

   We believe that these distinctions between rural and urban adolescents mark another aspect of diversity about which little is known. We would encourage scholarship in this area and financial investments to enable these families to raise their children successfully.

to successfully raise their children. Involvement with schools is also characteristic of the parents of socially mobile youths. It enables parents to not only monitor their child's educational progress but to advocate for her/his needs when necessary.

Finally, *adult-sponsored development* involves adult encouragement of certain skills and competencies. For example, adolescents may be encouraged to assist their parents in managing the household. In brief, by weeding out undesirable influences, protecting the adolescent from neighborhood dangers, and giving that person positive sources of support, Black adolescents can be helped to succeed.

Black families are not alone in their use of the extended family to foster success among its members. While emphasizing different features, Latino and Asian families are also very family focused. For example, while the male-dominated (patriarchical) nuclear family may be the archetypal Latino family form, recent evidence points to an emerging egalitarian family structure within Latino families (Chilman, 1993). Whether patriarchical or egalitarian, the Latino family includes extended family and godparents (Lum, 1996). Like many successful Black families, Latino Americans turn to these extended family members when help is needed, even when other sources of support are available (Lum, 1996). Further, Chilman (1993) states that the Latino extended family (parents, grandparents, aunts, and uncles) is a major support system for Latino children.

Like many Latino families, Asian-American families tend to be male dominated (patriarchical) with family roles and relationships clearly defined (Harrison et al., 1994; Lum, 1996). Within many Asian-American families, the father's role is to provide leadership, and the mother's role is to provide nurturance and caretaking to her husband and children (Lum, 1996). Obedience from children is expected. In return for their obedience, parents provide the child with a strong moral upbringing, academic training, and emotional support. There is a high regard and concern for children in Asian-American families (Lum, 1996). Importantly, fulfilling one's appropriate role in the family is a sign of family group loyalty, which is more highly valued than individual independence.

Socialization of Collectivist and Communal Ideals

In contrast to the individualism found in many European-American families, many diverse families, as we have noted, emphasize collectivist values. This is especially true of Japanese-, Hawaiian-, and Mexican-American family cultures where affiliation, cooperation, and interpersonal relationships are highly prized. While neither set of family values is superior to the other, it does set groups apart. One set of values esteems the accomplishments and achievements of the individual. The other appreciates the interconnection of the person to the group and that his/her identity is rooted in that group (Harrison et al., 1994).

Generally, the traditional values of Asian-American (especially Japanese and Chinese) cultures favor a group orientation. Nagata (1989) states that traditional Japanese values for in-group unity, group consensus, and the discouragement of individuality are responsible for the behavior of many Japanese-American families. To illustrate, Feldman and Quatman (1988) find that in contrast to

European-American parents Asian-American parents expect their adolescent children to be compliant longer and engage in less autonomous behavior longer.

Evidence for collectivism is also found within the child-rearing disciplinary practices of Black-American families. Drawing from evidence that Black mothers discipline early adolescents more strictly than White mothers, Portes, Dunham, and Williams (1986) speculate that living in a historically oppressive and prejudicial society has encouraged Black families to emphasize that their children behave, particularly in public. It also might be argued that more strict disciplinary Black parenting styles are the result of parenting practices that stress connecting to others. Thus, the importance of learning proper social behavior is given greater emphasis.

Differences in family interactional patterns among ethnic groups can also be the result of nuclear and extended family parenting practices. For example, Hsu, Tseng, Ashton, McDermott, and Char (1985) explored family interactions in Japanese-American and White families with adolescents. They noted that the two groups differed in the amount of autonomy extended to family members. For example, the Japanese were more reluctant to express individual thoughts and feelings. Furthermore, the Japanese were found to be less willing to accept responsibility for their own thoughts, feelings, and actions, and were more meddling in their interactions with other family members. In individual communication, family members frequently spoke for each other. These findings may represent the Japanese culture's value of striving to maintain harmonious interpersonal relationships.

What may further strengthen an ethnic group's sense of collectivism are those aspects that make them unique. These aspects can include language, religion, and other practices including food and family members' roles. For example, for Mexican Americans, a strong sense of family, a unique Mexican-Catholic ideology, and the use of Spanish set Mexican Americans apart from other groups (Buriel, 1987). Indeed, Diaz-Guerrero (1987), summarizing the research on Mexican-American youths, concludes that they are more family centered and cooperative in their interpersonal activities than White youths.

To sum up, the stricter and more authoritarian parenting styles found in some diverse families may reflect a desire to socialize children toward communal roles (relatedness). Socialization practices that encourage group values and interdependent behaviors suggest that independence (individuality) may not be of central importance to diverse families.

SUMMARY

From presenting parenting styles and reviewing several of the many changes occurring to North American families to showing the uniqueness of the many diverse people that live here, this chapter has covered a wealth of material. Hopefully, you'll agree with us that the historical evidence we reviewed moderated evidence suggesting the modern family is in trouble. Next, did you see the influence of context on the developmental pathways for child and their families? Incidentally, when it was appropriate, we drew upon our clinical training and expertise to offer advice on how to best weather distressing family storms. In your opinion, did you agree with our understanding of how to best help children and families in distress? Finally, we hope you've used your highlighter or a pencil to mark words and phrases that will trigger these recollections for you at a later date.

MAJOR POINTS TO REMEMBER

1. The generation gap is more a figment of imagination than reality. Peers do have a great deal of influence on their fellows during adolescence, but that does not mean that parents or schools have none.
2. The family serves certain basic functions. It provides cohesion or emotional bonding, a model of adaptability, and a network of communication experience.
3. All parenting styles differ, but research on families has identified four main types. These are warm and loving, hostile and cold, controlling and restrictive, and permissive and undemanding. It is highly unlikely that one would find many pure examples of one parenting type. Many families show degrees of each style.
4. The family exercises strong influence, even in adolescence, on such factors as personality development and social competence.
5. Many ethnic minority family environments are characterized by extended-family networks and shared parenting responsibilities between members of the network. Adolescents benefit from these family types in respect to having a large number of adult caregivers who provide social support and socialization.
6. Socialization among many ethnically diverse groups includes components of collectivist and communal ideals. These ideals are in conflict with the independent, self-oriented practices of the larger culture.
7. Were this 1950, the very thought of mothers in the work force would be condemned. As the percentage of working mothers has grown beyond 30% in 1956 to over 70% in the 1990s, society has learned to accept the idea and to be aware of the benefits and occasional problems that accompany this family style.
8. The involvement of the father in family life falls short of the mother's involvement.
9. When discussing divorce, we have been increasingly inclined to comment that three things in life are now certain: death, taxes, and divorce. The divorce rate is rapidly approaching the level in which one in two marriages ends up in court.
10. Research suggests that while the process is difficult, painful, and emotionally bruising, young people can, with love and help, make it through their parents' divorce.

11. This balancing process can be made easier by the divorced parents working together to raise their children.

12. The most important part of working with families is to build on strengths. Because there are so many family styles, the goal of intervention is to help the family find the style that is most comfortable for that particular family. So long as that style does not harm family members or other families, it should be considered functional for that family.

Peer, Leisure, and Work Experiences

TIMES WERE THAT children worked at the sides of their parents or learned a trade from another adult. Times were that as many hands as could be found cultivated crops, cared for animals, and prepared for that time of year when the fields rested beneath a blanket of frost and snow. Times were that motherhood came early and often until death or old age stopped the flow of life.

You'll remember that earlier in this book we talked about adolescence as a social invention. That is, as the need for young people to move into adult roles declined, childhood was extended. This extension was called adolescence. Since young people are no longer needed to harvest crops and care for animals or to marry at a young age and produce children, adolescence provides a hiatus between childhood and adult responsibilities. These role changes are clearly evident in the way in which young people have related to adults over time. Before the mid-1800s, the vast majority of young people across North America either remained at home, actually on the farm, working beside their parents, or were apprenticed so that they constantly lived under the direction of an adult. However, after the 1850s, with greater migration to the cities—the centers of industrialized activity—and with more parents working away from home, young people increasingly came to be on their own. Beginning then and extending to the present, decreasing adult supervision, increasing autonomy, and an educational system built on the "peer culture" (Coleman, 1961) gave rise to concerns about who is and what is influencing the development of young people. For while in theory adolescence provides an interval between childhood and adulthood, most young people, encouraged by the society around them, loathe this delay in accessing adult rights of freedom to dress, look, and act as they wish. This chapter looks at some of the who's and what's that are influencing youth. We discuss peer groups and their influence on adolescent behavior. We also take up the adolescent's use of leisure time to watch television, listen to music, play video games, interact in cyberspace, and participate in sports. Finally we examine adolescents at work.

PEER GROUPS

Group Formation

Take a moment and think about your middle and high school friendships. Now consider this question. Did your peer group provide a framework for your social and personal interactions? For example, if your friendship group was very interested in school- based social activities but not at the expense of grades then the framework for values and behavior would have encouraged you to participate in school activities while maintaining good grades. As you think about your adolescent peer group, can you identify the values of your peer group and see how those values influenced your behavior? Drawing on material from the second chapter, we can look at the writings of scholars representing different theoretical perspectives and observe that from a psychosocial perspective peer groups offer feedback and information on defining the self in the process of identity formation (Erikson, 1968). Behavioral theorists see peer groups as important sources for reinforcing behaviors and values (McCandless, 1970). And sociologists like Kingsley Davis (1940) contend peer groups form because of intergenerational conflicts. Thus, depending on your understanding, the formation of the peer group assists in the formation of identity; it encourages certain norms and mores and it speeds the process of becoming independent parents and other significant adults. If your experience is like ours, the peer group did all this and more.

Regardless of why peer groups emerge, it is clear that in early adolescence young people prefer to be in the company of other young people (Brown, Eicher, & Petrie, 1986; Montemayor, Adams, & Gullotta, 1994; Reisman, 1985). For example, a 2-year study of 335 early adolescents from grades 6 to 8 found that as these young people grew older, groups formed, telephone usage increased, and, by the 8th grade, dating began. Nearly half the males and females in this study acknowledged having "made out" by the 8th grade (Crockett, Losoff, & Petersen, 1984). Beyond the obvious attraction for young people in discovering each other's sexuality, there are other reasons for peer relations. One is the mutual support and guidance that the peer group offers adolescents in contrast to the adolescents' perceived view of their parents as rule-makers (Moran & Eckenrode, 1991). It is this gradual process of acquiring autonomy, distance, and emancipation from parents that enable youth to mature (Cooper, 1994).

Some Determinants of Friendship

Having determined that peer groups speed the process from adolescence to adulthood, think again about your friendship group. Why did you choose this peer group, and why do you think you were accepted into this group? If your response is because of common interests, then a large body of research would support your observation. Friendship groups form around similar interests, values, and opinions (Whitbeck, Simons, Conger, & Lorenz, 1989). Further, they most often occur among youths who are of similar age, the same sex, and race (Brown, Mory, & Kinney, 1994; Kandel, 1981b). Thus, involvement and behavior in school—namely, educational expectations, grades, frequency of cutting classes, number of days absent, and time spent doing homework—are similar for close friends. Indeed, one recent study reports similar identity statuses for close friends (Akers, Jones, & Coyl, 1998). This extends also to illicit activities (Kandel, 1973; Whitbeck, Simons, Conger, & Lorenz, 1989). On this last point, engaging in delinquent acts

The peer group provides a framework for friendship values and beliefs.

attracts peers with similar interests. Likewise, young people who smoke marijuana or tobacco, drink alcohol, or use psychedelic drugs are more likely to have friends who do the same, lending credence to the old statement "You can tell a lot about people by the friends they keep."

Friendship Formation and Peer Behavior

Friendships occur where feelings of closeness, support, attachment, love, esteem, and acceptance exist (Montemayor & Gregg, 1994). Reflect again on the past and consider present friendships. We suspect that your close lasting friendships have an unconditional acceptance element to them. That is, while you may recognize faults in a friend you choose to overlook them in favor of other redeeming qualities. Friendships may develop because of (1) assortative pairing in which friends are selected on the basis of similarity and/or (2) a socialization process in which friends influence each other (Kandel, 1981b). In fact, both factors are at work in most relationships. The sharing of same interests or qualities contributes to friendship formation, while the socialization process deepens the friendship over time.

While young people are peer focused, their peer interactions are often self-centered. For example, in one naturalistic observation study of male adolescents, the author found most of the adolescents' comments reflected joking, exaggeration, elaborations on truth, or tales of perceived invulnerability. However, when these adolescents interacted with an adult leader, many of their remarks showed discouragement and a belief that adults did not take them seriously (Newman, 1976). Another researcher has elaborated on this point in a study of several hundred early adolescents who were asked to identify socially supportive adults. In this study, young people identified such supportive behaviors as affection, nurturance, and useful help coming most from their mothers, significantly less from their fathers, and "uniformly" withheld by their teachers (East, 1989).

The Emergence of Groups

To understand why groups emerge during adolescence we need to appreciate the psychosocial nature of adolescence. With the social invention of adolescence, emphasis shifted from an adult-focused to a youth-focused world in which adolescents spend most of their time interacting with other youths. Even in settings like schools where adults are expected to influence young people, teacher behavior generally favors peer over adult–youth interactions. For example, one study observed that high school teachers overwhelmingly used lectures to teach. This study reported that less than 1% of instructional time "required some kind of open response involving reasoning or perhaps an opinion from students" (Goodlad, 1984, p. 299). Indeed, it has been observed that teachers passively accept students' membership in almost any peer group without making serious attempts to influence friendship patterns (Newman & Newman, 1976). On the other hand, teachers actively solicit youths with specific characteristics for membership in certain school-related groups. Have you ever thought about the common characteristics of adolescents who are office helpers, hall monitors, teachers' assistants, and so forth? Contrast these characteristics with those of adolescents assigned the role of class stooge or resident J.D. (juvenile delinquent).

Thus, social environments encourage group identity over social alienation. This social process can be viewed in terms of psychosocial conflict. That is, young people are pushed by individual and social needs to identify with a social group or experience feelings of alienation and isolation. For example, if an adolescent chooses to identify only with the family, there is the potential for a self-perceived perennial childhood. If not attached to a social group, the adolescent is likely to experience the distress of isolation. Thus, the group is a natural outcome of a social structure that encourages youths to identify with at least one peer group (see Box 8–1 for social processes that influence peer group formation). Having examined the "why" of groups, let's next examine some of the interpersonal influences within peer groups.

Interpersonal Influence

You need only to look around you to recognize that adolescents influence each other. One form of learning theory offers a framework for understanding this influence. Social-cognition theory sees this interpersonal influence emerging from (1) imitation, in which one person observes the behavior of another and copies it, and (2) social reinforcement, in which a person is rewarded for adopting the behaviors or values of another.

B O X **8-1**   The Social Psychology of In-Groups and Out-Groups

---

Same-sex, same-age, and same-race are the three most common characteristics of adolescent friendships (Kandel, 1981b). One way to examine the dynamics of race and ethnicity in peer relations is through in-group and out-group comparisons. When an individual is born into a group or affiliates with a group as a child, adolescent, or adult, he or she is a member of an in-group. Similarity is a factor that strengthens in-group connections. Out-groups are those groups of which the individual is not a member.

There are many positive aspects of in-group membership. For example, a sense of who you are comes from membership in social groups (Hinkle & Brown, 1990). Members of in-groups typically develop positive feelings of belonging, solidarity, and group pride. On the other hand, the tendency may be for in-groups to feel superior and to express prejudice toward out-groups. Discrimination is a common occurrence between in- and out-groups.

In reality, people are members of a variety of in-groups based on factors like race and ethnicity, gender, religion, interests and hobbies, athletic activities, and educational level. The more groups of which a person is a member, the greater the potential for contact with out-group members. Thus, one way to minimize prejudice and discrimination among adolescents would be to provide multiple opportunities for interaction and cooperation between out-groups. But, in order to be effective, certain favorable conditions are necessary for between group contact. Brigham (1986) has identified five of these key conditions:

1. *Participants need to have equal status with one another.* Brigham (1986) notes, however, that equal status has not characterized interracial contact in the United States. One implication of this point is to strive for equality in as many settings as possible.
2. *Competition increases group hostilities; thus, intergroup contact should include opportunities for mutual interdependence and cooperation.* The introduction of common goals is an effective way to enhance interdependence between groups that formerly have been in conflict.
3. *Personal relationships and the development of friendships should be encouraged by social norms and authorities.* In-group adolescents can be taught that many of their needs and interests are shared with out-group adolescents and vice versa. Emphasizing communality provides the basis for building friendship.
4. *Characteristics of group members do not reinforce negative stereotypes of the groups.* Emphasize the many attributes of individuals that challenge common stereotypes.
5. *Encourage generalization of changed attitudes to new people and situations.* Once adolescents have been exposed to the misleading nature of stereotypes with respect to one out-group, encourage them to explore misconceptions they may hold about other out-groups.

We can use this understanding to predict and then test a concern that parents have regarding the influence older youth exercise over younger adolescents. This concern has legitimacy in that many school districts place younger youths with older adolescents. For example, some elementary schools are K–8. In other communities, secondary schools are 7–12. The developmental differences between young people in these settings can be vast.

Testing the impact of placing younger students with older students, one research study found that younger students experienced damaging effects when placed with older students. When 9th-graders were moved into a high school containing 9th and 10th grades, they were found to show more worry about their school environment, increased drug use, and increased concern about victimization. Similar, but less obvious, effects were noted when 7th- and 8th-graders were educated in the same building with 9th-graders (Blyth, Hill, & Smyth, 1981). A second study by Gifford and Dean (1990) found that 9th-grade students in junior high school settings were more involved in extracurricular school activities than their counterparts in senior high school settings. In addition, these young people had better attitudes toward school and higher grades than 9th-graders in 9–12 school settings.

To ease the transition from one school setting to another, one group of community psychologists has designed an effective prevention program that increases parent–child tutorial involvement, heightens teacher awareness, and uses peer mentors (Jason, Kurasaki, Neuson, & Garcia, 1993). Preventive interventions of this nature that sensitize school officials and that educate, support, and guide the new student hold promise for reducing the stress of school change. Involved teachers, in caring youth-focused schools that actively involve parents in the educational process, can also significantly reduce these stresses.

DEVELOPMENTAL CHANGES IN INFLUENCE AND INVOLVEMENT

Parental and Peer Influence

For all of the influence of the peer group, several studies have documented the less than all-powerful effect peers have on behavior (Collins & Repinski, 1994; Sebald, 1989). For example, in one study young people were asked to whom they would turn to for advice. On issues like education, careers, and money matters, adolescents sought advice from parents. On subjects like dress, dating, drinking, and other social activities peer influence prevailed (Sebald, 1989). This measured influence of peer groups on adolescent behavior has been demonstrated by others (Berndt, Miller, & Park, 1989). For example, Berndt et al. found that on matters of attitudes toward school and behavior in school settings that parents were reported to be more influential than peers. In short, parents matter in the lives of their offspring.

Another study of 272 12- to 15-year-old English girls provides cross-cultural support for these findings. On moral issues, parental values dominated. In contrast, on issues such as grooming and social activity, peer values dominated (Niles, 1981). These findings are consistent with J. C. Coleman's (1978) beliefs about adolescent development. According to Coleman, differing themes associated with parental and peer influence on adolescent behavior occur at different ages. For example, Coleman provides evidence that fear of peer rejection, which peaks about age 16, influences adolescent decision-making. In view of this last statement, it is easy to imagine that parents and their children will disagree on issues. Several authors build on this observation and note that among the developmental tasks facing adolescents is the paradoxical situation of achieving independence while maintaining an affectionate and supportive relationship with parents (Rice & Mulkeen, 1995; Youniss, Mclellan, & Strouse, 1994).

Clearly, the parent–adolescent relationship is an important factor in understanding the varying influence of peers on adolescent behavior. In one such study, adolescents who reported a high-quality relationship with their parents had fewer peer contacts, reported less reliance on peers, and claimed more overall auton- omy (Iacovetta, 1975). A second investigation suggests that parental qualities are stronger predictors of peer-group involvement than peer characteristics (Smith, 1976). Thus, the degree of peer-group influence is more associated with the quality of the parent–adolescent relationship than with the lure of peer groups themselves.

From Same-Sex Involvement to Opposite-Sex Involvement

For most youth, adolescence is not only a time of increasing peer influence but also a period of change from same-sex friendships to heterosexual involvements. When examined from a group-formation perspective, peer relations emerge in crowds and cliques. A *crowd* is a large group of youths who connect with one another through the identification of a common leader or idol. Membership in a crowd does not assure a close relationship among all the members; rather, a crowd is a collection of smaller groups referred to as cliques. A *clique* is composed of several youths who are very close friends. In contrast to membership in a crowd, belonging to a clique means keeping a close relationship with all the other mem- bers. The initiation and development of peer groups is a gradual social process involving both cliques and crowds.

A classic field observation study by Dexter Dunphy (1963) in Australia offers insight into this process (see Figure 8-1). In early adolescence (Stage 1), boys and girls maintain small, same-sex cliques. Over time, these same-sex cliques begin to interact. Gradually the leaders and higher-status group members form addi- tional cliques based on heterosexual relations. Next, the newly formed heterosex- ual cliques come to replace the same-sex cliques. Furthermore, these heterosexual cliques relate with each another in a larger crowd during group functions and social activities. In late adolescence the crowd begins to break-up into small cliques or couples. While the crowd loses its utility as couple relationships form, friendships made earlier can continue for life.

We suspect you noticed that this section focused on heterosexual youths. For homosexual or bisexual youth, this period of life is often filled with loneliness. Peer interaction and the forming of friendships are important elements in the healthy social and emotional development of the adolescent. As we noted in Chapter 5 on sex roles, for most youths adolescence is accompanied by an exaggeration of sex-typed behavior. Thus, homosexual or bisexual youths are likely to expe- rience rejection by peers anxious about their own sexuality and, sadly, by others who can neither understand nor accept this sexual orientation (Savin-Williams, 1994).

Social Interaction between Ethnic Groups

Many Canadian and U.S. cities are ethnically, racially, and religiously diverse communities. Due to the multicultural richness of this experience, we suspect that

FIGURE 8.1

The development of heterosexual cliques, crowds, and couples. Individual sets without an arrow are noninteracting. Sets with arrows are interacting groups. Overlapping sets are interacting between included figures only.

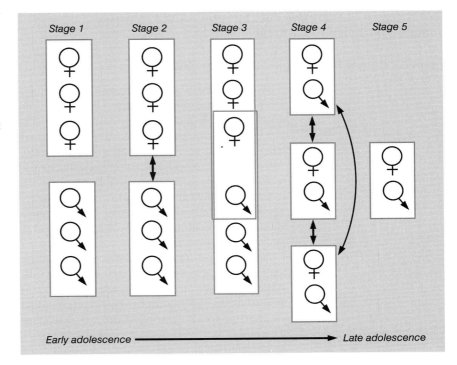

young people living in Edmonton, Quebec, Toronto, Portland, Tucson, Baltimore and elsewhere are likely different from youth living in less diverse communities. In this section we examine the nature and context of social interactions between racial and ethnic peers.

To begin, differences in ethnic and racially diverse adolescents' associations with peers can be understood by their reference-group orientation. What's a *reference-group orientation*? It refers to the way in which we choose to define ourselves and includes the "labels, values, attitudes, preferences, and behaviors specific to particular ethnic groups" (Rotheram-Borus, 1990, p. 1075). Rotheram-Borus (1990) identifies three main reference groupings—mainstream, strongly ethnically identified, and bicultural. *Mainstream* ethnic youths view themselves in accord with the values of the broader society. *Strongly ethnically identified* adolescents adopt values of their ethnic group. *Bicultural* youth bridge mainstream and ethnic cultures pulling values and practices from each.

Some individuals, like the Nation of Islam religious leader Louis Farrakhan, would argue that a strong ethnic identity is best for the social adjustment of young people and for their larger minority group interests. Others, including ourselves, believe that greater interpersonal involvement and understanding will move us closer together as a people living under the same flag and system of government.

PEER RELATIONS AMONG ETHNIC AND RACIAL MINORITY ADOLESCENTS

Ethnic/Racial Mixing among Peer Groups

An increasingly culturally rich North American society is reflected in the ethnic and racial compositions of many of its schools. The impact of this diversity on peer relations is of obvious interest to scholars, school officials, and community leaders.

Our understanding of adolescent ethnic intermixing can be helped by examining Canadian society. In contrast to the United States, which views itself as a "melting pot," Canadians see themselves as living in a "cultural mosaic." But with recent increases in non-European immigration and the growth of ethnic diversity in Canada, this "cultural mosaic" is being challenged. Examining this dynamic, a research team studied the perceptions and attitudes among French, Italian, and Haitian adolescents attending a Montreal school (Laperriere, Compere, D'Khissy, Dolce, & Fleurant, 1994).

Young people for their study were drawn from a predominantly French (65%) high school that included an Italian minority (15%) and a more newly immigrated Haitian minority (15%). Three age groups (12–13, 14–15, and 16–17) were examined for age differences in interethnic attitudes and behaviors. For the youngest group (the 12- to 13-year-olds), cultural characteristics were of little importance to the French Quebec adolescents, and they felt that their social relations with Italian and Haitian youths were positive. Interestingly, however, the Italian and Haitian youths thought of themselves first as members of their ethnic groups and saw the French youths as discriminating against them.

In contrast, the 14- to 15-year-old French adolescents showed greater awareness of cultural differences and placed a higher value on the unique features of their own groups. For example, French youths recognized their cultural uniqueness, and the Italian and Haitian youths were more open about their cultural practices and traditions.

Among the 16- to 17-year-old French youths three groups emerged holding different views about intergroup contact. One group of French youths was socially involved with ethnically different youths. The second group retreated into their own culture and placed less emphasis on cross-cultural contacts, while the third group of French youths displayed racist behavior toward others, in particular, the Haitians. Italian and Haitian 16- to 17-year-olds also displayed a continuum of attitudes toward French and others ranging from separatist preferences of cultural superiority to values supportive of and respectful toward cultural plurality (Laperriere, Compere, D'Khissy, Dolce, & Fleurant, 1994). Clearly, the reference-group orientation discussed earlier in this chapter is evident in this study.

Maharaj and Connolly (1994) also were interested in social interaction among peer groups in the Canadian multicultural context. Their sample was drawn from a middle-income suburban high school. Of the nearly 900 participants, approximately 400 were grouped as belonging to the acculturated North American group with the remaining students belonging to Asian, West Indian, and other groups. In forming peer groups, each ethnocultural group selected peers from their own group in greater numbers than the relative proportion of that group to the total school. Although ethnocultural peer preferences were shown, patterns of peer segregation were not strongly observed.

In summary, research using a reference-group model indicates that the acceptance of bicultural values enhances social involvement for some youths. While some may argue that a strong ethnic identification is most desirable for social adjustment, others believe that greater interpersonal involvement and cross-group understanding resulting from a bicultural orientation is preferable. The authors of this book subscribe to the second position. We believe that drawing upon ones own heritage and borrowing aspects from other groups not only enhances growth but enriches the overall experience of life.

Peer Support among Diverse Adolescents

The strong social supports found in many racially and ethnically diverse families is also evident in close networks of friends and peers. For example, Coates (1987) writes that social support serves as a buffer against stress and as a facilitator of competence in adolescence. Social support is particularly important for Black and other diverse youths because it aids in the accomplishment of goals that might be otherwise blocked by social prejudice and injustice.

But peer support systems may not be the same for both sexes. For instance, Black females' social networks appear to be more intimate than males. Summarizing the literature on interpersonal relations among Black youths, Gibbs (1989) notes the presence of strong same-sex peer groups. In particular, Black female peer groups serve as social support networks in communities characterized by many single-parent families and having few community resources.

Other differences between Black males and females also exit. For example, Coates (1987) shares that Black female adolescents believe they know more persons than do Black male adolescents. However, females report less contact than do males with their social networks. Still, females report that they meet members of their social networks in more intimate settings than do males. Further, a higher proportion of Black females than Black males report having small friendship groups (less than five persons). In short, social support networks are important to both male and female Black adolescents, but the degree of intimacy with friends and the size of friendship groups vary for the females and males (Coates, 1987).

Strong peer social support is linked to positive emotional ties between friends. The unwelcome counterpart of social support happens when friendship bonds influence young people to behave in destructive ways (Gibbs, 1989). Resistance to joining a negative peer group and refusing to participate in antisocial behavior can result in social isolation and ridicule for adolescents. In keeping with our earlier discussion on similarity between adolescent friends, it is clear that similarity in the willingness to engage or to not engage in deviant behavior is a factor worth consideration.

For example, in one study of friendship dyads the authors reported that White adolescents were similar to their friends in respect to the number of cigarettes smoked in the last week, attitudes toward smoking, and the importance of activities related to misconduct and school. On the other hand, Black friendships were not based on similarity in attitudes and behaviors toward certain activities. In contrast to White youth, Black youth reported: (a) giving more importance to parent and school activities, (b) assigning less importance to peer involvement and misconduct activities, (c) giving less dispositional compliance to friends, and (d) being less likely to have ever smoked or currently smoked (Tolson & Urberg, 1993). For this one sample, it is evident that close friendships of Black adolescents were not dependent on any degree of willingness to engage in deviant behaviors; degree of importance of activities; or attitudinal similarity in respect to peers, family, and school.

While it was not clear in the Tolson and Urberg (1993) study what factors of similarity in respect to deviance tied some Black adolescents to each other, the psychosocial friendship characteristics between delinquent Puerto Rican adolescent males was explored by Pabon, Rodriguez, and Gurin (1992). The subjects consisted of 11- to 19-year-old lower-income Puerto Rican males living in the South Bronx of New York City. This study reported that association with delinquent peers was predicted by time spent together with friends especially in the evening. In contrast, emotional closeness did not predict delinquency.

Another aspect of complying to peer pressure may be related to the degree to which diverse adolescents have accepted White middle-class norms. Evidence exists that the more mainstream-acculturated ethnic adolescent is at greater risk for negative peer conformity than less acculturated adolescents. Why would this be the case? We'll use a study of susceptibility to delinquent peer pressure according to degree of acculturation to explain this statement. In this study, the subjects were mostly low-income urban Latino high school students. Susceptibility to delinquent peer pressure was predicted by: (1) school grades, (2) sex (males), and (3) a more acculturated perspective. In respect to the last finding, it may be that the more acculturated adolescent had adopted an European-American orientation toward peer-versus-parental involvement. That is, peer influence ranked more strongly than family influence. In contrast, the less acculturated Latino adolescent may have been more strongly tied to values of family and parental authority and, therefore, was less susceptible to negative peer influence. Interestingly, these findings are comparable to similar studies on European Americans (Wall, Power & Arbona, 1993).

To summarize, the realities of social support from peers for ethnically and racially diverse adolescents are twofold. On the positive side, many diverse youths live in strongly connected social worlds that are filled with broad-based social support from friends and peers. Although the degree of connection may vary for females and males, this broad connection provides a wide network of concern and caring. However, if the network is defiant, norm-breaking, or delinquent, the influence may be socially or psychologically harmful. Indeed, the nature of social support among delinquent peers may be less associated with emotional bonding and more strongly related to convenience in respect to time and opportunity. Degree of acculturation is another important variable to consider on this topic. Ethnically and racially diverse adolescents most protected from negative peer influence are those who: (1) are less acculturated to European-American norms of independence and individuation from family and (2) are more adhering to values of emotional support and family ties. In the next section, we move from examining the interplay between peers and others to how young people use their leisure time.

ADOLESCENTS, PEER GROUPS, AND THEIR USE OF LEISURE TIME

Frankly, we are not sure whether society influences adolescent tastes, adolescents influence adolescent tastes, or adolescents influence society's tastes. We do suspect that the interactions are complex and revolve around archetypal themes of individuality and independence. We have selected several of the most interesting and explore them in the remainder of this chapter (see Table 8-1).

Television: Surfing Them Channels

In exhaustive reviews of the literature on the effects of television on youth, Jason, Hanaway, and Brackshaw (1998), Leibert and Sprafkin (1988), Murray (1980), and Strasburger (1995) provide information gathered from 4 decades of research in the area. The picture that emerges from their work is disturbing because of the tremendous impact on our attitudes and behavior that we have permitted television to have.

Television viewing begins as early as the first year of life. Most children begin watching television before they are walking, talking, and playing with other children. It is estimated that U.S. and Canadian youth consume 18,000 hours of television during their adolescent years (Carruth, Goldberg, & Skinner, 1991). Few of us can probably remember a time when a television set was not in our homes. But for those few who can, the arrival of a set meant that as preadolescents we spent less time reading, listening to the radio, visiting friends, or going to the movies. We used television for emotional release, to engage in fantasy, and to be informed of micromachines, light bulb powered ovens, "Barbies," and "My Little Ponies" (whose long nylon hair could be combed endlessly). We used television to have something to talk about with our friends and to compare ourselves against some idealized version of family life appearing in shows like *"Lassie," "The Brady Bunch," "The Cosby Show," "The Wonder Years,"* or *"Family Ties."*[1] This is in decided contrast to today's dysfunctional television families which portray parents as absent, bungling, or grosssly unfit. For example, consider *"Grace Under Fire,"* which illustrates the absent parent; the bungling parent can be found on *"Home Improvement;"* and the parents on *"Married With Children"* are unfit at best. Interestingly, although children and adolescents are major consumers of this

---

[1] The cable channels TV Land and Nickelodeon have reintroduced todays adolescents and Generation Xers to "Lassie," "The Brady Bunch," and "Dobie Gillis"—the adolescent of the early 1960s. Now, if only they'd bring back "Howdy Doody."

T A B L E 8-1   Daily Leisure Activities of High School Seniors by Type of Activity and Sex

Activity and sex	Percentage participating in activity each day								
	1976	1980	1984	1985	1986	1987	1988	1989	1990
Watch television	71	72	73	72	74	71	73	71	72
Males	71	72	76	74	77	74	74	77	74
Females	71	73	69	69	71	69	71	66	70
Read books, magazines, or newspapers	59	59	53	51	50	48	46	47	47
Males	58	59	52	50	50	49	47	48	50
Females	62	59	54	52	51	48	46	46	46
Get together with friends	52	51	48	47	49	47	50	51	49
Males	55	55	51	52	52	49	54	56	52
Females	48	47	43	43	46	45	48	46	45
Participate in sports and exercise	44	47	44	43	44	44	44	44	46
Males	52	57	54	53	54	55	57	55	56
Females	36	38	33	34	36	34	31	33	34
Spend at least one hour of leisure time alone	40	42	44	42	42	43	42	42	41
Males	39	40	42	40	40	44	41	44	40
Females	41	44	45	45	43	44	42	41	42
Work around house, yard, or car	41	40	41	35	34	33	32	29	28
Males	33	30	35	28	27	27	25	24	22
Females	49	49	47	42	41	38	37	34	35
Ride around in a car for fun	—	33	34	35	36	36	37	36	34
Males	—	38	40	39	41	40	41	42	36
Females	—	28	27	31	31	32	33	31	32
Play a musical instrument or sing	28	29	30	29	27	28	27	27	28
Males	22	25	24	24	22	24	23	23	26
Females	35	34	37	35	32	32	31	30	31
Do art or craft work	12	13	12	11	14	14	13	13	15
Males	10	12	14	12	14	15	12	13	15
Females	13	14	10	10	13	13	12	13	14
Do creative writing	6	5	6	6	7	6	6	6	7
Males	4	4	6	4	6	6	6	5	6
Females	6	6	6	7	7	7	6	7	8

— Data not available.

Source: U.S. House of Representatives. Select Committee on Children, Youth, and Families. *U.S. Children and Their Families: Current Conditions and Recent Trends,* 1992, page 120.

medium, they are depicted as characters in shows less than 10% of the time (Huston, Donnerstein, Fairchild, Katz, Murray, Rubenstein, Wilcox, & Zuckerman, 1992).

Television and Adolescence

The effect of television on the academic performance of young people is in most cases damaging. Researchers report that, as a general rule, as nightly viewing time exceeds 1 to 2 hours, grades decrease (Strasburger, 1993). Young people of lower socioeconomic status appear to watch television more than do those of higher economic status. Also Blacks spend more time with television and radio than Whites (Brown, Childers, Bauman, & Koch, 1990). An additional finding is that as intelligence decreases, viewing time increases. Adolescents with high self-esteem watch less television than those young people who think poorly of themselves (Gerbner, Gross, Morgan, & Signorielli, 1984; Leibert & Sprafkin, 1988; Murray, 1980; Tucker, 1986). Cross-cultural studies show that television viewing by a majority of 13-year-old students in many nations exceeds 3 hours a day (see Box 8-2). In the United States 73% of 13-year-olds watch more than 3 hours of television daily. Viewing time for the youth in the United States has been rising. In the 1960s 17% of young people watched 3 hours of television a day; this figure increased to 29% in the 1970s and to 73% in 1988 (Lawrence, Tasker, Daly, Orhiel, & Wozniak, 1986; U.S. Department of Education, 1989). It should be noted that television watching peaks during early adolescence and declines sharply thereafter. The preadolescent and the early adolescent appear to use television as a companion. As adolescents grow older, they seek out places to meet and socialize with other youths.

BOX **8-2** **Watching the Tube: A Cross-Cultural Perspective**

The following are the percentages of 13-year-old students by amount of time per day spent watching television in five countries and in the Canadian provinces of Ontario and Quebec for the year 1988.

Why do you think viewing habits are so similar in so many countries? What may account for Korea's and Quebec's lower viewing times? Are we becoming a world of one visual image? (U.S. Department of Education, 1989).

Country or Province	0–2 hrs	3–4 hrs	5 hrs or more
United States	27	42	31
United Kingdom	28	45	27
Ireland	45	41	14
Spain	46	41	13
Korea	49	44	7
Ontario (English)	35	43	22
Quebec (French)	49	40	11

Television as Reality

The overwhelming weight of evidence indicates that television strongly shapes adolescents' attitudes toward people, places, and things. If they see it on television, they tend to believe it. If you accept this statement, for a moment, as truth (you can't believe everything you read), then you can view television as a means for shaping public opinion and behavior. For example, consider the clothing that young people wear. Studies suggest that as adolescents increase in age, peer influence in their choice of clothing increases (Eicher, Baizerman, & Michelman, 1991; Koester & May, 1985; Littrell, Damhorst, & Littrell, 1990). Studies report that adolescents are drawn to designer labels (Lennon, 1986). Studies also report that young women spend an incredible 4 billion dollars a year on cosmetics (Brown, Greenberg, & Buerke-Rothfuss, 1993). While no comparable data are available for males, we suspect they equally invest in creams and fragrances that hide the smells and blemishes caused by the hormonal changes triggered by the physical changes that accompany puberty. Where did this awareness of designer labels originate? How do fashions, creams, and fragrances move from relative obscurity to popularity? The answer, of course, can be found on the commercial breaks between music videos.

Television's critics might be more forgiving if it were not for other issues, such as the sexual exploitation of women that routinely fills the airwaves or the televised encouragement of violence. Literally scores of reports have documented the damaging effects of watching excessive televised violence (for example, Bandura, 1965; Berkowitz, 1962, 1964; Comstock & Strasburger, 1993; Murray, 1980; Sege, 1998; Shanahan, 1995).

For example, studies find that as television viewing increases so too does authoritarian world views (Shanahan, 1995). Television creates an artificial reality. This is a fictional world in which ineffective screenplay justice is replaced by the vigilante whose scripted violence is viewed as a legitimate solution to wrongful acts. Violence and crime is a television constant. It is estimated that by adolescence young people have witnessed 200,000 violent acts. Huston et al. (1992) report that the average prime-time television show or movie contains five violent acts per hour. For male youths who excessively watch television, it is this repeated exposure to televised violence that is believed to be responsible for increased aggressive behavior (Sege, 1998; Strasburger, 1993).[2] As an aside, successful action films, like *Lethal Weapon*, *Die Hard*, and *The Terminator*, that spawn sequels have more in common than not much dialogue. Subscribing to a scriptwriting formula that more is better, all of these films, which regularly appear on television, dramatically increased the level of violent behavior in their sequels. As if 32 killings were not enough, the viewer of *Robo Cop II* saw 81. In *Die Hard*, 18 individuals met their demise but in *Die Hard II*, the viewer was treated to 264 deaths before the final credits rolled (Comstock & Strasburger, 1993). While this next statement falls into the category of pure author speculation, we believe that the

---

[2]Communication scholars refer to this form of learning as the "drip" model. That is, televised violent act by televised violent act, behavior is shaped (Huston et al. 1992).

court trials of the youths accused of recent school killings in the U.S. will find them out to be fans of this film slaughter genre. If that is the case, do not be surprised if the defending attorneys use the "drip" model to explain how their clients stepped over the line from fantasy to the destruction of their fellow classmates and teachers.

Finally, evidence suggests that lack of access to parents due either to maternal employment or to parental absence is associated with increased viewing time by adolescents (Brown et al., 1990). Thus, absence of effective monitoring of viewing time by parents or substitution of alternative activities may be a factor in understanding likely negative influences.

Music

Any parent will tell you that musical taste emerges during adolescence. It has been estimated that young people listen to more than 10,500 hours of music during their adolescent years—a figure roughly equivalent to 12 years of schooling (Brown & Hendee, 1989). Indeed, a strong argument can be made that rock music provides the very foundation of what adolescence is all about. It may provide the peer-cultural expectations of adolescent behaviors in such matters as love, activism, values, parent relations, and even aggression.

Music offers its young listeners the chance to be conformingly "with it" in the pop top 40 or to be nonconformingly cool in the counterculture, whether it's rap, heavy metal, punk rock, or good old rock-and-roll. Incidentally, the next time your grandparents extol the virtues of performers like Little Richard, Chuck Berry, or Elvis Presley, you might want to remind them that the emergence of

Contemporary music is the language of youth—where better celebrated than at the concert?

rock-and-roll in the 1950s was met with as much concern as rap music is today. For its time, the words and subject matter of rock-and-roll were considered as sensual and provocative as any of today's lyrics. Indeed, the name "rock-and-roll" refers directly to a rhythm and blues phrase meaning "sex" (Palladino, 1996). And Elvis Presley, the "King of Rock-and-Roll" certainly contributed to its degenerate image. His patented waist and hip movements were, for their time, as shocking and sexually provocative as the suggestive movements of any of today's music stars.

Interestingly, the influence of music and the message it carries to young people has not been intensively studied by the academic community. According to an investigation of the relationship between time spent listening to music and academic behavior by adolescents in grades 7 to 9 (Burke & Grinder, 1966), the more time spent listening to youth-culture music, the lower the grade-point average, the less time spent in studying, and the lower the academic aspiration. It is unclear from this and other investigations (see Strasburger, 1995) whether time spent listening to music actually lowers academic standards or whether poor students listen to more youth-culture music.

LaVoie and Collins (1975) also attempted to assess the effects of music listening on adolescents' academic behavior. Adolescents in grades 9 to 12 were asked to complete study units dealing with either literature, mathematics, physical science, or social science while listening to either rock, classic, or no music. Follow-up testing for retention of material clearly indicated that listening to rock music interfered with both immediate and longer-range recall of information. LaVoie and Collins argue that rock music has its own rewarding power, "since its informational value for the adolescent provides a source of identification with peers" (p. 64). Therefore, when intellectual activities must compete with rock music, the music, with its strong reward power, will provide a stronger reinforcing effect.

Recent studies have concluded that most youth (and as you'll shortly see adults as well) do not understand the lyrics of the songs they heard (Greenfield et al., 1987; Hendren & Strasburger, 1993; Thompson, 1993; Wanamaker & Reznikoff, 1989). To illustrate this point consider the Bruce Springsteen song "Born in the U.S.A." This popular recording with its strong refrain and driving rhythmic rock beat was praised by President Regan as an example of the new American patriotism in 1984. Only problem was the song was a bitter commentary on American life that discussed nonexisting life opportunities, legal hassles, and unemployment. Even if adolescents can repeat the lyrics to a song, many of them, and apparently their elders, cannot explain their meaning.[3]

[3] Readers who can remember the song "*Louie Louie*" by the Kingsmen should recall the controversy when it appeared. The concern was that the lyrics described an act of fornication. No one could be sure of this, of course, because no one could understand the lyrics. Given this situation, today's college youths should know that their parents and grandparents rushed out to buy millions of copies of this 45-rpm recording and hid away in their bedrooms to play it at 33-1/3 rpm in a futile attempt to understand it. Recently, the Kingsmen revealed that the lyrics were not obscene, but that the recording equipment was so bad that no one would have been able to tell anyway. Incidentally, the lyrics by the late Richard Berry tell the story of a sailor pining for his girlfriend and relating his misery to a bartender (Rockwell, 1990).

The marriage of video to music nearly 2 decades ago has significantly changed the relationship of youth to music. MTV is telecasted to 55 million North American homes. MTV Europe reaches another 24 million homes in 27 countries. And the MTV viewing audience is growing at the rate of 5 million homes a year (Strouse, Buerkel-Rothfuss, & Long, 1995). One indicator of the power of music video is the estimate that 43% of all adolescents in the United States view MTV at least once a week (Thompson, 1993). Mental images once formed to rhythm, beat, and perceived lyrics are now created by a video mixer and special effects. Research has found that those images more often than not are violent or sexually suggestive. The majority of concept videos studied portrayed women in stereotyped fashion as weak and sexually provocative (Brown & Hendee, 1989; Jason et al., 1998; Sun & Lull, 1986; Vincent, Davis, & Bronszkowski, 1987).

The influence these video images have on adolescents is uncertain. Has Michael Jackson's video behavior increased the sale of crotch supports, "Quell," or nonbinding underwear? Or for that matter, does gangsta rap encourage city street violence or does it give voice to a hidden subculture that we would rather ignore? Scholars continue to debate whether these performers and countless other have encouraged poor behavior or provided healthy outlets for fantasy and aggressive feelings.

Finally, in work with delinquent and hospital populations, scholars (Gold, 1987; King, 1988; Shatin, 1981; Waite, Foster, & Hillbrand, 1992) have found that music could encourage behavior that was counterproductive to the therapeutic process. Music, particularly heavy metal, that glorifies sadistic, violent, or drug-using behavior can work to the detriment of such patients. Interestingly, in one study with an adolescent hospitalized population when MTV was removed from the floor there was a significant decrease in aggressive behavior on the unit (Waite, Foster, & Hillbrand, 1992).

In some sense we are not surprised by this last finding. The music of rap and heavy metal is purposely inciting (Took & Weiss, 1994). Whether it is Guns 'N' Roses wailing "I used to love her but I had to kill her," Ice T proclaiming " 'bout ready to dust some cops off," or 2 Live Crew being obscene merely to be obscene, this is the adolescent protest music of this generation. Elvis shook his hips, crooned about hound dogs, and sent parents into a fright in the 1950s. The Beatles pushed the envelope of social mores again in the 1960s with long hair, electric guitars, and gurus. Today's antiestablishment musicians, like their predecessors, need to reject the status quo and hang on the edge of poor taste shocking the older generation with their clothes, their jeweled decorated body, and their music.[4] Like others before them (Janis Joplin, Jim Morrison, and Jimi Hendrix) who abused alcohol and drugs, todays artists (Kurt Cobain and Tupac Shakur) will see their lives ended early by similar forces—whether driven by internal anger expressed in substance abuse or externally vented in violent behavior that inevitably invites retaliation.

As we watch this adolescent behavior, we travel back in time to our youth to remember vacant-eyed, rocking, moaning teens going through some ancient, mystic ritual of adoration of a rock idol. This sort of behavior has appeared with

---

[4]As an aside, have you ever wondered how some of these folks get through airport metal detectors?

each new generation of young people and will continue into the future. Indeed, we can't wait for the day to arrive when those of today's heavy metal groups who actually possess the ability to play their instruments appear some Saturday evening on PBS—that's PBS, not MTV—and play their ear-deafening numbers to a 50-year-old-plus audience that once upon a time in the 1990s wore oversized grunge jeans, sprayed their coiffured hair fluorescent colors, and wore body rings in the most amazing locations.

Implications

The influence of both television and music on young people is unmistakable. Both have significantly enlarged adolescents' knowledge of the world, in one sense creating a global village, but they have also restricted it by monopolizing young people's attention. At their best these media inform, entertain, and enrich. At their worst, they encourage racism, sexism, and violence. The answer to curbing these abuses rests, in our minds, not in V-chips or increased legislation but in parental action. Parents need to become aware of the music young people listen to and the programs they watch. We do not encourage adults to censor but to become actively involved in discussing the messages these media impart to young people. To do so, of course, takes time, time with young people, and that is something we very strongly encourage.

Video Games

Before we begin this section we feel the need to remind the older returning student with adolescents at home that video games are not new to this generation of youth. The first ones appeared in the early 1970s and enjoyed initial financial success until the latter part of that decade only to reemerge in the mid-1980s. The lineage of the video game can be traced back to that of the pinball machine, which occupied the leisure time of previous generations of youth dressed in turned-up blue jeans, white socks, and penny loafers in the bowling alleys and soda shops that today are malls. This seemingly reassuring news provides little comfort to many parents, however, who worry about the influence these games may have on today's youth (Garver, 1990). Indeed, given that one cable network has a contest show with a video game theme, that magazines are bought to outwit computer foes, and that none other than PBS airs "*Where in the World is Carmen Sandiego?*" (a popular computer program, now a game show), maybe they have a point.

It is estimated that 90% of adolescents in the United States and Canada play video games. The typical video game player has been described in studies as young, male, and bright. The game is seen as an electronic friend, suggesting that some of these youths may have difficulty creating friendships. Interestingly, players are not perceived as being in trouble with authorities more than nonplayers. The stronger interest males have in video games has been explained by the fact that most games involve violent or aggressive acts like escaping from danger, pursuing some evil creature, or waging warfare. We believe the powerful reinforcing element found in video games can be explained by their interactive capabilities. Regardless of one's size, strength, age, or agility a youth can pit himself or herself against another human player or the machine with color, 3D action, and stereo sound thrown in for good measure. Further, unlike friends who can tire of an activity, these games can continue so long as the batteries or power pack operate. Given the hostile nature of most of these games, it is not surprising to find studies showing increased levels of aggressive feelings in young people after a game. Whether these games are helpful in letting off steam or in encouraging hostile behavior remains uncertain (Cooper & Mackie, 1986; Funk, 1993; Griffiths, 1991; Schutte, Malouff, Post-Gorden, & Rodasta, 1988).

Cyberspace

The growth of home computers has been phenomenal in recent years. The U.S. Census Bureau estimates that nearly 23% of the U.S. households owned a computer in 1993. That's nearly 23,000,000 home computers (U.S. Census Bureau, 1997, Chart 1207 p. 732). Incidentally, that is up 7% from the previous year or 8 million computers. Once used for such mundane activities as typing manuscripts for ever-demanding publishers, employers, or teachers, the computer now offers entertainment, information, and, oh yes, word processing. Connected to a modem, as 11% of American households with computers are, the computer through a server can access an ever-growing number of similarly linked computers across Canada, the United States, and the world through the Internet (Kim, 1996).

Like all other mediums before it (the printed word, radio, television), the development of this technology was heralded as the great new educator. An ever-friendly, patient machine, the computer could assist the learning-disabled individual. It could give access to libraries and learning institutions. It could link individuals in study groups called list-serves, and it could efficiently transmit messages via e-mail. Indeed, it does all of this and more. It is the "more" part that is troublesome.

With the growth of the home computer industry and the corresponding increase in the use of the Internet, young people have found new ways to satisfy what Freud once described as humankind's two instinctual urges—sex and aggression. Media reports reveal that youths are visiting World Wide Web (WWW) sites and receiving pornographic images and literature. Chat rooms located on popular commercial access providers are being used to lure youths into sexual encounters. These concerns reached such a level that the U.S. Congress in 1996 passed telecommunications legislation attempting to regulate sexual information on the Internet.[5] Despite this

[5]We suspect that, as with other new technologies, concern over sexually explicit material on the Internet will fade with time. Why do we have this opinion? As part of a continuing study on sexual behavior, the first author monitors pornographic material on the Internet. Tom is not impressed. Most suppliers of pornographic pictures want money for their material. Most adolescents we know don't have the credit cards to obtain this access. For the material that is freely available, the same material is more readily available at the mall bookshop (download times are a drag) or in moving, moaning images on late-night cable television which can be saved on the family's VCR for replay when parents are not home.

concern, a computer literature search done from the home computer of one of the authors of the National Institute of Health's library failed to uncover a single published academic study on this topic.

Sports

Involving 20 million youths between the ages of 6 and 15 and costing an estimated $17 billion a year, the sheer popularity of athletic activity among family members suggests it to be a positive outlet for young people (Danish, Petitpas, & Hale, 1990). In fact only family, television, and school activities take up more of a young person's time (Danish, Nellen, & Owens, 1996). Sports are seen by many as an important factor in the development of the adolescent's social competency (Kleiber & Kirshnit, 1991). Most young people enjoy sports activities but for reasons other than competition. Those reasons are having fun, creating friendships, and building skills (Hodge & Danish, 1998). School personnel, less glowingly but nevertheless strongly, support athletics though they voice concern that parents are a primary problem with athletics (Maresh, 1992; Yaffe, 1982). Many school personnel see parents as unruly spectators and poor coaches because they are overdesirous of having their children win.

The thought of a coed pick up basketball game was unheard of a generation ago.

But not all views of sports are as laudatory. For example, Sabo and Runfola (1980) describe sports activities as "the most crucial socializing forces in the development of the superman syndrome in American society" (p. ix). They blame the "association between [sports], violence, and masculinity" for encouraging "the prevalence of rape and wife- beating, the rising tide of sadomasochistic sexual images in men's magazines, and the eroticized violence against women in television and cinema productions" (p. xiii). The authors conclude the preface to their thought-provoking book *Jock: Sports and the Male Identity* with a quote from Marie Hart (1971) that states that despite women's entry into the field of athletic activity, "American society cuts the penis off the male who enters dance and places it on the woman who participates in competitive athletics" (p. xiv). In a similar theme, Mariah Nelson (1995) in *The Stronger Women Get, the More Men Love Football: Sexism and the American Culture of Sports* decries the relegated status of women as cheerleaders or as providers of sexual favors.

Finally, high school athletes have brought deserved criticism on themselves. The reason for this is the rise in student athletic violence. From student fights on the playing field to striking game officials, the increase in game violence has moved several states to impose sanctions as in Alaska's 1-year probation on interscholastic hockey or in Iowa's rating schools on sportsmanship. As one Michigan official aptly phrased it, "Lest we forget, this is supposed to be educational athletics" (Diegmueller, 1996, p. 8).

Clearly, here are two rather different views of sports and their role in society. In this section we examine each argument more closely with an eye toward gauging the impact this leisure-time activity has on the social and emotional development of the adolescent.

Proponents

Summarizing the findings of authors and researchers who support competitive sports, Dowell (1970) and others like Pressley and Whitley (1996) report that the benefits of such sports are found in four broadly defined areas: physical development, emotional development, social development, and miscellaneous benefits. Some of the benefits of competitive sports in the physical area are the development of motor ability and body strength. In the emotional domain, advocates argue sports can improve self-concept (Kishton & Dixon, 1995; Salokun, 1994). Further, sports teach self-control and are an outlet for nervous energy (Dowell, 1970; Pressley & Whitley, 1996). Within the social domain, Dowell (1970) finds evidence from various sources to suggest that sports teach citizenship, encourage social acceptance of the athlete by his or her peers, and contribute to later educational and financial success. In the fourth, miscellaneous category, sports advocates state that athletics reduce delinquency, encourage fitness, increase sportsmanship, and are a better use of leisure time than watching television, for instance (Pressley & Whitley, 1996). Further, for a few young people, it is an opportunity to attend college. That opportunity, if not squandered, can lead to a college education as it is highly unlikely to lead to a career in professional sports (Sellers, Kupermine, & Damas, 1997).

While supportive of athletic activity, other scholarship is more restrained on the benefits of sports activity. For example, for those youths with a high self-concept of ability in sports, it is a significant factor in identity development, the promotion of self-esteem, and social standing among one's peers (Fejgin, 1994). Through sports activity that emphasizes skill development and fair play, personal character and sportsmanship are developed (Lumpkin, Stroll, & Beller, 1994).

Not surprisingly, among males 12 to 16 years old sport activity is more highly valued than school. The reason for this is that sports is a primary context by which friendships develop for male adolescents (Roberts, 1993). Because society values athletic ability, it becomes a means to social acceptance. For those who would doubt the truth of this last statement, consider the visibility, wealth, and attention given to professional athletes. Many of these individuals are sorely lacking in education and some in social grace or manners. Do you think that without their athletic ability, they would receive any attention? In the next section the critics of team sports argue their case.

Opponents

> To play this game you must have fire in you, and there is nothing that stokes fire like hate
> (Vince Lombardi, football coach, cited in Freischlag & Schmidke, 1979, p. 183).

If this quote suggests an overemphasis on winning, and encouragement of violence, and a stance that the end justifies the means, then you already have a good idea of the arguments against competitive sports (Spencer, 1996). For example, many critics contend that the body of the young athlete is overtaxed. This demand to perform too often results in permanent damage to the adolescent's young body (such as to knee ligaments) that will rule out sports activity later in life.

Consider for a moment the most recent summer Olympic games and the performance of U.S. gymnast Kerri Strug in that competition. Having seriously injured her ankle, she defied that pain to perform a vault that enabled the U.S. team to achieve a gold medal. But was that act truly necessary? Was the example she set the example we want for young athletes who may choose to ignore their own injuries for a moment of glory on a town soccer field, a city recreation league's basketball court, or a high school wrestling mat? Is that moment of glory really worth a serious lifelong injury (Dalton, 1996)?

Rowley (1987) questions whether a negative stigma is attached to females who participate in sports activities. His studies challenge findings that peer cooperation and social relationships improve. Rather, he notes an increase in antisocial behavior and aggressive acts. And although athletes may express higher educational aspirations, his work cannot establish an actual relationship between that aspiration and higher academic results. Developing this last point, Shields and Bredemeier (1995) state that sports do not build character. Their review of the literature suggests that most athletes operate on a "game reasoning" level. That is, unless the referee observes unsportsmanlike conduct, it didn't occur and that winning at all costs matters most.

Misused, sports can harm social development.

Freischlag and Schmidke (1979, p.184) and others (Coakley, 1990) contend that sports are a legal war in which "athletes are encouraged to nail, crush, crucify, and stick opponents. Blitzes, bombs, sacks, and kills are recorded in team statistics." This idea that one's opponent is the enemy and that the coach is a general leading his troops conjures up images of war, of the Christians and the lions, of the Roman arena and the gladiators. It should be noted that this image is further encouraged by the television networks, which open these gladiatorial battles with adrenaline-stimulating music, cut-away film footage of the athletes donning their gear, and loud boisterous threats directed at an opponent.

These issues concern females as well as males, critics contend. Although at one time society may have considered the "weaker sex" unfit for the rigors of sport, that view is now nearly extinct. Since the federal government's long-overdue Title IX regulation ordered schools to provide equal opportunity for women to participate in sports, women have demonstrated their sports abilities. As Nelson (1995) points out meaningful differences between males and females are culturally constructed—not biologically driven. Achieving equity on the playing field is a step toward reaching equity in others spheres of life. The issue that we address in the conclusion of this section is whether sports for both females and males need be this way.

Implications

The evidence is clear that athletic activity exerts an extremely powerful influence on young people's lives. The proponents of sports assume that the current socialization process is positive. The critics of team sports are not as convinced. These critics are not against sports per se but against what they see sports as having become.

BOX 8-3 Sports and Social Competency—An Intriguing Integration

Each semester, students—especially female athletes—will ask, "How can people be so critical of sports? I just know that it has helped me develop all kinds of new skills, and I don't identify myself as a (fe)male jock!" Given the frequency with which this question is raised, the good teacher (and the better researcher) searches for a response that satisfies the discrepancy between these students personal experiences and the research which generally does not rank sports activity highly.

We think the answer to this question can be found in a fascinating chapter by Martin Bloom (2000) that explores the relationship between sports, after-school activities, and social competency. Bloom, one of North America's premier health-promotion scholars, begins his discussion by offering his understanding of the term *social competency*. He understands it to mean working, playing, loving, thinking, and serving others well. So what does the word "well" mean? It means doing things like work, play, or serving others correctly, nicely, properly, and with justice.

Now, against this standard of social competency, Bloom identifies four levels of physical activity. He terms the first level sports, which he considers to be structured (rules), competitive, and organized into teams (tennis, basketball, or a high school golf team for example). Team membership is time limited, lasting through high school, college, community recreation leagues, or, very rarely, in semiprofessional or professional league play. The next level of physical activity is *games*. While games are structured, they have consensual rules often made up on the spot. They can be competitive, but do not have to be, and team membership is momentary (a pick up game of tag football for example). The third level of sports activity is *play*. Play is personally structured and is rarely competitive with no concept of teams (playing catch for example). The fourth level of sport is *exercise*. Exercise is individually structured, noncompetitive, and, Bloom states, intended to strengthen body and mind.

Using these understandings of social competency and athletic activity, Bloom constructs a table of values that compares the overlapping characteristics of each. This imaginative and creative approach yields the following results. Sports, with its structure and emphasis on competition, has the least overlap with the characteristics Bloom uses to understand social competency (work, play, love, thinking, and serving others *well*). Play followed by games rank slightly better, suffering on the dimensions of work and thinking. It is exercise that scores highest in Bloom's analysis. With its individual purposive noncompetitive focus, exercise (like walking, swimming, etc.) can be enjoyed across the lifespan.

"But wait a minute," our student athlete says, "how does this explain my satisfaction with sports." We would ask, "Is it *sports* that you find so satisfying? Or is it the *higher level of skills* you've developed over the years? Is it the competition against others you enjoy or is it the improvement in yourself that is satisfying?" Depending on your responses to these questions, your involvement in sports might be better understood as exercise.

Curing society's ills through violent conflict between two teams is not the answer, these individuals suggest (see Box 8-3).

If we give serious consideration to these critics' arguments, what changes could be encouraged in sports? First, coaches and parents have a major responsibility for deemphasizing winning and emphasizing skill development. One outstanding example of this approach is Going for the Goal (Danish, 1997). This program uses sport activities as a means to encourage young people to learn life skills. The program emphasizes goal-setting and problem-solving. It strives for sport to achieve, as Steve Danish has so eloquently phrased it, an activity where one need

---

BOX **8-4**   **The Cost of Winning**

The need to win, regardless of the cost, is no better illustrated than by the common practice of wrestlers to cut their weight or, to use the vernacular, "suck down." The principle behind the act is to shed enough pounds to allow a wrestler to compete in a lower weight class. Experience suggests that the athlete who can manage the weight loss and compete in the lower weight class will win. The following comments by two young men who engage in this behavior, with the knowledge of their parents and coaches, illustrate critics' charges that many in society have lost sight of the purpose of athletic activity.

My preseason weight is a bit over 130 pounds, but I wrestle at 118 pounds. I want to wrestle at 114 pounds,

because I know I could win all the time because I'd fight smaller kids. . . . I'd lose the weight and then gain it all back and then have to lose it all over again. One time I had trouble making the weight. I took a laxative and got real sick. I thought I would die.

I normally weigh 158 pounds but wanted to wrestle at 132 pounds. I had problems though, because I wouldn't do it right. I'd go up and down with my weight. I'd starve for a day, make weight, wrestle—a few times I though I'd throw up right on the mat—and come home and pig out, you know, eat everything in sight. I knew it wasn't good for me, but it's part of wrestling.

"It's part of wrestling"—but we wonder, does it really need to be?

---

not continue "to have to prove oneself, it can be a place where one begins to know oneself. When knowing becomes as important as proving, sport becomes an essential vehicle for developing personal competence" (Danish et al., 1990, p. 190).

Second, sports activity should be encouraged not in one or two areas but in several, and it should be integrated with other leisure activities, particularly the arts. Exposing young people to the intricacies and physical demands of dance, for instance, would serve to broaden young people's experience beyond these small social groups. Finally, society needs to value, recognize, and emphasize other ways in which young people can achieve feelings of self-worth (see Box 8-4).

One example of such a program that has achieved success in this area is in operation in Connecticut. Called "Creative Experiences," the program uses the arts to develop physical, social, and emotional skills while giving young people an opportunity to experience feelings of recognition, self-worth, and importance. The program is intergenerational in that it encourages adults to participate in its activities for young people and is built on the philosophy that all members are equal and important to the group (Gullotta & Plant, 2000; Smith, Goodwin, Gullotta, & Gullotta, 1979).

Another example of a competency enhancement program is ROPE (Rite of Passage Experience). Founded on the belief that young people are not provided with clear pathways into adolescence and later early adulthood, ROPE integrates group "Outward Bound"-type challenge activities with peer and adult involvement in exercises that create a deeper awareness and respect for self and others. Like

Young people should be encouraged to explore a variety of after school activities ranging from sports and dance to music and theatre.

Creative Experiences, the program believes that young people succeed when they give to others. Thus, a community improvement project is an integral part of the ROPE graduation exercise (Blumenkrantz & Gavazzi, 1993).

These programs are two of many experiments occurring around the United States and Canada that emphasize the promotion of social competency in youths. The application of these principles to sports and other leisure-time activities could foster the type of socioemotional growth that critics feel is lacking in sports activities today. Each of these programs balance the need for individuality and the need for social relatedness. In turn, they enhance individuality and social connection that nourish identity formation.

ADOLESCENTS AND WORK

The history of unemployment for adolescents mirrors that of the U.S. and Canadian economy. Generally speaking, when economic times are good employment opportunities are available. When the economy is in recession, unemployment figures for youths rise. The phrase "generally speaking" is used because Black adolescents are significantly more likely to be unemployed than are White youths. Still, even in this unprecedented decade of low unemployment, the unemployment rate of youths 16 to 24 is many times higher than the U.S. national rate of 5.4% for 1996. The 1996 unemployment rate for White male youths 16 to 19 years old was 14.2%; it was 33.6% for Blacks and 23.6% for Latino youths. This pattern continued into early adulthood. Unemployment rates for 1996 for White 20- to 24-year-olds was 7.8% and for Blacks, 18.8%. For young adults ages 20 to 24, Latino unemployment rates were only slightly higher than White young adult unemployment rates (11.8% vs 7.8%). Unemployment rates for women observed similar racial/ethnic patterns (U.S. Census Bureau, 1997, Chart 652, p. 418).

Today as in the past, chronic youth unemployment affects only a small percentage of U.S. teenagers. Estimated to be about 10% of the total, these unemployed youths are most often city dwellers who belong to ethnic or racially diverse groups

(Eberly, 1991; Rodriquez, 1980; W. T. Grant Foundation, 1988). Among this group, those most likely to remain unemployed are youths who have dropped out of school (Eberly, 1991; Congressional Budget Office, 1980; Hamilton, 1982; Rist, 1982; W. T. Grant Foundation, 1988).

Family background, too, seems to exercise some influence over an adolescent's success in finding a job. Those with the greatest success are from middle-class, well-educated families. Those with the least success are lower-class and poorly educated. The influence of the family is not direct but, rather, indirect in that education is ultimately related to occupation and thus to income:

> For both Blacks and Whites, family background has a strong effect on the amount of education young people receive; this in turn has considerable impact on the types of jobs they get. For white young men parental occupation is as important as the young man's I.Q. in predicting educational attainment. For Blacks, although parental occupation is not so strong a factor, the size of the family is. Black young men from very large families receive less education, and education in turn affects wages" (Hill, Shaw, & Sproat, 1980, p. 2).

How the relationship between poverty and unemployment is translated into social costs is examined next.

The Social Costs of Unemployment

Employment is necessary for survival. In fact, many researchers would suggest that it is necessary for one's positive mental health. Adolescent unemployment has been linked to lower levels of self-esteem and higher degrees of emotional stress including depression and family unrest (Hammarstrom & Janlert, 1997; Patton & Nolles, 1991; Prause & Dooley, 1997). As one group of researchers studying youth unemployment in Ireland so aptly phrased it, "unemployed youth appear to be people with a problem rather than problem people" (Hannan, O'Riain, & Whelan, 1997, p. 307). Without a job or some other legitimate means of support, people have no way to acquire food, clothing, and shelter and must make a decision about how to obtain money in other ways. The unemployed adolescent is at particular risk for becoming engaged in illegal activities for money (Swinton, 1980). Prostitution, drug dealing, robbery, and other forms of unsanctioned or illegal behavior often have just one purpose: obtaining money.

This consequence of unemployment is clearly shown in Harvey Brenner's (1980) analysis of the social costs of youth unemployment. He writes that the ratio of youths unemployment to the total unemployment rate is (statistically) significantly related to motor vehicle fatalities, mental hospital admissions, and narcotics law violations and to nearly all major crimes, including criminal homicide, rape, assault, robbery, auto theft, and prostitution. With each additional percentage-point rise in youth unemployment, Brenner estimates, there is a corresponding rise in arrests for those crimes.

According to Bowman (1990) chronic joblessness is a major challenge for Black youths in the United States. Discouragement steming from not finding a job is very severe and continues into adulthood. Discouragement and self-blame can increase maladaptive responses. However, Bowman indicates that many Black youths diminish maladaptiveness by relying on strong kinship bonds, religion, and ethnic coping orientations (specific ethnic behaviors that facilitate coping). In particular, Black cultural resources appear to nurture a general sense of personal efficacy. Self-empowerment, together with family and kin encouragement of cultural pride and school success, helps some Black youths beat the odds of unemployment and associated discouragement.

The Value of Employment

From the Great Depression until recently, research suggested that work enhances adolescent development. Work, according to the Kettering Foundation report on youth employment, teaches responsibility and instills discipline in the adolescent (Brown, 1980). It creates a sense of social identification with society. It uses the adolescent's time and energy in a productive capacity for which the adolescent receives financial compensation. Employment in U.S. society is essential for feeling meaningful, having self- respect, and being able to express oneself.

Thus, it is with interest that scholars have looked at reports suggesting that these aforementioned ennobling aspects of work during adolescence may no longer apply. Greenberger, Steinberg, and their associates contend that, whereas in the past work and responsibility were related, this relationship no longer exists for the vast majority of American youths. Rather, large numbers of youths are employed in positions requiring no independent decision-making (Greenberger & Steinberg, 1981, 1986). For example, consider the grocery checkout clerk. With the optical scanner and the computerization of inventory, the counter clerk's skills, never terribly complicated to begin with, have been reduced to passing a universal product code bar over a scanner beam.

These authors suggest that the belief that work exposes adolescents to positive adult role models is no longer true. Indeed, their studies suggest that while the time spent with family and other adults decreases, time spent with peers does not change (Greenberger & Steinberg, 1981; Greenberger, Steinberg, Vaux & McAuliffe, 1980). Finally, they suggest that the employment opportunities available to young people are boring, repetitive, and dull. Rather than encouraging an interest in work, they produce apathy (Greenberger & Steinberg, 1986). Consider, for example, fast-food clerks who push a button that dispenses a predetermined amount of soda into a cup. Think about their other job functions. Is there any aspect of their automated activity that varies? Is there any variation on the theme? These authors would answer "no."

Somewhat moderating this dismal view is a study that reports young people perceiving benefits from working under certain circumstances. In contrast to jobs that require little intellectual stimulation, the authors find that when job skills are related to a young person's future career aspirations, benefits result. They also report a powerful relationship between job stress and students' mental health status with emotional health declining as stress increases (Mortimer, Finch, Shanahan,

& Rhu, 1992). However, although this study provides some hope, the intriguing unanswered question is, How many opportunities of this type are available to young people or, for that matter, adults?

For example, in a recent study examining job growth from 1983 to 1993, Rosenthal (cited in Bracey, 1996) provides evidence that it is the lower-skilled end of the job market that is growing the fastest. Indeed, 60% of the job growth that occurred during the sampled years were jobs like teacher's aide, general office clerk, and, returning to our button-pushing, soda-dispensing friend, the food preparer. These poor paying positions require the employee "to work more jobs or more hours to make ends meet" (Bracey, 1996, p. 385). During these same years, the United States lost over 400,000 manufacturing jobs. During this period of time and carrying into the present, we have been exchanging $30,000-a-year positions with $18,000-a-year service sector jobs—regardless of education. As Bracey (1996, p. 385) so bitingly puts it "an education is no longer a guarantee of getting a good job, although a lack of education is a virtual guarantee of not getting one."

Implications

As we examine the issue of work in adolescence, we are torn between two persuasive arguments. The first notes the importance of employment; the second notes the dehumanizing aspects of that work for adolescents and, increasingly, for adults. Nevertheless, in our opinion, employment and job experience are important. The failure to gain work experience during adolescence appears to adversely affect people in later life.

We could call for a new commitment to education. Despite Bracey's (1996) sharp observation, there is clearly a powerful relationship between educational achievement and ultimate job attainment, and that approach should not be discounted. But the problem of unemployment really weights most unfairly on only one segment of society. No minor adjustment in educational funding, student work attitudes, or the like will alter the fact that discrimination is a factor in youth unemployment. Until we come to grips with this issue, unemployment will continue to exacerbate the problems that confront many young people.

SUMMARY

Let's look at the material you've just read against the four themes of this book. First, the origin of leisure time and the power of the peer group clearly have historical roots in the social invention of adolescence. Next, the varying influences of race, class, and family repeatedly illustrate contextualism for Latino, White, Black, and other youths and how developmental paths to adulthood can be shaped. Third, the power of kinship and friendship networks was demonstrated for diverse youths in studies that showed some of these young people protected from potentially deviant peer temptations. Finally, in several areas like school transitions, television viewing, and sports we offered our thoughts on reducing negative consequences.

Before you call it a night, take a moment and consider what other actions might be taken to promote positive peer relationships, strengthen adolescent family supports, and improve the use of leisure time. You can do this as you pack your books for tomorrow's class or down a Coke—better yet a fruit juice.

MAJOR POINTS TO REMEMBER

1. Peer groups influence adolescents' preparation for adult roles as well as the youth culture itself.
2. These groups constitute a highly reinforcing setting for specific adolescent behaviors.
3. Peer groups do not replace parental influence, but they do supplement it.
4. A generational consciousness, or identification with one's youthful reference group, is an important influence on values and behaviors.
5. Television has a tremendous impact on young people. Research has shown that it can affect academic performance, shape attitudes, and influence behavior. Music and video games have a similarly powerful effect for good or evil.
6. Proponents believe that sports encourage physical health, promote body development, and strengthen emotional and social development.
7. Opponents believe that sports, in their most excessive and violent forms, harm physical health, encourage violence, and diminish concern for others.
8. Unemployment is one of the most pressing problems for minority youths.
9. Chronic unemployment affects only a small minority of teenagers in our society. The chances for unemployment increase when an adolescent has a poor education and few financial resources and is a member of a minority ethnic or racial group.
10. Crime and mental illness are significantly related to unemployment. As unemployment rises, homicide and other crimes, motor vehicle fatalities, and admissions to mental hospitals rise as well.

EDUCATION

IT HAS BEEN said that if you added together all of the money spent on all of the schools in the United States, it would far surpass the budget of any single group of industries. For the year 1996 that funding amounted to nearly $514 billion for elementary, secondary, and postsecondary education (U.S. Census Bureau, 1997, Chart 234, p. 153). Certainly, the growth of education in the United States and Canada over the past 100 years suggests a strong commitment to the belief that knowledge is the key to success. Given the tools to work with, any number of immigrant or native-born youngsters who applied themselves could reasonably expect to get their fair share of the pie. Thus, through the years, parents have dressed their children; equipped them with lunch pails, pencils, and rulers; and sent them off to school to learn. But to learn what?

There has never been disagreement that young people should learn to read. In the United States, the debate has been over what they should read. Is *Huckleberry Finn* (Clemens, 1884/1962), with its "N"-word, suitable for a multicultural society striving to get beyond a time when slavery existed within its borders? Or is *Catcher in the Rye* (Salinger, 1951) appropriate reading for impressionable youth given Holden Caulfield's emotional breakdown, his encounters with a prostitute, and the homosexual advances of his former English teacher? There has never been disagreement that young people should learn arithmetic. The dispute began when it was applied to problems that calculated waste emissions rather than to how interest compounds on an initial cash investment. There has never been a disagreement over the important role educators play in shaping the moral values of youth. The quarrel arose when religion was removed from the classroom. It has been said and it is true that knowledge is power. But to harness that power, ideology is necessary. It is the application of knowledge through a philosophy (world view) that determines the decisions that are made.

Education is not value free. For example, instructors who use this book want you to appreciate the cultural diversity evident in Canada and the United States. Your instructor wants you to appreciate theory, research, and how that information can be applied to improve health. These are values. Other textbooks on adolescence may share some of these values and have other points they want to emphasize. To appreciate the educational debates underway in Canada and the United States, it is important for the student to take the long view of the evolution of educational practices.

In taking that long view, we must first recognize that prior to this century education was made *fully* available only to middle-class White men. It was not available to minorities, to women, and not readily available to poor White men. The education of women, for example, involved domestic instruction in managing the home and in providing "moral guardianship" for the family. Similarly, Blacks were deprived of educational opportunities or, if instructed, were taught the need for obedience. Like Blacks, poor Whites found themselves barred from education not by prejudice and discrimination but by poverty.

The school is a miniature social system in which people learn to function in society. It is that educational experience that strongly shapes future beliefs. Students spend 12 years encountering authority figures (in the form of teachers), rules, other students, and peer pressure. As they progress through the educational maze from elementary to junior high to high school, they will be expected to assume the responsibilities of becoming independent, contributing members of society. In this chapter we explore how education developed. We examine the social structure of the adolescent's life in school and the influence of family background in acquiring an education, as well as the problems of truancy, dropping out, and school violence. Finally, we look at the discussions and modest attempts being undertaken to improve the North American secondary educational experience.

THE DEVELOPMENT OF THE U.S. SCHOOL SYSTEM

According to *The Student and the Schoolmate*, circa 1858, "As a general rule, the more schoolhouses there are, the fewer prisons there will be." In light of recent observations that it costs more to house an individual in a prison than to send that person to college, it underscores the wisdom of this nearly 150-year-old axiom. But we're getting ahead of ourselves. First, we need to understand that there are two views of the history of U.S. education, and they are radically different. According to the first, the passing of education laws to eradicate ignorance as early as 1642 in the Massachusetts Bay Colony was indicative of the colonists' "sense of mission . . . that they would need not only educated leaders and clergy, but an educated populace as well" (Hechinger & Hechinger, 1975, p. 17). Historians subscribing to this view believe that education emerged as a positive force promoting those aspects of the new republic considered to be most attractive. Education encouraged self-sufficiency and promoted social and economic mobility.

Listing the accomplishments of the school movement, the early historians saw education as promoting social progress. Schools were credited with taking children out of the sweatshops and the fields. Schools were said to encourage class mobility and equality of opportunity. Reason was triumphing over the forces of ignorance (Cubberley, 1934; Monroe, 1940).

A second view of education, emerging from the writings of Katz (1973, 1975), Nasaw (1979), Kett (1977), and others, is not as laudatory. Interest in education is not viewed as a way to encourage egalitarianism but as a way to exercise continued control over a rapidly growing number of "foreign" immigrants. In response to a fear of losing control, Nasaw argues, the privileged classes sought to indoctrinate the new arrivals with a healthy does of republican thinking.[1] The wealthy, he reports, funded a number of social experiments through such organizations as the Society for the Prevention of Poverty to remedy the growing "problems" occurring with the influx of new immigrants into the cities.

One such experiment was the introduction of the Lancaster system of education. The Lancaster system used a special classroom-seating plan and student assistants to instruct large numbers of pupils in a single classroom. Nasaw (1979) describes the system as "more appropriate to a feudal kingdom than to a New World Republic" (p. 23). The instructor sat like an overseer above the pupils while the student assistants roamed throughout the classroom enforcing order and discipline. Punishment for such crimes as talking, being out of one's chair, or truant did not involve the birch switch so common in the one-room schoolhouse. Instead, punishment involved stooping for hours in a corner of the room or serving as a footstool (Kett, 1977).

Barbaric as this may appear, it received resounding praise from its wealthy financial backers. Here was a system that encouraged discipline among the young hoodlums roaming the streets of the new cities. Moreover, here was a system that was "both economical and effective [using the same principles of] labor saving machinery [that had been] pioneered in the production of factory goods" (Nasaw, 1979, p. 21). Nevertheless, this system of privately financed education would slowly die out as the movement for common schools gained momentum.

The movement to create publicly supported schools was fueled by several factors. One of these, the influx of immigrants, seems to have been the most important influence in winning the taxation battles that had spelled defeat for the common school before 1875. The revisionist historians argue that these new waves of Irish Catholics overwhelmed the capacity of the private sector to accommodate their "Americanization." Faced with wandering youths who appeared to be without proper supervision and moral direction, first the more industrialized states and later the agricultural states passed taxation laws to support local public education.

The movement of young people into these institutions was encouraged from 1851 onward by compulsory education laws. First enacted in Boston and then spreading to other cities and then to entire states, these laws served several purposes. Not only did they provide enforcement powers to move the "ruffians" off the streets, through the schools, and into reformatories, but they enabled a struggling economy to create more employment opportunities for adults at the expense of young people. Young people's participation in society was gradually being redefined from provider to consumer, from worker to learner (Katz, 1975; Kett, 1977).

Which of these two perspectives is accurate? To accept the revisionist view of U.S. education is to accept education without a future or hope for reform. If all reform movements in education have been attempts to sort out individuals, to

---

[1] For a further description of the social forces at work here, see Chapter 13 on Crime and Delinquency.

The view of revisionist historians is that North American education served to maintain the status quo.

categorize and stigmatize others, and to continue the status quo, what faith can one invest in the leaders of new movements to change the educational system? On the other hand, the evidence that the revisionists have gathered in defense of their argument cannot be easily swept aside. The comments of American leaders in education show a concern for promoting education not only as a worthwhile endeavor but also as a means of social control:

> No one at all familiar with the deficient household arrangements and deranged machinery of domestic life, of the extreme poor and ignorant . . . can doubt that it is better for children to be removed as early and as long as possible from such scenes and such examples and placed in an infant or primary school (Barnard, 1851, cited in Katz, 1975, p. 10).

We suspect that both views are partly accurate depictions of the development of the U.S. educational system. The privileged classes supported the educational movement partly because the Industrial Revolution demanded a new breed of worker—one who would surrender "republican" defiance for compliance to work rules and work hours (see Box 9-1).

Yet the idea that education offers a promise of a different life was embraced by the masses. Clearly, there were individuals who had used their schooling opportunities to rise above their station and succeed. This belief was also shared by the privileged classes as they sought, with some of the common people, to deny education to certain elements of society. For example, even as late as 1875, when President Ulysses S. Grant introduced legislation to support a free public school system, a coalition of southern politicians and Catholics defeated the measure. For Catholics, they feared that public education was nothing more than a Protestant attempt to steal their children from their religious teachings. Southern interests understood the power of education and that making education readily and freely

B O X **9-1** A Woman's Place

The revisionist historians argue that education was used not to stimulate social change and mobility but to maintain class, racial, and ethnic distinctions. Textbooks of the 18th and 19th centuries provide one means of investigating this charge. The following is a short "moral" lesson that 19th-century instructors used in class to improve the elocution of their students. Does it support the argument of the revisionist historians?

A WORLD OF TROUBLE
Characters—Thomas Basswood, a mechanic; Susan Basswood, his wife; Uncle John, one who gives good advice.

Scene I—A room. Susan sewing.

Susan: O, dear me! I believe no woman ever had half so much to do as I have. It is drudge, drudge, drudge, from morning till night. This is a world of trouble.

[Enter Thomas Basswood.]

Thomas: Well, Susan, how are all the children?
Susan: They are all well, You don't ask how I am. You never think what a slavish life I lead.
Thomas: Slavish life?
Susan: I have to drudge like a slave from morning till night. No sooner is one thing done than another must be begun. I wonder how I have stood it as I have.
Thomas: It is just the same with me, Susan. I have to work all day. But I do not regard that as a hardship.
Susan: You never regard anything as a hardship. Your work is different from mine. This is a world of trouble. (Sighs.)
Thomas: Nonsense! This is a very good world, Susan. The people in it make it bad.
Susan: That means me, I suppose.
Thomas: Come, come, Susan; don't grumble all the time.
Susan: Who is grumbling? I cannot speak a word lately without being accused of grumbling.
Thomas: Because, my dear, you seldom utter a sentence which does not contain a complaint. If you would be a little more cheerful, things would go much better with you.
Susan: How can a body be cheerful with as many troubles as I have?

Thomas: Your troubles are very few and very insignificant. They exist in your own imagination.
Susan: Just what you always say.
Thomas: I must say one word more, Susan. I am heartily disgusted with this continued fault-finding. My home has become a very gloomy and disagreeable place lately.
Susan: I suppose I make it so.
Thomas: You do, Susan. I have not seen a smile on your face, nor heard a pleasant word from your lips, for a year. It is enough to wear a man out. I can't stand it.
Susan: (Cries.) You have no sympathy for me in my trials and troubles.
Thomas: You don't have any trials and troubles. It is all nonsense! You have a good house, well furnished; plenty to eat, drink, and wear. You have to keep busy; so do I. So do your father and mother. Your little crosses are not worthy to be called trials and troubles. I haven't come into the house for six months without being told that this is a world of trouble, and being compelled to listen to a long list of grievances, which are too trivial to be mentioned.
Susan: I am a monster. I suppose. (Cries.) (Exeunt.)

[Lapse of One Year]

Scene II—Susan, seated at a table.
Susan. O, dear me! This is a world of trouble, and every year brings some new trial. My husband, who used to be a steady and industrious man, has taken to drinking, and he hardly ever comes home sober now. O, dear! This is a real trouble.

[Enter Thomas, slightly intoxicated.]

Thomas: Well, wife, is supper ready?
Susan: Not yet, Thomas.
Thomas: What's the reason it isn't ready? I'm in a hurry. There's to be a turkey raffle at the tavern tonight, and I'm going.
Susan: Don't go, Thomas.
Thomas: Yes, I will.
Susan: You never stay home evenings now. Do stay with me this evening.
Thomas: No, I won't.
Susan: It didn't use to be so. You never stay at home now.

Thomas: I don't mean to. Do you think (staggers) I'd stay here and hear you grumble and growl all the evening? I won't d'zo it.

Susan: O, Thomas! You are—(Pause.)

Thomas: Well, what am I?

Susan: O, dear me!

Thomas: What am I?

Susan: You are—

Thomas: I'm drunk. Why don't you say it right out? I'm drunk. (Staggers.) I used to be a respectable man. I ain't now.

Susan: Why do you drink?

Thomas: Because you grumble—that's why I drink— why I get drunk. Supper ain't ready, you say. I'll go without supper then.

Susan: Stay at home tonight.

Thomas: I won't d'zo it. (Staggers off.)

Susan: A drunkard's wife! Alas, that I should come to this! (Weeps.) I shall die, I know I shall.

[Enter Uncle John.]

Uncle J: Ah, Susan, in tears?

Susan: O, Uncle John! My husband has just left me—and he is intoxicated. He never says at home now.

Uncle J: You don't wonder at that—do you? How often have I told you that your complainings would bring about some great calamity? It has come, I fear. You have made his home a place of misery, and he flies from it to the tavern.

Susan: I, Uncle John?

Uncle J: Yes, you, Susan. (She reflects.)

Susan: May Heaven forgive me! You are right. But what can be done?

Uncle J: Perhaps nothing. It may be too late. But, Susan, promise not to grumble any more, and I will talk with Thomas. He is a good-hearted man, and I think will reform if you will do so.

Susan: I will—O, how gladly!

Uncle J: Wives should never grumble. It makes home so unpleasant that husbands prefer the tavern. (Exeunt.)

(Source: The Student and Schoolmate, Scientific Pursuits, circa 1858, pp. 200–207.)

available to Blacks and poor Whites meant the demise of the post-war servitude (tenant farming) that chained both groups to financial servitude.[2]

THE SOCIAL FABRIC OF THE SCHOOL

Why go to school? For decades the reason given by parents to their children has been "So you'll learn to read and write and get a good job." The understanding of the parents in this communication is that education translates at some point into an opportunity for a better life. But as with most things, the agendas of students, parents, and schools do not always mesh. James S. Coleman (1961), E. E. Snyder (1969), and John Goodlad (1984) observe, for instance, that the social structures of schools most often emphasize values other than education. The status systems of some high schools place considerable value on athletics for males and social success for females. For example, in one recent study the authors collected data from recently

[2]The failure to pass this legislation is a clear example of the view that education is power, and the fear in one case that a Protestant world view would ideologically separate Catholic parents from their newly educated offspring and, in the other case, that the promise equality of opportunity would spell the demise of the financial servitude found in sharecropping.

Surprisingly, in the 1990s, research continues to show that the pathway of success for girls is sociability and appearance, not intellectual scholarship.

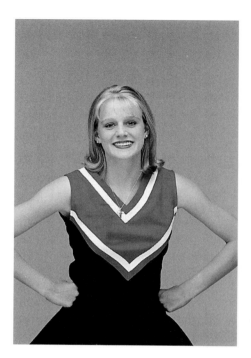

graduated high school students and asked graduates to list five ways in which males and female students could have achieved status in their former high school. The findings suggest not much has changed since the 1960s. As the authors state, "boys continue to acquire prestige primarily through participation in sports and school achievement, while girls continue to acquire prestige primarily through a combination of physical appearance, sociability, and school achievement" (Suitor & Reavis, 1995, p. 265).

In addition to the content of what qualities or characteristics acquire status among peers, two status-system attributes influence peer recognition. One of these is the ascriptiveness of the system. Coleman finds evidence that, depending on the school, high status may be awarded because of who a person is rather than what that person does. It appears, for instance, that schools with a student body that is predominantly upper middle class tend to place a higher value on the socioeconomic indicators of success than do schools without a large number of wealthy students. Finally, how content and ascriptiveness interact affects the range of attributes that will be rewarded with status by the student body. In some schools, sports like football and basketball completely dominate the status system. In other schools, combinations of these factors work to dictate who receives recognition.

As one example of how this process works, indulge the first author of this text as he remembers that social status in his high school was dominated by a combination of variables. In content, sports were relatively unimportant. The small size of the school prohibited a football team, and soccer, the sport played at the school, had not yet achieved a U.S. following. Furthermore, winning seasons at this small, private preparatory school were rather unusual. Scholarship was recognized. Savoir faire with the opposite sex was recognized. This was an all-male school. Perhaps, though, the most important characteristic was the car one drove. We shall push aside the Freudian interpretation that, deprived of a coeducational experience, we advertised our sexual prowess through our cars. At any rate, we religiously spent lunch hours staring under the hoods of vehicles. Not a single one of us knew a thing about caring for a car, but stare we did. This was an era when gasoline cost 28.9¢ a gallon; songs like "Little Deuce Coupe", "409", and "Little GTO" filled the airwaves; the lowly "Beetle" was scorned; and the "'vette" was elevated to goddess stature. As can be imagined, the ascriptiveness of the system was directly related to socioeconomic status. The range of recognition on the scale of peer status found the semiathletic type who had good grades, an attractive girlfriend, a fast car, and money to be a school social leader. Depending on how much a student deviated form this ideal pattern, his membership in the controlling elite diminished to nonexistence.

As Coleman (1961) observes, because adolescents are deprived of the power to "dispense material rewards," the social statuses that adolescents confer on their peers "show the patterns of rewards and punishments dispensed by the adolescent society" (p. 314). In inner-city schools gang membership may be an important element in achieving social recognition, while clothes and SES may matter in another setting.

Interestingly, status issues strongly affect student motivations for attending school. Once the student voices the two most often-heard reasons for attending high school ("earn more money" and "get a better job"), a fascinating assortment of other reasons emerges for attending high school—and, for that matter, college. In our discussions with students over the years, the following statements frequently surfaced: I go to school to party; to find somebody to marry; because I don't know what I want to do; to be with my friends; and, rarely, because I enjoy learning.

The social fabric we have described thus far is the one created by the students. There is a second social fabric that intertwines with that of the adolescents: the social structure of the school. The school is expected by society to impart knowledge and encourage good citizenship, "ethical character," sound bodies, proper use of leisure time, and skills sufficient to acquire employment (Hawby, 1990). The means to achieve these goals has been the comprehensive high school. In a rejection of specialized schools that would channel students into specific careers, the comprehensive high school evolved to encompass the educational needs of both vocation-oriented and college-bound youths. This multipurpose institution can be considered a uniquely American institution in which students from all types of backgrounds come together and experience different kinds of learning, including not only academic courses but extracurricular activities as well.

The system is not without its critics, who contend that it is no more humane or democratic than Lancaster's academic factories. They observe that in adolescence, when young people most need adult relationships for guidance, support, and understanding, we strip them of that support (Gullotta, 1983). They are moved from elementary school, in which contact with teachers is high and intimate, to an assembly-line system in which they receive 45-minute doses of knowledge from specialists who are remote and focused in content. In contrast to learning environments in which questioning students seek knowledge, Sarason (1997) reports that on average in a 45-minute class students ask 2 questions to the teacher's 40 to 150 questions. Gregory and Smith (1987) contend that the large comprehensive high school is a basically flawed institution whose very size breeds dehumanization, and, as Sarason (1997, p. 772) states, "schools [are] problem producers and not problem preventers." Underscoring this point are Sizer (1983), who observes that the U.S. high school system is essentially unchanged from 1880, and Goodlad (1984), who points out that total direct teacher/pupil interaction in a typical high school amounts to a measly 7 minutes a day. According to Childress (1998), the high school breeds frustration. Like Sarason and Goodlad, he sees students as passive recipients who are channeled into failure by forces other than their lack of ability.

SCHOOL AND FAMILY INFLUENCES ON LEARNING

As we have noted, the school system is not without critics charging it with creating an environment of failure, not an environment of success. The source of much of this disillusionment can be traced to a study commissioned by Congress in passing the Civil Rights Act of 1964:

> Sec. 402. The Commission [of Education] shall conduct a survey and make a report to the President and Congress, within two years of the enactment of this title, concerning

the lack of availability of equal educational opportunities for individuals by reason of race, color, religion, or national origin in public educational institutions at all levels in the United States, its territories and possessions, and the District of Columbia (Mosteller & Moynihan, 1972, p. 4).

The intent of Section 402 was to document for all time the gross inequality of educational opportunities that existed between minorities and Whites and between the middle class those trapped in poverty. Everyone, including Coleman, the principal investigator in the study, assumed that "the study will show the difference in the quality of schools that the average Negro child and the average White child are exposed to. You know yourself that the difference is going to be striking" (cited in Mosteller & Moynihan, 1972, p. 8).

The study that resulted was one of the largest social science research projects ever undertaken. It involved nearly 4,000 schools, more than 60,000 teachers, and 570,000 students. Miraculously, it was delivered within its 2-year deadline. In 1966 Congress was able to look at a study that has been described by some as a breath of fresh air in a locker room of myths and by others as the most damaging indictment of public education ever produced.

This study generated both passionate anger and passionate praise. Essentially, the report, Equality of Educational Opportunity (EOEO), offered five major findings. First, and not unexpectedly, the Untied States was found to be a segregated society. Of the White students in the nation, 80% attended schools that were 90 to 100% White. Next, and as expected, minorities were found to be learning less than Whites, and the poor, less than the middle and upper classes. The third finding, which also received much attention, was that minority students with feelings of control over their environment (an internal locus of control) and a positive self-concept performed at a higher academic level than White students. Up to this point EOEO had confirmed the suspicions of its creators: schools were segregated, the poor and minorities were learning less than Whites, and those like Kareem Abdul-Jabbar and Joycelyn Elders, capable of seeing the space between the bars of prejudice, succeeded (Abdul-Jabbar & Steinberg, 1996; Elders & Chanoff, 1996). What was not expected were the next two findings. School facilities (that is, books, the number of teachers, teacher training and experience, the school's physical plant and its equipment) were not found to be unequal. Furthermore, the variable that contributed most to a young persons learning was family background (education, socioeconomic status, ethnic group).

What is so disturbing about these last two findings is that, according to the report, spending programs to improve schools, to train teachers, and to purchase additional equipment would not significantly improve a student's learning. The country and the educational world, which had been expecting a call to launch a Marshall Plan of school reconstruction, were rocked by these findings. Reanalysis of the data by others found errors in EOEO, but these errors only diminished the importance of variables outside the family (Mosteller & Moynihan, 1972).

In the years that followed EOEO, additional arguments were introduced to account for the disparity in achievement levels between the poor and the middle class. One of these reaffirms the importance of family background by noting that if unlimited funds were spent on equalizing high school facilities, the equalization would reduce the standard deviation of achievement scores among seniors by no more than 1% (Jencks et al., 1972). Jencks and his associates contend that if the United States is truly committed to achieving equality of opportunity, emphasis should be shifted from the educational front to correcting social, racial, and economic inequalities. They state that such an effort, if successful, could eliminate as much as 20% of the difference between Blacks and Whites on achievement tests.

The general ineffectiveness of the high school for redressing social inequality is reexpressed by Jencks and Brown (1975) in a study contending that characteristics typically associated with "good" comprehensive high schools have little consistent effect in raising students' achievement scores. They find that at least for Whites, "more money, more graduate courses for teachers, smaller classes, socioeconomic, desegregation, and other traditional remedies" (p. 320) are not likely to decrease the disparities between successful and unsuccessful students.

The image of education fared no better with the publication of Rosenthal and Jacobson's book *Pygmalion in the Classroom* (1968). Investigating the impact of teacher expectations on grades, the authors devised an ingenious experiment in which they selected by chance students to be academically successful. They informed these student's teachers that these pupils had received high scores on Rosenthal's "late bloomers' test" (in actuality a commonly used IQ test). With no other intervention in the system, these students 1 year later were reported by their teachers to have "blossomed." Rosenthal and Jacobson argue that teacher expectations can contribute strongly to a student's failure. Clearly, this report did not sit well with the embattled educational community and with the failure of more than a score of attempts to replicate the findings of the study, a sinister mood emerged among educators, with some suggesting that Rosenthal and Jacobson's work be rejected.

The negative influence of teacher expectations on students' academic behavior was confirmed, however, with the publication of a research report by R. Rist (1970). Rist followed a group of elementary school students from kindergarten into the third grade as they underwent a process of labeling and stigmatization. He found that social position (that is, similarity to the teacher's socioeconomic status) had a greater influence on learning than any other variable. Kindergarten teachers, Rist observed, spend the greatest amount of instructional time with and give more positive reinforcement to children most like themselves. As the socioeconomic gap widens between the student and the teacher, the more likely it is that the student will be ignored. Rist found that this type of treatment influences children to misbehave and that the misbehavior confirms the labels attached to them and stigmatizes them from that time forward.

In the meantime, ignoring the policy implications of EOEO, a well-meaning Congress and President Johnson's administration had embarked on a series of compensatory education programs, of which Head Start is probably the best known.

Based on the work of M. Deutsch, I. Katz, and Jensen (1968) and others, these programs attempted to provide an educationally enriched environment for minority youngsters. However, as reports of failure emerged (some of which, as with Head Start, were incorrect), attention shifted to a question of genetics instead of to the policy implications of EOEO.

The trigger for this shift was a paper by Arthur Jensen published in the *Harvard Educational Review* in 1969. Beginning his argument with the long-known fact that Blacks score about one standard deviation (15 points) below Whites, Jensen stated that genetics might contribute to the lower IQ scores of Blacks as a group. Now doesn't this have a familiar "ring" to it? We'll see shortly how this issue was revisited by Hernstein and Murray in their 1994 book *The Bell Curve*. But before we do that it is insightful to see how scholars responded 30 years ago.

The reaction of the academic community to Jensen's monograph was swift and negative. J. S. Kagan (1969) found Jensen's work to be filled with "major fallacies" involving such points as his "inappropriate generalization from within-family IQ differences to an argument that separate racial gene pools are necessarily different" (p. 274). Kagan pointed out that Jensen had ignored evidence of the strong impact that environmental influences have on intelligence and noted that compensatory education programs had not been evaluated enough to allow one to categorically dismiss their potential impact on raising IQ scores.

Some researchers (for example, Bodmer & Cavalli-Sforza, 1970) argue that in a nation inherently unequal because of years of racism and oppression, it is impossible to compare Blacks and Whites fairly. Others find strong evidence to support an argument that environmental influences contribute strongly to IQ scores. For example, in a study of Black children adopted by White parents, Blacks adopted by upper-middle-class White families had higher mean IQ and achievement scores than White students in their schools (Scarr & Weinberg, 1976).

Thomas Sowell (1981), a Black economist with the Hoover Institute, offers yet another possible explanation for this IQ gap. He states:

> History shows there is nothing unique about the Black IQ level . . . . Group IQ averages at or below 85 have been common in history and currently. In the 1920's . . . numerous studies showed these kinds of IQ averages for such American ethnic groups as the Italians, Greeks, Poles, Hispanics, Slovaks, and Portuguese. A more recent study shows Mexican-Americans with lower average IQ's than Blacks in the 1940's, 1950's and 1960's, and Puerto Ricans with lower average IQ's than Blacks in the 1970's (p. 753)

The people Sowell (1981, 1986) is talking about were recent immigrants. We suggest that these individuals then and Blacks, Puerto Ricans, and other groups now have an important element in common. The element is poverty. And new research on the brain and its early development holds significant implications for learning in the adolescent years. It has been demonstrated that poor prenatal nutrition increases by 25% a baby's chances of falling at least 250 grams below the normal 1400 grams in brain weight by age 6 (Hodgkinson, 1979, 1995). Neuron development is essentially completed in the first several years of life. Deprive the young child of adequate nutrition and the adolescent is deprived of the necessary raw material (brain cells) needed to learn. This is not genetic. This is the environment, and we believe with others (Hodgkinson, 1989; 1995) that rather than solely genetic factors, it is the environmental condition of poverty that largely accounts for the difference in IQ scores.

One of the by-products of the publication of EOEO is an emergent and controversial understanding of the differences in U.S. society. The idea of the "melting pot" is being replaced by a recognition of the pluralistic nature of U.S. society. Whether that multicultural concept takes hold is another issue.[3]

IQ achievement tests are recognized as being culturally biased. Language differences are recognized, and in many parts of the country bilingual programs have been started. The work emerging from the publication of EOEO also indicates that the school is not all-powerful.

Finally, we come to a recognition that the family is the major influence on young people and their ultimate success in society. Not only do socioeconomic factors influence grades but so too do parent's involvement and disciplinary and decision-making styles matter. For example, parental monitoring of a young person's school homework and daily performance can have a positive effect on grades, particularly if that person is Mom (Bogenschneider, 1997). Harsh discipline negatively affects academic performance, while joint parent–youth decision-making appears to improve school performance (Dornbusch, Ritter, Mont-Reynaud, & Chen, 1990; Wentzel, Feldman, & Weinbeger, 1991). Furthermore, if the family is the victim of racism and oppression, it will not be able to provide its children with the same life chances that an advantaged family can. The policy implications of this view remain untouched as issues too sensitive to deal with, for ultimately the problem becomes one of investing in families—a decidedly different view than the pioneer "rugged individualism" that was thought to have built Canada and the United/break States.

Still, as we'll see next, the acknowledgement of these factors does not mean their acceptance. These same issues of genetics, ineffective teaching, and (supposedly) failed remedial programs will be joined by other issues like the United States' lagging in world educational achievement to give credence to the observation that "if ya hang around long enough you'll catch it all over again."[4]

---

[3]Canadians are struggling with the same dilemma. In 1971 Pierre Elliot Trudeau announced the intention of creating a multicultural bilingual nation. Citizens of Canada and the U.S. are increasingly questioning how nationalism can be reconciled with multiculturalism. At what point can one expect the immigrant (recognizing that except for Native Americans we are all immigrants) to lay aside old behaviors for Canadian or U.S. living practices (McConaghy, 1995)?

[4]From Jensen, wide ties, short skirts, tie-dyed clothing, and Nehru jackets in the 1960s and 1970s to *The Bell Curve*, wide ties, short skirts, tie-dyed clothing, and shirts without collars in the 1990s, it amazes us how the world goes 'round. From decade to decade, fashions go in and out of style—with both clothing and theories. Now where was it we put those bell bottom pants, that flowered shirt, and those platform shoes?

TWENTY-FIVE YEARS LATER: A NATION AT RISK AND THE BELL CURVE

Two decades after the publication of EOEO, a new series of educational reports appeared. Focusing less on differences between the classes and races, these studies looked at the growing inability of the U.S. secondary school system to educate its students. The most ambitious of these reports was a multimillion-dollar, 8-year study of that system by Goodlad (1984).

Analyzing voluminous data from over 27,000 interviews and classroom observations, Goodlad concluded that the educational system was in need of a drastic overhaul. Specifically, schools need to be made smaller. The sprawling comprehensive high school is an impersonal, dehumanizing institution. Next, a core curriculum needs to be developed that will provide all students with a common frame of reference to prepare them to be participating members of society. Third, the common practice of tracking students into high-, average- and low-ability classes is destructive and should be abolished. Goodlad's observations reaffirm the earlier works of Rosenthal and Jacobsen (1968) and R. Rist (1970). Finally, with regard to secondary education, a career track for teachers other than one leading into administration needs to be developed to keep bright instructors in the classroom.

Sizer (1983) sounds a similar theme. His work examining secondary schools concludes that they have remained essentially unchanged since the 1880s. Yet

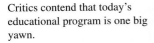

Critics contend that today's educational program is one big yawn.

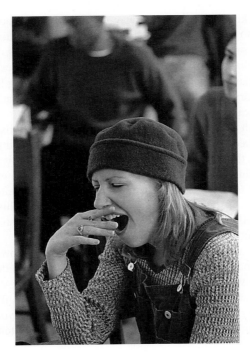

although the institutions have remained unchanged, their goals have grown exponentially. The result, he finds, is that after 12,000 hours of inhabiting school buildings young people are only marginally literate and are unprepared to accept their responsibilities in the wider world.

Underscoring these points, Powell (1985) study of high school students suggests that the average student is lost in the modern high school. Using the analogy of the shopping mall, Powell reports that many students wander aimlessly for 4 years up and down the corridors of education. Not unhappy with their educational program but intellectually unchallenged for most of the time, they blunder into the English store or the social science store to sample a course here or taste a subject there.

Almost 2 decades after changing our understanding of the factors that primarily account for academic achievement, James S. Coleman and his associates (1982, 1987) added their insight to this issue. After comparing public and private schools, this research team concluded that private schools did a better job of educating young people than did public schools. The private school climate, they found, is more orderly, the enrollment in academic courses is higher, and performance expectations are greater than in public schools.

Finally, add to these legitimate studies popular media reports of school failures and the breakdown of school discipline, and you create an environment of heightened concern among the American people. In circumstances like these, it is not unusual to see exaggerations emerge. For example, we suspect many readers have heard the story that a survey of teachers in the 1940s identified the following as the pressing problems of the day: (1) talking in class, (2) chewing gum in school, (3) making noise in the hallway, (4) running in the halls, (5) getting out of turn in line, (6) wearing improper clothing, and (7) not putting paper in the wastebasket. These problems are then compared to the problems of today: (1) drug abuse, (2) alcohol abuse, (3) teen pregnancy, (4) suicide, (5) sexual assault, (6) robbery, and (7) assault. How the authors of this book would long for the good old days, if only this story were true; this survey was a total fabrication. It was never done. The story was made up (O'Neill, 1994).

With these ringing indictments, similar in the disappointing mood to studies described in the previous section, and with misleading information being disseminated, the stage was set yet again for a genetic thesis to be put forward to explain the failure of the American educational system to educate the underprivileged. In *The Bell Curve*, Hernstein and Murray (1994) reintroduced the argument that genes, to use the colloquial, ruled. They reached this conclusion after using the first half of *The Bell Curve* to establish a relationship between intelligence and socioeconomic status (SES).

The authors informed us, not surprisingly, that low intelligence was associated with a number of poor life conditions including low educational achievement, poor jobs, low incomes, family difficulties, high crime, welfare dependency, and low levels of community involvement. The issue: Was this the result of inequality? That is, lost opportunities in schooling, access to vocational training with a future, and residence in stable communities and not tenant neighborhoods with an ever-shifting populace. Or was this the inevitable outgrowth of life among those unable to be taught?

In the third part of their work, the authors began to address this issue by presenting data that indicated Blacks scored about 15 points below Whites on standardized IQ tests. The authors also shared data that Asians scored higher that European Americans on these tests and that high-SES Hispanics scored closely to Whites.[5] From this data, the authors inferred that the testing gap between the studied groups led to the reasonable assumption that intelligence and the cognitive differences between the groups was genetic. Having drawn this inference, the authors concluded *The Bell Curve* by calling for a retreat. That is, a retreat from Head Start and other educational remedial efforts and a retreat from social programs that provide other services to the less fortunate. And having retreated from these modestly successful programs, where does one then invest educational and social resources? Those investments should be invested with intelligent youth.

As with Jensen's genetic argument published in 1969, reaction to *The Bell Curve* (1994) from scholars across many different disciplines was highly critical (see Jacobby & Glauberman, 1995 and Kincheloe, Steinberg, & Gresson, 1996 for extensive critiques on the book). Edmund Gordon (1995, p. 9) viewed their work as in tune with the current political movement that supported "selfishness . . . It makes a case for circling the wagons so as to protect the 'threatened' resources of the privileged few." Nancy Cole (1995, p. 30), president of the Educational Testing Service, writing in *Education Week* stated, "I am particularly disturbed that the authors treat the Scholastic Assessment Test as if it were an IQ test, which it clearly is not, and then use the results as if they provided proof of inherited intelligence, which is by any standard bad science." Andrews and Nelkin (1996, p. 13) observed that the studies Hernstein and Murray drew upon have "significant methodical difficulties . . . If anything, the lack of predictability from genetic information has become the rule rather than the exception." Finally, Siegel (1995), writing in the *Alberta Journal of Educational Research*, notes that general intelligence is not easily measured and increasingly of less use as educators in Canada and the U.S. recognize theories of multiple intelligences and adjust their instruction accordingly.

As we'll see throughout this book claims for the genetic origins of all sorts of behaviors are made. Some of these claims may well be true (as, we suspect, with persistent clinical depression). But even if those claims have validity, genes alone do not make the person. For example, it is true intelligence is in part a question of genes just as height is predicted in part by genes. Why do we use the words "in part"?

Arthur Jensen (1995), certainly no proponent of nurture/environment interventions, in defending the work of Hernstein and Murray speculates that 70%

---

[5]This brings up the interesting point of exactly what is a "Hispanic?" The term "Hispanic" denotes neither ethnicity nor race. "Hispanics," some of whom are very very dark indeed, are grouped typically with Caucasians. The term "Hispanic" is an invention of the U.S. Census Department to enable them to count people whose family origins are south of the United States.

of IQ is hereditary. Assuming that Jensen is correct in his speculation, this still leaves 30% of an individual's IQ subject to the environment. This is a significant percentage for positive intervention and should not be ignored. Of course, Jensen may be wrong and the influence of the environment may be even greater. For example, deprive the child of exposure to language and beyond some critical threshold, regardless of intelligence, the child will not learn to speak. Expose the young brilliant child to lead and watch her intellectually wither. Rob the child of adequate nutrition and see body, height, and mind waste. In the opinion of the authors of this book, the environment and, in particular, families matter. Indeed, recall that using the statistical technique of a meta-analysis, Devlin and his associates (1997) demonstrated that genes account for less than 50% of the factors that determine IQ (see Box 9-2 on Family Practices to Improve Learning).

B O X 9-2   Family Practices to Improve Learning

Drawing from research, we have made the argument that families are the major factor in predicting young people's success in school. While having an adequate income, a good secure job, and clean affordable housing in a crime-free neighborhood are conditions we would wish for all families, this is not the reality for many. But does that mean the young people in those families are doomed to failure? Obviously, the answer is no. Many examples exist in which youths from abysmal circumstances succeed. Sometimes, it is finding a mentor who offers the young person a vision that provides the pathway out of poverty and ignorance. Many times, it is the parents or guardians of these youth who serve that role.

In an important monograph titled "The Family Is Critical to Student Achievement," Henderson and Berla (1994) review the numerous studies that have established this truth. They conclude that seven factors promote student achievement. Those factors are:

1. Families that promote student achievement have an established daily routine. That is, there is a quiet place for a student to study; there is a defined and adhered to sleep and wake-up schedule; sleep time is adequate; and young family members have responsibilities.

2. Families monitor school work. Families that help youths succeed place limits on television viewing; they know what their children are doing after school; and if not able to be home, these families have developed systems of responsible supervision for those young people.

3. Families model learning. Young people who achieve live in families that exercise self-discipline, that read, and that communicate with each other.

4. Families express high but achievable academic expectations. It is important to these families that their youths learn.

5. Families support the learner. Families with learners are connected to the school that their child attends. When possible, these families provide assistance with homework.

6. Families read together. They discuss news or magazine articles; share opinions about books; and if the child is young, they read to the child.

7. Finally, these are families that use community resources. That is, they involve younger family members in community activities like sports, music, or theatre groups that offer both additional positive role models and experiences.

These are important achievable objections that need to be put more into practice.

AND THEN THERE WAS PROJECT 2000 . . . WELL KIND OF

In a recent speech, President Clinton, like President Bush before him, dedicated himself to creating an educated populace second to none. Interestingly, the plan outlined in his address closely parallels a program called Goals 2000. Goals 2000 was devised in 1989 when then-President Bush and the nation's governors, including Bill Clinton, then governor of Arkansas, agreed to several national goals for U.S. education that, if reached, would improve student achievement by the end of this decade. In the third edition of this book we examined four of these goals, asking the question how the United States might ever achieve them. In rewriting this chapter, we initially dropped this section when a highly politicized Goals 2000 was eviscerated by Congress (Broder, 1996). But in light of continued widespread public concern with each of the goals, we think it is useful to examine them and judge, as best we can, how U.S. youths are learning.

Goal 1. By the year 2000, all children in the United States will start school ready to learn.

This first goal is eloquent in its simplicity. But how do you prepare children for school? Is the question the readiness of children for education or parents for parenthood? Is the question one of access to health care, adequate nutrition, clothing, and housing? Or is the question one of access to quality early child care? The authors would agree all children should be ready for education. And yet, even though the effectiveness of the early childhood program Head Start has been established, it remains that 80% of the children eligible for Head Start are not enrolled for lack of adequate funding. Regarding housing, there are an estimated 8 million low-income individuals seeking affordable housing. And yet, the low-income housing supply has been estimated at 4 million housing units (Hodgkinson, 1989, 1995). Of the estimated 37 million people in the United States without health insurance, 12 million are children. Twenty-five percent of the pregnant women in the United States receive no medical care during the first trimester of their pregnancy (Hodgkinson, 1989, 1995) (see Box 9-3).

Finally, while the incidence of poverty has declined for the elderly, it has increased for young people. Illustrating this last point is the following data from the U.S. Census Bureau. In 1970, 24.6% of persons 65 years of age and older were living below the poverty line. By 1995, this had declined to 10.5% (U.S. Census Bureau, 1997, Chart 740, p. 476). In contrast, in 1970, 14.9% of youths under the age of 18 lived below the poverty line. By 1993, this figure had grown to 20% (U.S. Census Bureau, 1997, Chart 737, p. 475). Incidentally, poverty is neither colored nor ethnically blind. Nevertheless, it extracts its worse punishment on diverse youths. For the year 1995, White children under the age of 18 had a poverty rate of 15.5%, Black youths 41.5%, and Latino youths 39.3% (U.S. Census Bureau, 1997, Chart 737, p. 475).

BOX **9-3**   School-Based Health and Social Services Centers

There were days that Marvin just ached all over. His joints would swell, and his energy level was nowhere. "Man, I'm 16 years old. I'm not supposed to feel this way. I need me some Geritol or something," he'd joke to his friends. At the urging of his father, Marvin visited one of the school-based health centers that the first author of this book administers. Enrolled by his parents for services at the center, Marvin saw a nurse practitioner, and after blood work on Marvin was completed and reviewed, antibiotic treatment for an acute case of Lyme disease was started. Marvin responded quickly to treatment, becoming in his junior and senior years a regular customer for sports physicals, throat cultures, and, tragically, after the violent death of an older brother, counseling services.

What is a school-based health center? It is a place in or near a school where a parent gives written permission to allow a young person to go to receive primary physical or mental health services confidentially. Staffed by physicians, nurse practitioners, and school workers, the center can provide routine services for a variety of common ailments, including sexually transmitted diseases. Centers work closely with parents, school officials, and the youth's pediatrician (should there be one) providing services that promote healthy lifestyles, and they discourage the development of harmful behaviors like smoking and eating disorders (Dryfoos, 1998, 1999).

In recent years, concern has been expressed over school-based health centers' prescribing or dispensing contraceptives. Actually, very few (<15%) of the estimated 1000 school-based health centers nationwide presently distribute or prescribe contraceptives (Gullotta & Letarte, 1995; Gullotta, Noyes, & Blau, 1996). What services do school-based health centers provide? Data for one state indicate that for the year 1995 the majority of mental health service requests made by young people were for family problems, problems with peers, and with school issues. This was followed by requests for help with stress management, drug use, depression, and handling violent circumstances. Principal physical health care issues included reproductive health education, physical exams, health screenings, the administration of medication, and reproductive health services. Reproductive health services included Pap smears and the diagnosis and treatment of sexually transmitted diseases (Dowden, Calvert, Davis, & Gullotta, 1997). From the Gullotta and Noyes (1995) study, 80% of secondary school students are enrolled in centers the Child and Family Agency operates. Fifty-five percent of these youths have no other source of medical care. Many are not poor enough for Medicaid and therefore have no medical insurance.

Dryfoos (1998, 1999) believes that school-based health services will become commonplace early in the next century. They provide ready access to quality care to a population of youths that are medically underserved. School-based health centers, she believes, are the start of a transformation that will see schools join in cooperative ventures with other agencies to serve the "whole" needs of children and adults in communities.

If this first goal is ever to be achieved then these issues will need to be addressed if children are to be ready for school.

Goal 2. By the year 2000, U.S. students will leave grades four, eight, and twelve having demonstrated competency in challenging subject matter, including English, mathematics, science, history, and geography; and every school in the United States will ensure that all students learn to use their minds well, so that they may be prepared for responsible citizenship, further learning, and productive employment in our economy.

Young people spend roughly 9% of their childhood years in school (Bracey, 1991). Many scholars would suggest that they spend much of that time in unchallenging classroom situations learning rote skills (Darling-Hammond, 1990). To best understand the progress that needs to be made in this area, it would be useful to examine the National Assessment of Educational Progress Tests (NAEP), which are administered each year to a representative sample of young people ages 9, 13, and 17 across the United States. Forget state mastery test scores, which are easier than the NAEP or College SATs that are not administered randomly. The NAEP is a well-kept secret that *is* the nation's report card. Proficiency is scored on a 0 to 500 scale. A score in the 150 range represents "rudimentary" reading ability; in the 200 range "basic" proficiency readers. "Intermediate" readers in the 250 range can search for specific information and make generalizations, while "adept" readers in the 300 range can find, understand, and explain complicated information like that found in an editorial of the *Wall Street Journal* or the *New York Times* (Ralph, Keller, & Crouse, 1994; U.S. Census Bureau, 1997).

As Table 9-1 demonstrates, the mean scores for early adolescents (13-year-olds) have not changed dramatically from 1979 to 1994. Modest growth trends over time in reading have declined slightly for the most recently reported data. Further, not a single group average broke the 300 range, enabling them to understand complex information. However, notice the impact parent education has on NAEP scores. As the parent's education increases so too does the student's score, a finding that should not escape your notice (U.S. Census Bureau, 1997, Chart 278 p. 178).

To improve these scores some people have endorsed the concept of choice (vouchers) or charter schools leading to a free market in what otherwise might be described as a monopoly. Others call for increased focused federal funding. Still others believe that the states should be left to develop their own solutions.

Goal 3. By the year 2000, U.S. students will be the first in the world in mathematics and science achievement.

For more than a decade students in the United States have not compared well against their counterparts in other nations. For example, in international comparisons of performances in science the Congressional Budget Office (1993) reported that 13-year-old U.S. youth lagged behind young people from Korea (1), Taiwan (2), Russia (3), Canada (4), France (5) and Spain (6). Similarly, in mathematics a similar rank order appeared. The one exception is that in contrast to the science ranking where Canadian youth ranked fourth, they lagged slightly behind French youth and ranked fifth.

Again, to have a perspective on this issue we use the NAEP proficiency scores for science and mathematics. This time, let's look at the performances of older adolescents (17-year-olds). As Table 9-1 illustrates, small movement in science has occurred over the last decade. Nevertheless, the trend has been generally positive with Black and Latino youths showing the greatest gains. The U.S. youth total score at age 17 (294) is roughly at the "adept" (score 300) level. Scores for males exceed those of females. White 17-year-old students exceed Black and Latino students by more than 30 points. Scores in mathematics, although higher, reflect the same trends (U.S. Census Bureau, 1997, Chart 278, p. 178; see Table 9-1). Again, notice the positive impact of parent's education on student's scores.

TABLE 9-1   Test Scores of High School Graduates: Proficiency Test Scores for Selected Subjects by Characteristic: 1977–1992[a]

| | | SEX | | RACE | | | Parental education | | More than high school | | |
| | | | | | | | Less than high school | High school | | | |
Test and year	Total	Male	Female	White[a]	Black[b]	Latino			Total	Some college	College graduate
Reading											
9 year olds:											
1979–80	215	210	220	221	189	190	194	213	225	NA	NA
1987–88	212	208	216	218	189	194	193	211	220	NA	NA
1989–90	209	204	215	217	182	189	193	209	218	NA	NA
1993–94	211	207	215	218	185	186	189	207	221	NA	NA
13 year olds:											
1979–80	259	254	263	264	233	237	239	254	271	NA	NA
1987–88	258	252	253	251	243	240	247	253	265	NA	NA
1989–90	257	251	253	252	242	238	241	251	267	NA	NA
1993–94	258	251	266	265	234	235	237	251	269	NA	NA
17 year olds:											
1979–80	286	282	289	293	243	261	262	278	290	NA	(NA)
1987–88	290	286	294	295	274	271	267	282	300	NA	(NA)
1989–90	290	284	297	297	267	275	270	283	300	NA	(NA)
1993–94	288	282	295	296	266	263	268	276	299	NA	(NA)
Writing[2]											
4th graders:											
1983–84	204	201	208	211	182	189	179	192	217	208	218
1987–88	206	199	213	215	173	190	194	199	212	211	212
1989–90	202	195	209	211	171	184	186	197	210	214	209
1991–92	207	198	216	217	175	189	191	202	212	201	214
8th graders:											
1983–84	267	258	276	272	247	247	258	261	276	271	278
1987–88	264	254	274	269	246	250	254	258	271	275	271
1989–90	257	246	268	262	239	246	246	253	265	267	255
1991–92	274	264	285	279	258	265	258	268	263	280	284
11th graders:											
1983–84	290	281	299	297	270	259	274	284	299	298	300
1987–88	291	282	299	296	275	274	276	285	298	296	299
1989–90	287	276	298	293	268	277	268	278	296	292	298
1991–92	287	279	296	294	263	274	271	278	295	292	296
Mathematics											
9 year olds:											
1977–78	219	217	220	224	192	203	200	219	231	230	231
1985–86	222	222	222	227	202	205	201	218	231	229	231
1989–90	230	229	230	235	208	214	210	226	237	236	238
1993–94	231	232	230	237	212	210	210	225	(NA)	239	238

(continues)

TABLE 9-1 *(continued)*

Test and year	Total	SEX		RACE			Parental education		More than high school		
		Male	Female	White[a]	Black[b]	Latino	Less than high school	High school	Total	Some college	College graduate
13 year olds:											
1977–78	264	264	265	272	230	238	245	263	280	273	284
1985–86	269	270	268	274	249	254	252	263	278	274	280
1989–90	270	271	270	276	249	255	253	263	279	277	280
1993–94	274	276	273	281	252	256	255	266	(NA)	277	285
17 year olds:											
1977–78	300	304	297	306	268	276	280	294	313	305	317
1985–86	302	305	299	308	279	283	279	293	310	305	314
1989–90	305	306	303	310	289	284	285	294	313	308	316
1993–94	306	309	304	312	286	291	284	295	(NA)	305	318
Science											
9 year olds:											
1976–77	220	221	218	230	175	192	199	223	233	237	232
1985–86	224	230	221	232	196	199	204	220	235	236	235
1989–90	229	235	227	238	196	206	210	226	236	238	236
1993–94	231	232	230	240	201	201	211	225	(NA)	239	239
13 year olds:											
1976–77	247	251	244	256	208	213	224	245	264	260	266
1985–86	251	256	247	259	222	226	229	245	262	258	264
1989–90	255	259	252	264	226	232	233	247	266	263	268
1993–94	257	259	254	267	224	232	234	247	(NA)	260	269
17 year olds:											
1976–77	290	297	282	298	240	262	265	284	304	296	309
1985–86	289	295	282	298	253	259	258	277	300	295	304
1989–90	290	296	285	301	253	262	261	276	302	297	306
1993–94	294	300	289	306	257	261	256	279	(NA)	295	311
History, 1993–94											
4th graders	205	203	206	215	177	180	177	197	(NA)	214	216
8th graders	259	259	259	267	239	243	241	251	(NA)	254	270
12th graders	286	288	285	292	265	267	263	276	(NA)	287	296
Geography, 1993–94											
4th graders	206	208	203	218	168	183	186	197	(NA)	216	216
8th graders	260	262	258	270	229	239	238	250	(NA)	265	272
12th graders	285	288	281	291	258	268	263	274	(NA)	286	294

NA   Not available.

[a] Non-Latino.

[b] Writing scores revised from previous years; previous writing scores were recorded on a 0 to 400 rather than 0 to 500 scale.

[c] Based on The National Assessment of Educational Progress Tests which are administered to a representative sample of students in public and private schools. Test scores can range from 0 to 500. For details, see source.

Source: U.S. National Center for Education Statistics, *Digest of Education Statistics,* annual.

NAEP and other scores would suggest that Canadian and U.S. youth are doing as well as might be expected.

Several explanations have been offered for these less-than-stellar performances. One explanation is that research design controls partly explain the poor performances. The problem is, or so it has been suggested, that the United States does not restrict students from taking the exam. Perhaps with a more discriminating pool of exam takers achievement scores would improve (Rotberg, 1990, 1995).[6] A second argument offered is that gender differences in these scores are not the result of genetic differences but rather the result of biased tests and gender tracking against women (Wellesley College Center for Research on Women, 1992). We are not sure that we would subscribe to sample-tailoring to improve the United States science and mathematics scores. Rather, it appears to us that science, mathematics, and reading need to be more fully integrated into a curriculum free of bias and free of steering to improve the achievement levels of all, not just some, youths (see Box 9-4.)

Goal 4. By the year 2000, every person in the United States will be literate and will possess the skills necessary to compete in a global economy and to exercise the rights and responsibilities of citizenship.

At present, about 40% of the U.S. public cannot find information in a newspaper article and 30% cannot write a simple letter to explain to a company that an error had occurred in a billing statement (Mikulecky, 1990). In part, this may explain why most popular magazines are written at a fourth-grade reading level with story lengths that rarely exceed a few hundred words. It may also explain the urging to

---

[6]Rothberg (1995, p. 1446) notes that some nations like Kenya encourage low-achieving youths not to take the exam, while up to 20% of Chinese youths "may be retained in grade in upper-middle school in order to increase scores."

B O X **9-4**   **Science and Adolescent Women**

For many years data have supported findings that adolescent females do not perform as well as males on tests that determine science and mathematical ability (Benbow & Stanley, 1980, 1983; Kramer, 1991; Steinkamp & Maehr, 1984). On Scholastic Aptitude Tests (SATs), for example, males have outscored females by more than 30 points for the past 2 decades. In 1996 male average SAT scores were 527 compared to female scores of 492. On other measures like the American College Tests, the NAEP, and the 3rd International Mathematics and Science study differences favoring males have been observed (U.S. Census Bureau, 1997, Charts 276, 277, and 278, pp. 177–178; Vogel, 1998). Collectively these examinations provide evidence that males score about one-half a standard deviation higher than do females.

Several arguments have been offered to explain these continuing differences. Camill Benbow and Julian Stanley (1980, p. 1264) suspect these differences result from "superior male mathematical ability, which may in turn be related to greater male ability in spatial tasks."

Reporting in *Science*, Holden (1998) cites evidence that math ability is a "stable trait." The study involved 276 academically gifted young children. Half were tutored in math; the other half received regular instruction. Regardless of the group, boys maintained an academic edge over girls in math.

Others believe that gender steering is occurring (Steinkamp & Maehr, 1984). That is, to be a scientist is to be masculine, and adolescent women should not be masculine. This argument has been further extended to imply that being successful in school is unfeminine. Several authors and groups like the American Association of University Women have decried this situation and called for an end to suspected tracking practices that steer women away from these courses and higher enrollment in high school math and science classes (Pallas & Alexander, 1983; Benz, Pfeiffer, & Newman, 1981; Wellesley College Center for Research on Women, 1992).

What do you think? Did your experiences in high school confirm the steering hypothesis? Are the sexes different in their ability?

dumb-down undergraduate textbooks and the growing tendency to hear headline or "sound bite" news.[7]

If we sidestep the issue of how we choose to define the term literate, than there is some encouraging data that suggest that most—but certainly not all—people in the United States are striving to improve their knowledge. For instance, 69% of adults 25- years of-age and older in 1996 had graduated from a 4-year high school (U.S. Census Bureau, 1997, Chart 49, p. 49).

Finally, adult educational services are more available and from more sources than ever before. For example, including all forms of continuing education, about 40% of the U.S. adult population (17 and over) took a course in 1995 for reasons that varied from personal enrichment (44%), job advancement (54%), and job training (11%) to the completion of a degree (10%) (U.S. Census Bureau, 1997, Chart 312, p. 196). It would seem the continuing accrual of practical knowledge our forefathers thought so valuable remains an important element of the American

[7]It might interest you to know that this volume is considered a "high-end" textbook. That is, it is written for an upper-level college audience. There are college textbooks on adolescence written for a 6th-grade reading audience. We suspect that in your instructor's choice of this book (s)he has high expectations for your work.

experience. Even though we believe the goal of literacy for everyone by the year 2000 is unattainable, for many improvement is under way.

SUMMARY

The cynical reader might say, "So what? More than 30 years ago we were provided with information that could have brought about change, but it was ignored. So here we are three decades later revisiting virtually the same script. Some researchers say schools don't work. Others say teachers don't care. Still others hint that some students are not worth teaching. They are genetically inferior. So what?" As that baseball sage Yogi Berra once remarked, "It's deja vue all over again." Why be concerned now?

For the cynical who would question the well-intentioned actions of others, one reason to care is demographic. As the U.S. birthrate declines to historic lows, the value of each child increases proportionately. Beginning with this decade, the overwhelming majority of new employment positions with a future will require education beyond high school. The number of young people in the work force between the ages of 16 and 24 will drop from 30% in 1985 to 16% in the year 2000. It is projected that 20% of the labor force will be Black, Asian, and of Latino heritage (Darling-Hammond, 1990; Wattenberg, 1987). In short, we do not have a single child to waste to ignorance if we expect to compete in the new "global" economy.

For the less cynical, these studies and statements are a mere continuation of the concern expressed for children and how best to raise them to be productive members of our society. The interest that society has in those children is clearly represented in the $514 billion the United States spent to educate their young people in 1996. It is represented in two U.S. Presidents wanting to be known as the "Education" President. Perhaps these calls for action will be heeded this time. If not, the problems will not disappear. Other individuals, in other years, will raise similar issues until the situation is finally corrected.

It would have been nice to end this section on a less decidedly sour note. In some regards, the educational system and the family have achieved positive changes. For example, the number of young people enrolled in high school grew from 6.7% in 1889 to 15.4% in 1909, from 73.3% in 1930 to 90% in 1958. This figure still remains in excess of 90% (U.S. Census Bureau, 1997, Chart 240, p. 1557). While we should remain highly concerned about the number of young people who leave school before graduating, still we can take heart that the drop-out rate has significantly dropped for Blacks and Latino youths over the years.

For example, in 1970, 10.8% of Whites failed to finish school. This declined ever-so-slightly to 9.7% by 1995. For Black students, the improvement has been significant. Twenty-two percent failed to complete high school in 1970 as compared to 10% in 1995. Keeping in mind that the term "Hispanic" is of recent invention, their initial measuring point was in 1980 when 29.5% dropped out. This initial figure declined to 24.7% in 1995 (U.S. Census Bureau, 1997, Chart 273 p. 171).

However, these are small victories that get lost in an increasingly bitter ideological struggle underway in both the United States and Canada. It is in many ways an ancient struggle played over who will have access to resources and who will determine the information that will be disseminated. Who should be educated, how should they be educated, and what should they be educated in are long running major issues in both countries. From cuts in the Alberta education budget (McConaghy, 1994) to attempts to shut down the U.S. Federal Department of Education, the spirit of the dialogue is, as it has always been, ideological.

POSITIVE EFFECTS OF SCHOOLING

Despite the discouraging evidence just put before you, there are data indicating that schools do impart knowledge. For example, a study of 18,000 adults showed that knowledge increases as level of education increases (Hyman, Wright, & Reed, 1975). This last point can be clearly seen by again referring to Table 9-1. As young people grew older and moved through the educational system, their proficiency increased. True, part of this increase was due to maturational effects, but part of it was also surely due to the sharing of knowledge that is the business of schooling.

In recent years, the decline in SAT scores has stabilized with average verbal scores in 1996 at 500 (males: 507; females: 503). Math scores averaged at 508 (males: 527; females: 492) (U.S. Census Bureau, 1997, Chart 276 p. 177). More interesting still is the fact that 1995 saw more students than ever scoring above 600 on the math portion of the SAT—23.4%. This declined slightly to 22.7% in 1996 (U.S. Census Bureau, 1997, Chart 276 p. 177). And while the number of students scoring below 400 on the verbal portion of the SAT was a disturbingly high 42.3% in 1994, Bracey (1995b, p. 154) was still able to report that U.S. youths are still among "the best teenage readers in the world . . . while the worst [U.S.] readers are no worse than their counterparts" in the other studied countries.

Finally, think back for a moment to your own educational experience. Most of the young people we have spoken with have warm and lasting memories of their school experience. Most students want school to be a friendly and relaxed place. And certainly Powell (1985) reports a "deep satisfaction" among most students with their educational setting. Indeed, as Erik Erikson (1968) has written so eloquently, for many of us a teacher has made all the difference in the world. Clearly, there is room for improvement in how the United States educates its youth, in particular, those young people who are not White males. Nevertheless, it would be unfair to ignore the progress that has occurred benefiting all youth in this country, particularly, when improvement efforts are underway.

For example, some social scientists are devoting their energies to clearly identifying those major influences that affect school learning (Wang, Haertel, & Walberg, 1993). With this knowledge, targeted efforts to improve learning can be undertaken. These researchers have categorized a list of influences under the headings of (1) state and district governance organization; (2) home and community educational contexts; (3) school demographics, culture, climate, policies and practices; (4) design and delivery of curriculum and instruction; (5) classroom practices; and (6) student characteristics. Each of these dimensions are defined in Table 9-2.

T A B L E   **9-2**   **A Description of Major Categories of Influences on School Learning**

State and district governance and organization
  These categories are associated with state- and district-level school governance and administration. They include
    state curriculum and textbook policies, testing and graduate requirements, teacher licensure, specific provisions
    in teacher contracts, and some district-level administrative and fiscal variables.

Category	Illustrative variable
District demographics	School district size
State and district policies	Teacher licensure requirements

Home and community educational contexts
  These categories are associated with the home and community contexts within which schools function. They include
    community demographics, peer culture, parental support and involvement, and amount of time students spend
    out of school on activities such as television viewing, leisure reading, and homework.

Category	Illustrative variable
Community	Socioeconomic level of community
Peer group	Level of peers' academic aspirations
Home environment and parental support	Parental involvement in ensuring completion of homework
Student use of out-of-school time	Student participation in clubs and extracurricular activities

School demographics, culture, climate, policies, and practices
  These categories are associated with school-level demographics, culture, climate, policies, and practices. They include
    demographics of the student body; whether the school is public or private, and levels of funding for specific categorical
    programs: school-level decision-making variables; and specific school-level policies and practices, including policies
    on parental involvement in the school.

Category	Illustrative variable
School demographics	Size of school
Teacher/administrator decision-making	Principal actively concerned with instructional program
School culture (ethos conducive to teaching and learning)	Schoolwide emphasis on recognition of academic achievement
Schoolwide policy and organization	Explicit schoolwide discipline policy
Accessibility	Accessibility of education program (overcoming architectural) communication, and environmental barriers)
Parental involvement policy	Parental involvement in improvement and operation of instructional program

Design and delivery of curriculum and instruction
  These categories are associated with instruction as designed and with the physical arrangements for its delivery. They include
    the instructional strategies specified by the curriculum, and characteristics of instructional materials.

Category	Illustrative Variable
Program demographics	Size of instructional group (whole class, small group, and one-on-one instruction)
Curriculum and instruction	Alignment among goals, contents, instruction, assignments, and evaluation
Curriculum design	Materials employ advance organizers

Classroom Practices
  These categories are associated with the implementation of the curriculum and the instructional program. They include
    classroom routines and practices, characteristics of instruction as delivered, classroom management, monitoring of
    student progress, quality and quantity of instruction provided, student/teacher interactions, and classroom climate.

(continues)

TABLE 9-2 *(continued)*

Category	Illustrative Variable
Classroom implementation support	Establishing efficient classroom routines and communicating rules and procedures
Classroom instruction	Use of clear and organized direct instruction
Quantity of instruction	Time on task (amount of time students are actively engaged in instruction
Classroom assessment	Use of assessment as a frequent integral component of instruction
Classroom management	Group alerting (teacher uses questioning/recitation strategies that maintain active participation by all students)
Student and teacher social interactions	Student responds positively to questions from other students and from teacher
Student and teacher academic interactions	Frequent calls for extended, substantive oral/written responses (not one-word answers)
Classroom climate	Cohesiveness (members of class are friends sharing common interests and values emphasizing cooperative goals)

Student characteristics

These categories are associated with individual students, including demographics, academic history, and a variety of social, behavioral, motivational, cognitive, and affective characteristics.

Category	Illustrative Variable
Student demographics	Gender and marker
History of educational placement	Prior grade retention
Social and behavioral	Positive, nondisruptive behavior
Motivational and affective	Attitude toward subject matter instructed
Cognitive	Level of specific academic knowledge in subject area instructed
Metacognitive	Comprehension monitoring (planning; monitoring effectiveness of attempted actions and outcomes of actions; testing, revising, and evaluating learning strategies)
Psychomotor	Psychomotor skills specific to area instructed

From "Toward a Knowledge Base for School Learning" by Margaret C. Wang, Geneva D. Haertel, and Herbert J. Walberg, *Review of Educational Research*, 1993, *63*, 249–294.

To understand the power of these many influences on school learning, the investigators completed a complex study that examined research "effect size" (the size or proportion of influence on school learning). From the most influential to the least were student characteristics, classroom practices, home and community educational contexts, design and delivery of curriculum and instruction, school demographics, and state and district governance and organization (Wang, Haertel, & Walberg, 1993). Ryan and Adams (1995) report a similar ordering of variables influencing school achievement (see also, Ryan, Adams, Gullotta, Weissberg, & Hampton, 1995). Notice that these findings are not remarkably different from Coleman's work discussed earlier.

In Table 9-3 the 30 most influential features on learning are listed from the most to the least powerful. In examining this list, it is clear that there are many places where interventions to improve the educational experience can occur. For example,

TABLE **9-3**   A Rank-Order of Influences on School Learning

Category	Content ratings	Expert ratings[a]	Meta-Analyses	Average
Classroom management	59.5	64.9	70.0	64.8
Metacognitive	60.0	68.0	61.1	63.0
Cognitive	55.5	58.1	70.2	61.3
Home environment and parental support	51.9	62.1	61.3	58.4
Student and teacher social interactions	57.3	56.1	—	56.7
Social and behavioral	55.5	55.0	—	55.2
Motivation and affective	53.3	64.9	46.2	54.8
Peer group	56.4	56.1	49.3	53.9
Quantity of instruction	57.3	50.2	53.7	53.7
School culture	49.2	57.7	52.8	53.3
Classroom climate	56.8	54.2	45.9	52.3
Classroom instructional	49.7	59.3	47.2	52.1
Curriculum design	51.0	51.0	52.0	51.3
Student and teacher academic interactions	51.5	41.9	59.3	50.9
Classroom assessment	51.5	52.6	47.3	50.4
Community	47.4	50.6	—	49.0
Psychomotor	71.2	36.3	39.3	48.9
Teacher/administrator decision-making	40.7	56.1	—	48.4
Curriculum and instruction	52.8	44.3	46.0	47.7
Parental involvement policy	41.6	43.1	52.6	45.8
Classroom implementation support	49.2	48.6	39.3	45.7
Student demographics	43.0	41.1	50.4	44.8
Student use of out-of-school time	53.7	46.6	32.6	44.3
Program demographics	55.1	39.5	33.9	42.8
School demographics	44.8	36.6	43.0	41.4
State and district policies	22.4	32.8	56.0	37.0
School policy and organization	29.5	39.1	40.8	36.5
District demographics	32.2	33.6	—	32.9
Accessibility	*	*	*	*
History of educational placement	*	*	*	*

[From "Toward a Knowledge Base for School Learning" by M. C. Wang, G. D. Haertel and H. J. Walberg, Review of Educational Research, 1993, 63, 249–294.]

cognitive development, critical thinking skills, and academic performance can be enhanced by improving students' developmental characteristics, by offering better or more efficient classroom practices, and by working with home and community educational contexts.

Using similar data, efforts at improving classroom instruction to better academic performance can be identified. For example, Wentzel (1997) observes that caring teachers can promote not only prosocial behavior but grades as well. In his study, he identifies four successful instructional characteristics. First, successful teachers use a democratic interactional style of instruction. This style encourages discussion and student questions, which in turn creates interest in the material. Next, these teachers tailor expectations to the learning styles of the students. Third, they model a caring attitude for their students. This attitude encourages respect for the subject and the students. Last, they provide their students with positive constructive feedback.

In another effort, David Perkins (1995) summarizes a number of proven educational programs that enhance intelligence and educational success. One interesting effort is Project Intelligence. Consisting of six instructional units, attention is given to the *how of thinking* rather than *what to think*. Units focus on: (1) foundations of reasoning (observation, classification, ordering, analogies, spatial reasoning); (2) understanding language (word relations, structure of language, reading for meaning); (3) verbal reasoning (assertions and arguments); (4) problem solving (mental simulations, trial and error, inference); (5) decision-making (systematic gathering and evaluation of information); and (6) inventive thinking (concepts, designs, and inventions).

To learn these skills involves instruction, discussion, practice, exercises, and learning how to engage in thoughtful analysis and broad thinking. According to the evidence, programs that focus on these fundamentals make a difference—academically and in intelligence. In the realm of offering a word of advice, for students pursuing an educational degree, a useful guide on improving multiple intelligences is David Lazear's (1991) *Seven Ways of Knowing: Teaching for Multiple Intelligences*. Next, let's see how all that new-found intelligence is applied.

EDUCATION, CAREERS, AND THE FUTURE

Myth has it that life used to be predictable. You were born in one community, grew up in one house, were educated in one school, married one person, worked in one job, and returned back to that house to eventually die at home. Look around you and the inaccuracy of that myth is readily apparent. What concerns us in this section is the issue of career education and its role in today's society.

U.S. and Canadian society has always experienced change. The difference between the recent past and the present is the rate of change. Needless to say, since World War II the rate of change has accelerated. This rapid change makes it extremely difficult to predict the future. For example, the first author remembers in 1973 purchasing his first calculator. "Miracles of technology," he thought, "a calculator with a square-root key for only $73." Today, as he walks through the enclosed suburban malls that did not exist when he was a youth, he could buy a programmable calculator with more more power than the computer aboard the ill-fated Apollo 13 mission for that amount of money. Consider another example. In the mid-1960s the American automobile industry was unrivaled. Car production was at historic highs. If a young person decided in 1965 to embark on a career as a spot welder for American Motors, his or her guidance counselor would have probably thought the decision was a wise one. Who would ever have thought that less than 25 years later spot welders would have been replaced by robots and that American Motors would have been bought and sold twice, losing its name in the process?

Thus, the traditional notion that career education introduces young people into established, lifelong occupational structures are no longer valid. Indeed, it has even been demonstrated that high school grades, class rank, and aptitude have no relationship to employment status (Bracey, 1992). Consequently, a new understanding of the role of career education is emerging. It is based on the following beliefs: First, throughout life, change will be the only constant. Next, during an individual's work life, he or she will probably have several jobs, very possibly in different employment fields. Last, successful career education programs need to expand young people's understanding of the multitude of options available to them.

Does career education alone influence the decisions that young people make regarding their ever-changing career paths? Obviously, the answer is "no." Several other significant forces exist:

1. Individual factors such as intelligence, work attitude, and ambition.
2. Family factors such as income, religion, race, and parental attitudes about the importance of education.
3. General societal factors such as current attitudes about gender roles, public aid for education, and levels of racism.
4. Changes in the world marketplace.
5. Chance.

The first three factors are self-explanatory, but the fourth and fifth deserve brief explanations.

What does the world market have to do with one's career? An example might be helpful. Look at the manufacturing label on the clothing you are wearing. What does it say? Chances are the article of clothing you are wearing was made in

Parent's education not only has a positive influence on a young person's test scores but is also an important factor in later career decisions.

China, Korea, or Bangladesh and not in either Canada or the United States. This is a real example of the "global marketplace" at work. Manufacturing shifts to those locations where the product can be produced at acceptable quality at the lowest possible cost. While this is providing needed employment in "Pacific Rim" nations, it has had disastrous consequences for the clothing manufacturing industry in North America.

Assuming trade barriers are not reestablished, the economies of the world's nations will blur over the next 50 years. With that blurring of national economic boundaries, today's well-paying jobs in North American industries like airplane manufacturing and system software development may very well move to other parts of the globe, and individuals in those occupations (who do not adapt to these shifting employment patterns) will join the ranks of previously displaced workers in clothing, steel, and electronic manufacturing who also saw their careers leave North America for other locations. Constant change, in unpredictable directions, is the new reality. To adapt to this condition, the young student needs to remain a student for life—ever learning new skills to earn a living.

Finally, it may be that despite all of the best intentions of educators and parents, young people begin their careers as much by chance as any other factor. A part-time college job may provide experience that leads to full-time employment after graduation. A friend of the family may know the personnel officer of a corporation. Or, perhaps, Mom owns 51% of it. The point is that chance rather than a deliberate planning effort may be the most important factor. To illustrate, for those Generation X youths growing up on the "Disney Channel," the actress Annette Funicello, of the original "Mickey Mouse Clubhouse" and beach-blanket-film fame, shares the story that Walt Disney by chance observed her performing in a dance recital. This accidental encounter provided her with the opportunity to establish a very successful career as an entertainer.

Even if we are correct that chaos and chance are significant factors, we do not mean that you should give up all career planning. Graduating from high school and joining that intellectual elite minority of American citizens who have graduated from college is, on average, a wise investment.[8] Data suggest that high school graduates earn half as much as nongraduates and that college graduates earn twice as much as nongraduates (see Table 9-4 for a selected list of the fastest growing and declining occupations in the U.S.).

TRUANCY, DROPPING OUT, AND SCHOOL VIOLENCE

For some young people formal education is a source of unhappiness, and for a variety of reasons they either avoid attending school whenever they can or leave before graduating. Others behave destructively at school, damaging property and threatening or attacking people.

[8]It is estimated that in 1996 nearly 24% of the U.S. population had graduated from college. This is up from 8% in 1960 (U.S. Census Bureau, 1997, Chart 243 p. 159).

TABLE **9-4**   Employment in the Fastest Growing and Fastest Declining Occupations Projected to 2005—Selected Examples

Growth 1992–2005	Percentage change
Fastest growing	
Home health aides	+106%
Computer engineers and scientists	+102%
Physical therapists	+84%
Electronic pagination systems workers	+88%
Fastest Declining	
Directory assistance operators	−69%
Data entry keyers	−66%
Machine tool setters and set-up operators	−30%
Typists and word processors	−30%

Adapted from: Chart No. 647, Civilian Employment in the Fastest Growing and Fastest Declining Occupations: 1994–2005, In: U.S. Census Bureau (1997). *Statistical abstract of the United States 117th ed.*, Washington, D.C., p. 414.

Truancy

Like running away, playing hooky is a national pastime. Neither behavior is particularly accepted—idleness has long been popularly thought to breed trouble—but until recently neither has been investigated by the scientific community.

There are essentially two kinds of explanation for truancy. The first can be described as a psychological explanation. According to this view, the influence of the school on truancy is less important than personal and family variables.

Most of the psychological research in this area focuses on the need of the mother to retard her adolescent's attempts to gain independence and shows that she must be helped to relax her grip on the young person's life and let the adolescent go. This point of view is illustrated by Sperling (1967) and C. Goldberg (1977), who suggest that truancy is the result of an excessively close mother/child relationship in which ambivalence over separation results in school abscence. They suggest that the return of the young person to school as soon as possible and family treatment are both needed to deal with truancy. According to Nielson and Gerber (1979), the problems of truants are often serious and longstanding. They found that truants were depressed and angry, with many committing delinquent acts. If the truant has older brothers and sisters, they, too, are often truants. The families of these young people experience many problems, with divorce, unemployment, illness, and alcoholism not uncommon (Sommer & Nagel, 1991). Although these young people see the value of school, few, if any, have a positive relationship with the school staff. The open hostility that these adolescents feel for the staff serves to fuel a cycle of increased truancy.

Not everyone agrees that truancy is the by-product of a struggle between parent and child. Some researchers, relying heavily on their observations of the social

FIGURE 9-1

Earnings and education (*Source:* U.S. Census Bureau (1991). Does Education really pay off? *Census and You, 26,* p. 8).

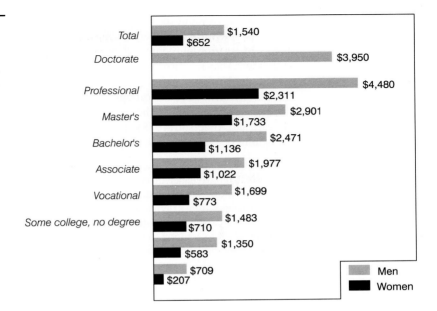

structure of the school, suggest that the system may work against some young people. For instance, Albert Cohen (1955) argues that the school is essentially a middle-class structure that frustrates lower-class individuals by denying them recognition. This frustration motivates young people to stay away from school and seek other means of recognition.

In view of our earlier discussion of the works of Rosenthal and Jacobson (1968) and Rist (1970), Cohen's argument is compelling. Deprived of the opportunity to feel worthwhile, to be valued, and to achieve status, the frustrated young person turns away from education in many instances. As the frustration grows, the probability of that young person's completing high school diminishes.

Dropping Out

In large U.S. cities, roughly 40% of the young people enrolled in high school will not finish (Hahn, 1987; Strother, 1986). Nationwide, this represented over 406,000 students between the ages of 16 and 17 in 1995 (U.S. Census Bureau, 1997, Chart 273, p. 176).[9] The consequences of this decision for young people are considerable. The drop-out has roughly a 1 in 3 chance of finding employment. If successful in the job search, those jobs pay the 18- to 24-year-old an average yearly salary of $6000 (Hayes, 1992) (see Fig. 9-1.)

[9]If young adults between the ages of 18 and 21 are added to this group the figure swells by nearly 2 million individuals.

Several reviews of the literature have identified the factors that predict which young people are most likely to leave school (Bracey,1996; Gage, 1990; Hahn, 1987). Many drop-outs come from impoverished families. The home life for many is strained. They have a history of truancy and trouble with school authorities. Their parents are likely not to have completed high school. Felice (1981) maintains that for many Black students, dropping out is a rejection of the school's racist and discriminatory behavior. The influence of culture is unmistakable, according to Howard and Anderson (1978). Echoing Cohen's (1955) observation that the school is essentially a middle-class institution, they assert:

> Whereas the middle class emphasis is on order and discipline, the lower class emphasis is on avoidance of trouble or involvement with authorities, development of physical prowess, skill in duping others, the search for excitement and a desire for independence from external controls. Thus, while socialization in middle class families prepares youths to compete successfully in school, lower class children are not prepared to conform to the academic and informal requirements of school. The lower class child, not prepared to be studious, obedient, and docile, comes into conflict with the middle class teacher. His language, poor social adjustment and "cult of immediacy" impair his chance of success (p. 225).

Other writers contend that peer influence also serves to accelerate the decision to leave school earlier (see, for example, Elliot, Voss, & Wendling, 1966; Parsons, 1959). Those at greatest risk are young people whose friends are no longer in school. Still other scholars observe that criminal behavior and dropping out of school are related (Thornberry, Moore, & Christenson, 1985) and that drop-outs are poorly motivated students (Richardson & Cerlach, 1980). In a recent study of French Canadian youths, a group of researchers identified a number of previously noted factors that contributed to the decision to leave school (Janosz, LeBlanc, Boulerice, & Tremblay, 1997). Of these factors, staying back, poor grades, and a lack of interest in school mattered most in the decision to drop out of school.

We propose two strategies for breaking the truancy/drop-out pattern. The first is based on Cohen's (1955) argument that the school denies the truant and the drop-out recognition. Providing recognition to more students is clearly in order. Schools need to broaden their curricula to include such ideas as expanded work/study options, credit-for-experience programs, and alternative learning centers to provide young people with an increased chance at recognition. Interestingly, a report by Shumer (1994) provides support for this last observation. In a project that provided at-risk youths with tutors, opportunities for volunteering, and community-based education, the incidence of leaving school was reduced.

The basis for the second strategy is EOEO. If truancy and dropping out are essentially problems of the poor, then change will not occur until we address the fundamental inequalities of poor housing, inadequate medical care, and poor nutrition that exist in our society. These same inequalities help to fuel the anger and hatred that provoke violence in schools and turn many of them into armed camps.

Finally, we need to recognize that educational timetable the United States has established may not be appropriate for all learners. Some young people will need more time to mature, to discover the need for education, and to want to learn. Concepts like the much-maligned Clinton National Youth Service Program, which would enable youths to stumble out of that psychosocial moratorium less hurriedly, are to be encouraged (Eberly, 1991; Woodring, 1989).

School Violence

In reading reports of school life in colonial times (before Lancaster introduced his school), one cannot help feeling that those quaint, one-room, stove-warmed buildings had more in common with *The Blackboard Jungle* than with *Little House on the Prairie*. Kett (1977) reports that it was not uncommon for an unpopular teacher to be seized in his classroom by the older, stronger boys, taken outside, and thrashed. Teacher turnover was, needless to say, high. Because the teacher was usually a traveling instructor who lodged in the homes of the villagers, the community more frequently sided with their children in disputes or instances of violence than with the teacher. Times have not changed much; Canadian and U.S. newspaper accounts of robbery, assaults, and even murder in our schools today are all too common.

Reacting to reports of increased school violence, Congress as long ago as 1974 called for a report determining the extent of "illegal and disruptive" activities in schools. This study, which became known as the Safe School Study, involved more than 4000 schools. The study reported that acts of violence against individuals and property rose steadily throughout the 1960s and into the 1970s but appeared to have leveled off. This study was the first to report that adolescents were at greater risk of violent injury in schools than anywhere else (Violent Schools, 1979).

More than 400,000 students were victims of violent crime during a 6-month period in 1988 and 1989. More than one-third of these incidents involved early adolescents (12- to 15-year-olds) inside or on school property. Early adolescents were more than twice as likely as older adolescents (16- to 19-year-olds) to be victimized at school. A close examination of the data found that 37% of violent crimes and 81% of thefts against early adolescents occurred at school, compared with 17% of the violent crimes and 39% of thefts against older adolescents (Whitaker & Bastian, 1991).

National data from 1991 indicate that almost 56% of the crimes committed against young people occurred in or on school grounds. Most thefts occurred in school (72%) and violent behavior was as likely to happen in school (23%) as at home (25%) (Snyder & Sickmund, 1995). More recent data find middle and junior high schools more violent places than either K–8 or K–12 schools (Anderman & Kimweli, 1997). Could it be that younger elementary-grade students have a calming effect on the boisterousness of early adolescence? In another study more than 50% of students in grades 6–8 reported being victimized (Kuther & Fisher, 1998).

Additional data from the National Crime Victimization Survey of 10,000 nationally representative youths between the ages of 12 and 19 found nearly a quarter of Black inner-city students worried about being attacked when going to and coming from school. Six percent of the sample reported avoiding some place in or around school (mostly restrooms) because they feared harm. Sixteen percent reported knowledge of either a threat or an attack against a teacher. Fifteen percent reported gangs at their school (Bastian & Taylor, 1991). In another study of U.S. 8th-graders, 10% stated they had been offered drugs for purchase (Hafner, Ingels, Schneider, & Stevenson, 1990) (see Table 9-5).

Although these are in actuality small percentages, the effects of these figures on the educational and social climate of schools are unmistakable. First there are the calls in the media and from local boards of education for security guards and increased discipline. Student's rights are assailed for contributing to the problem. Accompanying the cry for increased discipline is a call for increased use of corporal punishment.

Twenty-nine states continue to have rules permitting school personnel to use reasonable physical force against students (Orentlicher, 1992).[10] Arguments that corporal punishment is "cruel and unusual" have not moved the U.S. Supreme Court to reverse the April 19, 1977, decision approving corporal punishment. In Ingraham vs Wright, the Court, in a 5-to-4 decision, held that the protections of the Eighth Amendment do not apply to young people except in the criminal justice process. The majority opinion of the Court was that as schools are not prisons but "open" institutions, "the school child has little need for the protection of the Eighth Amendment" (Flygare, 1978). However, many people, including the U.S. Advisory Board on Child Abuse and Neglect (1991), would dispute the Court's contention that the school is an open institution. Hampton, Jenkins, and Gullotta (1996) contend that violence in any setting encourages violence in return. For example, the assistant principal of an Atlanta high school was critically wounded and paralyzed by a gun-wielding 15-year-old boy. The enraged student shouted, "You are not going to whip me anymore!" (Welsh, 1978, p. 341). Supporting Hampton's et al. contention are studies showing that mothers who use severe punishment have more aggressive children than mothers who do not (Sears, Maccoby, & Levin, 1957; Bauer, Dubanoski, Yamauchi, & Hunbo, 1990) and that children rated by their peers as being physically aggressive in the classroom have parents who use corporal punishment more often than other parents (Eron, Walder, & Lefkowitz, 1971). Why do schools use punishment? Surveying school administrators in South Carolina which has the 9th highest rate of physical punishment in the nation, two researchers reported that force was most commonly used against youths when students were (1) fighting, (2) using profanity, or (3) disrupting the classroom (Medway & Smircic, 1992).

In recent years fighting has taken on new meaning as firearms appear to be the weapon of choice to right perceived wrongs against teachers and classmates or to bring certain conclusion to a dispute. The use of firearms in and around schools is

---

[10]States prohibiting corporal punishment are: Alaska, Arizona, California, Connecticut, Hawaii, Iowa, Maine, Massachusetts, Minnesota, Montana, Nebraska, New Hampshire, New Jersey, New York, North Dakota, Oregon, Rhode Island, South Dakota, Vermont, Virginia, Wisconsin, and the District of Columbia (Orentlicher, 1992).

T A B L E **9-5**   Students Reporting at Least One Victimization at School by Personal and Family Characteristics

Student characteristic	Total number of students	Percent of students Reporting victimization at school		
		Total	Violent	Property
Sex				
Male	11,166,316	9	2	7
Female	10,387,776	9	2	8
Race				
White	17,306,626	9	2	7
Black	3,449,488	8	2	7
Other	797,978	10	2*	8
Latino origin				
Latino	2,026,968	7	3	5
Non-Latino	19,452,697	9	2	8
Not ascertained	74,428	3*	—	3*
Age				
12	3,220,891	9	2	7
13	3,318,714	10	2	8
14	3,264,574	11	2	9
15	3,214,109	9	3	7
16	3,275,002	9	2	7
17	3,273,628	8	1	7
18	1,755,825	5	1*	4
19	231,348	2*	—	2*
Number of times family moved in last 5 years				
None	18,905,538	8	2	7
Once	845,345	9	2	7
Twice	610,312	13	3*	11
3 or more	1,141,555	15	6	9
Not ascertained	51,343	5*	5*	—
Family Income				
Less than $7,500	2,041,418	8	2	6
$7,500–$9,999	791,086	4	1*	3
$10,000–$14,999	1,823,150	9	3	7
$15,000–$24,999	3,772,445	8	1	8
$25,000–$29,999	1,845,313	8	2	7
$30,000–$49,999	5,798,448	10	2	8
$50,000 and over	3,498,382	11	2	9
Not ascertained	1,983,849	7	3	5
Place of residence				
Central city	5,816,321	10	2	8
Suburbs	10,089,207	9	2	7
Nonmetropolitan area	5,648,564	8	1	7

Source: From L. D. Bastian & B. M. Taylor (1991), p. 1. *School Crime* (NCJ-131645) (Washington D.C.: U.S. Justice Department, 1991), 1.

not new. It has been several years since the U.S. Congress passed PL103-382, better known as the Gun-Free School act. Essentially, the bill requires local school systems to implement a zero-tolerance policy regarding students possessing firearms on school property or lose federal educational support (Pipho, 1998). Clearly, despite this legislation, the use of firearms on school property has not abated.

In those very few highly publicized schools where a young person has used a weapon to kill classmates and teachers, we can only conjecture that these are lonely alienated youths whose membership in the school was marginal at best. As we speculated in the previous chapter, we would not be surprised if these youths were heavy viewers of the slaughter genre of films and video games. As we'll discuss in the next chapter, the surest pathway to problem behavior is to not belong, to not be valued as a group member, and to be denied the opportunity to make a meaningful contribution to the group's existence. Combine these factors with the desensitizing that occurs watching the slaughter genre. Mix in the heavy media coverage of these events. And the result can be the copycat killings of others on school grounds.

The problem of school violence is not easily solved. Calls for increased discipline (Bauer, 1985) and stronger leadership by principals (Ianni & Reusslanni, 1980) skirt the real issue: violent schools are not positive places. Increased security guards, metal detectors, identification cards, fences, and closed-circuit televisions are band-aids, not solutions. In the last section of this chapter, we examine the success of some possible alternatives to the present educational system. But first, let's look more closely at the experiences of diverse youths in North American school settings.

SCHOOL CONTEXTS AND ETHNIC AND RACIALLY DIVERSE YOUTH

With the ideological disputes raging in North America about Black English (or ebonics), bilingual education, boys- or girls-only academies with school uniforms, and charter schools with ethnocentric missions, effective schooling in a multicultural society means many different things to different people. Against this backdrop, let's examine several aspects of the educational experience of diverse youths.

Integration and Social Relations

In Brown vs the Board of Education, the Supreme Court found that separate but equal schools for White and Black youths were *constitutionally* unequal. In redressing the issue of inequality of opportunity between the races, this decision opened the door to possibly improving race relations (Hallinan & Smith, 1985).

There are two hypotheses that apply to cross-racial friendships in desegregated classrooms. According to the *opportunity hypothesis*, the smaller racial group has more possibilities for cross-race contacts than the larger group. Furthermore, as the number of class members of one group increases, opportunities for interaction with these students also increase. To state the obvious, contact is necessary for friendships to occur. Thus, the smaller ethnic/racial group will have a larger number of cross-race or ethnic friendships (Hallinan & Smith, 1985). The second hypothesis states that *cross-race contacts* in the classroom are influenced by student's sticking to issues of social status. The thought here is that lower-status youths are victims of prejudice and are at-risk (as a result) for lower self-esteem. In this scenario, lower-status youths turn to each other for social support and reject interaction with the larger group. Thus, cross-racial friendships do not occur.

By asking students to identify their best friends in the classroom (a sociometric measuring technique) several studies have tested these assumptions. For example, Hallinan and Smith (1985) found support for the opportunity hypothesis among Black and White adolescents in interracial classrooms. Cross-racial friendships increased for Black and White youths as the proportion of the other-race peers increased and the proportion of same-race peers decreased. Being in either a Black or White minority did not diminish the friendliness of minority students. They also reported that interracially balanced classrooms maximized cross-race friendships for both Blacks and Whites.

Similarly, DuBois and Hirsch (1990) examined friendship patterns in a junior high school in which nearly a quarter of the students were Black. The proportion of White and Black students in this school reflected the racial make-up of the community and was not the result of desegregation efforts. Most of the students reported having an other-race school friend (over 80%). This figure declined when students were asked if that other-race school friend was a close friend (23% White and 47% Black). Thus, having a friend of another race is quite common in mixed-race school settings, but cross-race friendships decline out of school. Supporting the opportunity hypothesis, Black students were more likely to maintain ties with their close other-race friends outside of the school context.

While these studies offer evidence for the opportunity hypothesis, it is important to understand the response of the majority White students to the friendliness of the minority Black students. Clark and Ayers (1988) addressed this topic in a study of 7th- and 8th-grade Black students who were attending a predominantly White school. Using a sociometric strategy, researchers asked students to rank their three best friends. Reciprocated friends were those students who were selected as a best friend by one of their best-friend choices. Nonreciprocated friends were those in which mutual selection did not occur. The authors reported that the Black students were significantly more likely to be in the unreciprocated group (40%) than were the White students (14%). They concluded that in desegregated classrooms, where Blacks were in the minority, they have more difficulty than Whites in forming reciprocated friendships.

Clearly students who find themselves in the minority must find adaptive ways to cope in the classroom. Addressing this issue, Miller (1989) identified four patterns of adaptive behavior among Black high school students who were bussed to wealthy suburban schools. Each observed pattern was linked to a specific style of social interaction. For example, some Black students adapted by becoming a model student. A second pattern of adaptation was to establish interracial friendships, which included strong participation in school events like dances, clubs, and sports events. A third adaptation pattern was seen with students who were highly involved and integrated in school activities, but did not date. The final coping style used by Black students was characterized by a philosophical agreement with the aims of desegregation. However, these students did not become directly involved in school activities.

While the opportunity to interact cross-racially is one outcome of the Brown vs Board of Education decision, why are race relations still so tense given these studies showing that friendships are possible? As this chapter has repeatedly pointed out, wealth and social class exercise powerful mediating influences. In the previously discussed study Miller (1990) later reported that significant income differences contributed to detrimental interracial interactions. In fact, he found evidence that the greater the income discrepancy, the less welcome were minority students. In Miller's (1990) opinion, to have positive experiences in desegregation the following factors were needed: (1) equivalent social class indicators between the groups (very low-income diverse students should not be bussed to highly affluent suburbs), (2) schools should have increased minority enrollment (in Miller's study 2.6 to 8.5% of the student body were Black minority students), (3) more minority staff are needed in desegregated schools, and (4) specific programs to meet the needs of minority students are necessary.

Academic Achievement

The landmark Brown vs the Board of Education decision was intended to narrow if not eliminate the learning gap between White and Black youths. As we discussed earlier in this chapter, for many reasons that gap has not been closed. What factors contribute to this educational gap? Authors such as Sharpton (1996) cite teacher and system-wide prejudice and discrimination as reasons for failure. Recall our earlier description in this chapter of Rist's study; the contention here is that the teaching style of middle-income staff is out of touch with the learning styles of some very poor ethnic and racial groups.[11] Further, the decaying inner cities, home to these poor ethnic and racial groups, lack the tax base necessary to adequately equip, maintain, and staff aging school buildings.

Two perspectives can be used to further our understanding of lowered academic achievement among some diverse adolescents. The first, called a *cultural difference approach*, focuses on microanalytic interactions in examining the classroom environment (Trueba, 1988). The belief is that differences in communication, motivation, and cognitive styles, along with classroom social organization and social relations, interaction style, and literacy and writing between White middle-income and other cultures contribute to school failure among diverse youths (Ogbu, 1987, 1997). Diverse students are taught in this learning environment that includes White middle-class values. Discrepancies between the student's upbringing and the expectation that (s)he conform to this manner of education result in a less than

---

[11] The teachers in Rist's study were Black. More important than race may be SES factors.

desirable educational experience for the minority student. Thus, lowered academic achievement occurs.

In the opening pages of this chapter, we shared that immigrant Irish Catholic parents were opposed to compulsory education. Their fear of losing their children to British Protestant teachers and their teachings is an example of this perspective. Take that image and now apply it to families whose American heritages are rooted in slavery and the same fears, albeit in a different time, emerge. Having maneuvered within the system for centuries to survive, to succeed now requires cooperating and trusting individuals who historically represent the oppressors.

A second view to understanding academic difficulties and successes among diverse youths is found in the *cultural discontinuity approach*. This approach examines broad patterns of activity at a societal (macroethnographic) level. One of its leading theorists is Ogbu (1987, 1997), who has identified three types of diverse groups in the United States. The underlying concept behind cultural discontinuity is that the history of each group's interaction with the broader U.S. society influences academic achievement of the group's members.

For example, *autonomous* diverse groups are minority groups primarily in a numerical sense. That is, they constitute a smaller percentage of the total number of people in a population. Such groups (for example, people of the Jewish faith) have cultural frames of reference that encourage its children to strive for academic success. Hence, these groups tend not to be characterized by problems in reading, writing, and other aspects of academic achievement.

Immigrant diverse groups (for example, West Indians) are those that have moved to the United States voluntarily. Similar to autonomous minorities, they do not exhibit lingering problems in school failure. Immigrant minorities, however, quite commonly experience prejudice and discrimination to a greater degree than autonomous minorities, who typically have more power. In contrast to autonomous and immigrant diverse groups, *castelike or involuntary groups* were brought into the United States through slavery, conquest, or colonization (for example, African Americans and American Indians). Castelike minorities exhibit the most difficulties in respect to school achievement and academic success. In *Black Profiles in Courage*, Kareem Abdul-Jabbar (Abdul-Jabbar and Steinberg, 1996, p. 23) has written eloquently of this last situation. Where all diverse groups live behind the bars of prejudice and discrimination, Abdul-Jabbar believes that because he is a West Indian he was able to succeed: "West Indians don't see the bars; they see the space between the bars." Until either the bars are removed through laws like affirmative action or castelike/involuntary diverse groups see enough space between the bars to move forward, there only will be the bars.

Given this background, let's next examine the factors associated with academic achievement among diverse adolescents.

Factors That Contribute to Academic Achievement

In Ogbu's model Asian Americans are representative of an immigrant diverse group that moved to the United States voluntarily. It is also an immigrant group that exhibits high academic achievement in this country. Several factors have been associated with their high academic achievement (Schneider and Lee, 1990). They are: (a) expectations of parents, teachers, and peers for academic success; (b) parental efforts to direct children's after school activities toward academic tasks; and (c) factors associated with Asian culture that are rewarded in White middle-income school environments (for example, children who are quiet, industrious, disciplined, and orderly).

An interesting study of academic achievement examined Asian-American, Caucasian-American, Chinese, and Japanese 11th-grade students in mathematics (Chen & Stevenson, 1995). In the test that was given to the four groups, the Chinese scored first, the Japanese second, the Asian Americans third, and the Caucasian Americans scored last. Test performance was then compared to a number of factors. In contrast to Caucasian Americans, the Asian-American students "attended good schools, had parents and peers who held high academic standards, believed that the road to success was through effort, had very positive attitudes about mathematics, were enrolled in more challenging courses, studied diligently, and experienced less interference with their schoolwork from jobs and informal peer interactions" (Chen & Stevenson, 1995, p. 1232). The authors of this study believe that cultural attitudes toward studying and education that prevail among the Japanese and Chinese are exhibited to a smaller degree by Asian Americans whose residence in the United States has weakened those strong cultural educational values (see Box 9-5).

In contrast to Asian Americans, poorer academic achievement has been associated with some diverse groups that fall into Ogbu's (1987) classification of castelike minorities. Of these groups, none has been more examined than Black Americans.

In one recent effort, Wilson and Wilson (1992) identified those factors that influenced educational aspirations among a large sample of Black and White high school seniors living in two-parent families. Grade performance is linked to higher educational aspiration, which encourages ever higher grade level attainment. Black youths had significantly higher aspirations than White youth. This finding is meaningful and is consistent with a pattern of higher grades and grade attainment discussed earlier in this chapter. Of special interest is that educational aspirations were enhanced through parental involvement and support in the school program of the Black adolescents. As with the previously mentioned Irish Catholics, once suspicion was replaced with belief in the system, young people learned.[12]

The findings of Wilson and Wilson (1992) are indicative of a growing interest in the role parents play in the academic achievement of adolescents. Reynolds and Gill (1994) explored this topic in a study of low-income Black families with 6th-grade youths. All of the young people had participated in government-funded early childhood programs. Interestingly, parents' satisfaction with the quality of education and parents' expectations for their children's levels of educational attainment served to predict academic achievement in the 6th grade as measured in higher

---

[12]Interestingly, that belief in the system resulted in parochial not public schools. The charter school movement is seen by some Black leaders as the way to give birth to a similar movement among Black Americans. More on that when we examine culturally specific education shortly.

BOX **9-5** A Cross-Cultural Perspective: Education in Japan

The spectacular success of the Japanese people in trade and scientific developments has led to a growing world influence. In the United States many critics, perceiving Americans doing business as usual, have argued that U.S. institutions should imitate the Japanese. Nowhere is this call greater than in education. Critics of American education point out the typical Japanese high school graduate has an educational level comparable to that of an American college graduate. An impressive 94% of Japanese students graduate from high school. Finally, on international science and mathematics tests Japanese low-scorers outperform American high-scorers.

Observers note that in contrast to the U.S. system's 180-day school year, the Japanese attend school 240 days, including a half-day of school on Saturdays. Course work is more difficult. Homework is mandatory. *Shiken jiqoko* (examination hells) are used to select only the best and brightest Japanese students for intensive advanced academic preparation. Many students attend after-hours schools. And in the ultimate contrast to American students, Japanese young people clean their own schools and serve their own lunches (Shimahara, 1985; White, 1987; Sato & McLaughlin, 1992).

Is this the answer to problems in American education? There is a price to pay for this structure and discipline as George (1995) discussed in *Japanese Secondary Schools: A Closer Look*. After spending a year observing the educational system and having his son enrolled in a Japanese high school, George observed that teachers' only instructional style was the lecture format. Questions were almost never asked. Concepts were almost never manipulated to find new understandings. The Japanese national curriculum was adhered to strictly.

Finally, as pleasant or frightening as these observations may sound, playing with the structure of the school system alone will not improve the U.S. educational system. As Shimahara and White point out, education is central to the Japanese culture. Few Japanese mothers are employed outside of the home. Rather, they are "employed" in preparing their children for education. Furthermore, the Japanese society is very homogeneous. Minorities constitute only 3% of the population. The divorce rate is one-third that of the United States, and only 5% of the population lives in single-parent families. Education involves more than schools. It involves families.

scores in reading, math, and competence behavior and lower scores in adolescents' problem behavior. Hence, rather than specific parental behaviors, attitudes and expectations were found to be most important in the academic achievement of these young adolescents.

To state the obvious, dropping out is a clear indicator of school failure. In light of the earlier discussion identifying poor diverse youths to be at particular risk, one research group sought to identify risk and promotive factors for this problem area (Connell, Halpern-Felsher, Clifford, Crichlow, & Usinger, 1995). Not surprisingly, factors like low attendance, low scores on standardized achievement tests, suspension, course failure, and being older than classmates were found to be counterproductive to staying in high school. However, these risk behaviors could be minimized by higher levels of students' commitment to school. In particular, the probability of engagement in school was maximized by perceived competence (believing that one is doing well in school and can excel) and perceived relatedness (experiencing connectedness and emotional security with others in the educational setting including both peers and adults). For females, perceived autonomy (individuality) predicted engagement in school. Perceived competence, autonomy, and relatedness (connectedness) were predicted by perceived support from teachers and adults from home. While economic factors influence the decision to remain in school, the Connell et al. (1995) study suggests that personal factors like competence, belief in oneself, and school investment when combined with support from teachers, parents, and other adults can minimize school failure.

Other studies offer similar insights into those factors that promote academic achievement among Black youths. Those factors are: (1) impressing on Black youths the connections between school performance and employment (DeSantis, Ketterlinus, & Youniss, 1990); (2) wakening parents to the positive influence they can have on their adolescent's academic career (DeSantis et al., 1990); (3) encouraging high academic standards (Kaufman & Rosenbaum, 1992); (4) providing students information and guidance on college enrollment (Kaufman & Rosenbaum, 1992); (5) providing additional teacher help and tutoring to students (Kaufman & Rosenbaum, 1992); (6) having positive role models for youths (Kaufman & Rosenbaum, 1992); and (7) instilling educational and achievement values (Ford, 1992).

In an qualitative study exploring similar factors leading to academic success, Gregory (1995) interviewed White and Latino youths 14 to 25 years of age who had experienced school difficulties but were presently performing at acceptable levels as shown by improved attendance, interest in doing required work, improved quality of work, and a more positive attitude toward school and future prospects in life. Youths were interviewed concerning their improvement and what led to their positive changes.

Students reported that remembering academic success in elementary school provided the motivation to turn themselves around from problematic behaviors in high school. Interestingly, students identified the transition to high school as a reason for not doing well. For example, very practical issues of having long commutes to attend the high school of a student's choice and dealing with territorialism and gangs posed real obstacles to academic success.

Decisions and motivations for turning around focused on students' taking responsibility for themselves and their futures (Gregory, 1995). Several participants in the study attributed their change to growing up. They felt that they gained new insights and awareness and that it was time to get on with their lives. Beginning to care about oneself also was evident in students' statements concerning the positive changes in their lives. Having an experience of success, like a high grade or having a positive internship experience, encouraged change for some youth. Pride was a motivating for others. The experience of a traumatic event frightened still other students into action. Supporting their efforts at change were caring teachers, counselors, peers, and family. It is important to again recognize the power of social support on youths. A caring adult can make all the difference in the life of a young person. *Please, never forget this last point—a caring adult really can make all the difference in the life of a young person.* Clearly, the findings of Gregory (1995) provide evidence of those effects.

Having positive role models that encourage educational aspirations is a factor for Latino youth remaining in school.

Less research is available on Latino and American Indian school success. In respect to Latinos, academic success has been linked with college-prep training stressing effective communication skills (Abi-Nader, 1990). Cardoza (1991) found that educational aspirations, role models, and choosing to delay marriage and childrearing were predictive of college attendance among Latino females. As with other groups, family support is a powerful factor for Latino youths staying in school (Delgado-Gaitan, 1988).

In a study identifying protective factors for Latino academic success, Alva (1995) sorted 10th-grade students into two groups. The first was classified as invulnerable (higher academic achievement). The second was identified as vulnerable (lower academic achievement) from scores on the Comprehensive Tests of Basic Skills (CTBS) and grades for two semesters in the 10th-grade. This study found invulnerable (successful) students: (1) experienced less stress with language issues, (2) had fewer family concerns, (3) perceived they were being readied for college, and (4) were more involved in school activities.

The role of culturally specific education in encouraging higher academic achievement is much debated. We have noted that when religious divisions between Protestants and Catholics were more acutely felt in the United States that Catholic families, through their churches, began a still-successful parallel school movement in the United States. Remembering that fact and understanding that culturally specific education requires a separate educational experience, this specialized program is not possible in most public schools. To provide a culturally specific education, the teacher utilizes instructional strategies and curricula that are relevant and appropriate for the group targeted in the educational experience. For example, the third author of this text observed at a Sioux tribal school in South Dakota that taught the language, history, and customs of their tribe in addition to basic skills. Youths were encouraged in the learning process through culturally appropriate teaching styles and classroom protocol. Since the young people were of the same racial group and teachers were committed to this teaching approach, the potential for a racially discriminating intragroup educational experiences was minimized. This educational experiment is being tried across the country with Black and Latino youths. Other alternatives are also being explored as we will see in the next section.

SOME ALTERNATIVES TO THE PRESENT EDUCATIONAL SYSTEM

This chapter concludes on a more optimistic note than earlier editions. We hold hope for three reasons. First, experiments in educating children differently are under way. Next, taxpayers across the country are rebelling against "business as usual." Finally, by the end of the first decade of the next century, demographics will reshape the relationship between schools and communities regardless of the efforts of people have committed to the status quo.

Experiments Under Way

For several years educators have attempted to identify characteristics of effective school programs. In a report to Congress by the General Accounting Office (1989) five of these features were identified:

1. Effective school programs have strong purposeful administrative and instructional leadership that creates community consensus on educational goals.
2. Programs focus instruction on higher-order not rote learning (like the Odyssey Program).
3. Schools are orderly and safe, allowing students and teachers to focus their attention on learning.
4. The expectation is that children can learn.
5. Continuous evaluation enables appropriate modifications of individualized educational programs and system efforts.

Emerging from these roots, efforts are under way to change the American educational experience. Here are some examples:

Smaller classes is one way to increase academic achievement.

In Tennessee the state legislature funded a 4-year study to determine the effect of class size on achievement. Project STAR (Student/Teacher Achievement Ratio) analyzed three classroom configurations: classes with one teacher and 13 to 17 students, one teacher and 22 to 25 students, and one teacher and an aide to 22 to 25 students. After 4 years, the study found that students in smaller classes scored significantly higher on achievement and basic skill tests than students in other settings. Consistent with findings presented in this chapter, children from more economically privileged backgrounds always outperformed students eligible for the free lunch program (Pate-Bain, Achilles, Boyd-Zaharias, & McKenna, 1992). The point is to remember that family variables like socioeconomic status (SES) and relationship instability (divorce, death, or serious illness) in the family matter! Equally, important to remember, however, is that the individualized attention found in small classes can result in dramatic academic growth. This growth contributes to feelings of success that can keep an at-risk young person involved in the educational process (Bracey, 1995c; Mosteller, 1995).

In Minnesota, Milwaukee, St. Louis, Missouri, Cambridge, Massachusetts, and elsewhere, pilot programs permit parents a choice in selecting schools for their children. Initial findings from these efforts were not particularly encouraging. For instance, in St. Louis when inner-city parents were provided an opportunity to send their children to suburban schools, few parents enrolled their children. In Milwaukee, 65% of parents who had enrolled their children in the program withdrew in the second year. Still, these efforts are significant in their attempt to break down the social stratification that permeates education systems across the United States (Bracey, 1993).

A recent study sheds additional light on these school choice efforts. Looking at five school choice plans, the authors reported that low-income parents who participated in these efforts were better educated than nonparticipating parents. Their incomes were higher, and they were more likely to be employed. Why did these families enroll their children in school choice programs? Participating parents believed their children would receive a better education and more discipline than if their offspring remained in their current academic setting (Martinez, Thomas, & Kemerer, 1994).

Because of housing prices and local zoning practices, the United States and its school districts are stratified by race and income levels. We reside, work, and educate our children in a segregated society. Some programs may help to erode the educational caste system that has developed. Again, it should not be expected that student achievement scores from low-income and middle-income families will achieve parity. They will not. Nevertheless, EOEO demonstrates that low-income youths benefit academically from educational placements with young people of higher socioeconomic status, provided (as we read earlier) that the discrepancy is not extreme.

Finally, the creation of the New American Schools Development Corporation (NASDC) and the initial funding of 11 projects are exciting developments. In many respects these programs are reminiscent of alternative education programs that briefly flourished 3 decades ago. For example, the Audrey Cohen College project intends to link the classroom with the "real world." Each semester, community projects will be interwoven with course work to demonstrate to the student the interconnectedness of the world in which the student lives.

The ATLAS project brings together James Comer of Yale, Theodore Sizer of Brown, and Howard Gardner of Harvard to implement the visions of these educational reformers. Schools under this model will be community-focused centers for active learning. They will also draw heavily on the knowledge and direct involvement of mental health professionals. This health-focused effort contrasts with historic understandings that schools are places of cognitive, not affective learning.

Finally, we mention Expeditionary Learning. Using many of the successful concepts previously developed by Outward Bound, this project involves students in such community activities as developing recycling centers and child care facilities and taps the talents of visiting artists, scholars, and business people. Against this stimulating backdrop, academic courses will be made "relevant" for students (Mecklenburger, 1993; Sherry, 1992).

Collectively, these efforts are not breakthroughs in the development of new learning systems. Indeed, these experiments have been discussed for years. Why, then, are we excited? First, a prolonged taxpayer revolt is in progress (Mathews, 1996). That revolt shows no sign of waning. In fact, given the expected increase in the number of families without school-aged children, the traditional voting constituency of education budgets (parents with school-aged children) will continue to decline. Unsuccessful schools—that is, schools that are not educating its youth, not building relationships with the parents of those youth (their voting constituency on budgets), and not demonstrating its relevancy to the wider community—will surely fail financially. Because we believe that schools that fail young people and their families should either change or go out of business, the failure of an individual school is not troubling to us. For too long too many students have been failed.

We believe demographics will significantly alter education in the United States in the next century. Population projections of adolescents ages 14 to 17 show a slight percentage rise from 5.3% of the total population in 1990 to 5.9% in 2005. This growth then declines to roughly 5.2% of the population through the year 2050. Correspondingly, individuals 85 years and older by the year 2050 are expected to make up 4.6% of the population (U.S. Census Bureau, 1993a). For a nation that at its birth had a populace with a median age of 18, this six-tenths of 1% difference is astonishing (Adams & Gullotta, 1983)![13]

We believe that schools as places of learning for only youths will cease to exist by the year 2010. Schools will be redefined as lifelong centers for community learning or they will go out of business. These new centers will become places in which public, private, and not-for-profit agencies will concurrently offer services. We expect that senior citizens, toddlers, and parents will freely wander school corridors receiving services ranging from child to family medical care, stopping, by the way, to dine on improved school meals that will include breakfast and dinner. What excites us about this vision (made possible by declining numbers of students against the backdrop of infrastructure expenditures) is the opportunity to rekindle a sense of community around learning. Will it happen? Stay tuned. The next century is nearly here.

SUMMARY

Take a moment and consider the material you've just read. This chapter had a very historical focus, didn't it? Why do you think the authors used the past to explain the current state of educational affairs? Was it because the promise and hope of education remains unaltered from the past? Was it because education has always threatened (but rarely delivered on that threat) to change the status quo? Or was it because the explanations for why some youths fail have not changed since the 1960s? Further, in contrast to earlier chapters, this one had a strong sociological perspective. Consider your own grade school/high school education. Was it grounded in best learning practices or was it rooted in other values reflective of group beliefs at that time?

But what about the other themes that are reflected in this book? Did you see how different circumstances can effect educational outcomes for different youths? If you did, that's an example of how development occurs in context. Further, did you see how the experiences of youths vary not only by socioeconomic class but by race and ethnicity? If these points are not clear to you then why not spend a

[13] At present, the median age is 34.3. In the United States, Utah is the "youngest" state with a median age of 26.8 and the "oldest" state is West Virginia at 37.4 (U.S. Census Bureau, 1996).

few moments with a fellow classmate and discuss these questions over a cup of coffee or, better yet, herbal tea. It's a great way to improve learning and make new friends at the same time.

MAJOR POINTS TO REMEMBER

1. Educational controversies develop not from what to teach (reading, writing, math, science) but how it is taught.
2. There are two views on the history of U.S. education. One sees the educational movement in a favorable light. The other is less kind.
3. There are two social structures in every school. Status within these two structures is assigned for rather different reasons. The school staff dispenses academic rewards, while the peer group dispenses social status within the group.
4. Why students go to school often differs considerably from why we think they do.
5. The comprehensive high school has been praised by some as a triumph of democracy. Others find that it provides only a mediocre education for those who are not college bound.
6. EOEO, better recognized by many as the Coleman Report, is considered to be one of the most important studies on education ever undertaken. Its findings radically changed our understanding of how the educational system affects learning.
7. Following the publication of EOEO, several explanations emerged for the school system's apparent failure to educate. These explanations include the self-fulfilling prophecy, the finding that cognitive deficits can be caused by poor nutrition, and the controversial argument that genetics may be a factor in the learning rates of certain groups of people.
8. Educational, individual, family, and societal factors, as well as chance, influence the changing career decisions individuals will make across the life span.
9. Explanations for truancy include the idea that parents and their children are overinvolved with one another and the belief that some young people are deprived of an opportunity to achieve recognition in schools.
10. School violence dates back to the nation's beginning. Interestingly, for young people between the ages of 12 and 15, school may be more dangerous than the streets. The response to this situation has been to increase security precautions at schools.
11. For demographic and financial reasons, schools will change in the next century.

Dealing with Issues of Concern: Prevention and Treatment

PART

FOUR

Dealing with Issues
of Concern:
Prevention and
Treatment

Helping Adolescents: Intervention and Prevention

NOT LONG AGO a major association of mental health professionals held a conference to discuss the proliferation of new therapies. In writing a chapter on therapy for adolescents, many authors might take a similar approach and simply describe the enormous variety of therapies now available. We have taken a different route. This chapter does not contrast the advantages of, say, structural family therapy to cognitive behavioral therapy, nor does it state that Maslow is inferior to Carl Rogers or he to Freud. Instead, we have drawn on our own experiences to share our beliefs about working with young people.

We have organized this chapter into three sections. The first section shares the secret of success in working not only with adolescents but with people of any age. The second section, on treatment and rehabilitation, describes what our society has emphasized for many years: the correction of already existing problems. In this section we briefly touch on the major types of therapies available but, as just promised, avoid the multitude of variations. Last, we examine the concept of prevention, an area of tremendous promise in the mental health field that is only now coming into its own alongside treatment and rehabilitation. Prevention programs aimed at alleviating or removing the causes of troubled adolescent behavior are now under way, and at the end of this chapter we look at the promise of such programs for reducing the need for treatment and rehabilitation. Indeed, for the remainder of this book, we'll use prevention's principles to accomplish the fourth theme of this book. That is promoting health while reducing the incidence of dysfunctional behavior.

CARDINAL RULES

The formula for success in working with adolescents is simple, although combining the ingredients in the proper amounts can at times be puzzlingly complex. There are six essential ingredients in helping adolescents decide to change their behavior. The first of these is *trustworthiness*. The adolescent must be able to trust the mental health worker, for young people do not share feelings that show their vulnerabilities and weaknesses with individuals who they feel will treat those feelings insensitively.

The second quality that a mental health professional must have is *genuineness*. We believe that no other age group is so perceptive in "reading" other people. If mental health workers are not genuine in their concern for and love of young people, their effectiveness will be severely impaired. Genuineness helps establish an atmosphere in which trust can grow. Feigning genuineness is more damaging to a therapeutic relationship than expressing the inability to be "real" with that adolescent and withdrawing from the relationship.

The third quality that a mental health worker must have is *empathy*, the ability to feel for the young person. Empathy, incidentally, is not to be confused with *sympathy*. The word *sympathy* implies agreement and commiseration with the individual's handling of a situation. *Empathy*, on the other hand, implies caring for the individual as a person but not necessarily condoning that individual's behavior in a given situation.

The fourth ingredient is *honesty*. Without honesty there can be no relationship. Honesty means that if the professional disapproves of an action by the client, the professional is able to express that feeling in a way that does not pull the relationship apart. The notion that any mental health worker can remain impartial in a therapeutic relationship is, in our estimation, simply bull. We believe that expressing sadness, dissatisfaction, worry, or pleasure over the behavior of a young person is far better than attempting to hide it, for we contend that such feelings cannot be hidden. We believe that professionals who fail to openly express these feelings work against themselves by building a barrier to the development of a trusting and genuine relationship.

Like the scarecrow in *The Wizard of Oz* you are probably thinking how simple this recipe is and thinking "Why, I should have thought of that myself." Without trustworthiness, genuineness, empathy, and honesty, behavioral change will not occur. However, these four ingredients are worthless without the fifth and sixth ones to hold them all together. The fifth ingredient is the adolescent's *perception* of the mental health worker as trustworthy, genuine, empathic, and honest. Our experience has shown that regardless of how trustworthy, genuine, empathic, and honest a mental health professional is, if the client does not perceive the professional as having those qualities, change will not occur (Rogers, 1965). The sixth ingredient is *self-efficacy*. Remember that phrase from earlier in the book? To refresh your memory, self-efficacy means having the ability to accomplish or achieve some act or goal and understanding that it is important to reach that level of performance (Bandura, 1982). It's not enough to be involved in a helping relationship. It's not enough to understand that the person wants you to succeed. You must want to succeed and succeed because it is important to you.

TREATMENT AND REHABILITATION

By merging two operational definitions that the federal government uses in mental health information systems, we can obtain a fairly inclusive definition of the term *therapy*. Therapy involves the ability to determine the mental health status of clients and provide them with the help necessary to improve their coping abilities. Therapy occurs in face-to-face encounters between a therapist and a client who suffers from some difficulty, according to the client or the therapist or both.

To work successfully requires trustworthiness, genuineness, empathy, honesty, and the adolescent's perception of those qualities in the teacher or youth worker.

Before we examine the major schools of treatment, it might be helpful to look at how this interaction takes place.

CATEGORIES OF THERAPY

There are four basic categories of therapy. The first and perhaps still the most common is *individual therapy*. The client and the therapist explore together in private the feelings, thoughts, behaviors, and attitudes of the client.

The second category of therapy, which has become the standard for nearly all interventions with young people, is *family therapy*. Depending on the circumstances, the therapy may be limited to the adolescent and his or her parents or it may include other family members as well. We admit to a bias in favor of this form of therapy. Our experiences in working with young people have demonstrated time and again the usefulness of being able to gather family members together to explore what are seen to be family, not individual, problems. In family therapy the difficulty is perceived to exist not solely with the individual but also with the system from which that individual comes.[1]

The third category is *group therapy*. Within a small group of people (normally no more than 10), the therapist interacts with each individual and encourages them

[1]Family therapy lends itself well to a developmental contextual perspective which just so happens to be a principle theme of this book.

to interact with one another. The groups usually, but not always, consist of clients experiencing similar problems.

The last category is *couple therapy*. Not really family therapy because other members of the family are not included, couple therapy is the working through of problems between two individuals (who need not be related) with a mental health worker.

It should be noted that each of the four categories may have literally hundreds of approaches that fit within the category. For example, cognitive behaviorism, which emerged out of social learning theory, is an approach often used by therapists today for a wide variety of dysfunctional behaviors. We have seen it used in each of the above categories. In contrast, structural family therapy, as its name implies, does not lend itself to a category other than family therapy.

THERAPY LOCATIONS, THE MEDICAL MODEL, AND GENES

The terms *treatment* and *rehabilitation* often relate to the locations in which therapy is undertaken. The first term suggests to most mental health workers an *outpatient* setting. This setting may be a child-guidance clinic, a youth-service bureau, a family-service agency, or a community mental health center. The second term suggests an *inpatient* setting, such as a hospital or a residential school.

The above remarks reflect an orientation influenced by what is commonly called the *medical* model. In this model emotional difficulties are treated as diseases. Although the model has justly come under severe criticism in recent years (Albee, 1980, 1996), it is still the most commonly used explanation of illness in the field of mental health. For that reason we briefly discuss it here.

The Medical Model

In the medical model dysfunctional behavior is considered to be a disease. From this perspective each dysfunctional behavior has a specific cause and a specific set of symptoms associated with it. Taken to an extreme, the medical model suggests that *all* dysfunctional behavior is biogenic: that is, all dysfunctional behavior can be explained by a physical malfunction within the body.

To see how the medical model works, let's for a moment examine the physical disease called a staphylococcal infection from this perspective. The staphylococcus is a bacterium frequently found in infections containing pus. If left untreated, it can result in life-threatening physical disorders. For example, the presence of a sore throat and a fever would provide diagnostic indications signaling a warning that the staphylococcus bacterium might be present. Using this information, the physician would swab the infected area and test for the presence of the bacterium, and if it was found, antibiotics would be prescribed.

Treatment in this model involves a diagnosis that the conditions present in a disease are evident in the individual. Our client would already be showing early clinical signs of the disease: fever, soreness in the infected area, or the appearance of a white milky pus in the throat. In this situation, efforts would be taken to confirm the diagnosis and to stop the disease before it progressed further. It is this action to stop the progress of the disease before its final stage that is called treatment.

Within the medical model, *rehabilitation* occurs after the disease has damaged the body. In our illustration, if the bacterium had not been detected and had resulted in nephritis (a potentially life threatening inflammation of the kidneys), efforts would be made to restore as much functioning as possible. This attempt to restore functioning is called rehabilitation.

The medical model operates on the principle that before actions can be taken to restore health, the cause of the illness must be understood. Once the defect, or malfunction, has been identified, it can be corrected. Operating from this premise, many within the medical community in the mid-19th century searched for germs in a futile attempt to find an explanation for dysfunctional behavior. This exploration was replaced in the 20th century by a search for viruses, chemical imbalances, and, presently, genes, which some researchers believe are responsible for all dysfunctional behavior.

There is a third level of intervention, which does not occur after the fact, or during the fact, but before the fact. This third level is *primary prevention*. But before we explore it, we need to look briefly at the groupings of therapies presently in use.

SCHOOLS OF THERAPY

Just as there are four categories of treatment (individual, group, family, and couple), there are five primary groupings of therapies: analytical, behavioral, humanistic, transpersonal, and biogenic. Although these groupings are by no means all-inclusive, they do provide a general way of categorizing the philosophical underpinnings of most therapies. One further note, most of these interventions are rooted in theories we reviewed in Chapter 2. It might be helpful if you quickly reviewed that material before reading this section.

Analytically Oriented Therapy

The first grouping is derived from classic psychoanalysis. This perspective focuses on the interactions of instinctual desires, anxieties, and defenses. It places considerable importance on the conflicts between opposing wishes, the anxiety caused by those wishes, and the defenses that arise against wishes that have created anxiety. Furthermore, it is believed that most of this process occurs without the individual's conscious knowledge.

According to psychoanalytic therapists, emotional difficulties arise out of early experiences buried in the unconscious and can be resolved by bringing these experiences into consciousness. Helping clients become more aware of themselves is thought to enable them to change their behavior. Thus, these therapists do not attempt to change their clients' behavior directly but to increase their understanding of themselves and, in so doing, allow behavioral change to occur through a gradual self-made transformation.

Psychoanalytic theory has literally changed our understanding of human behavior. For example, it was psychoanalysts who first suggested how past experiences could explain an individual's present behavior. It provided the first explanation of dysfunctional behavior that did not have biogenic origins, and it introduced a whole new set of meanings into Western society (for example, concepts such as repression, rationalization, and libido).

However, even though the contributions of psychoanalytic theory to the understanding of human behavior are many, this therapy is not without serious problems. First, there is the lack of experimental support for many of its tenets. It is a theory whose assumptions rest on a limited number of clinical cases. Second, it is a therapeutic intervention that often takes considerable time, and more cost-effective interventions have been developed.

Next, there is an overdependence on inference. To illustrate this last point, there is a story that the founder of the psychoanalytic movement, Sigmund Freud, was once confronted by a follower who declared that one of Freud's favorite pastimes, smoking a cigar, was a phallic activity. It is reported that Freud responded, with cigar in hand, "Sometimes a good cigar is just a good cigar" (Meltzer, 1987, p. 215). A theory that assumes that obvious behavior does not represent obvious behavior is prone to error. Finally, the view that all human behavior is driven by the deterministic instinctual drives of sex and aggression or that early childhood experience sentences a person to an inescapable adult life outcome has found little favor in recent years.

Behavior Therapy

There are four basic tenets underlying behavioral psychology. First, behaviorists view their role as studying the responses people make to the stimuli in their environment. Second, behaviorists use empirical methods to gather data in order to study human behavior. Next, they believe that all behavior can be predicted and ultimately controlled. This belief is rooted in the fourth tenet, that the primary component of all human behavior is learning. Thus, behavioral therapists are not concerned with their clients' self-awareness but with their overt behavior. Using learning theory, behaviorists study the events that lead to and directly follow a maladaptive behavior and attempt to intercede in that course of events to break a learned response pattern.

The behavioral model has made important contributions to the understanding and treatment of dysfunctional behavior. The most important contribution has been the establishment of research protocols in assessing treatment protocols. The establishment of these protocols has introduced the scientific method into treatment. Phrases such as treatment goals and baseline counts of behavior are examples of the behaviorists' influence on treatment. Behaviorists can justly lay claim to being responsible for providing the means by which all treatment plans are now held accountable.

Nonetheless, the behavioral model is not without its critics. Where the medical model sees dysfunctional behavior as biogenic in origin and the psychoanalytic

---

BOX **10-1**   Cognitive Developmental Behaviorism and Its Application to
Intervention and Prevention

In recent years mental health professionals have turned with increasing interest to attempting to understand the interrelatedness among behaviorism, cognition, and human development. Cognitive developmental theorists such as Mischel (1973, 1979) and Bandura (1977, 1982) contend that people react less to external stimuli in the environment than to their individual processing of those stimuli. This theoretical offshoot of behaviorism offers a more intricate and complex view of human behavior than traditional stimulus/response theory.

Mischel, for example, suggests that five mediating variables help shape a response to a given stimulus. The first variable, *competencies*, represents the past repertoire of skills that individuals call on when dealing with both familiar and novel situations. The second, *encoding*, involves the manner in which young people perceive and categorize their life experiences. The next, *expectancies*, represents the predicted outcome (whether pleasant or unpleasant) of some event based on previous learning. The fourth, *values*, stands for the different weights that individuals assign to life events. And the last, *plans*, governs the rules that humans use to lead their lives.

Rather than the five mediating variables Mischel proposes, Bandura suggests that expectations govern an individual's response to a particular situation. Expectations can take one of two forms. The first, an outcome expectation, is the belief that a certain behavior will lead to a person's predicted outcome of that event. The second, an efficacy expectation, involves a person's belief that he or she will be able to execute the behavior successfully.

The premise of mental health professionals using these models is that behavior results from not only external but also internal reinforcers. Thus, to change behavior external as well as internal contingencies need to be manipulated. From an interventionist's position, this manipulation involves the use of social learning models. From a preventionist's position, it involves the application of each of prevention's four tools: education, promotion of social competency, community organization/systems intervention, and natural care giving. Both approaches are directed toward a cognitive restructuring of a young person's understanding of events and his or her self-reinforcing behaviors. In the chapters that follow, examples of these applications will appear.

---

model views this behavior as rooted in unconscious childhood experiences, the behaviorist sees learned habits. This world view expressed as "what you see is what is there" has been criticized as being oversimplified. For example, Watson's (1914) view that behaviorists would someday be able to take society's worst social failure, "pull him apart, psychologically speaking, and reconstruct him anew" is not widely shared today. The second major criticism is that behavioral theory is deterministic. If all behavior is in response to the stimuli present in the environment, free will does not exist. This is a world view that also is not currently held in favor (see Box 10-1 which describes an increasingly popular form of learning theory called cognitive behaviorism which does take meaning into account).

Humanistic Therapy

Humanistic approaches to treating dysfunctional behavior emerge from a basic belief in the goodness of humans. Rather than viewing dysfunctional behavior as a physical disease or viewing humans as being driven by instinctual urges or as being merely reactors, humanists understand people to be basically good, rational, and interested in that collective community known as society. They believe that conflicts in life occur when people cannot realize their potential. Accordingly, therapists try to help their clients achieve self-acceptance, self-satisfaction, and their own potential as fully functioning individuals. Humanistic therapy and analytically oriented therapy both emphasize self-discovery, but the kinds of discovery differ. At the risk of some legitimate criticism, one might think of humanists as focusing on humanity's most positive attributes and of psychoanalysts as tending to focus on the more base instinctual drives.

Perhaps the single most important contribution that the humanist model has made to our understanding of dysfunctional behavior is its firm belief that humans are actors. We can change our lives. This perspective has encouraged therapists to urge clients to take control of their lives and destinies.

Given the humanistic view that the focus in treatment is what the client thinks about his or her own life, it is not surprising that critics contend that humanists ignore the science of human behavior. For example, how can one ignore the wealth of scientific information about the uniqueness of individuals that places the person outside of the common?

Transpersonal Therapy

The fourth grouping is "not content with the aim of integrating one's energies and expanding the awareness of oneself as an entity separate from the rest of the universe [as are humanists]" (Parloff, 1977, p. 8). Rather, transpersonal therapists, or existentialists, focus their attention on the major challenge facing humanity in the 21st century: living in an amoral, technological society. Transpersonal therapy is concerned with a search for meaning and the ability of people to live their lives according to their own principles. Whereas humanists focus on individuals and their needs, existentialists are concerned with the individual's relationship to the human condition and the question of individual responsibility. Transpersonal approaches do not share a common set of theoretical concepts. Rather, they assume that all humans have large untapped pools of spiritual abilities. Examples of transpersonal approaches include Zen, psychosynthesis, yoga, Buddhism, and transcendental meditation.

The primary contribution that transpersonal therapy has made is in raising issues of major human concern. We live in a time when genocide, in the guise of "ethnic cleansing," occurs with regularity. We prize concepts like free will; yet we shop at chain stores in nondescript malls eating standardized foods dispensed in foam containers. Where can we find meaning is one of the central issues transpersonal therapy strives to answer. Like the humanists, existentialists are accused of an unscientific approach. Nevertheless, as we near the next milenium and disillusionment about science grows, these *New Age* beliefs have gained favor as individuals search for spiritual meaning.

Biogenic Therapies

This final grouping focuses on biological explanations for dysfunctional be-havior and on the use of genetic research, pharmacology, or surgical interventions to understand or treat those dysfunctions. It contains several widely varying and often competing approaches to treating dysfunctional behavior. Nevertheless, they all view the problems that humans experience from a biological perspective.

The first of these perspectives focuses on genetics. This perspective maintains the position that genes, not the environment, control behavior. Scientists search the human genome for possible DNA (deoxyribose nucleic acid) aberrations that might explain dysfunctional behaviors like alcoholism, criminal misconduct, the affective disorders, or schizophrenia. The primary methods to undertake these investigations are the use of twin and adoptee studies.

In the first instance, if a genetic marker exists for some behavior, then identical twins, who have the same genes, would be expected to exhibit similar histories for developing (or not developing) that specific dysfunctional behavior. The second method is to study the adopted children of parents who suffered from the dys-functional behavior under investigation. Again, if a genetic marker exists, then in numbers higher than would otherwise be expected by chance the adopted child of that affected biological parent should develop similar behaviors. Of course (and geneticists admit) living conditions complicate the picture considerably, and twin studies have difficulty accounting for varying environmental conditions. "Heri-tabilities for behavior [in the best of studies] seldom exceed 50%," thus providing enormous opportunities for living situations to affect the ultimate outcome (Plomin, 1990, p. 187).

It is reasonable to believe that genetic errors increase the risk of some individuals for certain behaviors. Mania, depression, obsessive compulsion, and schizophrenia certainly appear to have genetic components. Many other hotly debated dysfunc-tional behaviors like attention deficit disorder may also have a genetic element. Nevertheless, confirming reports locating specific genes for specific behaviors have routinely failed to withstand replication. Furthermore, even if a specific gene were identified, the fact that countless "at risk" individuals never proceed to develop the dysfunctional behavior suggests that a complex interaction of environment and chemistry are under way.

Given that at present no engineered retrovirus exists to alter DNA for behavioral purposes, attention, we believe, needs to be focused on the factors explaining how individuals "escaped" the DNA script provided them at conception. For those indi-viduals who suffer from these emotionally wrenching disorders, interventions that strengthen the surrounding environment should be undertaken. That is, strengthen the family's ability to be supportive, provide the appropriate educational and ther-apeutic learning, and use, when necessary, pharmacological treatment.

The second perspective is biochemical neurology. This approach maintains that dysfunctional behavior is the result of chemical imbalances within the brain. These imbalances are thought to occur in the chemical messengers that serve the brain's neurons. It believes that medications can correct these chemical imbalances. For example, a common salt, lithium, has been successfully used with many individuals suffering from manic depressive episodes. Other drugs called tricyclic antidepressants (for example, Imipramine) or serotonin reuptake inhibitors (for example, Prozac) have been found effective in treating depression. Still, other drugs called neuroleptics like Thorazine, Melleril, and Haldol have shown effectiveness in decreasing the excitement and racing thoughts associated with schizophrenia. Each of these medications act on one or more of the brain's three principal nuerochemical messengers. It appears that it is these three principal neurotransmitters (dopamine, norepinephrine, and serotonin) that regulate mood.

Medications like those just described have helped to revolutionize treatment for many individuals in our society. In combination with other forms of therapy discussed in this chapter, individuals who might otherwise have found themselves in institutions have been able to lead productive lives. Still, there are reasons for mental health professionals, educators, and others to be concerned.

The first concern is a growing mistaken belief by some that medication alone can address the needs of individuals. We and others believe this to be wrong. The use of medications has had dramatic effects on reducing the symptoms associated with many disorders. But studies repeatedly find that when medication alone is compared with medication and some form of mental health intervention, the second condition (medications + the mental health intervention) is preferable (Bolinger, 1999; Plant, 1999). The second concern is whether, in some instances, medications are helping individuals or merely masking ineffective schools or poor parenting behaviors instead?

The final perspective is psychosurgery. This perspective maintains that surgical removal or destruction of brain tissue will correct dysfunctional behavior (for a fascinating but deeply disturbing history of psychosurgery, read *Great and Desperate Cures* by Elliot Valenstein, 1986).

With the exception of psychosurgery, whose popularity waned with the introduction of the neuroleptics (Thorazine, etc.) in the 1960s, biogenic approaches are attracting increasing attention. These approaches can be credited with drawing the public's attention to the fact that the mind and the body reside in the same space and interact. They can also be credited with helping the public better understand that in many circumstances behavior *is* beyond the control of an individual. Just as society does not condemn the person suffering from cancer or diabetes nor should it ostracize individuals who struggle to control thoughts which lead them to dysfunctional behaviors.

Nevertheless, as critics point out, the evidence for attributing *all* dysfunctional behaviors *solely* to organic causes is weak. Further, critics question whether society should seek the Brave New World that the biochemical-neurology approach promises to deliver.[2] What is the difference, they ask, between plucking out portions

---

[2]The novel *Brave New World*, by Aldous Huxley (1936/1958), examines the incompatibility of individual freedom and a society made "trouble-free" by science.

of the brain tissue (lobotomy or psychosurgery) and chemically straight-jacketing individuals?

DIVERSITY AND MULTICULTURALISM IN THE THERAPEUTIC SETTING: PSYCHOTHERAPY WITH ETHNICALLY DIVERSE GROUPS

Until very recently, therapeutic interventions were developed without regard to the special needs that exist for the ethnically and racially diverse groups that reside in North America. This section examines some of the efforts underway to bring greater sensitivity to our treatment of those children and their families.

Respect for another includes, among other things, care in understanding and using a person's culture to assist in the healing and recovery process. From this understanding, the American Psychological Association (1990) approved guidelines for working with ethnic minorities. These guidelines urge mental health providers to accept the responsibility for (1) educating their minority clients about the intervention process; (2) being personally informed of the relevant research and therapeutic practices for minority groups; (3) recognizing the importance of culture and ethnicity in understanding psychological processes; (4) respecting the roles of family, community, values, and beliefs of the minority client's culture; (5) respecting minority religious and spiritual beliefs and their role in psychological recovery; (6) considering the sociopolitical factors of each person's case in making assessments and designing interventions; and (7) striving to eliminate forms of prejudice, bias, or discrimination in therapeutic practice.

When one considers that 25% of the United States population is of non-European ancestry and that by the year 2056 the average citizen will trace his or her descents to almost anywhere but White Europe, the need to develop ethnic and racially appropriate interventions becomes evident (Henry, 1990).

The growing cultural revolution associated with the browning of America is bringing increased attention to *transpersonal* therapies discussed earlier in this chapter (Gibbs & Huang, 1989). Comas-Diaz (1992) suggests that in the coming years a shift in therapeutic values and foci are likely to come from the ethnocultural backgrounds of ethnic minorities.

For example, instead of setting a premium on independence, greater attention will be given to the importance of interdependence. More attention will be given to the role of coping through faith and prayer. The concept of health will incorporate notions of balance and harmony within the different aspects of self (for instance, yin and yang). The value of developing the self through spirituality, social, physical, or emotional dimensions will become more broadly recognized and implemented. The theme of interconnectedness, family, community, and even cosmos will be expanded and a broader contextual definition of self will become prominent in therapy for diverse ethnic groups. This definition will include elements of the self in relationship with others, self in relationship with the world, and self in relationship with the cosmos.

To work successfully with diverse youth requires culturally appropriate helping.

THE NEED FOR THERAPEUTIC MULTICULTURAL SENSITIVITY

Intolerance among Practitioners

Culturally appropriate helping requires that counselors be sensitive to the life experiences of their clients. Counselors can sometimes hold biases toward groups other than their own (Whaley, 1998). This interpersonal intolerance operates in very subtle ways and is linked to prejudicial and discriminatory practices. In this regard, Camino (1995) identifies five processes of interpersonal intolerance that operate among practitioners. They are discussed below.

Processes of Interpersonal Intolerance

Dysfunctional rescuing contains an implicit assumption that diverse individuals cannot help themselves. Therefore, the helper fails to challenge and encourage the diverse person to discover his or her own strengths and potentials. A response to dysfunctional rescuing is *system beating*. The recipient of dysfunctional rescuing learns how to manipulate the system to meet his or her wants and needs. Hence, adolescents own competencies and strengths remain underdeveloped.

The second process, *blaming the victim*, is a form of intolerance that blames the diverse person for his or her difficulties. Attempts to understand historical, cultural, social, political, and economic influences on the young person's condition are not taken into account. Negative stereotypes about the group remain unchanged. The minority adolescent's response may be a failure to take responsibility for his or her actions. Blaming others and the system are typical patterns of response.

In *avoidance of contact* there is an absence of involvement with members of the diverse group, and there is lack of effort in trying to learn anything about the group. The result is similar avoidance on the part of the diverse person. A distrust of all members of the majority group is likely to occur. In this pattern, as well, the adolescent's development may be constrained because he or she has learned to shut out other groups as well as opportunities that could foster healthy development and positive outcomes.

When practitioners are "color-blind" or attempt to ignore or minimize the cultural heritage of their adolescent clients, *denial of cultural differences* exist. The counselor may choose to deny such differences in an effort to promote egalitarian values or may simply not want to consider the complexities of race and culture. Unfortunately, the result for the diverse adolescent is that he or she may overidentify with the majority group and accept the derogatory opinions against his or her own group. A poor sense of ethnic identity is a likely outcome.

Finally, *denial of the political significance of intolerance and oppression* operates to produce a less effective therapeutic or helping process for diverse youths. Powerful messages from the dominant culture that deny prejudice, discrimination, and intolerance lead to feelings of hopelessness and anger that can result in displaced frustration (Camino, 1995).

DOES THERAPY WORK?

In light of our earlier expressed concern that a movement for medication-only intervention was emerging, is there any evidence to support our belief that counseling works? Several recent reviews of treatment outcome studies with children and adolescents provide some clues as to the effectiveness of psychotherapy with young people (Kazdin, 1987; Keith & Matthews, 1993; Mann & Borduin, 1991; Marelich & Rotheram-Borus, 1999; Plant, 1999; Rivera and Kutash, 1994; Rotheram-Borus, 1997; Weisz, Weiss, Alicke, & Klotz, 1987). Collectively these studies find evidence to suggest that psychotherapy works. Mann and Borduin (1991), for example, conclude that insight therapies such as analytically oriented or humanistic treatment models can be successful with adolescents who have developed formal operational thinking skills. Approaches that use behavioral techniques can be effective in improving social skills, problem-solving, and communication abilities of young people. It should be noted that Mann and Borduin encourage multisystem approaches to improving the functioning of dysfunctional youths. This suggestion is made because no single therapeutic model was found to be successful for all youths in all circumstances.

This last statement underscores the cardinal rules described in this chapter. It may not be so much the theoretical underpinnings of the therapeutic approach as the interpersonal relationship between client and therapist that matters. This alliance, founded on mutual agreement regarding goals, behavior changes, and respect for each other, spell, in our experience, the difference between change and stagnation (Marziali & Alexander, 1991).

PRIMARY PREVENTION AND ITS TECHNOLOGY

The concept of prevention is far from new. The thought that emotional distress might be avoided and mental health encouraged can be traced back to the ancients. However, the idea of prevention as an attainable goal emerged only recently as the result of the inability of the treatment model to reduce the ever-growing number of seriously emotionally ill individuals in our society (Albee, 1980, 1985a; Albee and Gullotta, 1997). What do we mean by that last statement? Consider this ongoing dilemma: studies on the incidence of serious mental illness in North America report that in any given year about 20% of Canadian and U.S. youths are in need of help. For the U.S., with a youth population of 63 million, that means over 12 million young people are in need of help yearly. Yet, the capacity to serve these youths is a small fraction of that number and is essentially unchanged from George Albee's (1959) first discussion of this issue in the 1950s!

Prevention has evolved since the early 1960s, when Gerald Caplan (1961, 1964, 1974) introduced a model suggesting that emotional illness could be prevented. That three-tier model of primary, secondary, and tertiary prevention, similar to the prevention model found in public health, has been refined. Secondary prevention activities—attempts to reduce the length of time an individual or family experiences an emotionally distressful situation—are now called *treatment activities*. Tertiary prevention activities—attempts to prevent the recurrence of a debilitating problem and to restore as high a level as possible of individual and family reorganization—are now called *rehabilitation activities*. Prevention has emerged in a hybrid form called *primary prevention*.

The goal of primary prevention remains basically unaltered from Caplan's (1974, pp. 189–190) original purpose of reducing "the incidence of new cases of mental disorder in the population by combating harmful forces which operate in the community and by strengthening the capacity of people to withstand stress." Parameters for this goal have now been established. Primary prevention focuses on groups (not individuals) and the specific problems those groups experience (Klein & Goldston, 1977). Prevention is proactive; that is, it builds new coping resources and adaptation skills therein promoting emotional health (Albee & Gullotta, 1986). Prevention programs are comprehensive, using at least three of prevention's four technologies at any one time; ideally those interventions extend over time (Gullotta, 1994). Finally, prevention activities are planned interventions that can be observed, recorded, and evaluated for effectiveness (Cowen, 1982b; Kelin & Goldston, 1977).

From this general conceptualization, different strategies emerge. They all involve each of us as an active participant in preventing illness and promoting health. Prevention advocates reject the claim "that major [emotional] illness is probably in large part genetically determined and is probably, therefore, not preventable, at most modifiable" (Lamb & Zusman, 1979, p. 1349). Rather, prevention takes the position that emotional problems are not *solely* diseases that can be traced to some microorganism or DNA thread, but are often problems in living often created by blows of fate. Prevention views dysfunctional behavior, whether

B O X **10-2**   Albee's Incidence Formula

What explains dysfunctional behavior and how might it be prevented? George Albee has studied that question for many years. His incidence formula remains one of the principle tools preventionists use in designing interventions (Albee, 1980, 1985). This formula is expressed as follows:

$$\text{Incidence} = \frac{\text{Organic factors} + \text{stress} + \text{exploitation}}{\text{Coping skills} + \text{self-esteem} + \text{support groups}}.$$

From this formula realize that factors that increase the size of the numerator will increase the incidence of dysfunctional behavior in society, and activities that reduce, modify, or eliminate those factors will diminish the incidence of dysfunction. Likewise, efforts that reduce the size of the denominator will increase the incidence, while efforts that increase the size of the denominator will reduce incidence.

What do the numerator terms represent? *Organic* refers to environmental factors like lead poisoning and genetic disorders like phenylketonuria, both of which are responsible for serious cognitive impairments in children. *Stress* can be understood to mean any perceived negative event in a person's life. These events can range from an argument to the loss of a loved one. *Exploitation* is repeatedly taking unfair advantage of another. For some groups this is a continual occurrence.

How should we understand the denominators? *Coping skills*, like a strong spiritual faith in God, are the available resources an individual has to handle distressful events. *Self-esteem* represents the respect individuals have for themselves. *Support groups* refer to the quality and depth of the caregiving that can be found around the individual.

By using this formula and the prevention tools described in this chapter, you'll be able to design very powerful interventions.

individual or family, as an outgrowth of multiple factors interacting to place groups of individuals at risk. One of these factors is the impact of stress on each person's life. From stress theory, the idea emerges that harmful stress (distress) might be managed, avoided, or eliminated. Thoughts also develop that you and I, our family, and our friends can gather strength to first cope with and then adapt to circumstances that cruel twists of fate fling across the paths that humans walk (Hollister, 1977). How might we handle these problems in living? The answer is found in the technology that preventionists use to promote emotional health and to discourage emotional illness in society (see Box 10-2).

The technology of prevention consists of four tools that are used to fashion a healthier environment (Gullotta, 1987, 1994; Albee and Gullotta, 1997). These tools are *education*, *Community organization/systems intervention*, *competency promotion*, and *natural care giving*. These tools have overlapping boundaries, and well-planned prevention programs practice elements of all four (see Table 10-1).

Education

Of all the tools of prevention, education is the most widely used. The belief behind education is that by increasing our knowledge we can change attitudes and behaviors that hurt ourselves or others. Education can be used to ease the passage from one life event to another; information can be given to individuals to enhance

T A B L E 10-1   **The Tools of Prevention: Selected Examples and Desired Outcomes**

Tool	Examples	Desired outcomes
Education		
Public information	Public-service announcement, Printed material, films, curricula	Avoid harmful stressors, manage stressors
Anticipatory guidance	Career guidance	Manage stressors, build resistance to a stressor, avoid harmful stressors
Behavioral approaches	Biofeedback, yoga, meditation	Manage stressors, avoid harmful stressors
Community organization/ systems intervention		
Modification or removal of institutional barriers	Institution of new practices such as pass/fail system to replace letter grades; or a change in old practices such as permitting pregnant adolescents to attend class	Eliminate stressors
Community resource development	Neighborhood associations, rehabilitation of housing stock	Eliminate stressors, manage stressors, avoid stressors
Legislative or judicial action	Civil rights legislation, consumer-protection laws	Avoid stressors, eliminate stressors, manage stressors
Competency promotion		
Active approaches	Wilderness schools: art, theater programs	Build resistance to a stressor
Passive approaches	Affective education, assertiveness training	
Natural care giving		
Indigenous care givers	Coaches, lawyers, friends	Manage stressors, build resistance to a stressor
Trained indigenous care givers	Clergy, teachers	Manage stressors, build resistance to a stressor
Mutual self-help	Alateen	Manage stressors, build resistance to a stressor

their well-being. Whether in the form of the spoken word, a visual image, or printed material, education uses three techniques.

The first of these is *public information*. This information awakens, alerts, and sensitizes us to hazardous situations that can affect our lives. For example, public-service announcements about cigarette smoking are attempts to enlighten the public and to promote health. Education also includes books (like this one) that encourage you to take responsibility for your own life while sharing with you the findings that the social sciences can offer about individuals, relationships, and the family.

George Albee's Incidence
Formula offers an explanation
not only of the origins of
dysfunctional behavior but how
it might be prevented.

Here, the intention is to alert you not only to potential hazards but also to health-promoting activities as well. Public information can include films, role plays, and classroom activities to impart to the learner new or improved skills for handling life.

Research is very clear on the point that all animals, including humans, desire some warning about an event before it happens (see Elliott & Eisdorfer, 1982). The time between the warning and the actual occurrence permits us to gather emotional resources to handle the event. Preventionists call the educational technique that builds these resources *anticipatory guidance*. Anticipatory guidance may take a form as simple as printed material that explains an upcoming life event, like the booklets that explain what to expect in the transition to college life. Or it may involve a mixture of print, film, and lecture material, like that used by health organizations teaching teenage expectant parents about childbirth and the infant.

Finally, some educational approaches use *behavioral techniques* to promote increased self-awareness. This category includes such approaches as visualization, biofeedback, progressive relaxation, and Eastern meditational philosophies. These techniques provide informational feedback that permits individuals to acquire the skills to cope and adapt to life.

Community Organization/Systems Intervention

The ability to live life effectively is sometimes impeded by forces beyond one's personal control. Such community forces limit access to life options and opportunities (Jason & Kobayashi, 1995). The second tool of prevention is used to redress these inequities. Obstructions can be removed in any of three ways. Where obstructions exist because of the institutional practices or policies of an organization, individuals can work to *modify or remove institutional barriers*.

One successful example has been the pressure exerted by health officials to include information about AIDS in the public school health curriculum. By lifting the veil of secrecy around this disease and explaining how it is transmitted, it is hoped that young people will adopt behaviors that will impede its spread.

A second area for community organization/systems intervention (CO/SI) is *community resource development*. Here the activity is focused on achieving a more equitable distribution of power to improve the standard of living of a group of people within a community. Neighborhood associations and community-owned, community-directed operations to rehabilitate housing stock are two examples.

The third activity within the domain of CO/SI activity is *legislative or judicial action*. This is the most controversial of the three approaches, because it involves a change in the balance of political power in the direction of empowering the weak. And lately the buzzword "empowerment" has fallen on hard times. Those who need to be "empowered" have fallen even harder. The preventionist recognizes that the young people who fill the rosters of clinics and hospitals come predominantly from the leagues of the powerless, the disenfranchised, the helpless, and the hopeless. Lack of power itself has been suggested as a major stress in these people's lives: "Every research study we examined suggested that major sources of human stress and distress generally involve some form of excessive power [over the powerless]. . . . It is enough to suggest the hypothesis that a dramatic reduction and control of power might improve . . . mental health" (Kessler & Albee, 1977, pp. 379–380). If one of the keys to explaining dysfunction is a lack of power, then organizing and mobilizing a group for the purposes of acquiring power in a free society is a necessary and legitimate function of prevention activity. Such initiatives have been undertaken by the American Civil Liberties Union, Mothers Against Drunk Drivers, the National Organization for Women, and the National Association for the Advancement of Colored People, among others. These organizations are attempting, through legislative and judicial means, to put teeth into the phrase *equality of opportunity*.

Competency Promotion

Competency promotion activities develop a feeling of being a part of, rather than apart from, society. They encourage feelings of worth, care for others, and belief in oneself. Encouraging such pride promotes increased self-esteem, an internal locus of control, and community interest rather than self-interest.

To be socially competent, three factors must be present. First, socially competent people *belong*. That is, they are members of a society and have recognized roles and positions in that society. Next, socially competent people are *valued*. That is, they have worth not in the sense of wealth but in respect for their individuality. They are desired members of that society. Third, they have the opportunity and exercise that opportunity to *contribute*. Unless people can add their thoughts, labor, and energy to the society they belong to, they cannot be considered a part of that

Well run programs that encourage belonging, valuing, and contributing promote social competency.

society (Gullotta, 1990). Activities such as affective education and assertiveness training are both education and competency promotion tools. They are also examples of *passive approaches* to competency promotion. Passive approaches involve group classroom activities. They differ from the activities typically undertaken by wilderness schools, Scouting, 4-H, and arts programs. These programs teach skills like climbing, canoeing, or stage-set construction and acting but emphasize, first and more importantly, interpersonal and community relationships. Because these activities involve action and are usually directed toward accomplishment of some task, they are called *active approaches*.

Natural Caregiving

On almost every issue, adults and youths turn not to professionals but to family members, friends, or others (coaches, the clergy, teachers, and so on) for advice and guidance. A recent study of Australian youths reconfirms this truism (Boldero and Fallon, 1995). The sample of more than 1000 youths reported that family members, friends, and teachers provided help when needed. Professionals were not seen as a resource to these young people. Of interest also was their report that many personal problems were handled without the help of another.

Natural caregiving recognizes the ability within each of us to help a fellow human being. It extends beyond activities like those of helping another in similar straits (mutual self-help groups) to acknowledge the responsibility each of us has to fellow human beings (Cowen, 1982a). Natural caregiving involves behavior such as the sharing of knowledge, of experiences, compassionate understanding, companionship, and, when necessary, confrontation. Such caregiving is a reference point for people to acknowledge that they are an important part of an emotional network that extends beyond family members and friends to all people.

Some of us may choose professions in which we become *trained indigenous caregivers*, such as teaching and in the clergy (Sutherland, Hale, & Harris, 1995). Others of us will at some time in our lives join a *mutual self-help group* to give and receive help from others who find themselves in similar straits—for example, as a child of an alcoholic parent or as an individual recovering from a serious physical or emotional illness. Regardless of the circumstance, it is vital to remember that each of us is an *indigenous caregiver* with a responsibility to assist his or her fellow human beings.

DOES PREVENTION WORK?

In 1981 the American Psychological Association created a task force to identify model primary prevention programs. The book *14 Ounces of Prevention: A Casebook for Practitioners* was the result of that effort (Price, Cowen, Lorion, & Ramos-McKay, 1988). From that effort, Conyne (1991) identified five common features of successful prevention programs. They are:

Real friendship that extends over time is a powerful caregiving tool that promotes emotional health.

- Establish an information base on the circumstances and problems experienced by the at-risk group;
- Design interventions that create long-term change;
- Teach new skills such as decision-making, communication, assertiveness, and other coping skills;
- Maintain sensitivity to cultural and ethnic variations within the population;
- Use research and evaluation techniques to document successful outcomes and program effectiveness.

Recognizing that recent studies suggest that 15 to 22% of the roughly 63 million children and adolescents in the United States experience mental health problems (National Advisory Mental Health Council, 1990), there is an obvious need for primary prevention efforts. Family, school, and community-oriented prevention efforts that have documented success can now be identified (Weissberg, Caplan, & Harwood, 1991), and many programs are sensitive to the needs of diverse youths (Cherry, Belgrave, Jones, Kennon, Gray, & Phillips, 1998; Stevenson, McMillan, Mitchell, & Blanco, 1998) (see Box 10-3 for information about prevention and refugee youth).

Since the publication of *14 Ounces of Prevention: A Casebook for Practitioners*, other works have added to the growing evidence that prevention programs can significantly improve health and reduce the risk of dysfunctional behavior. The first, *Reducing Risks for Mental Disorders* (Mrazek & Haggerty, 1994), was commissioned by the Congress of the United States to recommend a prevention research agenda. This volume identified not only that specific agenda but also successful efforts of health promotion and illness prevention across the life span. Not surprisingly, those that succeeded contained multiple elements from each of prevention's four technologies.

B O X **10-3**   Primary Prevention among Adolescent Refugees

Refugees are immigrants who have had to flee their homes because of religious, political, or ethnic persecution. Many have experienced war, hunger, and other horrific life events. In countries like the United States and Canada, which are open to refugees, the need to assist them in their transition to the "New World" is evident. The work of a Canadian/United States research team provides a model for professionals to use in encouraging immigrant acculturation and adaptation (Williams & Berry, 1991).

Acculturation and adaptation deal with changes that individuals must make when they move to another culture. It focuses on differences between cultures and the individual changes in behavior, values, attitudes, and social identity that an immigrant needs to make to integrate into that new group. To facilitate acculturation, professionals need to adopt a cross-cultural perspective that includes the understanding of the immigrant's sociocultural history. Further, the acculturation process should be viewed as an "interaction" between cultures—not just a process within the ethnic minority/refugee group. Finally, it needs to be recognized that there are wide individual differences in stress and adjustment.

Adapting to another culture can enrich one's life or it can disrupt one's physical and emotional well-being. When acculturative stress is high, the individual may experience societal disintegration. With former patterns of authority and relationships gone, it is likely the individual will feel angry, uncertain, depressed, or confused in identity. Feelings of marginality and alienation, anxiety, and psychosomatic complaints are common among refugee family members. Williams and Berry (1991) suggest the following chain of reactions in their model of acculturative stress:

Acculturation experience > Stressors > Acculturative stress

The degree to which an adolescent copes with this chain of events and processes is based on a series of complex factors including (1) degree of loss of status to the family due to socioeconomic factors; (2) the tolerance for or acceptance of the culture of the group within the new community; (3) the availability of a network of social and cultural group support for the refugee; (4) the occurrence of prejudice, discrimination, or exclusion as barriers to acculturation; (5) prior intercultural exposure or encounters; (6) attitudes toward the acculturation process; and (7) skills in coping strategies.

Professionals working with adolescent refugees have significant challenges. However, models of primary prevention for working with refugees provide a starting foundation for the effective application of psychological theory and practice.

The second work, *Prevention Works* (Albee & Gullotta, 1997), focuses attention of the National Mental Health Association's Lela Rowland Award recipients. These award recipients have demonstrated their ability to significantly improve parenting skills, enhance social skills among youth, prevent depressive episodes among those at risk, and moderate painful life stressors.

Among the book's many lessons is a warning that education efforts alone will neither prevent illness nor promote health. The authors caution that education almost always increases knowledge, occasionally changes attitudes, but almost never changes behavior. All four tools of prevention's technology must be employed if lasting behavioral change is to occur. The book also warns about unanticipated consequences. That is, the preventionist should appreciate that an action for good may result in less than a desirable outcome. For example, in an attempt to get tough on drug pushers, the federal government increased penalities against these individuals. This action had the unanticipated consequence of transferring drug trafficking from adults to youths! (See Chapter 13 for details.)

The third, *Primary Prevention Practices* (Bloom, 1996b), is a thoughtful exhaustive examination of the effectiveness of strengthening individual, social, and societal supports while decreasing the factors that impede the practice of healthy behaviors. It is an outstanding volume that carefully demonstrates how the ecological model is applied in prevention.

Finally, two recent research reviews support the effectiveness of primary prevention interventions. The first is a meta-analysis of 177 primary prevention mental health programs involving children and adolescents. The researchers find strong evidence to support preventive interventions (Durlak and Wells, 1997). Their review reports that not only were risks reduced in most cases but that youths had measurably increased competencies. Even more impressive is that the strengths of these findings match or exceed those found in medical studies. For example, aspirin has been found to be effective in preventing heart attacks with an effect size of 0.07. Yet, Joseph Durlak and Anne Wells reviewed studies successfully preventing cigarette and alcohol use with far more powerful effect sizes of 0.29 and 0.36. The second meta-analysis by Tobler and Stratton (1998) examines 120 school-based drug prevention programs across Canada and the U.S. These authors report that when the students had the opportunity to discuss material, brainstorm solutions, and practice new behaviors the preventive intervention again statistically exceeded the power of aspirin. Does prevention work? The answer most decidedly is "yes"!

THE PROMISE OF PREVENTION IN WORKING WITH ADOLESCENTS

The goal of prevention is not to eliminate all stresses. Life without any stress is death. Each of us experiences stress with every life change. The goal of prevention is to help ensure that stress does not create distress, which contributes to emotional suffering. Prevention specialists should work to help people manage stress, avoid or eliminate those stresses that are distressful, and strengthen stress-resistance abilities (Albee & Gullotta, 1997).

In recent years the strengthening of stress-resistant abilities has been the focus of several investigations (Anthony, 1987, Bloom, 1990, 1996a,b; Downs, 1990; Grossman, Beinashowitz, Anderson, Sakurai, Finnin, & Flaherty, 1992; Luthar & Zigler, 1991; Schinke, McAlister, Orlandi, & Botvin, 1990; Work, Cowen, Parker, & Wyman, 1990). The riddle these scholars have sought to solve may be expressed as follows: Who becomes dysfunctional? Who doesn't? Why?

Their preliminary findings suggest that nonsupportive families and institutions with failure experiences in settings such as school place youth at risk—particularly young people who are temperamental and male. Stress-resilient youths use a variety of mechanisms to succeed, including humor; intelligence; an internal locus of control; and involvement with supporting, caring, and empathic adult role models.

BOX **10-4**   What Makes an Intervention or a Relationship Work

Let's review again time the points made in this chapter about successful treatment and preventive interventions. If you take these points seriously, remember them, and work hard to implement them in your life, we believe you'll be successful in teaching, counseling, or any other helping profession.

First, successful relationships require that you be trustworthy, genuine, empathic, and honest. Most important is that these attributes are seen in you by those with whom you are working. Further, the individual must see the value in change and want change to occur. Next, every human being needs to belong, to be a valued member of a group, and be able to make a meaningful contribution to the group's continuance. If you can generate the feeling that people really matter, the chances of your success are very high. Third, we have seen the healing power one single human being can make in the life of another person over time. Never underestimate your ability for good in the life of another. Never shut the door on a young person. Search for the good in that adolescent and remind that child-adult called an "adolescent" of their potential.

Remember that change most likely will occur when all of prevention's technology is applied. Education informs, occasionally changes attitudes, but rarely changes behavior. Education is strengthened when social competency is promoted. Promoting social competency increases self-worth, responsibility for self, and concern for others. This intervention is made even more powerful when caring for others is encouraged. Natural caregiving acknowledges that each of us has a responsibility for the welfare of others. The most successful programs ask the questions: How are the institutions around us contributing to dysfunctional behavior, and how can we change those dysfunctional practices? These community organization/systems interventions ask that we examine the social institutions around us and look for ways to promote healthy institutional behavior which could be as simple as measuring academic ability (testing) in different ways for different students. Finally, for good to happen, new behavior must be practiced.

We believe these points are the essence of any successful intervention. Use them with the primary prevention work sheet in Box 10-5 to create interventions that will promote health and reduce the incidence of dysfunctional behavior.

Importantly, these supporting adults are involved with a young person *over time*. The power of simple caring and practicing Carl Roger's (1965) relationship principles matter. They can make all the difference in the world for some young person (see Box 10-4).

In adolescence the circumstances under which a particular stress occurs may change, but the stresses themselves remain constant. Pause for a few moments to consider how you might use each of the tools of prevention to improve the conditions under which each of these stresses occurs. Are some of the stresses imposed by the structure of society? (For instance, would the passage of the Equal Rights Amendment have removed stress on women that is structurally imposed by society?) If so, can they be eliminated through political action? Are other stresses inevitable? If so, can we help adolescents at highest risk avoid them, those at lesser risk manage them, and still others combat them successfully? As you read the rest of this text, ask these questions about each of the issues we raise, and don't be afraid to work out possible answers where we have not (see Box 10-5).

BOX **10-5** A Primary Prevention Worksheet

The following worksheet was first used by Klein and Goldston (1977) at an NIMH-sponsored workshop and then adapted by George Albee for use in teaching students about prevention. We have refined it further and encourage you to use it after reading each of the remaining chapters in this book. The task at the end of each chapter is to design for yourself or an "at-risk" group a prevention program to promote health and reduce distress.

1. If this is a program for an "at-risk" group, describe why an intervention is necessary.
2. In this exercise, list the major stressors affecting you or the "at-risk" group.
3. In this exercise, what problems do you wish to manage, avoid, or eliminate? What competencies do you wish to develop or strengthen that will build resistance to the stressors identified in question 2?
4. Describe the prevention initiatives you would use to address the problems and promote the competencies identified in question 3. Remember that a good program will use all of prevention's technology.
5. Do your initiatives have ethical or political implications? Are some initiatives easier to implement than others?
6. Taking into account the ethical and political implications of your initiatives, combine those initiatives that appear most feasible and describe your prevention program.

SUMMARY

In this chapter we've given you a broad overview of both treatment and prevention. The importance of appreciating that development occurs in context appeared several times in this chapter, as did the need to be conceptually and programatically responsive to the needs of diverse youths, Finally, you were encouraged to use history to gain insight into their own cultural upbringing and that of others.

In the chapters that follow we will examine typical and atypical adolescent development. We will refer to the material in this and earlier chapters in an attempt to make sense of acts that sometimes are merely foolish but at other times harm not only oneself but others as well. We hope that you will apply the information found in this chapter to the life events that fill the rest of this book. We also hope that you will use this information to promote your health and that of others.

MAJOR POINTS TO REMEMBER

1. The secret of working with adolescents is being trustworthy, genuine, empathic, and honest. For this formula to work, the adolescent must perceive the mental health worker as having these qualities.

2. Therapy involves diagnosing a client's emotional problem and, where appropriate, acting to correct that problem by increasing the individual's capacity to cope with life.

3. The four basic categories of therapy are individual, family, group, and couple therapy. The two primary locations in which therapy takes place are treatment (outpatient) settings and rehabilitation (inpatient) settings.

4. The medical model is a disease-based model in which illness passes through certain predictable stages. Although useful for physical illness, this approach has certain inherent weaknesses when applied to emotional problems.

5. Most of the many kinds of therapies can be grouped into five schools: analytically oriented therapy, behavioral therapy, humanistic therapy, transpersonal therapy, and biogenic therapies.

6. In primary prevention, emotional illness is avoided and mental health encouraged. Prevention is proactive and emphasizes groups rather than individuals.

7. There are four prevention tools: education, community organization/systems intervention, competency promotion, and natural care giving.

8. Stress accompanies any change in life. Excessive stress causes distress, which contributes to emotional suffering.

9. The tools of prevention help individuals manage stress, avoid or eliminate stresses, and strengthen stress-resistance skills.

10. Prevention's promise for working with adolescents is that it can help to ease the life-transition points.

Adolescent Sexuality: Issues for Concern

$\mathbf{T}$HE TOPICS FOR this chapter remind us of those classic horror films. You remember: Dracula, Frankenstein, and Dr. Jekel and Mr. Hyde in which the monster is hidden from view during the day but emerges at night to stalk his victims. Roaming without restraint, he remains loose until morning breaks the grip of night and then, unable to stand the sun's penetrating and purifying light, withdraws into his shelter until dusk again falls. We admit that this sounds flowery and moralistic, but then all horror films and most sexual advice are flowery and moralistic.[1]

In the past, each issue we examine in this chapter was considered to be relevant to only a few young people who hung on the fringes of society. Over the past decade, we have begun to appreciate that adolescent pregnancy, sexually transmitted diseases, and other problem behaviors are not unique to a few but are experienced by millions of sexually active young people in North America each year. In this chapter we examine these problems and, where appropriate, discuss what actions can be taken to prevent or treat them.

ADOLESCENT PREGNANCY

When the traditional or double standard of sexual behavior was still in vogue, the teenage couple who had conceived a child had few choices, and all of them difficult. Although the couple could marry, most often the girl quietly withdrew from school and, amid neighborhood rumors, disappeared to stay with a relative or at a home for unwed mothers to await the birth of the infant. Once delivered, the infant was given up for adoption. This pattern has changed considerably; and although the choices remain difficult, there are more options than existed in 1970.

Some of these changes involve better methods of preventing conception (the Pill, foam). Others involve wider accessibility to already known birth control devices (condoms). There has also been a liberalization of our attitudes. We are now able to openly discuss some sexual issues, and old standards for women are gradually giving way to new codes of sexual conduct. Some groups argue that these changes have resulted in an epidemic of adolescent pregnancies. The term epidemic can be understood to have several meanings. Among these would be births to unmarried adolescents.

[1] Notice the next time you go to the movies, who escapes the clutches of evil. We guarantee you that it will be the character who is pure in body, mind, and spirit.

In 1960, for example, 85% of births to adolescent women were to married teenagers. In contrast, by 1988 this percentage had decreased to fewer than 33% (Jorgensen, 1993). Several researchers argue, in response, that there has been no increase in the number of adolescent women giving birth to children (Chilman, 1983; Vinovskis, 1981). Rather, they contend, the issue is one of demographics; that is, fewer women above the age of 20 are having children than in the past. The result is that it appears that adolescent birthrates are on the rise when, in fact, births to adolescents have declined.

To illustrate, in 1952 the overall U.S. birthrate was 86 in 1000 among women 15 to 19 years old. In 1972 the rate was 62 in 1000. In 1983 there were 52 births per 1000. During the 1980s the rate per thousand hovered in this 52 per 1000 range. Interestingly, as we entered the 1990s two additional drops have occurred. For the latest year for which data is available, 1994, the figure stood at 36 per 1000 (U.S. Census, 1997, p. 81, Chart 102). Recently, the news media have picked up on this several-year decline with headlines that adolescent pregnancy rates are dropping. The tone of these articles is that this is a recent occurrence, which clearly is not the case.

Regardless of one's position on whether the adolescent pregnancy rate is high, there is no disagreement that an estimated 1 adolescent female in 10 will conceive this year. That's about 1 million pregnancies. Of this number about half of these young women are expected to carry the fetus to term. For the year 1994, this means that of the total number of live births that occurred to all women (3,953,000), 13.1% (518,000) were to women less than 20 years of age (U.S. Census, 1997, p. 75, Chart 90).[2] Finally, two other changes are occurring. Fewer young women are leaving home to have their babies. More interesting still is that fewer young women are giving up their infants to family agencies for adoption (Farber, 1991; Kalmuss, Namerow, & Bauer, 1992). Can we conclude that society has cast off its prohibitions and embraced these young people? Is adolescent pregnancy less stigmatizing than it was 10, 15, or 300 years ago?

To be frank, we find it hard to imagine that any behavior associated with media headlines involving words like "casualty figures," "epidemic," or "national disaster" can be considered desirable in society's eyes. Proponents of the welfare reform act, recently passed in the United States, used stories of promiscuous teenagers having babies at taxpayer's expense as an argument in urging the bill's passage. Information that the cost to the United States of children born to teenage mothers is $7 billion in welfare payments, Medicaid, and food stamps does little to endear these teenagers and their children to the public ("Cost of Teen Pregnancy Put at $7 Billion a Year," 1996). Nor do we find evidence to suggest that the immediate family has become any more understanding of the problems these young people face. The consequences of adolescent pregnancy clearly remain painful (Dryfoos, 1990; Hechinger, 1992; Jorgensen, 1993; Sagrestano & Paikoff, 1997; Terre and Burkhart, 1996).

---

[2]Of the 518,000 live births to young women in 1994, 12,000 were to females under the age of 15 (U.S. Census Bureau, 1997, p. 79, Chart 97).

For the majority of young women who have a baby, life's opportunities decline.

Many young pregnant women drop out of school, and few ever return to complete their education. Handicapped by a poor education, few are ever satisfied with the jobs they are capable of getting. Most find their freedom severely limited by their new family responsibilities. For those who marry the father of the infant, marital satisfaction is lower than in nonadolescent marriages, and the divorce rate is twice as high. Further, family size tends to be larger than with other marriages, with the children of adolescent parents experiencing greater health risks, such as low birth weight and premature birth. As those children grow older, they are more likely than other youths to do poorly in school, to display disruptive behaviors, to live outside their homes sooner than other young people, and to become parents in their own adolescent years (Aquilino, 1996; Cooksey, 1997; Dryfoos, 1990; Hechinger, 1992; Jorgensen, 1993; Office of Technology, 1991).

Yet, we should note that Cooksey (1997), Timms (1996), and others appropriately caution that these negative outcomes are not a wholesale condemnation of adolescents as mothers. Rather, given their young age and inexperience, life stresses have a way of piling on these youths. It is this stacking of life stresses that produce the negative findings detailed earlier. If these are the unpleasant consequences of adolescent pregnancy, what, then, are the antecedents? In the following sections we examine the literature on the teenage girl/mother, her family, the child's father, and adolescent marriage.

The Girl/Mother

From a historical perspective, given that Sigmund Freud presumed the sex drive to be one of two instinctive universal human urges (the other being aggression), it is certainly understandable that there are numerous psychoanalytic explanations for adolescent pregnancy dating before the mid-1970s. One of the most common themes is the Oedipal nature of intercourse for adolescent girls. Several studies using clinical populations suggest that the adolescent girl, desiring sexual relations with her father, pushes back those incestuous feelings and engages in sexual intercourse with a surrogate (Babikian & Goldman, 1971; LaBarre, 1968). Other psychoanalytic explanations that stretch one's imagination are that pregnancy is a struggle against a pre-Oedipal, homosexual liaison with the mother (Blos, 1967) and that pregnancy is a substitute for the female's missing penis (Clothier, 1943).

Beginning in the 1970s studies started to offer more than a one-dimensional view of adolescent pregnancy. For example, half of one research sample showed few, if any, signs of deviancy; these girls were typical outgoing, open, and enthusiastic adolescents (Kane, Moan, & Bolling, 1974). A more recent study of middle-income adolescents yielded very few differences between pregnant and nonpregnant youths leading the authors to speculate that "the lack of major psychological or demographic differences between pregnant and nonpregnant sexually active adolescents is of interest. It is possible that few differences exist, and chance plays a large role in accounting for whether [a sexually active female] becomes pregnant" (Morgan, Chapar, & Fisher, 1995, p. 287). Several reviews of the literature reinforce the suggestion that there may be no psychological differences between pregnant and nonpregnant girls (McKenry, Walters, & Johnson, 1979; Phipps-Yonas, 1980; Shaffer, Pettigrew, Wolkind, & Zajicek, 1978).

Some of the work on pregnant adolescents shows that some may have deep emotional problems. However, many of the authors of these studies properly caution their readers that the sample for observation was drawn from a small, highly selective group, so that the findings cannot be generalized to the overall population. Are all pregnant adolescents emotionally disturbed? We believe not. There is a growing body of evidence to support a finding that often the caring relationship between two people simply ends unexpectedly in pregnancy. The reactions of the girl's family to this news and their contribution to this situation are investigated next.

The Girl/Mother's Family

There is greater agreement in the literature on the families of most pregnant adolescents. Several common themes emerge from these studies. The home is described as a very stressful place, with the parents reported in some cases to be alcoholics or assaultive (Franklin, 1988; McCullough & Scherman, 1991; Ravert & Martin, 1997; Science, 1991a). Single-parent families abound (Barnett, Papini, & Gbur, 1991; Gilmore, Lewis, Lohr, Spencer, & White, 1997). Mother/daughter relationships, at least before pregnancy, are often described as strained (Babikian & Goldman, 1971; LaBarre, 1968). Other reports indicate that physical or emotional illness marks many of these families (LaBarr, 1968; Russ-Eft et al., 1979).

Because of the suggestion that adolescent pregnancy may be the result of an unresolved Oedipal conflict, the descriptions of mother/daughter relationships before and after conception are particularly interesting. Most studies report a vast improvement in tense and conflict-ridden relationships after conception. The grandmother-to-be in these reports seems to, midway through the pregnancy, share in her expectant daughter's experience. In one recent study 60% of the adolescent mothers continued to live at home with their mother. Although the new grandmothers reported becoming upset at learning of their daughter's pregnancy and younger grandmothers in their 20s and 30s reported the role as burdensome and stressful, these women still extended help and support to their daughters and grandchildren. This help and support could be considered vital to the well-being of the infant for, in the opinion of the researchers, these new grandmothers were more responsive to the child's needs and caring than the adolescent mother (Chase-Lansdale, Brooks-Gunn, & Palkoff, 1991). Whether the adolescent's mother is reliving her own pregnancy, or whether this situation creates an environment in which daughter and mother can share experiences and in so doing improve their relationship, is unclear (Townsend & Worobey, 1987; Wise & Grossman, 1980).

What is clear, however, is that the mother of the pregnant adolescent plays a very important continued role in her life. In many instances the adolescent mother remains home and shares the parenting responsibilities of the new infant with her mother. When the new grandmother is able to provide help without criticism, she is viewed as a significant source of social support (Nitz, Ketterlinus, & Brandt, 1995; Samuels, Stockdale, & Crase, 1994). When the grandmother strays from this supportive role, she is viewed as less helpful and more interfering (Richardson, Barbour, & Bubenzer, 1995; Samuels, Stockdale, & Crase, 1994).

In general, the picture that develops of the girl/mother and her family suggests a fair amount of family stress. Several studies have found a higher incidence of separation or divorce and strained mother/daughter relationships. Until recently, little attention was paid to the child's father. In the next section we look at him and their marriage.

The Child's Father and Adolescent Marriage

Perhaps it is society's double standard that has allowed males to be ignored in studying the problems created by adolescent pregnancies. Society has tended to view the male's involvement in this situation as one of sowing wild oats. Although the male bears the responsibility for planting the seed, society has reasoned that it is the girl who allows it to be planted. Further, should conception occur, it is she, of course, and not the male, who carries the unmistakable signs of pregnancy. Finally, it is also clear that when marriage has not been an option, the girl's family has taken every measure available to separate the young lovers.

Few research reports exist on the boy/father (Meyer, 1991). In large part, this is because the fathers of children born to adolescent women are often not adolescents but older men (Hardy & Duggan, 1988; Males, 1994; Sagrestano & Paikoff, 1997). For example, examining census data, Males (1994) finds that 77% of the births to women between the ages of 16 and 18 have fathers who are several years older than the mother. For adolescent mothers under the age of 15, 51% of the fathers are adults. Examining the most recent census data available indicate that in 1992, 518,000 women under the age of 20 gave birth to a child. If adolescent males are primarily responsible for these births there numbers should approximate this number. In fact at 129,000, the "age of the father" numbers fall far short of the threshold figures necessary to suggest that adolescent males are, to borrow a phrase from Margaret Mead, "driving" the adolescent pregnancy rate (U.S. Census Bureau, 1996, p. 75, Chart 92).[3] It is adult males who are principally the mates for adolescent females. This reality has led former Surgeon General Jocelyn Elders to wonder aloud why society has not been more aggressive in charging these adult males with rape (personal communication, 1994).

The few studies that do exist portray a young man in many ways less prepared than the adolescent mother for the responsibilities of parenthood. Although several early reports describe him as involved with and concerned over his family's welfare (Cannon-Bonventure & Kahn, 1979; Connally, 1978; Earls & Siegel, 1980), others describe him as flighty, childish, and irresponsible (Thornberry, Smith, & Howard, 1997; Walters & Walters, 1980). In either description the young man is less than fully prepared to assume the responsibilities of a father. Poorly educated with few, if any, financial resources, the boy/father in any case is an inadequate family provider (Dryfoos, 1990; Hardy & Duggan, 1988; Smollar & Ooms, 1987; Thornberry, Smith, & Howard, 1997). For example, one study reports that adolescent fathers have fewer years of education, poorer jobs, and lower incomes than other young men. Further, in this study these young men appear to be at higher risk for involvement in deviant activities like gangs and the selling of drugs (Thornberry, Smith, & Howard, 1997).

Thus, it probably should not be too surprising to learn that adolescent marriages have a greater chance than others of ending in divorce (Dowling, 1987; Furstenberg, 1976; Russ-Eft et al., 1979). Nor should it be surprising that financial problems in part related to poor education and inadequate job skills plague these marriages (Cannon-Bonventure & Kahn, 1979; Dowling, 1987; Nye & Lamberts, 1980; Office of Technology, 1991).

Still, in two urban samples of Black pregnant adolescents, most boy/fathers did not desert the girl/mothers but remained involved with the mother and child (Lorenzi, Klerman, & Jekel, 1972; Smith, Munford, & Hammer, 1979). Other studies report the majority of males willing to provide financial child support (Robinson, 1988; Westney, Cole, & Munford, 1986) and anxious not to leave the decision of parenthood solely to the girl/mother (Redmond, 1985). Not surprisingly, an involved and helpful boy/father to an adolescent mother can be a strong source of emotional support while a nonsupportive boy/father can be a source of considerable emotional distress (Nitz et al., 1995; Samuels et al., 1994). Although unquestionably these young people, married or not, face overwhelming problems in maintaining their relationship, it is important to note that at least in some of these studies, many of the couples report caring for each other.

There can be no doubt that adolescent marriages begin with a poor prognosis for success. Nor can there be any doubt that the burden of pregnancy still descends heavily on the female. What does begin to emerge in all these studies is some appreciation of the factors weighing against the young couple.

[3]Census data for "age of the father" was not available for years after 1992.

Finally, two other longitudinal studies provide additional insight on the long-term prospects of early childbearing. The first, a 17-year longitudinal study of slightly more than 300 mostly Black women who became pregnant in the mid-1960s, provides small encouragement to the belief that early adversity can be overcome later in life. Compared to the 5-year follow-up in 1972, when one-third were receiving welfare and only half had graduated from high school, the 1984 data reported that significantly more women had returned to finish high school or its equivalent. Similarly, many more had left welfare programs and were employed in stable jobs. Even so, only slightly more than one-third were married and, in comparison to other groups of Black women who had delayed childbearing, these individuals were not as successful (Furstenberg, Brook-Gunn, & Morgan, 1987).

The second study was a 20-year follow-up of 154 Black women who also became pregnant as teenagers in the 1960s. The researchers reported that at the follow-up 62% had completed a high school education or its equivalent and were either employed or married. Using this standard as a "success" measure, the researchers were interested in understanding what factors enabled success. Five common elements were identified.

First, successful subjects were further along in their high school studies when they became pregnant. Next, women who succeeded had participated in life skills training sessions during their initial pregnancy (see Box 11-1). These women returned to school after the birth of the first child and importantly avoided a second pregnancy for at least 2 years after the birth of the first child. Fourth, they were

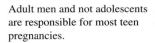
Adult men and not adolescents are responsible for most teen pregnancies.

BOX **11-1**   Young Parents Programs

Barbara Sheffey has been a community worker for Child and Family Agency for more than 2 decades. This gracious, lovely grandmother has worked during those years with young teenage women who become pregnant and decide to carry to term. She exemplifies the best characteristics of a helping professional. Warm, trustworthy, empathic, and no-nonsense, Barbara has seen hundreds of young women enter adulthood prematurely and has held their babies as they struggled to complete their education.

Barbara is employed in a service called the Young Parents Program. Located in the high school, young women are able to continue with their education after their pregnancy while their infants are cared for at a nursery located in or near the school. Primary medical care for the infants and mothers is provided by the school-based health center located at that site. Mental health counseling services, should they be needed, are also provided by the school-based health center. "Concrete" social service help in

enrolling for city, state, and federal aid programs is also provided on-site by Barbara, who will transport child-mother and infant, if necessary, to ensure both receive quality care.

In contrast to the experiences of many young mothers, teenagers enrolled in young parent programs finish high school. Further, as Higginson (1998) notes, programs for young mothers seem to encourage an increased concern for and interest in their infants.

Barbara Sheffey would agree. She feels the Young Parents Program offers these young women the social support and child development information needed to have a better chance at making it. Quiet talks, tears, and laughter make up Barbara's day. That also includes following up on child-mom and infant when they fail to arrive at school on a given day. "Can't miss school, you know, too much at stake for that little baby," she'll say—a statement we would all agree with.

---

not socially isolated after the first pregnancy and were able to reintegrate quickly into society. Finally, successful women had smaller families than unsuccessful subjects. Family size for successful women numbered two to three children as compared to several children for other subjects (Horwitz, Klerman, & Jekel, 1991).

Ethnic Differences

Attitudes about childbearing are related to both socioeconomic status and race. Examining data on middle to late adolescents from the National Longitudinal Surveys of Labor Market Experience of Youth, Trent (1994) observed that poor adolescents were more likely to expect to become pregnant than middle-income youths. In respect to race, Blacks were more likely to expect early childbearing and without marriage than White youths.

In contrast to Black adolescent mothers, White adolescent mothers are more likely to marry (National Research Council, 1993). However, whether a teenager is likely to marry depends on a number of factors including mate availability. White women have a higher percentage of marriage before the birth of their first child than Black women, and Black women have a higher probability of having a child prior to marriage (South, 1996). One of the reasons for this is demographic. That is, Black women have fewer eligible partners for marriage than do White women. Further, among the available men, Black males are less likely to be employed than White males. South (1996) reported that for White and Black women, both availability of men and employment status of men were marriage factors.

Important qualitative research has identified themes associated with teenage pregnancy among Black (Boxill, 1987) and Latino (de Anda, Becerra, & Fielder, 1990) youths. Confirming earlier statements about an impaired family life, Boxill's research with Black adolescent females indicated these youths felt let down by their parents, having experienced consistent conflict, fighting, and avoidance between themselves and their parents. Although they love their parents, these Black youths viewed their parents as ineffective. These pregnant or parenting Black teenagers saw their personal relationships as losing propositions. They indicated they avoided committing to lasting relationships because of a history of unhappiness and broken expectations. Relationships with peers and parents were viewed as punitive, insincere, and ineffective. Most youths viewed themselves as caught in a life transition where they were either too young or too old:

> I am too young to have to make all these decisions. I am too old to have to ask for advice. I should be able to figure things out on my own. I am too young to have to be in control of everything. I am too old to have to depend on my parents. I am too young to get a job. I am too old to take hand-outs. I am too young to have to be grown-up. I am too old to do childish things. I am too young to know the answers. I am too old to be so confused. I am too young to be a mother. I am too old to be told what to do (Boxill, 1987, p. 47).

Collectively, feelings of family conflict and disappointment, dissatisfaction about personal relations with peers, and the perceptions of being marginalized leave pregnant Black youths unprepared for parenting.

Pregnant Mexican-American teenagers portray a somewhat different picture (de Anda et al., 1990). Interviews with Mexican-American adolescents reveal warm recollections of early childhood, damaged by the loss of a parent due to divorce or death. Perceptions of loss of a special person and loss of protection permeate these adolescents' images. Conflict over the choice of friends, based on parental wishes, is commonly observed—particularly with mothers. Relationships with fathers are generally conflict free but are distant and alienated nevertheless. Therefore, the lives of these pregnant teenagers are filled with arguments, name-calling, and disobedience between mother and daughter, with running away common. The social lives of these youths are usually filled with continuous involvement in peer activities, like hanging around, cruising, shopping, going to movies or beaches, and attending parties or dances. Most pregnant Latino youths report having limited prior experience with males. They tend to have relatively few sexual encounters and are involved in a meaningful and reasonably committed relationship. Usually when they discover they are pregnant, their boyfriends propose marriage and assume some responsibility for their sexual behavior.

According to Zayas, Schinke, and Casareno (1987), parental commitment by Latino fathers may be due, in part, to the gender-specific role of machismo. To add to the earlier discussion in Chapter 5, to be *machismo* also means to be an adequate and gentle protector, provider, and nurturer of one's children. This involves assuming responsibility for one's masculine (sexual) behavior. Likewise, the macho role compels the male adolescent to avoid bringing shame (*verguenza*) to the family by neglecting one's duties and responsibilities to one's mate, offspring, and mate's family. Therefore, in contrast to Black females, who might experience sexual demands with marginal responsibility for parenting (due to economic limitations and other problems) from their male partners, Latino females may experience greater paternal support and involvement by their mates.

Thus, differing social and cultural conditions surround teenage pregnancy for adolescents from different ethnic groups. Cultural values, varying degrees of parental support/conflict, and paternal involvement by boyfriends vary for each group, making it important for youth workers to consider these sociocultural factors in working with pregnant youths from different racial or ethnic groups.

Implications for Treatment and Prevention

Two treatment approaches can be used to improve the life conditions of these young people once conception has occurred. Both are highly controversial and emotionally charged. The first is to provide easily accessible, low-cost or no-cost abortions to young people without the need for parental consent. Since 1973, when the U.S. Supreme Court legalized the procedure (with some restrictions), millions of unwanted pregnancies have been terminated by young people who felt that they could not properly care for a child (see Box 11-2).

BOX **11-2** A Decision on Abortion

Since the U.S. Supreme Court decision of 1973, an abortion during the first few months of pregnancy is a personal matter between a woman and her doctor in most states. Abortion differs from contraception in that abortion terminates a pregnancy, while contraception prevents it. Studies suggest women experience the greatest psychological distress before an abortion occurs. Severe negative psychological responses have not been reported frequently in the literature (Adler, David, Major, Roth, Russo, & Wyett, 1990). Latest available data for the year 1992 report that 20% of the 1,529,000 abortions were performed on women under the age of 19. For all women seeking abortions 83% were not married. Sixty-two percent were White (U.S. Census Bureau, 1997, p. 86, Chart 115). Nevertheless, the decision to terminate a pregnancy is always a very difficult one for any woman but is more so for the adolescent.

The adolescent is confronted not only with the pro-life movement's argument against abortion but with tremendous personal stress, as the following case of one of the authors illustrates:

> Sherry was a 17-year-old who became pregnant a few months into her senior year of high school. When she came to my office seeking help in deciding what to do, she was, by her best estimate, 5 to 6 weeks pregnant. She informed me that she and Donald, her boyfriend, had been going steady for a year but had no plans to marry. Both wanted to go to college. Since he had learned about the pregnancy (which she had confirmed for herself by using an over-the-counter pregnancy-testing kit), Donald had been encouraging her to have an abortion. According to Sherry, their relationship was not going well; she felt that he did not care about her but was worrying only about himself. (I had no chance to meet with Donald, but Sherry did tell me later that they had broken up.) Sherry

(continues)

(continued)

said she had not been able to discuss her problem with her parents, whom she described as rather strict religious types. She remarked, "If my parents knew, they would die!"

Sherry was clearly under tremendous stress. She had not been sleeping well and had lost weight. She also reported feeling depressed and "crying for no reason." I asked what she wanted to do. She said she had thoroughly researched the issue herself at the library and had concluded that having a child would not be a good decision at this time. After further exploring this issue with her, I felt that she had, as best one could, reached a difficult decision that for her was correct.

I transferred this case to the local Visiting Nurses Association, which had a nurse specialist in adolescent health problems. In our particular area, doctors would not perform an abortion on a minor without parental permission. As Sherry absolutely refused to inform her parents of her situation, arrangements were made to have the operation performed out of state with continuing care done through the VNA.

The treatment Sherry received was a suction abortion, or vacuum curettage. This technique is the procedure of choice for abortions in the first months of a pregnancy. It involves the insertion of a flexible tube into the uterus. Suction from the tube gently loosens the fetal tissue from the uterine wall and removes it. This type of procedure can be performed in a doctor's office, as was done in Sherry's case. She experienced some discomfort for the next few days, but it was relieved with medication.

If Sherry had waited beyond the 10th to 12th week to have the abortion, the procedure would have been much more complex, and the possibility of complications would have increased tremendously. Abortions performed after this period involve the use of vaginal suppositories of prostaglandin E2 or the injection of a saline solution into the uterus to induce labor. These procedures require a short stay in a hospital. The period of recovery is longer, and most clinicians find the emotional trauma more pronounced. We strongly encourage young women having an abortion in the second trimester to accept the follow-up care offered for assistance in dealing with the natural feelings of anger and depression that follow many abortions performed during this stage of pregnancy.

Sherry's situation mirrors some of the findings of a group of researchers who studied the communication patterns of adolescents seeking an abortion (Resnick, Bearinger, Stark, & Blum, 1994). They found that when a young woman realizes she is pregnant she is most likely to discuss the matter with her male partner (83%), followed by her mother (56%), friends (50%), and father (22%). These authors reported that if a young person feels that a person can be trusted and relied upon then the adolescent will confide in them. It is when parents and others shut the door on communication that adolescents retreat to silence.

Do you believe that it was the correct decision to support Sherry's decision to terminate her pregnancy? What other interventions might have been used? What are the ethical and moral issues involved in handling a case like this?

The second approach involves society's revaluing all children, but particularly the children of adolescents, as national resources and providing them with the means to grow up in a healthy home environment. We have noted the problems that the adolescent faces in attempting to rear a child. Support programs and financial aid would be necessary to ensure that the mothers and fathers could complete their own educations and provide food, shelter, clothing, and medical attention for their infant above today's rapidly shrinking welfare standards. Although many opponents of this suggestion would argue that we would be rewarding adolescents for their irresponsible behavior, we argue that we should not be destroying their lives—and, more important, the lives of their children—because they had a child in adolescence.

Prevention is no less controversial. First, think of prevention's technology. Remember that it has four principal tools. One of those tools is education and (not surprisingly) we believe that sex education should be a mandatory part of all school curricula. It should begin in elementary school and should be directed at more than simply providing information. Courses should attempt to encourage young people to be more comfortable with their sexuality. This increased level of comfort is not intended to encourage sexual behavior. Rather, it is to encourage the discussion of sexual behavior between a couple considering sexual behavior. Our desire is to reduce the incidence of the following statements: "I just got carried away"; "I didn't know what I was doing"; "It just happened." Pregnancies shouldn't "just happen." Couples that discuss their actions *before* taking those actions are making decisions—not merely casting their fate and seed to the wind. Further, we believe these courses should include substantial information on family life, child care, responsible decision-making, and practical parenting skills. Indeed, we are encouraging schools to reintroduce many features of the home economics courses that seemingly lost their relevance in the 1970s. Skills of meal preparation, cleanliness, and promoting child development still have a place in the educational curriculum as we enter the next century. Incidentally, encouraging responsible decision-making is promoting social competency and caring couple discussions is natural caregiving.

Finally, we need to make available to sexually active young people the means to prevent conception (an example of system change). Again, this is not a condoning of their sexual activity. It would be marvelous if all young people were to delay becoming sexually active until marriage, but that is not the case. The first step is to inform them of birth control methods in school or other community settings. The next is to make sure that young people have access to them.

These are not easy or uncontroversial proposals, particularly at a time in our society in which anger is being directed increasingly at young people. But if we are serious about wanting to diminish the number of unwanted pregnancies and improving the life chances of infants born to adolescent parents, the solution is not moralistic platitudes. One cannot expect platitudes that have been unsuccessful in the past to succeed now.

CONTRACEPTION

The desire to prevent conception dates back thousands of years. The means to do it effectively and safely, however, have been available to adults only since the 1960s and to many adolescents only since 1977 (Beiswinger, 1979). We can vividly remember from our own adolescence the unsuccessful attempts by friends to purchase condoms and the use of clear plastic wrap as a substitute. Girls fared no better; their contraceptive knowledge was based largely on hearsay offering such bits of wisdom as that douching with soft drinks after intercourse prevented conception (see Box 11-3).

BOX **11-3**   The Spermicidal Effectiveness of Coca-Cola

Since its introduction in 1886 as a patent medicine reputedly able to cure the world's ills. Coca-Cola has been used, among other things, as a contraceptive. Its use as a birth control douche continues to this day in some Third World nations. Thus, it was only a matter of time before science would ask the question "Is Coke the real thing?" In a letter to the editor of the *New England Journal of Medicine*, a group at Harvard Medical School reported the results of mixing sperm samples with Diet Coke and Classic Coke. The researchers found that no sperm were swimming after a 1-minute exposure to Diet Coke and 8.5% were still moving upstream after a 1-minute exposure to Classic Coke. Apparently, Pepsi is not interested in the douche possibilities of its product and has not challenged Coke's supremacy in this area. (*Source:* S. A. Umpierre, J. A. Hill, & D. J. Anderson, "Effect of 'Coke' on Sperm Motility," *New England Journal of Medicine*, 1985, **313** (21), p. 1351.)

It was not until 1977, when the U.S. Supreme Court overturned New York's law prohibiting the sale of birth control devices to minors, that the means of birth control were accessible to many young people. Why, then, with the means available to prevent unwanted births, are we experiencing a so-called epidemic of adolescent pregnancies? In this section we examine some of the possible reasons that many adolescents do not use contraception.

Factors Involved in Not Using Contraceptives

Given that it is possible to prevent conception, why are young people becoming pregnant? Four general explanations have been proposed for why some adolescents do not use contraceptives. Prudence Rains first suggested in her book *Becoming an Unwed Mother* (1971) that the primary reason most young women do not use contraceptives is that they have not accepted their sexual behavior as correct. The second explanation is that young people do not have adequate access to either birth control information or contraceptive devices. The third explanation is that the depth of the relationship may determine whether contraceptives are used. Thus, couples who have been going together and are "serious" are more likely to use contraceptives than are people in a relationship that could be categorized as a one-night stand. The final perspective is that contraceptive nonusage is intentional. A closer look at each of these perspectives is warranted in order to gain a fuller appreciation of how these factors operate independently and collectively to effect a conscious or an ignorant decision not to use contraceptives.

The Emotional Development Perspective

The results of several studies support Rains's (1971) suggestion that contraceptive usage is a function of accepting one's own sexuality (Goldsmith, Gabrielson, Gabrielson, Matthews, & Potts, 1972; Reiss, Banwart, & Foreman, 1975; Reiss & Reiss, 1997; Schneider, 1982). Ira Reiss and his associates (1975) suggest that young women who use contraceptives believe that it is their right to choose their own sexual lifestyle. They also appear to view themselves as more attractive than nonusers do. This positive self-image, the researchers believe, acts to encourage "one to be contraceptively safe, perhaps because one expects that attractiveness to males will lead to full sexual relationships" (p. 625). Expanding on the influence of self-image, Plotnick and Butler (1991) found that higher self-esteem, positive attitudes about school, and future thoughts about college decrease the risk for pregnancy.

Some authors suggest that the inability to accept one's sexuality may be a function of age. Using a cognitive development model, they point out that the young adolescent is in between concrete and formal operations. The ability to look at the future and take the necessary precautions to avoid pregnancy is a characteristic of formal operations. Thus, caught between formal and concrete operations, young adolescents are hindered in making decisions on sexual matters (Cobliner, 1974; Cvetkovich, 1975; Dembo & Lundell, 1979; Franklin, 1988; Gullotta, Adams, & Alexander, 1986; Hart & Hilton, 1988; Pestrak & Martin, 1985). Indeed, in one study even having had a pregnancy or a "pregnancy scare" did not improve contraceptive usage. Only with the passage of time did contraceptive usage improve for these young women (Orcutt & Cooper, 1997).

Still others suggest that societal expectations strongly influence female sexual behavior. Although we may be gradually changing to a more egalitarian system of male/female sex roles, this change is not yet complete. Thus, for many young females, planning their sexual encounters is unacceptable, for this sexual aggressiveness might be perceived by their partner (or in their own minds) as suggesting loose morals (Chilman, 1973, 1980; Dembo & Lundell, 1979). A recent Australian study lends support to this belief (Hillier, Harrison, & Warr, 1998). Questioning over 500 senior students, the researchers find that preparing for sexual relations can give a female a bad reputation or as the title of their paper so aptly phrases it, "When You Carry Condoms All the Boys Think You Want It."

Lack of Information

Ignorance of one's own body, of how it functions, and how pregnancy occurs is another cited reason for adolescent pregnancy rates. A number of early studies have documented that adolescents operate under a large number of misconceptions about sexual issues. These include: pregnancy cannot occur in the middle of the menstrual cycle (Babikian & Goldman, 1971; Kanter & Zelnick, 1972); pregnancy occurs only to those who want to become pregnant (Babikian & Goldman, 1971; Zelnick, 1979); and pregnancy cannot occur if one is too young (Furstenberg, 1970; Kanter & Zelnick, 1973). These misconceptions, coupled with studies showing that adolescents have little factual information on childbearing (Walters, McKenry, & Walters, 1979) and that males express the belief that contraceptives are her problem (Finkel & Finkel, 1978), underscore the need for education on sexual matters (Freeman et al., 1980; Blau & Gullotta, 1993).

Relationship Factors

Several studies indicate that contraceptive use increases as the relationship lengthens. One reason may be the couple's realization that the frequency of their sexual relations increases the probability of conception and that precautions should be taken (DeAmicis, Klorman, Hess, & McAnarney, 1981; Jorgensen, King, & Torrey, 1980; Kanter & Zelnick, 1973; Reiss et al., 1975).

Other motivations as well may encourage contraceptive use by adolescents. According to one study, such internal variables as the stability of the relationship, strong feelings for the partner, and self-esteem may influence the female to use contraceptives (Hornick, Doran, & Crawford, 1979). Adolescent females most likely to use them come from well-educated, middle-class families and have stable dating relationships. Those least likely to use them are young women who date several people. In contrast, contraceptive use by adolescent males is affected by external forces related to parental permissiveness and dating experience. The earlier a male dates, the more likely it is that he will use a contraceptive. Males with parents who would not be upset by learning that their sons are sexually active are reported to use contraceptives least. As parental permissiveness decreases and the attitude that planning intercourse is acceptable increases, male contraceptive use increases. A study of 283 college students confirms many of these findings (Lowe & Radius, 1987). The authors suggest that easy access to contraceptives, open couple communication, and a liberal ideology encourages use. Disturbingly, 57% of this college sample reported not using

Many couples do not use contraceptives until the relationship lengthens. This can lead to certain outcomes.

a contraceptive at the time of first coitus in a new relationship. A more recent study of college students found that while 88% of men and 51% of women used condoms at least once, only 35% used them *all* the time. More disturbing still was that withdrawal as a means of contraception was practiced by 22% of this population (Murstein & Mercy, 1994). In another college sample about half (49%) used a condom at the time of first coitus in a new relationship (Poppen, 1994).

Similar reports of contraceptive nonuse can also be found in Jorgensen's (1993) review of the literature. He estimates that only 48% of sexually active adolescents regularly use contraceptives. Even this disappointing figure may be optimistically high. One study of 1880 15- to 19-year-old males reported that roughly one-third of these adolescents used condoms. Of additional concern was the finding that 73% of the female partners in this study did not expect contraceptives to be used. Factors determining male condom use were fear of pregnancy, fear of AIDS, and respect for the sexual partner (Pleck, Sonenstein, & Kie, 1991).

Intentional Contraceptive Nonusage

Given the availability of condoms and foam in drug stores, supermarkets, and discount stores, unintended pregnancies need not occur and yet they do. Many scholars believe that a percentage of these pregnancies are intentional. That is, the young woman wanted to become pregnant. The reasons to explain this behavior can be found in deprived childhoods filled with abuse, emotional neglect, and troubled families (Jorgensen, 1993; Miller, Christopherson, & King, 1993; Rickel & Hendren, 1993). These young women have histories of poor school performance, truancy, drug use, running away from home, and fights (Elster, Ketterlinus, & Lamb, 1990). With a low sense of self-esteem and depression (*Science*, 1991a), early sexual behavior becomes, as one young woman of 12 once told one of the authors, "a feeling"—a feeling, we would observe, that for her occurs in a world devoid of success, social support, and emotional love. In such a world, the temporary physical pleasure of sex poorly replaces the emotional needs of the adolescent. In such a world, having a baby is something to love, to cherish, and to establish an identity around. Tragically, for the child and its child-mother these hopes for identity are rarely, if ever, fulfilled.

Summary

Clearly, no single explanation accounts for all lack of contraceptive use among adolescents. However, when taken together, the four explanations discussed in this section provide a picture of young people who are poorly informed or misinformed about their sexuality and who are uncomfortable with themselves as sexual beings. Conditions such as these contribute not only to unwanted pregnancies but to disease as well. In the next section we examine a problem more serious than not using contraceptives—sexually transmitted diseases.

SEXUALLY TRANSMITTED DISEASES

Sexually transmitted diseases are infections almost always transmitted in sexual intercourse (vaginal, anal, and oral are all included). The organisms that cause sexually transmitted diseases are extremely sensitive to light, air, and the absence of moisture. Only in dark, warm, moist areas can the organisms survive. (Thus, stories of contracting AIDS from toilet seats are sheer fantasy.) As luck would have it, the human body offers perfect conditions for this group of diseases to flourish. Once inside the body, syphilis, gonorrhea, herpes simplex virus types 1 and 2, chlamydia, and the human immunodeficiency virus (HIV-1 and HIV-2) have an ideal environment in which to grow and multiply. Unchecked, these diseases can cause serious and permanent damage or even death. In pregnant women these diseases can be passed on to the unborn child (see Table 11-1).

Why should this be of concern to students of adolescence? It is of concern for two very simple reasons. First, recall that earlier in this book we established that while many adolescents are sexually active, very few take the precautions necessary to prevent sexually transmitted diseases. Indeed, the studies just discussed and in Chapter 6 report that few college students practice safe sex. Second, this failure to practice safe sex results in reports that 25% of all sexually transmitted diseases occur to adolescents (Luster & Small, 1994; Remez, 1996). In light of these findings, we ask that you to carefully read the following material.

Syphilis

Referred to by adolescents as "bad blood," "syph," and "the pox," syphilis may havebeen a gift from the New World. There is no evidence that syphilis existed in Europe before Columbus' voyage, but by 1497 the disease was running rampant, decimating the population. Columbus himself is believed to have died of the disease. At that time the names given to the disease represented a kind of political slur against a neighboring state. The French called it the "Neapolitan disease." The citizens of Naples returned the favor by referring to it as "the French pox." It was not until 1530 that an Italian physician, Hieronymus Fracastorius, gave this disease its present name in a poem in which a shepherd named Syphilus was struck with the plague that came to bear his name. The infectious agent that causes syphilis was discovered in 1905. It was a discovery that at the time was equivalent in magnitude to the finding of the retrovirus responsible for AIDS. At the turn of the century one-third of all hospital beds in the United States were filled with patients suffering from syphilis. Indeed, so serious was the threat of this disease that in 1918 the United States imprisoned 20,000 suspected prostitutes in a futile attempt to reduce the military's exposure to the disease (Brandt, 1988).

Syphilis is caused by a very tiny, slender, corkscrew-shaped bacterium (*Treponema pallidum*) called a spirochete. It is nearly always spread by direct contact from a carrier of the disease to a noncarrier by sexual intercourse. When a noninfected individual's broken skin touches a syphilitic lesion, syphilis can

TABLE **11-1**   Overview of Selected Sexually Transmitted Diseases and Syndromes

Agent	Disease or syndrome	Typical presenting signs and symptoms	Examples of potential complications/sequelae
Bacterial agents			
Neisseria gonorrhoeae	Gonorrhea	Abnormal vaginal or penile discharge, abdominal pain; may be asymptomatic	Disseminated gonococcal infection (e.g., blood infection, pelvic inflamatory disease, infertility, infection of the male reproductive organs
Chlamydia trachomatis	Chlamydial infections: Nongonococcal urethritis	Dysuria, urinary frequency, abnormal penile discharge; may be asymptomatic	Urinary narrowing and infection
	Mucopurulent cervicitis	Abnormal endocervical discharge; may be asymptomatic	Infection of the lining of the uterus, infection of the fallopian tubes, infertility, adverse obstetric outcomes
Treponema pallidum	Primary syphilis	Chancre	Late (teriary) syphilis and sequelae, neuro-syphilis
	Secondary syphilis	Skin rash, mucous patches, lymphadenopathy, condyloma lata	
Viral agents			
Herpes simplex virus (HSV) 1	Nongenital herpes	Blisters on eyes or other facial regions	Inflamation of the brain and spinal cord, recurrent HSV infection
Herpes simplex virus (HSV) 2	Genital herpes	Blisters, genital ulcers, stomatitis, and oral lesions	Disseminated infection, recurrent HSV infection
Human immunodeficiency virus (HIV)	HIV infection	Generalized lymphadenopathy, weight loss, night sweats, intermittent fever, malaise, drar rhea; may initially be asymptomatic	Full-blown AIDS
	Acquired immunodeficiency syndrome (AIDS)	Symptoms of opportunistic infections such as pneumocystic pneumonia, or Kaposi's sarcoma	Death

Source: Office of Technology Assessment, 1991, based on U.S. Department of Health and Human Services, Public Health Service, Centers for Disease Control, "Sexually Transmitted Disease Summary: 1990." Atlanta, GA, June, 1990.

be transferred. Once infected, the individual, if left untreated, goes through three stages of the illness plus a latent period.

The first, or primary, stage appears 3 or 4 weeks after exposure to the disease in the form of a hard, often painless, open sore called a chancre. Chancres can appear singly or in groups. Ranging from one-eighth of an inch to an inch in diameter, they look like small craters. The surfaces of these craters appear red, raw, and at times crusted. In men they appear most often on the shaft of the penis, and in women they appear (without their notice) within the vulva, on the walls of the vagina, or on the cervix. Typically, these chancres disappear a few weeks after their first appearance, leading the infected individual to believe that the problem has gone away. It has not! The disappearance of these painless sores signals the entrance of the disease into its second stage. In the second stage, the effects of syphilis on the body are more pronounced. Two to six months after exposure, the individual may complain of fever, loss of appetite, headaches, or a sore throat. However, the symptom most significantly associated with secondary syphilis is one of two types of skin rashes called macular syphilide and papular syphilide. In the first type small, round, shiny, red spots appear on the upper body and arms. These spots may be so light that they are hardly noticeable, and they may disappear in a few days. The second type is more prominent. Papular syphilide appears as raised red spots and covers the entire body, including the soles, palms, and face. Hair loss can occur, with hair falling out in patches. But even in this most infectious stage of syphilis, the symptoms disappear after several weeks. Syphilis now enters the latent period.

In this period all symptoms disappear as the disease becomes spontaneously cured, remains latent, or invades the others organs of the body, such as the eyes, heart, brain, and spinal cord.[4] In the latent period, the disease can no longer be transmitted from one sexual partner to another, but pregnant women can transmit it to the fetus. After one or several years, if the disease has been invading other body tissues, the last stage occurs.

In this late, or tertiary, stage extremely serious health problems appear. Depending on which body organ has been attacked, the individual may experience blindness, insanity, paralysis, or severe heart problems. It is the heart problems that most frequently cause death (Ammer, 1983; Leukenfeld & Haverkos, 1993; McCammon, Knox, & Schacht, 1993; Nettina, 1990). For the year 1995, 69,000 cases of syphilis were diagnosed and reported in the United States. Encouragingly, this continues a 6-year decline in yearly reported incidences and nearly matches rates in 1985 when cases dipped to a record low of 68,000 (U.S. Census Bureau, 1997, p. 141, Chart 213).[5]

[4]Spontaneous cures resulted from patients' experiencing an extremely high fever. It appears that the fever and the body's reaction to it often destroyed the spirochete. From the 1920s into the 1940s syphilitic individuals were intentionally infected with a mild form of malaria to induce this condition (Valenstein, 1986).

[5]Data given is for the most recent year for which information is available. Researchers suspect that most STDs are underreported and that rates may be two or three times higher. Nevertheless, these reported figures are useful as they help to discern trends.

Gonorrhea

Called, among other things, "the drip," "clap," "dose," or "strain," gonorrhea infected more than 393,000 individuals in 1995. Of this number more than two-thirds are estimated to be either adolescents or young adults (Masters, Johnson, & Kolodny, 1994). Until 1994, gonorrhea held the dubious distinction of being the most reported sexually transmitted disease in the country (U.S. Census Bureau, 1997, p. 141, Chart 213). It is caused by the bacterium *Neisseria gonorrhoeae* and affects the mucous membranes of the genitalia, throat, or rectum.

After sexual contact (anal, oral, or vaginal) with an infected individual in which the bacterium finds a small break in the skin or other tissue by which to enter the bloodstream, the disease appears in 1 day to 2 weeks in its first form. In males this is a yellowish, pus-like discharge from the penis. Other symptoms include a burning sensation when urinating and a sensation of itching within the urethra. Symptoms in women may be nonexistent in the earliest stage of this disease. As many as 80% of the women infected with gonorrhea have no early symptoms. Those who do have a yellowish-green vaginal discharge. If unnoticed or left untreated in this early stage, gonorrhea may affect other parts of the body.[6]

In its most advanced stages the disease in males can cause chronic infection of the urethra, resulting in the inability to urinate, or it can cause sterility. In women the disease can spread through the uterus and Fallopian tubes, causing sterility. Infections resulting from this disease can lead to heart problems, blindness, and arthritis in both males and females. Until recently, infants could be contaminated by the disease at birth in their passage through the infected birthcanal. The result of this passage through the infected area was blindness. This problem has been successfully prevented by the application of small amounts of silver-nitrate drops or penicillin ointment to the eyes of these infants (Ammer, 1983; Masters, Johnson, & Kolodny, 1994; McCammon, Knox, & Schacht, 1993).

Herpes

Herpes takes its name from "herpein" (Greek), "to creep." In its latent stage, the herpes virus most often resides at the base of the spine or recessed in the fifth cranial nerve. When the carrier's resistance is lowered by fatigue, stress, or illness, the virus creeps down the nerve fibers at the rate of 1 inch in 16 hours and erupts in a painful sore that appears most often on the lips, inside the mouth, or on the genitals. The sexually transmitted forms of the virus are herpes simplex virus type 1 (HSV-1) and herpes simplex virus type 2 (HSV-2). There are more than 50 kinds of herpes viruses. The most common are herpes simplex types 1 and 2, which infect the genitals, skin, eyes, mouth, and brain; herpes zoster, which causes shingles and chicken pox; cytomegalovirus, which causes blindness or mental retardation in babies; and Epstein–Barr virus, which causes mononucleosis and some forms of

---

[6]It has been estimated that a single unprotected coital experience exposes a male to a 25% risk of gonorrhea and a woman to a 50% chance of infection. This risk increases to roughly 90% for both sexes after four exposures (Masters, Johnson, & Kolodny, 1994).

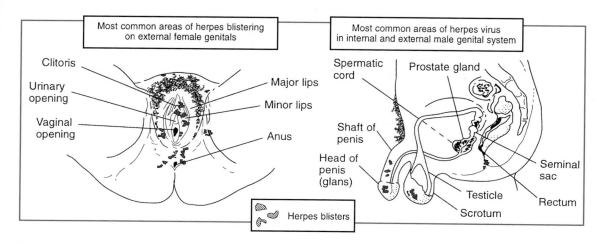

Most common areas of herpes blistering on external female genitals

Most common areas of herpes virus in internal and external male genital system

Clitoris
Urinary opening
Vaginal opening
Major lips
Minor lips
Anus

Spermatic cord
Prostate gland
Shaft of penis
Head of penis (glans)
Seminal sac
Testicle
Scrotum
Rectum

Herpes blisters

FIGURE 11-1

Areas of female and male genitals commonly infected with herpes simplex types 1 or 2. (*Source:* Zelnick, M., & Kantner, J. F. (1980). Sexual activity, contraceptive use and pregnancy among metropolitan-area teenagers: 1971–1979. Family Planning Perspectives, 12, 230–237.)

cancer. The herpes simplex virus (HSV-1 and -2) is very contagious, with a single risk exposure for infection for males estimated to be 50% and for females at nearly 90% (Masters, Johnson, & Kolodny, 1994; McCammon, Knox, & Schacht, 1993).

It was once incorrectly believed that herpes type 1 occurred only above the waist and type 2 only below the waist. Because of oral contact with various parts of the body, both types are increasingly found almost anywhere.

Herpes simplex type 2 blisters (often accompanied by a fever and chills) appear anywhere from 1 day to about 3 weeks after contact (Fig. 11-1 shows the most common locations). The sores and flu-like symptoms disappear over the course of a few days to several weeks, as the virus retreats along the nerve fibers to wait to erupt again at some future date. During an outbreak of HSV-1 or -2 the disease is highly contagious because the sore or sores are constantly shedding the virus. Caution needs to be exercised at this time, because one can inadvertently give the virus to others or spread it to other parts of one's own body. For example, inserting contact lenses after touching a herpes sore without washing one's hands with soap and water may transmit billions of active viruses to one's eyes (Bettoli, 1982). Medical reports also suggest that it is possible to experience an asymtomatic shedding of the virus. That is, the virus may be present and active without noticeable side effects. Thus, caution must be exercised by known carriers of the virus (Brock, Selke, Benedetti, Douglas, & Corey, 1990; Masters, Johnson, & Kolodny, 1994).

Unlike other sexually transmitted disease organisms, which cannot live outside the body, HSV-1 and -2 can survive for several hours on such surfaces as the human skin, clothing, and plastic (Turner, Shehab, Osborne, & Hendley, 1982). In fact, the National Institutes of Health once reported that three elderly women had contracted the disease while soaking in a hot tub. Although viruses cannot live in the chemically treated water in a hot tub, they did survive long enough on the tub rim to infect these three individuals (Highlights, 1984).

Additional concern is warranted for pregnant women who have genital herpes. For instance, genital herpes increases the risk of spontaneous abortion or premature delivery. There is also a risk of 40 to 60% that a woman delivering vaginally who is experiencing an outbreak of genital herpes at the time of delivery will infect her infant (Bettoli, 1982). Transmitted infections occur roughly once in every 3500 deliveries (Masters, Johnson, & Kolodny, 1994).[7]

Although genital herpes cannot be cured at this time, it can be managed. The drugs acyclovir, valacyclovir and famciclovir have been approved for topical and oral applications and have been shown to be effective in speeding the healing of HSV sores (Corey & Holmes, 1983; Journal of the American Medical Association, 1998, September).

Meanwhile, the following suggestions will minimize discomfort for the herpes sufferer and reduce the probability of spreading the disease to others. During an outbreak of genital sores, avoid intercourse (oral, anal, or vaginal) for 14 days. When the HSV is active, take particular care not to touch the sores. Should you touch a sore, wash your hands immediately, and do not touch your eyes. To prevent recurrences, get ample rest and good nutrition and engage in stress-reduction techniques. Herpes, though painful for one's body and soul, can be lived with successfully with some care and effort (Lenard, 1982; Masters, Johnson, & Kolodny, 1994).

Chlamydia

This little-known disease has the dubious distinction of being the most reported STD in the U.S. In 1995 478,000 cases of chlamydia were reported (U.S. Census Bureau, 1997, p. 141, Chart 213). It is suspected that several million Canadians and U.S. citizens are infected each year. Once believed to be a virus, it is a highly contagious infection caused by obligate, intracellular organisms classified as bacteria (Leukenfeld & Haverkos, 1993). Chlamydia is transmitted through sexual intercourse. It is a difficult disease to diagnose because it often produces no symptoms in its early stages. If symptoms appear (approximately 3 weeks after exposure), the most often-reported complaints are, for women, a slight vaginal discharge and pain during coitus and, for men, pain on urination and a urethral discharge. To complicate matters further, if symptoms do appear, they are often mistakenly attributed to some other malady.

Chlamydia is responsible for about half of the cases of pelvic inflammatory disease in women. In addition the disease can be transmitted to infants as they pass through the birth canal. Roughly 120,000 infants in the United States each year

---

[7] A woman with genital herpes need not fear infecting her unborn infant provided she fully informs her physician of her condition. Should an outbreak of HSV occur near or during the birth process, the child can still be safely delivered by a cesarean section.

develop eye infections or pneumonia as a result of chlamydia. Left untreated, a male may become sterile.

Chlamydia can be treated successfully in its early stages with antibiotics. More important, it can be prevented. The use of condoms and spermicidal foam offers excellent protection against the disease (Ammer, 1983; Kronholm, 1986; Leukenfeld & Haverkos, 1993; Lumiere & Cook, 1983).

Acquired Immune Deficiency Syndrome (AIDS)

The story of this final sexually transmitted disease begins in March, 1981, when a group of epidemiologists at the Centers for Disease Control in Atlanta noticed something unusual. In the Los Angeles area five homosexuals had died during the previous 18 months of a rare protozoan infection that causes pneumonia. Intrigued by their finding, the researchers were also surprised, on further investigation, to discover that an unusually large number of homosexuals had died from a very rare skin malignancy called Kaposi's sarcoma. Both diseases had been known to strike people undergoing immunosuppressive therapy (typically to prevent the body's rejection of a transplanted organ). But why would these diseases attack these two groups and, as time went on, other people? The answer to this riddle, called acquired immune deficiency syndrome (AIDS), can be found in a retrovirus (HIV) that destroys the body's ability to ward off disease (Leukefeld & Fimbres, 1987; Leukefeld & Haverkos, 1993; West, 1983).[8]

HIV is a retrovirus. Regular viruses, like the ones that cause the flu, are made of DNA (deoxyribonucleic acid), the genetic material that is the building block of all living things. DNA viruses operate by infecting the body, penetrating a cell, and using the cell's machinery to make more viruses. Eventually the cell bursts, sending additional virus copies into the body to infect other cells. This process continues, causing the misery we all associate with colds and the flu, until the body's immune system stops the viral infection (Weiss, 1993).

Retroviruses differ from regular viruses in a significant, insidious, and disturbing way. Rather than being composed of DNA, retroviruses are made up of RNA (ribonucleic acid). RNA serves as DNA's messenger in communicating the instructions that determine the makeup of every cell in our body. Thus a retrovirus—unlike a regular virus, which the immune system of the body can detect, attack, and destroy—alters the original DNA blueprint to become a part of the cell's genetic code. As part of the genetic DNA blueprint, the retrovirus will continue to multiply, spreading throughout the body, and will appear in varying concentrations in its fluids (i.e., in semen, blood, saliva, tears, and other body fluids).

Whether that is a permanent part of the cell's genetic code is, for the first time, open to speculation. A recent report in the *New England Journal of Medicine* raises hope that if the disease is detected early enough the use of interleukin-12 can

---

[8]There are actually two HIV retroviruses, HIV-1 and HIV-2. The second appears to be less virulent than the first (Cohen, 1995).

stimulate the production of helper T cells. It appears interleukin-12 "jump starts" the battery of immune resistance and encourages the body to fight the infectious agent in *some* individuals. The *untested* belief is that if this drug and others can be administered early in the course of the infection when the T cell count is still high and, hopefully, the retrovirus has not made its way into certain difficult-to-reach body tissues, such as the brain, the body might, and we emphasize the word *might*, be able to rid itself of the retrovirus or at least stop its insidious destructive progress (Hall, 1995). While we hope that this line of clinical research proves fruitful, until many more successful trials are held, common opinion remains that a retrovirus infection is lifelong. Thus, an AIDS infection is lifelong. Indeed, recent reports in *Science* gives discouraging news that the powerful so-called "cocktails" being used to treat AIDS are not proving as effective as originally thought for three very different reasons. First, the difficulty of taking numerous pills several times a day means some individuals simply do not comply with the treatment program. Next, this retrovirus mutates with alarming speed. Thus, it outwits the drugs intended to suppress it. Last, early media reports of HIV-positive individuals testing negative after treatment with the powerful new drug combinations were hasty. As ever-more-sensitive testing has developed, researchers are finding that HIV was not totally eliminated from the body (Balter, 1997; Balter & Cohen, 1998; Cohen, 1997; Ho, 1998; Perrin & Telenti, 1998).

The retrovirus that is responsible for AIDS is so deadly because it sets up home in the T blood cells that orchestrate the body's immune defense system. By attaching itself to the CD4 protein receptor and other spots on the T cell (i.e., chemokine receptors), the HIV retrovirus enters its T cell host (Cohen, 1996a,c). These T cells are gradually destroyed by still unknown processes as the disease progresses, making its victims vulnerable to a host of cruel opportunistic diseases (Balter, 1998b; Curran et al., 1985; Runck, 1986).

Despite the intensive efforts of hundreds of research centers around the world, no cure or preventive vaccine has been developed yet to control one of the deadliest diseases that humankind has ever encountered. HIV has been reported in every country. U.S. Census data indicate that from 1985 to the close of 1995, over 426,000 people have been diagnosed with AIDS (U.S. Census Bureau, 1997, p. 141, Chart 213). Of that number, 305,843 have died (U.S. Census Bureau, 1997, p. 100, Chart 133). One need not be a mathematician to realize how deadly AIDS is.

Examining AIDS cases by age distribution for 1996 reveals that 1041 individuals (1.5% of new cases) were under the age of 19 when diagnosed with the disease. For 1996 and historically, it is the age groups 20 to 29 (14.6% of new cases) and 30 to 39 (44.8% of new cases) that AIDS strikes hardest. In light of the 3 to 15 years it takes for the HIV infection to lower the T cell count and thus expose the individual to harm, this finding is not surprising. What is very distressing, however, is the thought that the HIV retrovirus was contracted during high school or college by many of these young adults (U.S. Census Bureau, 1997, p. 142, Chart 215).

AIDS occurs more frequently among Black and Latino adolescents than White youths because of unprotected heterosexual practices and the use of dirty needles.

AIDS is not transmitted by casual contact.

In respect to Black adolescents, DiClemente (1993) notes that 13- to 19-year-old Black youths are 5 times more likely to have been diagnosed with AIDS than White youths. For Black females, in particular, who are 11 times more likely than White adolescent females to be diagnosed with AIDS, the problem is particularly alarming. Latinos are also at greater risk for AIDS. The spread of HIV to Latinos occurs through the typical methods of exchange of bodily fluids through unprotected sex and sharing needles (Nyamathi and Vasquez, 1995; Yep, 1995).

Both Yep (1995) and Nyamathi and Vasquez (1995) suggest that culturally appropriate AIDS prevention is missing for Latinos because current efforts are not reducing the rapid increase in the AIDS rate among this group. A similar argument has been made for Black adolescents. Effective AIDS prevention must take into account cultural factors that heighten risk related to unprotected sex and sharing needles.

For example, one culturally relevant characteristic of Blacks and other ethnic diverse groups is social support. This positive characteristic has been found to play a significant role in low-income Black adolescents' engagement in risky sexual behavior. In general, Black adolescents, particularly males, with lower social support engaged in more risky sexual behaviors (St. Lawrence, Brasfield, Jefferson, Allyene, & Shirley, 1994). Black adolescents reporting lower social support: (a) were unlikely to believe that condoms had a positive effect on relationships or sexual behaviors, (b) had less confidence in their self-control, (c) had more negative attitudes toward condom usage, (d) perceived that they were at less risk when engaging in sexual encounters, (e) were more reluctant to address the subject of condom usage in a sexual relationship, (f) were more likely to believe that those who use condoms are more promiscuous, and (g) placed less importance on safety in a relationship (St. Lawrence et al., 1994).

Why is low social support associated with greater risk in respect to sexual activity and what are the dynamics that serve as protective factors against engagement in risky sexual behaviors? St. Lawrence et al. (1994) suggest that adolescents with fewer social supports have fewer sources from whom they can learn about safe vs unsafe sex. Since learning the facts about protecting oneself in sexual encounters is a prerequisite to actual behavior, having reliable sources of information about protective actions is critical. The more sources from whom adolescents can draw knowledge, the greater the likelihood of responsible outcomes. However, knowledge alone cannot create safe sexual practices. Adolescents must feel that they are capable to take protective actions and that the actions they take can protect them from HIV infection. Lack of social support might undermine youths' feelings of confidence and adequacy in themselves and the actions they take.

In contrast, high social support aids adolescents in the development of social competency skills, which in turn can help them exhibit more safe sexual practices through the use of assertiveness, communication, and problem-solving skills (St. Lawrence et al., 1994). Greater social competency has a circular function; that is, it is developed through interactions with others and then serves to build and strengthen one's social support network. It can be concluded from the findings of St. Lawrence et al. (1994) that in addition to heightened social support, Black adolescents can benefit from increased knowledge about the consequences of unprotected sex and how they can protect themselves.

Currently, it is estimated that 1.5 million people in the U.S. have been infected by HIV (Rosenberg, 1995). This number is certain to grow in the coming years. Although the risk to heterosexuals is increasing as the disease spreads beyond the high-risk populations, the majority of reported North American AIDS cases remain either intravenous drug users or homosexual/bisexual males and their partners. The remaining at-risk population includes recipients of contaminated blood transfusions and infants born to infected mothers (Booth, 1988; Leukenfeld & Haverkos, 1993; Runck, 1986; U.S. Census Bureau, 1997, p. 142, Chart 215).

HIV is transmitted in the following ways: by sexual intercourse, the sharing of unsterilized needles between drug users, contaminated blood transfusions, and an infected mother's giving birth or breast feeding. HIV *may* also be transmitted through oral–genital sex. We make this last statement cautiously as it is based on a single study of primates (monkeys) exposed to HIV-1 and anecdotal clinical reports. In the primate study, varying concentrations of the retrovirus were administered orally to the primates. All developed AIDS at HIV concentrations less than would be experienced in anal sex but more than in needle IV transmission. The authors note that kissing, sharing food utensils, or toothbrushes "have not been associated with HIV-1 transmission." The needed concentration to infect the primates (and possibly humans) would be found in blood or the semen of an HIV-positive individual (Baba, Trichel, An, Liska, Martin, Murphey-Corb, & Ruprecht, 1996, p. 1488).

HIV progresses in the following manner. In the beginning, an exposed individual tests positive for AIDS antibodies but otherwise appears healthy. At one time the word "dormant" was used. However, recent research suggests that the retrovirus is multiplying rapidly in sites within the lymph nodes and related organs like the spleen, tonsils, and adenoids (Ho, 1996). As the disease weakens the immune system, individuals begin to experience noticeably swollen glands, near-constant fevers in excess of 100°, persistent diarrhea, and chronic fatigue.

As the disease destroys the immune system, the body becomes vulnerable to any number of opportunistic diseases. It is these infections that kill an AIDS carrier. Currently, there is no reliable estimate of how many individuals infected with the HIV retrovirus will develop AIDS. The most recent data place the risk of developing AIDS from the date of an HIV-positive test at 2% after 2 years, 35% from 2 to 7 years, and 50% after 10 years (Brookmeyer, 1991). After 20 years, 15% of HIV-positive individuals remain without the AIDS diagnosis. It has been suggested that these individuals may be infected with a less virulent form of HIV (HIV-2) or that they may have special characteristics certainly deserving study (Haynes, Pantaleo, & Fauci, 1996).

As there is a latent period from a few months to several years between testing HIV-positive and the onset of symptoms, individuals may transmit the disease without realizing that they are carriers (Centers for Disease Control, 1983a,b; Runck, 1986). Although the retrovirus has been found in tears and saliva, these fluids apparently do not carry the retrovirus in sufficient quantity to cause an infection. Blood and semen can carry the viral load in sufficient quantity to infect others. The key to infection, of course, is the entry of the retrovirus in sufficient quantity through a break in the skin or other bodily tissue to permit the entry of HIV into the bloodstream. Thus behaviors that expose an individual to high concentrations of the retrovirus are ill advised. These are the sharing of needles, anal sex, or ingesting semen. *No evidence exists to suggest that AIDS can be transmitted by casual or even close daily contact with AIDS victims.* Various drugs, such as AZT, Videx (ddI), DDC (zalcitabine), and interleukin-12 are being used to provide help to patients struggling with AIDS (Kolata, 1987a; *Science,* 1991b; Hall, 1995; Johnston and Hoth, 1993). Until such time as a cure or vaccine is developed, we strongly urge sexually active individuals to take the following steps to help prevent the spread of this fatal disease (Koop, 1987; Leukenfeld & Haverkos, 1993; Runck, 1986):

1. Avoid sexual contact with persons who are HIV-positive or have AIDS.
2. Avoid engaging in sex with multiple partners or with others who have multiple partners.
3. Avoid sex with intravenous drug users.
4. Homosexuals (or anyone for that matter) should not use amyl nitrate to facilitate lovemaking. This drug is an immunosuppressant, the worst possible agent to have in your body.
5. Avoid sexual practices that damage body tissues (for example, anal intercourse).
6. *Insist that you and your sexual partner use latex condoms and spermicidal foam!*

The Treatment and Prevention of Sexually Transmitted Diseases

Before the development of penicillin and other antibiotics, syphilis and gonorrhea sufferers were treated with mercury, arsenic, and other assorted home remedies. Syphilis, gonorrhea, and chlamydia can be successfully treated. That is, if the infected individual cooperates with the treatment process. This means completing the required course of medication. Failure to do so results not only in the risk of continued infection and the spread of that infection to others but also in making that infection resistant to medications. Herpes, while it has no known cure, can be treated to reduce the uncomfortable effects of an attack and prevent a secondary infection. These diseases need not be damaging, even to the fetus, if the sexually active adolescent who has the slightest suspicion of sexually transmitted disease seeks medical help. It is natural for adolescents to be embarrassed over suspecting themselves of being infected, but with helpful, youth-oriented programs in family-planning clinics, local health departments, and Planned Parenthood offices, they need not fear ostracism or unsympathetic care. These organizations recognize and appreciate the adolescents' dilemma and treat their their clients with respect and dignity.

The astute reader will have noticed that we have not included AIDS in the above paragraph. Adolescents must recognize that *the only way to beat AIDS is to prevent AIDS*. In the process of preventing AIDS, the adolescent will also prevent other sexually transmitted diseases. It is nice to encourage, and we certainly would encourage young people to consider, sexual abstinence. Assuming one is not an illegal IV drug user, abstinence is the only 100% guaranteed method for avoiding sexually transmitted disease. However, until such time as the majority of the adolescents in the United States and Canada who are sexually active elect abstinence, we will urge that sexually active adolescents practice safer sex. Safer sex is more than latex condoms. Safer sex is latex condoms and foam. The condom works by providing a barrier to keep infected and uninfected areas from touching. In the event that the condom fails, foams such as Delfen, Emko, Ortho, Conceptrol, and others, used before intercourse, reduce the chances of becoming infected with sexually transmitted bacteria. The effectiveness of these foams on viruses is uncertain. But safer sex is more than latex condoms and foam; it is knowing your partner and your partner's sexual history. The mind set for adolescents to have is that they are having sex not only with their partner but also with whomever their partner has ever had sex. Incidentally, that mind set tends to encourage condom and foam use. Finally, adolescents need to learn to check sexual partners for signs of sexually transmitted disease before engaging in intercourse. We encourage foreplay, mutual showers, and a thorough exploration of each other's bodies before intercourse. If something doesn't look right, we urge you to ask about it. We want you to remember that if you decide to become sexually active, it is your responsibility to protect yourself. Those are our thoughts. What would you propose to do? Take a moment and think of prevention's technology. How would you use education, the promotion of social competency, natural caregiving, and community organization/systems intervention to reduce the incidence of sexually transmitted diseases? (see Box 11-4.)

BOX **11-4** **AIDS: Questions and Answers**

In 1981, we began to include in our class lectures a brief discussion about AIDS. Needless to say, as HIV began to threaten humanity, the amount of time we devoted to the subject grew. The following are the most frequently asked questions that come out of those classes and our responses.

Q: What are my chances of contracting AIDS?

A: One study has calculated the risk from a single act of intercourse at one in five billion, assuming that a latex condom is used and the sexual partner is "low risk." The risk increases dramatically if the partner is a prostitute, bisexual, homosexual, an IV drug user, or if a condom is not used.

Q: If I test positive for the retrovirus, does that mean I will die?

A: Frankly, no one knows for sure. One study in *Science* reported that a sample of 84 homosexual and bisexual men who had tested positive for HIV all went on to develop AIDS. Discouraging as this information is, it cannot be generalized to the entire HIV-positive population. It is believed that nearly 1.5 million people in the United States and millions worldwide currently are carrying the virus. Most of these people are now healthy. It is important to understand that a positive test result is not a diagnosis of AIDS. Furthermore, it does not mean the individual will develop AIDS. Rather it is a sign that the individual has been exposed to the retrovirus. For example, it appears that in the two forms that HIV appears one form (HIV-2) is less virulent than the other. Studies are reporting that individuals carrying HIV-2 have remained AIDS free for up to 25 years in some cases. Further, there may be individual factors involving lifestyle, heredity, or something else that provide immunity against the virus for that individual. The important thing to remember is that once infected, always infected. Caution must be exercised to ensure that the virus is not spread further.

Q: Why don't we quarantine HIV-positive people and AIDS victims from the rest of society? Aren't they a health risk?

A: Providing the HIV-positive individual or AIDS victim is not engaging in illegal IV drug use or unsafe sexual practices, there is no need to remove him or her from society. The retrovirus is very difficult to contract. It requires direct contact between HIV-carrying fluids and the blood of another individual. In fact, as of the summer of 1998 there had been no reports of any one contracting the retrovirus from any activity short of blood-to-blood contact. Having said this, there is a concern that oral–genital sex may also be a means of transmitting the retrovirus. Therefore until more is known, oral intercourse is being discouraged by health authorities.

Q: Can oral–genital sex give you the HIV retrovirus?

A: First, it should be noted that this concern emerges from a single monkey study in which concentrated HIV was administered orally to the primates. Each primate became infected with HIV that developed into AIDS. Taking this laboratory study and applying it to humans, the transmission vehicle would be the semen the male ejaculates and the vaginal fluids the female emits during oral–genital sex. While the good news is that human saliva has a chemical composition that destroys the HIV, the sheer amount of semen or vaginal fluids ingested may overwhelm the capacity of the salvia to do this. For oral–genital sex, the suspected entry points of HIV into the bloodstream are the tonsils or bleeding gums (i.e., gingivitis).

Q: Could I become infected with HIV by sharing a water bottle with someone?

A: As we noted earlier, HIV is present in all body fluids. The concentration of the retrovirus in saliva or tears is quite low in comparison to the concentration in either blood or semen. In studies of health workers and family members in "casual" contact with an AIDS victim, there does not exist a single case of transmission. The few reports that do exist of health workers who have tested positive for the retrovirus are the result of blood-to-blood exposure in which the worker was exposed to large amounts of retrovirus-carrying material. By that we mean needle pricks where the risk has been calculated at 1 in 200 episodes, exposure in the research laboratory by spilling retrovirus samples on broken skin, or exposure in an emergency situation in which the health worker trying to control a victim's bleeding had a break in the skin that came in contact with the victim's blood. These facts are extremely encouraging and support the contention that this is a very difficult disease to catch. Again, however, until more is known regarding the pathogenicity of the retrovirus, health officials advise avoiding the exchange of bodily fluids including the fluids generated in oral sex for the reasons cited above.

Q: I've heard that you can go crazy from AIDS.

A: Sadly, the retrovirus does travel to the brain. The term "AIDS dementia complex" describes the condition that results from that infection. Symptoms range from forgetfulness and a loss of balance to severe depression and incontinence (loss of bladder control).

Q: I heard that the virus was a biological warfare experiment that got out of hand. Is this true?

A: It is true that some elements in the former Soviet Union had reported that AIDS was a U.S. biological warfare experiment gone wrong. However, there is no evidence to support this contention. The evidence strongly suggests that AIDS originated in Africa. It has been found that the African green monkey carries a retrovirus almost identical to HIV. Some suggest that this retrovirus crossed the species barrier and infected humans. Of particular interest are published reports of serum and tissue samples collected from Africans in the 1970s and as early as 1959 that have tested positive for HIV. In large part this would explain the pandemic spread of the disease in central Africa. For example, it is presently estimated that 25% of the adult population in Botswana and Zimbabwe are HIV-positive.

Q: If the retrovirus has been found in frozen serum and tissue samples dating back 30 years, why has it only recently appeared in developed nations?

A: Recognizing that we are now speculating and that no one knows for sure, we surmise that the retrovirus may have been spread from infected Africans to French-speaking Haitians who went to central Africa to work in the 1960s after the colonial powers withdrew. Infected Haitians returning home may have passed the retrovirus to vacationing homosexuals from the United States. The disease spread rapidly among homosexuals because they tended to maintain a closed community and because many had numerous sexual partners. The second possible explanation is that for many years the United States purchased human blood from Africa.

Q: I heard AIDS came from a polio vaccine. Is this true?

A: In the March, 1992 issue of *Rolling Stone*, Tom Curtis reported the theory of Blaine Elswood and Raphael Stricker that the AIDS virus might have crossed the species barrier from monkeys to people through a tainted polio vaccine. It is a fact that some early polio vaccines were manufactured using monkey tissue. It is also true that simian immunodeficiency virus (SIV) is a relative to the human AIDS virus. Furthermore, in the July 31, 1992 issue of *Science*, it was reported that the Centers for Disease Control has identified two cases in which SIV had infected laboratory workers. It should be noted that in both instances the contact was blood-to-blood.

Q: Does this mean science fiction has become science fact? We've created the seeds of our own self-destruction as a species!

A: Whoa, don't go "B" movie quite yet. First, it is a hypothesis that has not been substantiated. Second, many authorities deny its feasibility. Third, other SIV possibilities also exist. For example, given that two laboratory workers contracted SIV after direct blood-to-blood exposure to contaminated blood products, why could that not have been the means for exposing countless others in Africa. Well, monkey meat is a food source in equatorial Africa. Contact with contaminated meat might have transmitted SIV to humans. A second possibility might be a bite from an infected monkey might have transmitted the disease. (Now wasn't there a movie using that as the premise for transmitting a rapidly spreading fatal virus?) If monkeys were the original host, once the species barrier was crossed, transmission between humans across the African continent was accelerated

(continues)

(continued)

by the common use of unsterilized needles during—get this—vaccination campaigns to reduce disease!

Q: Are adolescents as a population really at risk for AIDS?

A: Most certainly, sexually active adolescents are at high risk for the disease given their failure to practice safe sex. It appears that at best 50% of sexually active adolescents practice partially safe sex with the use of a condom. Disturbingly, some studies report that as high as three-quarters of sexually active adolescent females do not insist on safe sex.

Q: If the HIV retrovirus is so dangerous, why don't we test everyone?

A: First, it would not be cost effective. Second, just because you tested negative for the virus today does not mean that if you have been exposed that 6 months from now you would not test positive. The better approaches to spending those dollars, providing you are not in a high-risk group, are for preventing the spread of the disease and for developing a vaccine and cure for this deadly disease.

Q: Does that mean no one should be tested?

A: If you believe yourself to be in a high-risk group (homosexual, bisexual, IV drug user, an individual with multiple sex partners who has not practiced safe sex, hemophiliac, or the partner of a member of the aforementioned groups) you should seriously consider being tested. Further, if you are a pregnant woman the Centers for Disease Control now recommend that you also be tested. Recent studies suggest that an infant born to an HIV-positive woman can be protected from that disease if the pregnant woman takes AZT.

Q: I have heard that my risk for HIV infection is not great if I am male and exclusively heterosexual. And yet I read about sports stars and others who have become infected with the HIV retrovirus. It doesn't make sense.

A: This is a difficult question to answer. If I told you your risk of receiving the AIDS retrovirus was 1 in 40,000, which is the latest estimate, then you would feel quite comforted. That is, unless you happened to be the 1 in 40,000. It appears that it is harder for a male to receive the retrovirus from a woman than it is for a woman to receive it from a man. However,

as you increase the number of sexual partners, the number of times unsafe sex occurs, and practices that increase the chance of the transmission of blood, risk increases.

Q: Why am I at greater risk if I am a female?

A: It is into your body the male ejaculates. This fluid, which may contain the retrovirus, has a longer opportunity to find damaged tissue than does the fluid your body deposits on the circumcised penis. Risk increased dramatically for males if they are not circumcised. Therefore, it is in your best interest to insist on safe sex or no sex.

Q: What if my male partner has the HIV retrovirus and I am pregnant by him or want to become pregnant by him? What is my risk and the risk for my baby?

A: First, please talk to your doctor. These are questions best answered by a medical expert. If your sexual experiences did not involve infected fluid-to-blood contact then there is a very good probability you are not infected. Can you carry a child from an HIV-infected individual? A report in *Science* suggests that it is the ejaculated fluid and not the sperm that carries the retrovirus. If this report is correct, then it is conceivable that someday sperm free of fluid could be artificially implanted. But again, these are tentative findings and should be discussed with your doctor.

Q: If my partner and I are infected with the virus will our child be infected?

A: Not necessarily. More than 40% of children born to HIV-infected individuals do not test positive for the virus. Further, it appears that taking AZT during pregnancy can prevent the transmission of the retrovirus to the unborn fetus. Even more interesting is a recent report in *Science* that some infants appear able to clear HIV from their bloodstream. However, again, we urge you to seek good medical advice before making any decisions.

Q: Can I become infected with HIV by French kissing?

A: How about a yes/no answer. Here's the yes part. The CDC reported in the summer of 1997 that an HIV-infected man who had bleeding gums and canker sores transmitted the retrovirus through a French kiss to a female who also had bleeding gums. The transmission path in this case was blood leaked from bleeding gums of the infected person to cracks in the gums of the other individual.

Here's the no part. Although the retrovirus can be found in low concentrations in saliva, it is considered unlikely. What works in your favor here is: (1) the low concentration of HIV in saliva and (2) the "killing" power of your own salvia to destroy HIV. Still, the CDC recommends that if a partner is known to have HIV French kissing should be avoided because of the possibility of bleeding gums.

Q: Why should I worry about AIDS? Modern medicine will develop a cure for this problem.

A: The most optimistic reports are that a vaccine might be developed by 2010. Furthermore, AIDS is caused by a retrovirus that appears in several genetic variations. Thus, one vaccine—even several vaccines—may not be enough to provide immunity. If you plan to become sexually active before a cure is found, we would encourage you to worry. Worry motivates you to exercise caution and motivates you to protect yourself and your partner.

Q: OK, I'm worried. What advice would you offer?

A: For those seeking complete protection, celibacy or practicing masturbation (providing you are not an illegal IV drug user) are the two most certain means of avoiding the retrovirus. As one strays from this path, the risk increases. Ways of reducing the risk are to know your partner's previous sexual history, avoid sexual practices that damage tissues (for example, anal sex), avoid the exchange of body fluids containing blood, and, most of all, use a latex condom and foam.

(Baba et al., 1996; Balter, 1998, 1998b,c; Buckingham & Van Gorp, 1988; Cohen 1995, 1996b, 1997; Curran et al., 1985; Kanki, Alroy, & Essex, 1985; Letvin, 1998; Lui, Darrow, & Rutherford, 1988; Marx, 1986, 1989; Piot et al., 1988; Price et al., 1988 Runck, 1986; Viscarello, 1990; Guilian, Vaca, & Noonan, 1990; New York Times Service, 1990; Davidson & Grant, 1988; Goodman & Cohall, 1989; Bloom & Glied, 1991; Science, 1989; Marx, 1989; Segest, Mygind, Harris, & Bay, 1991; Moore & Rosenthal, 1991; Palca, 1991; Catania et al., 1992; Fox, 1992; Curtis, 1992; Select Committee on Children, Youth, and Families, 1992; Thompson, 1996).

Adolescent Prostitution

North Americans are apparently fascinated with adolescent prostitution, given the constant stream of films and cyberporn sites devoted to the subject. Other than these Hollywood and Internet versions of life on the streets, what do we know of prostitution? First, it is as old as recorded history. Second, child prostitution is not unique to this century. In England before 1814, for example, girls were officially allowed to become prostitutes at the age of 12; the age was changed to 13 in 1875 and to 16 in 1885 (Baizerman, Thompson, & Stafford-White, 1979; Downs & Hillje, 1993; Zacks, 1994). The circumstances of one child prostitute can be found in DeQuincey's (1856/1950) *Confessions of an English Opium-Eater*. In that classic tale of addiction and redemption, he describes his caring relationship with the "peripatetic" (street-walker) Ann, a homeless girl of 16 who prostitutes in London's backalleys.

Then as today, young people exchanged sexual services for money, with the fee dependent on the service rendered. Today in some parts of the United States manual masturbation (a "hand job") might cost as little as $25 while on either coast the charge may be as high as $50. A "French massage" (oral sex) can

As in the past, the majority of johns are middle-aged, middle-class males. Prostitution offers a quick means to cash.

vary from $60 to $75, and "half and half" (a progression from manual stimulation to oral or vaginal intercourse) can cost from $80 to several hundred dollars.

In a review of the literature Rickel and Hendren (1993) and others (Brown, 1979; Caplan, 1984; Newton-Ruddy & Handelsman, 1986; Vitaliano, Boyer, & James, 1981) suggest several explanations for juvenile prostitution. Rickel and her associate Hendren report that family relationships are strained and that parental sexual abuse is common. They speculate that normlessness, poor education, and poor employment prospects also help to push a young person onto the streets. Other factors may contribute to a decision to stay there. For example, Caplan (1984) observes that pimps often fulfill parental needs for these young girls, and Brown (1979) notes that an element of adventure is involved and that the financial rewards of prostitution can be high. Few other jobs pay from $200 to $1000 a day tax-free, and for the adolescent on the run who needs cash quickly, prostitution offers a means to acquire it:

> Listen, man, I'm 14 years old. Can't even work yet. But I gotta have money. Nobody's gonna take care of me. So I visit Danny [a store manager] and look, you know, sexy. Well, he gets turned on and starts squeezing me. So I says, "I'll let ya touch me if I can have those jeans over there." Christ, he threw the stuff I wanted at me—he wanted it so bad.

Other factors, such as early forced sexual relations, association with delinquent peers, and drug abuse, can combine with a sense of powerlessness, anger, and hatred to push an adolescent into prostitution. Many studies report strong antifather feelings expressed by female prostitutes who, in these authors' judgment, are "symbolically castrating them" (Brown, 1979, p. 672).

Baizerman, Thompson, and Stafford-White (1979), in an article based on their professional contacts with teenage prostitutes, provide support for Brown's (1979) observations. To the possible surprise of many, they note that many young prostitutes, without their parents' knowledge, service businessmen after school.

In a study of Canadian youth similar findings appear. In a sample of 100 male and female prostitutes, young people reported very negative feelings toward their families. These feelings contributed to their decision to leave home at an early age. In the case of females, that average age was less than 14 years old. This unhappiness with family life in many instances involved sexual abuse by a close family member. Finally, the authors suggest that different motivational factors may affect the decision of males to enter into prostitution. They raise the question for further study of whether "for males, sexual preference [homosexuality] may influence entry into prostitution" (Earls & David, 1990, p. 10).

For males, it appears the pathways to prostitution are similar. Most are school dropouts. There is a history of early physical or sexual abuse. Broken homes are common. Entry into prostitution frequently occurs between the ages of 11 and 25, with older males between the ages of 30 to 50 serving as clients. In one study 60% of the youth interviewed had experienced an STD (Markos and Wade, 1994). In another study of New Orleans adolescent males, 66% acknowledged they turned tricks not using condoms. When this high-risk behavior is combined with the admission that 45% were IV drug users, it should not be surprising that 25% at the time of the study were HIV-positive (Simon, Morse, Osofsky, & Balson, 1994).

Brown (1979) and Baizerman and his colleagues (1979) do not find the outlook for preventing teenage prostitution particularly bright. They note that such factors as societal rejection, poor family life, and the plain fact that prostitution pays so well combine to encourage rather than discourage it. Baizerman and his associates propose a combined approach of education and shelter homes to help young people in or at risk of prostitution. Education would focus on a "nonscare approach" of information and discussions with teenage prostitutes. Shelter homes would offer girls wanting to get out of prostitution the medical, legal, and educational/vocational help necessary to work in some other area.

SUMMARY

Consider for a moment the themes that emerged from this chapter. First, we saw that none of the behaviors discussed were recent to this time. Whether adolescent pregnancy, sexually transmitted diseases, or prostitution, each has been part of the human saga since that story was first told. Second, we saw how each of these issues are woven into that story in interconnecting ways. Remember that development occurs in context. Next, we saw how in several instances diverse youths differed from White youths in sexual behavior and attitudes. Finally, we discussed prevention initiatives that use education, natural caregiving, and community organization/systems change to improve the life circumstances of these young people.

Finally, we need to recognize that the solutions to the problems described in this chapter are not simple, nor are they easy. Attacking these situations constructively calls first for a realization that such behaviors exist and cannot be stopped with moralistic statements. Only then can society begin to address the needs of these young people.

MAJOR POINTS TO REMEMBER

1. Although birth control methods are widely available, this year more than 1 in 10 adolescents will become pregnant this year. About half that number will carry to term.
2. The problems facing the expectant teenager are many, including poor future educational employment prospects, lower marital satisfaction, and a high divorce rate.
3. Researchers are divided on why some adolescents become pregnant and others don't. Some investigators find evidence for psychological explanations, while others state that it is really nothing more than dumb, blind, unfortunate luck.
4. The family life of many adolescents who become pregnant has been described as very stressful before the pregnancy, but the relationship between the adolescent and her mother is thought to improve during the time the adolescent is pregnant.
5. Until recently, little attention has been paid to the adolescent father. Although he appears to be less prepared than his sexual partner for parenthood, he has been found to be caring and concerned in most studies.
6. Most of the fathers of children born to adolescent mothers are not adolescents.
7. Social support appears to be a supportive factor for African-American adolescent mothers. However, the potential for conflict and exhibition of negative parenting behaviors exist particularly when mothers and grandmothers share parenting responsibilities.
8. Although contraceptive knowledge dates back thousands of years, it is only in the past few decades that many adolescents have had access to birth control devices. Even so, few teenagers use them.
9. Explanations for not using contraceptives include feeling uncomfortable about one's sexuality, lack of information, relationship factors, and a desire to become pregnant.

10. The organisms that cause sexually transmitted diseases are highly vulnerable to light, air, and dryness. As luck would have it, the human body is dark, without air, and moist, providing the perfect incubator for the growth of these extremely harmful diseases.

11. Sexually transmitted diseases could be brought under control if only sexually active individuals would combine the use of condoms with vaginal foams.

12. African Americans and Hispanics are at heightened risk for HIV infection. Since it appears that current prevention efforts among these groups are not effective, it is necessary to design prevention programs that are culturally relevant.

13. Social support is a factor that can serve a protective function against HIV, while use of alcohol and drugs heighten risk for HIV infection.

14. Sexual responsibility is a shared responsibility.

15. Strained family relationships, often including parental sexual abuse, the desire for adventure, and the economic lure are some of the factors that draw young people into prostitution.

Substance Use and Abuse in Adolescence

The recovery of the sick is often delayed, sometimes entirely prevented, by the habitual use of tobacco or opium.... The use of tobacco is a pernicious habit in whatever form it is introduced into the system. Its active principle, Nicotine, which is an energetic poison, exerts its specific effect on the nervous system, tending to stimulate it to an unnatural degree of activity, the final result of which is weakness, or even paralysis... Tobacco, when its use becomes habitual and excessive, gives rise to the most unpleasant and dangerous pathological conditions, oppressive stupor, weakness or loss of intellect, softening of the brain, paralysis, nervous debility, dyspepsia, functional derangement of the heart, and diseases of the liver and kidneys.... Dr. King says, "A patient under treatment should give up the use of tobacco, or his physician should assume no responsibility in his case...." The opium habit, to which allusion has also been made, is open to the same objections (Pierce, 1895, pp. 384–385).

THE PRECEDING PASSAGE illustrates one of the problems in writing a chapter on substance use. The author of that passage, R. V. Pierce, M.D., of the Invalid's Hotel and Surgical Institute and president of a mail-order patent-medicine firm specializing in such remedies as Dr. Pierce's Favorite Prescription and Dr. Pierce's Compound Extract of Smartweed, is not unlike many writers and researchers both then and now who carry their personal convictions about substance use over into their work. The result is confusion, misrepresentation, and the creation of a credibility gap so wide that many young people beginning to experiment with alcohol or drugs reject any and all findings that portray one or the other in an unfavorable light.

In this chapter we attempt to unravel myth from reality and fantasy from fact for the substances alcohol, tobacco, marijuana, inhalants, steroids, hallucinogens, stimulants, barbiturates, cocaine, and heroin. In the process we examine the factors that influence some young people to use, others to abuse, and still others to become psychologically and/or physically dependent on alcohol and drugs. Finally, we examine the implications for treating and preventing substance abuse and dependence.

HISTORICAL OVERVIEW

Although today's newspapers and magazines constantly run headlines expressing fear and consternation over the use and abuse of drugs and alcohol by adolescents, the use of these and other substances by young people has never been uncommon. This behavior was not condoned or accepted, but the problem was viewed more as a moral or legal concern rather than as a mental health issue. In fact, much of the addiction to narcotics by youths in the 19th century (and addiction was common) can be traced to the family and its use of store-bought patent-medicines or home-brewed recipes. Most of these contained liberal amounts of opium, which was then easily obtainable (Gullotta & Blau, 1995; Gullotta, Hampton, Senatore, & Eismann, 1998; Jaffe, 1979).

For instance, sandwiched between the "saloon department" and "the Tanner's, Shoe, and Harness Maker's department" in the 1866 edition of *Dr. Chase's Recipes; or Information for Everybody: An Invaluable Collection of about Eight Hundred Practical Recipes*, the good doctor offered this morphine-rich recipe to mom for her family:

> For Nervousness—Nervous Pill—Morphine 9 grs.; extract of stramonium and hyoscyamus, of each 18 grs.; form into pill-mass by using solution of gum arabic and tragacanth, quite thick. Divide into 40 pills. Dose—In case of severe pain or nervousness, 1 pill taken at bedtime will be found to give a quiet night of rest. The advantage of this pill over those depending entirely upon opium or morphine . . . is that they may be taken without fear of constipation (Chase, 1866, pp. 149).

Until well into this century, morphine and other highly addictive substances were easily attainable from a druggist either by direct purchase or through a doctor's prescription. The ease by which these substances could be acquired is made abundantly clear in Eugene O'Neill's (1955/1984) painful depiction of the disintegration of his morphine-addicted mother in the autobiographical play *Long Day's Journey Into Night*.

But before we begin to examine individual substances, we need to clarify some terms. By *substance use* we mean the infrequent and limited intake of alcohol or drugs. *Substance abuse* is the frequent and excessive use of alcohol or drugs such that there is an impairment in the physical, mental, or social functioning of the individual. *Substance dependence* is synonymous with addiction. It is characterized by the need to use alcohol or drugs on a continuous basis to meet psychological or physical needs and to avoid the discomfort of its absence (withdrawal).

ALCOHOL

Consider the following facts:

1. The National Institute on Alcohol Abuse and Alcoholism (NIAAA) estimates that 4.6 million U.S. teenagers ages 14 to 17 experience serious alcohol-related problems (Johnston, O'Malley, & Bachman, 1991).

2. In college, 47% of the student population drinks heavily (Johnston, O'Malley, & Bachman, 1996b).

3. Motor vehicle accidents involving alcohol are the leading cause of death for young people in the United States ages 15 to 19, accounting for 45% of fatalities in this age group (U.S. Department of Health and Human Services, 1985).

4. In the 1997 U.S. senior class, roughly 82% reported using alcohol at least once in their life (Johnston, O'Malley, & Bachman, 1997). In Ontario, Canada for the same year 75% of the senior class made this admission (Paglia & Room, 1999).

5. Twenty-five percent (25.2%) of the U.S. 8th-graders in 1997 reported becoming drunk (Johnston, O'Malley, & Bachman, 1997).

Given these findings, why, to paraphrase an advertising campaign, is drinking so "downright upright"? If the federal government's estimates of the enormous cost of alcohol-related problems are accurate, then society lost nearly $99 billion in 1995 alone (Rouse, 1995). These data certainly lend a second, more serious meaning to W. C. Field's famous film short *The Fatal Glass of Beer.*

At one time alcohol consumption was prohibited in the United States, but that well-known 13-year experiment in sobriety failed. It failed because the simple truth is that drinking makes most people feel good. Furthermore, most people do not abuse or become dependent on alcohol (Nicholson, 1995). Given its unique status in our society (the cocktail hour, the Sunday champagne brunch, the Western saloon, wine tasting parties, the corner bar of countless television shows), it is understandable, but not pardonable, that most North Americans view other drugs as evil or corrupting and alcohol as acceptable despite overwhelming evidence to the contrary.

Initiation into Drug Use: The Alcohol Connection

A popular belief spurred by anxious and well-meaning individuals suggests that a causal relationship exists between the use of marijuana and the pathway to other drugs such as cocaine and heroin. For example, in a recent issue of *Science* two study groups demonstrate that marijuana has addictive qualities related to its ability to stimulate the production of the nuerochemical dopamine (Rodriquez de Fonseca et al., 1997; Tanda et al., 1997).[1] This laboratory evidence, using rats as subjects, is then used to argue that the use of marijuana inevitably creates the need to use a second drug and then a third drug and so on. Interestingly, while proponents of this stage theory begin their argument with marijuana, they ignore the fact that most marijuana users first used alcohol.

In a series of articles Kandel (1981a) and her associates (Kandel, & Faust, 1975; Kandel, Yamaguchi, & Chen 1992; Yamaguchi & Kandel, 1984) have repeatedly

[1]Grinspoon and his associates (1997) caution that while marijuana (and more specifically THC) does activate the dopamine reward system so too do sex and chocolate. These researchers point out that marijuana is about as addictive as caffeine with less of a withdrawl reaction (Grinspoon, Bakelar, Zimmer, & Morgan, 1997).

Alcohol and cigarettes are the pathway drugs into the use of illegal substances.

demonstrated that drug use starts with beer and wine. If there is an entrance drug into the continuum of drug use then it is alcohol. One of their early studies established an order that most adolescents follow in using drugs. This model suggests that the adolescent begins to experiment with socially approved drugs such as beer and wine. For many young people, this first level is the last level; no further drug use occurs. Other young people take a second step to cigarettes and hard liquor. Interestingly, evidence on the tobacco/alcohol connection suggests that those who begin with cigarettes are likely to use hard liquor but those who begin with hard liquor are very unlikely to begin cigarette smoking. "Thus, while drinking can proceed without smoking, smoking is almost always followed by drinking hard liquor. Joint use of hard liquor and cigarettes is associated with the highest rates of entry into illicit drugs" (1975, p. 931). This last point was recently reemphasized by the principal investigator of a longitudinal study of adolescent drug use in the United States. He noted, "Learning to smoke cigarettes is excellent training for learning to smoke marijuana [as] marijuana smoking is almost always preceded by smoking cigarettes" (Johnston, 1996, p. 4).

Kandel and Faust emphasize that while "the data show a very clear-cut sequence in the use of various drugs, they do not prove that the use of a particular drug infallibly leads to the use of other drugs higher up in the sequence" (1975, p. 931). Many youths in their study stopped at one of the three lower levels of involvement, with only a minority proceeding to drugs beyond marijuana. This fact has led Paglia and Room (1999) to challenge the concept of pathways.

Table 12-1 compares the use of alcohol and other drugs between 1975 and 1997. The table shows the percentage of U.S. high school students who reported having used the listed drugs at any time during their lifetime. Alcohol received by far the heaviest use (81.7%), followed by cigarettes (65.4%) and marijuana (49.6%). In

T A B L E   **12-1**   **Long-Term Trends in *Lifetime* Prevalence of Use of Various Drugs for 12th-Graders**

	Class of 1975	Class of 1976	Class of 1977	Class of 1978	Class of 1979	Class of 1980	Class of 1981	Class of 1982	Class of 1983	Class of 1984	Class of 1985
Approx N =	9400	15400	17100	17800	15500	15900	17500	17700	16300	15900	16000
Any illicit drug[a,b]	55.2	58.3	61.6	64.1	65.1	65.4	65.6	64.4	62.9	61.6	60.6
Any illicit drug other than marijuana[a,b]	36.2	35.4	35.8	36.5	37.4	38.7	42.8	41.1	40.4	40.3	39.7
Marijuana/hashish	47.3	52.8	56.4	59.2	60.4	60.3	59.5	58.7	57.0	54.9	54.2
Inhalants[c]	—	10.3	11.1	12.0	12.7	11.9	12.3	12.8	13.6	14.4	15.4
Inhalants, adjusted[e,d]	—	—	—	—	18.2	17.3	17.2	17.7	18.2	18.0	18.1
Amyl/butyl nitrites[e,f]	—	—	—	—	11.1	11.1	10.1	9.8	8.4	8.1	7.9
Hallucinogens	16.3	15.1	13.9	14.3	14.1	13.3	13.3	12.5	11.9	10.7	10.3
Hallucinogens, adjusted[g]	—	—	—	—	17.7	15.6	15.3	14.3	13.6	12.3	12.1
LSd	11.3	11.0	9.8	9.7	9.5	9.3	9.8	9.6	8.9	8.0	7.5
PCP[e,f]	—	—	—	—	12.8	9.6	7.8	6.0	5.6	5.0	4.9
MDMA (ecstasy)[a]	—	—	—	—	—	—	—	—	—	—	—
Cocaine	9.0	9.7	10.8	12.9	15.4	15.7	16.5	16.0	16.2	16.1	17.3
Crack[h]	—	—	—	—	—	—	—	—	—	—	—
Other cocaine[i]	—	—	—	—	—	—	—	—	—	—	—
Heroin[j]	2.2	1.8	1.8	1.6	1.1	1.1	1.1	1.2	1.2	1.3	1.2
Other opiates[k]	9.0	9.6	10.3	9.9	10.1	9.8	10.1	9.6	9.4	9.7	10.2
Stimulants[b,k]	22.3	22.6	23.0	22.9	24.2	26.4	32.2	27.9	26.9	27.9	26.2
Crystal meth. (Ice)[l]	—	—	—	—	—	—	—	—	—	—	—
Sedatives[k,m]	18.2	17.7	17.4	16.0	14.6	14.9	16.0	15.2	14.4	13.3	11.8
Barbiturates[k]	16.9	16.2	15.6	13.7	11.8	11.0	11.3	10.3	9.9	9.9	9.2
Methaqualone[k,m]	8.1	7.8	8.5	7.9	8.3	9.5	10.6	10.7	10.1	8.3	6.7
Tranquilizers[k]	17.0	16.8	18.0	17.0	16.3	15.2	14.7	14.0	13.3	12.4	11.9
Alcohol[n]	90.4	91.9	92.5	93.1	93.0	93.2	92.6	92.8	92.6	92.6	92.2
Been drunk[l]	—	—	—	—	—	—	—	—	—	—	—
Cigarettes	73.6	75.4	75.7	75.3	74.0	71.0	71.0	70.1	70.6	69.7	68.8
Smokeless tobacco[a,o]	—	—	—	—	—	—	—	—	—	—	—
Steroids[l]	—	—	—	—	—	—	—	—	—	—	—

[a]Use of "any illicit drug" includes any use of marijuana, LSD, other hallucinogens, crack, other cocaine, or heroin, *or* any use of other opiates, stimulants, barbiturates, methaqualone (excluded since 1990), or tranquilizers not under a doctor's orders.

[b]Beginning in 1982 the question about stimulant use (i.e., amphetamines) was revised to get respondents to exclude the inappropriate reporting of nonprescription stimulants. The prevalence rate dropped slightly as a result of this methodological change.

[c]Data based on four of five forms in 1976–88; N is four-fifths of N indicated. Data based on five of six forms in 1989–97; N is five-sixths of N indicated.

[d]Adjusted for underreporting of amyl and butyl nitrites. See text for details.

[e]Data based on one form; N is one-fifth of N indicated in 1979–88 and one-sixth of N indicated in 1989–97.

[f]Question text changed slightly in 1987.

[g]Adjusted for underreporting of PCP.

[h]Data based on one of five forms in 1986; N is one-fifth of N indicated. Data based on two forms in 1987–89; N is two-fifths of N indicated in 1987–88 and two-sixths of N indicated in 1989. Data based on six forms in 1990–97.

[i]Data based on one form in 1987–89; N is one-fifth of N indicated in 1987–88 and one-sixth of N indicated in 1989. Data based on four of six forms in 1990–97; N is four-sixths of N indicated.

[j]In 1995 the heroin question was changed in half of the questionnaire forms. Separate questions were asked for use with injection and without injection. Data presented here represent the combined data from all forms.

(continues)

TABLE 12-1 (*continued*)

Class of 1986	Class of 1987	Class of 1988	Class of 1989	Class of 1990	Class of 1991	Class of 1992	Class of 1993	Class of 1994	Class of 1995	Class of 1996	Class of 1997	'96–'97 change
15200	16300	16300	16700	15200	15000	15800	16300	15400	15400	14300	15400	
57.6	56.6	53.9	50.9	47.9	44.1	40.7	42.9	45.6	48.4	50.8	54.3	+3.5s
37.7	35.8	32.5	31.4	29.4	26.9	25.1	26.7	27.6	28.1	28.5	30.0	+1.5s
50.9	50.2	47.2	43.7	40.7	36.7	32.6	35.3	38.2	41.7	44.9	49.6	+4.7ss
15.9	17.0	16.7	17.6	18.0	17.6	16.6	17.4	17.7	17.4	16.6	16.1	−0.5
20.1	18.6	17.5	18.6	18.5	18.0	17.0	17.7	18.3	17.8	17.5	16.9	−0.6
8.6	4.7	3.2	3.3	2.1	1.6	1.5	1.4	1.7	1.5	1.8	2.0	+0.2
9.7	10.3	8.9	9.4	9.4	9.6	9.2	10.9	11.4	12.7	14.0	15.1	+1.1
11.9	10.6	9.2	9.9	9.7	10.0	9.4	11.3	11.7	13.1	14.5	15.4	+0.9
7.2	8.4	7.7	8.3	8.7	8.8	8.6	10.3	10.5	11.7	12.6	13.6	+1.0
4.8	3.0	2.9	3.9	2.8	2.9	2.4	2.9	2.8	2.7	4.0	3.9	−0.1
—	—	—	—	—	—	—	—	—	—	6.1	6.9	+0.8
16.9	15.2	12.1	10.3	9.4	7.8	6.1	6.1	5.9	6.0	7.1	8.7	+1.6s
—	5.4	4.8	4.7	3.5	3.1	2.6	2.6	3.0	3.0	3.3	3.9	+0.6s
—	14.0	12.1	8.5	8.6	7.0	5.3	5.4	5.2	5.1	6.4	8.2	+1.8s
1.1	1.2	1.1	1.3	1.3	0.9	1.2	1.1	1.2	1.6	1.8	2.1	+0.3
9.0	9.2	8.6	8.3	8.3	6.6	6.1	6.4	6.6	7.2	8.2	9.7	+1.5ss
23.4	21.6	19.8	19.1	17.5	15.4	13.9	15.1	15.7	15.3	15.3	16.5	+1.2
—	—	—	—	2.7	3.3	2.9	3.1	3.4	3.9	4.4	4.4	0.0
10.4	8.7	7.8	7.4	7.5	6.7	6.1	6.4	7.3	7.6	8.2	8.7	+0.5
8.4	7.4	6.7	6.5	6.8	6.2	5.5	6.3	7.0	7.4	7.6	8.1	+0.5
5.2	4.0	3.3	2.7	2.3	1.3	1.6	0.8	1.4	1.2	2.0	1.7	−0.3
10.9	10.9	9.4	7.6	7.2	7.2	6.0	6.4	6.6	7.1	7.2	7.8	+0.6
91.3	92.2	92.0	90.7	89.5	88.0	87.5	87.0	—	—	—	—	—
							80.0	80.4	80.7	79.2	81.7	+2.5ss
—	—	—	—	—	65.4	63.4	62.5	62.9	63.2	61.8	64.2	+2.4
67.6	67.2	66.4	65.7	64.4	63.1	61.8	61.9	62.0	64.2	63.5	65.4	+1.9
31.4	32.2	30.4	29.2	—	—	32.4	31.0	30.7	30.9	29.8	25.3	−4.5
—	—	—	3.0	2.9	2.1	2.1	2.0	2.4	2.3	1.9	2.4	+0.5

[k] Only drug use which was not under a doctor's orders is included here.

[l] Data based on two of six forms; N is two-sixths of N indicated. Steroid data based on one of six forms in 1989–90; N is one-sixth of N indicated in 1989–90. Steroid data based on two of six forms since 1991; N is two-sixths of N indicated since 1991.

[m] Sedatives; Data based on five forms in 1975–88, six forms in 1989, one form in 1990 (N is one-sixth of N indicated in 1990), and six forms of data adjusted by one-form data beginning in 1991. Methaqualone: Data based on five forms in 1975–88; six forms in 1989, and one of six forms beginning in 1990 (N is one-sixth of N indicated beginning in 1990).

[n] Data based on five forms in 1975–88 and on six forms in 1989–92. In 1993, the question text was changed slightly in three of six forms to indicate that a "drink" meant "more than a few sips." The data in the upper line for alcohol came from the three forms using the original wording (N is three-sixths of N indicated), while the data in the lower line came from the three forms containing the revised wording (N is three-sixths of N indicated). Data for 1994–97 were based on all six forms.

[o] Prevalence of smokeless tobacco was not asked of 12th-graders in 1990 and 1991. Prior to 1990 the prevalence question on smokeless tobacco was located near the end of one 12th-grade questionnaire form, whereas after 1991 the question was placed earlier and in a different form. This shift could explain the discontinuities between the corresponding data.

Note: Level of significance of difference between the two most recent Classes: s = .05, ss = .01, sss = .001. —indicates data not available.

Source: The Monitoring the Future Study, the University of Michigan.

T A B L E **12-2**   **Long-Term Trends in *Annual* Prevalence of Use of Various Drugs for 12th-Graders**

	Class of 1975	Class of 1976	Class of 1977	Class of 1978	Class of 1979	Class of 1980	Class of 1981	Class of 1982	Class of 1983	Class of 1984	Class of 1985
Approx N =	9400	15400	17100	17800	15500	15900	17500	17700	16300	15900	16000
Any illicit drug[a,b]	45.0	48.1	51.1	53.8	54.2	53.1	52.1	49.4	47.4	45.8	46.3
Any illicit drug other than marijuana[a,b]	26.2	25.4	26.0	27.1	28.2	30.4	34.0	30.1	28.4	28.0	27.4
Marijuana/hashish	40.0	44.5	47.6	50.2	50.8	48.8	46.1	44.3	42.3	40.0	40.6
Inhalants[c]	—	3.0	3.7	4.1	5.4	4.6	4.1	4.5	4.3	5.1	5.7
Inhalants adjusted[e,d]	—	—	—	—	8.9	7.9	6.1	6.6	6.2	7.2	7.5
amyl/butyl nitrites[e,f]	—	—	—	—	6.5	5.7	3.7	3.6	3.6	4.0	4.0
Hallucinogens	11.2	9.4	8.8	9.6	9.9	9.3	9.0	8.1	7.3	6.5	6.3
Hallucinogens, adjusted[g]	—	—	—	—	11.8	10.4	10.1	9.0	8.3	7.3	7.6
LSD	7.2	6.4	5.5	6.3	6.6	6.5	6.5	6.1	5.4	4.7	4.4
PCP[e,f]	—	—	—	—	7.0	4.4	3.2	2.2	2.6	2.3	2.9
MDMA (Ecstasy)[a]	—	—	—	—	—	—	—	—	—	—	—
Cocaine	5.6	6.0	7.2	9.0	12.0	12.3	12.4	11.5	11.4	11.6	13.1
Crack[h]	—	—	—	—	—	—	—	—	—	—	—
Other Cocaine[i]	—	—	—	—	—	—	—	—	—	—	—
Heroin[j]	1.0	0.8	0.8	0.8	0.5	0.5	0.5	0.6	0.6	0.5	0.6
Other Opintes[k]	5.7	5.7	6.4	6.0	6.2	6.3	5.9	5.3	5.1	5.2	5.9
Stimulants[b,k]	16.2	15.8	16.3	17.1	18.3	20.8	26.0	20.3	17.9	17.7	15.8
Crystal meth. (Ice)[l]	—	—	—	—	—	—	—	—	—	—	—
Sedatives[k,m]	11.7	10.7	10.8	9.9	9.9	10.3	10.5	9.1	7.9	6.6	5.8
Barbiturates[k]	10.7	9.6	9.3	8.1	7.5	6.8	6.6	5.5	5.2	4.9	4.6
Methaqualone[k,m]	5.1	4.7	5.2	4.9	5.9	7.2	7.6	6.8	5.4	3.8	2.8
Tranquilizers[k]	10.6	10.3	10.8	9.9	9.6	8.7	8.0	7.0	6.9	6.1	6.1
Alcohol[n]	84.8	85.7	87.0	87.7	88.1	87.9	87.0	86.8	87.3	86.0	85.6
Been drunk[l]	—	—	—	—	—	—	—	—	—	—	—
Cigarettes	—	—	—	—	—	—	—	—	—	—	—
Smokeless tobacco[a,o]	—	—	—	—	—	—	—	—	—	—	—
Steroids[l]	—	—	—	—	—	—	—	—	—	—	—

[a]Use of "any illicit drug" includes any use of marijuana, LSD, other hallucinogens, crack, other cocaine, or heroin, *or* any use of other opiates, stimulants, barbiturates, methaqualone (excluded since 1990), or tranquilizers not under a doctor's orders.

[b]Beginning in 1982 the question about stimulant use (i.e., amphetamines) was revised to get respondents to exclude the inappropriate reporting of nonprescription stimulants. The prevalence rate dropped slightly as a result of this methodological change.

[c]Data based on four of five forms in 1976–88; N is four-fifths of N indicated. Data based on five of six forms in 1989–97; N is five-sixths of N indicated.

[d]Adjusted for underreporting of amyl and butyl nitrites. See text for details.

[e]Data based on one form; N is one-fifth of N indicated in 1979–88 and one-sixth of N indicated in 1989–97.

[f]Question text changed slightly in 1987.

[g]Adjusted for underreporting of PCP.

[h]Data based on one of five forms in 1986; N is one-fifth of N indicated. Data based on two forms in 1987–89; N is two-fifths of N indicated in 1987–88 and two-sixths of N indicated in 1989. Data based on six forms in 1990–97.

[i]Data based on one form in 1987–89; N is one-fifth of N indicated in 1987–88 and one-sixth of N indicated in 1989. Data based on four of six forms in 1990–97; N is four-sixths of N indicated.

[j]In 1995 the heroin question was changed in half of the questionnaire forms. Separate questions were asked for use with injection and without injection. Data presented here represent the combined data from all forms.

(continues)

TABLE 12-2 (*continued*)

Class of 1986	Class of 1987	Class of 1988	Class of 1989	Class of 1990	Class of 1991	Class of 1992	Class of 1993	Class of 1994	Class of 1995	Class of 1996	Class of 1997	'96–'97 change
15200	*16300*	*16300*	*16700*	*15200*	*15000*	*15800*	*16300*	*15400*	*15400*	*14300*	*15400*	
44.3	41.7	38.5	35.4	32.5	29.4	27.1	31.0	35.8	39.0	40.2	42.4	+2
25.9	24.1	21.1	20.0	17.9	16.2	14.9	17.1	18.0	19.4	19.8	20.7	+0
38.8	36.3	33.1	29.6	27.0	23.9	21.9	26.0	30.7	34.7	35.8	38.5	+2
6.1	6.9	6.5	5.9	6.9	6.6	6.2	7.0	7.7	8.0	7.6	6.7	−0
8.9	8.1	7.1	6.9	7.5	6.9	6.4	7.4	8.2	8.4	8.5	7.3	−1
4.7	2.6	1.7	1.7	1.4	0.9	0.5	0.9	1.1	1.1	1.6	1.2	−0
6.0	6.4	5.5	5.6	5.9	5.8	5.9	7.4	7.6	9.3	10.1	9.8	−0
7.6	6.7	5.8	6.2	6.0	6.1	6.2	7.8	7.8	9.7	10.7	10.0	−0
4.5	5.2	4.8	4.9	5.4	5.2	5.6	6.8	6.9	8.4	8.8	8.4	−0
2.4	1.3	1.2	2.4	1.2	1.4	1.4	1.4	1.6	1.8	2.6	2.3	−0
—	—	—	—	—	—	—	—	—	—	4.6	4.0	−0
12.7	10.3	7.9	6.5	5.3	3.5	3.1	3.3	3.6	4.0	4.9	5.5	+0
4.1	3.9	3.1	3.1	1.9	1.5	1.5	1.5	1.9	2.1	2.1	2.4	+0
—	9.8	7.4	5.2	4.6	3.2	2.6	2.9	3.0	3.4	4.2	5.0	+0
0.5	0.5	0.5	0.6	0.5	0.4	0.6	0.5	0.6	1.1	1.0	1.2	+0
5.2	5.3	4.6	4.4	4.5	3.5	3.3	3.6	3.8	4.7	5.4	6.2	+0
13.4	11.2	10.9	10.8	9.1	8.2	7.1	8.4	9.4	9.3	9.5	10.2	+0
—	—	—	—	1.3	1.4	1.3	1.7	1.8	2.4	2.8	2.3	−0
5.2	4.1	3.7	3.7	3.6	3.6	2.9	3.4	4.2	4.9	5.3	5.4	+0
4.2	3.6	3.2	3.3	3.4	3.4	2.8	3.4	4.1	4.7	4.9	5.1	+0
2.1	1.5	1.3	1.3	0.7	0.5	0.6	0.2	0.8	0.7	1.1	1.0	−0
5.8	5.5	4.8	3.8	3.5	3.6	2.8	3.5	3.7	4.4	4.6	4.7	+0
84.5	85.7	85.3	82.7	80.6	77.7	76.8	76.0	—	—	—	—	—
							72.7	73.0	73.7	72.5	74.8	+2
—	—	—	—	—	52.7	50.3	49.6	51.7	52.5	51.9	53.2	+1
—	—	—	—	—	—	—	—	—	—	—	—	—
—	—	—	1.9	1.7	1.4	1.1	1.2	1.3	1.5	1.4	1.4	0

[k] Only drug use which was not under a doctor's orders is included here.

[l] Data based on two of six forms; *N* is two-sixths of *N* indicated. Steroid data based on one of six forms in 1989–90; *N* is one-sixth of *N* indicated in 1989–90. Steroid data based on two of six forms since 1991; *N* is two-sixths of *N* indicated since 1991.

[m] Sedatives; Data based on five forms in 1975–88, six forms in 1989, one form in 1990 (*N* is one-sixth of *N* indicated in 1990), and six forms of data adjusted by one-form data beginning in 1991. Methaqualone: Data based on five forms in 1975–88; six forms in 1989, and one of six forms beginning in 1990 (*N* is one-sixth of *N* indicated beginning in 1990).

[n] Data based on five forms in 1975–88 and on six forms in 1989–92. In 1993, the question text was changed slightly in three of six forms to indicate that a "drink" meant "more than a few sips." The data in the upper line for alcohol came from the three forms using the original wording (*N* is three-sixths of *N* indicated), while the data in the lower line came from the three forms containing the revised wording (*N* is three-sixths of *N* indicated). Data for 1994–97 were based on all six forms.

[o] Prevalence of smokeless tobacco was not asked of 12th-graders in 1990 and 1991. Prior to 1990 the prevalence question on smokeless tobacco was located near the end of one 12th-grade questionnaire form, whereas after 1991 the question was placed earlier and in a different form. This shift could explain the discontinuities between the corresponding data.

Note: Level of significance of difference between the two most recent Classes: s = .05, ss = .01, sss = .001. — indicates data not available.

Source: The Monitoring the Future Study, the University of Michigan.

examining Table 12-1 note the reported difference between admitting to having ever consumed alcohol (81.7%) and the lower percentage of youth who drank to the point of intoxication (64.2%).

A developmental model to account for adolescent drug use has been derived from Kandel and her colleagues work (Kandel, 1981a; Kandel & Logan, 1984; Kandel, Treiman, Faust, & Single, 1976). Denise Kandel and her associates propose that young people who begin to use alcohol are more socially advanced than their peers. They have adopted adult standards of social behavior and are imitating their parents' drinking behaviors. Adolescents who make the step from alcohol to marijuana do so with their peers. These young people are described as having anti-establishment feelings toward their parents, school, church, and community. The final move from marijuana to other drugs occurs for those who experience strong feelings of depression and alienation from family, friends, and the community.

In brief, it appears that the chances are good that the illicit-drug user first experimented with beer or wine, tobacco, and hard liquor. This finding does not, however, establish a causal connection between the use of these substances and the use of other drugs. Substance use on one level does not necessarily suggest movement to other illicit drugs. In the next section we take a closer look at the research in an attempt to explain why young people drink.

Sociological and Psychological Viewpoints

By the time U.S. students graduate from high school, nearly 82% will have tried alcohol and 64% will have gotten drunk at least once (Johnston, O'Malley, & Bachman, 1997). About 5% will continue to get drunk frequently throughout adolescence. Despite these statistics, studies show, most of these youthful drinkers will not become alcohol abusers or dependent in the future (Daugherty & Leukefeld, 1998; National Institute on Alcohol Abuse and Alcoholism, 1984).

Table 12-2 compares drug use by U.S. high school seniors from year to year. Note the differences in levels of use from the lifetime use recorded in Table 12-1 and the use of substances from 1996 to 1997.

In one often-cited study 44% of a college sample were described as problem drinkers—that is, substance abusers. Two decades later, of the 200 college students involved in that study, the number of problem drinkers had decreased to 19% (Fillmore, 1974). This and other studies with similar findings have led some researchers to conclude that drinking is a normal part of adolescence and decreases with age (Duncan & Petosa, 1995). It is with some individuals (estimated to be 10%) that drinking becomes problematic (Daugherty & Leukefeld, 1998) (see Table 12-3, which presents use over a 30-day period by the U.S. Class of 1997).

A number of reasons have been suggested for becoming intoxicated. These include such "healthy" purposes as occasional desires to escape responsibilities as in "letting off steam," celebrating a special event such as a sports victory or holiday, or the wish to have a pleasant sensation. Less healthy or justifiable reasons include the desire to avoid the emotional pain associated with growing up, to encourage sexual misconduct, or to compensate for feelings of inadequacy.

The drinking behavior of adolescents can be viewed as being in step with the increased permissiveness of the times. Nevertheless, whether the figure is 19, 10, or 5%, tens of thousands of young people become alcohol dependent each year and seriously harm their health (see Table 12-4, which presents the daily use of alcohol and other drugs by the U.S. senior Class of 1997).

A great deal of research has been conducted on the factors that contribute to making a young person vulnerable to becoming alcohol dependent. For instance, the results of a longitudinal study that followed several hundred male children over 30 years (M. C. Jones, 1968) suggest that those who become alcohol dependent are extroverted and worried over their masculinity and were rebellious as children. Karl Menninger (1965) and others (C. A. Johnson et al., 1990; Newcomb & Bentler, 1986) viewed the alcohol-dependent individual as a depressed failure seeking to escape the problems of living. In fact, Menninger speculated that alcohol dependence was a subtle form of suicidal behavior.

Numerous reports show that alcohol-dependent adolescents do poorly in school (Dryfoos, 1990; Johnson et al., 1990; Newcomb & Bentler, 1989; Scheier & Botvin, 1998). They are likely to be involved in deviant activities including violent crime (Dawkins, 1997; NIAAA, 1997b; Palmer & Liddle, 1996; Rua, 1990). Alcohol-dependent adolescents are nonreligious or at least less religious than their peers (Thomas & Carver, 1990), are likely to be using other illicit drugs (Vicary & Lerner, 1986), and, for White youths are influenced more by their peer group than by their families (Barnes, Farrell, & Banerjee, 1994; Department of Health and Human Services, 1991a; Selnow & Crano, 1986; Stein, Newcomb, & Bentler, 1987; Swaim, Oetting, Edwards, & Beauvais, 1989). It is estimated that for youths with drinking problems more than half have a cooccurring emotional disorder (Greenbaum, Foster-Johnson, & Petrila, 1996). This last point is of particular interest. It may be that young people are using alcohol and other drugs to numb the emotional suffering associated with disorders like depression. Indeed, we know that the consumption of alcohol frequently precedes suicidal behavior (King, Hill, Naylor, Evans, & Shain, 1993; NIAAA, 1997a).

A composite picture, then, of alcohol-dependent adolescents is one of low-achieving, delinquent individuals. Not highly religious, they are likely to be using other drugs and those who are White are influenced more by their peers than by their families. Having feelings of rootlessness, depression, and failure, alcohol-dependent adolescents are seen as committing a form of suicide by their use of alcohol. Many have accompanying emotional disorders that may exacerbate their drinking.

A Family Perspective

There is considerable evidence that parents have a strong influence on the drinking habits their children acquire. As discussed earlier in this text the family is the primary socialization agent for young people. No other institution maintains the length or depth of contact that the family does with its children. And yet we need to remain cautious in attributing the substance abuse problems of adolescents

T A B L E **12-3**   **Long-Term Trends in *Thirty-Day* Prevalence of Use of Various Drugs for 12th-Graders**

	Class of 1975	Class of 1976	Class of 1977	Class of 1978	Class of 1979	Class of 1980	Class of 1981	Class of 1982	Class of 1983	Class of 1984	Class of 1985
Approx N =	9400	15400	17100	17800	15500	15900	17500	17700	16300	15900	16000
Any illicit drug[a,b]	30.7	34.2	37.6	38.9	38.9	37.2	36.9	32.5	30.5	29.2	29.7
Any illicit drug other than marijuana[a,b]	15.4	13.9	15.2	15.1	16.8	18.4	21.7	17.0	15.4	15.1	14.9
Marijuana/hashish	27.0	32.2	35.4	37.1	36.5	33.7	31.6	28.5	27.0	25.2	25.7
Inhalants[c]	—	0.9	1.3	1.5	1.7	1.4	1.5	1.5	1.7	1.9	2.2
Inhalants adjusted[e,d]	—	—	—	—	3.2	2.7	2.5	2.5	2.5	2.6	3.0
amyl/butyl nitrites[e,f]	—	—	—	—	2.4	1.8	1.4	1.1	1.4	1.4	1.6
Hallucinogens	4.7	3.4	4.1	3.9	4.0	3.7	3.7	3.4	2.8	2.6	2.5
Hallucinogens, adjusted[g]	—	—	—	—	5.3	4.4	4.5	4.1	3.5	3.2	3.8
LSD	2.3	1.9	2.1	2.1	2.4	2.3	2.5	2.4	1.9	1.5	1.6
PCP[e,f]	—	—	—	—	2.4	1.4	1.4	1.0	1.3	1.0	1.6
MDMA (Ecstasy)[a]	—	—	—	—	—	—	—	—	—	—	—
Cocaine	1.9	2.0	2.9	3.9	5.7	5.2	5.8	5.0	4.9	5.8	6.7
Crack[h]	—	—	—	—	—	—	—	—	—	—	—
Other cocaine[i]	—	—	—	—	—	—	—	—	—	—	—
Heroin[j]	0.4	0.2	0.3	0.3	0.2	0.2	0.2	0.2	0.2	0.3	0.3
Other opiates[k]	2.1	2.0	2.8	2.1	2.4	2.4	2.1	1.8	1.8	1.8	2.3
Stimulants[b,k]	8.5	7.7	8.8	8.7	9.9	12.1	15.8	10.7	8.9	8.3	6.8
Crystal meth. (Ice)[i]	—	—	—	—	—	—	—	—	—	—	—
Sedatives[k,m]	5.4	4.5	5.1	4.2	4.4	4.8	4.6	3.4	3.0	2.3	2.4
Barbiturates[k]	4.7	3.9	4.3	3.2	3.2	2.9	2.6	2.0	2.1	1.7	2.0
Methaqualone[k,m]	2.1	1.6	2.3	1.9	2.3	3.3	3.1	2.4	1.8	1.1	1.0
Tranquilizers[k]	4.1	4.0	4.6	3.4	v3.7	3.1	2.7	2.4	2.5	2.1	2.1
Alcohol[n]	68.2	68.2	71.2	72.1	71.8	72.0	70.7	69.7	69.4	67.2	65.9
Been drunk[i]	—	—	—	—	—	—	—	—	—	—	—
Cigarettes	36.7	38.8	38.4	36.7	34.4	30.5	29.4	30.0	30.3	29.3	30.1
Smokeless tobacco[a,o]	—	—	—	—	—	—	—	—	—	—	—
Steroids[i]	—	—	—	—	—	—	—	—	—	—	—

[a] Use of "any illicit drug" includes any use of marijuana, LSD, other hallucinogens, crack, other cocaine, or heroin, *or* any use of other opiates, stimulants, barbiturates, methaqualone (excluded since 1990), or tranquilizers not under a doctor's orders.

[b] Beginning in 1982 the question about stimulant use (i.e., amphetamines) was revised to get respondents to exclude the inappropriate reporting of nonprescription stimulants. The prevalence rate dropped slightly as a result of this methodological change.

[c] Data based on four of five forms in 1976–88; *N* is four-fifths of *N* indicated. Data based on five of six forms in 1989–97; *N* is five-sixths of *N* indicated.

[d] Adjusted for underreporting of amyl and butyl nitrites. See text for details.

[e] Data based on one form; *N* is one-fifth of *N* indicated in 1979–88 and one-sixth of *N* indicated in 1989–97.

[f] Question text changed slightly in 1987.

[g] Adjusted for underreporting of PCP.

[h] Data based on one of five forms in 1986; *N* is one-fifth of *N* indicated. Data based on two forms in 1987–89; *N* is two-fifths of *N* indicated in 1987–88 and two-sixths of *N* indicated in 1989. Data based on six forms in 1990–97.

[i] Data based on one form in 1987–89; *N* is one-fifth of *N* indicated in 1987–88 and one-sixth of *N* indicated in 1989. Data based on four of six forms in 1990–97; *N* is four-sixths of *N* indicated.

[j] In 1995 the heroin question was changed in half of the questionnaire forms. Separate questions were asked for use with injection and without injection. Data presented here represent the combined data from all forms.

(continues)

TABLE 12-3 *(continued)*

Class of 1986	Class of 1987	Class of 1988	Class of 1989	Class of 1990	Class of 1991	Class of 1992	Class of 1993	Class of 1994	Class of 1995	Class of 1996	Class of 1997	'96–'97 change
15200	*16300*	*16300*	*16700*	*15200*	*15000*	*15800*	*16300*	*15400*	*15400*	*14300*	*15400*	
27.1	24.7	21.3	19.7	17.2	16.4	14.4	18.3	21.9	23.8	24.6	26.2	+1.6
13.2	11.6	10.0	9.1	8.0	7.1	6.3	7.9	8.8	10.0	9.5	10.7	+1.2
23.4	21.0	18.0	16.7	14.0	13.8	11.9	15.5	19.0	21.2	21.9	23.7	+1.2
2.5	2.8	2.6	2.3	2.7	2.4	2.3	2.5	2.7	3.2	2.5	2.5	0.0
3.2	3.5	3.0	2.7	2.9	2.6	2.5	2.8	2.9	3.5	2.9	2.9	0.0
1.3	1.3	0.6	0.6	0.6	0.4	0.3	0.6	0.4	0.4	0.7	0.7	0.0
2.5	2.5	2.2	2.2	2.2	2.2	2.1	2.7	3.1	4.4	3.5	3.9	+0.4
3.5	2.8	2.3	2.9	2.3	2.4	2.3	3.3	3.2	4.6	3.8	4.1	+0.3
1.7	1.8	1.8	1.8	1.9	1.9	2.0	2.4	2.6	4.0	2.5	3.1	+0.6s
1.3	0.6	0.3	1.4	0.4	0.5	0.6	1.0	0.7	0.6	1.3	0.7	−0.4
—	—	—	—	—	—	—	—	—	—	2.0	1.6	−0.4
6.2	4.3	3.4	2.8	1.9	1.4	1.3	1.3	1.5	1.8	2.0	2.3	+0.3
—	1.3	1.6	1.4	0.7	0.7	0.6	0.7	0.8	1.0	1.0	0.9	−0.1
—	4.1	3.2	1.9	1.7	1.2	1.0	1.2	1.3	1.3	1.6	2.0	+0.4
0.2	0.2	0.2	0.3	0.2	0.2	0.3	0.2	0.3	0.6	0.5	0.5	0.0
2.0	1.8	1.6	1.6	1.5	1.1	1.2	1.3	1.5	1.8	2.0	2.3	+0.3
5.5	5.2	4.6	4.2	3.7	3.2	2.8	3.7	4.0	4.0	4.1	4.8	+0.7s
—	—	—	—	0.6	0.6	0.5	0.6	0.7	1.1	1.1	0.8	−0.3
2.2	1.7	1.4	1.5	1.2	1.3	1.8	2.3	1.8	2.3	2.3	2.1	−0.2
1.8	1.4	1.2	1.4	1.3	1.4	1.1	1.3	1.7	2.2	2.1	2.1	0.0
0.8	0.6	0.5	0.6	0.2	0.2	0.4	0.1	0.4	0.4	0.6	0.3	−0.3
2.1	2.0	1.5	1.3	1.2	1.4	1.0	1.2	1.4	1.8	2.0	1.8	−0.2
65.3	66.4	63.9	60.0	57.1	54.0	51.3	51.0	—	—	—	—	—
						48.6	50.1	51.3	50.8	52.7		+1.9
—	—	—	—	31.6	29.9	28.9	30.8	33.2	31.3	34.2		+2.9
29.6	29.4	28.7	28.6	29.4	28.3	27.8	29.9	31.2	33.5	34.0	36.5	+2.5s
11.5	11.3	10.3	8.4	—	—	11.4	10.7	11.1	12.2	9.8	9.7	−0.1
—	—	—	0.8	1.0	0.8	0.6	0.7	0.9	0.7	0.7	1.0	+0.3

[k] Only drug use which was not under a doctor's orders is included here.

[l] Data based on two of six forms; *N* is two-sixths of *N* indicated. Steroid data based on one of six forms in 1989–90; *N* is one-sixth of *N* indicated in 1989–90. Steroid data based on two of six forms since 1991; *N* is two-sixths of *N* indicated since 1991.

[m] Sedatives; Data based on five forms in 1975–88, six forms in 1989, one form in 1990 (*N* is one-sixth of *N* indicated in 1990), and six forms of data adjusted by one-form data beginning in 1991. Methaqualone: Data based on five forms in 1975–88; six forms in 1989, and one of six forms beginning in 1990 (*N* is one-sixth of *N* indicated beginning in 1990).

[n] Data based on five forms in 1975–88 and on six forms in 1989–92. In 1993, the question text was changed slightly in three of six forms to indicate that a "drink" meant "more than a few sips." The data in the upper line for alcohol came from the three forms using the original wording (*N* is three-sixths of *N* indicated), while the data in the lower line came from the three forms containing the revised wording (*N* is three-sixths of *N* indicated). Data for 1994–97 were based on all six forms.

[o] Prevalence of smokeless tobacco was not asked of 12th-graders in 1990 and 1991. Prior to 1990 the prevalence question on smokeless tobacco was located near the end of one 12th-grade questionnaire form, whereas after 1991 the question was placed earlier and in a different form. This shift could explain the discontinuities between the corresponding data.

Note: Level of significance of difference between the two most recent Classes: s = .05, ss = .01, sss = .001. —indicates data not available.

Source: The Monitoring the Future Study, the University of Michigan.

TABLE **12-4** **Long-Term Trends in Thirty-Day Prevalence of** *Daily* **Use of Various Drugs for 12th-Graders**

	Class of 1975	Class of 1976	Class of 1977	Class of 1978	Class of 1979	Class of 1980	Class of 1981	Class of 1982	Class of 1983	Class of 1984	Class of 1985
Approx N =	9400	15400	17100	17800	15500	15900	17500	17700	16300	15900	16000
Marijuana/hashish	6.0	8.2	9.1	10.7	10.3	9.1	7.0	6.3	5.5	5.0	4.9
Inhalants[c]	—	*	*	0.1	*	0.1	0.1	0.1	0.1	0.1	0.2
Inhalants adjusted[e,d]	—	—	—	—	0.1	0.2	0.2	0.2	0.2	0.2	0.4
amyl/butyl nitrites[e,f]	—	—	—	—	*	0.1	0.1	0.0	0.2	0.1	0.3
Hallucinogens	0.1	0.1	0.1	0.1	0.1	0.1	0.1	0.1	0.1	0.1	0.1
Hallucinogens, adjusted[g]	—	—	—	—	0.2	0.2	0.1	0.2	0.2	0.2	0.3
LSD	*	*	*	*	*	*	0.1	*	0.1	0.1	0.1
PCP[e,f]	—	—	—	—	0.1	0.1	0.1	0.1	0.1	0.1	0.3
MDMA (Ecstasy)[a]	—	—	—	—	—	—	—	—	—	—	—
Cocaine	0.1	0.1	0.1	0.1	0.2	0.2	0.3	0.2	0.2	0.2	0.4
Crack[h]	—	—	—	—	—	—	—	—	—	—	—
Other cocaine[i]	—	—	—	—	—	—	—	—	—	—	—
Heroin[j]	0.1	*	*	*	*	*	*	*	0.1	*	*
Other opiates[k]	0.1	0.1	0.2	0.1	*	0.1	0.1	0.1	0.1	0.1	0.1
Stimulants[b,k]	0.5	0.4	0.5	0.5	0.6	0.7	1.2	0.7	0.8	0.6	0.4
Crystal meth. (Ice)[i]	—	—	—	—	—	—	—	—	—	—	—
Sedatives[k,m]	0.3	0.2	0.2	0.2	0.1	0.2	0.2	0.2	0.2	0.1	0.1
Barbiturates[k]	0.1	0.1	0.2	0.1	*	0.1	0.1	0.1	0.1	*	0.1
Methaqualone[k,m]	*	*	*	*	*	0.1	0.1	0.1	*	*	*
Tranquilizers[k]	0.1	0.2	0.3	0.1	0.1	0.1	0.1	0.1	0.1	0.1	*
Daily[n]	5.7	5.6	6.1	5.7	6.9	6.0	6.0	5.7	5.5	4.8	5.0
Been drunk daily[i]	—	—	—	—	—	—	—	—	—	—	—
5+ drinks in a row in last 2 weeks	36.8	37.1	39.4	40.3	41.2	41.2	41.4	40.5	40.8	38.7	36.7
Cigarettes Daily	26.9	28.8	28.8	27.5	25.4	21.3	20.3	21.1	21.2	18.7	19.5
Half-pack or more per day	17.9	19.2	19.4	18.8	16.5	14.3	13.5	14.2	13.8	12.3	12.5
Smokeless tobacco[a,o]	—	—	—	—	—	—	—	—	—	—	—
Steroids[i]	—	—	—	—	—	—	—	—	—	—	—

[a] Use of "any illicit drug" includes any use of marijuana, LSD, other hallucinogens, crack, other cocaine, or heroin, *or* any use of other opiates, stimulants, barbiturates, methaqualone (excluded since 1990), or tranquilizers not under a doctor's orders.

[b] Beginning in 1982 the question about stimulant use (i.e., amphetamines) was revised to get respondents to exclude the inappropriate reporting of nonprescription stimulants. The prevalence rate dropped slightly as a result of this methodological change.

[c] Data based on four of five forms in 1976–88; *N* is four-fifths of *N* indicated. Data based on five of six forms in 1989–97; *N* is five-sixths of *N* indicated.

[d] Adjusted for underreporting of amyl and butyl nitrites. See text for details.

[e] Data based on one form; *N* is one-fifth of *N* indicated in 1979–88 and one-sixth of *N* indicated in 1989–97.

[f] Question text changed slightly in 1987.

[g] Adjusted for underreporting of PCP.

[h] Data based on one of five forms in 1986; *N* is one-fifth of *N* indicated. Data based on two forms in 1987–89; *N* is two-fifths of *N* indicated in 1987–88 and two-sixths of *N* indicated in 1989. Data based on six forms in 1990–97.

[i] Data based on one form in 1987–89; *N* is one-fifth of *N* indicated in 1987–88 and one-sixth of *N* indicated in 1989. Data based on four of six forms in 1990–97; *N* is four-sixths of *N* indicated.

[j] In 1995 the heroin question was changed in half of the questionnaire forms. Separate questions were asked for use with injection and without injection. Data presented here represent the combined data from all forms.

[k] Only drug use which was not under a doctor's orders is included here.

(continues)

TABLE 12-4 *(continued)*

Class of 1986	Class of 1987	Class of 1988	Class of 1989	Class of 1990	Class of 1991	Class of 1992	Class of 1993	Class of 1994	Class of 1995	Class of 1996	Class of 1997	'96–'97 change
15200	*16300*	*16300*	*16700*	*15200*	*15000*	*15800*	*16300*	*15400*	*15400*	*14300*	*15400*	
4.0	3.3	2.7	2.9	2.2	2.0	1.9	2.4	3.6	4.6	4.9	5.8	+0.9s
0.2	0.1	0.2	0.2	0.3	0.2	0.1	0.1	0.1	0.1	0.2	0.1	−0.1
0.4	0.4	0.3	0.3	0.3	0.5	0.2	0.2	—	—	0.4	0.2	−0.3s
0.5	0.3	0.1	0.3	0.1	0.2	0.1	0.1	0.2	0.2	0.4	0.1	−0.3s
0.1	0.1	*	0.1	0.1	0.1	0.1	0.1	0.1	0.1	0.1	0.3	+0.1s
0.3	0.2	*	0.3	0.3	0.1	0.1	0.1	—	—	0.4	0.4	−0.1
*	0.1	*	*	0.1	0.1	0.1	0.1	0.1	0.1	*	0.2	+0.1s
0.2	0.3	0.1	0.2	0.1	0.1	0.1	0.1	0.3	0.3	0.3	0.1	−0.2s
—	—	—	—	—	—	—	—	—	—	0.0	0.1	+0.1
0.4	0.3	0.2	0.3	0.1	0.1	0.1	0.1	0.1	0.2	0.2	0.2	−0.1
—	0.1	0.1	0.2	0.1	0.1	0.1	0.1	0.1	0.1	0.2	0.1	0.0
—	0.2	0.2	0.1	0.1	0.1	*	*	0.1	0.1	0.1	0.1	−0.1
*	*	*	0.1	*	*	*	*	*	0.1	0.1	0.1	−0.1
0.1	0.1	0.1	0.2	0.1	0.1	*	0.1	0.1	0.1	0.2	0.2	0.0
0.3	0.3	0.3	0.3	0.2	0.2	0.2	0.2	0.2	0.3	0.8	0.3	0.0
—	—	—	—	0.1	0.1	0.1	0.1	*	0.1	0.1	0.1	0.0
0.1	0.1	0.1	0.1	0.1	0.1	0.1	0.1	*	0.1	0.1	0.1	0.0
0.1	0.1	*	0.1	0.1	0.1	*	0.1	*	0.1	0.1	0.1	0.0
*	*	0.1	*	*	*	0.1	0.0	0.1	0.1	0.0	0.1	+0.1
*	0.1	*	0.1	0.1	0.1	*	*	0.1	*	0.2	0.1	−0.1s
4.8	4.8	4.2	4.2	3.7	3.6	3.4	2.5	—	—	—	—	—
							3.4	2.9	3.5	3.7	3.9	+0.2
—	—	—	—	—	0.9	0.8	0.9	1.2	1.3	1.6	2.0	+0.4
36.8	37.5	34.7	33.0	32.2	29.8	27.9	27.5	28.2	29.8	30.2	31.3	+1.1
18.7	18.7	18.1	18.9	19.1	18.5	17.2	19.0	19.4	21.6	22.2	24.6	+2.4s
11.4	11.4	10.6	11.2	11.3	10.7	10.0	10.9	11.2	12.4	13.0	14.3	+1.3
4.7	5.1	4.3	3.3	—	—	4.3	3.3	3.9	3.6	3.3	4.4	+1.0
—	—	—	0.1	0.2	0.1	0.1	0.1	0.4	0.2	0.3	0.3	0.0

[l] Data based on two of six forms; *N* is two-sixths of *N* indicated. Steroid data based on one of six forms in 1989–90; *N* is one-sixth of *N* indicated in 1989–90. Steroid data based on two of six forms since 1991; *N* is two-sixths of *N* indicated since 1991.

[m] Sedatives; Data based on five forms in 1975–88, six forms in 1989, one form in 1990 (*N* is one-sixth of *N* indicated in 1990), and six forms of data adjusted by one-form data beginning in 1991. Methaqualone: Data based on five forms in 1975–88; six forms in 1989, and one of six forms beginning in 1990 (*N* is one-sixth of *N* indicated beginning in 1990).

[n] Data based on five forms in 1975–88 and on six forms in 1989–92. In 1993, the question text was changed slightly in three of six forms to indicate that a "drink" meant "more than a few sips." The data in the upper line for alcohol came from the three forms using the original wording (*N* is three-sixths of *N* indicated), while the data in the lower line came from the three forms containing the revised wording (*N* is three-sixths of *N* indicated). Data for 1994–97 were based on all six forms.

[o] Prevalence of smokeless tobacco was not asked of 12th-graders in 1990 and 1991. Prior to 1990 the prevalence question on smokeless tobacco was located near the end of one 12th-grade questionnaire form, whereas after 1991 the question was placed earlier and in a different form. This shift could explain the discontinuities between the corresponding data.

Note: Level of significance of difference between the two most recent Classes: s = .05, ss = .01, sss = .001.— indicates data not available.

'*' Indicates less then .05%. Any apparent inconsistency between the change estimate and the prevalence estimates for the two most recent classes is due to rounding error. Daily use is defined as use on 20 or more occasions in the past 30 days except for 5+ drinks, cigarettes, and smokeless tobacco, for which actual daily use is measured.

Source: The Monitoring the Future Study, the University of Michigan.

solely to family factors (Stice & Gonzales, 1998). Individual, community, and other factors can negate even the best of families.

In a classic paper G. M. Barnes (1977) uses a family perspective to suggest that "problem drinking is a manifestation of incomplete, inadequate socialization within the family" (p. 573). Two studies support this conclusion. The first, by Vicary and Lerner (1986), draws from a 30-year longitudinal study of 133 White, middle-class subjects and their parents. It documents abuse of alcohol by those subjects who were rejected by their mothers or whose families experienced conflict over childrearing practices or exercised inconsistent or restrictive discipline. The second study, by Hundleby and Mercer (1987), draws on a Canadian sample of 2048 Ontario school children. In this sample lack of parental affection, concern, or involvement in these young people's lives significantly contributed to their substance misuse.

The profile of the alcohol-dependent adolescent's family that emerges from these and other reports is of poor parental control over the adolescent and a distant relationship between the teenager and his or her and parents (Foxcroft & Lowe, 1995; Newcomb & Bentler, 1986; SAMHSA, 1996; Turner, 1995). These are often families in turmoil with parents who abuse alcohol (Sher, Gershuny, Peterson, & Raskin, 1997). Families with affectionate, authoritative, child-centered parents, on the other hand, are much less likely to have adolescents who use illegal substances (Brook, Gordon, & Brook, 1980; Peterson, Hawkins, Abbott, & Catalano, 1994; Stice & Gonzales, 1998; Turner, 1994).

Despite the poor relationship between alcohol-dependent adolescents and their parents, these researchers have found that the parents often condone, if not encourage, their adolescents' drinking (Barnes & Welte, 1986; McDermott, 1984). Seligman (1986) illustrates this last point in his clinical report of working with such a family. He reports that the family arrived at the second session amused, reporting that their son had taken the money that his father had given him and "'blown it on a boozing binge with his friends.' Father's complaint, made in a half-jocular indulgent tone, was that Ricky had stayed out without telephoning to say where he was" (p. 234).

Finally, in a society in which baby-boomer parents now have adolescent children, researchers are finding a strong positive relationship between parental use of alcohol and other drugs and use by their children (Anderson & Henry, 1994; U.S. Department of Health and Human Services, 1991a; Hussong & Chassin, 1997; Newcomb, Huba, & Bentler, 1983). Indeed, as readers review Tables 12-1 to 12-4, notice that the gradual declines from 1979 to 1992 in drug use have been replaced with a gradual increase in the use of many drugs since 1993. It is believed that this increase in drug use can be traced in part to a generation of parents who are the founding mothers and fathers of the 1960s "counter culture," who used drugs heavily and frequently. Their example of drug use now or admission to their children that they once used drugs are contributing factors to the growth in drug use in recent years.

Here's how this example of role modeling works. It was possible for the wife of the then-President of the United States, Nancy Reagan, to tell young people to "Just

Say No!" There is no public record of either Mr. or Mrs. Reagan having ever used illegal drugs. This is not the case with President Clinton. Having admitted to illegal drug use, is the message: "taste but don't swallow" or "smoke but don't inhale"? Humor aside, today's parents and youth are confronted with that age-old situation of "do as I say not as I did." Frankly, this is a message with little impact. If this is the case, and we suspect it is, then the authors of this book can only project an increased use of alcohol and other drugs by adolescents over the next decade as parents present a less-than-ideal behavioral role model to their children on this matter.

The Biological Connection

In many of these studies, at least one parent of the alcohol-dependent adolescent was also alcohol dependent. Whether there is a genetic predisposition to dependency is difficult to assess. Certainly, the family conditions we have described provide one convincing social explanation for an adolescent's drinking. Nevertheless, the results of several studies support a partial genetic explanation. For example, Bohman (1978) found that adopted sons with alcoholic biological fathers were three times as likely to become alcoholic as were the adopted sons of nonalcoholic fathers. Adopted sons whose mothers were alcoholic were twice as likely to become alcoholic as were the adopted sons of nonalcoholic mothers. Additional research tends to support a general finding that children of alcoholic parents stand a greater chance of becoming alcoholics than children whose parents are not (Cadoret, Cain, & Grove, 1980; Cotton, 1979; McCaul, Srikis, Turkkan, Bigelow, & Cromwell, 1990). Indeed, in a study that has been likened to the Manhattan Project, the National Institute on Alcohol Abuse and Alcoholism currently has under way a "massive" study to "crack the biological riddles of the disease" (Holden, 1991, p. 163). This venture represents a selectionist's view of behavior in which the gene operates totally independent of other factors (see Chapter 2).

Whether this research undertaking will find *the* alcoholism gene is questioned by an increasing numbers of critics. Their skepticism is fueled by the failure to establish biological connections (deWit & McCracken, 1990) and only occasional reports, the last appearing in the *Journal of the American Medical Association* (Blum & Noble, 1990) announcing the long-awaited discovery of that gene. As in every other previous announcement of a genetic explanation for human behaviors like substance abuse and delinquency, the initial report of the finding has not been upheld (Holden, 1991, 1994). As Holden (1991, p. 163) reports, increasingly "scientists are beginning to suspect that there may be no genes for alcoholism per se, but rather for a general susceptibility to compulsive behaviors whose specific expression is shaped by environmental and temperamental factors." More recently, a number of the researchers involved in this "Manhattan Project" called the "Collaborative Study on the Genetics of Alcoholism" acknowledged this reality. As Enoch Gordis, NIAAA director noted, "Alcoholism genes are many, they interact in unknown ways, and they have complete penetrance, which means you can have the genes but not be an alcoholic .... These are genes for risk, not for destiny" (cited in Holden, 1998, p. 1349). This is an instructional model of gene operational theory that recognizes that development occurs in context and context, in all of its biological, sociological, and psychological complexity, determines development.

Representing the environment-only position, Peele (1986) points out that alcoholism rates vary significantly among ethnic groups, genders, and social classes. Further, methodological problems seriously compromise most studies. These problems lead Peele to conclude that genetic models by themselves are inadequate to explain alcohol abuse.

To summarize, the family appears to be a major influence on adolescent drinking. Studies suggest that the alcohol-dependent young person comes from a strained home environment, and many researchers find similar drinking habits in parents and children. Finally, researchers continue their attempts to discover biological explanations for alcoholism.

TOBACCO, MARIJUANA, INHALANTS, STEROIDS, LSD, STIMULANTS, BARBITURATES, COCAINE, AND HEROIN

Tobacco

Consider the following:

1. In the U.S. senior high school class of 1997, 14.3% smoked a half-pack or more a day. This continues a 5-year pattern of growth in the percentage of adolescent heavy smokers (Johnston, O'Malley, & Bachman, 1997).
2. In Ontario, Canada 50% of the 1997 senior class reported using tobacco at least once in their lives. This figure was 65.4% for seniors in the U.S. (Johnston, O'Malley, & Bachman, 1997; Paglia & Room, 1999).
3. More than 47% of the U.S. 8th-grade class in 1997 tried tobacco and nearly 17% used smokeless tobacco (Johnston, O'Malley, & Bachman, 1997).
4. In 1988 then-Surgeon General C. Everett Koop cautioned that "the pharmacologic and behavioral processes that determine tobacco addiction are similar to those that determine addiction to drugs such as heroin and cocaine" (Byrne, 1988, p. 1143).
5. Tobacco addiction is killing 400,000 Americans each year (Centers for Disease Control, 1989).

Tobacco (*Nicotiana tabacum*) was, along with syphilis, one of the many "gifts" from the New World. As with every other substance described in this chapter, tobacco was assumed to have healing powers. In England, for example, from 1573 to 1625 it was believed to be a useful drug for heart pains, snake bites, chills, fatigue, and had the "singular and divine virtue" of reducing individual risk to the Black Plague (Austin, 1979, p. 1). It was popularized in England by Sir Walter Raleigh for recreational use and, despite royal attempts to discourage its use, by 1575 tobacco was literally worth its weight in silver.

In the American colonies, tobacco was embraced by Virginia, which used it as currency until the early 1700s, and rejected by the Massachusetts Bay Colony, which prohibited smoking in 1632. Interestingly, it was U.S. travelers returning home from England who first introduced America to the cigarette in the 1850s. By 1885, cigarette production in the U.S. had reached 1 billion cigarettes a year and rapidly grew to 80 billion by the 1920s. Currently, over 575 billion cigarettes are sold each year (Centers for Disease Control, 1989). The first (dare we say) serious medical evidence (beyond Dr. Pierce's protestations) of the harmful effects of cigarette smoking and lung disease was published in 1939. A quarter of a century later, the 1964 Surgeon General's Report established that relationship permanently. Even so 51 million Americans continue to use tobacco products (Austin, 1979; Gullotta & Blau, 1995; Resnick, 1990; Slade, 1989).

Substance Characteristics

Although it can be chewed, tobacco is generally smoked. The active ingredient in tobacco is nicotine, which is readily absorbed from tobacco smoke into the lungs. Interestingly, it is believed that the mildness of cigarette tobacco smoke is responsible for the increases in deaths due to lung cancer since the 1920s. Because of its mildness, cigarette tobacco smoke is more deeply inhaled than either cigar or pipe smoke (Centers for Disease Control, 1989). This smoke then passes quickly into the blood stream and to receptor sites in the brain. Its psychoactive effects include, at low doses, increasing attention and vigilance and, at higher levels, inducing relaxation and lowering perceived stress. Like cocaine, nicotine blocks the reuptake of the brain chemical dopamine—the chief neurotransmitter in what is believed to be the brain's pleasure center. This blocking action prolongs nicotine's euphoric effects (Nowak, 1994).

Withdrawal from the substance typically causes a decreased heart rate and thyroid functioning, weight gain, increases in anger and anxiety, restlessness, and impatience. Interestingly, nicotine accumulates in the body during the day and lasts overnight. Thus, regular smokers are continually exposed to its mood-altering effects. Nicotine is considered to have a high potential for creating a physical dependence such that the drug has been likened to cocaine and heroin. To illustrate its addictive qualities, consider the fact that 50% of smokers who lose a lung to cancer continue to smoke afterward (Nowak, 1994)! Tolerance (the need for increasing amounts of a drug to maintain its effect) is quite high (Benowitz, 1990; Cherek, Bennett, Roache, & Grabowski, 1990; Hughes, 1990; Schelling, 1992; Villanueva et al., 1990).

In recent years, the United States Food and Drug Administration (FDA) has attempted to regulate tobacco as a drug (Nowak, 1994). The fierce struggle with the tobacco industry over whether the FDA has that authority is under negotiation. It appears that the FDA and other U.S. Federal regulatory bodies may have a greater say in the marketing, sales, and distribution practices of this substance.

Young people who smoke are under greater stress than those who do not.

User/Abuser Characteristics

Studies of adolescents who begin to use tobacco find that parental smoking behavior strongly correlates with adolescent use of the substance. Adolescents who use tobacco tend to have parents who use tobacco. As we noted in the last section on alcohol, individuals who smoke are very likely to use alcohol (80 to 95%) (NIAAA, 1998). Adolescents who use tobacco report fewer plans to attend college (Johnston, O'Malley, & Bachman, 1996b). In addition, studies suggest these adolescents have lower self-esteem and perceive themselves to be under greater stress than do nonsmoking adolescents (U.S. Department of Health and Human Services, 1991b; Bauman, Fisher, Bryan, & Chenoweth, 1984; Foshee & Bauman, 1994; Jackson, Henriksen, Dickinson, & Levine, 1997; Kandel & Wu, 1995; Murphy & Price, 1988; Reppucci, Revenson, Aber, & Reppucci, 1991).

Marijuana

Consider the following:

1. In comparison to the U.S. high school class of 1979, when 60.4% admitted to using marijuana at least once in their lifetime, 49.6% of the class of 1997 made this admission. The U.S. class of 1997 continues a 5-year trend beginning in 1992 of increased lifetime use of this drug with the increase between 1996 and 1997 reaching statistical significance (Johnston, O'Malley, & Bachman, 1997).
2. Of the graduating U.S. class of 1997, 49.6% had used marijuana at some time in their lives, 38.5% had used it in the last year, and 23.7% had used it in the previous month (Johnston, O'Malley, & Bachman, 1997).

3. In Ontario, Canada 30% of the 1997 senior class reported using marijuana at least once in their lives (Paglia & Room, 1999).
4. Nearly 23% of the U.S. 8th-grade class of 1997 reported trying marijuana at least once (Johnston, O'Malley, & Bachman, 1997).
5. In 1977 then-President Jimmy Carter said that although "we can and should continue to discourage the use of marijuana.... [I support] legislation amending federal law to eliminate all federal criminal penalties for the possession of up to one ounce of marijuana" (President Carter's Address, 1977, p. 6). Currently, two states permit marijuana use for medicinal purposes (Arizona and California) (Grady, 1996). Eleven states have decriminalized marijuana by making the possession of small amounts a misdemeanor (*New York Times*, March 7, 1993).
6. In 1992 then-candidate for President, Bill Clinton, acknowledged experimenting with marijuana but not inhaling. He later lamented that oversight on MTV.
7. In 1993 then-Surgeon General Elders made the following remark on the legalization of drugs, "Many times [drug users are] robbing, stealing, and all of these things to get money to get drugs. I do feel that we would markedly reduce our crime rate if drugs were legalized" (*USA Today*, 1993).

The history of marijuana (*Cannabis sativa*) in North America is a curious one involving a king, an American president, ethnic prejudice, and the Great Depression. To begin at the beginning, the earliest English settlements in America raised a form of marijuana (hemp) as a cash crop. The hemp plant was extremely useful. Its fibers could be turned into sails, linens, paper, blankets, clothing, flags, and, most important of all, rope. So important was this commodity to England that King James I ordered the settlers of Virginia to produce hemp for the mother country (Austin, 1979; Grinspoon, 1971; Sloman, 1979).

Production of marijuana continued after the colonial revolution of 1776 without concern for its intoxicating qualities.[2] In fact, first drafts of the U.S. Declaration of Independence were written on hemp. Even George Washington cultivated the plant. Like many other gentlemen of the time, Washington raised hemp to be sold for making cloth and rope. At the time of the Civil War, the growing of marijuana as a cash crop declined. Other parts of the world, notably Russia and the Philippines, produced a product superior to that grown here.

Like many now-illegal substances, marijuana was used from the 1800s to the 1930s for medicinal purposes. However, it never captured the support other drugs were able to attract. The lack of medical enthusiasm for marijuana was due to the variable quality of the psychoactive substance found in the plant, THC (delta-9-tetrahydrocannabinol).

Several social histories of marijuana published in recent years suggest that the events that moved marijuana from being considered a relatively harmless plant to the status of "killer weed" began with the Great Depression. The circumstances

---

[2]*Cannabis sativa* is the name given to two plants. One intoxicates. The other is said to cause headaches. It is the second that is called hemp. Both are illegal.

surrounding this redefinition include the migration of Mexicans into the United States and the scarcity of work. It appears that in the late 1920s and early 1930s the largest group of users of marijuana for recreational purposes was Mexican Americans. Ethnic prejudices against this immigrant group fueled by the high unemployment of the Great Depression evidently encouraged federal authorities to not only label marijuana a narcotic but to encourage an illegal state effort to repatriate an estimated 500,000 Mexican Americans to Mexico. Many of those repatriated were not illegal immigrants but citizens of the United States (Austin, 1979; Grinspoon, 1971; Mintz, 1997; Novas, 1994; Sloman, 1979)!

Does marijuana offer "one moment of bliss and a lifetime of regret"? Is it "the new drug menace destroying the youth of America" or "a violent narcotic. . . the real Public Enemy Number One"? In the 1938 cult classic *Reefer Madness*, the answer to these film-posed questions is an unqualified "Yes!" The likely response of many people educated in the 1970s through the mid-1990s would be "No!" What is the truth?

Substance Characteristics

Although it can be ingested, marijuana is usually smoked. The effects range from mild euphoria to shifting sensory images to hallucinations. Depending on the potency of the sample, the effects are usually experienced within 10 minutes and can last for several hours. The potency of marijuana is dependent on the concentration of THC in the plant. Over the past 2 decades the potency or concentration of THC has increased from 1.5% in the 1970s to 4% today and in some instances to as high as 12%. Hashish and hashish oil, both derived from the marijuana plant, contain far greater amounts of THC, so that the "mind-altering" effects of these two drugs are substantially greater. Marijuana is generally considered to have a low potential for creating psychological dependence (National Institute on Drug Abuse, 1987b; U.S. Department of Health and Human Services, 1991b). But as noted earlier in this chapter, this finding is now under review with the publication of two studies using mice that demonstrate that chronic substantial marijuana use has strong addictive qualities (Rodriquez de Fonseca et al., 1997; Tanda et al., 1997). Tolerance can occur but is unusual when used infrequently or in small doses.

User/Abuser Characteristics

Studies of the motivations and personal characteristics of marijuana users and nonusers show no differences. Occasional marijuana users are not seen as maladjusted or psychopathological in their use of this substance (Jessor, 1979; Pascale, Hurd, & Primavera, 1980; Zimmer & Morgan, 1997).

In contrast, according to reports funded by the Substance Abuse and Mental Health Services Administration (SAMHSA) and the National Institute on Drug Abuse, the homes and personal lives of *marijuana-abusing* adolescents are conflict ridden. This report described the relationships between parents and adolescents as severely strained. Marijuana-abusing adolescents acted-out at home and were frequently disruptive in school and other settings (Hendin, Pollinger, Ulman, & Carr, 1981, SAMHSA, 1996).

Youth who abuse marijuana report serious strain within their families.

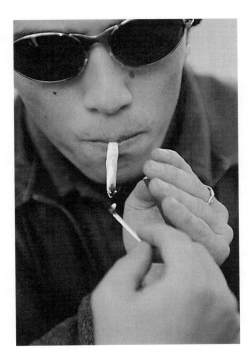

The young people described in these reports viewed their parents as insensitive and uncaring toward them. In the opinion of these researchers, marijuana served several important functions in these young people's lives. The first was a public expression of defiance against parental and community authority. Second was the self-destructiveness that seemed to mark the life of each participant. Third was the use of marijuana to numb the intense anger these young people felt toward their parents. Next, it appeared to the authors that these young people used marijuana to compensate for feeling "that they amounted to nothing within the context of their own families" (Hendin, Pollinger, Ulman, & Carr, 1981, p. 76). Finally, marijuana permitted these adolescents to escape the competitive academic and peer pressures around them (SAMHSA, 1996).

We would suggest that, in those situations in which marijuana use becomes abuse, it is very difficult to attribute the decrease in personal functioning solely to the drug. The findings of a sense of alienation (Jessor et al., 1980); less religiosity (Jessor et al., 1980; Perry & Murray, 1985; Thomas & Carver, 1990); lower academic grade expectations (Kandel, 1981a); and weak parental control, affection, and support (Frauenglass, Routh, Pantin, & Mason, 1997; Vicary & Lerner, 1986) for both marijuana-abusing youths and alcohol-dependent adolescents raise a real question of whether it is the drug or the young person's life environment that precipitates increased use. Furthermore, since both alcohol-dependent and marijuana-abusing youths are likely to be abusing other drugs, attributing decreased personal functioning to marijuana alone is unrealistic (Jessor et al., 1980).

Such a position does not mean that marijuana is without negative effects. Quite the contrary: it has been clearly shown, for instance, that marijuana and driving do not mix (Pace, 1981) and that smoking it is more harmful than cigarette smoking (Kozel & Adams, 1986; Department of Health and Human Services, 1991b). In particular, marijuana smokers inhale about four times the amount of tar into their lungs as cigarette users (Brown, 1996). This leads to a significantly higher rate for chronic bronchitis and in time will lead, we expect, to higher rates of lung and throat cancer. Marijuana has been shown to impair short-term memory and motivation (National Institute on Drug Abuse, 1982), and in persons with a history of emotional illness it may produce an acute toxic psychosis, including delusions, hallucinations, and agitated behavior (Jones, 1980; National Institute on Drug Abuse, 1987b; Weller & Halikas, 1985).

Inhalants

Consider these facts:

1. Twenty-one percent (21%) of the U.S. 8th-grade class of 1997 have used inhalants. Fortunately, inhalant use decreases with age (Johnston, O'Malley, & Bachman, 1997).
2. Of the graduating U.S. high school class of 1997, 16.1% had used inhalants at some time in their lives, 6.7% had used it in the last year, and 2.5% had used it in the previous month (Johnston, O'Malley, & Bachman, 1997).[3]
3. Inhalant abuse (daily use) by the U.S. class of 1997 was almost statistically nonexistent (1/10 of 1%) (Johnston, O'Malley, & Bachman, 1997).

The inhaling of model-airplane glue, gasoline, paint thinner, and other substances to achieve an intoxicating effect seems most prevalent among males aged 10 to 14. The young adolescent may turn to solvents because of a lack of access to other substances. Thus, the decline in solvent use as the adolescent grows older is thought to be related to increasing access to other intoxicants (alcohol, sedatives, and so forth). According to one researcher, no other category of substances discussed in this chapter poses such danger to physical health as solvent abuse (Cohen, 1979; NIDA, 1995).[4]

Substance Characteristics

Solvent inhalers generally place the substance in a plastic bag, pour it onto a rag, or sniff it directly from the original container. The effects, ranging from alcohol-like intoxication to severe disorientation to unconsciousness, are usually experienced

---

[3]Note that 8th-graders use exceeded the lifetime use of 12th-graders in 1997. This insures that the class of 2001 will exceed the class of 1997 in their lifetime use of inhalants.

[4]In recent years amyl and butyl nitrates have been included in this category and as a result the usage of inhalants has statistically increased. The popularity of these nitrates is linked to their over-the-counter availability and in their use to facilitate lovemaking in relationships in which anal intercourse is practiced. As we have said, nitrates are immunosuppressants and thus compound the problems of AIDs sufferers.

within a few minutes after inhaling the solvent. The degree of effect is determined by the nature of the solvent, its strength, and the length of time it is inhaled. Because some solvents, such as tetrachloride and benzene, are poisons, the solvent abuser does run a risk of severe injury or death. Even those chemicals such as toluene that are considered relatively safe have been associated with disorders of the kidneys, nervous system, and bone marrow (Cohen 1979, 1981; National Institute on Drug Abuse, 1987b, 1995; Sharp, Beauvais, & Spence, 1992). Tolerance varies with the substance inhaled. Although only a minority of young people experiment with solvent use and most of those who do experiment do so for only a short time and incur no lasting health damage, solvent use must be considered as having a high potential for physical damage to the user.

User/Abuser Characteristics

Studies report solvent use to be higher among Latinos and Native Americans than among either Blacks or Whites in the United States (Barnes, 1979; Cohen, 1979; Rodriguez-Andrew, 1985). Barnes attributes the higher incidence of solvent use among the first two groups to the greater stress and alienation they experience within our society. The solvent abuser is pictured as male; a poor student; and depressed, anxious, and alienated (Barnes, 1979; Cohen, 1979; Sharp, Beauvais, & Spence, 1992). The influence of the peer group is a major factor in solvent abuse (Cohen, 1979; Sharp, Beauvais, & Spence, 1992). The family is also a primary contributor. Studies show that poor parent/child relationships, divorce, alcoholism, and other problems are common in families with solvent-abusing adolescents (Barnes, 1979; National Institute on Drug Abuse, 1978a, 1995; Sharp, Beauvais, & Spence, 1992).

Anabolic Steroids

Consider the following:

1. Of the U.S. graduating high school class of 1997, 2.4% had used steroids at some time in their lives, 1.4% had used it in the last year, and 1% had used it in the previous month (Johnston, O'Malley, & Bachman, 1997).
2. Steroid abuse (daily use) by the class of 1997 was almost statistically nonexistent (three-tenths of 1%) (Johnston, O'Malley, & Bachman, 1997).
3. In the U.S. 8th-grade class of 1997, the use of steroids was statistically nonexistent (Johnston, O'Malley, & Bachman, 1996).
4. Steroids do not increase or enhance athletic ability (Cicero & O'Connor, 1990).

Attempts to improve athletic performance predate the Greek Olympiads. In recent years a group of drugs first developed in Europe in the 1930s has been used and abused by athletes trying to gain an edge on their competition. Those drugs, anabolic steroids, are synthesized derivatives of the male hormone testosterone (Kochakian, 1990). It has been estimated that there are more than

1 million regular steroid users in North America and that 96% of professional football players may have used the drug, as well as 80 to 99% of bodybuilders (Goldstein, 1990). Among all American adolescent athletes, it is estimated that 7% of the males and 1% of the females may have used the drug (Yesalis, Anderson, Buckley, & Wright, 1990). It has also been estimated that nearly 80% of the steroids produced in the United States are not used for legitimate purposes and that black market sales of the drug presently exceed $400 million a year (Goldstein, 1990).

Substance Characteristics

Anabolic steroids are injected into the body in the belief that they will improve muscular development and athletic performance. Users report euphoria, a sense of well- being, increased energy, aggressive and invincible feelings, and tenseness (Cicero & O'Connor, 1990; Katz & Pope, 1990). Interestingly, most studies do not find evidence to support the contention that steroids improve either male muscular development or athletic performance (Cicero & O'Connor, 1990; Lombardo, 1990). Steroid use by female athletes has not been as well studied. However, as these drugs are testosterone variants, it is reasonable to believe that they would increase a female's strength. This is, of course, at the cost of creating females who develop many of the secondary sex characteristics of males as a result of their steroid use.

The abuse of steroids by adolescents can result in endocrine disturbances, cardiac and liver problems, stunted growth, testicular atrophy, impotency, and acne (Cicero & O'Connor, 1990).

Steroids do have legitimate medical uses in preventing muscular atrophy in injured individuals, in treating males with testosterone deficiency, and in treating abnormally delayed sexual maturation in adolescent females. There is no evidence that tolerance of the drug develops.

User/Abuser Characteristics

Unlike other substances in this chapter that are taken for their psychoactive effects, users of steroids take the drug to enhance athletic ability. They are achievers, individuals who commit themselves to rigorous training schedules in order to further their athletic ability.

Nevertheless, the drug does have psychoactive side effects. Individuals using steroids may become more aggressive and engage in irrational destructive behavior sometimes referred to as "roid rage" in response to even minor frustrations (Cicero & O'Connor, 1990). Reports suggest users may experience paranoid episodes and depression (Tennant, Black, & Voy, 1988). In one study, for example, Katz and Pope (1990) interviewed 41 male bodybuilders and football players who admitted using steroids. They found that more than 1 in 5 reported experiencing depression after steroid use. Twelve percent (5) reported psychotic symptoms.

LSD

Consider the following:

1. Of the U.S. high school class of 1997, 13.6% at some time in their lives had used LSD (Johnston, O'Malley, & Bachman, 1997). This is record use for this hallucinogen.
2. In Ontario, Canada 10% of the 1997 senior class reported the lifetime use of LSD (Paglia & Room, 1999).
3. LSD abuse (daily use) by the U.S. class of 1997 was almost statistically nonexistent (two-tenths of 1%) (Johnston, O'Malley, & Bachman, 1997).
4. In the U.S. 8th-grade class of 1997, 4.7% have tried LSD (Johnston, O'Malley, & Bachman, 1997).
5. Prior to its regulation in the 1960s, "all one had to do was send a little note to Sandoz Pharmaceuticals and tell them you would like some LSD. . . . and they would send it wholesale" (Burnham, 1993, p. 124).

The LSD antics of the Door's lead singer Jim Morrison to the Jefferson Airplane's "White Rabbit" and Peter Fonda's "acid dropping" on film in the late 1960s replaced the more innocent antics of the *Beach Blanket Bingo* gang for many adolescents 3 decades ago. With the high priest of the psychedelic movement, Timothy Leary, urging young people to "turn on, tune in, and drop out," many adolescents—possibly disillusioned with the Vietnam War and the assassinations of John and Robert Kennedy and Dr. Martin Luther King, Jr.—may have followed Leary's advice. Present-day experimentation with these mind-altering substances by youths whose interest in retro-1960s music and clothing seemingly extends to the drugs as well has increased the lifetime use of LSD to record levels.

Lysergic acid diethylamide or "Electric Kool-aid," as it was known to a generation of youths whose children are now in college, is ingested, usually in the form of tablets, small squares of gelatin, or impregnated paper (Medrow, 1995). Similar substances are found naturally in, for example, the ergot fungus, which grows on rye and other cereal grasses, and in morning glory seeds.[5] Its effects range from time/distance distortions and hallucinations to psychotic episodes. The drug typically takes effect within 30 minutes, and the effects last 8 to 12 hours in most cases, depending on the dose. Flashbacks (the reentry into a hallucinogenic state without taking the substance) are reported in some instances, and for some young people, the psychotic behavior resulting from the ingestion of LSD has continued for much longer than 12 hours. Users do not become physically dependent. Psychological dependence on LSD is considered highly unlikely (Lin & Glennon, 1994).

Research on LSD consumers has focused on the abuser of LSD, not the user. With this qualifier in mind, we can describe LSD abusers as often coping poorly with a disorganized and confused personal life and as in search of some meaning to

---

[5]For those interested in swallowing a packet of morning glory seeds or brewing a cup of tea with them, the advice is "don't." For several years seed companies have been spraying the seeds with chemicals that cause vomiting and diarrhea.

their existence (Jones, 1973; NIDA, 1995; Smart & Jones, 1970). Family hardships, such as broken homes, alcoholic parents, and poor parent/adolescent relationships, are frequently present (NIDA, 1995; Welpton, 1968). Abuse of more than one drug is very likely to occur with the LSD user (Seffrin & Seehafer, 1976).

Stimulants

Consider these facts:

1. Stimulants are one of two drugs more often used by females than males (Johnston, O'Malley, & Bachman, 1996b).
2. Of the U.S. graduating class of 1997, 16.5% had used stimulants at some time in their lives, 10.2% had used it in the last year, and 4.6% had used it in the previous month (Johnston, O'Malley, & Bachman, 1997).
3. Stimulant abuse (daily use) by the U.S. class of 1997 was almost statistically nonexistent (three/tenths of 1%) (Johnston, O'Malley, & Bachman, 1997).
4. Less than 13% (12.3%) of the U.S. 8th-grade class of 1997 have tried stimulants (Johnston, O'Malley, & Bachman, 1997).

Some of the more commonly known stimulants are nicotine, caffeine, cocaine, and methamphetamine or "ice." Our interest here is in amphetamines, known popularly as "speed."

Substance Characteristics

Amphetamines can be taken orally or injected. Users report effects varying from increased alertness, insomnia, loss of appetite, and euphoria at medically prescribed levels to agitation, depression, confusion, hallucinations, paranoia, and, in some situations and at higher levels, convulsions. The effect of amphetamines increases directly in proportion to the level of usage involved. Unless they are injected into the bloodstream, their effects are felt in about 30 minutes. Although the possibility of physical dependence on amphetamines is low to moderate, the chances of psychological dependence are high. Tolerance can occur very rapidly. For example, abusers have been known to inject 1000 milligrams of amphetamines into their bodies at one time, whereas a prescribed dose is between 2.5 and 15 milligrams per day.

User/Abuser Characteristics

Millions of adolescents and adults have used amphetamines over the years. From the struggling dieter to the student "pulling an all-nighter" and the sleepy truck driver to the professional football player, they have used amphetamines to lose weight, to stay awake, or to stimulate alertness and increase aggression. Their availability in medicine cabinets across the country (thus permitting "closet" drug use) helps to explain their popularity with females (National Institute on Drug Abuse, 1987b).

Amphetamine abusers including those same medicine-cabinet borrowers, sleepy students and truck drivers, and athletes report anxiety, depression, mood swings, and paranoid feelings as their use of the drug reaches serious proportions (Williamson, Gossop, Powis, Griffiths, Fountain, & Strang, 1997). In other regards, they are similar to other drug abusers. Likely to be multiple-drug abusers, they are described as failures in school and at personal relationships. The family again emerges as a primary contributing factor, with the home environment described as a cold, unfeeling, and uncaring place (Brook, Kaplum, & Whitehead, 1974; Yeh, Chen, & Sim, 1995).

Barbiturates

Note the following findings:

1. Approximately 81 million prescriptions for barbiturates are written each year (Department of Health and Human Services, 1991b).
2. Of the U.S. high school graduating class of 1997, 8.1% had used barbiturates at some time in their lives, 5.1% had used it in the last year, and 2.1% had used it in the previous month (Johnston, O'Malley, & Bachman, 1997).
3. Barbiturate abuse (daily use) by the class of 1997 was almost statistically nonexistent (one-tenth of 1%) (Johnston, O'Malley, & Bachman, 1997).
4. Of the U.S. 8th-grade class of 1997, 4.8% had tried tranquilizers (Johnston, O'Malley, & Bachman, 1997).
5. Adolescent use of these drugs is higher for females than for males (Johnston, O'Malley, & Bachman, 1996b).

Booze and pills have caused the deaths of many a creative artist, from Elvis Presley to Margeaux Hemingway. The combination of too much alcohol and too many barbiturates (or just too many barbiturates alone) drastically lowers blood pressure and respiration, resulting in the loss of life.

Substance Characteristics

Barbiturates are most frequently taken orally, but they can be dissolved in water and injected. Injected, they produce the warm, sleepy sensations commonly associated with a "rush." Taken orally, the drug takes effect in about 30 minutes. In low doses, barbiturates produce a mild sedation. As the amount increases, the effects range from a sense of well-being to depression to alcohol-like intoxication marked by slurred speech and impaired motor coordination to unconsciousness, coma, and/or death resulting from an overdose. Tolerance to barbiturates builds rapidly, resulting in the increased danger to the barbiturate abuser of reaching unsafe or lethal doses of the drug in a relatively short time. Barbiturates are regarded as having a moderately high potential for creating a physical and/or psychological dependence (Coupey, 1997; National Institute on Drug Abuse, 1987b; U.S. Department of Health and Human Services, 1991b).

We should note before we conclude this section that barbiturate abusers should *never attempt to quit the habit without medical supervision.* Not all barbiturates are alike in their effect on the individual attempting to quit. The barbiturate abuser runs a real risk of life-threatening convulsions, delirium, and grand mal seizures during withdrawal. To avoid these withdrawal symptoms, the abuser is best advised to find the proper medical care to ensure that a bad experience is not the last experience (Coupey, 1997; National Institute on Drug Abuse, 1987b).

User/Abuser Characteristics

The typical barbiturate user who appears in the emergency room of a hospital is White, female, and between the ages of 20 and 40 (U.S. Department of Health and Human Services, 1991b). Although nearly all barbiturate abusers are aware of the dangers of combining alcohol and pills, they do it anyway. This behavior leads some researchers to conclude that barbiturate abusers have suicidal personalities. Anxious, depressed, with low self-esteem, and viewing themselves as failures (Lech, Gary, & Ury, 1975), abusers mirror the alcohol-dependent personality in many aspects of personal, school, and family life.

Cocaine

Here are four interesting facts:

1. Of the U.S. high school graduating class of 1997, 8.7% had used cocaine at some time in their lives, 5.5% had used it in the last year, and 2.3% had used it in the previous month (Johnston, O'Malley, & Bachman, 1997).
2. Cocaine abuse (daily use) by the U.S. class of 1997 was almost statistically nonexistent (two-tenths of 1%) (Johnston, O'Malley, & Bachman, 1997).
3. Of the U.S. 8th-grade class of 1997, 4.4% had tried cocaine (Johnston, O'Malley, & Bachman, 1997).
4. Mark Twain relates in his autobiography that "I had been reading Lieutenant Herndon's account of his explorations of the Amazon and had been mightily attracted by what he said of coca. I made up my mind that I would go to the head-waters of the Amazon and collect coca and trade in it and make a fortune" (Neider, 1959, p. 98). Mark Twain never got there.

With published reports of its abuse by athletes, movie stars, and the wealthy, cocaine has acquired a degree of notoriety. Its history is particularly fascinating, for its use reaches back hundreds of years, to before the Incan Empire, and involves a pope, a soft-drink company, and the founder of the psychoanalytic movement.

Cocaine is found in the leaves of a South American plant, the coca shrub (*Erythroxylon coca*). Possessing religious significance for the Incan Empire, coca was controlled directly by the Incan emperor, and its use was limited to the privileged nobility of that society. This restricted use changed with the invasion of the Spanish, who liberally distributed coca among the South American natives once they discovered that its stimulant effect resulted in higher worker productivity with lower food rations (Inglis, 1975).

Coca did not become popular in Europe until the mid-1850s, when it was introduced into a number of products ranging from patent-medicines to wine. The wine, in particular a variety called Mariani's Wine, won a number of high endorsements, including one from Pope Leo XIII. The popularity of coca spread back overseas, this time to North America, where in Atlanta in 1886 a druggist introduced a patent-medicine containing coca. Claimed to be a remedy for a number of troublesome ailments, Coca-Cola, as it was called, gained widespread popularity. One additional note on this patent drug is warranted: long before the 1906 Pure Food and Drug Act was passed, the makers of this no-longer-popular patent-medicine but now-popular soda-fountain beverage had replaced coca with other substances (Grinspoon & Bakalar, 1976).

The isolation of the "kick" in coca, cocaine, occurred in Germany, where it was used as a stimulant and as an anesthetic in eye surgery. The medical popularity of cocaine as an anesthetic, a reliever of depression, and a substitute for morphine in treating cases of morphine addiction spread quickly. With none other than Dr. Sigmund Freud describing it as a "magical drug," the popularity of cocaine moved from the medical to the public arena (Brecher, 1972).

Portrayed as a quick pick-me-up for the tired of mind or body, more enjoyable than alcohol and without the side effects, cocaine was widely used by the public for several years. Interest in cocaine diminished as reports began to come in that it produced strong psychological dependence, created severe mental disturbances, and in some cases even led to death. Freud's own defense of cocaine abruptly ended with the emotional breakdown of a close friend, Dr. von Fleischl-Marxow. Marxow's use of the drug to treat his morphine addiction had reached outlandish proportions, and he developed a paranoid psychosis marked by formication. (Formication is the belief that insects or snakes are crawling on or under the skin.) This incident

Cocaine floods the brain with dopamine, making it a highly-addictive drug.

had such a profound impact on Freud that he foreswore the use of cocaine from that time forward both in his personal life and in his medical practice (Grinspoon & Bakalar, 1976).

Substance Characteristics

Cocaine can be injected but is more frequently inhaled ("snorted"). In its freebase form it can be smoked. Its effects on the user range from excitement and increased alertness to, in very large doses or with prolonged use, hallucinations and convulsions. Death can result from an ingested overdose of 1.2 grams or from applying 20 milligrams to the mucous membranes (American Society for Pharmacology, 1987; Gay, Sheppard, Inaba, & Newmeyer, 1973; Jones, 1987; Siegel, 1987).

The powerful addictive ability of cocaine is explained by its effect on the dopaminergic synapse of the brain. Cocaine prolongs the activity of dopamine in the synapse by flooding it with the neurotransmitter. If given unlimited access to the drug, cocaine has the ability to dominate instinctual behaviors like eating, sleeping, and the sexual drive (Gawin, 1991; Holden, 1989; Wise, 1987). This has made the treatment of cocaine addiction particularly difficult. Encouragingly, a recent report in *Science* suggests that a chemical enzyme is under development that may speed the breakdown of cocaine in the bloodstream, thus robbing the drug of its powerful "rush" effect before it reaches the brain (Morell, 1993).

Psychological dependence is very high, and tolerance builds rapidly. Although in the past the high cost of cocaine made it difficult for adolescents to develop a habit (dependence), the appearance of a freebase form of cocaine called "crack" in a 65- to 100-milligram dose for $10 has placed the drug "temporarily" within the price range of young people. The word temporarily is used because the cost of maintaining a crack habit will rapidly escalate, forcing the young person into either treatment or illegal activity (U.S. Department of Health and Human Services, 1991b) (see Box 12-1).

User/Abuser Characteristics

It is highly unusual to find a pure cocaine abuser. Rather, research and clinical evidence suggests, the so-called cocaine abuser is in fact a polydrug user (Adams & Kozel, 1985; Wesson & Smith, 1985). Not surprisingly, the cocaine abuser has been found to be involved in illegal activities—many of which are violent (Denison, Paredes, & Booth, 1997). Likely to be fatigued, depressed, and impotent, the cocaine abuser is, given the cost of supporting a cocaine habit, in serious financial trouble (Clayton, 1985; Johanson, Duffy, & Anthony, 1996; Gold, Washton, & Dackis, 1985; Siegel, 1987; Wesson & Smith, 1979, 1985). In turn, the abuser's financial difficulties understandably contribute to strained family relations. As the availability of cocaine has increased a clearer and sadder picture of the cocaine abuser has developed. Because of cocaine's addictive power, the drug has the ability to dominate an individual's life. For those few individuals who are able to "contain" their use of the substance, evidence suggests that they appear as emotionally healthy as the next person (Grinspoon & Bakalar, 1976; Siegel, 1987).

BOX **12-1**   Crack: Cheap Thrills

Cocaine that has been chemically altered, using baking soda and heat, into a "base" is called crack. The origin of the word can be traced to the tendency of the substance to crackle when it is heated. Processed crack looks like small lumps or soap shavings, with a porcelain-like texture. In 1997, 3.3% of the U.S. senior class admitted to ever using crack; 2.4% used it in the last year; <1% used it in the last month; and one-tenth of 1% used it daily (Johnston, O'Malley, & Bachman, 1997). Of concern, the U.S. 8th-grade class of 1997 reported lifetime use of crack at 2.7% (Johnston, O'Malley, & Bachman, 1997). Unless these early crack users leave school before graduation, which is highly likely given that crack users have the lowest psychosocial functioning of all drug users (Kandel & Davies, 1996), it appears that by the time they reach their senior year in 2001 they will have exceeded the lifetime use of the senior class of 1997.

There is no question but that cocaine can be addictive. The experiences of Dr. von Fleischl-Marxow described earlier in this section certainly confirm that observation. What has controlled the incidence of cocaine dependence since the 1950s has been its high cost. The appearance of crack is deeply disturbing for two reasons. First, its price per "hit" places the substance within the means of nearly everyone. Second, crack is the most potent form of cocaine. Smoking the substance produces an immediate "high" of short duration that is followed by an intense "low" that leaves the user wanting more. Given crack's low cost, that need for more can be satisfied—again and again and again until the individual is addicted. The dependence is so intense that a cocaine-addicted individual will prefer the drug over all else (Adams & Durell, 1987).[6]

The powerful addictive ability of the drug and its initial low cost have created an economic job market albeit fraught with danger for many unemployed city youths (Johnson, Williams, Sanabria, & Dei, 1990). These young people either sell the drug on the streets or steer individuals to places where the drug can be purchased and used. These "crack houses" are reminiscent of the opium dens that catered to the addicts of the 19th century and similar to the "shooting galleries" found in most cities today, where heroin addicts can rent the works to inject themselves with a nickel bag of dope. Whether it be a crack house, opium den, or shooting gallery, its customers have become slaves to a substance (National Institute on Drug Abuse, 1987a).

[6]Smoking cocaine is not new to our time. At the turn of the century the respected pharmaceutical firm of Parke, Davis & Co. manufactured two such cocaine products— coca cheroot and coca cigarettes—for sale. Each is thought to have contained between 0.5 to 1% cocaine (Jones, 1990).

Heroin

Consider these facts:

1. Only 2.1% of the U.S. high school class of 1997 have ever used heroin (Johnston, O'Malley, & Bachman, 1997).
2. Disturbingly, 2.1% of the U.S. 8th-grade class have used heroin. This insures that the rate of use for the senior class of 2001 will exceed that of seniors in 1997. (Johnston, O'Malley, & Bachman, 1997).
3. Heroin abuse (daily use) by senior classes since 1975 has never exceeded one-tenth of 1% (Johnston, O'Malley, & Bachman, 1997).

Heroin has a special meaning in the hearts of most Americans. Through such television shows as "Chicago Hope," "ER," and "NYPD Blue" and such films as *Trainspotting*, *The Doors*, and Andy Warhol's *Trash*, the American public has come to fear the drug known on the street as Aunt Hazel.

The opium poppy (*Papaver somniferum*) grows in many areas of the world— from Southeast Asia to India, Turkey, Hungary, Yugoslavia, and Mexico—to name just a few. Its use as a medicine to ease pain and to treat dysentery, malaria, and other ailments dates back to before the birth of Christ. Opium and its chief constituent, morphine (from which heroin is synthesized), were easily obtained in the 19th century throughout North America, as we showed at the beginning of this chapter, and much of the rest of the world as well.[7] Heroin was first produced in 1898. The availability of all three drugs in the United States was not really limited until the Harrison Narcotic Act of 1914.

Substance Characteristics

Heroin can be sniffed, smoked, or consumed as a beverage, but it is most commonly injected.[8] The warm rush that comes moments after the injection has been reported to feel like a whole-body orgasm. This sensation is soon followed in most cases by lethargy and the need to sleep. The potential for physical and psychological dependence is high, and tolerance builds rapidly. Street heroin is sold in bags (a single dose) of 100 milligrams. Of this amount, perhaps 5% is heroin. The remainder may be sugar, starch, powdered milk, quinine, or some other substances. Occasionally, heroin users purchase a bag containing a much higher percentage of heroin than they have been accustomed to using. The result of injecting this higher percentage of heroin is an overdose, often resulting in death (National Institute on Drug Abuse, 1987b; Department of Health and Human Services, 1991b).

A second threat to the IV heroin user is the development of AIDS. The use of contaminated needles is rapidly spreading this deadly viral infection among heroin users (Kozel & Adams, 1986). Nearly 31% (and that figure is increasing) of all AIDS victims are IV drug users (U.S. Census Bureau, 1997, 142, Chart 215).

User/Abuser Characteristics

Although it is possible to use heroin and not become addicted, the tendency is for users to become abusers and then dependent in a relatively short time (Zinberg, 1979). Part of the reason is the rapid build-up of tolerance to the drug.

Although a heroin-dependent individual can come from any socioeconomic group, the poor are disproportionately represented. Coming from a background of poverty, hopelessness, and conflict, these heroin addicts are viewed as feeling worthless, being manipulative, and unable to handle frustration (Collum & Pike, 1976; Craig, 1986; Kurtines, Hogan, & Weiss, 1975; SAMHSA, 1997). They are

---

[7]China's attempt to stop the British importation of opium into China for use by the populace created the opium War of 1839–1842. The Chinese government's loss of that war ensured the populace an adequate supply for the next sevral decades.

[8]In *Confessions of an English Opium-Eater*, Thomas DeQuincey consumed opium in a beverage probably mixed with alcohol.

The use of unsterilized needles is a sure way of contracting several deadly diseases, including AIDS.

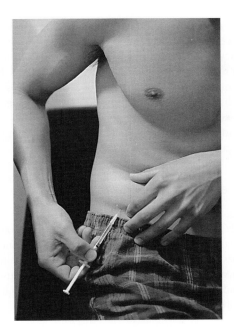

also seen as depressed, aggressive, self-destructive, unable to cope with stress, and escaping reality through denial, rationalization, and drug dependence (Craig, 1986; SAMHSA, 1997; Woody & Blaine, 1979). The addict is likely to come from a poor home situation marked, again, by family turmoil, parental rejection, and loose supervision. It also appears that (as with the alcohol-dependent individual) the addict is likely to have a parent or parents who abuse alcohol or other drugs (Braucht, Brakarsh, Follinstad, & Berry, 1973; Woody & Blaine, 1979).

Summary

One substance, solvents, emerges as the greatest immediate threat for serious physical or psychological damage to the user.[9] Although a small minority of adolescents become drug abusers or dependent, those who do are most frequently multiple-drug users. The factors contributing to abuse or dependence include personality, family, and community variables. Most studies show drug-abusing or drug-dependent individuals as having low self-esteem and feelings of helplessness (Paglia & Room, 1999). They are anxious, depressed, restless individuals

[9]This statement assumes that the other drugs purchased on the street are in fact the drugs the buyer has asked for and that, in the case of injectable substances, the user is using "clean works." Since there are no consumer laws protecting the illcit drug user and since quality control has been known to slip on occasion, wisdom would suggest that one should not expriment. But in wisdom's absence, *caveat emptor* ("let the buyer beware")!

who internalize their anger and depression in self-destructive drug use. Likely to be delinquent and heavily influenced by their peer group, these young people use delinquency and relationships with their friends as attempts to secure replacements after their rejection of—and rejection by—family, school, and community.

The families of these adolescents are viewed as contributors to their use of drugs. Loose parental control, poor parent/adolescent relationships, high family discord, and divorce are common. There is also evidence that parental abuse of alcohol and other drugs sets an early and poor example for the child to follow in adolescence (Paglia & Room, 1999).

Substance Use among Ethnic and Racial Groups

European Americans and ethnically and racially diverse groups in the United States and Canada consume drugs differently. For example, while Whites are most likely to use alcohol or marijuana, Blacks, Latinos, and American Indians are more likely to use alcohol and drugs other than marijuana (McWhirter et al., 1993). These consumption patterns are influenced by factors like social class, cultural beliefs, and experiences of prejudice and discrimination. Given these variations, let's explore them.

Black Americans

In comparison to Whites and other diverse groups, there is evidence that alcohol and drug usage is lower among Black adolescents. Welte and Barnes (1987) reported that Black youths, when compared to five other ethnically diverse groups, had the lowest percentage of drinkers among 7th- to 12th-grade adolescents (with the exception of Asians). Further, there was a lower percentage of heavy drinkers among Black youths in contrast to the other groups. On the other hand, for those Black adolescents who did drink, they had a higher number of alcohol-related problems than other groups. This pattern of behavior was also observed by Barnes, Farrell, and Banerjee (1994), who found that 13- to 16-year-old Blacks had significantly lower levels of overall drinking, frequent heavy drinking, drunkenness, and overall deviant behaviors in contrast to their White counterparts.

Drug use patterns of Blacks have been found to be similar to alcohol use behavior (Welts & Barnes, 1987). Newcomb, Maddahian, Skager, and Bentler (1987) reported that use of drugs among Blacks was less than that of American Indians and Whites, but not as low as Asians. However, Poulin (1991) noted that the gap in drug use between Blacks and Whites closed after the age of 20.

Families can exert strong influences that discourage substance use. Family behavior related to lower alcohol abuse among Black youths included higher levels of religiosity, higher levels of maternal support, parental monitoring, and positive communications with the mother (Barnes et al., 1994). Religious involvement is a strong deterrent to alcohol and drug use among Black adolescents (Wallace & Bachman, 1991; Obot, 1996). Emotional support from fathers has been found to be related to lower marijuana use among Black adolescents (Zimmerman, Salem, &

Maton, 1995). And contrary to common belief, living in a single-mother household has not been found to be related to higher alcohol and substance abuse among Black adolescents (Barnes et al., 1994; Zimmerman et al., 1995).

In contrast, several factors have been associated with problem drinking among older Black adolescents and adults. They are: (1) being male, (2) living in an urban area, (3) having less than 12 years of education, and (4) living in a poor neighborhood (Obot, 1996). Despite this, Black adolescents have been shown to have higher resistance to peer and adult role modeling of substance abuse in comparison to Whites, Latinos, and Asians (Newcomb & Bentler, 1986).

North American Indians

Strong evidence exists that alcohol- and drug-use problems occur at greater levels with American Indian adolescents than with other youths (Beauvais & LaBoueff, 1985; Cockerham, Forslund, & Raboin, 1976; Oetting & Beauvais, 1982; Porter, Vieira, Kaplan, Heesch, & Colyar, 1973). For example, Welte and Barnes (1987) found that American Indian students in grades 7 to 12 were highest in per capita alcohol consumption, had the highest percentage of heavy drinkers, reported the highest number of times of being drunk, had the highest number of alcohol-related problems, and were highest on illicit drug use in comparison to White, Asian, Black, West Indian, and Latino youths. Others have reported that the use of alcohol and drugs (with the exception of hard drugs) was highest among American Indian students in grades 7, 9, and 11 as compared to other youths (Newcomb et al., 1987).

Among high school females, Riley, Barenie, Mabe, and Myers (1990) found that American Indians reported higher use of chewing tobacco. Further, American Indian early adolescents were active abusers of inhalants with alcohol frequently replacing inhalants by mid-adolescence (Berlin, 1986). Berlin (1986) also noted high usage of marijuana by some American Indian youths and observed that this drug and others were readily available on many reservations. Greater accessibility thus contributed to higher usage by American Indian adolescents. Findings among Native Canadians reveal similar patterns of alcohol and drug use (Gfellner, 1994).

Many reasons have been offered to explain the high misuse of substances by some American/Canadian Indian youths (Royce, 1981). These theories contain cultural, social, economic, biological, and psychological elements. It appears that both *intrapsychic* (internal to the individual) and *extrapsychic* (stemming from sources outside of the individual) factors are active in the substance use of American Indians. For instance, as an intrapsychic factor, Berlin (1986) has identified depression as common among American Indian adolescents and noted that depression was linked to the misuse of drugs and alcohol. On many Indian reservations, depressed males, on a daily basis, congregate in groups and abuse inhalants and alcohol (Berlin, 1986). The fact that alcohol is used as a symbol for social connection and solidarity between friends and family members compounds the problem for American Indians (Welte & Barnes, 1987).

Extrapsychic explanations also require consideration in understanding the substance misuse of American Indians. North American Indians have experienced a 500-year-old history of prejudice and discrimination (that includes attempts at genocide) from European Americans. Discrimination against and prejudice toward American Indians are still common occurrences. Consistent with this argument, Westermeyer (1974) noted that the alarming rate of alcoholism among American Indians is not the largest problem of Indians nor the cause of other problems. Rather, social and economic difficulties play strong contributing roles to high rates of substance use and abuse among American Indians. Beauvais and LaBoueff (1985) affirm this view by stating "failure to understand the social, cultural, and geopolitical realities of American Indian life leads to inappropriate, and thus ineffective, solutions to social problems including alcohol and drug abuse" (p. 139).

The role of culture in substance use has additional relevance to the discussion of intrapsychic and extrapsychic factors. For instance, it is suggested that *biculturalism* (defined as an orientation toward both one's own culture and the dominant culture), *cultural identification* (identifying oneself as part of an ethnic group), and *acculturation* (the degree of adoption of the dominant culture's values and practices) are related to substance use among some American Indian adolescents. American Indian adolescents holding a bicultural orientation reported the lowest usage of alcohol and drugs, while those identifying only with the European-American culture had the highest rates of drug usage (Oetting & Beauvais, 1982).

Latinos

Alcohol and drug use among Latino youths is higher than some groups and lower than others. For example, for 7th- to 12th-grade students, Latino alcohol and drug usage is reported to be less than those of Whites and American Indians, but higher than those of Blacks and Asians (Welte & Barnes, 1987). Similarly, Newcomb and Bentler (1986) reported 7th- to 9th-grade Latinos drinking patterns to be similar to those of Whites, but higher than those of Blacks and Asians. Heavier drinking was more common among Latino males than females.

What factors influence substance use among Latino youths? Schinke and his associates (1988) have linked psychosocial and urban environmental stress related to substance abuse among Latino youths. In respect to psychosocial factors, Latino junior high alcohol users and nonusers were compared by Alva and Jones (1994). Significantly more alcohol users had gotten into trouble, felt pressure by friends to get into fights, could not communicate well with parents, had experienced other students making fun of them for the way they spoke English, and felt excluded from school because of their cultural background.

Additional psychosocial predictors of early Latino adolescent substance use were identified by Flannery, Vazsonyi, and Rowe (1996). Sixth- and seventh-grade Latino and White adolescents were examined in respect to parenting, personality, and school adjustment in relation to substance use. Few ethnic and gender differences were found. However, it was shown that lower levels of illicit drug use and experimentation with substances were directly linked to school adjustment. Feeling good about school was related to lower levels of dysfunctional personality variables like aggression, depression, and withdrawal. Lower drug use was also related to higher levels of positive parental support and effective supervision in their lives.

In regard to parental support, one group of researchers report that Latino youths who perceive their parents as supportive are less influenced by peers and better able to resist peer pressures to use drugs (Frauenglass, Routh, Pantin, & Mason, 1997). The word "perceived" should remind the reader of Carl Rogers (1965) observations made earlier in this book (Chapter 10). Remember, it is not enough that we be honest, genuine, trustworthy, and empathic with young people for change to occur, but they must see us as possessing these qualities. Further, as Bandura (1982) has observed, these youths must see themselves as capable of achieving that change.

Asian Americans

Of the ethnic/racial groups discussed in this section, Asian Americans have the lowest rates of alcohol and drug usage. Welte and Barnes (1987) reported that Asian-American 7th- to 12th-grade students were lowest in terms of percentage of drinkers and had the lowest number of alcohol-related problems in comparison to Whites and four other diverse groups. However, among those Asians who did drink, their average consumption was highest among the groups that were compared. Newcomb and associates (1987; Newcomb and Bentler, 1986) reported that Asian youths were lowest on drug use in comparison to American Indians, Blacks, Latinos, and Whites.

One factor that may account for lower Asian adolescent usage of substances may be the lack of peer relations. Asian youths appear to spend less time in peer activities and more time in family activities (Wallace & Bachman, 1991). Furthermore, Newcomb and Bentler (1986) reported that Asian adolescents had the lowest incidence of both peer and adult role modeling of substances. Oetting and associates (1988) have argued that peer involvement directly impacts alcohol use. Thus, less peer contact among Asian adolescents results in lower rates of substance usage. Related factors that have been linked to lower rates of substance use among Asians include a strong commitment to education and academic success (Wallace & Bachman, 1991).

To summarize, this section demonstrates that culture and racial factors effect patterns of drug use. In light of this information, the best efforts to treat and prevent drug abuse will capitalize on the positive aspects of racial and ethnic groups in the design of the intervention to lower drug use.

IMPLICATIONS FOR TREATMENT AND PREVENTION

Treatment

Increasingly, substance abuse professionals believe that "addiction is . . . a chronic, relapsing illness, characterized by impulsive drug seeking and use"

(Leshner, 1997, p. 45). From this perspective, it is believed that repeated drug use eventually changes the brain's structure to "crave" a drug, and individual choice is no longer an option—ever. Thus, the battle for the "former" substance abuser is a lifelong struggle against relapsing into reuse. If this understanding is correct then the importance of treatment and, more importantly, prevention is obvious.

For nearly all drug-dependent youths, kicking the habit begins with detoxification. Detoxification involves hospitalization to eliminate the acute physical or psychological dependence on the drug. The primary goal of the detoxification program is to provide the medical care necessary to relieve the physical discomforts that accompany withdrawal. A secondary goal is to assist the drug-dependent individual in finding the most suitable treatment program to help prevent the recurrence of substance dependence.

Therapeutic Communities

Once detoxification has occurred, the drug-dependent individual may decide in favor of a group home for treatment. One type of group home is a residence staffed by recovering alcoholics or ex-drug abusers. The therapeutic community uses group pressure and support, remedial education, or employment to help the dependent individual change his or her behavior.

The therapeutic community views the addict's actions as a lifelong destructive pattern of behavior. To change this pattern, the community often demands a complete alteration of the addict's lifestyle. Drug abstinence, the elimination of criminal behavior, obtaining a job or more education, and the development of such traits as self-reliance and honesty with oneself and others are encouraged in a 24-hour-a-day program that attacks old behaviors.

The intensity of the program is so great that only a small number (10 to 15%) of all those who are admitted to therapeutic communities can complete it. The program is considered effective for those who can. Follow-up studies 1 to 5 years later show that most former members are able to hold jobs, stay off drugs, and stay out of trouble with the authorities (DeLeon & Rosenthal, 1979; Lipton, 1996; Tims, DeLeon, & Jainchill, 1994).

Methadone Treatment for Heroin Addiction

For an estimated 115,000 former heroin addicts in North America today, the treatment program used to prevent the recurrence of heroin addiction is methadone (O'Brien, 1997). Methadone is itself a narcotic that in the proper dose acts to block heroin withdrawal's effects. This blocking action occurs because methadone has a cross-tolerance with heroin; that is, the drug neutralizes the effects of heroin. Additionally, methadone, when taken in regular, prescribed, oral doses, does not produce the "high" commonly associated with narcotics.

Methadone is not an answer in itself to drug rehabilitation, and other services must be provided if the former addict is to achieve a new life without drugs. Most clinics offer job training, remedial education, and counseling.

BOX **12-2** **Sometimes Drugs Are Medicine**

There are many reasons for taking drugs. For many young people, it's the challenge, the risk, the excitement of a new thrill. For others, it's an expression of anger, hatred, protest, or desperation. For still others, it is an attempt to hang on to sanity—an attempt at self-medication to get from today to tomorrow in the only way they know how, as the following case study illustrates.

Jimmy was a dirty, greasy, unattractive 15-year-old who hung around the center of town watching (nothing more—just watching). My contact with him resulted from a conversation I had with one of his former elementary school teachers. She had begun to suspect Jimmy of being the obscene phone caller whose nightly calls had begun to terrorize her. The suspicion was confirmed a few days later when she confronted him in school.

Jimmy begged her not to tell his parents and promised to do anything in return. She insisted he seek help and referred him to my office. In the days that followed, I saw a young, deeply troubled adolescent whose sexual interest in a stepsister had created tremendous inner conflict and guilt. To focus his attentions away from her, he had begun to phone other women, follow them home, and begin to plan to assault them. He recognized the wrongness of his behavior, and,

torn between his desire to follow through on his fantasies and his guilt over those fantasies, he had begun to increase his drug usage considerably. Jimmy's unconscious solution to controlling these very frightening feelings was to medicate himself with illicit drugs to the point where he could not act out his desires.

I saw Jimmy for several weeks. I concentrated on helping him recognize and verbalize his need for help. During that time I made no attempt to limit or influence Jimmy's drug use but worked to have him realize why he was medicating himself.

Jimmy eventually admitted his need for help and told his parents about his thoughts, feelings, and fears. Both parents and Jimmy agreed with me that hospital treatment was most appropriate. He checked in several days later, where his illegal self-medication was stopped and replaced with still other medication. Only this time it was prescribed by a physician.

Do you think it was correct to let Jimmy continue his drug abuse? Should Jimmy have been reported to the authorities to protect society? How do you balance the client's right to confidentiality with other people's right to be safe? For that matter, should clients have a right to confidentiality?

Whether methadone is an acceptable treatment for drug addiction is subject to heated debate. Proponents of methadone treatment point to its low cost and its success in enabling many former heroin addicts to return to school or work and to live otherwise normal lives. Opponents counter that substituting a legal narcotic for an illegal one accomplishes little or nothing. Abuse of methadone to achieve a "high" is possible, and opponents point out that the lifestyle of drug use has not been changed. Finally, opponents take a page from history and argue that not long ago heroin was used to combat morphine addiction. Is it not possible, they suggest, that today's cure for heroin dependence will become a problem in itself? (See Box 12-2.)

AA and Other Self-Help Groups

Extending a helping hand to a fellow human being in the same situation is the essence of the self-help group. Founded by former substance abusers, Alcoholics Anonymous (AA) and other programs operate under the belief that the recovering alcoholic or ex-drug abuser is in the best position to understand and help the individual struggling with an alcohol or a drug problem.

In some respects the programs of the therapeutic community and the self-help group are similar. Both rely upon ex-users, not professionals, to provide help. Both focus on completely changing the behavior of the user. Both demand abstinence from alcohol or drugs. Through weekly (or nightly) meetings, group members in both programs attempt to support one another in their goal of abstinence. Should temptation on the street become too great, each program uses a "buddy system"; that is, members are matched to other members to provide extra support for one another outside the meetings.

The success of self-help groups is difficult to determine. Although reports have been enthusiastic, these studies suffer from several problems in design. Nevertheless, given the growing popularity of the self-help movement with the general public, it would seem that the principle of neighbor helping neighbor is, from the public's point of view, effective.

Psychotherapy

Individual counseling can happen in many different settings. But whether it occurs in a hospital ward, in a methadone clinic, at a youth-service agency, or in a physician's office, therapy is directed at discussing the abuser's problems and attempting to resolve them.

This can take many different forms. Therapy styles can range from motivational approaches, which encourages the client to seek the strength and reasons to change behavior, to cognitive behavioral therapy, which uses systems of modeling, rewards, and negative reinforcements to change meaning and behavior into new lifestyle patterns (Birmingham, 1986).

Recent evidence suggests that matching patients to particular therapies is not necessary for effective treatment to occur (NIAA, 1997). However, cognitive behavioral approaches do show promise in treating adolescent substance abusers. Importantly, the treatment modality being used must be age appropriate if understanding is to occur. Further, given the complex multiple pathways that interact to lead a young person to abusing substances, it is doubtful that therapy alone will be successful. It is when therapy is used in conjunction with other treatment forms (methadone, self-help groups, job training, and so on) that it will be most useful (Palmer & Liddle, 1996; Wesson & Smith, 1979).

Family Therapy

One reason that individual psychotherapy often fails to help the substance-dependent individual may be that these approaches do nothing to change the system from which the individual has come. For the adolescent, this system is the family. We have already noted that parental drinking and drug use seem to have a strong influence on adolescent attitudes toward drugs and alcohol. We have also pointed out that poor parenting practices and poor parent/adolescent relationships seem to contribute to youthful drug abuse and dependence. Proponents of family therapy argue that changing the adolescent's behavior entails changing the family system.

In order to do so, the therapist helps family members solve their problems and achieve more positive and constructive ways of relating to one another. By focusing on the family as a whole and not on the "identified problem" (the drug-using adolescent), the therapist is able to avoid the pitfalls of the family's viewing the problem as only the adolescent's. Instead, this approach encourages the family to examine its own behaviors and the ways in which they contribute to the use of illegal substances by one of its members. In recent years comprehensive family-focused techniques have evolved. Called multisystemic family interventions, these interventions seek to strengthen family parenting practices, more closely monitor the peer friendships of youth, change parents' use of alcohol and other drugs, and strengthen the adolescent's social competency. These interventions are successful for both drug-abusing and delinquent youths (Borduin & Schaeffer, 1998; McCreary, Maffuid, & Stepter, 1998; Palmer & Liddle, 1996).

This treatment approach, while promising, is not without its problems. These problems involve the family's motivation for and commitment to changing its behavior. Many adolescents who abuse alcohol or drugs serve very useful functions in the family, such as keeping the parents from divorce or acting-out one parent's depression. If disrupting this delicate balance is too threatening, the family will resist and will maintain more familiar and comfortable ways of behaving. The message to the adolescent is then to continue to abuse drugs or alcohol (Palmer and Liddle, 1996).

Prevention

In a society that bombards its members with promises of instant relief from headaches, common-cold symptoms, dandruff, sleeplessness, and constipation, it is highly unlikely that drug use among the young can be prevented. Similarly, when drinking is considered so "downright upright," and alcohol is associated by advertisers with every social event from family reunions to job promotions, it is highly unrealistic to believe for a moment that drinking among youths can be delayed until they reach adulthood. We think prevention in the alcohol and drug arena should be directed not toward stopping their use ("Just Say No" efforts) but toward preventing abuse and dependence. Rather than zero-tolerance, this is a harm-reduction approach (Lewis, Duncan, & Clifford, 1997). The tools available to achieve this goal are education, promotion of social competency, community organization/systems intervention, and natural care giving.

Education

Under the umbrella of education, prevention can take the form of school activities, media announcements, and the distribution of materials. Many states require junior high school students to take at least one course in drug and alcohol education. The courses vary from school to school, but most of the programs currently in use combine factual information with social skills training in an effort to provide the adolescent with the ability to reject any drug use. This approach is best illustrated by the "Just Say No" drug campaigns of the 1980s.

In recent years scholars have challenged the "Just Say No" campaigns as being ineffective. In a society in which alcohol and cigarettes are both legal and heavily advertised to youths, the belief that young people will take "Just Say No" efforts seriously is doubtful. What is reemerging is a focus on harm reduction. That is, helping individuals understand the very real dangers drugs may present to them and assist them in developing informed decisions about their use. Thus, these drug-education programs are less interested in preventing all drug use as they are in encouraging responsible choices regarding the use of drugs at any age. In this model, a responsible choice for a young person may be not to use any drugs outside of medical prescriptions. For others, the choice may be to use potentially less-harmful drugs (Daugherty & Leukefeld, 1998; Meyer, 1995).

Finally, we warn individuals wanting to prevent drug abuse to recognize that by itself the prevention tool of education is not effective. A study by Fischer, Richards, Berman, and Krugman (1989) underscores this point. These authors were interested in the recall and eye-tracking behaviors of adolescents viewing tobacco advertisements. Their findings suggest that the warnings that appear in every advertisement are rarely, if ever, read. As noted in Chapter 10, education will nearly always increase knowledge; it will occasionally change attitudes; but it will rarely change behavior. It is only when education is used with prevention's three other tools that program effectiveness increases (Albee & Gullotta, 1997).

At a minimum this means that for drug prevention curricula to be effective they must involve the participant in an active way. Role plays, classroom discussions, and the encouragement of self-efficacy ("I can do this") must accompany the educational effort (Tobler & Stratton, 1997). Incidentally, engaging in these activities couples education with actions that are often used to promote social competency, but before you begin the next section consider what educational activities you would undertake to prevent drug use.

Promotion of Social Competency

Closely allied with education is the concept of promoting social competency. Social competency can be fostered through educational activities such as clarification of values and the encouragement of self-understanding and self-acceptance. It can be promoted through programs conducted by the YMCA, YWCA, and youth-service agencies; by church programs to improve parent/adolescent relationships through building communication skills; by peer counseling (which is more properly categorized as a tool not of competency promotion but of natural care giving); or by assertiveness training. Social competency promotion includes involvement in theatre, wilderness courses, boating, boxing, and innumerable other recreational or sports activities that meet the adolescent's social and emotional needs in socially acceptable ways (Emshoff, Avery, Raduka, Andersom, & Calvert, 1996; Johnson, Bryant, Strader, Bucholtz, Berbaum, Collins, & Noe, 1996).

The persuasive argument in favor of promoting social competency is that if the adolescent is given opportunities for personal and social growth and if these opportunities provide a feeling of worth, of importance, and a sense of being an *asset* to society, then drug or alcohol abuse and dependence will diminish. One final observation on the word *asset*.

Martin Bloom (2000), in an excellent review of the literature on promoting social competency through out-of-school activities, concludes that the ability of youths *to give back* mattered most in developing their sense of personal competency. For the authors of this book, who have spent their lives working with young people, we are not surprised. The *act of returning*, whether it is a theatre performance, volunteering at the library book sale, or doing some other civic duty, reaps praise, attention, and respect from the surrounding adult community. It is that valuing that youths seek and so desperately need in order to succeed in their lives. Again, we want you to pause here. Martin Bloom's observation is very insightful. Imagine yourself as a middle school teacher. How might you promote this youthful giving and as importantly adult recognition of that gift?

Natural Care Giving

Caring for oneself, for another, for others—that is the essence of natural care giving. For young people a spring of emotional support and strength to avoid substance abuse can flow from several sources.

One form of self-help is found in the numerous peer-leadership, counseling, and cross-age tutoring programs around the United States. These programs recognize that adults are often the last people whom young people consult about sensitive matters such as substance use. Thus, programs that provide youths with factual information and training in the use of that information with peers can be a useful tool in reducing drug usage. Preventionists believe that by extending honest, accurate information through peers, they can increase the probability that adolescents will make informed, responsible decisions (Gullotta & Adams, 1982b). The provision of such information offers an opportunity for young people to explore with one another the motivations behind substance use and to decide not to be users. Further, do you see that this is another example of "giving back" to another that is so important for healthy development?

A second form of caring, even more powerful than the first, is the power of a caring relationship *over time*. As the authors of this book examine the life stories of successful individuals, we are reminded repeatedly that those who get through adolescence and prosper in later life can identify a meaningful adult role figure during those years. It was this person the youth modeled herself or himself after. It was this person that bluntly but caringly told the youth to shape up when that was needed. It was this person who, when others were ready to throw in the towel, believed in the adolescent's potential. Programs like Big Brothers and Big Sisters are attempts to extend indigenous caregiving in planned ways.

By combining education, social competency, and natural caregiving, powerful programs can be developed to minimize alcohol, tobacco, and other drug use. Proof of this can be found in a recent meta-analysis of school-based drug prevention programs by Nan Tobler and Howard Stratton (1997). These researchers report that programs containing elements of these tools and used in an interactive format in which role playing and the practice of new skills occurs results in statistically powerful findings of minimized drug use. Indeed, the power of these programs equals and in many cases exceeds statistically the benefits of aspirin to prevent a heart attack. Further evidence for the effectiveness of combining these approaches can also be found in special issues of the *Journal of Adolescent Research* (Blakely, Coulter, Gardner, McColgan, & Gullotta, 1996), *The Journal of Early Adolescence* (Blakely, Coulter, Gardner, Jansen, & Gullotta, 1997), and *The Journal of Primary Prevention* (Blakely & Gullotta, 1998). Reviewing the funded research and development grants from the United States Federal Center for Substance Abuse Prevention, the editors for these special issues worked with successful grantees to publish their findings. A reoccurring theme was that single-focused single-tool approaches do not work. Approaches that work are comprehensive and targeted at the multiple systems (contexts) that impact youths. Noticeably absent from these federally funded projects were CO/SI initiatives. In a sense, this should not be surprising because macrolevel changes are very difficult to implement in the short period of time demonstration grants operate. Still, CO/SI interventions are very powerful methods of changing behavior, as we shall see.

Community Organization/Systems Intervention

More controversial than prevention's other tools is using legislation to prevent drug and alcohol abuse. Past attempts to legislate social behavior have proved unsuccessful.[10] Prohibiting the sale of cigarettes to young people under the age of 18 has not stopped smoking among this age group. Estimates that 70 million Americans have tried marijuana hardly strengthen the case for additional legal constraints, as supporters of the movement to decriminalize it are quick to point out (see Box 12-3).

Nevertheless, for some readily available substances—amphetamines, barbiturates, solvents, and alcohol—increased social action in the form of legislation may be an effective tool for decreasing their abuse by adolescents. For amphetamines and barbiturates, society needs to address the following issues. First, is the number of pills manufactured by U.S. firms warranted? Second, are these types of medication overprescribed by physicians? Finally, do the benefits of these drugs outweigh their disadvantages? Answers to these questions might produce enough evidence to warrant increased regulation of these substances. Similarly, regulatory control over the chemical content of solvents would provide the means of banning certain poisons and saving lives. Using the "distribution of consumption" model, which states that the availability of a substance is directly related to its incidence of abuse, Gullotta and Adams (1982b) and others (National Institute of Alcohol Abuse and Alcoholism, 1996; Wagenaar & Perry, 1994) suggest that alcohol abuse can be reduced. They encourage the use of such approaches as: (1) increasing the price of alcohol, (2) prohibiting the advertising of drugs and alcohol through the media,

---

[10]John Burnham (1993), in *Bad Habits*, would take issue with this last point. He contends that prohibition worked very well in reducing not only alcohol consumption but also alcohol-related illnesses. He argues it was the lure of huge profits that encouraged companies to effectively lobby Congress for change.

BOX **12-3**   Should Drugs Be Legalized?

What do Carl Sagan, William F. Buckley, Jr., Nobel laureate economist Milton Friedman, former Secretary of State George Shultz, and former Surgeon General Joycelyn Elders have in common? All of these noted individuals have spoken in favor of the legalization of one or more presently illegal drugs (Nicholson, 1989; *USA Today*, 1993). Why would these people and others speak in favor of substances that are harmful when abused?

These are several reasons. One reason is the economic cost of the war on drugs. An estimated $8 billion a year are being spent in a seemingly fruitless struggle to keep illegal substances out of this country. Drug-related arrests presently totaling more than 750,000 a year are clogging the courts and overcrowding the prisons such that "real time" is but a small fraction of assigned time (Nadelman, 1992). The profits from the illegal sale of drugs have financed a huge criminal element within this country whose power as a result of those profits can reach into the highest levels of state and federal governments.

Next, there are the social costs. The poor have disproportionately suffered under current drug control policies. It is their homes, their neighborhoods, and their children that are caught in the crossfire for the control of the drug trade (Clifford, 1992).

Third, there is the realization that the overwhelming majority of drug users are not and never will become drug dependent. Their use of substances is for the purpose of enjoyment (Nicholson, 1992). Furthermore, as Duncan (1992) points out, is it not hypocritical to selectively choose some drugs as being permissible like tobacco and alcohol and others like marijuana as being illegal? Reflect for a moment on material in this chapter concerning the "healthy" reasons for drinking alcohol. Are there not "healthy" reasons for using other drugs? And if there are not "healthy" reasons for using alcohol and tobacco, then should they not be made illegal also?

Finally, there is the opportunity to control the quality, access, and profits of illegal substances, if they were legalized. For example, drugs like LSD have been laced on occasion with substances like PCP to ensure the unknowing user a mind-altering experience that would be frighteningly memorable. Licensed substances with today's quality control methods and layers of packaging materials would be less likely to experience this problem. In addition, licensed substances can be controlled for potency. We noted that the percentage of the psychoactive drug THC in a marijuana cigarette had increased over the last decade. If legalized, this psychoactive agent and the levels of others could be controlled. Last but certainly not least, this multibillion-dollar-a-year industry would produce tax revenue that currently supports crime syndicates.

Opponents of those who would legalize drugs have several powerful counterarguments. Clayton and Leukefeld (1992) and others (Jarvik, 1990) dispute the contention that the war on illegal substances is being lost. They note that public opinion polls do not support a lessening of drug control efforts. The general public seems to support the cost of the war on drugs. Further, rather than loosening controls on illegal substances, Clayton and Leukefeld support increasing controls on tobacco and alcohol, agreeing that there are very few "healthy" reasons for any drug use.

Other authors (Goldstein & Kalant, 1990; Wilson, 1990) question whether legalizing drugs would result in savings. With reports that 15% of the nation's health bill is spent on alcohol and alcohol-related problems (Holden, 1987) and sobering information on the low to moderate success of drug treatment programs (Holden, 1987), legalization would worsen an already sad situation. Society, they believe, has not only the right but also the obligation to restrict individuals from potential harm. It is ultimately society and not the wasted individual that incurs the cost of caring for that person.

(3) labeling substances such as alcohol and drugs with warnings of their possible damage to health, (4) increasing taxes on substances, (5) increasing the legal drinking age, (6) reducing local tavern hours while stiffening zoning practices and increasing legal holidays when public tavern drinking and purchase of alcohol is

prohibited, (7) reducing the alcohol content of beverages, (8) reducing the level of blood alcohol content for a drunk driving arrest, (9) making servers (bartenders) liable for the actions of their customers, and (10) increasing penalties and instituting mandatory treatment for individuals convicted of drunk driving charges.

Some of these CO/SI activities have been implemented. Others continue to be hotly debated on grounds that they infringe on free will, are to costly to implement, or harm a special interest group like beer distributors, bartenders, tobacco growers, or drug manufacturers.

We concede that legislation in itself is not, nor has it ever been, the answer to drug and alcohol abuse. Used in an enlightened fashion, however, it can provide the necessary motivation for society to reduce its consumption of amphetamines, barbiturates, and alcohol and ensure that solvent manufacturers use the least harmful chemicals whenever possible.

SUMMARY

Let's step back for a moment and consider the major themes that emerged in this chapter. First, we saw repeatedly that attitudes toward tobacco, alcohol, and other drugs ebbed and flowed with the historical time. We observed that substance misuse does not have a straight trajectory. That is, multiple pathways involving families; peers; academic success; and biological, psychological, and other community factors interact to cause some youths to abuse substances. Next, we saw that ethnic and racial differences exist and that these differences can be either circumstantial (poverty) or cultural (time spent with peers, for example). Finally, we saw that there are treatment and prevention efforts that can help young people to stop abusing substances and, better yet, help them prevent or minimize their use of substances. Given the length of this chapter, we wouldn't be surprised if you suffered from a case of information overload. Take a break from your studying—you deserve it.

MAJOR POINTS TO REMEMBER

1. Many of the illegal substances discussed in this chapter were commonly used by the public as recently as 80 years ago.
2. Alcohol consumption is associated with a number of serious problems (traffic deaths, fetal alcohol syndrome). Alcohol-related problems cost the U.S. economy many billions of dollars a year.
3. The so-called marijuana stepping-stone theory can really be more accurately applied to alcohol. Alcohol is the entry drug into the use of other substances.
4. Studies show that adolescents who drink are imitating their parents' behavior, but marijuana use is peer influenced.

5. Most young people drink, and many of them drink too much too often. Yet many never develop into alcohol abusers. Those who do appear to have problems with school, with the community, and with their families.

6. In general, the family of the substance-abusing young person is characterized by weak parental control and poor parent/child relationships.

7. There is some evidence that alcoholism has a genetic component.

8. At least 70 million Americans have tried marijuana at least once. Many users are emotionally "well-adjusted" individuals. Some are not, but it is not possible to establish a causal link between their emotional "maladjustment" and marijuana. Still, we do know that driving under the influence of marijuana is unsafe and that marijuana may well be associated with health problems (cancer and damage to a fetus, for example).

9. Inhalants are most commonly used by younger adolescents. Inhaling solvents poses a serious health risk, since most contain poisons that can cause permanent damage to the user.

10. Anabolic steroids synthesized from the male hormone testosterone have not been found to increase athletic ability.

11. Female use of stimulants exceeds male use.

12. Barbiturate abusers are at high risk of physical harm. Some researchers believe that the barbiturate abuser has a suicidal personality.

13. Of all the drugs discussed in this chapter, cocaine has the most interesting history. It has been used as a religious drug, a medicine, and a popular pick-me-up and is now the preferred illegal "high" of the wealthy.

14. Daily use of heroin by adolescents is almost nonexistent. Those few who do abuse the drug are described as angry, helpless, manipulating individuals who have turned their anger away from their social condition and their family situation inward against themselves.

15. Substance use patterns among ethnically and racially diverse groups vary and are influenced by a host of factors including poverty and social class; cultural beliefs and practices; experiences of prejudice and discrimination; history of a group's involvement with substances; relationship patterns; and norms, values, and beliefs concerning alcohol and drug usage

16. The treatment of drug-abusing and drug-dependent adolescents often starts with detoxification and can then lead to a number of alternative outpatient treatments. These treatments include (depending on the substance abused) therapeutic communities, methadone treatment, self-help groups, individual psychotherapy, and family therapy.

17. Substance use cannot be prevented. In many respects, minimization of alcohol or drug use is a far better goal than prevention. Drug education with values clarification has been found to be one way to help young people decide for themselves whether to use drugs. Promotion of social competency, community organization/systems intervention, and natural care giving are the other ways for reducing new incidents of substance misuse.

Crime and Delinquency

THERE MAY BE no behavior that more excites the passions of adults than youths misbehaving. Each new generation of parents raises the cry against juvenile mischief through the media, at local school board meetings, and over the evening meal. Their comments range from pronouncements on the need for stricter controls and more discipline to such observations as "I never did that at your age!"

When that mischief crosses some unclear boundary, it is called delinquency. It may very well be that we can define *delinquency* as knowingly *committing acts that are illegal*. However, whether that has much bearing on who is considered delinquent is quite another matter. Delinquency has been confused with sin, poverty, urban growth, racism, and sexism, all played against a backdrop of punishment, reform, and, lately, more punishment. In this chapter we examine the curious history of delinquency, the various explanations for the deviant young mind, and the development of the juvenile court and the controversies now surrounding it. Finally, we examine violent juvenile crime, treatment approaches to delinquency, and the question of whether delinquency can be prevented.

HISTORICAL OVERVIEW

The laws governing children in the Massachusetts Bay Colony were straightforward. Disobedient or delinquent children could be severely punished or even put to death by their parents for their misbehavior. Even though rarely enforced, these early codes governing the behavior of the young in New England society were grounded in English common law and the Bible. Gradually, as time passed, the terms "delinquent" and "disobedient," which had been applied to all children who misbehaved, came to be associated with crime and the conditions of the poor in cities.

In many respects, to understand this change, one needs first to understand the climate in which it originated. The time was the early 1800s, and the places were large, new Eastern port cities—New York, Boston, and Philadelphia. Into these cities came waves of new immigrants—the Irish. As immigrants do now in large urban areas, they were met with overcrowding, an insufficient number of jobs, and an established community with a different ethnic background and religion.

The reaction of the established middle-class community (or, as they considered themselves, God's elect) to this incoming flood of humanity was determined by their fear that these immigrants had brought with them the seeds of social revolution. The community's response to this threat was to create a set of new institutions to educate these ruffians in the ways of the New World. In his seminal book on the subject, *Thorns and Thistles: Juvenile Delinquency in the United States* (1973), Mennel views this movement to establish "refuge homes" as the best attempt the established community could make to exercise continued influence in the rapidly growing and changing coastal cities.

In pursuing this mission of exercising influence, the early American reformers were not overly particular about whom the refuge houses sheltered. The orphan, the "artful dodger," and the pauper were all equally embraced for assistance in their individual journeys to reformation. In fact, Mennel (1973) and others (Eddy & Gribskov, 1998; Friedman, 1993; Levine & Levine, 1992) suggest it was not so much crime that was the villain to the middle class as it was pauperism. To the established community, crime, drunkenness, ignorance, or gambling were merely symptoms of the disease of poverty.

With missionary zeal the philanthropists of this time were quick to seize the young immigrant. They did not wish to wait until the child was actually a delinquent but would rather "snatch him as a 'branch from the burning' . . . [and] rescue him from the yawning gulf of poverty, drunkenness, and crime, into which he is about to fall" (Mennel, 1973, p. 12). This missionary fervor was not reserved only for male immigrants; it applied equally to females (Brenzel, 1980; Friedman, 1993).

The path to redemption for these young sinners combined large doses of religious teaching with equal amounts of time in what would be considered sweatshops today. Needless to say, discipline was strict, and punishment was liberally applied to those who dared misbehave. Boys spent their days caning chairs or manufacturing simple goods, while the girls perfected their skills doing household chores.

To understand the concept of delinquency at this time, it is essential to perceive the city as sinful and religion as needed for salvation. As the recorded sermons of ladies' groups to the young inhabitants of the refuge houses indicate, the established community left no stone unturned in attempting to educate the young in the ways of God. These young "sinners" provided ample evidence, to these reformers' Calvinist way of thinking, of humanity's fallibility and weakness of the flesh. With stories of looseness among girls in their ears and a proper sense of indignation on their tongues, they might—as one did—address "the girls feelingly on the necessity of a preparation for death and mention the sudden decease of a religious child, and . . . her happy close" (Mennel, 1973, p. 17). And if these young people responded by attempting to escape or to burn down the refuge house, was that not more confirmation of their sinfulness and need for salvation?

Increasing urbanization was seen as a major corrupter of the young. In the minds of these social reformers, the city bred indolence, poverty, and crime. Purifying these youths, and instilling middle-class values in them, called for a return to a simpler life. Thus, it was not unusual for these and later social reformers to separate children permanently from their families and apprentice them to farmers in the hope of changing their lives.

One of the most fervent believers in the practice of "placing out" was Charles Loring Brace. From the 1850s to nearly the close of the 19th century, the agency he helped found, the New York Children's Aid Society, placed hundreds of young children on westbound trains. At each farmtown whistle stop these children climbed down from the train to be inspected by the townsfolk and in some cases "adopted" on the spot. Viewing the solution to delinquency to be in the West's ability to absorb those who did not quite fit into Eastern Establishment ways, Brace was typical of the progressive thinkers of the time. In these reformers' minds the frontier and its rural farming life held the moral, social, and economic solution to the problematic Irish, Italians, and those other "worse than heathen Roman Catholics" (Mennel, 1973, p. 63).

When removal was not an option, schooling was. And conflicts between the established Protestant order and Catholic immigrants led to many serious confrontations. In fact in their outstanding history of the development of social services for children, Levine and Levine (1992, p. 11) contend it was Catholic immigrants desire "to have their own parochial schools . . . which contributed to the passage of compulsory education laws."

To summarize, until the late 19th century the word "delinquency" was synonymous with poverty. Those who were labeled delinquent were most likely to be orphans, Blacks, immigrants, and male, though less-than-virtuous females were as quickly confined. These young people were viewed as residing in a breeding ground for sin and as too weak to resist it. Their salvation rested not only in strict religious discipline but in a chance to escape from urban life. Once in the countryside, they would purge their bodies and souls of the poisons leading to damnation. Thus, to remedy the problems of crime in the cities, 19th-century social reformers applied liberal doses of religion, discipline, and parent/child separation. As the 19th century closed, this hopeful view of delinquency and redemption gave way to more scientific explanations with less optimistic outcomes.

PERSPECTIVES ON THE CAUSES OF DELINQUENCY

Although the link between poverty and crime remains a popular explanation for delinquency, some find physiological sources of criminal behavior, others stress psychological causes, and still others blame society for its failure to provide young people with adequate and acceptable opportunities.

Biological Explanations

Perhaps the most famous of all biological explanations for criminal behavior is Cesare Lombroso's. First described in a pamphlet published in 1876, his theory states that a criminal is physically different from a noncriminal. Criminal types can be identified by such physical traits as a slanting forehead, a jutting jaw, heavy eyebrows, and either excessive hairiness or no body hair at all. Although today most of us would consider Lombroso's theory preposterous, it stimulated countless attempts by other scholars to establish a causal relationship between appearance and criminal behavior.

Earnest Hooton, for instance, a professor of physical anthropology at Harvard University, studied the bodily characteristics of thousands of criminals during the 1920s and 1930s. He concluded that criminals and noncriminals differ significantly on such measurements as chest size, head circumference, ear length, nose size, and forehead height. Hooton did not stop at that point, however. He related physical types to ethnic and racial backgrounds and concluded, for example, that southern Europeans are more likely to commit crimes of violence and force, such as armed robbery, rape, or murder. Northern Europeans were said to be more likely to commit nonphysical crimes, such as fraud or forgery.

Despite the many years separating Lombroso's and Hooton's work, the influence of Charles Darwin's (1859) *Origin of Species* is evident in their thinking. Although both Lombroso and Hooton restrained themselves from suggesting, as Thomas Travis did, that reshaping the faces of delinquents would reshape their criminal minds (Mennel, 1973, p. 89), both clearly moved the proposed reasons for criminal behavior out of the realm of environmental conditions and religious infidelity and into the realm of physical characteristics.

The arguments for biological determination are still with us in the writings of genetic selectionists. That is, researchers who believe that all human behavior is "hard-wired" in the brain. Rather than concentrating on external characteristics, selectionists have studied possible relationships between chromosomal or neurological abnormalities and antisocial behaviors. The contention of these researchers is that genes shape physiology which in turn molds behavior. By understanding the physiology of all behavior—but in particular violent behavior—it might be possible to treat it from a biological perspective. Others contend that this is nothing more than "racist pseudoscience" (Roush, 1995, p. 1809). However, whether the argument is constitutional factors, intelligence, or XYY and XXY chromosomal errors, the evidence that biological factors *alone* explain criminal behavior is both contradictory and inconclusive.

In an exhaustive review of the literature, for example, Wilson and Herrnstein (1985) conclude in *Crime and Human Nature* that genetic and familial elements play a primary role in explaining criminal behavior. Using studies of adoptive twins, Wilson and Herrnstein conclude that genetically transmitted biological predispositions are involved in the etiology of most criminal behaviors. Powerful as the argument may seem that children of criminals, even if reared in adoptive homes, are more likely than other children to engage in criminal activity as they grow up, it remains specious. First, as discussed in the Chapter 2, correlative data can never establish causality. Next, in the best of these studies the correlations rarely account for 20% of the variance, leaving environmental factors to account for the remainder. Finally, given the retrospective nature of adoptive twin studies, researchers have never been able to control for selective placement, discrimination, or self-fulfilling expectancy effects that may have produced or significantly contributed to the child's behavior.

We contend that within every genetic explanation, one finds environmental influences. For example, Raine, Brennan, and Sarnoff (cited in Mann, 1994a, p. 1375) presented data suggesting birth complications may lead to cognitive or neuropsychological impairments which may in turn contribute to social dysfunctional behavior. This social dysfunctional behavior may place a youth at risk for violent behavior. Their study drew upon a data pool of 4269 unwanted Danish infants. The researchers reported that a small percentage of the infant population who experienced *both* birth problems and early rejection were most likely to engage in violent behavior later in life. Importantly, these researchers note that "neither variable—birth complications or early rejection—by itself was associated with high levels of violent criminality, but together they were strongly correlated with later violent crime". This and other studies suggest to the authors of this textbook that an unpredictable dynamic and fluid interaction exists between biology and life circumstance.

Similarly, although reports by some scholars may give the impression that low intelligence and criminal behavior go hand in hand (Moffitt, Gabrielli, Mednick, & Schulsinger, 1981; Wilson & Herrnstein, 1985), evidence to support this position is weak. Although it may be appealing to imagine most criminals as bumbling idiots (and those who are caught and thus constitute the available data pool may well be), the available sample is almost devoid of the highly educated, often undetected white-collar criminals who, through insider trading, embezzlement, and other financial manipulations, bilk the naive public of billions each year.

Finally, are chromosomal malformations and criminal behavior related? For a brief period in the late 1960s and early 1970s researchers excitedly reported findings that XYY and XXY chromosomal errors appeared with regularity in criminals (Price, Whatmore, & McClemont, 1966; Telfer, Baker, Clark, & Richardson, 1968). However, as work in this area continued, studies reported the same incidence of chromosomal errors in noncriminal populations and the absence of these chromosomal errors in criminal populations (Baker, Telfer, Richardson, & Clark, 1970; Clark, Telfer, Baker, & Rosen, 1970; Ferrier, Ferrier, & Neilson, 1970).

We reject any suggestion that a slanting forehead, ethnic background, genetics, intelligence, chromosomal differences, or any other biological characteristics *immediately* mark an individual as a criminal. As we review the history of biological explanations for criminal behavior, we are reminded constantly of the use to which proponents would use those explanations against the alleged perpetrator. For example, in the late 1960s at the height of the racial unrest that marked the end of that decade, one group of researchers in a letter to the *Journal of the American Medical Association* suggested that race riots were caused by violent slum dwellers suffering from focal brain lesions. The authors of this letter implied that the solution to correcting these misfiring synapses was psychiatric neurosurgery (Mark, Sweet, & Ervin, 1967). As we noted earlier, psychiatric neurosurgery is the polite phrase used to describe a lobotomy. Interestingly, for at least a while in the early 1970s (an era marked by a high degree of civil and social discord) the National Institute of Mental Health underwrote activity in this area. Today the mere suggestion that parts of the brain should be plucked out of the heads of dissidents would itself land the originator of the thought in a residential treatment facility.

Furthermore, criminal activity occurs at higher rates in early and middle adolescence, decreasing rapidly as individuals age. Is there some undiscovered retrovirus that is secretly altering the structure of DNA within most older adolescents, thus sparing them from a lifetime of crime? We think not. Rather, the explanations for criminal behavior are found elsewhere in this chapter.

Psychological Explanations

Psychological explanations focus not on the physical composition of the individual, as biological theories do, but on the internal drives and motivations that influence behavior. One psychological explanation for antisocial behavior is based on Sigmund Freud's psychoanalytic theory.

In his work Freud attempted to explain human social development from infancy to adulthood. In his framework early childhood experiences (before the age of 6) leave a lasting impression, for it is in these first years that the child moves from the oral to the genital stage. During this time the child must come to grips with two instinctual urges, the sexual and aggressive drives. Both of these urges create a constant state of tension in which the body seeks pleasure and satisfaction. Freud conceptualized this tension as resulting from the interaction of three forces, the id, the ego, and the superego. As we discussed in Chapter 2, the development of a strong superego is necessary to influence the ego to restrain the drives of the id. A weak superego will not be able to control the primitive drives of the young person entering adolescence. In this model these primitive drives revolve around the sexual desire of the male for his mother or those of the female for her father. If this desire (the Oedipus or Electra complex) is not successfully resolved early in the childhood, it reemerges in adolescence and creates tremendous stress in the individual. To relieve this stress, the adolescent may resort to delinquency as a defense mechanism (that is, a way in which to relieve emotional stress and maintain emotional stability). Thus, delinquency in a psychoanalytic model becomes an adaptation to intolerable stress. It is the best attempt a young person can make to balance a weak superego against the demands of the id for sexual gratification with a parent.

Considered to be in the psychoanalytic tradition, Erik Erikson has expanded on Freud's model to include the concept of social interaction. His stage theory (see Chapter 2) suggests that the development of identity is closely related to antisocial behavior. For Erikson, delinquency occurs in those young people who are without a strong sense of identity. They experience "role diffusion" and struggle during their teenage years to resolve the questions "Who am I?" "Why am I?" and "What am I?" During this process of resolving role diffusion, it is likely that young people will commit illegal acts or develop severe emotional problems—neither of which, Erikson notes, need be of a lifelong, crippling nature if appropriate intervention occurs.

Still considered as belonging to the family of psychological explanations but emerging out of the laboratory and not "off the couch" is the learning theory explanation. Learning theorists disclaim any need for the concepts of the id, the ego, and the superego. They suggest that a stimulus/response model provides a clearer explanation of delinquent behavior.

There are two important principles in a learning theory model. The first, reinforcement, can be understood to be some behavior or event occurring after a response that will either increase or decrease the chances of the response occurring again. In positive reinforcement the addition of a positive stimulus is likely to increase the chances that the response will recur. In negative reinforcement the removal of an unwanted stimulus is likely to increase the chances that the response will recur. In punishment the addition of an unwanted stimulus (for example, pain) or the removal of a desirable stimulus is likely to decrease the chances that the response will recur.

The second important learning principle is the concept of modeling. In modeling the young imitate the behavior of other individuals whom they admire or respect. One example of youthful modeling behavior that should be familiar to today's

Copying the dress and behavior of another person is called role modeling. Ouch, bet that hurt!

college student is the copying of Madonna's habit of wearing her underwear as outerwear during the 1980s and early 1990s. More recently, young people are copying singers who adorn their bodies with piercing jewelry and tattoos. Males may have avoided wearing their underwear as outerwear, but they are not immune to being influenced as the makers of men's cosmetics and four-wheel-drive vehicles well know.

But not all role models are positive, and when a role model's behavior is antisocial, the young person will be tempted to imitate it. When the model is also successful either monetarily or socially, the temptation is extremely strong. If a deviation into criminal activity brings wealth, status, prestige, or peer recognition, the behavior is likely to increase. If the foray into criminal activity is unsuccessful or if the adolescent loses face in the eyes of his or her peer group or in the eyes of significant others (parents, girlfriend/boyfriend), chances are that the behavior will diminish. Next, we discuss the other explanations for delinquency and then look at the psychological research on this problem.

Social-Control Explanations

Social-control perspectives are concerned with the individual's degree of belonging to society. The thinking is that the more involved an adolescent is with parents, school, and other socially accepted institutions, such as church, school clubs, or athletic activities, the less likely it is that this individual will become involved in delinquent activity. When these bonds do not exist, the chances are greater that deviant behavior will occur. Each of the following explanations attempt to answer why these bonds do not exist or have been broken.

Social control theory understands deviant behavior to be the result of failed socialization efforts.

Merton's (1937) *structural-disorganization theory* suggests that lack of equal access to financial, educational, or social resources explains delinquent behavior. Being denied the same economic and social goals that others, because of their status, can attain creates tremendous frustration. Thus, deprived of the legitimate means of obtaining the fruits of the good life because of socioeconomic status, ethnic background, or other factors, the individual resorts to illegal means to obtain them (see Box 13-1 for an example of how far disenfranchised youths are willing to go to obtain status).

A. K. Cohen (1955) expands on Merton's ideas by suggesting that adolescents are less concerned with wealth than with status. He notes that the major institution with the power to grant status to young people is the school system. From nursery school on, it provides young people with continual feedback about how their intellectual, physical, and social abilities compare with those of their classmates. The school is the fortress of middle-class values, Cohen would argue. The young person who does not look, dress, speak, or act like the middle-class model is likely to receive less than a fair share of positive recognition in school. Cohen believes that because lower-class youngsters start school with numerous economic and social disadvantages, by the time they have reached adolescence they have been alienated from school and thus alienated from society's greatest socializing mechanism.[1]

In its simplest form social-control theory states that delinquency occurs because a breakdown of the personal and social restraints on the individual permits it to occur. For Hirschi (1969), young people with caring parents, a good school record, positive relationships with their teachers, healthy peer relationships, and educational and vocational opportunities are very unlikely to become delinquents. Hirschi argues that it is these bonds of family, school, peers, and employment that permit socialization to occur. As each of these factors sours, the bonds between conventional morality and the adolescent weaken. Without those bonds, deviant behavior eventually will occur.

Deviance Explanations

There are essentially two schools of thought in the deviance category of explanations for antisocial behavior. The first is Émile Durkheim's (1958) observation that society needs criminal activity. He comments that even in the perfect society, one inhabited by saints, some action will occur that will bring ridicule, scorn, and rejection on the perpetrator: "Imagine a society of saints, a perfect cloister of exemplary individuals. Crimes, properly so called, will there be unknown; but faults which appear venial to the layman will create there the same scandal that the ordinary offense does in ordinary consciousness" (pp. 68–69).

---

[1] Recall the Rist (1970) study from Chapter 9 and how teachers unconsciously discriminated against young children from lower social classes.

BOX **13-1**   Violence and Gangs

From the *Blackboard Jungle* to *West Side Story* to *Colors*, from the large urban communities of Toronto, Los Angeles, Chicago, and Atlanta to smaller cities like Bridgeport, Salt Lake City, St. Paul, and Quebec City the scope and seriousness of youth gangs have grown dramatically since the late 1970s. Increasingly violent and engaged in illegal money-making activities like street-level drug-trafficking, these groups have turned many inner-city neighborhoods into battlegrounds pockmarked with seemingly random deadly shootings. For example, in 1990 youth gang killings accounted for 11% of all homicides in Chicago and for 34% in Los Angeles. The average age of the killer in these crimes was 20 (Sweet, 1990).

Why do gangs behave so violently over issues so seemingly unimportant as a club's colors? Yablonsky's (1970) typology of three gang types offers some valuable insights. The *social gang* forms around such activities as sports, cars, motorcycles, or dances. Membership in this group is relatively stable, and friendships can last into adulthood. The *delinquent gang* basically agrees with the materialistic and status values of society, but chooses illegal methods to get what it values. Despite their illegal behavior and occasional violence, Yablonsky believes that members of delinquent gangs are emotionally stable. It is the *violent gang*, however, that best describes the groups emerging from city neighborhoods in recent years to capture the media headlines. This type of gang functions in a psychopathic manner, with members using violence for emotional gratification. According to Yablonsky, "the gang's activity is dominated by sociopathic themes of spontaneous prestige-seeking violence with psychic gratification as the goal." This characterization helps, then, to explain the violent overreaction of gang members to seemingly minor events, such as wandering into another gang's territory or insulting a gang's colors. This group does not exercise its violence to protect its drug trade; rather, it acts to preserve its status and territory (Snyder & Sickmund, 1995).

Scholars suggest that the young people between 13 and 24 years of age who engage in violent delinquent gang activity abandon their poor family, school, and other community associations for a new identity (Fagan, Piper, & Moore, 1986; Flannery, Huff, & Manos, 1998; Huff,

1990; Spergel & Chance, 1991; Gardner & Resnick, 1996). The assumption of this identity may be assisted by the problems of depersonalization that occur in aging cities (Laub, 1983; Reiss & Roth, 1993). Because it provides its members with status, recognition, and a sense of purpose and belonging, the gang can be viewed as a family—although not, in some ways, for females who make up about 6% of the membership of gangs (Flannery, Huff, & Manos, 1998; Snyder & Sickmund, 1995).

The position of women within the male-dominated gang, as least until recently, is anything but equal. They have a low status within the male-dominated group and are excluded from most decision-making sessions. Interestingly, some researchers have found that their presence appears to diminish the gang's violent activity (Bowker, Gross, & Klein, 1980). However, this desire to subjugate women into inferior roles has resulted in the dramatic growth in recent years of independent and more violent female youth gangs. Trapped in the same cycle of poverty and societal and familial rejection, these female youths, like their male counterparts, are drawn together into a communal identity (Bowker, Gross, & Klein, 1980; Campbell, 1990).

However, as the essence of the violent gang is violence and not some other communal value, it becomes understandable, too, that to maintain group cohesiveness a constant state of tension must be maintained. Thus, warfare between clubs, internal violence against fellow club members, and other criminal activities serve "to maintain the continuity of the group, to give it structure, and to symbolize the gang's power of life and death over others" (Friedman, Mann, & Adelman, 1976, p. 532).

What factors lead a young person to gang membership? Staub (1996) offers a development pathway that steers youths to gang membership. Gang members are characterized as having negative attitudes toward others. Their hostile attitudes were formed from childhood interactions with parents who were negative, hostile, and overly permissive. These negative parenting experiences were strengthen by childhood observations of violence in the home, the community, and on television. Exposure to violence in these multiple contexts leads to a perception

(continues)

(continued)

that aggression is both normal and acceptable. Thus, aggression toward peers commonly occurs and creates problems in peer relationships which, in turn, contributes to poor school adjustment. This lack of connection to school and to other societal institutions intensifies the problem. Young people displaying these aggressive, poor adjustment, and alienating behaviors turn to peers with similar backgrounds (Flannery, Huff, & Manos, 1998; Staub, 1996).

Gangs appeal to these troubled youths because gang membership meets the needs of marginalized youths. Those needs are to belong, to be valued, and to be able to make a meaningful contribution to the group. As one youth shared with us, "When I put on the colors, I'm somebody. I get respect. I would die for my brother and he would die for me." Clearly, for this young person the gang provides an identity, value, and belonging. Disturbingly, however, gangs encourage in-group and out-group feelings which play out in violence toward others. Staub (1996) likens these in-group and out-group gang attitudes and behaviors to the dogmatism found with the Nazis or the KKK. He notes that youths joining gangs have experienced humiliation and shame. Gang membership suppresses these feelings because gangs provide a climate that emphasizes respect and honor. Unfortunately, gang members and their victims pay a high price for the maintenance of respect and honor.

What factors influence ethnically diverse adolescents toward or against gangs and youth violence? Staub (1996) states that diverse cultures have both protective or facilitative effects. Protective effects are characteristics of ethnic groups that prevent youth involvement in gangs. Facilitative effects enhance the likelihood of gang membership. In Latino cultures, for example, values of family, social collectivism, and respect for authority can protect youths from gangs. In contrast, the presence of family dysfunction and harsh parenting can serve as facilitative factors of gang membership. Staub (1996) also notes the difficulties ethnic minority youths face in respect to living

in two cultures—the dominant culture and that of the diverse adolescent. Values and practices of the two groups sometime conflict, which then presents a confusing set of options for ethnically diverse adolescents who are struggling with their identity.

A growing level of community concern with gang violence and the apparent randomness of its application have resulted in community attempts to curb gang activity. Spergel and Chance's (1991) national survey of youth gang problems and programs identified five such strategies. The first and most frequently used was suppression. Forty-four percent of the 254 respondents described increased police activity, arrest, and surveillance as a strategy for controlling gang activity. Social intervention services, which included crisis intervention, outreach, and treatment services for youths was in use by 31.5% of the respondents. The third most widely used strategy (10.9%) was court and police organizational responses like special prosecution and probation units. Community mobilization activities like joint policy and program development work between local community groups ranked fourth (8.9%) in practice. Finally, social opportunities like basic education, job training, and work incentives was the preferred strategy in 4.8% of the communities. Spergel and Chance (1991, p. 23) conclude from their survey that in communities with serious chronic gang activity that "several variables were found to be strongly associated with effectiveness in dealing with the gang situation: (1) the use of community mobilization and social opportunity as primary strategies, (2) community consensus on the definition of a gang incident, and (3) the proportion of agencies or organizations that had an external advisory group."

In the meantime, as adolescents in these communities struggle for recognition and for purpose, the number of dead youths will grow. Some of them will be gang members, while others will be innocent young people who unknowingly made the mistake of wandering into their path.

The second school of thought involves the ways in which one comes to acquire and retain a delinquent reputation. Playwrights and sociologists have observed for years that people are often judged unfairly based on factors unrelated to their behavior. In the words of Eliza Doolittle:

In recent years, female gang membership has been on the rise.

You see, really and truly, apart from the things anyone can pick up (the dressing and the proper way of speaking, and so on), the difference between a lady and a flower girl is not how she behaves, but how she's treated. I shall always be a flower girl to Professor Higgins, because he always treats me as a flower girl and always will; but I know I can be a lady to you, because you always treat me as a lady, and always will (Shaw, 1957, p. 270).

Crime in Durkheim's (1958) model is a glue holding society together. It is "an integral part of all healthy societies" (p. 67) serving to pull people together in a common sense of indignation and rage over some travesty. In *Wayward Puritans*, an outstanding book on the subject, Kai Erikson (1966) follows Durkheim in explaining deviance as being

conduct which the people of a group consider so dangerous or embarrassing or irritating that they bring special sanctions to bear against the persons who exhibit it. Deviance is not a property inherent in any particular kind of behavior; it is a property conferred upon that behavior by the people who come into direct or indirect contact with it (p. 6).

This perspective allows us to observe that not all unruly students are sent to the principal and not all pot-smoking teenagers caught by the police are referred to court. We can further observe that the definition of crime changes with the shifting opinions of society. Thus, alcohol may be prohibited in one decade but not in the next. Marijuana users may be described as emotionally disturbed individuals in one decade and in the next decade be described as normal, healthy, but foolish youths. It is possible to call running away an epidemic, pour millions of dollars into attempts to decrease it, and then virtually ignore this behavior a few years later only to rediscover it as "lost or missing children."

The deviance perspective says that crime is a part of life, a necessary thread in the fabric of society without which people could not judge who is good and who is bad. Without the knowledge of who is good and who is bad, society could not function and would begin to disintegrate. The interest of the labeling theorist is in understanding not only society's need for crime but how and why it is that certain groups are likely to be considered deviant rather than others.

Labeling theorists note that those least able to protect themselves are those most frequently labeled deviant. Into this category fall the mentally ill, the poor, minorities, and children. Belonging to more than one of these groups, such as being poor, an ethnic minority, and a child, increases the likelihood of being considered deviant.

Labels can be acquired even in the process of attempting to shed or avoid them. For example, the child who goes to a child-guidance clinic is considered by the family, the school, and the social agency to be receiving help. Help in this context implies weakness and fault. Something is not right with the child. Even if this treatment (the word itself suggests correction) is successful, the labeling theorist would argue, a stigma has been attached to that child. This stigma will reappear whenever the school or family needs it to reappear:

Mother: You must appreciate the fact that Johnny has had problems for years.
Therapist: What do you mean?
Mother: Well, even as a little child he was, you know, difficult to get along with. We had to take him to see a doctor several times. And now that John and I are getting a divorce, he has begun to act up on us again. I just can't understand what's wrong with that child.

This conversation is not atypical of parents' comments. It illustrates that even when Johnny's behavior has at least one good explanation in the environmental changes occurring around him, his parents will choose to ignore that explanation and focus instead on his earlier problems. Similarly, the "Huck Finn" who commits

> behaviors which [he] considers to be fun and part of play may be considered undesirable and bad by parents, police officers and others, who attempt to suppress them. If the behavior and its negative social reaction continue, the youth may begin to view himself as a bad person rather than [to see] that the problem is just his immediate behavior. He may feel set apart from. . . "good children" and seek companions who seem to enjoy the same sort of behavior and who do not act disapprovingly (Waugh, 1977, p. 136).

Thus, in his own eyes and in the eyes of others, he is a delinquent.

The Delinquent within the Psychological Model

The literature on delinquency in the fields of psychiatry and psychology is extensive. Although views differ somewhat on the factors responsible for delinquency, certain schools of thought can be discerned. For example, Bloch and Niederhoffer (1958) echo Erik Erikson in viewing delinquency as one of the normal problems of adolescence. Understanding delinquents, they argue, entails examining their identity problems and their attempts to escape from parental authority. In their rejection of parental values and in their experimentation with new roles, it is inevitable that the young will engage in deviant acts at some time.

Other writers adopt a more traditional, Freudian perspective that ties male delinquency to problems of sexual identification. They suggest that the delinquent identifies with his mother. In the attempt to establish a masculine identity, the adolescent turns to delinquency as a way of rejecting the earlier feminine identification and the socially accepted behavior associated with it (Bailey, 1996).

Between these two positions are numerous descriptions of the delinquent as possessing a weak ego; being asocial; having poor peer relations; suffering from social isolation; or being disorderly, nervous, confused, neurotic, or pathological (Howell, 1995; Jenkins & Hewitt, 1944; Leukefeld et al., 1998; Marcus, 1996; Reiss, 1952). Further, it appears that the earlier in a child's life that antisocial behavior appears, the more likely the child is to be antisocial later in life (Loeber, 1982; Hampton, Jenkins, & Gullotta, 1996; Reiss & Roth, 1993).

The Family of the Delinquent

Research suggests that the families of delinquents experience a multitude of problems, including marital strife, transience, unemployment, serious illness, and alcoholism and that the parents are inconsistent, uncaring, or even hostile in their treatment of their children (Goetting, 1994; Seydlitz & Jenkins, 1998; Widom, 1989, 1996). According to many studies on the families of delinquents:

1. There is a positive relationship between broken homes and delinquency (Farrington, 1990; Glueck & Glueck, 1950; Howell, Krisberg, Hawkins, & Wilson, 1995; Seydlitz & Jenkins, 1998).

2. Discipline is inconsistent in the homes of delinquents (Farrington, 1990; Glueck & Glueck, 1950; Howell et al., 1995; McCord & McCord, 1964; Nye, 1958; Seydlitz & Jenkins, 1998).

3. There has been a lack of affection between delinquents and their parents (Farrington, 1990; Glueck & Glueck, 1950; Howell et al., 1995; McCord & McCord, 1964; Seydlitz & Jenkins, 1998).

4. Marital discord is commonplace in the homes of delinquents (Farrington, 1990; Glueck & Glueck, 1950; Hagell & Newburn, 1996; Howell et al., 1995; Klein, Forehand, Armistead, & Long, 1997; Seydlitz & Jenkins, 1998).

5. A father's hostility or absence encourages delinquency (Heaven, 1994; Hirschi, 1969; Nye, 1958; Peiser & Heaven, 1996).

6. As parental support declines, peer influence and delinquent behavior increase (Howell et al., 1995; Seydlitz & Jenkins, 1998).

7. Emotional neglect and physical abuse are commonplace in the homes of delinquents (Crespi & Rigazio, 1996; Widom, 1989, 1996).

Other researchers have, however, disputed each of these positions. For instance, L. Rosen (1985), in identifying the contribution of familial variables to delinquency, concludes that the absence of father/son interactions in Black families encourages delinquency. For White adolescents, however, the socioeconomic status of the family emerges as a more powerful predictor of delinquent activity. In his study of 734 adolescents, R. E. Johnson (1986) finds little evidence that a broken home per se is a significant factor in the development of delinquency. Rather, it appears that interactional variables (communication patterns between males and stepfathers or discrimination by society against females and their single mothers) account for delinquency.

Finally, in an ongoing longitudinal study on child abuse and increased risk for delinquency, adult criminal behavior, and violent criminal behavior, Widom (1989) noted that although abused children are at risk the majority during adolescence did not become delinquent, criminal, or violent. She reported that even though a significant number of abused children had juvenile offenses (26%), nearly three times that number (74%) did not.

Recently, in a published continuation study with this now-adult population, Widom (1996) sadly reported that nearly 50% of the population had been arrested, 18% for violent offenses. She reports that emotional neglect in childhood is as damaging as physical abuse in influencing later socially dysfunctional behavior for *some* individuals. Despite these discouraging findings of increased antisocial and sociopathic behaviors among males and substance abuse and prostitution behaviors among females, we still must recognize that one-half of the sample did not succumb to this outcome. This is an important observation that deserves attention as it challenges the belief that the intergenerational transmission of violence is inevitable. Rather, other environmental and individual factors can compensate for early negative life experiences, and individuals can and do succeed.

We suggest that in combination with personal and environmental factors, one or more of these family variables identify adolescents at high risk of delinquency. It is clearly true that not all young people who fail to have a positive relationship with their parents are doomed to delinquency. Nevertheless, when other factors are added to their lives—poverty, uncertainty over who they are, school problems, or deviant peers—the chances of delinquency increase tremendously.

THE JUVENILE COURT

The notion of a juvenile court came from liberal reformers who possessed the same sense of conviction that moved the supporters of refuge homes to action. Before the establishment of the juvenile court in 1899, the judicial system operated under common-law principles that considered a youth's age in determining criminal responsibility. Children under 7 were not held responsible for their behavior. Children between the ages of 7 and 14 could be tried for their misdeeds, but before they could be convicted the prosecutor had to prove that they understood the meaning of their behavior. Youths over the age of 14 were considered responsible for their conduct and treated as adults. Subject to these few considerations, all juveniles over the age of 6 incurred the same penalties as adults for criminal behavior and were incarcerated in the same jails and prisons (Googins, 1998).

Much of the movement to establish the juvenile court system was in reaction to the imprisonment of youthful offenders with adults. Or, for the more cynically inclined, consider the argument that convicted young criminals were not imprisoned but allowed to roam the streets. There is evidence that many juries chose to release young criminals rather than imprison them with adults. This tendency to release youths may have been what really moved reformers to establish the separate court system (Gullotta, 1978). Either way, passionate arguments, accompanying moralistic stories of impressionable young children being schooled in the ways of crime, sin, and degradation, moved legislatures in most states in a very few years to establish a juvenile court system.

One of the most colorful and forceful proponents of this new system was Judge Ben Lindsey of Denver, Colorado. At the beginning of this century, he was placing delinquent youths on probation and urging the development of community detention homes as an alternative to jails (Levine & Levine, 1992, p. 119). Lindsey and his fellow reform-minded colleagues across the country did not see themselves as instruments of societal justice determining innocence or guilt. Rather, the prevailing view was one of a friendly but stern helper. Clearly, the court was to be unlike the adult courts: "The fundamental concern of the court regarding a child is what is he, how has he become what he is, and what had best be done in his interest and in the interest of the state to save him from a downward career" (McCarthy, 1977, p. 197) (see Table 13-1, which draws distinctions between the juvenile justice system and the adult courts. Source: Snyder and Sickmund, 1995, p. 74–75).

This statement clearly does not imply the adversarial relationship that exists in the adult courts. It implies that the judge is a kind, compassionate soul—although a stern parental figure when necessary—whose judgments will always be in the best interests of the child. To accomplish this goal, the court needs more resources than an adult court. Staff members are needed to perform such duties as gathering information on court-referred youths from parents, teachers, and others before these young people appear in court.

Leaning heavily on the legal doctrines of *parens patriae* and *in loco parentis*, the juvenile court attempted to find the best possible disposition for a referred case. Interestingly, the power to make dispositions did not reside with the judge alone. Probation officers funneled out of the system large numbers of court-referred youths for simple judicial supervision. These young people and their parents were advised of what actions the probation officer felt were necessary to prevent the recurrence of criminal activity.

From a historical perspective it is not possible to identify which offenses were diverted away from the court by the probation officer. In some states, shoplifting was a divertible offense; in others it was not. Moreover, in some states some judges considered shoplifting to be a divertible offense, while other judges serving in the

T A B L E **13-1** **Distinctions between the Juvenile Justice System and the Adult Courts**

Juvenile justice system	Common ground	Criminal justice system
	Operating assumptions	
Youth behavior is malleable. Rehabilitation is usually a viable goal. Youth are in families and not independent.	Community protection is a primary goal. Law violators must be held accountable. Constitutional rights apply.	Sanctions proportional to the offense. General deterrence works. Rehabilitation is not a primary goal.
	Prevention	
Many specific delinquency prevention activities (e.g., school, church, recreation). Prevention intended to change individual behavior—often family focused.	Educational approaches to specific behaviors (drunk driving, drug use).	Generalized prevention activities aimed at deterrence (e.g., Crime Watch).
	Law enforcement	
Specialized "juvenile" units. Some additional behaviors prohibited (truancy, running away, curfew violations). Limitations on public access to information.	Jurisdiction involves full range of criminal behavior. Constitutional and procedural safeguards exist. Both reactive and proactive (targeted at offense types, neighborhoods, etc.).	Open public access to all information.
↓		↓
Diversion—A significant number of youth are diverted away from the juvenile justice system—often *into* alternative programs.		**Discretion**—Law enforcement exercises discretion to divert offenders *out* of the criminal justice system.
	Intake—Prosecution	
In many instances, juvenile court intake, not the prosecutor, decides what cases to file. Decision to file a petition for court action is based on both social and legal factors. A significant portion of cases are diverted from formal case processing.	Probable cause must be established. Prosecutor acts on behalf of the State.	Plea bargaining is common. Prosecution decision based largely on legal facts. Prosecution is valuable in building history for subsequent offenses.
↓		↓
Diversion—Intake diverts cases from formal processing to services operated by the juvenile court or outside agencies.		**Discretion**—Prosecution exercises discretion to withhold charges or divert offenders out of the criminal justice system.
	Detention—Jail/lockup	
Juveniles may be detained for their own or the community's protection. Juveniles may not be confined with adults without "sight and sound separation."	Accused offenders may be held in custody to ensure their appearance in court.	Right to apply for bond.

(continues)

TABLE 13-1 *(continued)*

Juvenile justice system	Common ground	Criminal justice system
Adjudication—Conviction		
Juvenile court proceedings are "quasi-civil"—not criminal— may be confidential. If guilt is established, the youth is adjudicated delinquent regardless of offense. Right to jury trial not afforded in all States.	Standard of "proof beyond a reasonable doubt" is required. Rights to a defense attorney, confrontation of witnesses, remain silent are afforded. Appeals to a higher court are allowed.	Constitutional right to a jury trial is afforded. Guilt must be established on individual offenses charged for conviction. All proceedings are open.
Disposition—Sentencing		
Disposition decisions are based on individual and social factors, offense severity, and youths' offense history. Dispositional philosophy includes a significant rehabilitation component. Many dispositional alternatives are operated by the juvenile court. Dispositions cover a wide range of community-based and residential services. Disposition orders may be directed to people other than the offender (e.g., parents). Disposition may be indeterminate— based on progress.	Decison is influenced by current offense, offending history, and social factors. Decision made to hold offender accountable. Victim considered for restitution and "no contact" orders. Decision may not be cruel or unusual.	Sentencing decision is primarily bound by the severity of the current offense and offender's criminal history. Sentencing philosophy is based largely on proportionality and punishment. Sentence is often determinate based on offense.
Aftercare—Parole		
A function that combines surveillance and reintegration activities (e.g., family, school, work).	A system of monitoring behavior upon release from a correctional setting. Violation of conditions can result in reincarceration.	Primarily a surveillance and reporting function to monitor illicit behavior.

same states required all shoplifters to appear before them in court. Thus, "even judges could be inconsistent parents" (Gullotta, 1979, p. 7).

The Gault Decision

From its creation in 1899 until 1967, in its zeal to "snatch . . a 'branch from the burning,' " the juvenile court used case histories, psychological data, and judicial "parental" judgment to act in the best interests of the child. In 1967 the U.S. Supreme Court decided in the *Gault* case that juvenile courts were acting in such a way as to deprive young people of certain constitutional protections. Box 13-2,

BOX **13-2**   **Excerpt from Supreme Court's Gault Ruling**

To think that a phone call in which a woman is asked, "Are your cherries ripe today?" and "Do you have big bombers?" eventually could change the way in which young people are handled by the courts (Snyder and Sickmund, 1995). To think that for making these statements a young person could be confined in jail for 6 years. To think these immature "horny" questions would lead to extending the United States Constitution and the Bill of Rights to Youths. The transcript and the legal decision that follows is one of the most important legal decisions ever made in the United States regarding the rights of young people.

On Monday, June 8, 1964, at about 10 A.M., Gerald Francis Gault and a friend, Ronald Lewis, were taken into custody by the Sheriff of Gila County (Arizona). Gerald was then still subject to a 6 months' probation order which had been entered on February 25, 1964, as a result of his having been in the company of another boy who had stolen a wallet from a lady's purse. The police action on June 8 was taken as the result of a verbal complaint by a neighbor of the boys, Mrs. Cook, about a telephone call made to her in which the caller or callers made lewd or indecent remarks. It will suffice for purposes of this opinion to say that the remarks or questions put to her were of the irritatingly offensive, adolescent sex variety.

At the time Gerald was picked up, his mother and father were both at work. No notice that Gerald was being taken into custody was left at the home. No other steps were taken to advise them that their son had, in effect, been arrested. Gerald was taken to the Children's Detention Home. When his mother arrived home at about 6 o'clock, Gerald was not there. Gerald's older brother was sent to look for him at the trailer home of the Lewis family. He apparently learned then that Gerald was in custody. He so informed his mother. The two of them went to the Detention Home. The deputy probation officer, Flagg, who was also superintendent of the Detention Home, told Mrs. Gault "why Gerry was there" and said that a hearing would be held in Juvenile Court at 3 o'clock the following day, June 9.

Officer Flagg filed a petition with the Court on the hearing day, June 9, 1964. It was not served on the Gaults. Indeed, none of them saw this petition until the habeas corpus hearing on August 17, 1964. The petition was entirely formal. It made no reference to any factual basis for the judicial action which it initiated. It recited only that "said minor is under the age of 18 years and in need of the protection of this honorable Court [and that] said minor is a delinquent minor." It prayed for a hearing and order regarding "the care and custody of said minor." Officer Flagg executed a formal affidavit in support of the petition.

On June 9, Gerald, his mother, his older brother, and Probation Officers Flagg and Henderson appeared before the Juvenile Judge in chambers. Gerald's father was not there. He was at work out of the city. Mrs. Cook, the complainant, was not there. No one was sworn at this hearing. No script or recording was made. No memorandum or record of the substance of the proceedings was prepared. Our information about the proceedings, and the subsequent hearings on June 15, derives entirely from the testimony of the Juvenile Court Judge, Mr. and Mrs. Gault, and Officer Flagg at the habeas corpus proceeding conducted 2 months later. From this, it appears that at the July 9 hearing Gerald was questioned by the judge about the telephone call. There was conflict as to what he said. His mother recalled that Gerald said he only dialed Mrs. Cook's number and handed the telephone to his friend Ronald. Officer Flagg recalled that Gerald had admitted making the lewd remarks. Judge McGhee testified that Gerald "admitted making one of these [lewd] statements." At the conclusion of the hearing, the judge said he would "think about it." Gerald was taken back to the Detention Home. He was not sent to his own home with his parents. On June 11 or 12, after having been detained since June 8, Gerald was released and driven home. There is no explanation in the record as to why he was released. At 5 P.M. on the day of Gerald's release. Mrs. Gault received a note signed by Officer Flagg. It was on plain paper, not letterhead. Its entire text was as follows:

> Mrs. Gault:
> Judge McGhee has set Monday June 15, 1964 at 11:00 A.M. as the date and time for further Hearings on Gerald's delinquency.
> /s/Flagg

At the appointed time on Monday, June 15, Gerald,

his father and mother, Ronald Lewis and his father, and Officers Flagg and Henderson were present before Judge McGhee. Witnesses at the habeas corpus proceeding differed in their recollections of Gerald's testimony at the June 15 hearing. Mr. and Mrs. Gault recalled that Gerald again testified that he had only dialed the number and that the other boy had made the remarks. Officer Flagg agreed that at this hearing Gerald did not admit making the lewd remarks. But Judge McGhee recalled that "there was some admission again of some of the lewd statements. He—he didn't admit any of the more serious lewd statements." Again, the complainant, Mrs. Cook, was not present. Mrs. Gault asked that Mrs. Cook be present "so she could see which boy had done the talking, the dirty talking over the phone." The Juvenile Judge said "she didn't have to be present at the hearing." The judge did not speak to Mrs. Cook or communicate with her at any time. Probation Officer Flagg had talked to her once—over the telephone on June 9.

At this June 15 hearing a "referral report" made by the probation officers was filed with the Court, although not disclosed to Gerald or his parents. This listed the charge as "Lewd Phone Calls." At the conclusion of the hearing, the judge committed Gerald as a juvenile delinquent to the State Industrial School "for the period of his minority [that is, until 21], unless sooner discharged by due process of law." An order to that effect was entered. It recited that "after a full hearing and due deliberation the Court finds that said minor is a delinquent child, and that said minor is of the age of 15 years."

No appeal is permitted by Arizona law in juvenile cases. On August 3, 1964, a petition for a writ of habeas corpus was filed with the Supreme Court of Arizona and referred by it to the Superior Court for hearing.

At the habeas corpus hearing on August 17, Judge McGhee was vigorously cross-examined as to the basis for his actions. He testified that he had taken into account the fact that Gerald was on probation. He was asked "under what section of . . . the code you found the boy delinquent?"

[The judge] concluded that Gerald came within ARS 8-201-6(a), which specifies that a "delinquent child" includes one "who has violated a law of the state or an ordinance or regulation of a political subdivision thereof." The law that Gerald was found to have violated is ARS 13-377. This section of the Arizona Criminal Code provides that a person who "in the presence of or hearing of any woman or child . . . uses vulgar, abusive or obscene language, is guilty of a misdemeanor. . . ." The penalty specified in the Criminal Code, which would apply to an adult, is $5 to $50 or imprisonment for not more than 2 months. The judge also testified that he acted under ARS 8-201-6(d), which includes in the definition of a "delinquent child" one who, as the judge phrased it, is "habitually involved in immoral matters."

Asked about the basis for his conclusion that Gerald was "habitually involved in immoral matters," the judge testified, somewhat vaguely, that 2 years earlier, on July 2, 1962, a "referral" was made concerning Gerald, "where the boy had stolen a baseball glove from another boy and lied to the Police Department about it." The judge said there was "no hearing" and "no accusation" relating to this incident "because of lack of material foundation." But it seems to have remained in his mind as a relevant factor. The judge also testified that Gerald had admitted making other nuisance phone calls in the past which, as the judge recalled the boy's testimony, were "silly calls, or funny calls, or something like that."

The Superior Court dismissed the writ, and appellants sought review in the Arizona Supreme Court. That court stated that it considered appellants' assignments of error as urging (1) that the Juvenile Code, ARS 8-201 to ARS 8-239, is unconstitutional because it does not require that parents and children be apprised of the specific charges, does not require proper notice of a hearing, and does not provide for an appeal; and (2) that the proceedings and order relating to Gerald constituted a denial of due process of law because of the absence of adequate notice of the charge and the hearing, failure to notify appellants of certain constitutional rights including the rights to counsel and to confrontation and the privilege against self-incrimination, the use of unsworn hearsay testimony, and the failure to make a record of the proceedings. Appellants further asserted that it was an error for the Juvenile Court to remove Gerald from the custody of his parents without a showing and finding of their unsuitability and alleged a miscellany of other errors under state law.

The Supreme Court handed down an elaborate and wide-ranging opinion affirming dismissal of the writ and

(continues)

(continued)

stating the Court's conclusions as to the issues raised by appellants and other aspects of the juvenile process. In their jurisdictional statement and brief in this Court, "appellants do not urge upon us all of the points passed upon by the Supreme Court of Arizona. They urged that we hold the Juvenile Code of Arizona invalid on its face or as applied in this case because contrary to the Due Process Clause of the Fourteenth Amendment, the juvenile is taken from the custody of his parents and committed to a state institution pursuant to proceedings in which the Juvenile Court has virtually unlimited discretion, and in which the following basic rights are denied:

1. Notice of the charges;
2. Right to counsel;
3. Right to confrontation and cross-examination;
4. Privilege against self-incrimination;
5. Right to a transcript of the proceedings; and
6. Right to appellate review."

Do you think that the Supreme Court acted properly in extending these "adult" rights to adolescents?

(Source: In re: Gault (Supreme Court of the United States, May 15, 1967). In Task Force Report: Juvenile Delinquency and Youth Crime. President's Commission on Law Enforcement and Administration of Justice, U.S. Superintendent of Documents (No. 0-239-116), 1967).

which contains an excerpt from the Supreme Court's opinion, presents the fascinating story of Gerald Gault's arrest and conviction. We urge you to read this excerpt from this landmark case that redefined society's relationship with minors.

In many respects the handling of the *Gault* case represents the completion of a circle started by reformers in 1899 with the founding of the juvenile court system. They created the system to protect children from injustice. In 1967 the Supreme Court acted to protect children from that same court system's injustice. Specifically, the Supreme Court decided that young people have a right to know the charges against them, to have an attorney represent them, and to have that attorney cross-examine witnesses. Further, young people cannot be deprived of the rights guaranteed by the Fifth Amendment or of the right to appeal a case to a higher court. Essentially the Supreme Court decision declared for the first time that young people are not property but human beings.

Issues in Juvenile Court Reform

When the Supreme Court decided that Gerald Gault could not be denied the protection of the U.S. Constitution, the decision not only freed Gerald from a 6-year prison sentence for an alleged obscene phone call but triggered national juvenile court reform. Further, it stimulated a vigorous examination of society's handling of juveniles charged with criminal activity. In the years that followed the Gault decision, four issues emerged.

The Ones That Got Away

The first issue challenges our basic understanding of delinquency. The old notion that most adolescents who commit delinquent acts are detected and referred to court has been proved to be largely a myth. Studies indicate that only 3 to 5% of all

FIGURE 13-1

Age and arrests per 100,000 in 1975 in the United States. (*Source:* Sykes, G. M. (1980). *The future of crime* (National Institute of Mental Health, DHHS Publication No. ADM 80-912. Washington, DC: U.S. Government Printing Office.)

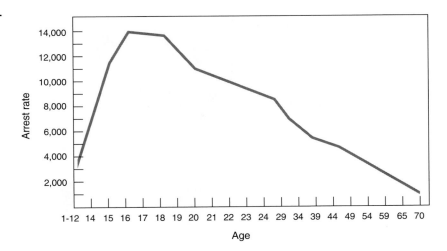

crime by youths is ever detected (Hindelang, Hirschi, & Weis, 1981; Mannarino & Marsh, 1978) and that adolescent crime levels off after age 16 (Farrington, 1983, 1990) (see Fig. 13-1). Furthermore, the overwhelming majority of delinquents are not "mentally ill" (Gibbons, 1986). More interesting still is the fact that most youths referred to juvenile court never return again (Snyder & Sickmund, 1995).

These studies indicate that almost all adolescents at one time or another commit acts that, if discovered, would be considered criminal. To illustrate, a U.S. Department of Justice study reports that in high-crime areas 94% of male youths and 90% of female youths admit to committing delinquent acts by age 18 (Snyder and Sickmund, 1995). But crime is not reserved for these areas only. *The Bureau of Justice Sourcebook of Criminal Justice Statistics for 1996* offers data that nearly 16% of the senior class of 1996 admits to hurting "someone badly enough to need bandages or a doctor" (Maguire & Pastore, 1996, p. 238). More than 27% admit to shoplifting, 24% to unlawfully entering a house, and 14% to damaging school property (pp. 239, 241).

Now having said this, it is vitally important to recognize that most serious adolescent crime is committed by a very small number of "chronic offenders" (Howell, 1995). Reviewing the studies on this matter, Snyder and Sickmund (1995) report that fewer than 10% of youths are responsible for 60 to 85% of serious crimes like rape, murder, and aggravated assault. So we are faced with a situation which finds many young people breaking the law at some point in adolescence and a very small number of young people repeatedly committing very serious offenses.[2] How

[2]Interestingly, that point in time for breaking the law is 3 P.M. for adolescents—right after school. It discourages the concepts of not only midnight basketball but also youth curfews (Snyder & Sickmund, 1995).

Even among those youth who are arrested, few ever make it to court.

one distinguishes the serious offender from the one-time foolish escapade offender is the challenge, as few youths launch their "criminal careers" with murder.

Furthermore, even those who are caught and referred to court stand a better-than-average chance of being released to the community. Court records clearly indicate that although thousands of young people are referred to juvenile court, few appear before a judge. Of those who do appear, few are deemed to warrant the close supervision of either probation or detention (Howell et al., 1995).

Examine Fig. 13-2, which follows the disposition of delinquency cases referred to the juvenile court for the most recent year for which data was available. Interestingly, as the reader will observe, out of 1000 referrals slightly more than half made it to court. Of those 506 cases, 41% were handled outside the courtroom. Of the remaining 299 cases, 8 were referred to adult criminal court; 11 were dismissed; and 197 were handled in ways not requiring imprisonment. Of the initial 1000 referrals, 91 cases or 9% (the 8 sent to adult court plus 83 juvenile cases) resulted in incarceration (Snyder & Sickmund, 1995, p. 134).

This evidence suggests that perhaps we are approaching the entire issue of delinquency incorrectly. The sheer numbers of young people who commit illegal acts indicate that at least one act of delinquency is normative behavior. For some young people, though, these occasional lapses into delinquent acts take a mean and habitual turn. Given that many violent offenders demonstrate their aggressive

FIGURE 13-2

Most delinquency cases never see a courtroom (*Source:* Snyder & Sickmund, 1995, p. 134).

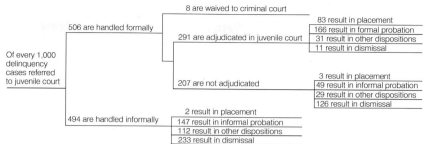

Most adjudicated delinquency cases received dispositions of formal probation or placement outside the home in 1992

- Of every 1,000 delinquency cases handled in 1992, 166 resulted in formal probation, and 83 resulted in residential placement following adjudication.
- Many delinquency cases that were handled formally in 1992 did not result in juvenile court adjudication. However, many of these cases still resulted in the youth agreeing to informal services or sanctions, including out-of-home placement, informal probation, and other dispositions.
- Although juvenile courts handled about half of all delinquency cases without the filing of a formal petition, more than half of these cases received some form of court sanction, including probation or other dispositions such as restitution, community service, or referral to another agency.

Source: Butts, J., et al. (1995). *Juvenile court statistics 1992.*

and impulsive behavior before age 8, it would seem not only appropriate and cost effective, but humane to intervene early in their lives to reduce the risk of this behavior developing (Gibbons, 1986; Gullotta, 1997; Hampton, Jenkins, & Gullotta, 1996; Lundman, 1984; Spergel & Chance, 1991).

Status Offenders

The second issue is the court's jurisdiction over status offenders. A status offense is an act that, if committed by an adult, would not be considered criminal. Behaviors such as truancy, indecent or immoral conduct, running away, incorrigibility, and school misconduct fall into the status-offense category. In recent years these offenses have made up 10% of the total juvenile court caseload. About 30% of those cases involve teenage drinking, 26% truancy, 17% runaways, 11% ungovernability, and the remaining 13% offenses like using tobacco and violating curfews (Snyder & Sickmund, 1995) (see Box 13-3).

Critics of the juvenile court argued successfully in the late 1970s and early 1980s that the court's jurisdiction over status offenders perpetuated the refuge-house mentality of imposing middle-class values on children by punishing the ones who challenge those values. They further contended that the court does more harm than good in labeling these young people criminals (Gullotta, 1979). Arguments such as these encouraged the federal government in the 1970s to use the threat of withholding law enforcement funds to force most states to decriminalize status offenses.

In recent years a rising chorus of criticism against these actions has been heard from court officials and youth workers. These individuals point out that without the power of enforcement the chronic status offender is very difficult to assist in community settings. This is particularly true when those youths may have serious

---

BOX **13-3**   **Runaway and Throwaway Youth in America**

Each year approximately 500,000 young people leave their homes. Another 128,000 young people are abandoned or "thrownaway" (Snyder & Sickmund, 1995). For some adolescents, running away will be a short-term romantic foray into a Tom Sawyer series of adventures ending when either boredom or an empty wallet dictates a return home. For others, it will be a desperate action to escape from family, school, or community crises with which they cannot cope. For still others, leaving home represents the only option; whether through implicit or explicit messages, these young people have learned that their families no longer want them.

There are several definitions of the term "runaway." The one we use is "a youth between the ages of 10 and 17, inclusive, who has been absent from home, at least overnight, without parental or guardian permission" (Opinion Research Center, 1976, p. 3). A throwaway or castaway is a young person who did not willingly leave home but was forced to do so by the attitudes or actions of his or her parents or guardian (Gullotta, 1978).

Why do young people leave home? In a classic article on the subject, running away was viewed by Gullotta (1979) "as a conflict between parent and child over a social control issue" (p. 113). The seemingly minor events that result in a young person's desire to leave home suggest that the major difficulty facing the family is a lack of trust and security. Thus, "disobedience over minor issues displaces the really significant issues, allowing for the displacement of intense anger to areas less likely to unsettle an already weak family structure" (p. 113).

In this model a lack of communication between parents and adolescents is the crucial factor in running away. The members of such families are temporarily estranged. Young people see their parents as unwilling to listen and as unable or unwilling to understand them. Parents, on the other hand, see their children as disrespectful, disobedient, and ungrateful. Because both parents and adolescents are uncertain about their roles in the family, each is unwilling to risk sharing. It is fear of rejection, not a lack of caring, "that paralyzes both parent and sibling and leads to subsequent conflict and struggle" and to finally running away.

In keeping with this perspective are the findings of Finkelhor, Hotaling, and Sedlak (1990). Their numbers

and characteristics study for the Office of Juvenile Justice and Delinquency Prevention suggests that a family argument about house rules, friends, school, or staying out late preceded a running episode about one-third of the time. Interestingly, only 28% of these homes could be described as intact (that is, both parents present) suggesting that parent–child role issues may well be a significant factor. Most runaways (94%) ultimately ran to a friend's or relative's house. Sixty-seven percent of caretakers knew the location of their child at least half the time, and the duration of the run was 2 days or less for 49% of the youth. As noted elsewhere in this chapter, when the runaway was an adolescent female the chances of referral to court for this status offense were significantly higher (Sickmund, 1990).

In contrast, the throwaway comes from a family in which the parents have cut all ties to the young person. The problem is not simply, "a weakening in a relationship but . . . a breakdown in the fabric of the family, a failure so severe, so emotionally tearing, that the bonds between parent and child are broken" (Gullotta, 1979, p. 113).

Several situations are capable of producing such a strong and complete rejection. One is the discovery of incest between parent and child or between children (Janus, McCormack, Burgess, & Hartman, 1987; Kurtz, Kurtz, & Jarvis, 1991). The abuse of drugs, criminal behavior, or promiscuity may result in the termination of the family relationship. Or after a divorce neither parent may want to care for the children. If the children are not simply deserted, life with either of the parents may become so unbearable that the young people leave (Radford, King, & Warren, 1989). In any case the breakdown of the family is complete and irreparable. In some cases it may be the end of repeated attempts "to stop some parentally perceived undesirable behavior. In other situations, it constitutes a scapegoating or desertion of the child" (Gullotta, 1979, p. 114).

Recent studies underscore this understanding as they describe young people fleeing untenable circumstances (Miller, Eggertson-Tacon, & Quigg, 1990) and of living isolated, depressed, antisocial lives (Adams, Gullotta, & Clancy, 1985; Hier, Korboot, & Schweitzer, 1990). Compared to other groups, runaway and homeless youths have the highest reported usage of tobacco, alcohol, and other drugs (Greene, Ennett, & Ringwalt, 1997). Finkelhor, Hotaling, and Sedlak (1990) report that 84% of these youth are over the age of 16 with nearly equal numbers of males and females. Only 19% come from intact homes. And in keeping with their earlier statement that family bonds were not merely strained but broken, 44% of their population was asked to leave home, 11% ran away and were refused permission to return home, and the remainder ran away and the "caretaker doesn't care" (p. 153).

The problems of throwaway youth are not easily addressed. Hurt, rejected, and filled with rage, they are by no means the easiest of youths with which to deal. The development of runaway shelters is a temporary stopgap measure. Such a shelter provides the youth with a clean bed and hot meal for a few days before that young person hits the road to some new destination. For youths willing to stay put, the use of independent living programs in which young people are provided with financial aid and social and emotional support is another attempt to bridge the gap in time from dependency to independent adult status. The use of foster homes and residential facilities has generally proven to be unsatisfactory, resulting in young people running away from these settings or needing to be frequently removed and placed in new settings because of unacceptable behavior. Society continues to struggle unsuccessfully in developing alternatives to the family for these youths.

mental health needs (Holden & Kapler, 1995). Supporters of the court and its jurisdiction over the status offender contend that parents need the court's help in controlling rebellious adolescents' behavior. They suggest that a poorly functioning family may itself endanger a young person's moral and social development. Proponents also argue that a status offense is often the only means by which a youth suspected of more serious criminal activity can be brought to justice. Without jurisdiction the court could not intervene on the young person's behalf. The issue of the court's jurisdiction over status offenses will continue to be debated heatedly for it involves the complex philosophical questions of what a society's responsibility is for guiding its young and how that responsibility compares to a youth's rights under the Constitution.

Sexism

The third issue is the differential treatment given female offenders. Evidence suggests that although girls primarily engage in status offenses rather than more serious violations (Steffensmeier & Steffensmeier, 1980), once arrested they are dealt with more harshly by society (Johnson, 1986). For example, while female adolescents are a small overall percentage of the juvenile justice system (about 15%), they represent 42% of the status offense cases (Snyder & Sickmund, 1995).

The work of Schwartz, Steketee, and Schneider (1990) continues to document findings that:

1. Girls are more likely than boys to be referred for status offenses involving sexually acting-out (Barton, 1976; Conway & Bogdan, 1977; Thornberry, Tolnay, Flanagan, & Glynn, 1991).

2. For the year 1987, girls were 10 times more likely to be incarcerated for status offenses than were boys in public training schools and 5 times more likely

to be incarcerated for status offenses than were boys in public detention centers (Schwartz et al., 1990).

3. Girls tend to receive severer sentences for status offenses than boys (Barton, 1976; Conway & Bogdan, 1977).

These ongoing circumstances lead Schwartz and associates (1990, p. 13) to conclude that "we need no longer wonder whether girls and boys are . . . confined . . . for similar offenses. The answer . . . is that they are not." Conway and Bogdan's (1977) observations regarding this disparity, made more than 2 decades ago, continue to ring true:

> Few incarcerated females are radicals; few are threats to the established order. Most are dupes of males who manipulate them to the point of social embarrassment. If we are not protecting society from these young girls, we must be expressing a Victorian demand that they be protected from their own stupidity (p. 134).

Why is a boy who loses his virginity held in esteem by friends and viewed indulgently by society, while a girl in the same situation is called "loose," "free with herself," an "easy lay," or other pejorative phrases? It does appear to us that the court tends to view female promiscuity unfairly in comparison with male promiscuity, making the court, in a sense, sexist. Sexism, we would argue, should not intrude on judicial matters (see Box 13-4 for the case of a young woman in this circumstance).

Racism

The last issue is whether racism permeates the juvenile justice system. According to several reports, the juvenile justice system is more likely to pick out Black, Latino, and other diverse youths for less-than-equal treatment under the law. The argument is that the police stop and search Black and Latino adolescents before they do White adolescents and are quicker to arrest them and refer them to court. Once in court, these young people receive harsher treatment than their White counterparts.

For example, although Black adolescent Americans (ages 10 to 17) comprise about 15% of the population of the United States, they represent 26% of all juvenile arrests. Nearly one-half of juvenile arrests for violent crime are Black youths. Almost one-third of referrals to juvenile court are Black teenagers. Forty-six percent (46%) of that nation's juvenile prison population is Black, and more than one-half (52%) of referrals to adult criminal court involve Black adolescents (Klein, Petersilia, & Turner, 1990; Langan, 1991; Snyder & Sickmund, 1995). As many Black leaders note, at present there are more Black males in prisons than are enrolled in colleges and universities in the United States. Nevertheless, the evidence for these contentions is inconclusive and contradictory. A review of the literature shows that

1. Some studies indicate that the police refer more Blacks than Whites to court, but by no means does this finding remain constant. Other research suggests that race is not a factor (see, for example, Barton, 1976).

BOX **13-4** Doing Nothing Is Sometimes Harder Than Doing Something

Pat was an attractive, sexually active 15-year-old whose arrest by the police motivated her mother to bring Pat to see me. Pat's father, a firm disciplinarian, had died suddenly less than a month before. Her relationship with her mother was positive.

Pat was arrested after a neighbor complained that a group of adolescent males were outside Pat's home. The police found several young males waiting to have sexual intercourse with her. They were sent home with no further action. Pat, however, was arrested and referred to juvenile court. In speaking with Pat, I saw a depressed, confused young woman searching for love. I believed that her father's death had precipitated much of her recent behavior. I did not see her as emotionally disturbed but as confused and in need of a supportive, caring environment. Pat's sexual activity considerably disturbed the juvenile justice authorities, and they proceeded to adjudicate her as a delinquent.

Not believing that this court action would be in her best interests, I worked out with her lawyer an arrangement with the court—not an ideal arrangement, in our opinion. Pat was placed on probation in a private coeducational school out-of-state. But Pat failed to last a year in the school. Her dismissal was related to her sexual activity.

The probation officer was eager at this point to commit Pat to state care. But we persuaded the court to return her, as I had initially encouraged, to her mother's care. Over the next several months I was successful in helping mother and daughter deal with their grief over the father's death, but I made little impression on Pat's need for sexual gratification. Her sexual activity did not essentially change. Nevertheless, I continued (at time with tremendous reluctance) to advocate her continued freedom in the community.

Pat graduated from high school and a local community college. She finished her undergraduate education. At 28 she is, by her own account, married, a parent, and working.

Frankly, I admit that my efforts to ease Pat's depression and thus modify her sexual activity can and should be judged mostly a failure. At many times I questioned my own sanity in encouraging Pat's remaining in the community when she made it a point to keep me vividly informed of her latest escapades. Nevertheless, judging by her performance today as a law-abiding citizen, a small dose of maturity and large injections of patience can be successful.

Was Pat's case handled correctly? How would you have dealt with this situation?

2. Probation officers tend to recommend Blacks more than Whites for incarceration. Whites are more likely to be referred for psychiatric examinations (Lewis, Balla, & Shanok, 1979).

3. The proportion of incarcerated youths who are Black and Latino is increasing, while the number of White incarcerated youths is decreasing (National Council on Crime and Delinquency, 1984).

Barton's review of the literature concluded that the available evidence did not support the finding that race was an important element in the juvenile justice process. A decade later McCarthy and Smith (1986) reached similar conclusions. Their study of 649 juveniles referred to court found that screening and detention decisions were not discriminatory. More recent efforts by Klein, Petersilia, and Turner (1990) continue to support this conclusion.

Their work (Klein et al., 1990) and that of L. E. Cohen and Kluegal (1978) help illuminate what factors do influence courts. The Cohen and Kluegal study of two juvenile courts revealed no evidence that race affected judicial decisions. Instead, they suggest that idleness (that is, lack of a job or of involvement in some other productive activity) and a prior record interact to produce the harshest sentences. The Klein et al. study found that rather than race, a history of previous convictions, being on probation, having been released from prison in the past 12 months, using a weapon, drug/alcohol use, not plea bargaining, failing to be released before the trial, and the lack of a private attorney accounted for 80% of imprisonment decisions in the State of California. Race as a variable in this study did not account for even 1% of the decisions.

A contrasting view is offered by Snyder and Sickmund (1995). Acknowledging that it is not possible to use existing national data to make judgements about the fairness of judicial decisions affecting Black youths in the United States, nevertheless, the authors find discrepancies in the way Black and White youths are handled. For example, convicted diverse youths are more likely to be housed in secure public institutions while White youths are found in private facilities. The authors refer to a second finding as "justice by geography" (Snyder & Sickmund, 1995, p. 92). Youths in urban areas are more likely to receive stricter treatment at every process point of the legal system than youths residing in rural or suburban areas. As most diverse youths live in urban areas, they obviously stand a higher chance for harsher outcomes (see Box 13-5).

B O X **13-5**   **Crime in the Future**

This box contains a prophecy that warns that unless we take action to educate and support young people today we shall surely witness a wave of violence early in the next century (Fox, 1996, p. 1).

Recent reports of a declining rate of violent crime in cities across the country would seem to be at odds with the growing problem of youth violence. The overall drop in crime hides the grim truth. There are actually two crime trends in America—one for the young and one for the mature—and they are moving in opposite directions.

The recent surge in youth crime actually occurred while the population of teenagers was on the decline. But this demographic benefit is about to change. As a consequence of the "baby boomerang" (the offspring of the baby boomers), there are now 39 million children in this country who are under the age of 10 more young children than we've had for decades. Millions of them live in poverty. Most do not have full-time parental

supervision at home guiding their development and supervising their behavior. Of course, these children will not remain young and impressionable for long; they will reach their high-risk years before too long. As a result, we likely face a future wave of youth violence that will be even worse than that of the past 10 years. . . .By the year 2005, the number of teens, ages 14–17, will increase by 20%, with a larger increase among Blacks in this age group (26%). . . .Even if the per-capita rate of teen homicide remains the same, the number of 14- to 17-year-olds who will commit murder should increase to nearly 5000 annually. . . .However, if offending rates continue to rise because of worsening conditions for our nation's youths, the number of teen killings could increase even more. (Source: J. A. Fox, Trends in juvenile violence: A report to the United States Attorney General on Current and Future Rates of Juvenile Offending. Bureau of Justice Statistics, Department of Justice. Washington, DC: U.S. Government Printing Office, March, 1996.)

This last point has been made by others. For example, the National Research Council (1993) and Taylor (1994) note that high rates of poverty, joblessness, and welfare dependency contribute to a subculture of violence found in inner cities. McWhirter et al. (1993) support these conclusions noting that increases in criminal behavior among ethnic groups can be attributed to poverty and alienation from society. They contend that economic and social inequities resulting from discrimination foster dissatisfaction and frustration that lead to antisocial acts.

Lewis, Balla, and Shanok (1979) have sought to explain why White youths are more frequently referred for psychiatric care than are Black youths. These authors contend that Black adolescents are being deprived of proper psychiatric care. They found numerous situations in which a Black youth's behavior was dismissed as "characteristically impaired" while a White youth displaying the same behavior was diagnosed differently. Lewis and her colleagues contend that in an attempt to avoid racism, mental health professionals are failing to diagnose the problems of Black youths accurately:

> Many seriously psychiatrically disturbed, abused, neglected Black children are being channeled to correctional facilities while their White counterparts are more likely to be recognized as in need of help and directed toward therapeutic facilities. The failure of White mental health professionals to recognize and treat serious psychopathology

Black youth are more likely to land in jail while white youth are referred to treatment programs.

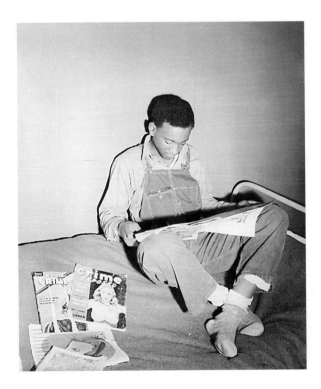

when it exists in the Black delinquent population accounts in part for the fact that our adult correctional facilities are becoming increasingly filled with members of minority groups (p. 60).

While this paper was written in 1979, the pattern persists. As Whaley (1998) notes, stereotypes continue to influence the way Black youths are treated. Perceiving them to be violent, streetwise, and ghetto youth it results in jail terms rather than treatment. Disturbingly, as one group of child advocates report, this focus on punishment means that in at least one state (Georgia) 60% of the youths in detention have an emotional illness that is not being properly treated (Faenza, Glover, Hutchings, & Radack, 1999). Minority youths find themselves in settings in which treatment and rehabilitation is not the institutional mission; rather, it is confinement.

Summary

Born in 1899 of good intentions, the juvenile court was to be a protective parent, helpful friend, and provider of justice. Over the years some but not all juvenile courts lost sight of these admirable goals. Court excesses were challenged in the landmark 1967 Gault case. In the Gault decision the U.S. Supreme Court extended to young people the protection of the Constitution.

At the same time revisionist views of the entire juvenile justice system began to appear in greater numbers than ever before and to command greater attention. The concepts of deviancy and labeling emerged. The questions of who is delinquent, how much delinquency exists, whether status offenders should be tried in court, and whether the courts are sexist or racist were addressed, albeit at times inconclusively. The issue of violent youth crime and questions of whether crime can be prevented and whether social deviants can be treated are the last subjects to be addressed in this chapter.

VIOLENT CRIME AND ADOLESCENCE

Not a day passes in which clans of youth, born not of blood but of circumstance, gather on street corners. They organize in long-forgotten shells of neighborhoods and in ignored public institutions like schools. They are there to defend their territory with all the meanings that can apply to that word. Elsewhere, an adolescent threatened by someone he dislikes intends to use the "equalizer" to level the playing field. Other angry disturbed young people with vivid imaginations, or poor impulse control, or flawed reality testing hyperreact to circumstances in their environment. The actions of these young people have helped to push the level of serious youth crime to alarming levels.

From a demographer's perspective the past 10 years should never have happened (Fox, 1996). With the smallest number of adolescents as a percentage of the population in North American history, crime rates should have plummeted. In fact, in most areas they did decline slowly. What skyrocketed statistically and onto the front page of every newspaper and magazine in the country and became the lead evening news story was violent crimes committed by youths—most often against other youths.[3]

Why Violent Crime?

The causes of violent behavior can be found throughout this chapter: frustration leading to aggression, lost opportunity, impaired ego functioning, and/or poor social bonds combined with media images and cultural values that numb offenders to the hurt and suffering others might experience (Borduin & Schaeffer, 1998).

The growth in violent crime is also related to the drug problem in North America. The influence is twofold. First, the disinhibiting features of most drugs (alcohol most certainly included) permit foolish, impulsive actions to occur (Gardner & Resnick, 1996; Leukefeld, 1997, Leukefeld et al., 1998). It is both significant and important to realize that 40% of youths in prison report that they were on drugs when criminal activity occurred (U.S. Bureau of Justice Statistics, 1995).[4] Does this mean that drugs "caused" the crime to be committed? No, the crime may have still occurred even if the individual was drug free. But as a contributing factor, the drug-distorted thinking may have influenced the commission of the crime in terms of actions and intensity.

The second thesis for the growth in youthful violent behavior is offered by Blumstein (1995). This noted criminologist tracks the rise in violence beginning in the mid-1980s to the growth of the cocaine "crack" trade and a constellation of sequential factors that placed youths at increased risk for violence. What were those factors? First was the recruitment of youths by the illicit drug marketers into the field. The cause for this recruitment can be traced to several variables. They are that in response to toughening federal drug enforcement actions youths became attractive couriers and distributors for drugs. To a group of disenfranchised adolescents perceived by most of society to be a sad lot of losers, the economic appeal of this "job" and its romantic "outsider" image were too attractive to resist. In fact, there were and continue to be no other competing job offers for these youths to entertain.

Having made the decision to participate in the business, young people were then faced with the reality that the only justice was street justice. A robbery of drugs or drug money by another individual could not be reported to the police. A bad batch of drugs could not be returned for replacement. State consumer protection offices are noticeably absent from these dealings. This meant that the young person

---

[3]While it should be noted that violent crimes have declined by 12% from 1994 to 1996, rates are still 50% higher than in 1987 (Washington Social Legislation Bulletin, 1998).

[4]Snyder and Sickmund (1995) report percentage data that incarcerated youths state they committed the following crimes while drug influenced: murder (43%), rape (34%), robbery (51%), and assault (49%).

needed to carry the means by which these circumstances could be resolved quickly and decisively. It meant carrying a weapon for protection and insurance.

The carrying of weapons generalized beyond drug market-involved youths and launched an arms race among young people living in vulnerable areas. Any arms race quickly escalates in intensity. It was not enough that one had access to a handgun. It became necessary to carry that weapon. Soon, it became necessary to use the weapon for cause. Real or imagined cause has become the standard that governs behavior today in many economically destitute neighborhoods such that, at this moment somewhere nearby there is a young suspicious frightened person worried about being victimized, with personal doubts of living beyond age 25, carrying a firearm for protection (DuRant, Getts, Cadenhead, & Woods. 1995). A recent Centers for Disease Control Study suggests that 20% of secondary school students carry a weapon during a 30-day period of time. One in 20 of those youths choose to carry a firearm (cited in Snyder & Sickmund, 1995).

Is There a Developmental Pathway to Violent Criminal Acts?

Whether there is a unique developmental pathway and are specific risk variables that lead to violent delinquency were examined in a study by Gorman-Smith, Tolan, Zelli, and Huesmann (1996). Youths in this study were classified as nonoffenders, nonviolent offenders, or violent offenders. The authors report that the two offending groups did not differ in the seriousness or frequency of their delinquent behavior. Next, the age at which delinquent activity began did not differ for violent and nonviolent offenders. Where differences were observed was in respect to parenting and family relations variables.

The rise in the use of firearms by black youth has its origins with changes in drug trafficking laws.

Specifically, the families of the violent offenders were characterized by: (a) poor parental monitoring of the adolescent's activities, (b) poor discipline, and (c) lack of family cohesion.

In short, parental involvement in the adolescent's life and providing effective and positive discipline are critical components in the prevention of violent delinquency. Emotionally close but not enmeshed families are an important factor in the prevention of youth violence (Jackson & Foshee, 1998).

The Means of Violent Crime

There are several instruments available to commit violent crimes. They include fists, feet, sharp or blunt instruments, and weapons that fire projectiles. If we could magically exclude the last category, violent crime ending in the death or serious injury of young people would dramatically decrease. While it is true that an individual can be beaten or stabbed resulting in their death, it is a different and more difficult kind of killing to complete than an attack with a firearm.[5] It is hard to imagine, for example, a drive-by beating.[6] Consider how doubtful it is that the arms of the attacker would reach the intended victim in the other car. Escape whether by car or foot would be more likely. The time necessary to execute the attack increases the possibility that others might intervene to stop the assault.

Consider also, the "equalizing" factor that firearms provide. Physical size, agility, strength, or accompanying companions do not matter. From a distance and for the time that the weapon can discharge, the attacker can fire deadly projectiles that will stop the other person or persons. For these reasons, the firearm and particularly the handgun became the weapon of choice for street protection.

The Demographics of Violent Crime

At present, seven adolescents are murdered each day. These are crimes that Black youths commit against other Black youths (92%) and that White youths commit against other White youths (93%). These are crimes committed by one family member against another (40%) (Snyder and Sickmund, 1995). One-quarter of nonfatal violent crimes (rape, robbery, and aggravated assault) are committed with a handgun. Fifty-seven percent (57%) of all homicides involve handguns (Zawitz, 1995).

The deaths and violent victimizations of youths are not evenly distributed across gender, racial, and ethnic groups. They disproportionately impact young Black males. For example, Black males between the ages of 16 and 19 experience victimization rates nearly twice as high as White males and three times as high as White females (Bastian & Taylor, 1994).

Not surprisingly, given the victimization and homicide rates of young Black males, their weapon arrest rates are significantly higher. Justice statistics indicate

[5]In 1991, 57% of all homicides were committed with a firearm, 17% with fists or feet, and 8% with a knife (Snyder and Sickmund, 1995).

[6]Drive-by shootings accounted for 12% of weapon-related crimes in 1994 (Zawitz, 1995).

that young Black males were arrested at a 221/100,000 rate compared to a 73/100,000 arrest rate for Whites. Most of these weapon arrests occurred in an urban setting (81%) compared to a suburban (14%) or rural (5%) location (Greenfield, 1995). Understandably, given the higher presence of firearms among Black males and firearms greater lethality, Black adolescent male arrest rates for murder and nonnegligent homicide are also higher (nearly 50/100,000 verus slightly more than 5/100,000 for White adolescents) (Snyder & Sickmund, 1995).

In Tables 13-2 and 13-3 the reader can examine murder and nonnegligent victimization and offender rates across age, gender, and racial groups (Maguire & Pastore, 1996, pp. 338, 340). Certain trends emerge during this examination. For example, for all children 13 years of age and younger victimization homicide rates have not changed dramatically since the late 1970s. It has grown by a factor of nearly 3 for youths 14 to 17 years of age. Significant growth also has occurred for

TABLE 13-2   **Who Gets Killed by Age, Sex, and Race in the United States**

		Age							Sex		Race	
	Total	13 years and younger	14 to 17 years	18 to 24 years	25 to 34 years	35 to 49 years	50 to 64 years	65 years and older	Male	Female	White	Black
1976	8.7	1.8	4.6	14.0	15.6	12.8	7.9	5.5	13.6	4.2	5.2	37.3
1977	8.8	1.9	4.9	14.5	15.7	12.5	7.8	5.1	13.7	4.2	5.4	36.3
1978	9.0	1.9	5.2	14.8	16.3	12.4	7.5	4.9	14.1	4.1	5.6	35.2
1979	9.8	1.8	5.3	16.9	17.8	13.0	7.9	5.4	15.4	4.4	6.1	37.6
1980	10.2	1.9	6.0	17.8	18.8	13.4	8.0	5.4	16.3	4.5	6.5	38.9
1981	9.8	1.9	5.1	16.3	17.8	13.2	8.3	5.0	15.6	4.3	6.2	36.6
1982	9.1	2.0	4.8	15.2	16.0	12.0	7.5	4.9	14.1	4.3	5.9	32.4
1983	8.3	1.8	4.5	14.0	14.8	10.7	6.5	4.4	12.8	3.9	5.3	29.5
1984	7.9	1.8	4.3	13.5	14.1	10.3	6.1	4.1	12.1	3.9	5.3	27.4
1985	8.0	1.8	5.0	13.5	14.2	10.1	6.0	4.1	12.1	4.0	5.3	27.7
1986	8.5	2.0	5.3	15.6	15.5	10.3	5.8	4.3	13.2	4.1	5.4	31.5
1987	8.3	1.8	5.8	15.7	14.9	9.5	5.5	4.4	12.5	4.2	5.2	30.8
1988	8.4	2.1	6.6	16.6	15.5	9.3	5.2	4.3	12.9	4.2	5.0	33.6
1989	8.7	2.1	8.0	18.4	15.7	9.3	5.4	3.8	13.6	4.0	5.0	35.2
1990	9.4	2.0	9.9	21.5	17.0	0.0	5.3	3.7	15.1	4.0	5.5	38.1
1991	9.8	2.1	11.3	24.4	17.0	0.1	5.5	3.6	15.7	4.2	5.6	39.6
1992	9.3	2.0	11.4	23.7	16.4	9.6	5.0	3.5	14.9	4.0	5.3	37.5
1993	9.5	2.2	12.3	24.7	16.3	9.6	5.1	3.5	15.1	4.2	5.3	39.0
1994	9.0	2.1	11.4	24.0	15.7	9.0	4.6	3.1	14.4	3.8	5.0	36.7
1995	8.2	1.9	11.2	21.8	14.1	8.3	4.7	3.0	12.9	3.7	4.8	13.9

Note. These data are from the Federal Bureau of Investigation's (FBI) Supplementary Homicide Reports (SHR), a component of the Uniform Crime Reporting Program. The SHR are incident-based reports, rather than the monthly aggregates that comprise the FBI Crime Index. Rates are calculated from U.S. Bureau of the Census population Ægures.Some data have been revised by the Source and will differ from previous editions of SOURCEBOOK.

Source: Table provided to SOURCEBOOK staff by James Alan Fox, College of Criminal Justice, Northeastern University.

TABLE **13-3**   Who Kills by Age, Sex, and Race in the United States

	Total	Age							Sex		Race	
		13 years and younger	14 to 17 years	18 to 24 years	25 to 34 years	35 to 49 years	50 to 64 years	65 years and older	Male	Female	White	Black
1976	9.5	0.2	10.6	22.4	19.4	11.1	5.2	2.3	16.3	3.1	5.1	44.7
1977	9.4	0.2	10.0	22.1	18.7	11.4	5.2	2.2	16.2	3.0	5.3	42.3
1978	9.6	0.3	10.1	23.1	19.0	11.4	4.9	2.2	16.8	2.8	5.5	42.3
1979	10.5	0.2	11.7	26.2	20.3	11.6	5.5	2.2	18.6	2.9	6.0	45.2
1980	11.6	0.2	12.9	29.5	22.2	13.3	5.1	2.0	20.6	3.1	6.7	49.9
1981	10.7	0.2	11.2	25.7	20.3	12.8	5.2	2.1	18.9	2.9	6.1	44.8
1982	9.9	0.2	10.4	24.2	19.0	11.3	4.8	1.8	17.4	2.8	5.8	39.8
1983	9.0	0.2	9.4	22.1	17.5	10.2	4.2	1.5	15.8	2.6	5.3	35.6
1984	8.6	0.2	8.5	21.5	16.9	9.5	4.0	1.7	15.2	2.3	5.3	32.8
1985	8.5	0.2	9.8	21.4	16.0	9.4	4.3	1.6	15.2	2.2	5.1	33.3
1986	9.2	0.2	11.7	23.4	17.6	9.9	4.1	1.6	16.5	2.3	5.4	36.8
1987	8.9	0.2	12.3	24.1	16.2	9.2	3.9	1.8	16.0	2.2	5.3	35.6
1988	9.3	0.2	15.5	26.9	16.5	8.9	3.6	1.7	16.8	2.2	5.0	40.3
1989	9.5	0.3	18.1	30.2	16.4	8.4	3.5	1.4	17.4	2.1	5.1	41.9
1990	10.6	0.2	23.7	34.4	17.6	9.5	3.5	1.4	19.6	2.2	5.6	46.9
1991	11.2	0.3	26.6	40.8	18.6	8.2	3.3	1.3	20.7	2.2	5.7	50.4
1992	10.4	0.3	26.3	38.4	16.8	7.7	3.3	1.3	19.3	1.9	5.2	46.8
1993	10.7	0.3	30.2	41.3	15.9	7.4	3.5	1.2	19.9	2.0	5.2	49.3
1994	10.2	0.3	29.3	39.6	15.2	7.4	2.9	1.0	18.8	1.9	5.0	46.1
1995	9.2	0.3	23.6	36.7	14.4	6.7	2.9	1.1	17.2	1.6	4.9	39.1

Note. See Notes, tables 3.129 and 3.131. Some data have been revised by the Source and will differ from previous editions of SOURCEBOOK.

Source: Table provided to SOURCEBOOK staff by James Alan Fox, College of Criminal Justice, Northeastern University.

young adults. Similar relatively stable findings can be observed for both gender and race. But in examining race, notice the extremely high incidence of death to Black males by homicide. It is more than twice as high as the White homicide rate.

Similar observations can be made about those who commit homicide. For children 13 years of age and under, the rate has remained relatively stable. Again, it is for youths between the ages of 14 to 17 and 18 to 24 that killing others has become too common an occurrence. Relatively stable findings again appear for both gender and race. But in examining race, notice for a second time the disturbingly high incidence of offending that occurs. Within our nations inner cities, Black people, and Black youths in particular, are destroying one another.[7]

[7]If any encouragement can be found in these numbers, it appears that from 1993 onward the rate of killing has slowed.

CAN DELINQUENCY BE TREATED OR PREVENTED?

The question of whether adolescent criminals can be treated rests on the individual's concept of delinquency. Depending on that conceptual framework, different solutions to the problem of adolescent crime can be recommended. Those who advocate a strict psychological interpretation of delinquency, for instance, argue for treatment approaches that focus on the individual or the individual's family (see Box 13-6).

The complete range of therapies (individual, group, and so on) has been used at one time or another with delinquent populations, but all have failed in varying degrees. Offer and his colleagues (1979) suggest that the failure of individual

---

BOX **13-6** Preventing Delinquency

In this last section "Can Delinquency be Treated or Prevented," we use the theories discussed in this chapter to develop approaches that should decrease delinquent behavior. As you read this section, think of these suggestions and ask yourself which tool of prevention does an intervention represent. Is it a tool of education, social competency promotion, natural caregiving, or community organization/systems intervention? Remember also that developing a program means little if it is not implemented well. What implementation factors matter?

Well, first, will the staff delivering the services be honest, trustworthy, empathic, and genuine? Without these staff characteristics, failure is assured. Next, how will the young people be given opportunities to belong, to be valued, and to make a meaningful contribution to the community? Remember that unless your effort creates this bonding, valuing, and contributing environment, positive results are very doubtful. Further, give careful consideration to the young person's understanding of this effort. Recall how important it is that young people perceive the person doing the intervention as sincere in order for success to occur. But in addition to perceiving the service provider as sincere, the young person must have a sense of self-efficacy. What's self-efficacy? It's a feeling that "I can do this successfully, and it matters in my life that I succeed."

Finally, two other elements need attention. The first of these is the *fidelity* of the intervention. What's fidelity?

It's how close your effort copies the original intervention. Let's assume you're using one of several effective educational curricula to promote social skills among a group of adolescents (for examples of successful programs see: Bierman, 1997; Bruene-Butler, Hampson, Elias, Clabby, & Schuyler, 1997; Danish, 1997; Weissberg, Barton, & Shriver, 1997). Let's also assume that this curriculum requires that the young people practice these skills in a number of interactive ways and that school teachers or parents are required to be involved. If in implementing the program, you choose to ignore the skill practice requirements, the teacher involvement component, or the parent involvement component, then the chance the program will work successfully is greatly reduced. Indeed, we know from the previous chapter that didactic-only instruction in substance abuse prevention programs is not effective. (Remember—that's the Tobler and Stratton (1997) meta-analysis of drug prevention programs.) The second element requiring attention is *dosage*. What's dosage? Dosage is the frequency and intensity of exposure the young person has to the intervention (Elias, 1997). For example, would you expect a child enrolled in swimming classes who missed half the course to know as much as the young person who attended all the classes? To achieve the maximum benefit of a program young people need to be drawn in to participate fully . . . and in a circular fashion we have just returned to the start of this box.

therapeutic approaches is partly related to inappropriate psychodynamic assessments. On the other hand, psychodynamic interventions for personality disorders historically have had a dismal record of success. Numerous studies suggest that antisocial, borderline, and sociopathic behavioral patterns do not respond to insight-focused therapeutic interventions.

Family therapy proponents emphasize that nearly all psychological theories stress the importance of the family as the primary socializer of the child. Although this influence diminishes as the child grows older, it nevertheless continues throughout adolescence. They argue that when a family experiences dysfunction, its members are likely to become dysfunctional as well. When an adolescent is in a dysfunctional state, the chances of criminal behavior increase. The efforts of family therapists to reestablish cooperative, supportive family units are thus likely to decrease delinquent misbehavior.

Encouragingly, three recent reviews of the literature identify multisystemic therapy as an effective intervention for delinquent youths. What is multisystemic therapy? It is an ecologically grounded approach that attempts to influence for good the many systems in which the youth lives. That is, the focus of intervention is the adolescent, his family, his peer system, his school, and his neighborhood. The intervention calls for intensive case management to insure that these systems are encouraging functional and not dysfunctional behaviors (Borduin & Schaeffer, 1998; Lausen & Rickle, 1998; Stanton & Meyer, 1998).

There are, however, disturbing reports that psychological interventions, unless carefully administered, may be more harmful than good for young people. For example, Joan McCord (1978) examined the life histories of 506 men who had been involved as children in the Cambridge–Somerville Youth Study. This study began in 1935 with several hundred boys described by schools, churches, or other organizations to be either "average" or "difficult." Some of these boys were used as a control group. The other boys and their families received visits from counselors for almost 5 years. The families were encouraged to call on the counselor for help when problems occurred, and "family problems [became] the focus of attention for nearly one-third of the treatment group" (p. 284). The treatment group received all kinds of services, ranging from tutorial help and medical care to summer-camp scholarships and involvement with scouting. Meanwhile, the control group received no such offers of help and participated only in providing information about themselves.

McCord's (1978) findings are remarkable. Nearly equal numbers of both groups committed crimes as juveniles. Furthermore, treatment for the "difficult" children did not prevent criminal activity; they were just as likely as the "average" children to commit illegal acts. Nor did these findings change with age; the treatment group and the control group showed similar rates of criminal activity in adulthood. Shockingly, it actually appears that the Cambridge–Somerville program did more harm than good. After 30 years the men in the treatment group had committed more crimes, showed more signs of alcoholism and serious mental illness, had a higher incidence of high blood pressure or heart conditions, had jobs with lower prestige, were less satisfied with their jobs, and died younger than the men in the control group. If anything positive can be said about the project, it is that the men in the treatment group fondly remembered their counselors.

There are several possible reasons for the treatment group's experiencing more problems than did the control group. McCord speculates that interacting with adults whose values are different from their parents' values creates later conflicts in children. Perhaps intervention breeds dependence or perhaps "the program [generated] . . . high expectations that later in life could not be fulfilled."

Finally, it may not matter whether children are "average" or "difficult"; if they are given special help, they will eventually believe that they need special help—another example of a self-fulfilling prophecy (Bloom, 1997).

Deviance theorists would support McCord's last observation. They would contend that by visiting these families and offering services, the counselors labeled these children as deviants. This argument is illustrated by the following hypothetical dialogue between a typical mother and son in the control group of the Cambridge–Somerville study:

Son: Mom, why can't I go to camp like Johnny?
Mother: You know we don't have the money. Times are hard, Tim.
Son: How come he gets to go, then?
Mother: Well, now, Tim, you know they got problems. You see that fella visit them, don't you? He's the one that's got the money for him to go. Now you just wash up and get ready for dinner. Do you hear me, Timothy?
Son: I still want to go—problems or no problems.

Labeling occurs not only in children's acceptance of their condition of helplessness but in their neighbors' attachment of the label to them. Some of the implications of this theory for the treatment and prevention of delinquency are:

1. Benign neglect, or radical nonintervention, should be practiced as far as possible in cases of delinquency. Delinquency is inevitable. Most young people commit illegal acts sometime during adolescence, but few become adult criminals. Many studies indicate that adolescent crime is highest between the ages of 13 and 16 but drops off rapidly after that age, whether or not a young person has been "treated." The point of the benign neglect, or radical nonintervention, position is to do as little as possible to treat delinquents differently from their nondelinquent peers.

2. As many young people as possible should be diverted away from the juvenile court system and into the least stigmatizing program available. The position of the deviance theorist is that the juvenile justice system is the most stigmatizing of the alternatives. Community-based programs are less so and should be used whenever possible.

3. Because juveniles are singled-out for special sanctions under the laws governing status offenses, the jurisdiction of the court should be limited. The argument here is that by limiting the court's jurisdiction to criminal cases and referring status offenders to community-based programs, the least amount of damage by labeling is done to the adolescent.

Structural-disorganization theorists would contend that although an adolescent may have personal problems and may be stigmatized by association, it is poverty and inequality that have produced these conditions. Poverty and inequality have deprived a young person of the means to achieve the material and social standards that have come to be associated with middle-class life. This deprivation produced the frustration that resulted in criminal activity. Correcting these social injustices demands direct social action programs and policies to provide equality of opportunity. Some of the implications of this model for the treatment and prevention of delinquency are:

1. All children should have the same chance at a good education. Educational opportunities can be equalized in a number of ways, some of which are equalization of per-pupil expenditures across communities, busing to achieve socioeconomic integration, federal aid for special remedial programs for all economically disadvantaged children, and affirmative-action enrollment programs for both undergraduate and graduate students at colleges and universities.

2. Housing and job opportunities should be equalized. Examples of efforts to accomplish this goal are affirmative-action hiring and housing programs.

3. Job-training and skills-improvement programs should be provided. Such programs as school-to-work training programs and the provision of federal youth-employment funds are examples of attempts to achieve equal opportunity in these areas.

Social-control theorists believe that if delinquency is to be controlled, the systems responsible for socializing the young person must be improved. It is their failure to provide adequate supervision and to instill the proper moral values in young people that encourages delinquency. Some implications of this theory for the treatment and prevention of delinquency are:

1. The childrearing practices of the family should be improved in ways that will develop greater self-control in the child.

2. Close identification with school, church, and other socially approved organizations should be encouraged in adolescents, since these organizations have value structures that discourage deviance.

3. The jurisdiction of the juvenile justice authorities should be strengthened. If more power is given to the court and the police, young people will gain greater respect for the law.

In the 1990s the issue of whether crime can be prevented or criminals treated has emerged with new intensity. The public is calling for and getting stiffer penalties and longer sentences against the young who commit criminal acts. Reports of the failure of previous treatment and prevention efforts have to some degree fueled this new get-tough attitude (Gibbons, 1986; Gibbons & Krohn, 1986; Polk, 1984). Thus, Langan's (1991) report that the soaring prison population in the United States could be explained by the greater likelihood of a prison sentence after conviction for nearly every type of crime should come as no surprise. What is intriguing is

Efforts to limit access to handguns has been shown to reduce crime.

his finding that with the phenomenal growth in prison beds, currently in excess of 610,000, there has been a corresponding reduction in U.S. crime rates according to crime victimization surveys. Could incarceration be working?

We suspect that the issue is more complicated than any quantitative study will ever be able to determine. The work of William McCord and José Sánchez (1982) impresses us with the complexity of the subject. The authors followed the lives of 340 juvenile offenders from the time of their incarceration to 25 years after their release. The subjects of this study had been sentenced for at least 18 months to one of two correctional institutions. One of these institutions used a therapeutic milieu of treatment and vocational training to rehabilitate. The other practiced punishment. The samples from each institution matched on several social-demographic variables, differing only in race. The institution emphasizing treatment was predominantly Black. The institution emphasizing punishment was predominantly White.

Five years after imprisonment, the graduates from the institution emphasizing treatment had a 9% recidivism rate. The institution emphasizing punishment had a 67% recidivism rate. By middle age, most men from both institutions had stopped their criminal activity, in essence supporting the view that for most individuals criminal activity is short-lived.

Disturbingly, while graduates of the treatment facility experienced lower recidivism 5 years after incarceration, their rate of recidivism increased after this period. Interestingly, graduates from the punishment facility experienced a lower recidivism rate 5 years after institutionalization. Does this finding suggest that punishment is preferable to other rehabilitation approaches?

McCord and Sánchez do not believe this to be the case. Rather, the authors focus on the racial composition of the two facilities to explain the difference in later recidivism rates. It is prejudice and discrimination, they suggest, that prevent Black youths from capitalizing on their positive institutional experience and escaping additional criminal acts. White youths, even when subjected to poorer rehabilitation experiences, eventually succeeded in greater numbers because of the color of their skin. Findings such as these that humane treatment can work encouraged Lundman (1984) to recommend:

- That traditional delinquency prevention efforts be abandoned
- That young people accused of status and minor offenses be diverted from the juvenile justice system
- That juvenile court judges use probation as the most frequent sentencing option
- That "scared straight" efforts, in which convicts visit schools and frighten young people with tales of prison life, be abandoned
- That community-treatment programs be expanded to include nearly all offenders
- That criminal institutions be reserved for chronic offenders who would be a danger to society

Supporting Lundman's position, authors like Lab (1984) maintain that the juvenile justice system should refrain from intervention in a young person's life until the third or fourth offense. Others like Gullotta and Adams (1982a) and Mulvey and LaRosa (1986), noting that most young people fall out of crime by their late teens, feel that adolescents need to be protected from the negative labeling process that accompanies a criminal conviction.

Finally, with the exception of violent crime, the trend since the late 1970s has been to see reduced levels of criminal behavior. As a general rule, the incidence of criminal behavior is a factor of the population age. The smaller the number of youths and young adults, the lower the incidence of crime. The exception to this rule, as noted earlier, was the rapid rise in the late 1980s of violent, often firearm-related, crimes committed by youths. The prevalence of handguns, the illicit drug economy, and the increasing hopelessness found in many urban ghettos combine to create an environment in which the callous disregard for human life flourishes.

As we again review these perspectives and the current literature in criminology, we see that different elements of each perspective can be useful with different adolescents in trouble (Bloom, 1997; Howell, Krisberg, Hawkins, & Wilson, 1995). We strongly advocate that the least restrictive setting and the least stigmatizing approach be used in juvenile housing, vocational training, and jobs. We believe that the family needs to be strengthened as an institution. We do not agree that police or court jurisdiction over young people should be strengthened. What needs to be strengthened are real alternatives to the money that young people can earn on the streets selling drugs for adults. What needs to be provided is hope for a generation of poor youths who do not see their lives extending beyond early adulthood.

Finally, we believe in the value of counseling, particularly family counseling, despite the disturbing findings of the McCord (1978) study. We find encouragement in reports about the successful use of multisystemic therapy for we believe that, in a time of need, extending a little friendly help that encourages individuals, families, and other systems to change has benefit.

SUMMARY

Consider your reading against the four principle themes of this book. To do this, read the next four sentences slowly pausing after each sentence to appreciate the new understanding you've gained as the result of your study. (1) Do you recognize how time and circumstances shaped understandings of delinquent behavior such that in the past poverty or an obscene phone call could warrant actions like removal to the countryside or imprisonment for several years? (2) From the multitude of explanations offered for delinquent behavior, do you see the numerous contextual pathways that can lead to delinquency? (3) From a multicultural perspective, do you see the risks and the protective factors that expose youths to danger and shelter them from trouble? (4) Using the theories discussed in this chapter, do you see how each theory can be used to generate approaches to treat or prevent delinquent behavior? This chapter was packed with information so if you're not clear on a particular point don't be afraid to revisit sections to clarify your understanding of each of these four themes.

MAJOR POINTS TO REMEMBER

1. Delinquency was redefined during the early 1800s to apply to a more limited number of people. Most often these were immigrants whose ethnic background, customs, and religion differed from those of the established community.
2. As the number of youths considered to be delinquents grew, society responded in a variety of ways. One of the most original was "placing out," or putting young immigrants, often without their parents' knowledge, on westbound trains.
3. Several theories have been proposed to account for criminal behavior. These include biological, psychological, social-control, and deviance explanations of crime.
4. Before the establishment of the juvenile court in 1899, age determined whether a young person was considered responsible for a criminal act.
5. Views differ on whether the juvenile court was established to promote a "parental" system of justice or to ensure that young people were sufficiently disciplined for their misbehavior.
6. The delinquent is often described in studies as having identity problems or as being neurotic or pathological. The delinquent's family is seen as inconsistent, uncaring, or hostile. These findings must be viewed with caution because research shows that many emotionally healthy young people from stable, caring families engage in delinquency.
7. The enormous popular support for the juvenile court was shattered by the 1967 Gault case in which abuses of the court were revealed and certain

constitutional protections were extended by the U.S. Supreme Court to young people charged with a crime.

8. An outcome of the controversy over the juvenile court's handling of young people was a new understanding of juvenile crime. Old notions on who commits crimes and the fairness with which the law is applied, particularly in regard to females and minorities, were reexamined and revised.

9. There are several strategies for treating or preventing delinquency. These include therapy, benign neglect or radical nonintervention, and strengthening of social control.

10. The prevention of delinquency involves changing the systems (community, school, and family) that fail to meet the social and emotional needs of young people while at the same time attempting to promote the social competency of youth.

Eating Disorders

$\mathbf{I}$MAGINE HAVING THE willpower to deny the need for food. Imagine being so repulsed after eating that you would have the willpower to induce vomiting. It is difficult for many of us to understand the motives and thought processes that enable a young person to reject the nourishment necessary for life or to choose the discomfort of vomiting. In this chapter we try to make some sense of why a small number of young people willingly endanger their health by starving or purging themselves. To comprehend these behaviors, called *anorexia nervosa* and *bulimia*, we draw from the fields of history, literature, and the social sciences. Then we look at how to help young people experiencing these problems.

FOOD (NOT SO) GLORIOUS FOOD

In the musical based on the Charles Dickens masterpiece *Oliver Twist*, the orphan Oliver approaches Mr. Bumble with an empty porridge bowl in hand and asks "Please, sir, more." The song in that musical, "Food Glorious Food," describes hot sausages, butter-laden muffins, and other high-fat, high-caloric treats. These are foods which in today's health-conscious society would be frowned upon, as they have been linked to heart disease and other life-shortening problems. North Americans live at a time in which the bounty of the earth has never been more available. Imagine living in Quebec City or Butte, Montana and in December eating cherries flown from Chile the night before to your supermarket. This marvelous food distribution system has contributed to a major North American concern—obesity.

If the foods adolescents ate were just fresh fruits, vegetables, and whole grains, the issue of obesity would be less pronounced. But that marvelous food distribution system has developed and heavily promoted empty calorie foods—high on taste but low in nutritious value. Young people (and the authors of this book) gulp down snack foods and sugar-laden fruit drinks (in which even the supposedly healthy beverages contain less than 10% real fruit juice) and later worry about our weight. We compare ourselves to ideal images appearing on television and in magazines in which every ounce of model body weight has been carefully sculpted through diet, exercise, and genes and collectively we sigh over the differences. Obesity has become a major public health concern with estimates that 55% of North Americans are currently overweight (Taubes, 1998). Of particular concern is that the number of youths who are clinically obese has grown significantly since the late 1970s. For example, in 1963 an estimated 2% of boys and 5.3% of girls 12 to 17 years of age were clinically obese. By 1991 this percentage had increased to 13.4% for boys and 16.2% for girls. About 23% of the North American population is clinically obese (Taubes, 1998). The cost of health problems associated with being overweight are estimated at $70 billion dollars a year in medical expenses and lost productivity (Wickelgren, 1998).

Not surprisingly, then, should there be studies that report young people, particularly females, are concerned about their weight by the age of 12 (Moreno & Thelen, 1995). In one English study of 126 early adolescents, the authors noted that concern for weight was particularly pronounced for early maturing females— especially when the weight gain was on the waist and hips (Fox, Page, Peters, Armstrong, & Kirby, 1994). In contrast to the times of Thackeray and Dickens, when women with ample thighs and hips were viewed as desirable, the small-waisted, long-legged female reflects the current ideal.

Those straying from that ideal suffer as one study has reported (Gortmaker, Must, Perrin, Sobol, & Dietz, 1993). Using a random sample of over 10,000 youths, these researchers followed the lives of these young people over 7 years. For females who had been overweight at the start of the study, they reported them completing fewer years of schooling than their female counterparts. They were less likely to have married. They had lower incomes and were more likely to have experienced poverty. Overweight young males 7 years later, on the other hand, were found to have been less likely to have married. Clearly, this study and antidotal reports underscore the difficulty overweight individuals confront in our weight-conscious society.

But is it possible to control your weight and body appearance? The easy answer on every televised late night infomerical is "yes"—apply the cream and watch cellulite melt away from your thighs, do "ab" tightening sit ups properly and reduce your waistline by inches, or cook your favorite foods using some new kitchen device and watch fat drain away. Purchasers of these and other products would challenge these claims. Nearly all of these products end up at "tag sales" or in the trash shortly after purchase. Even most folks who diet successfully see the weight return in 1 to 5 years. This is because obesity may be a polygenetic condition. That is, the affected individual may have inherited a genetic predisposition for weight gain on a high-fat diet. This genetic susceptibly may account for 40 to 70% of the problem of obesity (Comuzzie & Allison, 1998). This is the so-called "fat gene." Initial excitement that this gene had been mapped on mice and the problem traced to an inactive hormone related to a defective protein (leptin) gave temporary hope to many that the "silver bullet" for obesity had been identified. While the injection of the protein worked wonders for the laboratory mice, decreasing their appetites while increasing their bodies rate of fat consumption, findings for humans have not been encouraging (Barinaga, 1995, 1996; Marx, 1994). Challenging the genetic position, Hill and Peters (1998) note that obesity has reached epidemic proportions since the 1970s. They contend that it is highly doubtful that our genes could have changed so dramatically in such a short period of time. Obesity is not

Being overweight means more than health problems—it has a decided impact on the social life of the individual.

a genetic problem but an environmental one. That is, North Americans' weight gain is related to lower levels of physical activity and increased consumption of "energy-dense food" (p. 1371). That's a researcher saying we're eating too many high-fat/high-sugar foods that are both abundantly available and consumed across Canada and the U.S. (Hill & Peters, 1998).

Can you lose weight? Yes, it is possible through exercise and proper diet. But it is a difficult lifelong struggle. For some, this struggle becomes an obsession driven by a multitude of factors that can eventually lead to their death.

THEORETICAL PERSPECTIVES ON EATING DISORDERS

Before examining anorexia nervosa and bulimia more closely, we believe it is useful to place these two disorders within a conceptual framework. There are five theoretical explanations for anorexic and bulimic behaviors, each reflecting its own unique view of the world (see Chapter 2).

Psychoanalytic theory suggests that people with eating disorders equate the act of eating with sexual activity. Thus, the refusal to eat in anorexia becomes a symbolic means by which impregnation can be avoided. Furthermore, the act of self-starvation permits the young person to literally turn back the biological clock from that of a sexually maturing young person to that of a prepubertal youth.

The behaviorist, on the other hand, is not concerned with the historical antecedents or symbolism that might explain this behavior. Rather, the refusal to eat may be a learned behavior, the result of positive environmental reinforcement ("You look much better now that you've lost some weight"). Purging may be a form of avoidance behavior—that is, an intense desire to avoid becoming overweight. Or it may be a form of modeling behavior ("I perceive that to be slim is to be seen as desirable. I want to be desirable. Therefore I will avoid things like food that would make me undesirable").

In contrast, the family perspective explains eating disorders within the context of interpersonal relationships rather than individual psychopathology. It holds that the young person exhibiting such behavior serves a useful role in enabling a family to avoid potentially destructive internal conflict. In this model the eating disorder focuses attention away from the family as a whole and onto the "disturbed" family member. In this way the family is able to continue an outward appearance of successful functioning.

Although the previous explanations were concerned with the individual's behavior in relationship to self or others, the sociologist examines eating disorders against the backdrop of the larger society. Media images of thin young people enjoying the good life and looking attractive in their clothing reflect a societal standard that all adolescents are expected to achieve. In such a world, beauty is a precious and highly valued commodity, and to be beautiful one must be thin. To deviate from this ideal is to be rejected by society.

The final perspective to consider is genetic. Suspicions have existed for decades that eating disorders can be explained by biological or genetic factors. At the turn of the century concern focused on the pituitary gland, without success. Attention has shifted to the hypothalamus, a part of the brain, and the role it may play in this behavior. It is known that the hypothalmus controls the endocrine system (see Chapter 6). It is also known that when the endocrine system detects a shortage of the nutrients needed to survive, it will adjust bodily functions accordingly. While medical interest continues with studying the hypothalmus, attention is also being focused on the brain's chemical neurotransmitters— particularly serotonin (Walsh & Devlin, 1998). As we now proceed to examine anorexia nervosa in detail, consider the usefulness of each of these theoretical perspectives in making sense of this behavior.

ANOREXIA NERVOSA

A Historical and Literary Perspective

As with so many other behaviors, anorexia nervosa has a rich historical past. For our purposes the story begins in Italy in the mid-1400s with a 15-year-old by the name of Catherine (Bell, 1985).

Until her 15th year of life, there was nothing particularly extraordinary about this young lady. She appeared to around her to be an obedient, healthy girl who would soon be ready for marriage. That is until her beloved sister died in childbirth; then a different Catherine emerged. For the next 3 years she existed on meager portions of bread, raw vegetables, and water. She dressed in extremely uncomfortable woolen garments and added to her suffering by wrapping an iron chain around her hips. During this period she hardly spoke, rarely slept, and routinely beat herself with a chain until her body was covered with wounds. After entering a convent at age 18 and despite the church's pleas that she alter her behavior, she changed little in this daily ritual of self-abuse. At the age of 33, Catherine died.

It is interesting to note that Catherine was canonized as Saint Catherine of Siena by the Roman Catholic Church in part for actions such as these, which were viewed as "holy." More interesting still, at least 20 other young Italian women who also achieved sainthood had exhibited similar actions, which by today's standards would be described as examples of anorexic behavior. Rudolph Bell (1985), from whose book *Holy Anorexia* the story of Catherine was taken, notes that these young women strove to exercise their will and independence over a church and a society that paid little attention to women and assigned little value to them. Through their "holy" behavior, Bell contends, these women pursued the goals of spiritual health, fasting, and self-denial.

It would be more than 200 years after the death of Catherine that a young person's denial of the need to eat would appear in the medical literature. In *Phyhisiologia: Or a Treatise of Consumption* Richard Morton (1720) described his unsuccessful attempts in 1686 to save the life of a young woman whose "appetite began to abate" (p. 8). And nearly 200 more years would pass before William Gull (1874) labeled this behavior *anorexia nervosa.* The word anorexia is derived from the Greek meaning "lack of appetite."

At roughly the same time, the Russian novelist Leo Tolstoy (1872/1952), in his classic work *War and Peace*, described the disorder, as had other authors before him. The character "pining away" through self-starvation in Tolstoy's novel was the lovely Natasha:

> [The disease] was so serious that . . . the consideration of all that had caused her illness, her conduct and the breaking off of her engagement, receded into the background. She was so ill that it was impossible for them to consider in how far she was to blame for what had happened. She could not eat or sleep, grew visibly thinner . . . and, as the doctors made them feel, was in danger (p. 372).

There are two conclusions that we believe can be drawn from this history. The first is obviously that anorexic behaviors are not recent to our time but clearly existed in the past. Second, these behaviors, while limited, were nevertheless evident enough to capture the attention of novelists.

Characteristics and Incidence

To be anorexic involves more than the ability to resist the urge to eat. Indeed, if anorexia were defined only by caloric intake, the 40 million Americans who are daily engaged in a struggle to control their weight (Smead, 1983) would need to be considered anorexic. To apply the term anorexia nervosa to describe an individual's behavior, we need to find several of the following characteristics (Weinstein, 1996):

1. Age: victims are under the age of 25 when they begin to severely limit the intake of food.
2. Weight loss: they lose at least 25% of their ideal body weight.

Young men involved in ballet or wrestling are at greater risk for an eating disorder.

3. Distorted understanding of behavior: victims, when confronted with their behavior, do not recognize the serious health risks associated with it. They maintain that refusing food brings personal satisfaction. They seek and find pleasure in maintaining an extremely thin body image. They handle food in unusual or bizarre ways.
4. Physical health: there is no medical explanation for the weight loss.
5. Mental health: there is no known psychiatric condition to explain the weight loss.
6. Appearance and behavior: victims demonstrate at least two of these symptoms—(a) the inability to menstruate, if female; (b) soft, fine hair; (c) a constant resting pulse of 60 beats per minute or less; (d) occasional periods of hyperactivity; (e) grossly excessive overeating; or (f) induced vomiting. (Incidentally, the last two symptoms are the two principal distinguishing characteristics of bulimia.)

Research studies suggest that, while both males and females can become anorexic, young women widely outnumber young men by factors ranging from 10 to 20:1 (Comerci, 1986). It appears that activities in which low weight is an important element draw higher numbers of young people with eating disorders. For example, young women interested in gymnastics or ballet and young men involved with wrestling or long-distance running are more likely to be diagnosed as anorexic. This problem behavior is also found most often among White young people in upper-middle-income homes (Wichstrom, Skogen, & Oia, 1994). Estimates of the incidence of this behavior range from 1 to 3% of the total adolescent population (Taub & Blinde, 1994; Walsh & Devlin, 1998).

Given the severity of the behavior and the potential harm that young people can inflict on themselves, it is disturbing to note that the anorexic does not respond readily to intervention. Reviews of the treatment literature indicate that one- to two-thirds of young people with anorexia continue to have problems after treatment (Agras, Schneider, Arnow, Rawburn, & Telch, 1989; Bemis, 1978; Felker & Stivers, 1994; Hsu, 1980; Schwartz & Thompson, 1981). Mortality rates are estimated to be from 1 to 3% (Comerci, 1986; Kronenberg, Nachshoni, Neuman, & Gaoni, 1994; Walsh & Devlin, 1998) with the most frequent cause of death being cardiac arrest (Muuss, 1985; Wickelgren, 1998).

Research on Anorexia Nervosa

The current research literature supports aspects of each of the five theoretical perspectives. For example, several researchers note that anorexics have seriously ego-impaired pictures of themselves, reflected in gross misunderstandings of their body image (Berel & Irving, 1998; Brumberg, 1997; Kalliopuska, 1982). Many have a morbid fear of fat (Attie & Brooks-Gunn, 1989; Hesse-Biber, 1996; Shestowsky, 1983). They tend to be obsessive/compulsive and hysterical individuals (Bemis, 1978) who engage in regressive behaviors (Kalliopuska, 1982). Most are depressed, introverted, stubborn, and perfectionists (Keel, Fulkerson, & Leon, 1997; Kronenberg et al., 1994; Shisslak, Crago, Neal, & Swain, 1987). Some are involved with such impulsive behaviors as substance abuse or self-mutilation (Garfinkel, Moldofsky, & Garner, 1980).

Evidence also supports a finding that the family plays an important role in the behavior of anorexics. Numerous reports find their families as enmeshed, overprotective, and unable to deal openly with conflict. Family members are described as striving for perfection in behavior, appearance, relationships, and careers. In this tightly regimented environment, anorexic individuals use their behavior to declare control over their own lives as well as to maintain homeostasis in the family (Carroll, 1986; Gilbert & DeBlassie, 1984; Lucas, 1986; McClure, Timimi, & Westerman, 1995; Muuss, 1985; Strober & Humphrey, 1987; Weinstein, 1996; Wonderlich & Swift, 1990).

Sociologists such as Hesse-Biber (1996), historians like Brumberg (1997), psychologists like Smead (1983), and feminist scholars like Berel and Irving (1998) note that Western society places a high value on attractiveness for women. Whether it is diet soda commercials, Hollywood films, or various magazine's models, thinness is the desired body state. For example, in one study a small group of undergraduate women were shown either a fashion magazine or a news magazine. Subjects were then questioned on their satisfaction with their own bodies. Interestingly, those students exposed to the fashion magazine were more concerned with their appearance (Turner, Hamilton, Jacobs, Angood, & Dwyer, 1997).

As a society we have attached particular stereotypes to certain body types. While the thin are our heroes and our romantic stars, those who are more ample portray comics, buffoons, and sidekicks with names like Pancho, Sancho, and Marcellus.[1] You will remember from Chapter 6 that research strongly supported the position

---

[1] Pancho was the sidekick of the Cisco Kid. Sancho was the trusted ally of Don Quixote, and Marcellus Washburn was the friend of the infamous Harold Hill of *The Music Man*.

that physical attractiveness dictated adolescent women's social status within the group. To be attractive in our society is to be thin. Not surprisingly, then, concerns of excessive weight relate to higher depression levels among early adolescent girls (Rierdan & Koff, 1997).

Finally, it is clearly evident that significant changes in body chemistry occur when a person engages in anorexic behavior (Attie & Brooks-Gunn, 1989; Casper, 1984; Lucas, 1986; Yager, 1982). What remains unclear is whether these changes existed before the condition or are the result of the behavior. Altshuler and Weiner (1985) appropriately caution that all of the physical and emotional changes observed in anorexics also are seen in people suffering from starvation due to other causes. The person dying from starvation in a famine will experience the same depression an anorexic will experience. That person's hypothalamus will react in the same manner. Thus, although no one will deny that physical changes are occurring, we cannot state with any certainty whether those changes contribute to the disorder. Indeed, one research team is skeptical of biological explanations for anorexia nervosa. This skepticism originates with knowledge that with the return of weight the gastrointestinal, pituitary, and hypothalamus problems that occur to anorexics correct themselves (Walsh & Devlin, 1998).

Nevertheless, it is interesting to note that the medications commonly used for eating disordered behavior target the neurotransmitter serotonin. The antidepressants (for example, Prozac and Zoloft) discussed earlier in this book have shown modest positive results with this population (Weinstein, 1996). These drugs have been combined with short-acting anti-anxiety medications like lorazepam and oxazepam to enable an anxiety-ridden individual to make it through a meal.

BULIMIA

Whereas anorexics deny themselves nourishment, bulimics engage in unrestrained eating sprees only to purge themselves after their indulgence. Indeed, the word "bulimia" is derived from Greek words meaning "hungry ox." Interestingly, examples of this type of behavior can be traced back to the mid-15th century and to several of the "holy" anorexics mentioned earlier in this chapter (Bell, 1985). Of concern to us in the next section are the characteristics and incidence of a behavior that is very closely related to anorexia nervosa.

Characteristics and Incidence

Bulimics are uncontrolled binge eaters. They consume enormous amounts of food at a single sitting. This gorging is followed by intense feelings of self-repulsion for having grossly overeaten and by actions to purge oneself of the food. Purging most often occurs by self-induced vomiting, but bulimics may also use laxatives, diuretics, or enemas. Sharing the same concern for body image as anorexics, bulimics are considered separately by mental health professionals because of the way in which they maintain their appearance—that is, their use of purging behaviors rather than self-starvation. Bulimia is diagnosed when a repeated pattern of this behavior occurs (Weinstein, 1996).

Although bulimia can affect both males and females, young women, again, are afflicted more often. Like anorexia, it appears to be a problem of White, middle-class, late adolescents. Those males most likely to be stricken are athletes with rigid weight requirements that must be met in order to enable them to participate. An estimated 1% of adolescent females and two-tenths of 1% of adolescent males are troubled with this problem (Drewnowski, Hopkins, & Kessler, 1988; Fairburn & Beglin, 1990; Muuss, 1986; Walsh & Devlin, 1998).

Repeated episodes of bulimic behavior can have serious consequences for physical health. For instance, frequent vomiting can erode the enamel of teeth, inflame the esophagus, and contribute to irregular heartbeat. The abuse of laxatives, enemas, and diuretics can damage the colon, impair the functioning of the kidneys, and contribute to urinary infections.

Research on Bulimia

For each of the theoretical causes of bulimia described earlier, there are supporting research data. For example, studies focusing on personality factors note a high incidence of depression in bulimics (Johnson & Maddi, 1986; Schlesier-Carter, Hamilton, O'Neil, Lydiard, & Malcolm, 1989; Smith, Hillard, & Roll, 1991; Weinstein, 1996; Williamson, Kelley, Davis, Ruggiero, & Blouin, 1985). A poor sense of self-esteem appears to be coupled with shame and guilt, low-frustration tolerance, high anxiety, and substance abuse (Frank, 1991; Johnson & Maddi, 1986; Lehman & Rodin, 1989; Mitchell, Hatsukami, Eckert, & Pyle, 1985). Johnson and Maddi (1986, p. 17) suggest that bulimic patients can eroticize binge eating episodes, thus offering an alternative response to sexual feelings if they are conflicted about masturbation or heterosexual activity. Similarly, binge eating and subsequent purging behavior can become an effective way for expressing aggressive feelings that research indicates these individuals have trouble stating.

One possible reason for conflicted sexual feelings may be the sexual abuse some women experienced before developing an eating disorder. Using three clinical case histories as examples, Goldfarb (1987) suggests that prior abusive experiences are an unrecognized factor in many young women suffering from bulimia. Partial support for this clinical report can be found in a recent review of eating disorder behavior which reports that 30 to 50% of adult women suffering an eating disorder had an unwanted earlier sexual experience. Weinstein (1996) cautions, however, that unwanted sexual contact in these percentages of 30 to 50% occurs also within the general psychiatric population making the link between unwanted sex and eating disorders difficult to determine.

Data on family characteristics echo earlier observations made on the family life of anorexics. For example, Johnson and Flach (1985) report that the overwhelming majority of the 105 patients they have treated for bulimia had family structures that were enmeshed and overprotective. Assertive, independent behaviors on the young person's part were discouraged by the parents. Other studies note that bulimics' families are disengaged, are under considerable stress, and have contradictory communication patterns (Attie & Brooks-Gunn, 1989; Williamson et al., 1985; Hesse-Biber, 1996; Johnson & Flach, 1985; Johnson, Lewis, Love, Lewis, & Stuckey, 1984; Weinstein, 1996).

Researchers examining the sociocultural factors contributing to bulimia focus their attention on the numerous and often contradictory changes that have occurred for women in Western society since the 1970s. Opportunities for careers and lifestyles exist today that did not exist in the past. And yet for all of this change, society retains a clear, identifiable prejudice against the physically unattractive woman (Brumberg, 1988; 1997).

For example, Wooley and Wooley (1979), in an exhaustive review of the obesity literature, note that overweight young people are viewed as being responsible for their condition. Studies find that young people describe those who are overweight as stupid, sloppy, and ugly. The social scientist observes that if thinness is the cultural ideal, it is no surprise that its pursuit would lead some to either anorexia or bulimia (Brumberg, 1997; Hesse-Biber, 1996; Johnson et al., 1984).

Finally, as with anorexia, the connection between bulimia and biogenic factors has been suggested. Some researchers are looking at whether bulimia and affective disorders are linked genetically. Johnson and Maddi (1986) caution that given the pattern of this behavior, it is highly unlikely that a biogenic relationship will be discovered. Their point is well taken, for it is hard to imagine that the population with the highest incidence of bulimia (White middle- and upper-income college women) are somehow genetically different from other women.

EATING DISORDERS AND DIVERSE YOUTH

Practically every eating disorder study has centered on White, middle- and upper- income youths (particularly females). Indeed, as we shared earlier, eating disorders have been viewed as a White youth problem, but there is some evidence suggesting that eating disorders may be on the rise with other groups. In the following section, we examine this scant literature.

Socioeconomic Status and Eating Disorders

As noted previously, a good family income is a factor found with many youths suffering from eating disorders (Osvold & Sodowsky, 1993). In contrast, obesity appears to more frequently afflict those of lower incomes, particularly women. Osvold and Sodowsky (in press) note that the obesity rates among lower socioeconomic (SES) samples are 40% among Black women and 38% among American Indian women. The obesity rate for the general population is 22.5% (Tauber, 1998). Similar tendencies for eating differences according to SES were found in data on Finnish women (Jalkanen, Tuomilehto & Tanskanen, 1986 as cited in Osvold &

Sodowsky, 1993). In this Finnish study, upper-class women were more concerned with thinness, while lower-class women were less interested in weight loss and were heavier. In the United States, as well, it is suggested that improvement in SES for any race creates a concern with weight and increased desire for thinness (Osvold & Sodowsky, 1993).

Ethnic/Racial Groups and Eating Disorders in the United States

In one study of bulimic behavior among high school and university students, more White females acknowledged this behavior than Black, Latino, or Asian adolescents (Howat & Saxton, 1988). Nevertheless, evidence shows that Black and American Indian females are still at risk for eating disorders (Hiebert, Felice, Wingard, Munoz, & Ferguson, 1988; Holden & Robinson, 1988; Rosen, Shafer, Dummer, Cross, Deuman, & Malmberg, 1988).

Several explanations have been offered for the lower incidence of eating disorders among Blacks (Osvold & Sodowsky, 1993; Smith, 1982). The first is that Blacks, who do not buy into this cultural ideal of "thin is beautiful," are less concerned about their weight. A related point is that Black women are more accepting of their bodies than White women. Another explanation for the lower incidence of bulimia and anorexia is that these problems most frequently begin in adolescence, and adolescence is a briefer period for Black women (particularly lower-income adolescents who attain adult status more quickly). It is also offered that expectations for greater academic success, career achievement, and higher levels of responsibility for Black females are factors for the lower incidence of anorexia and bulimia among this group.

In spite of these "protective" factors against eating disorders among Black women, studies suggest that as Black women achieve higher income levels they are more likely to accept White values and behaviors, including the cultural ideal of thinness. Indeed, Osvold and Sodowsky (in press) found that acculturated Black and Native American females scored significantly higher on three subscales of the Eating Disorders Inventory than their less-acculturated counterparts. It also has been suggested that there may be a later onset for eating disorders among Black women (Osvold & Sodowsky, 1993).

Few studies have been conducted on eating disorders among Native Americans. However, Osvold and Sodowsky (in press) summarize from available data that these disorders may be more prevalent than previously believed. In an interesting comparison of eating attitudes of Native American and Black females, these authors found that the Blacks women scored significantly higher on three subscales of the Eating Disorders Inventory. Native Americans scored higher on one subscale of this measure. The authors note the importance of income in this study. As the socioeconomic status of diverse women drew closer to middle-class levels, attitudes regarding eating and thinness resembled those of White women.

IMPLICATIONS FOR TREATMENT AND PREVENTION

Treatment

Using the five theoretical views of disorders, it is possible to design therapeutic interventions to help young people demonstrating anorexic or bulimic behavior. For example, several treatment approaches have been formulated from psychodynamic theory. Some of these therapeutic techniques use free association, dream interpretation, and possibly hypnosis to help the young person confront unresolved conflicts. Within a framework of ego psychology, others use a warm, nurturing, supportive counseling relationship to focus attention on what is believed to be a dysfunctional mother/child relationship. And still others use a nondirective, client-centered approach to help young people redefine a flawed image of self and improve painful interpersonal relationships. The effectiveness of these approaches is not clear. Published clinical studies do report modest success. Since these case studies often involve only small numbers of clients and lack follow-up mechanisms, however, they must be treated cautiously (Bayer, 1984; Bemis, 1978; Carroll, 1986; Pettinatti & Wade, 1986; Weinstein, 1996).

From a behavioral perspective, the treatment literature contains numerous reports of the use of operant techniques to treat these dysfunctional behaviors. The typical treatment protocol takes place in a hospital and involves the removal of all the rights and privileges of the young person. Behavior that increases the young person's weight—that is, eating—may be rewarded by the return of rights such as increased staff attention, visiting privileges, and access to radio, television, or records. The failure to increase or maintain weight results in the removal of rights and privileges. Although this technique is successful in the short term in restoring weight to the young person experiencing an eating disorder, the literature suggests that a large number of young people fall back into the condition after a few years. Consideration must also be given to the confounding effects of the inpatient setting and the use of medications on reported success (Bemis, 1978; Kreipe, 1986; Ohlrich & Stephenson, 1986).

Agras and associates (1989) describe the use of an outpatient cognitive behavioral program to reduce bulimic behaviors. Their study used a control group and three treatment approaches to reduce bulimic behaviors in 77 women. They reported the most successful treatment approach used individual therapy with cognitive restructuring exercises directed toward altering food and body images of the subjects. Of the 22 women receiving this treatment approach 56% were able to stop their bulimic behaviors.

A third treatment approach, family therapy, is receiving considerable attention. If this theoretical perspective is correct, the eating-disordered individual is playing a role in a dysfunctional family system that can be changed. If the role is changed and if the family's functioning can be improved, the young person's eating disorder should diminish. The family therapist works to improve the family's communication patterns and to help the family learn how to openly express its anger.

BOX **14-1**   **Cindy: The Perfect Daughter**

"Cindy was the perfect daughter."

"You mean she is, don't you, Jim?"

"I don't know what I mean anymore about anything. Why is she doing this thing, this crazy thing, to us?"

Jim and his wife, Sally, were in my office to discuss their daughter's behavior. In the previous few months a healthy, physically active, "perfect" child who had never been a problem to anyone had gone on an incredibly regimented diet. Cindy, who at 5 feet 5 inches had weighed 120 pounds, now weighed less than 90 pounds. Her once long, dark, thick hair was now thin. Her menses had stopped, and she had developed health problems. Her condition had so deteriorated that she had been hospitalized for a while and had been tube-fed.

"I just don't understand it," Jim said. "I mean she never ever caused any trouble. She tried to please us in everything she did. It didn't matter what it was. She did everything we asked."

"I remember when she was ten and wanted to take trumpet lessons," Sally said. "Remember, Jim? We thought that wasn't appropriate for a young lady, you know, so Jim and I suggested the piano. There was no argument on her part, no pouting, no temper tantrums. She agreed. I just can't understand why she won't listen to us now. Why is she being disobedient?"

In the weeks that followed, during which I met with Cindy and her parents, the theme of control continually emerged. I was struck with the way in which Cindy had triumphed over her dominating parents. For no matter how they pleaded, threatened, cried, or bribed, their dominance had, in an indirect but very effective way, been broken forever. The image of Cindy in my office remains vivid to this day: a young woman sitting opposite her parents, showing little emotion save for an occasional slight smile, and controlling, by her silence, the events before her. Our sessions over those 8 months focused on separation, power, and role issues in the family, and Cindy's parents were somewhat successful in altering their behavior. I am uncertain whether my efforts helped Cindy. Although she did regain some of her lost weight, she remained an extremely thin young woman. The last time we met, she had completed college and was looking for employment as a teacher.

The therapist helps the family members let go of their need for perfection, let go of their need for control, and let the young person with the eating disorder achieve independence without resorting to starvation. Initial reports of the results of using this treatment are encouraging. But again these reports involve case studies and lack follow-up components (Bemis, 1978; Carroll, 1986; Weinstein, 1996) (see Box 14-1).

The fourth treatment intervention is, in our opinion, an adjunct therapy. That is, the use of medications have not been effective when used alone to treat these dysfunctional behaviors. But, when antidepressants and antianxiety medications are used in combination with a "talk" therapy, improvement sometimes occurs (Walsh & Devlin, 1998). The final theoretical approach discussed in this section does not offer a treatment intervention. The sociocultural perspective is more suited to efforts at preventing eating disorders.

In summary, there are several interventions for working with the young person with an eating disorder. However, none of these approaches has proven completely successful. Indeed, regardless of the treatment intervention about half of these young people return to these destructive behavioral patterns within several years

Young women vastly outnumber young men with the eating disorders of anorexia and bulimia

(Walsh & Devlin, 1998). Given this reality, most treatment teams working with victims of eating disorders use a combination of approaches.

Prevention

How might the incidence of eating disorders be reduced? Let's consider how each of the tools of prevention could be used.

Education

The use of information to alert, inform, and sensitize each of us to an issue of importance is the function of prevention's first tool. In reviewing the material in this chapter, one must realize that societal forces contribute to the problem. Using public-service announcements and family-life education programs, one can begin the exceedingly slow process of helping men and women understand that women should be judged by the same multiple standards that are used to judge men. Still, we know that education-only efforts will increase knowledge, sometimes change attitudes, but rarely, if ever, change behavior. For those attempted preventive interventions that used an education-only approach, behavioral change could not be measured (for example, see Paxton, 1993; Smolak & Levine, 1996).

Competency Promotion

It is clear from the research and clinical data presented in this chapter that young people with a poor self-image are at risk for this dysfunctional behavior. Given the role that parents play in the formation of self-esteem and in the development of this problem behavior, the focus for our use of this tool might be on them. Improving parents' skills in family communication and in enabling young people to achieve independence could significantly contribute to a reduction in eating disorders.

Natural Care Giving

To care, to love another, and to be able to give help as well as to receive help are the essence of this tool. If care giving can be done within the context of the family, the research in this chapter would predict a reduction in this problem. If it cannot occur within that context, the development of self-help groups can help fill an existing void. Such groups are testimony to the need all humans have for emotional support and caring.

Community Organization/Systems Intervention

As we mention earlier, we suspect that Western society plays a role in the incidence of anorexia and bulimia. CO/SI efforts are directed at structural changes within an organization, a community, or a society. If one considers the problem to be a failure to recognize young women for their talents and intelligence rather than for their body, a plan for a possible intervention emerges. To illustrate, in a forthcoming publication, Piran (2000) describes a 10-year intervention study to reduce eating disorders among students attending a ballet school in Toronto, Canada. What makes this intervention unique is that the author focused on systemic change. Piran worked with school staff to insure students would feel positive about their bodies regardless of shape and size. As she writes:

> There were multiple changes made at the [ballet school], including the replacement of the emphasis on body shape with an emphasis on stamina and body conditioning, prohibiting teachers from making any evaluative comments about body shape to their students, and the introduction of a staff member who could be contacted by students regarding concerns about body shape. Educational sessions with staff ... addressed prejudices about body shape, adults' responsibility to students' self- and body-esteem, the crucial processes of growth and puberty, and ways to protect students from harsh pressures in the larger dance world (pp. 8–9).

In addition to these system interventions, the program incorporated other prevention tools like addressing peer relations (education, natural caregiving) and encouraging a dynamic rather than a static informational format (education). Program results showed significant reductions in problem eating patterns and attitudes about physical appearance. This program is an example of how multiple tools can be used creatively to effect improved health among young people.

SUMMARY

Across 14 chapters and 400 pages of text, we've asked you to recognize four reoccurring themes. As the semester nears its inevitable close, consider that eating disorders were here long before *Vogue, Cosmopolitan,* and diet soft drink ads. Recognize also that not one but several rationales exist to explain eating disorders, and there's no reason why elements of several couldn't combine to result in an eating disorder for an individual—that's contextualism. Note also that differences between diverse groups exist but that as income increases diversity decreases. Finally, using prevention's technology, we hope you identified approaches to reduce the incidence of eating disorders.

MAJOR POINTS TO REMEMBER

1. Obesity has reached epidemic proportions across North America.
2. Obesity is caused by a variety of factors including lack of exercise, high-fat/high-sugar diets, and heredity.
3. Regarding heredity, 40 to 70% of weight gain may be due to genes that turn rich diets into body fat.
4. Obesity is responsible for many health problems that cost society an estimated $70 billion dollars a year.
5. Five theoretical perspectives that try to explain eating disorders are the psychoanalytic, behavioral, family, sociological, and biogenic explanations.
6. As with many other behaviors, there is historical evidence that eating disorders existed before modern times.
7. To apply the term anorexia nervosa to an individual's behavior, practitioners must find some of the following characteristics: (a) age under 25; (b) weight loss equal to 25% of ideal body weight; (c) a distorted understanding of that weight loss; and (d) no known physical or mental health reason for the weight loss.
8. More women than men suffer from eating disorders.
9. Research suggests that several factors contribute to eating disorders. These include individual, family, and societal factors.
10. Unlike anorexics, who simply deny themselves nourishment, bulimics engage in unrestrained eating sprees only to purge themselves in guilt.
11. A wide range of treatment modalities have been tried with eating disorders, with modest success.
12. Prevention approaches for this problem focus on improving individual self-esteem as well as working to change society's and institution's images of thinness.

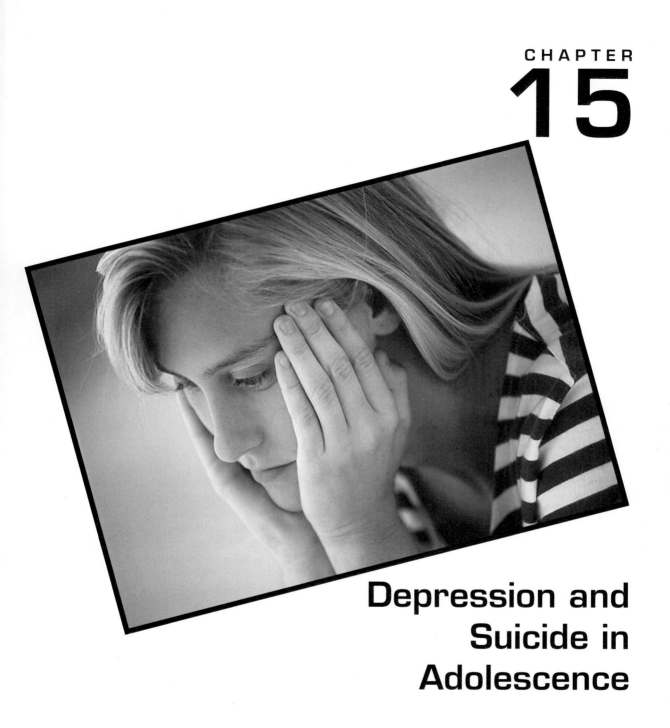

Depression and Suicide in Adolescence

$\mathbf{I}$MAGINE SADNESS SO profound that eating doesn't matter, that no amount of rest brings either wanted sleep or energy to an exhausted body. Imagine swinging from the depths of this depression to the heights of mania with a sense of euphoria that leads to grandiose thoughts and rash behaviors only to crash again into the hellish darkness of despair. Imagine alternating between sadness and anger go great that life itself has no value. These are the topics for this chapter. We'll use history, borrow from literature, and examine the social sciences for clues to understanding depression and suicide and how it might be treated and prevented.

DEPRESSION

Depression: Definition and History

Who among us has not at some time in life felt sad, unhappy, or discouraged? Who among us has not shed a tear over disappointment, in frustration, or the loss of a dream unfilled? What, then, separates these normal behaviors associated with depression from being "clinically" depressed? The answer to that question is essentially time. And time is a subjective factor. Thus, mental health professionals approach this subject cautiously—and with good reason. For while most clinical training would understand depressed mood and associated symptoms (insomnia, tearfulness, lack of appetite) lasting for more than 2 weeks that interfered with ordinary activities as "clinical" depression, there are instances, as in the loss of a loved one, when this diagnosis would be inappropriate.

Interestingly, these definitional issues troubled scholars less in the past. In ancient times, clinical depression was called *melancholia*. For the Greeks, who believed the body produced four "humors," fluids that influenced temperament and behavior, it was an excess of black bile that caused depression. Indeed, the word "melancholia" means "black bile" in Greek. During the Middle ages, depression, still called melancholia, was considered a problem of demonic possession solved by aggressive and often invasive religious intervention (an understanding we suspect that is still favored by much of Hollywood's film-making community).

Depression and Genetics

In the 19th century, it was suggested by the psychiatrist Kraepelin that recurrent depression was hereditary (Jackson, 1987). Currently, most scholars take an instructionist or contextual position and believe that "clinical" depression is caused by a combination of biological, environmental, social, and intrapsychic factors (Whybrow, 1997).

For the selectionist who believes the brain is preprogrammed, depression is the result of a serotonin and norepinephrine deficiency linked to an as-yet-unidentified malfunctioning gene (Asberg, 1989; Egeland et al., 1987). As we noted earlier in Chapter 2, serotonin is one of the three known principal neurochemical transmitters in the brain. It is commonly referred to as the controller of mood. But as we have cautioned throughout this book, the findings of one group of researchers like Egeland et al. (1987) who reported chromosome 11 as the marker gene for depression have not been confirmed by others, and Holden (1991, p. 1451) warns that depression may be "caused by a maladaptive response to stress, with concomitant disruption of many mechanisms, including serotonin and norepinephrine transmission."

Further, while twin and adoptive studies indicate that as much as 50% of the variance for "clinical depression" may be attributed to genetics, this still leaves 50% to be accounted for by other factors (Birmaher, Ryan, Williamson, Brent, Kaufman, Dahl, & Nelson, 1996). Clearly, one cannot and should not discount the importance of genetic susceptibility to "clinical" depression. However, as the biological instructionists or social science contextualists would remind us, family, social factors, intrapersonal characteristics, and life events matter greatly in determining whether depression will ever occur and, if it does, what its severity and duration will be (Moscicki, 1995).

Types

Among mental health professionals "clinical" depression is synonymous with the phrase affective disorders. The most common affective disorders are major depression, unipolar depressive disorder, dysthymic disorder, manic episode, bipolar disorder, and cyclothymic disorder. *Major depression* is characterized by a depressed mood. The individual often appears tense, nervous, and miserable. Feeling helpless and hopeless, apathy and thoughts of suicide are common. These episodes may last from several weeks to a year. The term *unipolar disorder* is used when major depressive episodes reoccur. *Dysthymic disorder* or *depressive neurosis* is used when the severity and duration of the depression is shorter than in the previously described conditions and psychotic symptoms like delusions or hallucinations are not present.

In contrast, *manic episodes* describe mood behavior that is excited and euphoric. Nervousness and irritability are often present. Manic individuals display hyperactive behaviors, such as the need for little rest, and often grandiose and delusional thinking. In a manic phase, it is not unusual that the manic individual

Major depression is characterized by feelings of helplessness and hopelessness.

will make rash and unwise decisions. These behavioral episodes may last from several days to months. The phrase *bipolar disorder* is used when an individual swings between periods of mania and depression. *Cyclothymic disorder* is applied when an individual displays a repeating pattern of numerous depressions with mild manic symptoms.

Feelings of hopelessness and helplessness (depression) are commonly associated with suicidal behavior (Rangell, 1988). Yet, as one Canadian study found, depression is not uncommon in adolescence (Ehrenberg, Cox, & Koopman, 1990). Surveying 366 Canadian high school students, their study reported that 31.4% of the sample were mildly to clinically depressed. Similar studies in the United States (Reed, 1994) and Ireland (Donnelly, 1995) have reported very comparable findings. Thus, other factors must be at work also, as we will see.

SUICIDE

"To be or not to be" is a question that most of us struggle to comprehend. And yet the question is so simple. The thought is so clear. Why, then, can we not understand adolescent suicide? Is it because we have forgotten some of the unique aspects of youth itself?

Attitudes about Suicide through History

Depending on the time and circumstances, suicide, a "conscious, deliberate attempt to take one's life quickly" (Farber, 1968, p. 4), was embraced or rejected by the Greeks, Romans, Jews, Christians, and others. For instance, in early Greek society the taking of one's own life was punished by mutilating the dead body. This punishment was not so much the result of a rejection of suicide per se as it was a determination that the individual had shown disrespect for the gods. "Heroic" actions or careful measures to ensure the gods' understanding made suicide more acceptable to the Greeks. Thus, the self-destruction of the sole surviving Spartan soldier of the battle at Thermopylae was cheered by the populace of Sparta, and we can observe how such famous personages as Socrates, Hannibal, and other citizens of the city-states of Athens, Massilia, or Keos could end their lives using hemlock (Alvarez, 1972).

The Roman Empire showed the same understanding of the role suicide played in society. For Roman citizens, suicide was considered a right and carried no penalties. Only those individuals who chose suicide "without cause" were punished, by denying them proper burial rights and thus condemning their souls to exile in the afterlife. Falling into this class were soldiers, slaves, and criminals. In each of these situations, suicide was punished because Roman society had been insulted or damaged. By committing suicide "without cause," the individual had cheapened the significance of the act for other Romans. The slave and the soldier were punished for depriving the empire of its assets. The slave was the property of the owner. The soldier was the property of the state. The loss of the slave was a financial burden for the master. The loss of the soldier weakened the empire. The criminal was punished for suicide for depriving the state of its right to extract its punishment from the individual (Alvarez, 1972).

The Greeks and Romans did not stand alone in endorsing suicide as an acceptable alternative to life. Incidences of self-destruction have been celebrated in many societies. The mass suicide of the Jews defending Masada to prevent their capture by Roman soldiers is just one example. The Japanese ritual of hara-kiri is another.

The history of early Christianity, too, is filled with examples of individuals' embracing suicide as a means of salvation. To the early Christians, life on earth was "at best unimportant" and filled with temptations to sin. Their kingdom was not of this world but of the next. Thus, given the opportunity to sever the tie with this world for eternal happiness in the next, it is understandable that many chose to do so. Alvarez, in his seminal work *The Savage God* (1972), writes that self-destruction, which was seen as the last option by the Roman citizen, was seized as the first choice by many of the early Christians. In a sense, then, the Romans' attempts to stamp out Christianity by putting its followers to death encouraged its growth. It would not be until 533 A.D. that the writings of Augustine against suicide would sway the church at the Council of Orléans to begin to consider suicide a sin. By 562 A.D., at the Council of Braga, the Fifth Commandment, "Thou shalt not kill," had been reinterpreted on the basis of Augustine's work to apply to the taking of one's own life as well (Alvarez, 1972).

The influence of this change on Western society was remarkable. From one European society to another, the bodies of people who had committed suicide were horribly mistreated. In France the body of an individual suspected of having committed suicide was dragged through the streets, burned, and then thrown on the village garbage heap. In areas where fear of the supernatural ran high, special but no less horrid precautions were taken with the body. These might include such special disposal methods as placing the body in a barrel and setting it adrift on a river or severing the hand responsible for the deed. Some sense of the cruelty of these people to their fellow human beings can be found in this account about the execution of a man for attempting suicide:

> A man was hanged who had cut his throat, but who had been brought back to life. They hanged him for suicide. The doctor had warned them it was impossible to hang him as the throat would burst open and he would breathe through the aperture. They did not listen to his advice and hanged their man. The wound in the neck immediately opened and the man came back to life again although he was hanged. It took time to convoke the aldermen to decide the question of what was to be done. At length the aldermen assembled and bound up the neck below the wound until he died (Alvarez, 1972, p. 45).

The fate of this poor creature's remains was no less gruesome. He was taken to a crossroads and there buried with a stake driven through his body! If this sounds like a sensible precaution against having a vampire haunt the living, understand that this procedure was practiced as late as the early 1800s, long after vampires ceased to exist in the imaginations of most people (Alvarez, 1972).

Thus, before the Council of Orléans, suicide was not considered inherently evil. For the Greeks, the Romans, and others with sufficient cause, suicide was an acceptable way out of an intolerable situation. With the Council of Orléans and subsequent religious councils, suicide came to be redefined as a sin against God and humanity.

Today, there are indications that this attitude may again be changing. Is this change a turning back to the Roman notion expressed by one Indian "that man's ability to destroy himself is his sole birthright" (Beaver, 1972, p. 17)? To answer this question, we must first recognize that self-destruction has been only selectively outlawed. History is full of examples of individuals or groups who committed suicide and have been revered as heroes for their behavior. Refusing to surrender to the enemy despite overwhelming odds, surrendering a safe existence for missionary service in disease-ridden parts of the world, or rushing into a burning building or leaping into a river to save another are all potentially suicidal. War itself is the pitting of one nation against another in a mass suicidal dance of destruction. Yet we have glorified in song and story, on stage and film, the defenders of Masada and the Alamo, and we celebrate their so-called noble destruction. No epic story is without its hero's or heroine's making a conscious decision to risk destruction for some altruistic purpose. It is this seemingly altruistic purpose that lifts these people above their self-destructive action and legitimizes their behavior.

Recently, society has begun to debate whether suicide can extend to other segments of the population without their being held in contempt and disgrace. For example, one Canadian study found adolescents more accepting of the act of suicide than their parents (Boldt, 1982). Rather than attributing responsibility for the act to the individual, as their parents did, the adolescents in this study viewed suicidal individuals as victims existing in a flawed society. A more recent study reported that Canadian youths see suicide as a call for help and, in contrast to their U.S. counterparts, "a more normal way to cope with problems" (Laenaars and Lester, 1995, p. 540).

Contributing to this discussion has been the public debate over physician-assisted suicide. In a physician-assisted suicide, a terminally ill individual is not simply asking to be allowed to die but to be assisted in hurrying the arrival of death. Opponents attack the concept on moral and religious grounds. Supporters argue that the technology of medicine has outpaced our capacity to handle the implications of life without life. It is possible to maintain a mechanical life—a beating heart, a breathing being—when there is no life. It is possible to lengthen terminal disease victims' existence by weeks, months, even years, but at what emotional and financial expense to the patients and their families? According to proponents, it returns the power of choice to the individual stricken with the terminal illness.[1]

We have defined suicide to be the "conscious, deliberate attempt to take one's life quickly." We argue that the "altruistic" suicide and assisted suicide are conscious decisions to destroy oneself. We do not know whether such an act is morally justifiable, but clearly the issue of who has control over one's own life has crept to center stage in the 1900s where, we suspect, it will remain for years to come. Suicide, once accepted and then rejected as a means to an end, is being reexamined. In this heated debate the adolescent is never mentioned. It remains inconceivable that a young person just coming into being would ever consider self-destruction. But adolescents are no less capable of committing suicide than are other people. In the next section we examine the demographics of suicide among the young.

Adolescent Suicide: Thoughts and Facts

Thoughts of death and dying are not strange or foreign to adolescents of this or past generations. In fact, teenagers confront death daily in the songs they listen to, the stories they read, and the movies they watch. We discuss throughout this book Erikson's concept of adolescence as a time of searching and exploring the unknown. Death is one such unknown. From our experience as adolescents, we remember trying unsuccessfully to conceptualize nonbeing. We were unsuccessful, for our minds, our bodies, and our energy spoke more to immortality than mortality. Those feelings of immortality create a kind of time distortion in young people. The distance from Monday to Friday is forever. Only when immortality passes (in our own cases in the early 20s or so) does time achieve its fatally excessive speed. As death is unreal in adolescence, so were our perceptions of death. We were part of the generation that grooved (yes, grooved) to such 45s as "Teen Angel," "Dead Man's Curve," and the classic "Leader of the Pack." We identified with James Dean in *Rebel Without a Cause* and later with Mel Gibson in *Mad Max*. We imagined ourselves in Susan Hinton's (1967) powerful novel of adolescent alienation *The Outsiders* and wondered whether we could ignore heat and flames to save another.

---

[1]Consider the steps the Greeks and others used to insure that their suicides were acceptable to society. Recognizing that taking ones own life is not mechanically difficult, we wonder if the physician suicide assistance movement is an attempt to develope "rites" about deliberately ending ones own life? What do you think?

Thoughts of death and dying
are not foreign to adolescents.

And empathized with Syliva Plath's (1963) torments in the semiautobiograhical novel of a college student in *The Bell Jar*.

In examining our experiences, we recognize a sort of death wish in ourselves and our friends. This death wish was not to die so much as it was to experience the sensation of death and then—as immortal beings—reverse time and situation. Thus, such ridiculous ballads as *Teen Angel*, in which a girl returns to a car stalled on the railroad tracks to search for her boyfriend's school ring only to be crushed by an oncoming train, or "Dead Man's Curve," in which a drag race on a wet, winding road ends in disaster, sent shivers up and down our spines. Maybe we identified with the survivors of these tragedies, who came so close to the experience themselves but returned to share their adventure in a 2-minute song, with sound effects included. Certainly, the excessive speed with which we drove our cars and the other life chances we took then were not the actions of individuals with a correct sense of their mortality.

Our experiences are supported by observations that young people have a distorted concept of death in which young people view it as a reversible event. Three factors are thought to influence this view of death. The first is that early in adolescence most young people have not yet reached the cognitive stage of formal operations and still deal with very complex issues in concrete terms. Unable to look beyond their immediate behavior or to understand the implications of their actions, young people can entertain thoughts of suicide. These thoughts are further stimulated by the cultural attitude that death is a taboo subject. Second, hearing euphemisms such as someone has "passed away" encourages the viewing of death as something other than harsh and unpleasant. Finally, television bombards young people with death and violence in a remarkably antiseptic fashion. The coyote in "Road Runner" cartoons suffers repeated physical catastrophes only to return moments later pursuing his dinner. Adolescents' favorite action film stars are clubbed, shot, stabbed, and beaten from the moment the house lights dim to the final roll of the film credits. Yet, these individuals never experience the massive swelling that results from a beating about the head, they never seem immobilized by the soreness in their muscles, and they never seem paralyzed by the pain of a puncture wound. These three factors of immature intellectual development, cultural taboos against talking about death, and the media's excessive and unrealistic portrayal of violence interact to encourage the attitude that death is trivial (Gould, 1965; McKenry, Tishler, & Christman, 1980; Sege, 1998).

These factors have come together on more than one occasion to result in the deaths of young people (see Box 15-1). Judas Priest was cleared of prompting two

---

BOX 15-1   Of Suicide, Rock Music, and Copycats

Music and images of death are not new, nor is the theme of suicide in music. To some of our previously mentioned favorite hits, we would share a number-one hit of 1961 *Moody River* sung by "no-more-mister-nice-guy" Pat Boone. In this song Pat sings about his girlfriend throwing herself into a river and perishing.

In contrast to today's slurred lyrics and subliminal suggestions that adolescents "do it" in Judas Priest's "Better by You, Better Than Me" or the alleged urging "to end your life" in Osbourne's "Suicide Solution," singers of the past were quite clear in their lyrical intentions. For example, in "Patches" Dickey Lee wails, "Patches, oh what can I do/I swear I'll always love you/It may not be right, but I'll join you tonight."

Why, then, the concern over music lyrics? The issue is contagion. Contagion is the phenomenon in which an individual exposed to a suggestion will act on it. Age offers no protective shield in this case. For example, consider the themes frequently found in heavy metal music. They are laments of sadness, drug misuse, alienation, and suicide. Recently, a group of researchers compared youth suicide rates to subscribers of heavy metal music magazines. Clearly, an individual who would invest their resources into a specialty topic magazine has a greater than average interest in that topic area. Controlling for other suicide predictors, the group found a strong correlation accounting for 51% of the variance between involvement in the heavy metal subculture and adolescent suicide (Stack, Gundlach, & Reeves, 1994).

In a second study, country western music was examined. Interestingly, the researchers found that the more air time given country western music in a listening area, the higher the white suicide rate in that area. They explain this phenomenon by noting the themes of many country western songs. Those themes deal with job loss, marital problems, and alcohol abuse. Those mournful country songs of lost love, taverns, and life's missed opportunities can be just as deadly for adults as screeching guitars can be for youths (Gundlach, 1992).

Several authors have documented also that attention given to adolescent suicides increases the frequency of suicidal attempts by that age group using the same means (Davidson & Gould, 1989; Phillips & Carstensen, 1988; Range, Goggin, & Steede, 1988). To discourage these so-called copycat deaths, Phillips and Carstensen recommend that (1) the media not dwell on the death of the adolescent; (2) the news article not appear on the front page; (3) the victim not be glorified; (4) the negative consequences of the action be shared; and (5) alternatives to suicide be stressed (available counseling services, crisis phonelines, and so on). These steps, it is hoped, will discourage adolescents from copying the behavior of rock musicians like Nirvana's Kurt Cobain, who ended his life with a firearm.[2]

[2]The press' response to the suicide of grunge rocker Kurt Cobain is believed to explain the almost nonexistent copycat deaths that followed his death.

fans to commit suicide by the use of subliminal messages on the band's "Stained Class" album. He joins Ozzy Osbourne, who was unsuccessfully sued by a California couple whose son had killed himself after listening to Osbourne's song "Suicide Solution." Osbourne, who once bit off a bat's head during a concert and, like Alice Cooper, has simulated onstage hangings, was accused of causing the boy's death with an alleged lyric urging young people "to end your life." Other young people have died trying to leap objects with motorcycles, jumping from high places into water, or driving at breakneck speeds. To cries that greater restraint must be exercised by entertainers and the media to avoid stimulating young people to end their lives, we must comment that times have certainly changed. With the advent of instant telecommunications we can watch, from the comfort of our homes, live and in color, butchery in places with names like the West Bank, Belfast, and Bosnia. Thus, it should not be too surprising that the music of the 1950s and early 1960s turned from the silly and frivolous (like "Itsy-Bitsy, Teeny-Weeny, Yellow Polka-Dot Bikini") to the quietly satirical "Suicide is Painless," to the heavy metal sound of "The End." Presently, the music industry caters to youthful feelings of alienation and rebellion with gangsta rappers and the "Antichrist Superstar" Marilyn Manson, whose adoring fans, we swear, dress like extras from Ed Wood's cult masterpiece *Plan 9 from Outer Space* and have been known to chant "We love hate! We hate love."

Interestingly, although the U.S. suicide rate climbed an astonishing 200% from 1955 to 1978 (Macdonald, 1987), it has since stabilized (Adams, Bennion, Openshaw, & Bingham, 1990; Bingham, Bennion, Openshaw, & Adams, 1994; Holinger & Offer, 1989; Holinger, Offer, Barrer, & Bell, 1994). More interesting still is that adolescent suicide is uncommon. For the most recent year for which data are available (1993), the number of suicides committed by young people between the ages of 15 and 19 was 1,965 or 10.9 per 100,000. For 10- to 14-year-olds, it was 322 or 1.7 per 100,000 (U.S. Bureau of Census, 1996, No 140, p. 102) Clearly, these are not statistically significant numbers, when the population of U.S. youths between the ages of 10 and 19 (an estimated 36 million) is considered. Still, the loss of any young life is heartbreaking.

What protective factors might be at work to reduce the risk of suicide for this age group? Fischer and Shaffer (1990) suggest three possible factors. The first is that the affective disorders, particularly major depression, most commonly appear in adult life. The next is that American youths have many opportunities to receive and benefit from social support systems. These systems may be found formally in churches, schools, and youth groups, and informally in peer and adult friendships. Finally, a degree of cognitive maturity is necessary, these authors believe, before psychological constructs like hopelessness and depression can occur.

Still, from another numerical standpoint, these figures are significant in that U.S. youths do not die in great numbers. Thus, even these small numbers of deaths elevate suicide to be the third leading cause of death among adolescents in the United States.[3] Finally, numbers are not people. Figures cannot express

---

[3]For 1994 for the age group 15 to 24, the leading causes of death were (1) accidents, (2) homicide and legal intervention, and (3) suicide (U.S. Census Bureau, 1997, Chart 130, p. 97).

the suffering these youths experienced that led them to conclude that life was not worth the trouble. Statistics cannot convey the anguish their premature deaths leave behind for their parents, their siblings, and their friends. Even though the facts of adolescent suicide may be clear, the reasons for overstepping the boundary between life and death remain clouded.

Sex Differences

Females attempt suicide more frequently than do males but are less successful in actually dying. Much of the explanation for this lies in the means the sexes use to end their lives. In 1993, for example, to commit suicide males used firearms 66% of the time, hanging (15%), and poisoning (14%), while females used firearms 39% of the time, poisoning (35%), and hanging (13%). Firearms are more lethal than other means, and their increased use by males resulted in a death rate for all ages almost six times higher than for females. Of concern should be the fact that over the past 2 decades the means by which females attempt to end their lives has changed with a nearly 10% increase in the use of firearms (U.S. Bureau of Census, 1996, Chart 139, p. 101).

Racial Differences

In the United States, Native Americans are 2.5 times more likely than Blacks to commit suicide. With a suicide rate half as high as that for Whites, some American Indian tribes have the highest suicide rate of all racial groups. Although general suicide rates among American Indian adolescents appear to be the highest, it is important to note that this is not the case for all American Indian tribes (LaFromboise & Bigfoot, 1988).

While females attempt suicide more than males; males use more lethal means.

Among American Indians, several factors have been associated with greater risk for adolescent suicide. First, American Indians who are adopted by White families have a suicide rate twice as high as that of American Indian adolescents living on reservations. Next, tribes with weak ties to tribal and religious traditions and characterized by high unemployment have higher rates of suicides. Third, suicide among American Indians is linked to depression and boarding school experiences. Fourth, suicide is more common among American Indian teenagers who belong to groups that abuse alcohol and hold feelings of anger, hopelessness, and helplessness. Fifth, for adolescent males who have lost a brother to suicide, anniversaries are periods of heightened vulnerability. Finally, higher suicide rates are found among American Indians who feel they have brought dishonor to their family (Berlin, 1986).

Adams, Bennion, Openshaw, and Bingham (1990) have examined data on adolescent suicide and other classifications of violent death from the National Center for Health Statistics. In comparing statistics from 1979 and 1984, they report that death by suicide decreases for Whites and Blacks, but increases for "others" (American Indians, Pacific Islanders, Asians, Latinos, and other diverse groups). Furthermore, while Blacks are at greater risk for death from homicides, Whites and "others" are at greater risk for death from suicide and motor vehicle accidents.

Adcock, Nagy, and Simpson (1991) examined attempted suicides and depressive symptoms in Black and White adolescents. While there were no differences between groups, Blacks were more likely to report feelings of sadness and hopelessness. Whites, in this study, were more likely to report feelings of having nothing to look forward to. Not surprisingly for both groups, those who were not sexually active or consumers of alcohol were significantly less likely to report attempted suicide. Why are we not surprised by this last statement? First, failed romances are often the "trigger" event that precipitates a suicide attempt. Second, alcohol is a disinhibiting beverage whose consumption is linked to suicide attempts and other harmful events (such as traffic accidents, drownings, and criminal acts).

A seeming anomaly arises when we examine these findings and compare suicide rates of White males 15 to 19 years old (18.5 per 100,000) and females (4.2 per 100,000) with Black males 15 to 19 years old (14.4 per 100,000) and females (the base figure is too small to report reliably). What factors cause Blacks to have a suicide rate less than that for Whites (U.S. Bureau of Census, 1996, Chart 140, p. 102)?

Fischer and Shaffer (1990) suggest that a history of oppression and racism against Black people has created an extended social support system that assists them. The availability of family and friends appears to be especially helpful for Black females whose suicide rate per 100,000 was too low to accurately calculate (Nisbet, 1996). Furthermore, it is thought that this history of external oppression pulls Blacks together as a people. Finally, anger not expressed inward tends to be expressed outward. And in this sense the issue of Black suicide rates may be one of interpretation (Braucht, Loya, & Jamieson, 1980). If we consider violent deaths, particularly homicide, to be equivalent to suicide, the figures change radically. For example between the ages of 15 to 24, Black men are more than twice as likely than White men to be murdered (242.2 per 100,000 compared to 99.1 per 100,000), and

Black women are also more likely than White women to be murdered (39.9 per 100,000 vs 28.2) (U.S. Bureau of Census, 1996, Chart 137, p. 101). Given these data, the authors of this book have long maintained that the Black suicide rate does not accurately reflect their suicidal feelings. Evidence in support of this position can be found in studies finding a link between violent behavior and suicide (Inamdar, Lewis, Siomopoulos, Shanok, & Lamela, 1982; Pfeffer, Plutchik, & Mizruchi, 1983; Shafii, 1985).

We believe that adolescent suicide rates for Blacks are low estimates because their suicidal tendencies are reflected in violent behavior. In addition, society's taboo against this behavior has encouraged many family doctors to report a suicide as an accident in order to protect the memory of the young person.

Homosexuality and Suicide

Although evidence is limited and existing studies have methodological flaws, gay and lesbian adolescents appear to be at higher risk for suicidal behaviors and suicidal ideation (Proctor & Groze, 1994). For example, Remafedi, Farrow, and Deisher (1991) found among a predominantly White gay and bisexual sample of males 14 to 21 years old that 30% had attempted suicide at least once and almost half of that number had made more than one attempt. Many of the suicide attempters (44%) attributed their attempts to family problems. Other reasons for suicide attempts were confusion regarding homosexual orientation, depression, conflict with peers, romantic problems, and the abuse of alcohol and other drugs. Further insight can be gained by comparing suicide attempters and nonattempters to several psychosocial variables. For example, reaching certain sexual milestones like experiencing homosexual feelings for another occurred at younger ages for suicide attempters than for nonattempters. Attempters were more likely to report having been sexually abused, arrested, having engaged in illicit drug use, and having undergone chemical dependency treatment. Further, suicide attempters scored higher on measures of depression, suicide ideation, and hopelessness. In respect to sex roles, suicide attempters were more likely to be classified as feminine or undifferentiated and less likely to be classified as masculine or androgynous. It may be that the feminine and undifferentiated sex roles heightened sad feelings of being different among these males (Remafedi, 1991). Collectively, these observations describe a group of behavioral, self-image, and psychosocial understandings that place some homosexual or bisexual males at greater risk for suicide. It is important to recognize that these characteristics are likely the result of stress associated with negative societal images about gays and lesbians and negative responses from family, peers, or community concerning the young person's sexual orientation.

What factors contribute to the higher rate of suicide attempts and suicide ideation among gays, lesbians, and bisexuals? One factor is the general negative attitude that exists in society toward gays and lesbians. Gays and lesbians are minorities in society and are faced with many stereotypes and prejudices about their actions. Next, distress very likely accompanies the individual's recognition that his or her homosexual preference will invite ostracizing behaviors from peers. If known, the homosexual or bisexual practices of the adolescent are likely to create family disruption (Garnets & Kimmel, 1991). Almost always, "coming out" is a stressful and difficult process for adolescent gays and lesbians because of the lack of proper guidance, social support, and coping skills youths have (due to age) to face internal and external stressors (Rotheram-Borus & Fernandez, 1995). Many gays and lesbians move between two different worlds—one in which their sexual orientation is known and the other where it is not.

There also is evidence that younger gay and lesbian adolescents may be at greater risk for suicide than older adolescents. Remafedi (1987) reported that adolescents who acknowledged homosexual or bisexual identities at younger ages were at greater risk for problems. Younger adolescents are more vulnerable because of psychological and social immaturity that affects their ability to cope with and accept a homosexual or bisexual orientation. Indeed, an awareness of sexual orientation frequently accompanies pubertal maturation in early adolescence (Petersen, Leffert & Graham, 1995). While biologically mature younger adolescents may be aware of their preference for the same sex, it has been suggested that younger adolescents should be encouraged to delay acting on these feelings until their development is more mature in other areas (Petersen et al., 1995).

Theoretical Perspectives on Suicide

Two principle groups of theories—one emerging from psychoanalytic thought, the other from sociological observations—have been proposed as explanations for suicide. The first set of explanations focuses on internal variables, while the second views external social forces as influencing the decision to take one's own life.

The Psychoanalytic Perspective

Although psychoanalytic theorists differ on the exact motivations of the individual who commits suicide, an essential element in each of their arguments is the concept of punishment. From a historical perspective, it is interesting to see how the instinctual urge of aggression represented by punishment and sex are represented in early Freudian writings. For example, Stekel (1967), a psychoanalyst writing in the latter half of the 19th century, expressed these concepts when he observed that "the punishment the child imposes upon himself is simultaneously the punishment he imposes on the instigators of his sufferings" (p. 89). For Stekel, the punishment was an act of revulsion against oneself for masturbating.

Alfred Adler (1967), a contemporary of Stekel, agreed that sexual issues are of major importance in pushing a young person to suicide but introduced the argument that other forces may be at work as well. For Adler, feelings of inferiority, revenge, and aggression interacted in such a way as to bring a wish for illness or death in order to punish loved ones for their real or imagined slights. This position was elaborated on by Karl Menninger (1938), who proposed that suicide is actually a displaced desire to kill or to be killed.

B O X **15-2**   **A Case Study of Suicide**

John was a 15-year-old honor student who had attempted for nearly all his life to match his father's expectation of him as a student and as an athlete. In his sophomore year John fell in love for the first time. She was a classmate named Susan. Although his grades remained high, John was no longer interested in participating in spring training for baseball: he wanted to be with Sue. John's father was not receptive to this idea, and as a result the relationship between the two deteriorated rapidly. Their arguments almost always ended with John's father saying "You care for her more than you care for me." Feeling tremendous pressure to break off the relationship, John did stop seeing Sue. Two days after breaking it off, John shot himself.

John's dilemma was a painful one. He loved and cared for both his father and Sue. He had tried to meet the standards his father had set for him, but at 15 he experienced his first love and a desire no longer to please his father. In the resulting family arguments John was torn between his father and his girlfriend. By ending his relationship with her, he lost an important person who could not be recovered. Furthermore, John now had strongly ambivalent feelings about his father, whom he held responsible for the breakup. John detested his father for making his life so miserable but loved him because he was his father. Torn between these conflicting emotions and feeling tremendous guilt, John decided to end his life.

It is, however, Sigmund Freud's (1957) conceptualization of suicide as resulting from the loss of a love object that is the most widely accepted of the psychoanalytic viewpoints. Interestingly, while psychoanalytic theory generally has fallen into disfavor, the concept of a lost love object remains a useful clinical viewpoint. In this explanation the suicidal person is seen as loving and then hating some object who has become lost or unavailable. Alternating between the desires to destroy and to cherish the object, the individual recognizes these hostile feelings and feels guilty about having them. This guilt turns the anger away from the object inward, and the anger against oneself is expressed by the act of suicide. There may be no better literary illustration of this concept than Shakespeare's tragedy of adolescent love *Romeo and Juliet*. Passion, anger, jealousy, and ultimately death as the lost love object remains forever from reach are the elements of this story (see Box 15-2).[4]

Other theories provide additional perspectives on suicide. M. L. Farber (1968) wrote that suicide results from a sense of hopelessness. The individual does not see any acceptable way out of an impossible situation and so chooses "a quick self-induced death . . . in preference to the certain prospect of an unbearable life" (p. 26). The trigger can be found in some life incident "that renders life more difficult to cope with and closes off any possibility of improvement in the situation" (p. 41) (see also Crumley, 1982; Tooley, 1980). In the case study described in Box 15–3, this life blow occurred with the ending of John's relationship with Susan. Unable to see an acceptable way out of his troubles, he selected the ultimate solution—suicide.

[4]Recall that Romeo ends his life mistakingly believing that Juliet has died. When Juliet reawakens from the sleeping potion she had taken and discovers her adolescent lover has killed himself, she too takes her life.

Shneidman (1976) describes suicide as a plea for help. The suicidal individual has come to the end of his or her emotional resources and through this act attempts to mobilize the support of others. Shneidman's view is supported by the fact that most suicide attempts do fail, thus providing the opportunity for assistance to emerge out of an attempt at self-destruction.

The Sociological Perspective

The other major group of explanations for suicidal behavior can be found in the sociological literature. Much of the work in this field is by Émile Durkheim, whose *Suicide: A Sociological Study* (1951, first published in 1897) is credited with stripping away much of the horror and fear that surrounded suicide until the late 1800s. Durkheim's conceptualization of suicide rests on the individual's integration into society. The individual who is poorly integrated into society commits an *egotistic* suicide. The controversial Thomas Hardy novel *Jude the Obscure* (1895/1967) well illustrates this form of suicide.

Jude is an adolescent whose ambitions of education and marriage are thwarted. He wanders the countryside uneducated and with the woman he earlier loved but is unable to wed. His unwanted nomadic lifestyle brings Jude no peace and the ostracizing of all those around him. His son, Little Jude, confronts the core dilemma of the family (that dilemma being belonging and being valued by society) when he confronts Jude's female companion:

It would be better to be out o' the world than in it, wouldn't it?
[She replies] It would almost, dear.
Tis because of us children, too, isn't it, that you can't get good lodging?
Well, people do object to children sometimes.
[Little Jude responds] Then if children make so much trouble, why do people have' em?

The individual who is poorly integrated into society is at risk to commit an egotistic suicide.

Oh—because it is a law of nature.

[Little Jude] But we don't ask to be born...I wish I hadn't been born!

You couldn't help it, my dear...

I think that whenever children be born that are not wanted they should be killed directly,

before their souls come to 'em,....

[The next morning Jude the senior and his companion find that Little Jude has hung himself and his two half-siblings. The note next to his body states] Done because we are too menny (Hardy, 1895/1967, pp. 355, 358).

While Little Jude commits suicide because he cannot integrate himself into a society that has no need for him, the individual who chooses a group identity over an individual identity in death commits an *altruistic* suicide. In this instance the death represents the sacrifice of the one for the many or for another. This theme of personal sacrifice, for those of you who are Star Trek fans, was explored several years ago in Spock's film death to save his comrades aboard the Starship Enterprise. For those of you who are readers of the penultimate, Charles Dickens, this sacrifice—this deliberate action of offering ones life knowingly for another—was represented in the actions of Sidney Carton, who substituted himself for Evremonde in the masterpiece *A Tale of Two Cities* (1859/1894). Consider these oft quoted words that Dickens used to describe Carton's feelings as he headed for the guillotine:

I see the lives for which I lay down my life, peaceful, useful, prosperous and happy, in that England which I shall see no more,... I see I hold a sanctuary in their hearts...[my offering my life for his] is a far, far better thing that I do, than I have ever done before (Dickens, 1859/1894, p. 373).

Finally, the individual caught in sudden societal or personal change that creates significant alienation or confusion in the individual commits an *anomic* suicide. While the data is not yet available, the recent changes in former communist countries like Albania would suggest an increase in the overall suicide rate in the coming years. For example, Kloep (1995) observed 121 Albanian 12-year-old females and reported on the tensions affecting them and their families. With the collapse of communist rule and the opening of this previously very isolated country to Western thoughts and lifestyles, his longitudinal study found decreased marital happiness in the families of these young adolescents. Lowered parental nurturing behaviors were accompanied by higher parental hostilities toward these youths. Challenging their parents—particularly their fathers—on the old ways, Kloep observed these young women engaging in antisocial behavior and reporting higher rates of depression. Proponents of Durkheim's model would speculate that in the near future the disruption Albania has experienced would express itself in a higher incidence of suicide among adolescents and in the general population. Or this depression will be turned outward and unrest and civil disturbances will occur.

Central to all three forms of suicide is Durkheim's (1897/1951) concept of anomie. The term *anomie* describes a society that is rootless, that is disintegrating because of some upheaval. As this society frays as a result of economic problems, revolution, value conflicts, or the like, individuals within that society experience increasing emotional difficulties, and as the cultural instability increases, the suicide rate increases. However, whether a suicide is egotistic, altruistic, or anomic, each represents a changing relationship with the environment. In the next section we examine the psychiatric and sociological theories in light of the research findings.

Psychological and Sociological Research on Suicide

What events come together to convince a young person to pursue so rash a course as suicide? A number of studies and clinical observations suggest that seemingly trivial events provoke the decision to attempt suicide. Several studies show, for instance, that fights with parents and the ending of a relationship with a boyfriend or girlfriend are the most frequent triggers. Certainly, these disputes with parents or breakups with friends are painful situations, but since they are near-universal adolescent experiences, much more must be going on (Blau, 1996; Birmaher et al., 1996; Butler, Novy, Kagan, & Gates,1994; Rubenstein, Heeren, Housman, Rubin, & Stechler, 1989).

Several studies show that young people who attempt suicide have extremely strained relationships with their parents. They report the following characteristics in many of these families. First, there is an absence of generational boundaries between the parents of these young people and their own parents. Next, spousal relationships are marked by dependency conflicts. These conflicts spill over onto the children as parental anger is inappropriately displaced onto them. Finally, maintaining the same symbiotic ties to their children as their parents maintain to them, the parents of these children discourage attempts at independence and, not surprisingly, live in a closed family system. Such a family environment, while smothering in one respect, is often emotionally detached from its children. This detachment results in most young people's feeling greatly unloved and unwanted. This theme emerges in almost every other study or review conducted on the subject (Birmaher et al., 1996; Compas, Connor, & Wadsworth, 1997; Moscicki, 1995; Pfeffer, 1981a).

This parental neglect can occur in one of two ways. Many authors note that young people are dependent on their parents for love and support. Parents inability to provide these essential elements for proper emotional growth places young people at risk (American Academy of Pediatrics, 1980; Compas, Connor, & Wadsworth, 1997; Pfeffer, 1981b). It is not surprising, then, that many studies report high marital discord or divorce in families with adolescents who attempt suicide (Allen, 1987; Paluszny, Davenport, & Kim, 1991; Strang & Orlofsky, 1990; Straus and Kantor, 1994; Tischler, McKenry, & Morgan, 1981). This conflict between the parents keeps the home in a constant state of tension and may carry over into their relationship with their children (Cohen-Sandler, Berman, & King, 1982; Orbach, Gross, & Glaubman, 1981; Paykel, 1989; Pfeffer, 1981a, 1989). In a few isolated cases the depth of parental rejection is so deep that researchers have gone so far as to suggest that one or both parents encouraged the young person to commit suicide (Molin, 1986; Pfeffer, 1981b; Rosenkrantz, 1978). In the "expendable child syndrome" (Sabbath, 1969) parents communicate to the

---

BOX **15-3**   The Cure for Love Melancholy

In this otherwise serious chapter, it might be good for all of us to take a breather and look again at the past—in this case at Robert Burton's *The Anatomy of Melancholy*, which was first published in the 17th century. In this monumental work such things as bad air, apples, beef, devils, kissing, pork, and witches are identified as causing melancholy. One serious form of melancholy affecting young people in particular is love melancholy. Burton offers the following advice for the cure and prevention of this illness:

1. The first rule to be observed in this stubborn and unbridled passion, is exercise and diet (p. 526).
2. Guianerius [an ancient medicine man, Burton reports, suggests that the sufferer of love melancholy] go with haircloth [wool] next [to] his skin, to go barefooted, and barelegged in the cold weather, to whip himself now and then, as monks do, but above all to fast (p. 526).
3. [Some sages suggest] bloodletting . . . as a principal remedy (p. 528).
4. [Of course, one should] avoid . . . kissing, dalliance, all speeches, tokens, love letters, and the like (p. 529).

5. As there be divers of this burning lust, or heroical love, as there be many good remedies to case and help: amongst which, good counsel and persuasion [are best] (p. 534).
6. [In what unquestionably was a period of high male chauvinism, to end his lovesickness, the male was urged to] see her undressed, see her, if it be possible, out of her attires . . . it may be she is like Aesop's Jay, or Pliny's Cartharides, she will be loathsome, ridiculous, thou wilt not endure her sight . . . As a posy she smells sweet, is most fresh and fair one day, but dried up, withered, and stinks another (p. 536).
7. The last and best cure of love-melancholy [Burton believes] is to let them have their desire. The last refuge and surest remedy, to be put in practice in the utmost place, when no other means will take effect, is to let them go together, and enjoy one another (p. 547).

(*Source:* R. Burton (1851). *The Anatomy of Melancholy* (4th ed.). Philadelphia, PA: J.W. Moore Publishers.)

---

adolescent that he or she is unwanted, is a burden to the family, and should never have been born. Recall in Chapter 13 our discussion of throwaway youths. Do you see the similarities that exist between the expendable child syndrome and throwaway youths? (see Box 15-3.)

The second kind of parental neglect is the result of the death of a parent. Research suggests that the earlier a child loses a parent, the more severe the effects will be (Glasser, 1978; Stanley & Barter, 1970). Stanley and Barter, who examined 38 hospitalized suicidal adolescents, report that they differed from a control group in having lost a parent before the age of 12. These authors speculate that the death of a parent at such an early age disrupts the proper resolution of dependency issues. Whether these findings continue to apply later in life is uncertain. For example, G. E. Barnes and Prosen (1985) found in a sample of 1250 outpatients seeking medical assistance from a general practitioner that the loss of the male parent contributed to depression in adulthood. However, they caution that this finding contributed only 2% to explaining the variance in the depression scores of adults (see Crook & Eliot, 1980; Paykel, 1989 for critical reviews of this literature).

Having made these statements about parental influences, a cautionary note is in order. We need to appreciate the interactive nature influencing individual and family behavior. What do we mean by interactive? It may be that some young people who may be biologically susceptible to depression interact with their families in ways that provoke the parental behaviors described in this section. It is also just as possible that the families are acting independently. The point is behavior occurs in a context that is unique for each individual, and it is that context that determines development.

Nevertheless, whether young people provoke their families to respond negatively or not, these studies suggest that the emotional needs of suicidal adolescents have not been met. Thus, it should not be surprising that these young people have been found to have poor self-esteem, poor social support, and problems with authority (Block, Block, & Gjerde, 1991; Butler, Novy, Kagan, & Gates, 1994; Capaldi, 1992; Daniels & Moos, 1990). They also experience higher levels of stress (Daniels & Moos, 1990; Kalafat, 1997; Rich, Sherman, & Fowler, 1990) and school difficulties (Farberow, 1989; Gispert et al., 1985; Kalafat, 1997). In addition, they have been described as angry, disagreeable, and impulsive (Gjerde, Block, & Block, 1991; Lehnert, Overholser, & Spirito, 1994; Newton, 1995) and as ego-brittle and lacking insight (Paluszny, Davenport, & Kim, 1991). The abuse of alcohol and other substances is common (Crumley, 1990; DeSimone, Murray, & Lester, 1994; Fischer & Schaffer, 1990; Klitzer & Blasinsky, 1990; Schuckit & Schuckit, 1989). Finally, youths who have been diagnosed with an affective disorder are at significant risk for attempting suicide. Indeed, 27 to 40% of suicides occur with individual suffering from an affective disorder (Compas, Connor, & Wadsworth, 1997) (see Table 15-1).

For a time, depression in the suicidal adolescent was a disputed issue. Although numerous studies reported depression as *the* principal contributing factor to attempted suicides (Cole, 1989; Daniels & Moos, 1990; Pfeffer, Klerman, Hurt, Lessor, Peskin, & Siefker, 1991), other studies reported that depression was not the primary factor (Glasser, 1981; Peck, 1987). Adolescent females in studies have appeared depressed and have reported depression, while males often have appeared aggressive, undercontrolled, and impulsive. We recognize today that depression in males or females is often hidden in disagreeable and antagonistic behaviors like temper tantrums, rebelliousness, and defiance.

As previously noted, the suicidal adolescent appears to have a poor family life and to experience considerable emotional deprivation (Corgrove, Zirinsky, Black, & Weston, 1995). As Teicher and Jacobs (1966) and others (Davidson, Rosenberg, Mercy, Franklin, & Simmons, 1989) describe it, the long-standing problems of the adolescent accelerate during a period in which parent and adolescent enter into a "squirrel cage" series of arguments ending with a complete "breakdown in communications." Desperate at this point to find meaning in life, the adolescent seeks close companionship. "The adolescent, already alienated to a great extent from the parents, seeks love, understanding, acceptance, reason, predictability—in short, a meaningful social relationship in one of the few remaining forms which allows for the intimacy implicit in such a relationship, i.e., a boyfriend or girlfriend"

T A B L E 15-1   Risk Factors for Increased, and Protective Factors for Decreased, Youth Suicidal Risk

Increased Suicidal Risk	← Risk Factors For: ←	Youth Suicidal Risk	→ Protective Factors For: →	Decreased Suicidal Risk
	1. Loss of Social Support 　a. Death 　b. Parental Separation/Divorce 　c. School Changes 　d. Peer Problems		1. Presence of Social Support 　a. Empathy 　b. Constant Availability 　c. Limit Setting 　d. Environmental Structure	
	2. Variability in Parental Functioning 　a. Affective Disorders 　b. Suicidal Tendencies 　c. Alcohol Abuse		2. Individual Adaptive Skills 　a. Appraisal of Stress 　b. Seek Alternative Solutions 　c. High Furstration Tolerance 　d. Self-esteem 　e. God Impulse Control	
	3. Violence 　a. Sexual Abuse 　b. Physical Abuse			

Source: C.R. Pfeffer (1989). Family characteristics and support systems as risk factors for youth suicidal behavior. In ADAMHA *Report of the secretary's task force on youth suicide:* Vol. 2: Risk factors for youth suicide. Department of Health and Human Services. publication ADM 89–1622. Washington. DC: U.S. Government Printing Office.

When a relationship sours for desperate youth, the risk for suicide increases.

(Teicher & Jacobs, 1966 p. 1255). In their attempt to gain this measure of satisfaction, young people invest all their remaining resources in this relationship, typically alienating themselves from school and other friends. When this relationship goes sour, they confront their loneliness and decide in desperation to attempt suicide.

Growing evidence suggests that this problem is more acute for some young people than for others. Young people with either an alcoholic parent or a depressed suicidal parent appear to be at significantly higher risk for suicide than their peers (Compas, Connor, & Wadsworth, 1997; Klitzner & Blasinsky, 1990; McKenry et al., 1980; Orbach et al., 1981; Pfeffer, 1981b; Tishler & McKenry, 1982; Tishler et al., 1981). Robins (1989) and Roy (1989) suggest this risk to be between four and five times the risk to their age cohort. This risk can be understood from a role model, a stress model, a biological model, or from a contextual perspective. In the first instance the young person is copying the parents' behavior. In the second instance, these parental behaviors place additional emotional stress on the adolescent's ability to cope with life. In the third instance, it may be a transferred biological susceptibility. From a contextual perspective, all of these factors are interacting with still other elements to shape and influence behavior.

Many of the writers we have cited believe that the young person in each of these situations is attempting to reclaim the loss of a love object. The findings of nearly all the studies reporting high levels of family discord, poor parent/child relationships, and emotional and physical child abuse lend themselves to this explanation. The young person attempting suicide is trying to recapture the emotional security that he or she so desperately wants.

Convincing as this argument may sound, sociologists say that committing suicide is far more complex than "simple" psychological constructs may suggest. For instance, as we have already noted, some Native American tribes have a suicide rate far higher than either Whites or Blacks do.[5] Can this high suicide rate be explained by assuming that their culture is marked by more family problems than others? Or are there other possible explanations?

Remembering Durkheim's conceptualization that suicide rests on the individual's integration into society, one group of scholars (Holinger, Offer, Barrer, & Bell, 1994) present data suggesting a significant relationship between increases in adolescent suicide rates and the size of the adolescent population. The authors suggest that as the relative number of young people in society increases, competition also increases. As opportunities are finite (the number of desirable jobs, scholarships, varsity positions), the chance for failure increases. They speculate that such failures contribute to a lower sense of self-worth and a gradual withdrawal of the individual from significant others, so that eventually some will commit suicide. Their model explains the dramatic increase in youth suicide during the 1970s and the leveling and decrease in incidence that began in the 1980s and continues to the present time. The authors speculate that rising numbers of adolescents from the mid-1990s to 2010 will result in a renewed rise in youth suicide.

---

[5]For example, the Apache nation has a very high suicide rate in contrast to the Pueblo nation.

TABLE **15-2**   Suicide Rates for Selected Countries by Sex and Age (15 to 24 Years Old) per 100,000

Male	
Canada	26.9
Italy	5.2
Japan	11.6
United Kingdom	9.3
United States	21.7
Female	
Canada	5.3
Italy	1.3
Japan	6.5
United Kingdom	2.1
United States	4.4
Total Average	
Canada	16.1
Italy	3.3
Japan	9.0
United Kingdom	5.7
United States	13.0

Source: U.S. Census Bureau (1991). *Statistical Abstract of the United States:* 1992 (112th edition). Washington, DC: U.S. Government Printing Office.

From a cultural perspective, Huffine (1989) and others (Lester, 1991; McAnarney, 1979; Stack, 1988) note that in societies in which family bonds are close (low anomie), suicide rates are low (see Table 15-2). In those societies experiencing changing family patterns (high anomie), suicide rates are higher. Religious beliefs also have an effect on reported suicide rates, with strongly religious nations reporting lower suicide rates than less religious nations (Hoelter, 1979). Further, the issue of transition, in general, affects the suicide rates of different nations. It appears that the more a nation experiences disruption and mobility, the higher the suicide rate is for that nation. For young people, the value a particular society places on achievement affects the suicide rate. Highly industrialized nations that place great importance on education, such as Japan and the United States, have significantly higher suicide rates than nations that do not. Finally, McAnarney (1979) notes that nations that encourage the suppression of aggression have higher rates of reported suicides than do nations that encourage the expression of feelings.

In applying these findings to Native Americans, we must recognize that some tribal lifestyles have been systematically attacked by the U.S. government and society in general for more than 300 years. Opportunities have been pervasively denied to Native Americans. Hollywood's movie-makers until recently portrayed some Native Americans as once noble and dignified savages. This same medium also portrays them as butchering heathens. Images and practices such as these have an insidious effect, conditioning these people to believe that they are little more than exces baggage in the 20th century. It is not surprising, then, to see a once so powerful people, who are now reduced in media portrayals and government handling to powerless positions, choose suicide as an acceptable alternative to an unacceptable life.[6]

But not all Native Americans attempt suicide, and more exceptions to Durkheim's rules of suicide have been found than affirmations, proving that complex behavior defies simplistic answers. We suggest that biological, personality, and social conditions interact in such a way as to select some young people for self-destruction. In the next section we look at what efforts can be made to treat or prevent suicidal behavior in young people.

Implications for Treatment and Prevention

Treatment

The treatment of suicidal behavior in young people demands that attention be paid to both the immediate crisis situation and the underlying problems that precipitated the attempt. Since the suicide attempt is a statement of the adolescent's abandonment of this world, friends and relatives must be mobilized to establish a lifeline of support, guidance, and friendship (Rosenbaum & Beebe, 1975). Schrut (1968) and others (Getz, Allen, Myers, & Lindner, 1983) emphasize that this alliance is critical for the therapist. They also suggest that if therapy is to be successful, the therapist must establish a relationship with the adolescent in which the young person can obtain "understanding, concern, and support" (see Box 15-4).

One of the first issues that must be addressed after a young person has attempted to take his or her life is whether hospitalization is advisable. Trautman (1989) and others (Blau, 1996; Blumenthal & Kupfer, 1989; Schrut, 1968) offer several guidelines for determining the answer to this question. Young people at lower risk of repeating the attempt are those whose precipitating circumstances suggest an impulsive action, who express a desire to continue to live, who do not show long-standing or presently severe depression, and who have a lifeline of family support available to them. At a higher risk of repeating the attempt to commit suicide are young people whose precipitating circumstances were "ordinary" life events (a family argument, for example), who are ambivalent about living after the attempt, who show present signs of severe depression or have a history of depression, and who, in the therapist's judgment, do not have the support of family and friends. Other factors, such as the means used to attempt suicide (firearms representing the most dangerous) and the young person's age and sex, must also be considered in determining whether the client is an acceptable risk for outpatient treatment.

[6]As one example of the humiliation Indians have experienced, consider the story of the Lone Ranger. His faithful Indian companion was named Tonto. In Spanish, *tonto* means "dopey" or "slow-witted." If you recall, Tonto called the Lone Ranger "Kimasabe." Himilce Novas (1994, p. 288) notes that Kimasabe appears to be a corruption of "quien mas sabe," which translated means "he who knows best."

B O X 15-4 Psychological First Aid

The following are action steps for the mature adult dealing with the suicidal young person:

Step 1: Listen. The first thing a person in a mental crisis needs is someone who will listen and really hear what he is saying. Every effort should be made to understand the feelings behind the words.

Step 2: Evaluate the seriousness of the youngster's thoughts and feelings. If the person has made clear self-destructive plans, the problem is apt to be more acute than when his thinking is less definite.

Step 3: Evaluate the intensity or severity of the emotional disturbance. It is possible that the youngster may be extremely upset but not suicidal. If a person has been depressed and then becomes agitated and moves about restlessly, it is usually cause for alarm.

Step 4: Take every complaint and feeling the patient expresses seriously: Do not dismiss or undervalue what the person is saying. In some instances, the person may express his difficulty in a low key, but beneath his seeming calm may be profoundly distressed feelings. All suicidal talk should be taken seriously.

Step 5: Do not be afraid to ask directly if the individual has entertained thoughts of suicide. Suicide may be suggested but not openly mentioned in the crisis period. Experience shows that harm is rarely done by inquiring directly into such thoughts at an appropriate time. As a matter of fact, the individual frequently welcomes the query and is glad to have the opportunity to open up and bring it out.

Step 6: Do not be misled by the youngster's comments that he is past his emotional crisis. Often the youth will feel initial relief after talking of suicide, but the same thinking will recur later. Follow-up is crucial to insure a good treatment effort.

Step 7: Be affirmative but supportive. Strong, stable guideposts are essential in the life of a distressed individual. Provide emotional strength by giving the impression that you know what you are doing and that everything possible will be done to prevent the young person from taking his life.

Step 8: Evaluate the resources available. The individual may have both inner psychological resources, including various mechanisms for rationalization and intellectualization which can be strengthened and supported, and outer resources in the environment, such as ministers, relatives, and friends whom one can contact. If these are absent, the problem is much more serious. Continuing observation and support are vital.

Step 9: Act specifically: Do something tangible; that is, give the youngster something definite to hang onto, such as arranging to see him later or subsequently contacting another person. Nothing is more frustrating to the person that to feel as though he has received nothing from the meeting.

Step 10: Do not avoid asking for assistance and consultation. Call upon whoever is needed, depending upon the severity of the case. Do not try to handle everything alone. Convey an attitude of firmness and composure to the person so that he will feel something realistic and appropriate is being done to help him.

Additional techniques for dealing with persons in a suicide crisis may require the following:

- Arrange for a receptive individual to stay with the youth during the acute crisis.
- Do not treat the youngster with horror or deny his thinking.
- Make the environment as safe and provocation free as possible.
- Never challenge the individual in an attempt to shock him out of his ideas.
- Do not try to win arguments about suicide. They cannot be won.
- Offer and supply emotional support for life.
- Give reassurances that depressed feelings are temporary and will pass.
- Mention that if the choice is to die, the decision can never be reversed.
- Point out that, while life exists, there is always a chance for help and resolution of the problems, but that death is final.
- Focus upon survivors by reminding the youngster about the rights of others. He or she will leave a

(continues)

(continued)

stigma on his siblings and other family members. He or she will predispose his friends and family to emotional problems or suicide.

- Call in family and friends to help establish a lifeline.
- Allow the youngster to ventilate his feelings.
- Do not leave the individual isolated or unobserved for any appreciable time if he is acutely distressed.

These procedures can help restore feelings of personal worth and dignity, which are equally as important to the young person as to the adult. In so doing, the adult helping agent can make the difference between life and death. A future potentially productive young citizen will survive.

Why do you think the phrase "mature adult" was used in the first paragraph? (*Source:* National Institute of Mental Health. (1977). Trends in mental health: Self-destructive behavior among younger age groups (DHEW Publication No. ADM 77–365). Washington, DC: U.S. Government Printing Office.)

From this and other epidemiological studies Robins (1989) has developed a table of correlates to suicide attempts (see Table 15-3). And Rotheram (1987) has proposed a screening procedure using two assessment interviews. The first, focusing on factors such as suicidal thoughts, history of past attempts, family history, evidence of clinical depression, and substance use, is used to determine potential risk. If risk is assessed to be high, the second diagnostic interview commences. In that interview the skilled clinician determines whether the adolescent is able to marshal enough coping resources to survive without being committed. For example, the clinician asks the adolescent to sign a written contract agreeing not to attempt suicide for a specified period of time. Depending on the adolescent's ability to agree and his or her answers to several other questions, the need for hospitalization is determined.

The use of medications is helpful with this population. Whether you prefer the word contextual, ecological, or instructionist, each term represents the belief that a dynamic fluid interaction between biology and environmental factors determines behavior. Medications that help regulate the neurotransmitter serotonin in the brain like the tricyclics (for example, imipramine or amitriptyline) or the selective serotonin reuptake inhibitors (for example, fluoxetine or sertraline) have been found to be ease persistent depression in most adolescents. For youths who alternate between mania and depression, mood stabilizers like lithium or valproate, which act on neuronal conduction, are generally effective (Birmaher, Ryan, Williamson, Brent, Kaufman, 1996; Bolinger, 1999; Whybrow, 1997).

But medication alone is not enough. These are not merely problems of brain chemistry. These are problems with multiple origins. Thus, regardless of medication or whether the adolescent is treated as an outpatient or an inpatient, family therapy in conjunction with individual or group therapy is recommended by most professionals. The psychological literature described earlier in this chapter presents a strong argument for the family's contribution to the life problems of the suicidal adolescent. If that young person is to stay with or return to the family, the therapist must help the family grow into a more supportive unit for the young person (Birmaher, Ryan, Williamson, Brent, & Kaufman, 1996; Walker & Mehr,

T A B L E **15-3** Predictors of Suicide Attempts in Adolescent Clinic Patients

5+ × population rate	Used barbs, PCP, hallucinogens, T's & blues, glue Wanted to die Thought of suicide
4–5 × population rate	Depressed two years or more Attempt before this year Hopelessness Four or more family diagnoses Runaway Alcohol problems this year Incarcerated this year Not living with relatives Psychiatric chief complaint
3–4 × population rate	Relative attempted Specific depressive symptoms ever 　loss of enjoyment 　felt slowed down 　felt wothless 　irritable Five or more depressive symptoms Ever incarcerated Three or more somatic symptoms not medically explained Four or more behavior problems Fighting at home involving patient this year Has been drunk at least three times in the last year Hurt or threatened this year Arrested this year
2–3 × population rate	White female aged 15 to 18 Has thought often about death Any depressive symptom ever Ever in trouble with the law Severe poverty Five or more posttraumatic symptoms

Source: L. N. Robins, (1989). Suicide attempts in teenaged medical patients. In ADAMHA *Report of the secretary's task force on youth suicide:* Vol. 4: Strategies for the prevention of youth suicide. Department of Health and Human Services publication ADM 89–1622. Washington. DC: U.S. Government Printing Office.

1983; Whybrow, 1997). In addition, the use of cognitive behavioral interventions have shown modest success with adolescents. These interventions typically combine relaxation training with cognitive restructuring, communication skills, and problem-solving techniques to effect behavioral change (Marcotte, 1997).

Simple human friendship is a powerful tool against suicide.

Prevention

The suicide prevention centers that started in England and were transplanted to North America in the 1960s represent a form of secondary prevention. Manned by trained professionals and volunteers, their hot lines provide a link between society and the individual contemplating suicide. The key to this form of crisis intervention is the caller's willingness to talk and share his or her feelings. The counselor encourages the ventilation of these emotions and tries to have the caller consider various alternatives to the present dilemma. Once a rapport has been established, the worker will volunteer to make arrangements for the caller to receive professional help. Some callers accept this invitation for help, while others do not (Potter, Powell, & Kachur, 1995).

The primary prevention of suicidal behavior must be aimed at the root causes of suicide. The theories examined earlier in this chapter provide suggestions for diminishing the prevalence of suicide (see Box 15-5).

Education   Arguments that suicide results from emotional deprivation and family neglect suggest that educational programs need to be developed to strengthen the family unit. We have urged repeatedly in this text that family life education be made an integral and important part of the young person's entire academic training. Such training could avert the ill-advised but growing popularity of pushing children at ever-earlier ages to achieve (Elkind, 1981). In addition, in recent

BOX **15-5** Prevention and Intervention Strategies: American Indian Adolescents

For several reasons, Native American youths are at greater risk for suicide than other youths. Knowing this, a preventionist works to reduce this risk for this population of youths. Drawing on Bandura's (1978) cognitive social learning theory, LaFramboise and Bigfoot (1988) suggest that identifying the thoughts, images, and inner conversations of Indian youths can be used to encourage healthy coping strategies. These authors identify four groupings of coping statements that can be used: (1) task-confidence statements, (2) perspective-keeping statements, (3) decatastrophizing statements, and (4) personal strength and determination statements. In their intervention program, statements illustrating each of these four categories are employed with other material to teach coping strategies to Native American youths.

Reviewing suicide treatment programs for American Indians, Berlin (1985) found that effective interventions included developing suicide prevention centers (containing inpatient facilities), providing education about suicide in school, engaging tribal healers and elders in prevention and intervention efforts, addressing issues related to suicide in programs designed for pregnant adolescents and new adolescent mothers and their infants, and incorporating suicide prevention and intervention strategies in alcohol and drug treatment programs.

In a review of suicide prevalence and prevention activities among Hopi youths, the authors concluded that suicide and alcohol abuse were linked for this population (Levy & Kunitz, 1987). In their work, youths most at risk were those whose parents married outside of the tribal group. A label of deviant was applied to these individuals and their children that increased their risk for alcohol abuse and suicide. From their study, Levy and Kunitz (1987) suggested several interventions that should be incorporated into Hopi suicide prevention programs. First, community strengths, rather than weaknesses, should be stressed. Next, prevention efforts should target younger adolescents. Third, prevention efforts and research should include individuals not currently believed to be at risk. Importantly, to avoid labeling those already defined as deviant, do not identify the program as suicide prevention. Finally, these authors suggest that a suicide prevention program among Hopi youths can be carried out with minimal cost and personnel, and argue for the use of volunteers from the community. The power of volunteers is an example of natural caregiving. One of prevention's more powerful tools.

years a number of highly effective social problem-solving skills programs have been developed to assist young people in their decision-making (Albee & Gullotta, 1997; Bloom, 1996b). We believe it vitally important that programs preparing college students for social service careers equip those students with problem-solving and conflict-resolution skills. So-equipped, the new teacher, case worker, minister, or recreational worker will be better able to assist young people in their care. The technology is there. We believe it incumbent upon institutions of higher learning to incorporate that learning into their education, recreational, religious, and social science curriculums.

Education can occur elsewhere than in the classroom. Commercial films like *Ordinary People*, *The Heart Is a Lonely Hunter*, and *The Bell Jar* sensitively portray the anguish that accompanies the decision to end one's life. And printed material like Jamison's (1994) *Touched with Fire: Manic-Depressive Illness and the Artistic Temperament* help all of us better understand the pressures these individuals face and how to provide them with the support necessary to cope with those stresses (see Box 15-6).

BOX **15-6** **Preventing Depression**

Earlier in this chapter we discussed depression and its link to suicide. Given this relationship, reducing the length and severity of clinical depression is an important preventive step to reducing suicidal behavior. One researcher has used learning theory to develop a successful intervention to prevent the onset of depression (Munoz, 1997). As Munoz has shared with the first author of this book, it is vitally important to shield, if possible, those most at risk from clinical depression because with each new depressive episode the chances of reoccurrence significantly increase (Munoz, personal communication, 1997).

Munoz describes The San Francisco Depression Prevention Research Project as an educational intervention that teaches mood management skills. Importantly, it does this in a way that enlists the participant as a partner—not a patient. This enlistment action makes the project more than an education only effort. In eight 2-hour small class sessions, participants were helped to identify mood states, how to recognize specific thoughts, and to recognize pleasant and unpleasant feelings connected to people and situations. Attention then focused on increasing thoughts related to positive mood and decreasing or reinterpreting negative mood feelings. In one trial of this project with a group of adolescents, Munoz reports that the incidence of new cases of depression was 15% for those who received the skill training vs 26% in the control group.

Given your understanding of prevention, how might you strengthen this intervention? What others tools would you use, and how would you use them?

Competency promotion   In this chapter, as in every other chapter devoted to discussing dysfunctional behavior in adolescence, we have observed a recurring pattern of personality development. Terms such as *low self-esteem* and *helplessness* continually appear. In fact, one might reasonably argue that given the similarity in family and personality types in all adolescent behavioral dysfunctions, chance as much as any other factor dictates which problems in living such adolescents will experience. The issue that must be grappled with is how to promote social competency. Education for expectant parents, stressing the crucial role they play in developing self-esteem and an internal locus of control in their children, is one approach. Another is providing opportunities through group activities such as Scouting, Outward Bound, and sports that develop a sense of power and accomplishment for young people. Perhaps most important is the need for us to remember that we should not by our individual interactions with others contribute to their sense of failure and inadequacy. We can and should each celebrate our racial, ethnic, and cultural heritage.

Community organization/systems intervention   Is it possible to build a utopia in which all individuals can feel worthwhile? Probably not. On the other hand, it certainly is possible to communicate a message through our schools and social programs that all individuals are valued. In other chapters we have argued for humane and sensitive educational environments for our children. We urge that services such as universal day care, adequate medical care, and food programs for young children either be developed or expanded. Our arguments are based on the belief that young children are too valuable a resource to risk neglect and abuse by any one segment of the population, whether that be the state or the parents. The programs and services we are talking about act as a check on the deprivation that may be occurring in a young person's life. They offer a statement of society's commitment to ensuring young people the opportunity to grow into healthy, contributing members of society.

On yet another level, we know that firearms kill very effectively. Reducing the access young people have to firearms will correspondingly reduce not only suicides but homicides. The Brady bill and local gun control ordinances like those in Washington, DC are examples of legislative *means restriction* efforts to reduce the number of children killing themselves and others.[7] We also know that alcohol or drugs are a deadly combination when used by a depressed or angry youth. These substances contribute mightily to reducing the inhibitions that may prevent an attempted suicide. Distribution of consumption actions to further restrict the availability of these harmful substances can and should be undertaken.

Natural care giving   How does a society care for itself? Durkheim's view that suicide is a function of the cohesiveness of society at any one time suggests two interventions. The first, focusing on relationships within the individual's family to promote membership and belonging, is more easily achieved than the second. That is, it is within our power to create and encourage a family environment or friendship environment in which individuals are valued and loved. It is within our power to let young people know that social support is there for them and that they need not face their problems alone. This would be, in contrast, to findings by a research group that reported 60% of the middle school and 40% of the high school sample population in their study did not know where to go for help (Culp, Clyman, & Culp, 1995). This caregiving response also acknowledges that peers are the individuals to whom other youth turn to in time of need. Thus, developing peer support networks offer opportunities to assist youth in need (Kalafat & Elias, 1995).

The second intervention, focusing on external relationships, is far more complex. For instance, do we encourage war or create the perception of an external threat to maintain social cohesiveness? Can we provide meaningful, worthwhile work to everyone who wants to work? Is it possible to bind together a nation in a single purpose without resorting to instinctual Rambolike aggression? Keeping a society healthy without destroying others is a challenge worthy of consideration. We encourage you to think how it might be done.

SUMMARY

Before we close this discussion let's take a moment and consider the material you've just read. Did you see how events in the past influenced attitudes toward those who either attempted or committed suicide? Did you see how current events

---

[7]Holinger et al. (1994) report that strict gun control laws in Washington, DC reduced suicide and homicide rates by roughly 25% during the first year the laws were in effect.

like modern medical technology can stimulate debates that may change attitudes and eventually laws regarding suicide? From the various theorists and research studies we reviewed, did you see the contextual pathways that can lead a young person to consider suicide? Were you struck with the differences in the incidence of suicide and homicide between White and Black youths and the factors that accounted for those differences? Finally, using prevention's technology, did you see ways to reduce the incidences of these destructive behaviors? If you did, job well done. Why not take a short break before calling it a night. Stretch those muscles for a few moments. The next time you return to this book, we'll look at adolescence in the year 2000 and beyond.

MAJOR POINTS TO REMEMBER

1. The onset of the affective disorders can be explained by biological, environmental, and intrapsychic factors.
2. Suicide is a "conscious, deliberate attempt to take one's life quickly."
3. Taking one's own life was not punished per se in earlier societies. Rather, the circumstances surrounding the suicide determined whether it was accepted or punished.
4. It was not until 533 A.D. at the Council of Orléans that the Christian Church began to view the taking of one's own life as sinful, and it was not until the Council of Braga in 562 A.D. that the Fifth Commandment, "Thou shalt not kill," was reinterpreted to apply to the taking of one's own life.
5. When an individual helps another to die, it is called "assisted suicide."
6. Many authors find that adolescents view death in a distorted and incomplete way. Death in many young people's eyes is not final but reversible. The factors contributing to this condition are the adolescent's immature intellectual development, cultural taboos against talking about death, and television's unrealistic portrayals of violence.
7. Females attempt suicide more frequently than males, but males are more successful.
8. If suicide rates are closely examined, the highest are found in some minority populations.
9. In very early psychoanalytic thought sexual repression was the cause of taking one's own life. This position has been considerably modified.
10. According to Menninger, suicide is a repressed desire to kill or to be killed.
11. Freud understood suicide to result from the loss of a love object.
12. Others see the taking of one's own life as the reflection of a sense of hopelessness or as a plea for help.
13. One of the most important conceptualizations of suicide is Durkheim's theory that the taking of one's life depends on the individual's integration into society.

14. In Durkheim's model, individuals who are loners, who have not integrated themselves into society, and who end their lives are said to have committed an egotistic suicide. Individuals who choose a group identity over their individual identities and end their lives are seen as committing an altruistic suicide. The last form of suicide in this model is anomic suicide. In this situation sudden societal or personal change so overwhelm the coping abilities of individuals that they end their lives.

15. Central to Durkheim's model is the concept of anomie. Anomie speaks of rootlessness, normlessness. As anomie increases in society, Durkheim suggests, suicide rates increase.

16. Studies show that many young people who attempt suicide feel unloved and unwanted. Family relationships are described as poor.

17. Toolan believes that adolescents attempt suicide to express anger, to control another, to call for help, to protect themselves, or to join a deceased relative.

18. Researchers exploring Durkheim's model have found cross-cultural evidence that where family bonds are close, belief in religion high, and societal disruption low (low anomie), suicide rates are low.

19. The first therapeutic effort that needs to be made to assist an individual who has attempted suicide is to extend a lifeline of support, guidance, and friendship.

20. Medications can be very helpful in assisting the depressed or suicidal adolescent.

21. Preventing the continuing increase of suicide among young people calls for strengthening the family and friendship units while at the same time building a sense of social cohesiveness.

FIVE

Parting Thoughts

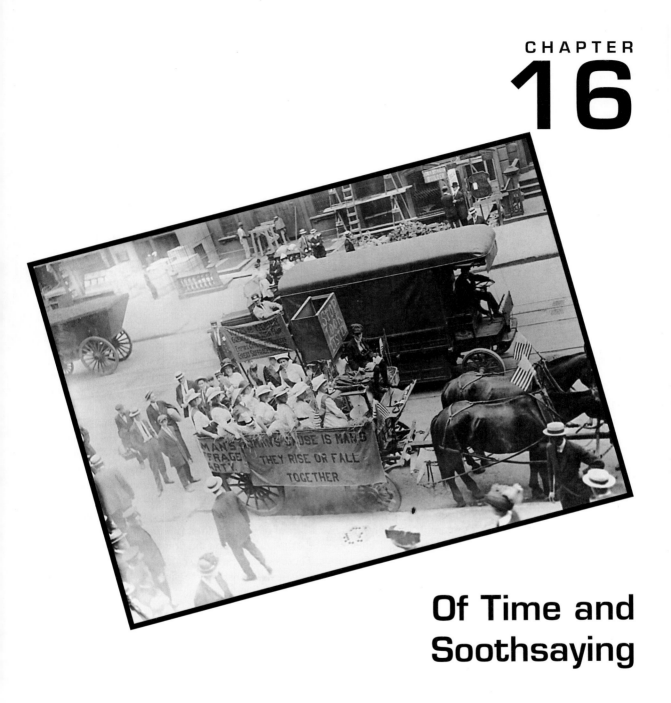

Of Time and Soothsaying

WHEN THE FIRST author was in high school he had a way of hurrying the eternity between Monday and Friday. It was the day-after approach. That is, on Sunday night he thought the day after tomorrow was Tuesday. On Tuesday the day after tomorrow was Thursday, and then the weekend was only a day away. But for reasons none of us fully comprehended, time accelerated after we left high school. Weeks passed with the speed of days, and semesters, well, you know. In this final chapter of a semester that seemed to begin only yesterday, we'll take a look at the future and project developments that will appear in future editions of this textbook.

Now, it is not with a little hesitancy that we venture into this last chapter. Remember, people were burned in the distant past for doing this future-looking stuff. Actually, in North America, witches were hung or, imagine this, pressed to death! The prophecies of these unfortunate souls and other soothsayers continue to haunt us. For example, at the turn of this century, some futurists predicted that every woman who wanted employment would find it, while others feared the literal burial of North American cities. On the basis of the information available at the time, both predictions could have come true. For example, at the turn of the century, telephone operators were needed to complete every phone call. As phone service was expected to grow and *only* women were phone operators, it made sense to predict a growth in the employment market for women. What about our compatriots who feared the burial of Quebec City, Edmonton, New York, and Washington, DC? They based their projections on the flow of horse-drawn traffic through these and other cities. These experts carefully calculated and recalculated a disturbing set of irrefutable statistics establishing the date at which the cities of North America would be buried under a sea of manure. Yes, that's right—horse manure.

These illustrations demonstrate the hazards of looking forward. Who in the 1890s, for example, could have predicted the invention of communication satellites, computers, lasers, and the host of technologies that have revolutionized communications and consequently limited employment opportunities for both women and men as phone operators? And can we really fault our turn-of-the-century futurists for not imaging a horseless carriage?

We must forgive these ancestral soothsayers, for as we now look forward to the beginning of the 21st century, who rightly knows whether the shadows we see are "the shadows of the things that *will* be, or are shadows of the things that *may* be"

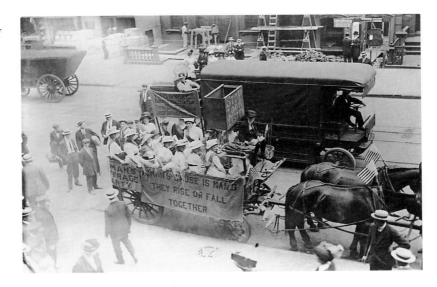

At the turn of the last century, futurists projected the burial of our cities under a see of manure.

(Dickens, 1843/1967, p. 128)? For as the great novelist once observed in a magical and wondrous tale of hope and redemption, "Men's courses will foreshadow certain ends, to which, if persevered in, they must lead. . . . But if the courses be departed from, the ends will change" (p. 128). Let's revisit Chapters 2 through 14 and see what the future might hold.

THE FUTURE AND ADOLESCENT ISSUES

Theories of Behavior

Our crystal ball does not foresee a new grand theory of human behavior emerging in the next century. Rather, we see a period of consolidation and integration occurring. Elements of the theories reviewed in Chapter 2 will be combined under current titles like ecological or contextual or given some new label. This forecast implies that the current "Decade of the Brain" will not identify particular genes for most problem behaviors. The instructionist position, to which we have shown partiality, will emerge as the dominant position. Remember that the instructionist position acknowledges a dynamic and fluid interaction between the environment and genes with each affecting the other over time. In essence this is developmental contextualism.

While the future looks bright for social learning theories that expand on the role of meaning and cognition for behavior, psychoanalytic theory will continue to diminish in importance. This is not to say that certain concepts like instinctual urges, the loss of a love object, or defense mechanisms will disappear. They will not. Rather, they will be incorporated, as they were in this book, into contextual explanations of behavior. Indeed, we are intrigued by a recent essay that states Freud had grown pessimistic about the clinical effectiveness of analytic therapy late in his life (Pollock, 1997). Further, given the rise in New Age thinking, psychoanalytic theory, with its focus on the unconscious and the psychic structure, will remain a rich vein of thought that writers, historians, and others will mine.

Intellectual Development

In this the "Decade of the Brain" some of the most exciting developments are occurring not with genes but with the environment. The first exciting development is a recent widespread recognition that the brain is a physically growing organ for several years after birth. Rather than a fixed entity, neurons by the tens of millions can be created with proper nutritional, social, and emotional stimulation. We believe research in the coming years will confirm many of the policy suggestions we have made in this edition. Namely, good nutrition, shelter, and care needs to be extended to both mother and child, particularly adolescent mothers. Home and school-based interventions that promote positive child development practices like parents reading to their children will be encouraged. We believe that special efforts will be made to change discouraging reports that while 77% of college-educated mothers read to their children only 37% of mothers with a grade school education read to their children (U.S. Census Bureau, 1997).

For seemingly a millennium, intelligence has been represented to be a relatively fixed biological trait. Indeed, the premise of a highly controversial book published earlier this decade was that upward of 80% of intelligence was inherited. This assumption was used in *The Bell Curve* (Hernstein & Murray, 1994) to argue that America was dividing into a two-tiered society. One tier occupied by brainy children born to bright, well-educated parents. The other occupied by dull youth born to poor and simple-minded parents. This impression was roundly discredited with the recent publication of Devlin and his associates' meta-analysis of the impact of the influence of heredity on intelligence (Devlin, Daniels, & Roeder, 1997).

Combining 212 previously published studies that compared the intelligence of children, especially twins, and their parents, these researchers searched for those variables that best explained intellectual growth. These authors found that intelligence was influenced by several factors including prenatal conditions, home environment, and genetic effects. In contrast to earlier studies, this meta-analysis attributes between 34 and 48% of intelligence to genetic factors. Thus, environment accounts for the remaining percentages. What appears in this study is evidence that exposure to environmental poisons like lead, tobacco smoke, and alcohol lowers intelligence. Inadequate nutrition lowers intelligence. Emotional and social deprivation lower intelligence. We believe this important study will be used in conjunction with brain growth studies to encourage *preventive* interventions to encourage the healthy development of youths.

Finally, with the rigid IQ framework less defensible, we see opportunities for other theories to emerge. For example, David Perkins' (1995) work, which

While society is increasingly coming to respect androgynous behavior, we suspect adolescence will continue to be a time of exaggerated behavior.

represents that the mind operates in three intellectual dimensions, may be more widely tested. We believe this same opportunity will be extended to Howard Gardner (1995), who sees intelligence as consisting of at least seven frames of reference ranging from the linguistic intelligence of writers and the spatial intelligence of painters and architects to the logical-mathematical intelligence of researchers to the bodily-kinesthetic intelligence of athletes and dancers.

Identity Development

Identity development owes much to the work of Erik Erikson. Writing at the end of the Second World War, his work was heavily influenced by the writings of Freud and a society that paid minimal attention to both women and diverse youths. While we see a universality in his writings that transcend gender, race, and ethnicity, we expect to see many more attempts made to delineate differences in the journey from childhood through adolescence to young adulthood.

Sex Roles

Despite heightened interest in androgynous behavior, we suspect that there will continue to be an exaggeration of masculine behaviors for males and feminine behaviors for females during the adolescent years. For young people uncomfortable with their sexual identity, this will continue to be a very painful time of life. While society has gradually come to applaud the accomplishments of exceptionally talented youths who cross gender boundaries like the male figure skater and the female basketball player, this will not generalize to a wider population of youths anytime soon.

Physical Development and Adolescent Sexuality

Biological advances in understanding the onset and course of development in adolescence will continue well into the next century. For a very small percentage of the population who suffer from very specific developmental disorders like precocious puberty wherein the gonads sexually mature in girls before age 8 and in boys before age 9, specific genes will be identified that are the cause of these disorders. Tests will be developed to identify these disorders *in utero*, leading to medical interventions before birth.

In matters of human sexuality, we suspect that the sexual standard of permissiveness with affection will continue to be the dominant form of expression for young people into the 21st century. The standard of abstinence has never been rigorously applied to males, and with gradual progress in North America toward equality between the sexes, we doubt that women will deny their sexual feelings as they did at the start of this century. Still, we do expect to see a slight increase in the percentage of females who delay sexual intercourse to early adulthood for fear of STDs.

Regardless of advances in the treatment of AIDS, we suspect that an effective preventive vaccine will not be developed for many years. Further, we suspect that powerful new strains of old sexually transmitted diseases will emerge, severely testing researchers abilities to develop new effective drug treatments. Despite this, the majority of youths will continue to be sexually active without taking precautions to insure their health. The reason for this, we believe, will be the continued inability of youths to accept their sexuality. In this regard, while actions taken by the American Psychiatric Association and the American Psychological Association to normalize homosexuality are helpful in removing the stigma associated with this sexual preference, exaggerated displays of masculine behavior by boys and feminine behavior by girls will continue to make adolescence a hellish time for bisexual and homosexual adolescents.

Adolescent Family Relations

In one sense the dramatic changes in America's families for the next century have already occurred. How so? It's demography or, if you prefer, the statistical study of human populations. From those numbers, you'd be amazed at how soothsayers can say, "demography is destiny." That is, by observing the number of births, deaths, marriages, divorces, and other life events predictions can be made.

For example, divorces have been a common part of the family life cycle since the late 1960s. In 1970, 85% of all children under the age of 18 lived with both parents. In 1995 that figure was 69%. Looking more closely at these figures reveals that in 1970, 90% of White youths 59% of Black youths and 78% of Latino youths lived with both parents. Twenty-five years later these figures were 76% (White), 33% (Black), and 63% (Latino) (U.S. Census Bureau, 1996, Chart 81, p. 65). Living in a single-parent home, more often than not, equates to poverty. Sixty percent (60%) of youths residing with their mother live in poverty, and mothers have custody of their children 96% of the time (U.S. Census Bureau, 1997b; U.S. Census Bureau, 1996, Chart 81, p. 65). But this is not the only change that has occurred. In 1960, fewer than 19% of married women and 41% of divorced, widowed, or separated women with children under the age of 6 worked. By 1995, these percentages had grown to 63.5 and 66.3%, respectively (U.S. Census Bureau, 1996, Chart 626, p. 400).

Taking these statistical snapshots and comparing them to the needs that families traditionally have fulfilled with adolescents, what can we say about the coming years? As families are under incredible stress to meet current obligations, we see the situation for the nuclear family becoming more difficult and for single-parent families, excruciating. Currently, parents joke about being sandwiched between two generations—one their children and their demands and the other their aging parents and their needs. The next generation of parents (and by the way that's all of you reading this text) will not only be pressured by these conditions but by time and work as well. To maintain that middle-class lifestyle most folks aspire to will require more labor effort on the part of the next generation. More work time means less time at home with other family members. Less time at home means youths will have more time alone or with peers. Now, we are well aware of statements that quality not quantity matters in instilling young people with values and fond remembrances. Nevertheless, our parenting experiences tell us that to get quality enough quantity needs to be there to make up for all those rotten family times. We suspect that additional efforts along the lines of the U.S. Family Leave Act will be passed in the coming years to enable parents to fulfill their obligations to both children and their aging parents.

Peers and Leisure Time

Given our earlier observations about future parents needing to hold more than one job to earn a comfortable living, it is very safe to say that in the next century young people will continue to be influenced by other young people. Now, whether these young people and their friends will continue to exercise a dominating influence over North Americans' tastes and habits is quite another matter. Changing demographic patterns pointing to a massive rise in the number of elderly in the first half of the next century make it unlikely that these youths will rule North America in the way the Baby Boomers did in the 1960s and 1970s. Indeed, the echo boom of children born to the Baby Boomers is exhausting itself in new births. The numerical decline of adolescents in North America reversed itself in the mid 1990s, and adolescents will grow as a percentage of the population for about a decade and then decline slowly thereafter.

So what does this hold for leisure activities? Will reruns of Mick Jagger and the Rolling Stones and the Barenaked Ladies dominate the air waves in 2040? We doubt it. Each generation of young people needs to find their own voice in music, film stars, and literature. Interesting, though, is the incredible current popularity of retro in music and television. Today's young people are being raised by the same "Lassie," "Mr. Wizard," and "Leave It to Beaver" shows that the authors of this book viewed as children. With reruns on cable channels like "Nick-at-Nite," "Disney," and "FX" and music video channels mixing the history of rock and roll with examples of that music, we find our students more than able to relate to the popular culture of our generation. In fact with the reappearance of bell bottoms, tied-dyed shirts, and love beads, we can't help but marvel at the ever returning patterns of taste and fashion. In another arena, we are very intrigued with the ways in which adolescents are using the internet—particularly the use of chat rooms. Indeed, one of the authors of this book can rarely be on-line for 20 minutes without a query asking whether his son is on-line. The interactive capabilities of this medium is only beginning to be explored, and it's influence will rival that of music and television in the next century.

Education

We noted earlier how demography is destiny. Consider how demography will affect education in the next century. Since 1985, the percentage of United States families without children under the age of 18 has exceeded those with under-18 children. This will continue into the future. While the number of adolescent youths will grow over the next several years, their numbers will peak by the middle of the next decade, and this will be followed by a slow decline in their numbers as a

Want to improve a child's academic performance? Read together!

TABLE **16-1** Percentage Distribution of the Population by Age (1990–2050)

	1990	1995	2000	2005	2010	2020	2030	2040	2050
Total	100.0	100.0	100.0	100.0	100.0	100.0	100.0	100.00	100.0
Under 5	7.6	7.4	6.9	6.6	6.6	6.6	6.4	6.4	6.4
5 to 13	12.8	13.1	13.1	12.5	11.9	11.8	11.7	11.5	11.6
14 to 17	5.3	5.6	5.7	5.9	5.7	5.2	5.3	5.3	5.2
18 to 24	10.8	9.5	9.5	9.8	10.1	9.2	9.1	9.2	9.0
25 to 34	17.3	15.5	13.6	12.7	12.9	13.3	12.4	12.4	12.5
35 to 44	15.1	16.2	16.3	14.8	13.0	12.3	12.9	12.1	12.2
45 to 64	18.6	19.9	22.2	24.9	26.5	24.9	22.1	22.5	22.5
65 & over	12.5	12.8	12.7	12.7	13.3	16.6	20.2	20.7	20.6
85 & over	1.2	1.4	1.6	1.7	1.9	2.0	2.4	3.6	4.6
100 & over	0.0	0.0	0.0	0.0	0.1	0.1	0.1	0.2	0.3

Source: *Census and you*, January 1993, 28(1), 2.
Note. Middle series consistent with 1990 census.

percentage of the population. Table 16-1 depicts this trend. While you're looking at this U.S. Census Bureau projection, look at the rise in the elderly population. Doing some quick mental math, you'll realize that in 1990 the percentage of young people under the age of 18 (25.7%) was nearly double that of individuals over the age of 65 (13.7%). Now look again at that chart and compare those between the ages of 14 to 17 (5.3%) to those 85 and over (1.2%). The gap is considerable, but notice what happens by 2050. By the middle of the next century, the percentage of those over 65 (25.5%) will exceed those under 18 (23.2%). More interesting still is our second comparison. The gap between 14- to 17-year-olds (5.2%) and those over the age of 85 (4.9%) narrowed in 1990. A slim three-tenths of 1% now separates these two populations—adolescents and the elderly elderly. Incidentally, those senior folks in 2050 just so happen to be you!

So, what does this have to do with education? Well, here are some of the issues. Will this large powerful block of elderly voters be willing to devote adequate resources to education when it likely will mean a decline in their own standard of living? Will they have an interest in the new "diverse" face of this nation? Which understanding of education's purpose will these elderly citizens support? Will they support the role of public education as encompassing the entire lifespan from cradle to grave or only the current K–12 model. Will they, like those before them, continue to support publicly administered education or will they want to see education privatized? These are just some of the issues that will play out during your lifetime.

Intervention and Prevention

At present, there is a heated debate going on between the providers of mental health services and the third-party payers of that care. Whether called an insurance company, health maintenance organization, or by some other name, these third-party payers are increasingly denying approval for the "talk" therapies discussed in Chapter 10 in favor of pharmacological-only approaches. We do not deny the usefulness of the new drugs that have been developed in recent years. Indeed, one of the most exciting areas for advancing treatment in the future is in pharmacology. However, as we have noted throughout this book, many of the problems young people are grappling with cannot be traced to biochemical or genetic malfunctions. They *are* problems in living. That is, problems of personal relationships, of inadequate caring (whether intentional or not) by adults, and of discrimination and prejudice. We expect that this debate will intensify over the next decade to ultimately be decided by government intervention. We expect that elected officials will agree with us that the counseling therapies are an important part of a multisystemic approach to addressing the problems discussed in this book.

Regarding prevention, we can only hope that the books and studies discussed in this textbook clearly establishing its effectiveness are read. In North America, we have the opportunity to improve the health status of children and adolescents across a wide range of areas from stimulating early brain growth to promoting social competency. The challenge becomes how to convince society to make an investment before dysfunctional behaviors appear. Hopefully, you will join us in taking that message forward.

Problems of Adolescent Sexuality: Issues of Concern

Life would be so much easier if young people were to delay sexual activity until marriage, if they were monogamous after marriage, and if prostitution did not exist. To the best of our knowledge no society has been able to sustain these conditions over time. Thus, we expect that adolescent pregnancies will continue, as will sexually transmitted diseases and prostitution. While in the United States welfare reform was passed to discourage adolescents from becoming pregnant, we do not believe it will be effective. Young women do not become pregnant for money. They become pregnant by mistake or intention. They continue their pregnancy because of philosophical beliefs or because they want to become a mother. On the other hand, were a particular culture to seriously frown on youth within their group becoming pregnant than this group pressure could push down pregnancy rates. For this to happen in the mosaic of cultures that is currently North America is doubtful.

In respect to sexually transmitted diseases, we have serious concerns about the future. From the first passing of a sexually transmitted disease from one person to another hundreds of thousands of years ago to the 1940s, these organisms not only survived but thrived. During the 1940s, a new class of drugs called antibiotics was developed. Penicillin and related medications radically transformed medicine making it possible to kill bacteria before that bacteria killed its host. Clearly, we have profited from those discoveries. Indeed, as many as one-third of your classmates might have died in childhood from septic infections related to a sore throat, a blood blister, or tuberculosis. Without antibiotics, syphilis and other STDs would be filling the beds of hospitals. Imagine then a new breed of killer bacteria immune to these drugs. There are superstrains of syphilis and gonorrhea, and no antibiotic is successful against a viral infection like herpes or HIV. Unless there is a major breakthrough in designing new antibiotics and developing the "penicillin" for viruses, we believe that within 30 years medical treatment for bacteria and killer viral infections will retreat to a darker time.

Finally, prostitution will continue because sex just feels too good. And anything that feels that good will have the purchaser spend whatever is necessary to secure the service whether it be from a male or a female. While we have sometimes been accused of being overly hard on Sigmund Freud, we concede that in his conceptualization of the two instinctual urges—sex and aggression—he really was on to something. From before the Old Testament to the current day, sex sells. It always has. It always will. (Just look at the sales of Viagra.) While not condoning cash for sex, during the 1970s when the Baby Boomer generation was at the height of their sexual prowess, North American attitudes seemingly tolerated this activity. As those Boomers now age that tolerance appears to be diminishing. Massage parlors, bathhouses, and alternative newspaper ads have declined. For those who would refer us to an earlier paragraph regarding our concern about STDs, we are not displaying hypocrisy when we lament the passing of this seeming window of tolerance. If these behaviors were tolerated as opposed to practiced secretly then it would be possible to regulate them. We take the position that regulating sexual activity is preferable to the current black market of sexual behaviors. Licensed and health-certified staff could go a long way toward managing a looming health crisis and insuring that minors are not active in the "oldest" profession. However, while some European countries—notably the Netherlands—and the state of Nevada have adopted this means control approach, it generally runs contrary to North American values.

Drugs

Having just lamented the decline of the quasi-brothel, where might we be heading in our discussion of drugs? Right back into controversy. Clearly, drugs are harmful when misused. For example, it is reported that a small glass of red wine a day may help protect against heart disease. On the other hand, a large bottle of red wine a day is a sure ticket to cirrhosis of the liver. Consider that for intolerable pain like that associated with terminal cancer, morphine extracted from opium is commonly prescribed. Still, in some litter-strewn back alley a person shooting morphine with dirty works is taking the fast track to hepatitis and AIDS. Finally, in the United States two states recently legalized the use of marijuana for certain medicinal purposes. Nevertheless, the chronic marijuana smoker rushes past the chronic cigarette smoker toward lung, throat, mouth, and tongue cancers.

Our current drug policies have made millionaires out of drug syndicates while enslaving others. Slavery takes several forms in the drug business. First, there is the abuser. Next, there is the small time—increasingly adolescent—dealer who risks his/her life selling drugs to a generally middle-class clientele. Finally, there is the neighborhood snared in fear and the violence that dealers need to protect territory and enforce rules of payment. There must be a better way. Nevertheless, we believe it is very doubtful that within the next 20 years we will see a change in North American drug policy. This is regrettable because we believe that this black market commodity will only grow as will sex-for-sale as individuals sorely in need of cash search for quick lucrative income. Because there are no green cards, social security taxes, federal or state taxes, or age restrictions on who can turn a trick or traffic in drugs, both offer youths income opportunities.

Crime

Despite recent get-tough legislative actions to treat juvenile offenders as adults, delinquency will continue unabated into the future just as Émile Durkheim would have predicted. Crime truly is an essential part of any healthy society. What concerns us is the growth in violent youth crime. Without changes in drug policies that would either eliminate or greatly curtail the current black market for drugs, we see more violent crime occurring in the next decade. Without an expansion of the Brady gun control bill to make the acquisition of firearms much more difficult, we see the number of violent deaths committed by juveniles rising as will the number of juvenile homicide victims.

Eating Disorders

Currently several theoretical models are vying for dominance. We do not believe that one will gain greater importance over another. Rather, we suspect that the development of anorexia or bulimia has several very different origins each with a different prognosis for successful treatment or prevention.

Improvement in treatment and pharmacology will improve outcome for individuals suffering from depression.

Depression and Suicide

If there is a bright spot in this book, it is with the affective disorders of which depression is one. We believe that over the next decade new medications will be developed. This adjunct therapy when combined with cognitive behavioral interventions will greatly improve treatment outcomes for this population. Improvement in the treatment of depression and wider prevention efforts will hold suicide rates at there present level. Recall that Holinger and his associates (1994) predicted that as the adolescent population rose over the next decade opportunity would decline and with that decline adolescent suicides would rise.

SUMMARY

On a personal note, we hope you've enjoyed this course and this book. We truly believe there is no more exciting time in life than adolescence. It is a time when mind and body, passion and intellect, emotion and spirit literally burst forth. There are two images we wish to leave with you. Please carry them in your thoughts long after this book fades from memory. The first is to never forget that with concerned nurturing *over time* and lots of patience, nearly all young people mature into responsible adults. Second, young people need to belong, to be valued, and to be able to make a meaningful contribution to their society. Give young people that opportunity.

Abdul-Jabbar, K., & Steinberg, A. (1996). *Black profiles in courage*. New York: Morrow.

Abernethy, V., & Abernethy, G. L. (1974). Risk for unwanted pregnancy among mentally ill adolescent girls. *American Journal of Orthopsychiatry, 44*, 442–450.

Abi-Nader, J. (1990). "A house for my mother": Motivating Hispanic high school students. *Anthropology & Education Quarterly, 21*, 41–58.

Abraham, K. G. (1983). The relation between identity status and locus of control among rural high school students. *Journal of Early Adolescence, 3*, 257, 264.

Abrahams, B., Feldman, S. S., & Nash, S. C. (1978). Sex role self-concept and sex role attitudes: Enduring personality characteristics or adaptations to changing life situations? *Developmental Psychology, 14*, 393–401.

Adams, E. H., & Durell, J. (1987). Cocaine: A growing public health problem. In J. Grabowski (Ed.) *Cocaine: Pharmacology, effects, and treatment of abuse*. Washington, DC: DHHS publication ADM 87-1326, U.S. Government Printing Office.

Adams, E. H., & Kozel, N. J. (1985). Cocaine use in America: Introduction and overview. In N. J. Kozel & E. H. Adams (Eds.), *Cocaine use in America: Epidemiological and clinical perspectives* (pp. 1–7). Washington, DC: NIDA research monograph No. 61, ADM 85-1414, U.S. Government Printing Office.

Adams, G. R. (1977a). Physical attractiveness, personality and social reactions to peer pressure. *Journal of Psychology, 96*, 287–296.

Adams, G. R. (1977b). Physical attractiveness: Toward a developmental social psychology of beauty. *Human Development, 20*, 217–239.

Adams, G. R. (1980). The effects of physical attractiveness on the socialization process. In G. W. Lucker, K. A. Ribbens, & J. A. McNamara (Eds.), *Psychological aspects of facial form* (Monograph 11, Craniofacial Growth Series). Ann Arbor, MI: Center for Human Growth and Development, University of Michigan.

Adams, G. R. (1981b).

Adams, G. R. (1985). Family correlates of female adolescents' ego-identity development. *Journal of Adolescence, 8*, 69–82.

Adams, G. R., & Gullotta, T. P. (1983). *Adolescent life experiences* (1st ed.). Monterey, CA: Brooks/Cole.

Adams, G. R., & Jones, R. M. (1983). Female adolescence identity development: Age comparison and perceived child-rearing experience. *Developmental Psychology, 19*, 249–256.

Adams, G. R., & Markstrom, C. M. (1987). Developmental issues in adolescent psychiatry. In G. Hsu & M. Hersen (Eds.), *Recent developments in adolescent psychiatry*. New York: Wiley.

Adams, G. R., & Marshall, S. (1996). A developmental social psychology of identity: Understanding the person-in-context. *Journal of Adolescence, 19*, 429–442.

Adams, G. R., & Montemayor, R. (1988). Patterns of identity development during late adolescence: A descriptive study of stability, progression, and regression. Unpublished manuscript.

Adams, G. R., & Schvaneveldt, J. D. (1985). *Understanding research methods.* New York: Longman.

Adams, G. R., & Shea, J. (1979). The relationship between identity status, locus of control, and ego development. *Journal of Youth and Adolescence, 8,* 81–89.

Adams, G. R., & Shea, J. (1981). Talking and loving: A cross-lagged panel investigation. *Basic and Applied Social Psychology, 2,* 81–88.

Adams, G. R., Abraham, K., & Markstrom, C. (1989). The association between identity development, self-consciousness, and self-focusing during middle and late adolescence. *Developmental Psychology, 23,* 292–297.

Adams, G. R., Bennion, L. D., Openshaw, D. K., & Bingham, C. R. (1990). Windows of vulnerability: Identifying critical age, gender, and racial differences predictive of risk for violent deaths in childhood and adolescence. *Journal of Primary Prevention, 10,* 223–240.

Adams, G. R., Bennion, L., & Dyk, P. (1990). Parent-adolescent relationships and identity formation. In B. Rollins and B. Barber (eds.) *Parenting.* NY: University Press of America.

Adams, G. R., Gullotta, T. P., & Clancy, M. A. (1985). Homeless adolescents: A descriptive study of similarities and differences between runaways and throwaways. *Adolescence, 79,* 715–724.

Adams, G. R., Marshall, S. K., Ketsetzis, M., Brusch, G., & Keating, L. (1996). Measuring individuality and connectedness in parent-adolescent interactions: A new clinical rating system. Presentation at the biennial meetings of the Society for Research on Adolescence, Boston, Massachusetts, March 7–10.

Adams, G. R., Montemayor, R., & Gullotta, T. P. (Eds.) (1996a). *Psychosocial development during adolescence: Progress in developmental contextualism,* Newbury Park, CA: Sage.

Adams, G. R., Montemayor, R., & Gullotta, T. P. (1996b). Psychosocial development during adolescence: The legacy of John Hill. In G. R. Adams, R. Montemayor, &

T. P. Gullotta (Eds.), *Psychosocial development during adolescence: Progress in developmental contextualism* (pp. 1–11). Thousand Oaks, CA: Sage.

Adams, G. R., Ryan, J. H., Hoffman, J. J., Dobson, W. R., & Nielsen, E. C. (1985). Ego identity status, conformity behavior and personality in late adolescence. *Journal of Personality and Social Psychology, 47,* 1091–1104.

Adams, G. R., Schvaneveldt, J. D., & Jensen, G. O. (1979). Sex, age and perceived competency as correlates of empathic ability in adolescence. *Adolescence, 14,* 811–818.

Adams, G. R., Shea, J. A., & Fitch, S. A. (1979). Toward the development of an objective assessment of ego-identity status. *Journal of Youth and Adolescence, 8,* 223–237.

Adcock, A. G., Nagy, S., & Simpson, J. A. (1991). Selected risk factors in adolescent suicide attempts. *Adolescence, 26,* 817–828.

Adler, A. (1967) [Untitled comments.] In P. Friedman (Ed.), *On suicide: With particular reference to suicide among young students.* New York: International Universities Press.

Adler, N. E. David, H. P., Major, B. N., Roth, S. H., Russo, N. F., & Wyatt, G. E. (1990). Psychological responses after abortion. *Science, 248,* 41–44.

Agras, W. S., Schneider, J. A., Arnow, B., Rawburn, S. D., & Telch, C. F. (1989). Cognitive behavioral response prevention treatments for bulimia nervosa. *Journal of Consulting and Clinical Psychology, 57,* 215–221.

Akers, J. F., Jones, R. M., & Coyl, D. D. (1998). Adolescent friendship pairs: Similarities in identity status development, behaviors, attitudes, and intentions. *Journal of Adolescence Research, 13,* 178–201.

Akhtar, S. (1984). The syndrome of identity diffusion. *American Journal of Psychiatry, 141,* 1381–1385.

Albee, G. W. (1959). *Mental health manpower trends.* New York: Basic Books.

Albee, G. W. (1980). A competency model must replace the defect model. In L. A. Bond & J. C. Rosen (Eds.), *Com-*

petence and coping during adulthood. Hanover, NH: University of New England Press.

Albee, G. W. (1985a, February). The answer is prevention. *Psychology Today,* 60–64.

Albee, G. W. (1985b). The argument for primary prevention. *Journal of Primary Prevention, 5,* 213–219.

Albee, G. W. (1996). Introduction to the special issue on social darwinism. *Journal of Primary Prevention, 17,* 3–16.

Albee, G. W., & Gullotta, T. P. (1986). Facts and fallacies about primary prevention. *Journal of Primary Prevention, 6,* 207–218.

Albee, G. W., & Gullotta, T. P. (Eds.) (1997). *Primary prevention works.* Thousand Oaks, CA: Sage.

Allen, B. P. (1987). Youth suicide. *Adolescence, 22,* 271–290.

Allport, G. (1964). Crises in normal personality development. *Teachers College Record, 66,* 235–241.

Almeida, D. M., & Galambos, N. L. (1991). Examining father involvement and quality of father-adolescent relations. *Journal of Research on Adolescence, 1,* 155–172.

Altshuler, K. Z., & Weiner, M. F. (1985). Anorexia nervosa and depression: A dissenting view. *American Journal of Psychiatry, 142,* 328–332.

Alva, S. A. (1995). Academic invulnerability among Mexican American students. In A. M. Padilla (Ed.), *Hispanic psychology: Critical issues in theory and research* (pp. 288–302). Thousand Oaks, CA: Sage.

Alva, S. A., & Jones, M. (1994). Psychosocial adjustment self-reported patterns of alcohol use among Hispanic adolescents. *Journal of Early Adolescence, 14,* 432–448.

Alvarez, A. (1972). *The savage god.* New York: Random House.

Amato, P. R., & Keith, B. (1991a). Parental divorce and the well-being of children: A meta-analysis. *Psychological Bulletin, 110,* 26–46.

Amato, P. R., & Keith, B. (1991b). Parental divorce and adult well-being: A meta-analysis. *Journal of Marriage and the Family, 53,* 43–58.

Amato, P. R., & Booth, A. (1996). A prospective study of divorce and parent–child relationships. *Journal of Marriage and the Family, 58,* 356–365.

American Academy of Pediatrics Committee on Adolescence. (1980). Teenage suicide. *Pediatrics, 66,* 144–146.

American Medical Association. (1990). America's adolescents: How healthy are they? In (J. E. Gans in collaboration with D. A. Blyth, A. Elster, and L. L. Gaveras, Authors), *Profile of Adolescent Health Series* (Vol. 1). Chicago, IL: American Medical Association.

American Psychological Association (1990) APA guidelines for providers of psychological services to ethnic, linguistic, and culturally diverse populations. Washington, DC: Author.

American Society for Pharmacology (1987). Scientific perspectives on cocaine abuse. *The Pharmacologist, 29,* 20–27.

Ammer, C. (1983). *The A to Z of women's health.* New York: Everest House.

Anderson, E. M., & Kimweli, D. M. S. (1997). Victimization and safety in schools serving early adolescents. *Journal of Early Adolescence, 17,* 408–438.

Anderson, A. R., & Henry, C. S. (1994). Family system characteristics and parental behaviors as predictors of adolescent substance use. *Adolescence, 29*(114), 405–420.

Anderson, J. L., Crawford, C. B., Nadeau, J., & Lindberg, T. (1992). Was the Duchess of Windsor Right: A cross-cultural review of the socio-ecology of ideals of female body shape. *Ethology and Sociobiology, 13,* 197–227.

Anderson, S. A., & Sabatelli, R. M. (1992) The differentiation in the family system scale. *The American Journal of Family Therapy, 20,* 77–89.

Andrews, L. B., & Nelkin, D. (1996). The bell curve: A statement. *Science, 271*(5245), 13–14.

Aneshensel, C. S., Fielder, S., & Becerra, R. M. (1989). Fertility and fertility-related behavior among Mexican-American and non-Hispanic White Female adolescents. *Journal of Health and Social Behavior, 30,* 56–76.

Angold, A., & Worthman, C. W. (1993). Puberty onset of gender differences in rates of depression: A developmental, epidemiologic and neuroendocrine perspective. *Journal of Affective Disorders, 29,* 145–158.

Ansuini, C. G., Fiddler-Woite, J., & Woite, R. S. (1996). The source, accuracy and impact if initial sexuality information on lifetime wellness. *Adolescence, 31,* 283–289.

Anthony, E. J. (1987). Risk, vulnerability, and resilience: An overview. In E. J. Anthony & B. J. Cohler (Eds.), *The invulnerable child* (pp. 1–48). New York: Guilford.

Aquilino, W. S. (1996). The life course of children born to unmarried mothers: Childhood living arrangements and young adult outcomes. *Journal of Marriage and the Family, 58,* 293–310.

Archer, S. L. (1989). Gender differences in identity development: Issues of process, domain and timing. *Journal of Adolescence, 12,* 117–138.

Archer, S. L., & Waterman, A. S. (1983). Identity in early adolescence: A developmental perspective. *Journal of Early Adolescence, 3,* 203–214.

Aries, P. (1962). *Centuries of childhood.* New York: Knopf.

Armistead, L., Wierson, M., & Forehand, R. (1990). Adolescents and maternal employment: Is it harmful for a young adolescent to have an employed mother? *Journal of Early Adolescence, 10,* 260–278.

Asberg, M. (1989). Neurotransmitter monoamine metabolites in the cerebrospinal fluid as risk factors for suicidal behavior. In *Report of the secretary's task force on youth suicide: Risk factors for youth suicide* (Vol. 2). Washington, DC: ADAMHA Report ADM 89-1623, U.S. Government Printing Office.

Asmussen, L., & Larson, R. (1991). The quality of family time among young adolescents in single-parent and married-parent families. *Journal of Marriage and the Family, 53,* 1021–1030.

Atkinson, D. R., Morten, G., & Sue, D. W. (1993). Counseling American minorities: *A cross-cultural perspective* (4th ed.). Dubuque, IA: Wm. C. Brown.

Attie, I., & Brooks-Gunn, J. (1989). Development of eating problems in adolescent girls: A longitudinal study. *Developmental Psychology, 25,* 70–79.

Austin, G. A. (1979). *Research Issues 24: Perspectives on the history of psychoactive substance use.* Washington, DC: DHHS Publication ADM 79-810, U.S. Government Printing Office.

Ausubel, D., & Ausubel, P. (1966). Cognitive development in adolescence. *Review of Educational Research, 36,* 403–413.

Ausubel, D. P., & Sullivan, E. V. (1970). *Theory and problems of child development* (2nd ed.). New York: Grune & Stratton.

Avery-Leaf, S., Cascardi, M., & O'Leary, D. (1994). Efficacy of a dating violence prevention program. Poster at the 102nd American Psychological Association, Los Angeles, CA.

Baba, T. W., Trichel, A. M., An, L., Liska, V., Martin, L. N., Murphey-Corb, M., & Ruprecht, R. M. (1996). Infection and AIDS in adult macaques after nontraumatic oral exposure to cell-free SIV. *Science, 272*(5267), 1486–1489.

Babikian, H. M., & Goldman, A. A. (1971). A study of teenage pregnancy. *American Journal of Psychiatry, 128,* 755–760.

Bailey, S. (1996). Adolescents who murder. *Journal of Adolescence, 19,* 19–39.

Baizerman, M., Thompson, J., & Stafford-White, K. (1979). Adolescent prostitution. *Children Today, 8,* 20–24.

Baker, D., Telfer, M. A., Richardson, G. R., & Clark, G. R. (1970). Chromosome error in men with antisocial behavior. *Journal of the American Medical Association, 214,* 869–878.

Balter, M. (1997). HIV survives drug onslaught by hiding out in T cells. *Science, 278,* 1227.

Balter, M. (1998a). Virus from 1959 sample marks early years of HIV. *Science, 279,* 801.

Balter, M. (1998b). Revealing HIV's T cell passkey. *Science, 280,* 1833–1834.

Balter, M. (1998c). HIV incidence: "More serious than we imagined." *Science, 280,* 1864.

Balter, M., & Cohen, J. (1998). International AIDS meeting injects a dose of realism. *Science, 281,* 159–160.

Bandura, A. (1960). *Relationship of family patterns to child behavior disorders: A progress report.* Stanford, CA: Stanford University Press.

Bandura, A. (1965). Vicarious processes: A case of no trial learning. In L. Berkowitz (Ed.), *Advances in experimental social psychology* (Vol. 2). New York: Academic Press.

Bandura, A. (1969). *Principles of behavior modification.* New York: Holt, Rinehart & Winston.

Bandura, A. (1977). Self-efficacy: Toward a unifying theory of behavioral change. *Psychological Review, 84,* 191–215.

Bandura, A. (1978). The self-esteem in reciprocal determinism. *American Psychologist, 33,* 344–358.

Bandura, A. (1982). Self-efficacy mechanism in human agency. *American Psychologist, 37,* 122–147.

Banks, J. A. (1988). Ethnicity, class, cognitive, and motivational styles: Research and teaching implications. *Journal of Negro Education, 57,* 452–466.

Barber, B. K. (1992). Family, personality, and adolescent problem behaviors. *Journal of Marriage and the Family, 54,* 69–79.

Barber, B. K. (1997). Adolescent socialization in context—The role of connection, regulation, and autonomy in the family. *Journal of Adolescent Research, 12,* 5–11.

Barinaga, M. (1995). "Obese" protein slims mice. *Science, 269,* 475–476.

Barinaga, M. (1996). Obesity: Leptin receptor weighs in. *Science, 271*(5245), 29–30.

Barnes, G. E. (1979). Solvent abuse: A review. *International Journal of the Addictions, 14,* 1–26.

Barnes, G. E., & Prosen, H. (1985). Parental death and depression. *Journal of Abnormal Psychology, 94,* 64–69.

Barnes, G. M. (1977). The development of adolescent drinking behavior: An evaluative review of the impact of the socialization process within the family. *Adolescence, 12,* 571–591.

Barnes, G. M., Farrell, M. P., & Banerjee, S. (1994). Family influences on alcohol abuse and other problem behaviors among blacks and white adolescents in a general population sample. *Journal of Research on Adolescence, 4,* 183–201.

Barnes, G. M., & Welte (1986). Patterns and predictors of alcohol use among 7–12th grade students in New York State. *Journal of Studies on Alcohol, 47,* 53–62.

Barnett, J. K., Papini, D. R., & Gbur, E. (1991). Familial correlates of sexually active pregnant and non-pregnant adolescents. *Adolescence, 26,* 457–472.

Bartle, S. E., & Rosen, K. (1994). Individuation and relationship violence. *The American Journal of Family Therapy, 22,* 222–236.

Bartle, S. E., & Sabatelli, R. M. (1989). Family system dynamics, identity development and adolescent alcohol use: Implications for family treatment. *Family Relations, 38,* 283–298.

Barton, W. H. (1976). Discretionary decision making in juvenile justice. *Crime and Delinquency, 22,* 470–480.

Bastian, L. D., & Taylor, B. M. (1991). *School crime.* Washington, DC: U.S. Department of Justice (NCJ-131645), U.S. Government Printing Office.

Bastian, L. D., & Taylor, B. M. (1994, December). Young black male victims. In *Crime Data Brief* (pp. 1–2). Washington, DC: U.S. Department of Justice (NCJ-147004).

Baucom, D. H., Besch, P. K., & Callahan, S. (1985). Relation between testosterone concentration, sex role identity, and personality among females. *Journal of Personality and Social Psychology, 48,* 1218–1226.

Bauer, G. B. (1985). Restoring order to the public schools. *Phi Delta Kappan, 66,* 488–491.

Bauer, G. B., Dubanoski, R., Yamauchi, L. A., & Hunbo, K. M. (1990). Corporal punishment and the schools. *Education and Urban Society, 22,* 285–299.

Bauman, K. E., Fisher, L. A., Bryan, E. S., & Chenoweth, R. L. (1984). Antecedents, subjective expected utility, and behavior: A panel study of adolescent cigarette

smoking. *Addictive Behaviors, 9,* 121–136.

Baumeister, R. (1986). *Identity: Cultural change and the struggle for self.* New York: Oxford University Press.

Baumeister, R., & Muraven. M. (1996). CH4 Identity as adaptation to social, cultural, and historical context. *Journal of Adolescence, 19,* 405–416.

Baumeister, R., Shapiro, J. P., & Tice, D. M. (1985). Two kinds of identity crises. *Journal of Personality, 53,* 407–423.

Baumrind, D. (1978). Parental disciplinary patterns and social competence in children. *Youth & Society, 9,* 239–276.

Baumrind, D. (1991). Effective parenting during the early adolescent transition. In P. A. Cowan & M. Heterington (Eds.), *Family transitions.* Hillsdale, NJ: Earlbaum.

Bayer, A. E. (1984). Anorexia and bulimia in adolescents. *Children Today, 13,*7–11.

Beauvais, F., & LaBoueff, S. (1985). Drug and alcohol abuse intervention in American Indian communities. *International Journal of the Addictions, 20,* 139–171.

Beaver, C. W. (1972). Hope and suicide in the concentration camp. In E. S. Schneidman (Ed.), *Death and the college student.* New York: Human Sciences Press.

Becker, W. C. (1964). Consequences of different kinds of parental discipline. In M. L. Hoffman & L. W. Hoffman (Eds.), *Review of child development research* (Vol. 1). New York: Russell Sage Foundation.

Beiswinger, G. L. (1979). The High Court, privacy, and teenage sexuality. *Family Coordinator, 28,* 191–198.

Bell, R. M. (1985). *Holy anorexia.* Chicago: University of Chicago Press.

Bem, S. L. (1974). The measurement of psychological androgyny. *Journal of Consulting and Clinical Psychology, 42,* 155–162.

Bem, S. L. (1981). Gender schema theory: A cognitive account of sex typing. *Psychological Review, 88,* 354–364.

Bem, S. L. (1993). *The lenses of gender.* New Haven, CT: Yale University Press.

Bemis, K. M. (1978). Current approaches to the etiology and treatment of anorexia nervosa. *Psychological Bulletin, 85,* 593–617.

Ben-Amos, I. K. (1995). Adolescence as a cultural invention: Philippe Aries and the sociology of youth. *History of the Human Sciences, 8,* 69–89.

Benbow, C. P., & Stanley, J. C. (1980). Sex differences in mathematical ability: Fact or artifact? *Science, 210,* 1262–1264.

Benbow, C. P., & Stanley, J. C. (1983). Sex differences in mathematical ability: More facts. *Science, 222,* 1029–1031.

Bennion, L. D., & Adams, G. R. (1986). A revision of the extended version of the objective measure of ego identity status: An identity instrument for use with late adolescents. *Journal of Adolescent Research, 1,* 183–198.

Benowitz, N. L. (1990). Clinical pharmacology of inhaled drugs of abuse: Implications in understanding nicotine dependence. In C. N. Chiang & R. L. Hawks (Eds.), *Research findings on smoking abused substances.* Washington, DC: U.S. Department of Health and Human Services publication ADM 90-1690, U.S. Government Printing Office.

Benz, C. R., Pfeiffer, I., & Newman, I. (1981). Sex role expectations of classroom teachers, grades 1–12. *American Educational Research Journal, 18,* 289–302.

Berel, S., & Irving, L. M. (1998). Media and disturbed eating: An analysis of media influence and implications for prevention. *Journal of Primary Prevention, 19,* 415–430.

Berg-Cross, L., Kidd, F., & Carr, P. (1990). Cohesion, affect, and self-disclosure in African-American adolescent families. *Journal of Family Psychology, 4,* 235–250.

Berkowitz, L. (1962). *Aggression: A social psychological analysis.* New York: McGraw–Hill.

Berkowitz, L. (1964). The effects of observing violence. *Scientific American, 210,* 35–41.

Berlin, I. N. (1985). Prevention of adolescent suicide among some Native American tribes. *Adolescent Psychiatry, 12,* 77–93.

Berlin, I. N. (1986). Psychopathology and its antecedents among American Indian adolescents. In B. B. Lakey & A. E. Kazdin (Eds.), *Advances in clinical child psychology* (Vol. 9). New York: Plenum.

Berndt, T. J., Miller, K. E., & Park, K. (1989). Adolescents' perceptions of friends' and parents' influence on aspects of their school adjustment, *Journal of Early Adolescence, 9,* 419–435.

Berne, L. A., & Berne, B. K. (1995). Sexuality education. *Phi Delta Kappan, 77,* 229–232.

Berzonsky, M. D. (1978). Formal reasoning in adolescence: An alternative view. *Adolescence, 13,* 279–290.

Berzonsky, M. D. (1992). A process perspective on identity and stress management. In G. R. Adams, T. P. Gullotta, & R. Montemayor (Eds.), *Identity formation during adolescence.* Newbury Park, CA: Sage.

Bettoli, E. J. (1982). Herpes: Facts and fallacies. *Journal of Practical Nursing, 32,* 17–21, 42.

Bierman, K. L. (1997). Implementing a comprehensive program for the prevention of conduct problems in rural communities: The fast track experience. *American Journal of Community Psychology, 25,* 493–514.

Billingham, R. E. (1987). Courtship violence: The patterns of conflict resolution strategies across seven levels of emotional commitment. *Family Relations, 36,* 283–289.

Billy, J. O., Rodgers, J. L., & Udry, J. R. (1984). Adolescent sexual behavior and friendship choice. *Social Forces, 62,* 653–678.

Bingham, C. R., Bennion, L. D., Openshaw, D. K., & Adams, G. R. (1994). An analysis of age gender and racial differences in recent national trends of youth suicide. *Journal of Adolescence, 17,* 53–71.

Bird, G. W., & Kemerait, L. N. (1990). Stress among early adolescents in two-earner families. *Journal of Early Adolescence, 10,* 344–365.

Birmaher, B., Ryan, N. D., Williamson, D. E., Brent, D. A., Kaufman, J., Dahl, R. E., Perel, J., & Nelson, B. (1996). Childhood and adolescent depression.

I. A review of the past 10 years. *Journal of the American Academy of Child and Adolescent Psychiatry, 35,* 1427–1435.

Birmaher, B., Ryan, N. D., Williamson, D. E., Brent, D. A., & Kaufman, J. (1996). Childhood and adolescent depression. II. A review of the past 10 years. *Journal of the American Academy of Child and Adolescent Psychiatry, 35,* 1575–1581.

Birmingham, M. S. (1986). An out-patient treatment programme for adolescent substance abusers. *Journal of Adolescence, 9,* 123–133.

Blakely, C. H., Coulter, J. B., Gardner, S. E., Jansen, M. A., & Gullotta, T. P. (Eds.) (1997). Center for substance abuse prevention: High risk youth programs—Special issue of the Journal of Early Adolescence. *Journal of Early Adolescence, 17,* 1–96.

Blakely, C. H., Coulter, J. B., Gardner, S. E., McColgan, B. R., & Gullotta, T. P. (Eds.) (1996). Preventing adolescent substance abuse: Special issue of the Journal of Adolescent Research. *Journal of Adolescent Research, 11,* 1–163.

Blakely, C. H., & Gullotta, T. P. (Eds.) (1998). Preventing adolescent substance abuse: Special issue of the Journal of Primary Prevention. *Journal of Primary Prevention, 18,* 247–388.

Blau, G. M. (1996). Adolescent suicide and depression. In G. M. Blau & T. P. Gullotta (Eds.) *Adolescent dysfunction behavior.* Thousand Oaks, CA: Sage.

Blau, G. M., & Gullotta, T. P. (1993). Promoting sexual responsibility in adolescence. In T. P. Gullotta, G. R. Adams, & R. Montemayor (Eds.), *Adolescent sexuality.* Newbury Park, CA: Sage.

Blau, G. M., Whewell, M., Gullotta, T. P., & Bloom, M. (1994). The prevention and treatment of child abuse in households of substance abusers: A demonstration progress report. *Child Welfare, 73,* 83–94.

Blee, K. M., & Tickamyer, A. R. (1995). Racial differences in men's attitudes about women's gender roles. *Journal of Marriage and the Family, 57,* 21–30.

Bloch, H. A., & Niederhoffer, A. (1958). *The gang.* New York: Philosophical Library.

Block, J. H. (1973). Conceptions of sex roles: Some cross-cultural and longitudinal perspectives. *American Psychologist, 28,* 513–526.

Block, J. H., Block, J. H., & Gjerde, P. F. (1991). Personality antecedents of depressive tendencies in 18 year-olds: A prospective study. *Journal of Personality and Social Psychology, 60,* 725–738.

Block, J. R., Von der Lippe, A., & Block, J. H. (1973). Sex role and socialization patterns: Some personality concomitants and environmental antecedents. *Journal of Consulting and Clinical Psychology, 41,* 321–341.

Bloom, D. E., & Glied, S. (1991). Benefits and costs of HIV testing. *Science, 252,* 1798–1804.

Bloom, M. (1990). The psychosocial constructs of social competency. In T. P. Gullotta, G. R. Adams, & R. Montemayor (Eds.), *Developing social competency in adolescence.* Newbury Park, CA: Sage.

Bloom. M. (1996a). Primary prevention and resilience: Changing paradigms and changing lives. In R. L. Hampton, P. Jenkins, & T. P. Gullotta (Eds.), *Preventing violence in America.* Thousand Oaks, CA: Sage.

Bloom, M. (1996b) *Primary prevention practices.* Thousand Oaks, CA: Sage.

Bloom, M. (1997). Preventing juvenile delinquency and promoting juvenile rightency. In T. P. Gullotta, G. R. Adams, & R. Montemayor (Eds.), *Delinquent violent youth* (pp. 256–308). Thousand Oaks, CA: Sage.

Bloom, M. (2000). The uses of theory in primary prevention practice. In S. Danish & T. P. Gullotta (Eds.), *Promoting socially competent youth: Sports and extra-curricular activities.* Washington, DC: Child Walfare Press.

Blos, P. (1962). *On adolescence.* New York: Free Press.

Blos, P. (1967). The second individuation process of adolescence. *Psychoanalytic Study of the Child, 22,* 162–186.

Blum, K., & Nobel, E. P. (1990). Allelic association of human dopamine D2 receptor gene in alcoholism. *Journal of*

the American Medical Association, 263, 2055–2060.

Blumenkrantz, D. G., & Gavazzi, S. M. (1993). Guiding transitional events for children and adolescents through a modern day rite of passage. *Journal of Primary Prevention, 13,* 199–212.

Blumenthal, S. J., & Kupfer, D. J. (1989). Overview of early detection and treatment strategies for suicidal behavior in young people. In *Report of the secretary's task force on youth suicide: Prevention and interventions in youth suicide* (Vol. 3), Washington, DC: U.S. Department of Health and Human Services publication ADM 89-1622, U.S. Government Printing Office.

Blumstein, A. (1995). Why the deadly nexus? *National Institute of Justice Journal, 229,* 2–9.

Blyth, D. A., Hill, J. P., & Smyth, C. K. (1981). The influence of older adolescents on younger adolescents: Do grade-level arrangements make a difference in behaviors, attitudes, and experiences? *Journal of Early Adolescence, 1,* 85–110.

Blyth, D. A., Simmons, R. G., Bulcroft, R., Felt, D., Van Cleave, E. F., & Bush, D. M. (1980). The effects of physical development on self-image and satisfaction with body image for early adolescent males. In R. G. Simmons (Ed.), *Handbook of community and mental health* (Vol. 2). Greenwich, CT: JAI Press.

Blyth, D. A., Simmons, R. G., & Zakin, D. F. (1985). Satisfaction with body image for early adolescent females: The impact of pubertal timing within different school environments. *Journal of Youth and Adolescence, 14,* 207–226.

Bodmer, W. F., & Cavalli-Sforza, L. L. (1970). Intelligence and race. *Scientific American, 223,* 19–29.

Bogenschneider, K. (1997). Parental involvement in adolescent schooling: A proximal process with transcontextual validity. *Journal of Marriage and the Family, 59,* 718–733.

Bohman, M. (1978). Some genetic aspects of alcoholism and criminality: A population of adopters. *Archives of General Psychiatry, 35,* 269–276.

Boldt, M. (1982). Normative evaluations of suicide and death: A cross-generational study. *Omega, 13,* 145–157.

Boldero, J., & Fallon, B. (1995). Adolescent help-seeking: What do they get help for and from who? *Journal of Adolescence, 18,* 193–209.

Bolinger, T. (1999). The psychopharmacologic revolution: Understanding its place in the treatment of childhood psychopathology. In T. P. Gullotta, G. R. Adams, R. L. Hampton, B. A. Ryan, & R. Weissberg (Eds.), *Children's health care: issues for the year 2000 and beyond.* Thousand Oaks, CA: Sage.

Booth, W. (1988). CDC paints a picture of HIV infection in U.S. *Science, 15,* 253.

Borduin, C., & Schaeffer, C. (1998). Violent offending in adolescence. In T. P. Gullotta, G. R. Adams, & R. Montemayor (Eds.), *Delinquent violent youth.* (pp. 144–174). Thousand Oaks, CA: Sage.

Bosma, H. A. (1992). Identity in adolescence: Managing commitments. In G. R. Adams, T. P. Gullotta, & R. Montemayor (Eds.), *Identity formation during adolescence,* Newbury Park, CA: Sage.

Bosma, H. A., & Gerrits, R. S. (1985). Family functioning and identity status in adolescence. *Journal of Early Adolescence, 5,* 69–80.

Bossard, J. H. S. (1954). *The sociology of child development.* New York: Harper & Row.

Bourne, E. (1978). The state of research on ego identity. I. A review and appraisal. *Journal of Youth and Adolescence, 7,* 223–252.

Bowen, M. (1976). Theory and practice in psychotherapy. In P. J. Guerin (ed.) *Family therapy: Theory and practice.* (pp. 42–90). New York: Gardner.

Bowen, M. (1978). *Family therapy in clinical practice.* New York: Jason Aaronson.

Bowker, L. H., Gross, H. S., & Klein, M. W. (1980). Female participation in delinquent gang activities. *Adolescence, 15,* 509–519.

Bowman, P. J. (1990). The adolescent-to-adult transition: Discouragement among jobless Black youth. *New Directions for Child Development, 46,* 87–105.

Boxill, N. A. (1987). How would you feel?: Clinical interviews with Black adolescent mothers. *Child & Youth Services, 9,* 41–51.

Boyd, R. D., & Koskela, R. N. (1970). A test of Erikson's theory of ego-state development by means of a self-report instrument. *Journal of Experimental Education, 38,* 1–14.

Bracey, G. W. (1991). Time outside of school. *Phi Delta Kappan, 73,* 88.

Bracey, G. W. (1992). Achievement and employment. *Phi Delta Kappan, 73,* 492–493.

Bracey, G. W. (1993). No magic bullets. *Phi Delta Kappan, 74,* 495–496.

Bracey, G. W. (1995a). Record-level SATs: Course related? *Phi Delta Kappan, 76,* 566.

Bracey, G. W. (1995b). The fifth Bracey report on the condition of public education. *Phi Delta Kappan, 77,* 149–160.

Bracey, G. W. (1995c). Research oozes into practice: The case of class size. *Phi Delta Kappan, 77,* 89–90.

Bracey, G. W. (1996). The rhetoric versus the reality of job creation. *Phi Delta Kappan, 77,* 385–386.

Bracey, G. W. (1996). Dropping out: A complex phenomenon. *Phi Delta Kappan, 77,* 386.

Brandt, A. M. (1988). The syphilis epidemic and its relation to AIDS. *Science, 239,* 315–380.

Braucht, G. N., Brakarsh, D., Follinstad, D., & Berry, K. L. (1973). Deviant drug use in adolescence: A review of psychosocial correlates. *Psychological Bulletin, 79,* 92–106.

Braucht, G. N., Loya, F., & Jamieson, K. J. (1980). Victims of violent death: A critical review. *Psychological Bulletin, 87,* 309–333.

Brayfield, A. (1995). Juggling jobs and kids: The impact of employment schedules on father's caring for children. *Journal of Marriage and the Family, 57,* 321–332.

Brecher, E. (1972). *Licit and illicit drugs.* Boston: Little, Brown.

Brenenson, J. F., & Benarroch, D. (1998). Gender differences in responses to friends' hypothetical gender success.

Journal of Early Adolescence, 18, 192–208.

Brenner, M. H. (1980). Estimating the social costs of youth employment problems. In *A review of youth employment problems, programs, and policies: The Vice President's Task Force on Youth Employment* (Vol. 1). Washington, DC: U.S. Department of Labor.

Brenzel, B. M. (1980). Domestication as reform: A study of the socialization of wayward girls, 1856–1905. *Harvard Educational Review, 50,* 196–213.

Brewster, K. L., Cooksey, E. C., Guilkey, D. K., & Rindfuss, R. R. (1998). The changing impact of religion on the sexual and contraceptive behavior of adolescent women in the United States. *Journal of Marriage and the Family, 60,* 493–504.

Brigham, J. C. (1986). *Social psychology.* Boston: Little, Brown.

Brock, B. V., Selke, S., Benedetti, J., Douglas, J. M., & Corey, L. (1990). Frequency of asymptomatic shedding of herpes simplex virus in women with genital herpes. *Journal of the American Medical Association, 263,* 418–420.

Broder, D. S. (1996, June 3). Back to the future. *Washington Post National Weekly Edition,* p. 4.

Brody, N. (1992). *Intelligence.* New York: Academic Press.

Bronfenbrenner, U. (1970). *Two worlds of childhood: U.S. and U.S.S.R.* New York: Russell Sage Foundation.

Bronfenbrenner, U. (1974). The origins of alienation. *Scientific American, 231,* 53–61.

Bronfenbrenner, U. (1989). Ecological systems theory. In R. Vasta (Ed.), Six theories of child development: *Annals of child development* (Vol. 6, pp. 187–249). Greenwich, CT: JAI Press.

Brook, J. S., Gordon, A. S., & Brook, D. W. (1980). Perceived paternal relationships, adolescent personality, and female marijuana use. *Journal of Psychology, 105,* 277–285.

Brook, R., Kaplum, J., & Whitehead, P. C. (1974). Personality characteristics of adolescent amphetamine users as measured by the MMPI. *British Journal of the Addictions, 69,* 61–66.

Brookmeyer, R. (1991). Reconstruction and future trends of the AIDS epidemic in the United States. *Science, 253,* 37–42.

Brooks-Gunn, J. (1986). Pubertal processes and girls' psychological adaptation. In R. M. Lerner and T. T. Foch (Eds.), *Biological psychosocial interactions in early adolescence: A life-span perspective.* Hillsdale, NJ: Erlbaum.

Brooks-Gunn, J., & Furstenberg, F. F. (1991). Adolescent sexual behavior. *American Psychologist, 44,* 249–257.

Brooks-Gunn, J., Newman, D. L., Holderness, C., & Warren, M. P. (1994). The experience of breast development and girls' stories about the purchase of a bra. *Journal of Youth and Adolescence, 23,* 539–565.

Brooks-Gunn, J., & Petersen, A. C. (Eds.). (1983). *Girls at puberty: Biological and psychosocial perspectives.* NY: Plenum.

Brown, B. B., Eicher, S. A., & Petrie, S. (1986). The importance of peer ("crowd") affiliation in adolescence. *Journal of Adolescence, 9,* 73–96.

Brown, B. B., Mory, M. S., & Kinney, D. (1994). Casting adolescent crowds in a relational perspective: Caricature, channel, and context. In R. Montemayor, G. R. Adams, & T. P. Gullotta (Eds.) *Personal relationships during adolescence* (pp. 123–167) Thousand Oaks, CA: Sage.

Brown, B. B., Mounts, N., Lamborn, S. D., & Steinberg, L. (1993). Parenting practices and peer group affiliation in adolescence. *Child Development, 64,* 467–482.

Brown, D. (1996, December 9–15). The marijuana riddle. *The Washington Post National Weekly Edition,* p. 35.

Brown, E. F., & Hendee, W. R. (1989). Adolescents and their music: Insights into the health of adolescents. *Journal of the American Medical Association, 262,* 1659–1663.

Brown, F. (1980). *Transition of youth to adulthood: A bridge too far.* Boulder, CO: Westview Press.

Brown, J. D., Childers, K. W., Bauman, K. E., & Koch, G. G. (1990). The influence of new media and family structure on young adolescents' television and radio use. *Communication Research, 17,* 65–82.

Brown, J. D., Greenberg, B. S., & Buerkel-Rothfuss, N. L. (1993). Mass media, sex and sexuality. *Adolescent Medicine, 4*(3), 511–525.

Brown, L. T., & Anthony, R. G. (1990). Continuing the search for social intelligence. *Personality and Individual Differences, 11,* 463–470.

Brown, M. E. (1979). Teenage prostitution. Adolescence, 14, 665–680.

Bruene-Butler, L., Hampson, J., Elias, M. J., Clabby, J. F., & Schuyler, T. (1997). The improving social awareness-social problem solving project. In G. W. Albee & T. P. Gullotta (Eds.), *Primary prevention works* (pp. 239–267). Thousand Oaks, CA: Sage.

Bruer, H. (1973). Ego identity status in late-adolescent college males, as measured by a group administered incomplete sentences blank and related to inferred stance toward authority. Unpublished doctoral dissertation, New York University.

Brumberg, J. J. (1988). *Fasting girls.* Cambridge, MA: Harvard University Press.

Brumberg, J. J. (1997). *The body project: An intimate history of American girls.* New York. Random House.

Buchingham, S. L., & Van Gorp, W. G. (1988). Essential knowledge about AIDS dementia. *Social Work, 33,* 112–115.

Buehler, C., Krishnakumar, A., Stone, G., Anthony, C., Pemberton, S., Gerard, J., & Barber, B. K. (1998). Interparental conflict styles and youth problem behavior: A two sample replication study. *Journal of Marriage and the Family, 60,* 119–132.

Buhrmester, D. (1990). Intimacy of friendship, interpersonal competence, and adjustment during preadolescence and adolescence. *Child Development, 61,* 1101–1111.

Bulcroft, R. A. (1991). The value of physical change in adolescence: consequences for the parent-adolescent exchange relationship. *Journal of Youth and Adolescence, 20,* 89–105.

Burgess, B. J. (1980). Parenting in the Native-American community. In M. D. Fantini & R. Cardenas (Eds.), *Parenting*

in a multicultural society. New York: Longman.

Buriel, R. (1987). Ethnic labeling and identity among Mexican Americans. In J. S. Phinney & M. J. Rotheram (Eds.), *Children's ethnic socialization: Pluralism and development.* Newbury Park, CA: Sage.

Burke, R. S., & Grinder, R. E. (1966). Personality-oriented themes and listening patterns in teen-age music and their relation to certain academic and peer variables. *School Review, 74,* 196–211.

Burnham, J. C. (1993). *Bad habits.* New York: New York University Press.

Burton, R. (1851). *The anatomy of melancholy* (4th ed.). Philadelphia, PA: J. W. Moore.

Butler, J. W., Novy, D., Kagan, N., & Gates, G. (1994). An investigation of differences in attitudes between suicidal and nonsuicidal student ideators. *Adolescence, 29* (115), 623–638.

Byrne, G. (1988). Nicotine likened to cocaine, heroin. *Science, 240,* 1143.

Cadoret, R. J., Cain, C. A., & Grove, W. M. (1980). Development of alcoholism in adoptees raised apart from alcoholic biologic relatives. *Archives of General Psychiatry, 37,* 561–563.

Camarena, P. M., Sarigiani, P. A., & Petersen, A. C. (1990). Gender-specific pathways to intimacy in early adolescence. *Journal of Youth and Adolescence, 19,* 19–32.

Camino, L. A. (1995). Understanding intolerance and multiculturalism: A challenge for practitioners, but also for researchers. *Journal of Adolescent Research, 10,* 155–172.

Campbell, A. (1990). Female participation in gangs. In C. R. Huff (Ed.), *Gangs in America.* Newbury Park, CA: Sage.

Cannon-Bonaventure, K., & Kahn, J. (1979). Interviews with adolescent parents. *Children Today, 8*(5), 17–19.

Cano, A., Avery-Leaf, S., Cascardi, M., & O'Leary, D. (1998). Dating violence in two high school samples: Discriminating variables. *Journal of Primary Prevention, 18,* 431–446.

Capaldi, D. M. (1992). Co-occurrence of conduct problems and depressive symptoms in early adolescent boys. II. A 2-year follow-up at Grade 8. *Developmental Psychopathology, 4,* 125–144.

Caplan, G. (Ed.) (1961). *Prevention of mental disorders in children: Initial explorations.* New York: Basic Books.

Caplan, G. (1964). *Principles of preventive psychiatry.* New York: Basic Books.

Caplan, G. (1974). *Support systems and community mental health.* New York: Behavioral Publications.

Caplan, G. M. (1984). The facts of life about teenage prostitution. *Crime and Delinquency, 30,* 68–74.

Cardoza, D. (1991). College attendance and persistence among Hispanic women: An examination of some contributing factors. *Sex Roles, 24,* 133–147.

Carroll, A. E. (1986). Individual and family therapy eating disorder patients. *Seminar in Adolescent Medicine, 2,* 57–64.

Carruth, B. R., Goldberg, D. L., & Skinner, J. D. (1991). Do parents and peers mediate the influence of television advertising on food-related purchase? *Journal of Adolescent Research, 6,* 253–271.

Casas, J. M., Wagenheim, B. R., Banchero, R., & Mendoza-Romero, J. (1995). Hispanic masculinity: Myth or psychological schema meriting clinical consideration. In A. M. Padila (Ed.), *Hispanic psychology: Critical issues in theory and research* (pp. 231–244). Thousand Oaks, CA: Sage.

Casper, R. C. (1984). Hypothalmic dysfunction and symptoms of anorexia nervosa. *Psychiatric Clinics of North America, 7,* 201–213.

Cassidy, L., & Hurrell, R. M. (1995). The influence of victims' attire and adolescents' judgements of date rape. *Adolescence, 30*(118), 319–323.

Catania, J. A., Coates, T. J., Stall, R., Turner, H., Peterson, J., Hearst, N., Dokini, M. M., Hudes, E., Gagon, J., Wiley, J., & Groves, R. (1992). Prevalence of AIDS-related risk factors and condom use in the United States. *Science, 258,* 1101–1106.

Cate, R. M., Henton, J. M., Koval, J., Christopher, F. S., & Lloyd, S. (1982).

Premarital abuse. *Journal of Family Issues, 3,* 79–90.

Ceci, S. J. (1990). *On intelligence . . . more or less.* Englewood Cliffs, NY: Prentice–Hall.

Centers for Disease Control (1983a). Acquired immune deficiency syndrome (AIDS) update: U.S. *Journal of the American Medical Association, 250*(3), 335–336.

Centers for Disease Control (1983b). Prevention of acquired immune deficiency syndrome (AIDS): Report of interagency recommendations. *Journal of the American Medical Association, 249*(12), 1544–1545.

Centers for Disease Control (1989). *Smoking, tobacco, and health.* Washington, DC: Public Health Service (CDC 87-8397), U.S. Government Printing Office.

Chaiken, S. (1979). Communicator physical attractiveness and persuasion. *Journal of Personality and Social Psychology, 37,* 1387–1397.

Chase, A. W. (1866). *Dr. Chase's recipes; or information for everybody: an invaluable collection of about eight hundred practical recipes.* Ann Arbor, MI: Author.

Chase-Lansdale, P. L., Brooks-Gunn, J., & Palkoff, R. L. (1991). Research and programs for adolescent mothers: Missing links and future promises. *Family Relations, 40,* 396–403.

Chen, C., & Stevenson, H. W. (1995). Motivation and mathematics achievement: A comparative study of Asian-American, Caucasian-American, and East Asian high school students. *Child Development, 66,* 1215–1234.

Cherek, D. R., Bennett, R. H., Roache, J. D., & Grabowski, J. (1990). Human aggressive and non-aggressive responding during acute tobacco abstinence. In L. S. Harris (Ed.), *Problems of drug dependence: 1989.* Washington, DC: U.S. Department of Health and Human Services publication ADM 90-1663, U.S. Government Printing Office.

Cherry, V. R., Belgrave, F. Z., Jones, W., Kennon, D. K., Gray, F. S., & Phillips, F. (1998). NTU: An Africentric approach to substance abuse prevention among

African American youth. *Journal of Primary Prevention, 18,* 319–340.

Cherlin, A. J., Furstenberg, F. F., Chase-Lansdale, P. L., Kiernan, K. K., Robins, P. K., Morrison, D. R., & Teitler, J. O. (1991). Longitudinal studies of effects of divorce on children in Great Britain and the United States. *Science, 252,* 1386–1389.

Childress, H. (1998). Seventeen reasons why football is better than high school. *Phi Delta Kappan, 79,* 616–619.

Chilman, C. (1973). Why do unmarried women fail to use contraception? *Medical Aspects of Human Sexuality, 7,* 167–168.

Chilman, C. S. (1980). *Adolescent sexuality in a changing American society.* Washington, DC: NIH Publication No. 80-1426, U.S. Government Printing Office.

Chilman, C. S. (1983). Social and psychological research concerning adolescent childbearing: 1970–1980. *Journal of Marriage and the Family, 43*(4), 793–805.

Chilman, C. S. (1990). Promoting healthy adolescent sexuality. *Family Relations, 39,* 123–131.

Chilman, C. S. (1993). Hispanic families in the United States. In H. P. McAdoo (Ed.), *Family ethnicity: Strength in diversity* (pp. 141–163). Newbury Park, CA: Sage.

Christopher, F. S., Madura, M., & Weaver, L. (1998). Premarital sexual aggressors: A multivariate analysis of social, relational, and individual variables. *Journal of Marriage and the Family, 60,* 56–69.

Cicero, T. J., & O'Connor, L. H. (1990). Abuse liability of anabolic steroids and their possible role in abuse of alcohol, morphine, and other substances. In G. C. Lin & L. Erinoff (Eds.), *Anabolic steroid abuse.* Washington, DC: U.S. Department of Health and Human Services publication ADM 91-1720, U.S. Government Printing Office.

Clark, G. R., Telfer, M. A., Baker, D., & Rosen, M. (1970). Sex chromosomes, crime, and psychosis. *American Journal of Psychiatry, 126,* 1659–1663.

Clark, M. L., & Ayers, M. (1988). The role of reciprocity and proximity in junior

high school friendships. *Journal of Youth and Adolescence, 17,* 403–407.

Clayton, R. R. (1985). Cocaine use in the United States: In a blizzard or just snowed? In N. J. Kozel & E. H. Adams (Eds.), *Cocaine use in America: Epidemiological and clinical perspectives.* Washington, DC: NIDA research monograph No. 61, No. ADM 85-1414, U.S. Government Printing Office.

Clayton, R. R., & Leukefeld, C. G. (1992). The prevention of drug use among youth: Implications of "legalization." *Journal of Primary Prevention, 12,* 289–302.

Clifford, P. R. (1992). Drug use, drug prohibition, and minority communities. *Journal of Primary Prevention, 12,* 303–316.

Clemens, S. (1884/1962). *The adventures of Huckleberry Finn.* San Francisco, CA: Chandler.

Clothier, F. (1943). Psychological implications of unmarried parenthood. *American Journal of Orthopsychiatry, 13,* 531–549.

Coakley, J. J. (1990). *Sport in society: Issues and controversies* (4th ed.). St. Louis, MO: Times Mirror.

Coates, D. L. (1987). Gender differences in the structure and support characteristics of black adolescents' social networks. *Sex Roles, 17,* 667–687.

Cobliner, W. G. (1974). Pregnancy in the single adolescent girl: The role of cognitive functioning. *Journal of Youth and Adolescence, 3,* 17–29.

Cockerham, W. C., Forslund, M. A., & Raboin, R. M. (1976). Drug use among white and American Indian high school youth. *International Journal of the Addictions, 11,* 209–220.

Cohen, A. K. (1955). *Delinquent boys: The culture of the gang.* New York: Free Press.

Cohen, J. (1995). Can one type of HIV protect against another type? *Science, 268*(5217), 1566.

Cohen, J. (1996a). Likely HIV cofactor found. *Science, 272*(5263), 809–810.

Cohen, J. (1996b). SIV data raise concern on oral-sex risk. *Science, 272*(5267), 1421–1422.

Cohen, J. (1996c). Investigators detail HIV's fatal handshake. *Science, 274,* 502.

Cohen, J. (1997). The daunting challenge of keeping HIV suppressed. *Science, 277,* 32–33.

Cohen, L. E., & Kluegal, J. R. (1978). Determinants of juvenile court dispositions: Ascriptive and achieved factors in two metropolitan courts. *American Sociological Review, 43,* 162–176.

Cohen, R. A. (1969). Conceptual styles, cultural conflict, and nonverbal tests of intelligence. *American Anthropologist, 71,* 828–856.

Cohen, S. (1979). Inhalants. In R. Dupont, A. Goldstein, & J. O'Donnell (Eds.), *Handbook on drug abuse.* Washington, DC: U.S. Government Printing Office.

Cohen, S. (1981). Adolescence and drug abuse: Biomedical consequences. In D. J. Lettieri & J. P. Ludford (Eds.), *Drug abuse and the American adolescent.* Washington, DC: NIDA research monograph No. 38, ADM 81-1166, U.S. Government Printing Office.

Cohen-Sandler, R., Berman, A. L., & King, R. A. (1982). A follow-up study of hospitalized suicidal children. *Journal of the American Academy of Child Psychiatry, 21*(4), 398–403.

Cole, D. A. (1989). Psychopathology of adolescent suicide: Hopelessness, coping beliefs, and depression. *Journal of Abnormal Psychology, 98,* 248–255.

Cole, N. S. (1995, January 11). Reacting to the bell curve. *Education Week,* pp. 29–32.

Coleman, J. C. (1978). Current contradictions in adolescent theory. *Journal of Youth and Adolescence, 7,* 1–11.

Coleman, J. S. (1961). *The adolescent society.* New York: Free Press.

Coleman, J. S., & Hoffer, T. (1987). *Public and private high schools: The impact of communities.* New York: Basic Books.

Coleman, J. S., Kilgore, S. B., & Hoffer, T. (1982). Public and private schools. *Society, 19*(2), 4–9.

Coleman, M., Ganong, L. H., & Ellis, P. (1985). Family structure and dating behavior of adolescents. *Adolescence, 20,* 537–543.

Collins, W. A., & Repinski, D. J. (1994). Relationships during adolescence: Continuity and change in interpersonal perspective. In R. Montemayor, G. R. Adams, & T. P. Gullotta (Eds.), *Personal relationships during adolescence* (pp. 7–36). Thousand Oaks, CA: Sage.

Collins, W. A., & Russell, G. (1991). Mother–child and father–child relationships in middle childhood and adolescence: A developmental analysis. *Developmental Review, 11,* 99–136.

Collins, W. A., Gleason, T., & Sesma, A., Jr. (1997). Internalization, autonomy, and relationships: Development during adolescence. In J. E. Grusec & L. Kuczynski (Eds.), *Parenting and children's internalization of values.* New York: Wiley.

Collum, J., & Pike, G. (1976). The borderline and the addict lifestyle. *Drug Forum, 5,* 39–44.

Coltrane, S., & Ishii-Kuntz, M. (1992). Men's housework: A life course perspective. *Journal of Marriage and the Family, 54,* 43–57.

Comas-Diaz, L. (1992). The future of psychotherapy with ethnic minorities. *Psychotherapy, 29,* 88–94.

Comerci, G. D. (1986). Preface. *Seminars in Adolescent Medicine, 2,* i–ii.

Compas, B. E., Connor, J., & Wadsworth, M. (1997). Prevention of depression. In R. P. Weissberg, T. P Gullotta, R. L. Hampton, B. A. Ryan, & G. R. Adams (Eds.), *Healthy children 2010: Enhancing children's wellness,* (pp. 129–174). Thousand Oaks, Ca: Sage.

Comstock, G., & Strasburger, V. C. (1993). Media violence: Q&A. *Adolescent Medicine, 4*(3), 495–509.

Comuzzie, A. G., & Allison, D. B. (1998). The search for human obesity genes. *Science, 280,* 1374–1377.

Congressional Budget Office (1980). *Improving youth employment prospects.* Washington, DC: U.S. Superintendent of Documents.

Congressional Budget Office (1993). *The federal role in improving elementary and secondary education.* Washington, DC: U.S. Government Printing Office.

Connally, L. (1978). Boy fathers. *Human Behavior, 7,* 40–43.

Connell, J. P., Halpern-Felsher, B. L., Clifford, E., Crichlow, W., & Usinger, P. (1995). Hanging in there: Behavioral, psychological, and contextual factors affecting whether African American adolescents stay in high school. *Journal of Adolescent Research, 10,* 41–63.

Conway, A., & Bogdan, C. (1977). Sexual delinquency: The persistence of a double standard. *Crime and Delinquency, 23,* 131–135.

Conye, R. K. (1991). Gains in primary prevention: Implications for the counseling profession. *Journal of Counseling and Development, 69,* 277–279.

Cooksey, E. C. (1997). Consequences of young mother's marital histories for children's cognitive development. *Journal of Marriage and the Family, 59,* 245–262.

Cooper, C. R. (1994). Cultural perspectives on continuity and change in adolescents' relationships. In R. Montemayor, G. R. Adams, & T. P. Gullotta (Eds.), *Personal relationships during adolescence* (pp. 78–100). Thousand Oaks, CA: Sage.

Cooper, C. R., & Grotevant, H. D. (1987). Gender issues in the interface of family experience and adolescents' friendship and dating identity. *Journal of Youth and Adolescence, 16,* 247–264.

Cooper, C. R., Grotevant, H. D., & Condon, S. M. (1983). Individuality and connectedness in the family as a context for adolescent identity formation and role-taking skill. In H. D. Grotevant & C. R. Cooper (Eds.), *Adolescent development in the family: New directions in child development* (No. 22). San Francisco: Jossey–Bass.

Cooper, J., & Mackie, D. (1986). Video games and aggression in children. *Journal of Applied Social Psychology, 16,* 726–744.

Copeland, E. P., & Hess, R. S. (1995). Differences in young adolescents' coping strategies based on gender and ethnicity. *Journal of Early Adolescence, 15,* 203–219.

Corey, L., & Holmes, K. K. (1983). Genital herpes virus infections: Current concepts in diagnosis, therapy, and prevention. *Annals of Internal Medicine, 98*, 973–983.

Corgrove, A., Zirinsky, L., Block, D., & Weston, D. (1995). Secondary prevention of attempted suicide in adolescence. *Journal of Adolescence, 18*(5), 569–577.

Cornwell, G. T., Eggebeen, D. J., & Meschke, L. L. (1996). The changing family context of early adolescence. *Journal of Early Adolescence, 16*, 141–156.

Cost of Teen Pregnancy Put at $7 Billion a Year (1996, June 19). *Education Week*, p. 4.

Costa, F. M., Jessor, R., Donovan, J. E., & Fortenberry, J. D. (1995). Early initiation of sexual intercourse: The influence of psychosocial unconventionality. *Journal of Research on Adolescence, 5*(1), 93–121.

Cote, J. E. (1996). Sociological perspectives on identity formation: The culture-identity link and identity capital. *Journal of adolescence, 19*, 417–428.

Cote, J. E., & Allahar, A. L. (1994). *Generation on hold: Coming of age in the late twentieth century*. Toronto: Stoddart.

Cotton, N. S. (1979). The familial incidence of alcoholism. *Journal of Studies on Alcohol, 40*, 89–116.

Coupey, S. M. (1997). Barbiturates. *Pediatric Review, 18*, 260–264.

Cowen, E. L. (1982a). Help is where you find it: Four informal helping groups. *American Psychologist, 37*, 385–395.

Cowen, E. L. (1982b). Primary prevention research: Barriers, needs and opportunities. *Journal of Primary Prevention, 2*, 131–137.

Craig, R. J. (1986). The personality structure of heroin addicts. In S. I. Szara (Ed.), *Neurobiology of behavioral control in drug abuse*. Washington, DC: NIDA Research Monograph No. 74, ADM 85-1506, U.S. Government Printing Office.

Craig-Bray, L., Adams, G. R., & Dobson, W. R. (1988). Identity formation and social relations during late adolescence. *Journal of Youth and Adolescence, 17*, 173–187.

Crespi, T. D., & Rigazio-DiGilio (1996). Adolescent homicide and family pathology: Implications for research and

treatment with adolescents. *Adolescence, 31*(122), 353–367.

Crockett, L., Losoff, M., & Petersen, A. C. (1984). Perceptions of the peer group and friendship in early adolescence. *Journal of Early Adolescence, 4*(2), 155–181.

Crook, T., & Eliot, J. (1980). Parental death during childhood and adult depression: A critical review of the literature. *Psychological Bulletin, 87*(2), 252–259.

Cross, J. H., & Allen, J. G. (1970). Ego identity status, adjustment, and academic achievement. *Journal of Consulting and Clinical Psychology, 34*, 288.

Cross, W. E. (1971). The Negro-to-Black conversion experience. *Black World, 20*, 13–17.

Crossman, S. M., Shea, J. A., & Adams, G. R. (1980). Effects of parental divorce during early childhood on ego development and identity formation of college students. *Journal of Divorce, 3*, 263–272.

Crouter, A. C., & Crowley, M. S. (1990). School-age children's time alone with fathers in single- and dual-earner families: Implications for the father-child relationship. *Journal of Early Adolescence, 10*, 296–312.

Crouter, A. C., Manke, B. A., & McHale, S. M. (1995). The family context of gender intensification in early adolescence. *Child Development, 66*, 317–329.

Crumley, F. E. (1982). The adolescent suicide attempt: A cardinal symptom of a serious psychiatric disorder. *American Journal of Psychotherapy, 36*(2), 158–165.

Crumley, F. E. (1990). Substance abuse and adolescent suicide. *Journal of the American Medical Association, 263*, 3051–3056.

Cubberley, E. P. (1934). *Public education in the United States* (2nd ed.). Boston: Houghton Mifflin.

Culp, A. M., Clyman, M. M., & Culp, R. E. (1995). Adolescent depressed mood, reports of suicide attempts, and asking for help. *Adolescence, 30*(120), 828–837.

Cunningham, M. R. (1986). Measuring the physical in physical attractiveness: Quasi-experiments on the sociobiology of female facial beauty. *Journal of*

Personality and Social Psychology, 50, 925–935.

Curran, J. W., Morgan, W. M., Hardy, A. M., Jaffe, H. W., Darrow, W. W., & Dowdle, W. R. (1985). The epidemiology of AIDS: Current status and future prospects. *Science, 229*, 1352–1357.

Curtis, T. (1992). Possible origin of AIDS. *Science, 256*, 1260.

Cutrona, C. E., Halvorson, M. B. J., & Russell, D. W. (1996). Mental health services for rural children, youth, and their families. In C. A. Heflinger & C. T. Nixon (Eds.), *Families and the mental health system for children and adolescents: Policy services and research* (pp. 217–237). Thousand Oaks, CA: Sage.

Cvetkovich, G. (1975). On the psychology of adolescent use of contraception. *Journal of Sex Research, 11*, 256–270.

Dalton, P. (1996, August 5–11). When play is no fun. *Washington Post National Weekly Edition, 13*(41), p. 22.

Damon, W. (1983). *Social and personality development: Infancy through adolescence*. New York: Norton.

Daniel, W. A. (1983). Pubertal changes in adolescence. In J. Brooks-Gunn & A. C. Petersen (Eds.), *Girls at puberty*. New York: Plenum.

Daniels, D., & Moos, R. H. (1990). Assessing life stressors and social resources among adolescents: Applications to depressed youth. *Journal of Adolescent Research, 5*, 268–289.

Danish, S. J. (1997). Going for the goal: In G. W. Albee, & T. P. Gullotta (Eds.), *Primary prevention works* (pp. 291–312). Thousand Oaks, CA: Sage.

Danish, S., Nellen, V., & Owens, S. (1996). Teaching life skills through sport: Community-based programs for adolescents. In J. Van Raalte & B. Brewer (Eds.), *Exploring sport and exercise psychology* (pp. 205–225). Washington, DC: American Psychological Association.

Danish, S. J., Petitpas, A. J., & Hale, B. D. (1990). Sport as a context for developing competence. In T. P. Gullotta, G. R. Adams, & R. Montemayor (Eds.), *Developing social competency in adolescence*. Newbury Park, CA: Sage.

Darling-Hammond, L. (1990). Achieving our goals: Superficial or structural reforms? *Phi Delta Kappan, 72*, 286–295.

Darwin, C. (1859). *On the origin of the species*. London: England.

Dash, L. (1996). *Rosa Lee: A mother and her family in urban America*. New York: Basic Books.

D'Augelli, A. R. (1993). Preventing mental health problems among lesbian and gay college students. *Journal of Primary Prevention, 13*, 245–262.

Daugherty, R., & Leukefeld, C. (1998). *Preventing alcohol and drug problems across the life span*. New York: Plenum.

Davidson, J., & Grant, C. (1988). Growing up hard in the AIDS area. *Maternal Child Care Nursing, 13*, 352–356.

Davidson, L., & Gould, M. S. (1989). Contagion as a risk factor for youth suicide. In *Report of the secretary's task force on youth suicide: Risk factors for youth suicide* (Vol. 2). Washington, DC: U.S. Department of Health and Human Services publication ADM 89-1622, U.S. Government Printing Office.

Davidson, L. E., Rosenberg, M. L., Mercy, J. A., Franklin, J., & Simmons, J. T. (1989). An epidemiologic study of risk factors in two teenage suicide clusters. *Journal of the American Medical Association, 262*, 2687–2692.

Davis, K. (1940). The sociology of parent-youth conflict. American *Sociological Review, 5*, 523–525.

Davis, L. L. (1984). Clothing and human behavior: A review. *Home Economics Research Journal, 12*, 325–339.

Dawkins, M. P. (1997). Drug use and violent crime among adolescents. *Adolescence, 32*, 395–405.

Day, R. D. (1992). The transition to the first intercourse among racially and culturally diverse youth. *Journal of Marriage and the Family, 54*(4), 749–762.

DeAmicis, L. A., Klorman, R., Hess, I. W., & McAnarney, E. R. (1981). A comparison of unwed pregnant teenagers and sexually active adolescents seeking contraceptives. *Adolescence, 16*(61), 11–19.

de Anda, D., Becerra, R. M., & Fielder, E. (1990). In their own words: The life experiences of Mexican-American and White pregnant adolescents and adolescent mothers. *Child and Adolescent Social Work, 7*, 301–318.

DeLeon, G., & Rosenthal, M. S. (1979). Therapeutic communities. In R. Dupont, A. Goldstein, & J. O'Donnell (Eds.), *Handbook on drug abuse*. Washington, DC: U.S. Government Printing Office.

Delgado-Gaitan, C. (1988). The value of conformity: Learning to stay in school. *Anthropology & Education Quarterly, 19*, 355–381.

de Mause, L. (ed.) (1974). *The history of childhood*. NY: Atcom.

Dembo, M. H., & Lundell, B. (1979). Factors affecting adolescent contraceptive practices: Implications for sex education. *Adolescence, 14*, 657–665.

Demetriou, A., & Efklides, A. (Eds.) (1994). *Advances in psychology: Intelligence, mind and reasoning: Structure and development* (Vol. 106). Amsterdam: North–Holland.

Demo, D. H. (1992). Parent–child relations: Assessing recent changes. *Journal of Marriage and the Family, 54*, 104–117.

Denison, M. E., Paredes, A., & Booth, J. B. (1997). Cocaine *Recent Developments in Alcohol, 13*, 283–303.

DeQuincey, T. (1856/1950) *Confessions of an English Opium-Eater*. New York: Heritage Press.

DeSantis, J. P., Ketterlinus, R. D., & Youniss, J. (1990). Black adolescents' concerns that they are academically able. *Merrill–Palmer Quarterly, 36*, 287–299.

DeSimone, A., Murray, P., and Lester, D. (1994). Alcohol use, self-esteem, depression, and suicidality in high school students. *Adolescence, 29*(116), 939–942.

Deutsch, M., Katz, I., & Jensen, A. R. (1968). *Social class, race, and psychological development*. New York: Holt, Rinehart & Winston.

DeVall, E., Stoneman, Z., & Brody, G. (1986). The impacts of divorce and maternal employment on pre-adolescent children. *Family Relations, 35*, 153–159.

Devlin, B., Daniels, M., & Roeder, K. (1997). The heritability of IQ. *Nature, 388*, 468–471.

deWit, H., & McCracken, S. G. (1990). Preference for ethanol in males with or without an alcoholic first degree relative. In L. S. Harris (Ed.), *Problems of drug dependence: 1989*. Washington, DC: U.S. Department of Health and Human Services publication ADM 90-1663, U.S. Government Printing Office.

Diaz-Guerrero, R. (1987). Historical sociocultural premises and ethnic socialization. In J. S. Phinney & M. J. Rotheram (Eds.), *Children's ethnic socialization: Pluralism and development*. Newbury Park, CA: Sage.

Dick, T. (1847). *On the mental illumination and moral improvement of mankind*. Hartford, CT: Sumner & Goodman.

Dickens, C. (1843/1967). *A Christmas carol*. New York: Heinemann.

Dickens, C. (1859/1893). *A tale of two cities*. Boston, MA: Houghton Mifflin.

Dickinson, G. (1978). Adolescent sex information sources: 1964–1974. *Adolescence, 13*, 653–658.

DiClemente, R. J. (1993). Confronting the challenge of AIDS among adolescents: Directions for future research. *Journal of Adolescent Research, 8*, 156–166.

Diegmueller, K. (1996, May 22). To stem violence, Alaska puts hockey on 1-year probation. *Education Week*, p. 8.

Dion, K. K., & Stein, S. (1978). Physical attractiveness and interpersonal influence. *Journal of Experimental Social Psychology, 14*, 97–108.

Doherty, W. J., Kouneski, E. F., & Erickson, M. F. (1998). Responsible fathering: An overview and conceptual framework. *Journal of Marriage and the Family, 60*, 277–292.

Donnelly, M. (1995). Depression among adolescents in northern Ireland. *Adolescence, 30*(118), 339–350.

Donovan, J. M. (1975a). Identity status and interpersonal style. *Journal of Youth and Adolescence, 4*, 37–56.

Donovan, J. M. (1975b). Identity status: Its relationship to Rorschach performance and to daily life patterns. *Adolescence, 10*, 29–44.

Dornbusch, S. M., Ritter, P. L., Mont-Reynaud, R., & Chen, Z. (1990). Family decision making and academic performance in a diverse high school population. *Journal of Adolescent Research*, *5*, 143–160.

Douvan, E. (1963). Employment and the adolescent. In F. Nye & L. Hoffman (Eds.), *The employed mother in America*. Chicago: Rand–McNally.

Douvan, E., & Gold, M. (1966). Model patterns in American adolescence. In L. M. Hoffman (Ed.), *Review of child development research* (Vol. 2). New York: Russell Sage Foundation.

Dowden, S. L., Calvert, R. D., Davis, L., & Gullotta, T. P. (1997). Improving access to health care: School-based health centers. In R. P. Weissberg, T. P. Gullotta, R. L. Hampton, B. A. Ryan, & G. R. Adams, (Eds.), *Establishing preventive services* (pp. 154–182). Thousand Oaks, CA: Sage.

Dowell, L. J. (1970). Environmental factors of childhood competitive athletics. *Physical Educator*, *27*, 17–21.

Dowling, C. G. (1987). *Teenage mothers: Seventeen years later*. New York: The Commonwealth Fund.

Downs, A. C. (1990). The social biological constructs of social competency. In T. P. Gullotta, G. R. Adams, & R. Montemayor (Eds.), *Developing social competency in adolescence*. Newbury Park, CA: Sage.

Downs, A. C., & Hillje, L. S. (1993). Historical and theoretical perspectives on adolescent sexuality: An overview. In T. P. Gullotta, G. R. Adams, & R. Montemayor (Eds.), *Adolescent sexuality*. Newbury Park, CA: Sage.

Drewnowski, A., Hopkins, S. A., & Kessler, R. C. (1988). The prevalence of bulimia nervosa in the U.S. college student population. *American Journal of Public Health*, *78*, 1322–1325.

Dryfoos, J. G. (1990). *Adolescents at risk: Prevalence and prevention*. New York: Oxford University Press.

Dryfoos, J. G. (1998). *Safe passage: Making it through adolescence in a risky society*. New York: Oxford University Press.

Dryfoos, J. G. (1999). School-based health and social service centers. In T. P. Gullotta, R. L. Hampton, B. A. Ryan, G. R. Adams, and R. P. Weissberg (Eds.), *Child*

health care: Issues for the year 2000 and beyond. Thousand Oaks, CA: Sage.

DuBois, D. L., & Hirsch, B. J. (1990). School and neighborhood friendship patterns of Blacks and Whites in early adolescence. *Child Development*, *61*, 524–536.

Duncan, D. F. (1992). Drug abuse prevention in postlegalization America: What could it be like? *Journal of Primary Prevention*, *12*, 317–322.

Duncan, D. F., & Petosa, R. (1995). Social and community factors associated with drug use and abuse among adolescents. In T. P. Gullota, G. R. Adams, & R. Montemayor (Eds.), *Substance misuse in adolescence*. Thousand Oaks, CA: Sage.

Dunphy, D. C. (1963). The social structure of urban adolescent peer groups. *Sociometry*, *26*, 230–246.

Dupold, J., & Young, D. (1979). Empirical studies of adolescent sexual behavior: A critical review. *Adolescence*, *14*, 45–63.

DuRant, R. H., Getts, A. G., Cadenhead, C., and Woods, E. R. (1995). The association between weapon-carrying and the use of violence among adolescents living in or around public housing. *Journal of Adolescence*, *18*, 579–592.

Durbin, D. L., Darling, N., Steinberg, L., & Brown, B. B. (1993). Parenting style and peer group membership among European-American adolescents. *Journal of Research on Adolescence*, *3*, 87–100.

Durkheim, E. (1897/1951). *Suicide: A sociological study*. New York: Free Press.

Durkheim, E. (1958). *The rules of sociological method* (S. A. Solovay & J. H. Mueller, translators). New York: Free Press.

Durlak, J. A., & Wells, A. M. (1997). Primary prevention of mental health programs for children and adolescents: A meta-analytic review. *American Journal of Community Psychology*, *25*, 115–152.

Dyk, P. H. (1993). How are rural families and youth "at risk"? Paper presented at the National Council on Family Relations, Baltimore, MD, November 14, 1993.

Eagly, A. H. (1987). *Sex differences in social behavior: A social role interpretation*. Hillsdale, NJ: Erlbaum.

Eagly, A. H., & Carli, L. L. (1981). Sex of researchers and sex-typed communications as determinants of sex differences in influenceability. *Psychological Bulletin*, *90*, 1–20.

Eagly, A. H., Ashmore, R. D., Makhijani, M. G., & Longo, L. C. (1991). What is beautiful is good, but. . . : A meta-analytic review of research on the physical attractiveness stereotype. *Psychological Bulletin*, *110*, 109–128.

Earls, C. M., & David, H. (1990). Early family and sexual experiences of male and female prostitutes. *Canada's Mental Health*, *38*, 7–11.

Earls, F., & Siegel, B. (1980). Precocious fathers. *American Journal of Orthopsychiatry*, *50*, 469–488.

East, P. L. (1989). Early adolescents' perceived interpersonal risks and benefits: Relations to social support and psychological functioning. *Journal of Early Adolescence*, *9*, 374–395.

Eberly, D. J. (1991). Education cost put at $308 billion in 1987–88. Washington, DC: National youth service, National Service Secretariat (1987, August 23). *New York Times*, 18.

Eddy, J. M., & Gribskov, L. S. (1998). Juvenile justice and delinquency prevention in the United States: The influence of theories and traditions on policies and practices. In T. P. Gullotta, G. R. Adams, & R. Montemayor (Eds.), *Delinquent violent youth* (pp. 12–52) Thousand Oaks, CA: Sage.

Egeland, J. A., Gerhard, D. S., Pauls, D. L., Kidd, K. K., Allen, C. R., Hostetter, A. M., & Housman, D. E. (1987). Bipolar affective disorders linked to DNA markers on chromosome 11. *Nature*, *325*, 783–787.

Ehrenberg, M. F., Cox, D. N., & Koopman, R. F. (1990). The prevalence of depression in high school students. *Adolescence*, *25*, 905–912.

Eicher, J. B., Baizerman, S., & Michelman, J. (1991). Adolescent dress. II. A qualitative study of suburban high school students. *Adolescence*, *26*, 679–686.

Eisikovts, Z., & Sagi, A. (1982). Moral development and discipline encounter in delinquent and nondelinquent adolescents. *Journal of Youth and Adolescence*, *11*, 217–230.

Elders, J. (1994). Personal communication.

Elders, J., & Chanoff, D. (1996). *Joycelyn Elders*. New York: Morrow.

Elias, M. J. (1997). Reinterpreting dissemination of prevention programs as widespread implementation with effectiveness and fidelity. In R. P. Weissberg, T. P. Gullotta, R. L. Hampton, B. A. Ryan, & G. R. Adams (Eds.), *Establishing preventive services* (pp. 253–289). Thousand Oaks, CA: Sage.

Elkind, D. (1967). Egocentrism in adolescence. *Child Development*, *38*, 1025–1034.

Elkind, D. (1981). *The hurried child: Growing up too fast too soon*. Reading, MA: Addison–Wesley.

Elliot, D. S., Voss, H. L., & Wendling, A. (1966). Capable dropouts and the social milieu of the high school. *Journal of Educational Research*, *60*, 181–185.

Elliott, G. R., & Eisdorfer, C. (Eds.) (1982). *Stress and human health: Analysis and implications of research*. New York: Springer-Verlag.

Elster, A. B., Ketterlinus, R., & Lamb, M. E. (1990). Association between parenthood and problem behavior in a national sample of adolescents. *Pediatrics*, *85*, 1044–1049.

Emshoff, J., Avery, E., Raduka, G., Anderson, D. J., and Calvert, C. (1996). Findings from SuperStars: A health promotion program for families to enhance multiple protective factors. *Journal of Adolescent Research*, *11*(1), 68–96.

Epstein, S., & Meier, P. (1989). Constructive thinking: A broad coping variable with specific components. *Journal of Personality and Social Psychology*, *57*, 232–350.

Erikson, E. H. (1954). Eight stages of man. In W. E. Martin & C. B. Standler (Eds.), *Readings in child development*. New York: Harcourt, Brace, Jovanovich.

Erikson, E. H. (1959). *Identity and life styles: Selected papers* (Psychological Issues Monograph Series I, No. 1). New York: International Universities Press.

Erikson, E. H. (1965). *The challenge of youth*. New York: Norton.

Erikson, E. H. (1968). *Identity: Youth and crisis*. New York: Norton.

Erikson, K. (1966). *Wayward Puritans*. New York: Wiley.

Eron, L., Walder, L. O., & Lefkowitz, M. M. (1971). *Learning of aggression in children*. Boston: Little, Brown.

Eskilson, A., Wiley, G., Muehlbauer, G., & Doder, L. (1986). Parental pressure, self-esteem and adolescent reported deviance: Bending the twig too far. *Adolescence*, *21*, 501–515.

Eyberse, W., Maffuid, J., & Blau, G. M. (1996). New directions for service delivery: Home-based services. In G. M. Blau & T. P. Gullotta (Eds.), *Adolescent dysfunctional behavior* (pp. 247–266). Thousand Oaks, CA: Sage.

Faenza, M. M., Glover, R. W., Hutchings, G. P., & Radack, J. A. (1999). Mental illness and violence. In T. P. Gullotta & S. McElhaney (Eds.), *Understanding violent behavior: Intervention and prevention*. Thousand Oaks, CA: Sage.

Fagan, J., Piper, E., & Moore, M. (1986). Violent delinquents and urban youths. *Criminology*, *24*, 439–468.

Fairburn, C. G., & Beglin, S. J. (1990). Studies of the epidemiology of bulimia nervosa. *American Journal of Psychiatry*, *147*, 401–408.

Farber, M. L. (1968). *Theory of suicide*. New York: Funk & Wagnalls.

Farber, N. B. (1991). The process of pregnant resolution among adolescent mothers. *Adolescence*, *26*, 697–716.

Farberow, N. L. (1989). Preparatory and prior suicidal behavior factors. In *Report of the secretary's task force on youth suicide: Vol. 2: Risk factors for youth suicide*. Washington, DC: U.S. Department of Health and Human Services publication ADM 89-1622, U.S. Government Printing Office.

Farrington, D. P. (1983). Offending from 10 to 25 years of age. In K. Van Dvaen & S. Mednick (Eds.), *Prospective studies of crime and delinquence*. Boston, MA: Kluwer-Nighoff.

Farrington, D. P. (1990). Implications of criminal career research for the prevention of offending. *Journal of Adolescence*, *13*, 93–113.

Fast, I., & Cain, A. C. (1966). The stepparent role: Potential for disturbances in family functioning. *American Journal of Orthopsychiatry*, *36*, 485–491.

Faust, M. S. (1977). Somatic development of adolescent girls. *Monographs of the Society for Research in Child Development*, *42*(1, Serial No. 169).

Faust, M. S. (1983). Alternative constructions of adolescent growth. In J. Brooks-Gunn & A. C. Petersen (Eds.), *Girls at puberty*. New York: Plenum.

Fejgin, N. (1994). Participation in high school sports: A subversion of school mission or contribution to academic goals? *Sociology of Sport Journal*, *11*, 211–230.

Feldman, S. S., & Quatman, T. (1988). Factors influencing age expectations for adolescent autonomy: A study of early adolescents and parents. *Journal of Early Adolescence*, *8*, 325–343.

Felice, L. G. (1981). Black student dropout behavior: Disengagement from school rejection and racial discrimination. *Journal of Negro Education*, *50*, 415–424.

Felker, K. R., & Stivers, C. (1994). The relationship of gender and family environment to eating disorder risk in adolescents. *Adolescence*, *29*(116), 821–834.

Fenwick, E., & Walker, R. (1994). *How sex works*. New York: Dorling Kindersley.

Ferrier, P. E., Ferrier, S. A., & Neilson, J. (1970). Chromosome study of a group of male juvenile delinquents. *Pediatric Research*, *4*, 205.

Fillmore, K. M. (1974). Drinking and problem drinking in early adulthood and middle age: An exploratory 20-year follow-up study. *Quarterly Journal of Studies on Alcohol*, *35*, 819–840.

Fine, M. A., & Kurdek, L. A. (1992). The adjustment of adolescents in stepfather and stepmother families. *Journal of Marriage and the Family*, *54*, 725–736.

Fine, M. A., McKenry, P. C., Donnelly, B. W., & Voydanoff, P. (1992). Perceived adjustment of parents and children: Variations by family structure, race, and gender. *Journal of Marriage and the Family*, *54*, 118–127.

Fine, M. A., Donnelly, B. W., & Voydanoff, P. (1991). The relation between adolescents' perceptions of their family lives and their adjustment in stepfather families. *Journal of Adolescent Research, 6*, 423–436.

Finkel, M. L., & Finkel, J. J. (1978). Male adolescent contraceptive utilization. *Adolescence, 13*, 443–451.

Finkelhor, D., Hotaling, G., & Sedlak, A. (1990). *Missing, abducted, runaway, and throwaway children in America*. Washington, DC: U.S. Department of Justice, U.S. Government Printing Office.

Fischer, J. L. (1981). Transitions in relationship style from adolescence to young adulthood. *Journal of Youth and Adolescence, 10*, 11–24.

Fischer, P., & Shaffer, D. (1990). Facts about adolescent suicide: A review of national mortality statistics and recent research. In M. J. Rotherham-Borus, J. Bradley, & N. Obolensky (Eds.), *Planning to live*. Tulsa, OK: National Resource Center for Youth Services.

Fischer, P., Richards, J. W., Berman, E. J., & Krugman, D. M. (1989). Recall and eye tracking study of adolescents viewing tobacco advertisements. *Journal of the American Medical Association, 261*, 84–89.

Fisher, T. D. (1989). An extension of the findings of Moore, Peterson, and Furstenberg (1986) regarding family sexual communication and adolescent sexual behavior. *Journal of Marriage and the Family, 51*, 637–639.

Fitch, S. A., & Adams, G. R. (1981, April). The identity-intimacy process revisited. Paper presented at the meeting of the Society for Research in Child Development, Boston.

Fitch, S. A., & Adams, G. R. (1983). Ego-identity and intimacy status: Replication and extension. *Developmental Psychology, 19*, 839–845.

Flannery, D., Huff, R., & Manos, M. (1998). Youth gangs. In T. P. Gullotta, G. R. Adams, & R. Montemayor (Eds.), *Delinquent violent youth* (pp. 175–204) Thousand Oaks, CA: Sage.

Flannery, D. J., Vazsonyi, A. T., & Rowe, D. C. (1996). Caucasian and Hispanic early adolescent substance use: Parenting, personality, and school adjustment. *Journal of Early Adolescence, 16*, 71–89.

Flewelling, R. L., & Bauman, K. E. (1990). Family structure as a predictor of initial substance use and sexual intercourse in early adolescence. *Journal of Marriage and the Family, 52*, 171–181.

Flygare, T. J. (1978). The Supreme Court approves corporal punishment. *Phi Delta Kappan, 59*, 347–348. .

Flynn, J. R. (1987). Massive IQ gains in 14 nations: What IQ tests really measure. *Psychological Bulletin, 101*, 171–191.

Forgarty, R. (1998). The intelligence friendly classroom. *Phi Delta Kappan, 79*, 665–667.

Ford, M. E. (1992). *Motivating humans: goals, emotions, and personal agency beliefs*. Newbury Park, CA: Sage.

Ford, M. E., & Tisak, M. S. (1983). A further search for social intelligence. *Journal of Educational Psychology, 75*, 196–206.

Forehand, R., McCombs, A., Long, N., Brody, G., & Fauber, R. (1988). Early adolescent adjustment to recent parental divorce: The role of interparental conflict and adolescent sex as mediating variables. *Journal of Consulting and Clinical Psychology, 56*, 624–627.

Forrest, J. D., & Singh, S. (1990). The sexual and reproductive behavior of American women, 1982–1988. *Family Planning Perspectives, 22*, 206–214.

Foshee, V., & Bauman, K. E. (1994). Parental attachment and adolescent cigarette smoking initiation. *Journal of Adolescent Research, 9*(1), 88–104.

Fowers, B. J., & Richardson, F. C. (1996). Why is multiculturalism good? *American Psychologist, 51*, 609–621.

Fox, C. H. (1992). Posssible origin of AIDS. *Science, 256*, 1259–1260.

Fox, J. A. (1996, March). *Trends in juvenile violence: A report to the United States Attorney General on current and future rates of juvenile offending*. Washington, DC: Bureau of Justice Statistics, Department of Justice, U.S. Government Printing Office.

Fox, K. R., Page, A., Peters, D. M., Armstrong, N., & Kirby, A. B. (1994). Dietary restraint and fatness in early adolescent girls and boys. *Journal of Adolescence, 17*(2), 149–161.

Foxcroft, D. R., & Lowe, G. (1995). Adolescent drinking, smoking and other substance use involvement. Links with perceived family life. Journal of *Adolescence, 18*(2), 159–177.

Frank, E. S. (1991). Shame and guilt in eating disorders. *American Journal of Orthopsychiatry, 61*, 303–306.

Frank, S. J., McLaughlin, A. M., & Crusco, A. (1984). Sex role attributes, symptom distress, and defensive style among college men and women. *Journal of Personality and Social Psychology, 47*, 182–192.

Franklin, C., Grant, D., Corcoran, J., Miller, P. O., & Bultman, L. (1997). Effectiveness of prevention programs for adolescent pregnancy: A meta-analysis. *Journal of Marriage and the Family, 59*, 551–567.

Franklin, D. (1988). Race, class, and adolescent pregnancy: An ecological analysis. *American Journal of Psychotherapy, 58*, 339–354.

Frauenglass, S., Routh, D. K., Pantin, H. M., & Mason, C. A. (1997). Family support decreases influence of deviant peers on hispanic adolescents' substance use. *Journal of Clinical Child Psychology, 26*, 15–23.

Freeman, E. W., Rickels, K., Huggins, G. R., Mudd, E. H., Garcia, C. R., & Dickens, H. O. (1980). Adolescent contraceptive use: Comparisons of male and female attitudes and information. *American Journal of Public Health, 70*, 790–796.

Freilino, M. K., & Hummel, R. (1985). Achievement and identity in college-age U.S. adult women students. *Journal of Youth and Adolescence, 14*, 1–10.

Freischlag, J., & Schmidke, C. (1979). Violence in sports: Its causes and some solutions. *Physical Educator, 36*, 182–185.

Freud, A. (1958). Adolescence. In A. Freud (Ed.), *The psychoanalytic study of the child*. New York: International Universities Press.

Freud, S. (1933). *New introductory lectures on psychoanalysis.* London: Hogarth Press.

Freud, S. (1953). *A general introduction to psychoanalysis.* New York: Permabooks.

Freud, S. (1957). Mourning and melancholia. In J. Strachey (Ed. and Trans.), *The standard edition of the complete psychological works of Sigmund Freud* (Vol. 14). London: Hogarth Press.

Freud, S. (1959). *Sigmund Freud: Collected papers.* New York: Basic Books.

Friedman, J., Mann, F., & Adelman, H. (1976). Juvenile street gangs: The victimization of youth. *Adolescence, 11,* 527–533.

Friedman, L. M. (1993). *Crime and punishment in American history.* New York: Basic Books.

Frisch, R. E. (1983). Fatness, puberty, and fertility: The effects of nutrition and physical training on menarche and ovulation. In J. Brooks-Gunn and A. C. Petersen (Eds.), *Girls at puberty.* New York: Plenum.

Frisch, R. E., & Revelle, R. (1971). Height and weight at menarche and a hypothesis of menarche. *Archive of Disease in Childhood, 46,* 695.

Funk, J. B. (1993). Video games. *Adolescent Medicine, 4*(3), 589–598.

Furstenberg, F. F., Jr. (1970). Premarital pregnancy among black teenagers. *Transaction, 7,* 52–55.

Furstenberg, F. F., Jr. (1976). The social consequences of teenage parenthood. *Family Planning Perspectives, 8,* 148–164.

Furstenberg, F. F., Jr. Allison, P. D., & Morgan, S. P. (1987). Paternal participation and children's well-being after marital dissolution. *American Sociological Reveiw, 52,* 695–701.

Furstenberg, F. F., Jr., Brooks-Gunn, J., & Morgan, S. P. (1987). Adolescent mothers and their children in later life. *Family Planning Perspectives, 19,* 142–152.

Furstenberg, F. F., Jr., Morgan, S. P., Moore, K. A., & Peterson, J. L. (1987). Race differences in timing of first intercourse. *American Sociological Review, 52,* 511–518.

Gage, N. L. (1990). Dealing with the dropout problem. *Phi Delta Kappan, 72,* 280–285.

Galambos, N. L., & Almeida, D. M. (1992). Does parent adolescent conflict increase in early adolescence? *Journal of Marriage and the Family, 54,* 737–747.

Galambos, N. L., Almeida, D. M., & Petersen, A. C. (1990). Masculinity, femininity, and sex role attitudes in early adolescence: Exploring gender intensification. *Child Development, 61,* 1905–1914.

Gardner, H. (1983). *Frames of mind.* New York: Basic Books.

Gardner, H. (1995). Reflections on multipe intelligences: myths and messages. *Phi Delta Kappan, 77,* 200–209.

Gardner, S. E., & Resnick, H. (1996). Violence among youth: Origins and a framework for prevention. In R. L. Hampton, P. Jenkins, & T. P. Gullotta, (Eds.), *Preventing violence in America.* Thousand Oaks, CA: Sage.

Garfinkel, P. E., Moldofsky, H., & Garner, D. M. (1980). The heterogeneity of anorexia nervosa. *Archives of General Psychiatry, 37,* 1036–1040.

Garnets, L., & Kimmel, D. (1991). Lesbian and gay male dimensions in the psychological study of human diversity. In J. D. Goodchilds (Ed.), *Psychological perspectives on human diversity in America* (pp. 143–189). Washington, DC: American Psychological Association.

Garnefski, N., & Arends, E. (1998). Sexual abuse and adolescent mal-adjustment: Differences between male and female victims. *Journal of Adolescence, 21,* 99–107.

Garske, D. (1996). Transforming the culture: Creating safety, equality, and justice for women and girls. In R. L. Hampton, P. Jenkins, & T. P. Gullotta (Eds.), *Preventing violence in America.* Thousand Oaks, CA: Sage.

Garver, L. (1990, June 11). No, you can't have Nintendo. *Newsweek,* 8.

Gavazzi, S. M., & Sabatelli, R. M. (1990). Family systems dynamics, the individuation process and psychosocial development. *Journal of Adolescent Research, 5,* 499–518.

Gawin, F. H. (1991). Cocaine addiction: Psychology and neurophysiology. *Science, 251,* 1580–1586.

Gay, G., Sheppard, C., Inaba, D., & Newmeyer, J. (1973). Cocaine in perspective: "Gift from the gods" to the rich man's drug. *Drug Forum, 2,* 409–430.

Gazzaniga, M. S. (1992). *Nature's mind: The biological roots of thinking, emotions, sexuality, language, and intelligence.* New York: Basic Books.

Ge, X., Conger, R. D., Cadoret, R. J., Neiderhiser, J. M., Yates, W., Troughton, E., & Stewart, M. A. (1996). The developmental interface between nature and nurture: a mutual influence model of child antisocial behavior and parent behaviors. *Developmental Psychology, 32,* 574–589.

Gecas, V. (1982). The self-concept. *Annual Review of Sociology, 8,* 1–33.

General Accounting Office (1989). *Effective school programs* (No. GAO/HRD-89-132BR). Washington, DC: U.S. Government Printing Office.

George, P. (1995). *Japanese secondary schools: A closer look.* Chicago, IL: National Middle School Association.

Gerbner, G., Gross, L., Morgan, M., & Signorielli, N. (1984). Facts, fantasies, and schools. *Society, 21*(6), 9–13.

Gersick, K. E., Grady, K., Sexton, E., & Lyons, M. (1981). Personality and sociodemographic factors in adolescent drug use. In D. J. Lettieri & J. P. Ludford (Eds.), *Drug abuse and the American adolescent.* Washington, DC: NIDA research monograph 38, ADM 81-1166, U.S. Government Printing Office.

Getz, W. L., Allen, D. B., Myers, R. N., & Linder, K. C. (1983). *Brief counseling of suicidal persons.* Lexington, MA: Lexington Books.

Gfellner, B. M. (1994). A matched-group comparison of drug use and problem behavior among Canadian Indian and White adolescents. *Journal of Early Adolescence, 14,* 24–48.

Gibbons, D. C. (1986). Juvenile Delinquency: Can social science find a cure? *Crime and Delinquency, 32,* 186–204.

Gibbons, D. C., & Krohn, M. D. (1986). *Delinquent behavior*. Englewood Cliffs, NJ: Prentice-Hall.

Gibbs, J. T. (1989). Black American adolescents. In J. T. Gibbs (Ed.), *Children of color: Psychological interventions with minority youth* (pp. 179–223). San Francisco: Jossey–Bass.

Gibbs, J. T., & Huang, N. (Eds.). (1989). *Children of color: Psychological interventions with minority youth*. San Francisco: Jossey–Bass.

Gilbert, E. H., & DeBlassie, R. R. (1984). Anorexia nervosa: Adolescent starvation by choice. *Adolescence, 19*, 839–846.

Gilligan, C. (1977). In a different voice: Women's conceptions of self and of morality. *Harvard Educational Review, 47*, 481–517.

Gilligan, C. (1982). *In a different voice: Psychological theory and women's development*. Cambridge, MA: Harvard University Press.

Gilmore, M. R., Lewis, S. M., Lohr, M. J., Spencer, M. S., & White, R. D. (1997). Repeat pregnancies among adolescent mothers. *Journal of Marriage and the Family, 59*, 536–550.

Ginsburg, S. D., & Orlofsky, J. L. (1981). Ego-identity status, ego-development and locus of control in college women. *Journal of Youth and Adolescence, 10*, 297–307.

Gispert, M., Wheeler, K., Marsh, L., & Davis, M. S. (1985). Suicidal adolescents: Factors in evaluation. *Adolescence, 20*, 753–762.

Gjerde, P. F., Block, J., & Block, J. H. (1991). The preschool family context of 18 year olds with depressive symptoms: A prospective study. *Journal of Research on Adolescence, 1*, 63–91.

Glasser, K. (1978). The treatment of depressed and suicidal adolescents. *American Journal of Psychotherapy, 32*, 252–269.

Glasser, K. (1981). Psychopathologic patterns in depressed adolescents. *American Journal of Psychotherapy, 35*(3), 368–382.

Glueck, S., & Glueck, E. T. (1950). *Unraveling juvenile delinquency*. New York: Commonwealth Fund.

Glueck, S., & Glueck, E. T. (1957). Working mothers and delinquency. *Mental Hygiene, 41*, 327–352.

Goetting, A. (1994). The parenting-crime connection. *Journal of Primary Prevention, 14*, 169–186.

Gold, B. D. (1987). Self-image of punk rock and non punk rock juvenile delinquents. *Adolescence, 22*, 535–544.

Gold, M. S., Washton, A. M., & Dackis, C. A. (1985). Cocaine abuse: Neurochemistry, phenomenology, and treatment. In N. J. Kozel & E. H. Adams (Eds.), *Cocaine use in America: Epidemiological and clinical perspectives*. Washington, DC: NIDA Research Monograph 61, ADM 85-1414, U.S. Government Printing Office.

Goldberg, C. (1977). School phobia in adolescence. *Adolescence, 12*, 499–509.

Goldfarb, L. A. (1987). Sexual abuse antecedent to anorexia nervosa, bulimia, and compulsive overeating: Three case reports. *International Journal of Eating Disorders, 6*, 675–680.

Goldman, J. A., Rosenzweig, C. M., & Lutter, A. D. (1980). Effect of similarity of ego identity status on interpersonal attraction. *Journal of Youth and Adolescence, 9*, 153–163.

Goldman, W., & Lewis, P. (1977). Beautiful is good: Evidence that the physically attractive are more socially skillful. *Journal of Experimental Social Psychology, 13*, 125–130.

Goldsmith, S., Gabrielson, M., Gabrielson, I., Matthews, V., & Potts, L. (1972). Teenagers, sex, and contraception. *Family Planning Perspectives, 4*, 32–38.

Goldstein, A., & Kalant, H. (1990). Drug policy: Striking the right balance. *Science, 249*, 1513–1521.

Goldstein, H. S. (1974). Reconstituted families: The second marriage and its children. *Psychiatric Quarterly, 48*, 433–440.

Goldstein, P. J. (1990). Anabolic steroids: An ethnographic approach. In G. C. Lin & L. Erinoff (Eds.), *Anabolic steroid abuse*. Washington, DC: U.S. Department of Health and Human Services publication ADM 91-1720, U.S. Government Printing Office.

Goodlad, J. I. (1984). *A place called School*. New York: McGraw–Hill.

Goodman, E., & Cohall, A. T. (1989). Acquired immunodeficiency syndrome and adolescents: Knowledge, attitudes, and behaviors in a New York City adolescent minority population. *Pediatrics, 84*, 36–42.

Googins, R. (1998). Reflections on delinquency, Dickens, and Twain. In T. P. Gullotta, G. R. Adams, & R. Montemayor (Eds.), *Delinquent violent youth* (pp. 1–11). Thousand Oaks, CA: Sage.

Gordon, E. (1995). Putting them in their place. *Readings, 10*(1), 8–14.

Gorman-Smith, D., Tolan, P. H., Zelli, A., & Huesmann, L. R. (1996). The relation of family functioning to violence among inner-city minority youths. *Journal of Family Psychology, 10*, 115–129.

Gortmaker, S. L., Must, A., Perrin, J. M., Sobol, A. M., & Dietz, W. H. (1993). Social and economic consequences of overweight in adolescence and young adulthood. *New England Journal of Medicine, 329*(14), 1008–1012.

Gottfried, A. E., & Gottfried, A. W. (1988). *Maternal employment and children's development*. New York: Plenum.

Gould, R. E. (1965). Suicide problems in children and adolescents. *American Journal of Psychotherapy, 19*, 228–246.

Grady, S. (1996, December 5). Common sense on legalizing pot. *The Day*, A10.

Greenbaum, P. E., Foster-Johnson, L., & Petrila, A. (1996). Co-occurring addictive and mental disorders among adolescents: Prevalence research and future directions. *American Journal of Orthopsychiatry, 66*(1), 52–60.

Greenberger, E., & Steinberg, L. D. (1981). The workplace as a context for the socialization of youth. *Journal of Youth and Adolescence, 10*(3), 185–210.

Greenberger, E., & Steinberg, L. (1986). *When teenagers work: The psychological and social costs of adolescent employment*. New York: Basic Books.

Greenberger, E., Steinberg, L. D., Vaux, A., & McAuliffe, S. (1980). Adolescents who work: Effects of part-time employment on family and peer relations. *Journal of Youth and Adolescence, 9*(3), 189–202.

Greene, A. L., & Grimsley, M. D. (1990). Age and gender differences in adolescents' preferences for parental advice. *Journal of Adolescent Research, 5,* 396–413.

Greene, A. L., & Wheatley, S. M. (1992). "I've got a lot to do and I don't think I'll have the time": gender differences in late adolescents' narratives of the future. *Journal of Youth and Adolescence, 21,* 667–686.

Greene, J. M., Ennett, S. T., & Ringwalt, C. L. (1997). Substance use among runaway and homeless youth in three national samples. *American Journal of Public Health, 87,* 229–235.

Greenfield, L. A. (1995, March). Weapons offenses and offenders. In *Selected Findings* (pp. 1–8). Washington, DC: NCJ-155284.

Greenfield, P. M., Bruzzone, L., Koyamatsu, K., Satuloff, W., Nixon, K., Brodie, M., & Kingsdale, D. (1987). What is rock music doing to the minds of our youth? A first experimental look at the effects of rock music lyrics and music videos. *Journal of Early Adolescence, 7,* 315–329.

Gregory, L. W. (1995). The "turnaround process": Factors influencing the school success of urban youth. *Journal of Adolescent Research, 10,* 136–154.

Gregory, T. B., & Smith, G. R. (1987). *High schools as communities.* Bloomington, IN: Phi Delta Kappan.

Griffiths, M. D. (1991). Amusement machine playing in childhood and adolescence: A comparative analysis of video games and fruit machines. *Journal of Adolescence, 14,* 53–74.

Grinspoon, L. (1971). *Marijuana reconsidered.* Cambridge, MA: Harvard University Press.

Grinspoon, L., & Bakalar, J. B. (1976). *Cocaine: A drug and its social evolution.* New York: Basic Books.

Grinspoon, L., Bakalar, J. B., Zimmer, L., & Morgan, J. P. (1997). Marijuana addition. *Science, 277,* 749–751.

Grossman, A. H. (1997). Growing up with a "spoiled identity": Lesbian, gay and bisexual youth at risk. *Journal of Gay & Lesbian Social Services, 6,* 45–55.

Grossman, F. K., Beinashowitz, J., Anderson, L., Sakurai, M., Finnin, L., & Flaherty, M. (1992). Risk and resilience in young adolescents. *Journal of Youth and Adolescence, 21,* 529–550.

Grotevant, H. D. (1983). The contribution of the family to the facilitation of identity formation in early adolescence. *Journal of Early Adolescence, 3,* 225–237.

Grotevant, H. D. (1992). Assigned and chosen identity components: A process perspective on their integration. In G. R. Adams, T. P. Gullotta, & R. Montemayor (Eds.), *Identity formation during adolescence.* Newbury Park, CA: Sage.

Grotevant, H. D., & Adams, G. R. (1984). Development of an object measure to assess ego identity in adolescence: Validation and replication. *Journal of Youth and Adolescence, 13,* 419–438.

Grotevant, H. D., & Cooper, C. R. (1985). Patterns of interaction in family relationships and development of identity formation in adolescence. *Child Development, 56,* 415–428.

Grunseit, A., Kippax, S., Aggleton, P., Baldo, M., & Slutkin, G. (1997). Sexuality education and young people's sexual behavior: A review of studies. *Journal of Adolescent Research, 12,* 421–453.

Guilford, J. P. (1967). *The nature of human intelligence.* New York: McGraw-Hill.

Guilian, D., Vaca, K., & Noonan, C. A. (1990). Secretion of neurotoxins by mononuclear phagocytes infected with HIV-1. *Science, 250,* 1593–1596.

Gull, W. W. (1874). Anorexia nervosa. *Transcript of Clinical Sociology, 7,* 22–28.

Gullotta, C. F., & Plant, R. (2000). Finding belonging, mastery, and meaning through a primary prevention program: Creative experiences. In T. P. Gullotta, R. Plant, & S. Danish (Eds.), *Promoting socially competent youth: Sports and extra-curricular activities.* Washington, DC: Child Welfare Press.

Gullotta, T. P. (1978). Runaway: Reality or myth? *Adolescence, 13,* 543–549.

Gullotta, T. P. (1978, November). The juvenile offender: The police, the courts, and the social agency. Paper presented at the meeting of the American Association of Psychiatric Services for Children, Atlanta.

Gullotta, T. P. (1979). Leaving home: Family relationships of the runaway child. *Social Casework, 60,* 111–114.

Gullotta, T. P. (1979, November). Should the juvenile court be continued, altered, or abolished? Paper presented at the meeting of the National Association of Social Workers, San Antonio, TX.

Gullotta, T. P. (1983). Early adolescence, alienation, and education. *Theory Into Practice, 22,* 151–154.

Gullotta, T. P. (1987). Prevention's technology. *Journal of Primary Prevention, 7*(4), 176–196.

Gullotta, T. P. (1990). Preface. In T. P. Gullotta, G. R. Adams, & R. Montemayor (Eds.), *Developing social competency in adolescence.* Newbury Park, CA: Sage.

Gullotta, T. P. (1994). The what, who, why, where, when, and how of primary prevention. *Journal of Primary Prevention, 15*(1), 5–14.

Gullotta, T. P. (1996). Selected theoretical frameworks of individual and group behavior for intervention and prevention. In G. Blau & T. P. Gullotta (Eds.), *Adolescent dysfunctional behavior* (pp. 11–36). Thousand Oaks, CA: Sage.

Gullotta, T. P. (1997). Operationalizing Albee's incidence formula. In G. W. Albee and T. P. Gullotta (Eds.), *Prevention works.* Thousand Oaks, CA: Sage.

Gullotta, T. P., & Adams, G. R. (1982a). Minimizing juvenile delinquency: Implications for prevention programs. *Journal of Early Adolescence, 2,* 105–117.

Gullotta, T. P., & Adams, G. R. (1982b). Substance abuse minimization: Conceptualizing prevention in adolescent youth programs. *Journal of Youth and Adolescence, 11*(5), 409–424.

Gullotta, T. P., & Blau, G. (1995). A social history of selected drug misuse in the United States. In T. P. Gullotta, G. R. Adams, & R. Montemayor (Eds.), *Adolescent substance misuse.* Newbury Park, CA: Sage.

Gullotta, T. P., & Noyes, L. (1995). The changing paradigm of community health: The role of school-based health centers. *Adolescence, 30,* 107–115.

Gullotta, T. P., Adams, G. R., & Alexander, S. J. (1986). *Today's marriages and families: A wellness approach.* Pacific Grove, CA: Brooks/Cole.

Gullotta, T. P., Adams, G. R., & Montemayor, R. (Eds.) (1993). *Adolescent sexuality.* Newbury Park, CA: Sage.

Gullotta, T. P., Adams, G. R., & Montemayor, R. (Eds.) (1997). *Delinquent violent youth.* Thousand Oaks, CA: Sage.

Gullotta, T. P., Hampton, R. L., Senatore, V., & Eismann, M. (1998). When pap gets too handy with his hick'ry: A selected literary and social history of substance abuse and child abuse. In R.L. Hampton, V. Senatore, and T. P. Gullotta (Eds.), *Substance abuse, family violence, and child welfare.* (pp. 1–17). Thousand Oaks, CA: Sage.

Gullotta, T. P., Noyes, L., & Blau, G. (1996). School-based health and social service centers. In G. Blau and T. P. Gullotta (Eds.), *Adolescent dysfunctional behavior.* Thousand Oaks, CA: Sage.

Gundlach, J. (1994). Country music and suicide. *Social Forces, 72,* 1245–1248.

Gwartney-Gibbs, P. A., Stockard, J., & Bohmer, S. (1987). Learning courtship aggression: The influence of parents, peers, and personal experience. *Family Relations, 36,* 276–282.

Hafner, A., Ingels, S., Schneider, B., & Stevenson, D. (1990). *A profile of the American 8th grader* (pp. 90–458). Washington, DC: U.S. Department of Education NCES.

Hagell, A., & Newburn, T. (1996). Family and social contexts of adolescents re-offenders. *Journal of Adolescence, 19*(1), 5–18.

Hahn, A. (1987). America's dropouts. *Phi Delta Kappan, 69,* 184–189.

Hall, G. S. (1904). *Adolescence: Its psychology, and its relations to physiology, anthropology, sociology, sex, crime, religion, and education* (2 vols.). New York: Appleton-Century-Crofts.

Hall, S. S. (1995). IL-12 at the crossroads. *Science, 268,* 1432–1433.

Hallinan, M. T., & Smith, S. S. (1985). The effects of classroom racial composition on students' interracial friendliness. *Social Psychology Quarterly, 48,* 3–16.

Halt, R. E. (1979). The relationship between ego identity status and moral reasoning in university women. *Journal of Psychology, 103,* 203–207.

Hamilton, S. F. (1982). Working toward employment. *Society, 19*(6), 19–29.

Hammarstrom, A., & Janlert, U. (1997). Nervous and depressive symptoms in a longitudinal study of youth unemployment—Selection or exposure? *Journal of Adolescence, 20,* 293–305.

Hampton, R., Jenkins, P., & Gullotta, T. P. (Eds.) (1996). *Preventing violence in America.* Thousand Oaks, CA: Sage.

Handelsman, C. D., Cabral, R. J., & Weisfeld, G. E. (1987). Sources of information and adolescent sexual knowledge and behavior. *Journal of Adolescent Research, 2,* 455–463.

Hannan, D. F., O'Riain, S., & Whelan, C. T. (1997). Youth unemployment and psychological distress in the Republic of Ireland. *Journal of Adolescence, 20,* 307–320.

Hanson, S. L., & Ooms, T. (1991). The economic costs and rewards of two-earner, two-parent families. *Journal of Marriage and the Family, 53,* 622–634.

Hardy, J. B., & Duggan, A. K. (1988). Teenage fathers and the fathers of infants of urban teenage mothers. *American Journal of Public Health, 78,* 919–922.

Hardy, T. (1895/1967). *Jude the obscure.* New York, Modern Library.

Harris, K. M., & Morgan, S. P. (1991). Fathers, sons, and daughters: Differential paternal involvement in parenting. *Journal of Marriage and the Family, 53,* 531–544.

Harris, S. M. (1992). Black male masculinity and same sex friendships. *The Western Journal of Black Studies, 16,* 74–81.

Harrison, A. O., Wilson, M. N., Pine, C. J., Chan, S. Q., & Buriel, R. (1994). Family ecologies of ethnic minority children. In G. Handel & G.G. Whitchurch (Eds.), *The psychosocial interior of the family* (pp. 187–209). New York: Walter de Gruyter.

Hart, B., & Hilton, I. (1988). Dimensions of personality organization as predictors of teenage pregnancy risk. *Journal of Personality Assessment, 52,* 116–132.

Hart, M. (1971, October). Sports: Women sit in the back of the bus. *Psychology Today,* 64–66.

Hartford, T. C., Willis, C. H., & Deabler, H. L. (1967). Personality correlates of masculinity–femininity. *Psychological Reports, 21,* 881–884.

Hartup, H. W. (1983). Peer relations. In P. H. Mussen (Series Ed.) & E. M. Hetherington (Vol. Ed.), *Handbook of child psychology: Socialization, personality, and social development* (4th ed., vol. 4, pp. 103–196). New York: Wiley.

Hauck, W. E., Martens, M., & Wetzel, M. (1986). Shyness, group dependence and self-concept: Attributes of the imaginary audience. Adolescence, *21,* 529–534.

Haveman, R., Wolfe, B. L., & Spauling, J. (1991). Educational achievement and childhood events and circumstances. *Demography, 28,* 133–157.

Hawby, R. A. (1990). The bumpy road to drug-free schools. *Phi Delta Kappan, 72,* 310–314.

Hayes, C. D. (Ed.) (1987). *Risking the future: Adolescent sexuality, pregnancy, and childbearing* (Vol. 1). Washington, DC: National Academy Press.

Hayes, L. (1992). The cost of dropping out. *Phi Delta Kappan, 73,* 413.

Haynes, B. F., Pantaleo, G., & Fauci, A. S. (1996). Toward an understanding of the correlates of protective immunity to HIV infection. *Science, 271*(5247), 324–328.

Hechinger, F. M. (1992). *Fateful choices.* New York: Carnegie.

Hechinger, F. M., & Hechinger, G. (1975). *Growing up in America.* New York: McGraw–Hill.

Henderson, A. T., & Berla, N. (1994). *The family is critical to student achievement.* Washington, DC: National Committee for Citizens in Education.

Henderson, V. L., & Dweck, C. S. (1990). Motivation and achievement. In S. S. Feldman & G. R. Elliott (Eds.), *At the threshold: The developing adolescent.* Cambridge, MA: Harvard University Press.

Hendin, H., Pollinger, A., Ulman, R., & Carr, A. C. (1981). *Research 40: Adolescent marijuana abusers and their families*. Washington, DC: DHHS publication ADM 81-1168, U.S. Government Printing Office.

Hendren, R. L., & Strasburger, V. C. (1993). Rock music and music videos. *Adolescent Medicine, 4*(3), 577–587.

Henry, W. A. (1990). Beyond the melting pot. *Time, 135,* 28–31.

Hernstein, R. J., & Murray, C. (1994). *The bell curve.* New York: Free Press.

Hershberger, S. L., Pilkington, N. W., & D'Augelli, A. R. (1997). Predictors of suicide attempts among gay, lesbian, and bisexual youth. *Journal of Adolescent Research, 12,* 477–497.

Hesse-Biber, S. (1996). *Am I thin enough yet?* New York: Oxford University Press.

Hetherington, E. M., & Furstenberg, F. F. (1989). Sounding the alarm. *Readings, 4,* 4–8.

Hiebert, K. A., Felice, M. E., Wingard, D. L., Munoz, R., & Ferguson, J. M. (1988). *International Journal of Eating Disorders, 7,* 693–696.

Hier, S. J., Korboot, P. J., & Schweitzer, R. D. (1990). Social adjustment and symptomatology in two types of homeless adolescents and throwaways. *Adolescence, 25,* 761–772.

Higginson, J. G. (1998). Competitive parenting: The culture of teen mothers. *Journal of Marriage and the Family, 60,* 135–149.

Higham, E. (1980). Variations in adolescent psychonormal development. In J. Adelson (Ed.), *Handbook of adolescent psychology.* New York: Wiley.

Highlights (1984, March). *Science,* 14.

Hill, J., Holmbeck, G., Marlow, L., Green, T., & Lynch, M. (1985a). Menarcheal status and parental–child relations in families of seventh grade girls. *Journal of Youth and Adolescence, 14,* 301–316.

Hill, J., Holmbeck, G., Marlow, L., Green, T., & Lynch, M. (1985b). Pubertal status and parental-child relations in families of seventh grade boys. *Journal of Early Adolescence, 5,* 31–44.

Hill, J. P., & Lynch, M. E. (1983). The intensification of gender-related role expectations during early adolescence. In J. Brooks-Gunn & A. C. Petersen (Eds.), *Girls at puberty: Biological and psychosocial perspectives.* New York: Plenum.

Hill, J. O., & Peters, J. C. (1998). Environmental contributions to the obesity epidemic. *Science, 280,* 1371–1374.

Hill, S. M., Shaw, L. B., & Sproat, K. (1980). Teenagers: What are their choices about work? In *A review of youth employment problems, programs and policies: The Vice President's Task Force on Youth Employment* (Vol. 1). Washington, DC: U.S. Department of Labor.

Hillier, L., Harrison, L., & Warr, D. (1998). "When you carry condoms all the boys think you want it": Negotiating competing discourses about safe sex. *Journal of Adolescence, 21,* 15–29.

Hillman, S. B., & Sawilowsky, S. S. (1991). Maternal employment and early adolescent substance use. *Adolescence, 26,* 829–837.

Hindelang, M., Hirschi, T., & Weis, J. (1981). *Measuring delinquency.* Beverly Hills, CA: Sage.

Hines, A. M. (1997). Divorce-related transitions, adolescent development, and the role of the parent-child relationship: A review of the literature. *Journal of Marriage and the Family, 59,* 375–388.

Hinkle, S., & Brown, R. (1990). Intergroup comparisons and social identity: Some links and lucunae. In D. Abrams & M. A. Hogg (Eds.), *Social identity theory.* New York: Springer-Verlag.

Hinton, K., & Margerum, B. J. (1984). Adolescent attitudes and values concerning used clothing. *Adolescence, 19,* 397–402.

Hinton, S. E. (1967). *The outsiders.* New York: Viking.

Hirschi, T. (1969). *Causes of delinquency.* Berkeley: University of California Press.

Hispanic Policy Development Project (1987). *The Research Bulletin, 1,* 1–12.

Ho, D. D. (1996). Viral counts count in HIV infection. *Science, 272,* 1124–1125.

Ho, D. D. (1998). Toward HIV eradication or remission: The tasks ahead. *Science, 280,* 1886–1887.

Hodge, K., & Danish, S. (1998). Promoting life skills for adolescent males through sport. In A. Horne & M. Kiselica (Eds.), *Handbook of counseling boys and adolescent males.* Thousand Oaks, CA: Sage.

Hodgkinson, H. (1979). What's right with education. *Phi Delta Kappan, 61,* 159–162.

Hodgkinson, H. L. (1989). *The same client.* Washington, DC: Institute for Educational Policy.

Hodgkinson, H. (1995). The future is already here! Presentation at the Hartman National Conference on Children and their Families, June, 1995, New London, CT.

Hodgson, J. W., & Fischer, J. L. (1979). Sex differences in identity and intimacy development in college youth. *Journal of Youth and Adolescence, 8,* 37–50.

Hoelter, J. W. (1979). Religiosity, fear of death, and suicide acceptability. *Suicide and Life-threatening Behavior, 9*(3), 163–171.

Holden, C. (1987). Is alcoholism treatment effective? *Science, 236,* 20–22.

Holden, C. (1989). Flipping the main switch in the central reward system. *Science, 248,* 246–247.

Holden, C. (1991). Depression: The news isn't depressing. *Science, 254,* 1450–1452.

Holden, C. (1991). Government launches study to alcohol gene. *Science, 254,* 163–164.

Holden, C. (1992). Twin studies link genes to homosexuality. *Science, 256,* 33.

Holden, C. (1994). A cautionary genetic tale: The sobering story of D2. *Science, 264*(5166), 1696–1697.

Holden, C. (1995). More on genes and homosexuality. *Science, 268*(5217), 1571.

Holden, C. (1998). Boys+girls+math. *Science, 279,* 1459.

Holden, C. (1998). A marker for female homosexuality? *Science, 279,* 1639.

Holden, C. (1998). New clues to alcoholism risk, *Science, 280,* 1348–1349.

Holden, G. A., & Kapler, R. A. (1995). Deinstitutionalizing status offenders: A record of progress. *Juvenile Justice, 11*(2), 3–10.

Holden, N. L., & Robinson, P. H. (1988). Anorexia nervosa and bulimia nervosa in British Blacks. *British Journal of Psychiatry, 152,* 544–549.

Holinger, P. C., & Offer, D. (1989). Sociodemographic, epidemiologic, and individual attributes. In *Report of the secretary's task force on youth suicide: Risk factors for youth suicide* (Vol. 2). Washington, DC: U.S. Department of Health and Human Services ADM 89-1622, U.S. Government Printing Office.

Holinger, P. C., Offer, D., Barter, J. T., & Bell, C. C. (1994). *Suicide and homicide among adolescents*. New York, Guilford Press.

Hollister, W. G. (1977). The management of primary prevention programs. In D. C. Klein & S. E. Goldston (Eds.), *Primary prevention: An idea whose time has come*. Washington, DC: National Institute of Mental Health, DHEW publication ADM 77-447, U.S. Government Printing Office.

Hornick, J. P., Doran, L., & Crawford, S. H. (1979). Premarital contraceptives usage among male and female adolescents. *Family Coordinator, 28*, 181–190.

Horwitz, S. M., Klerman, L. V., & Jekel, J. F. (1991). School-age mothers: Predictors of long-term educational and economic outcomes. *Pediatrics, 87*, 862–868.

Howard, W. L. (1911). *Confidential chats with boys*. New York: Edward J. Clode.

Howard, M. P., & Anderson, R. J. (1978). Early identification of potential school dropouts: A literature review. *Child Welfare, 57*, 221–231.

Howat, P. M., & Saxton, A. M. (1988). The incidence of bulimic behavior in a secondary and university school population. *Journal of Youth and Adolescence, 17*, 221–232.

Howell, J. C. (1995). *Guide for implementing the comprehensive strategy for serious, violent, and chronic juvenile offenders*. Washington, DC: U.S. Department of Justice, NCJ-153681, U.S. Government Printing Office.

Howell, J. C., Krisberg, B., Hawkins, J. D., & Wilson, J. J. (1995). *Serious, violent, and chronic juvenile offenders*. Thousand Oaks, CA: Sage.

Hsu, J., Tseng, W. S., Ashton, G., McDermott, J. F., & Char, W. (1985).

Adolescent development and minority perspectives. *American Journal of Psychiatry, 142*, 577–581.

Hsu, L. K. G. (1980). Outcome of anorexia nervosa. *Archives of General Psychiatry, 37*, 1041–1046.

Huff, C. R. (Ed.) (1990). *Gangs in America*. Newbury Park, CA: Sage.

Huffine, C. L. (1989). Social and cultural risk factors for youth suicide. In *Report of the secretary's task force on youth suicide: Vol. 2: Risk factors for youth suicide* (Vol. 2). Washington, DC: U.S. Department of Health and Human Services publication ADM 89-1622, U.S. Government Printing Office.

Hufton, O. (1995). *The prospect before her: A history of women in western europe 1500–1800*. New York: Knopf.

Hughes, J. R. (1990). Nicotine abstinence effects. In L. S. Harris (Ed.), *Problems of drug dependence: 1989*. Washington, DC: U.S. Department of Health and Human Services publication ADM 90-1663, U.S. Government Printing Office.

Humphrey, L. (1970). Tearoom trade: Impersonal sex in public places. *Transaction, 7*, 10–25.

Hundleby, J. D., & Mercer, G. W. (1987). Family and friends as social environments and their relationship to young adolescents' use of alcohol, tobacco, and marijuana. *Journal of Marriage and the Family, 49*, 151–164.

Hussong, A. M., & Chassin, L. (1997). Substance initiation among adolescent children of alcoholics: Testing protective factors. *Journal of Studies on Alcohol, 58*, 272–279.

Huston, A. C. (1983). Sex-typing. In E. M. Hetherington (Ed.), *Handbook of child psychology*. New York: Wiley.

Huston, A. C., Donnerstein, E., Fairchild, H., Feshbach, N. D., Katz, P. A., Murray, J. P., Rubinstein, E. A., Wilcox, B. L., & Zuckerman, D. (1992). *Big world, small screen*. Lincoln, NE: University of Nebraska Press.

Huxley, A. (1936/1958). *Brave new world*. New York: Bantam.

Hyde, J. S., Krajnik, M., & Skuldt-Niederberger, K. (1991). Androgyny

across the life span: A replication and longitudinal follow-up. *Developmental Psychology, 27*, 516–519.

Hyde, J. S., & Phillis, D. E. (1979). Androgyny across the life span. *Development Psychology, 15*, 334–336.

Hyman, H., Wright, E., & Reed, J. S. (1975). *The enduring effects of education*. Chicago: University of Chicago Press.

Iacovetta, R. G. (1975). Adolescent–adult interaction and peer group involvement. *Adolescence, 10*, 325–336.

Ianni, F. A., & Reuss-Ianni, E. (1980). School violence. *Today's Education, 4*, 20G–23G.

Inamdar, S. C., Lewis, D. O., Siomopoulos, G., Shanok, S. S., & Lamela, M. (1982). Violent and suicidal behavior in psychotic adolescents. *American Journal of Psychiatry, 139*(7), 932–935.

Inglis, B. (1975). *The forbidden game: A social history of drugs*. New York: Scribner's.

Inhelder, B., & Piaget J. (1958). *The growth of logical thinking from childhood to adolescence*. New York: Basic Books.

Institute for Social Research (1992). *Monitoring the future*. Ann Arbor, MI: Author.

Jackson, B. (1975). Black identity development. *MEFORM: Journal of Educational Diversity & Innovation, 2*, 17–25.

Jackson, C., & Foshee, V. A. (1998). Violence related behaviors of adolescents: Relations with responsive and demanding parenting. *Journal of Adolescent Research, 13*, 343–359.

Jackson, C., Henriksen, L., Dickinson, D., & Levine, D. W. (1997). The early use of alcohol and tobacco: Its relation to children's competence and parents' behavior. *American Journal of Public Health, 87*, 359–364.

Jackson, D. (1975). The meaning of dating from the role perspective of nondating pre-adolescents. *Adolescence, 10*, 123–125.

Jackson, D., & Huston, T. L. (1975). Physical attractiveness and assertiveness. *Journal of Social Psychology, 96*, 79–84.

Jackson, L. A., Hodge, C. N., & Ingram, J. M. (1994). Gender and self-concept: A reexamination of stereotypic differences and the role of gender attitudes. *Sex Roles, 30,* 615–630.

Jackson, S. W. (1987). *Melancholia and depression: From hippocratic times to modern times.* New Haven, CT: Yale University Press.

Jacoby, R., & Glauberman, N. (1995). *The bell curve debate.* New York: Times Books.

Jaffe, J. H. (1979). The swinging pendulum: The treatment of drug users in America. In R. Dupont, A. Goldstein, & J. O'Donnell (Eds.), *Handbook on drug abuse.* Washington, DC: U.S. Government Printing Office.

Jalkanen, L., Tuomilehto, J., & Tanskanen. (1986). Survey of weight reduction attempts in a Finnish population sample. *International Journal of Eating Disorders, 4,* 247–257.

Jamison, K. R. (1994). *Touched with fire: Manic-depressive illness and the artistic temperament.* New York: Free Press.

Janus, M. D., McCormack, A., Burgess, A. W., & Hartman, C. (1987). *Adolescent runaways: Causes and consequences.* Lexington, MA: Lexington Books.

Janosz, M., LeBlanc, M., Boulerice, B., & Tremblay, R.E. (1997). Disentangling the weight of school dropout predictors: A test on two longitudinal samples. *Journal of Youth and Adolescence, 26,* 733–762.

Jarrett, R. L. (1995). Growing up poor: The family experienced of socially mobile youth in low-income African American households. *Journal of Adolescent Research, 10,* 111–135.

Jarvik, M. E. (1990). The drug dilemma: Manipulating the demand. *Science, 250,* 387–392.

Jason L. A., & Kobayashi, R. B. (1995). Community building: Our next frontier. *Journal of Primary Prevention, 15*(3), 195–208.

Jason, L. A., Hanaway, L. K., & Brackshaw, (1998). *Remote control: A sensible approach to kids, t.v., and the new electronic media.* Chicago, IL: Professional Resource Exchange.

Jason, L. A., Kurasaki, K. S., Neuson, L., & Garcia, C. (1993). Training parents in a preventive intervention for transfer children. *Journal of Primary Prevention, 13,* 213–227.

Jencks, C. S., & Brown, M. D. (1975). Effects of high schools on their students. *Harvard Educational Review, 45,* 273–324.

Jencks, C. S., Smith, M., Acland, H., Bane, M. J., Cohen, D., Gintis, H., Heyns, B., & Michelson, S. (1972). *Inequality: A reassessment of the effect of family and schooling in America.* New York: Basic Books.

Jenkins, R. L., & Hewitt, L. (1944). Types of personality structure encountered in child guidance clinics. *American Journal of Orthopsychiatry, 14,* 84–94.

Jensen, A. R. (1969). How much can we boost IQ and scholastic achievement? *Harvard Educational Review, 39,* 1–123.

Jensen, A. R. (1995). Paroxysms of denial. In R. Jacoby & N. Glauberman (Eds.), *The bell curve debate.* New York: Times Books.

Jessor, R. (1979). Marijuana: A review of recent psychosocial research. In R. Dupont, A. Goldstein, & J. O'Donnell (Eds.), *Handbook on drug abuse.* Washington, DC: U.S. Government Printing Office.

Jessor, R. (1993). Successful adolescent development among youth in high-risk settings. *American Psychologist, 48,* 117–126.

Jessor, R., Chase, J. A., & Donovan, J. E. (1980). Psychosocial correlates of marijuana use and perhaps drinking in a national sample of adolescents. *American Journal of Public Health, 70,* 604–612.

Jessor, R., Costa, F., Jessor, L., & Donovan, J. E. (1983). Time of first intercourse: A prospective study. *Journal of Personality and Social Psychology, 44,* 608–626.

Jessor, S. L., & Jessor, R. (1975). Transition from virginity to nonvirginity among youth: A social-psychological study over time. *Developmental Psychology, 11,* 473–484.

Johanson, C. E., Duffy, F. F., & Anthony, J. C. (1996). Associations between drug use and behavioral repertoire in urban youths. *Addictions, 91,* 523–534.

Johnson, B. D., Williams, T., Sanabria, H., & Dei, K. (1990). Social impact of crack dealing in the inner city. In L. S. Harris (Ed.), *Problems of drug dependence: 1989,* Washington, DC: DHHS publication ADM 90-1663.

Johnson, C., & Flach, A. (1985). Family characteristics of 105 patients with bulimia. *American Journal of Psychiatry, 142,* 1321–1324.

Johnson, C., & Maddi, K. L. (1986). Factors that affect the onset of bulimia. *Seminars in Adolescent Medicine, 2,* 11–19.

Johnson, C., Lewis, C., Love., S., Lewis, L., & Stuckey, M. (1984). Incidence and correlates of bulimic behavior in a female high school population. *Journal of Youth and Adolescence, 13,* 15–26.

Johnson, C. A., Pentz, M. A., Weber, M. D., Dwyer, J. H., Baer, N., Mackinnon, D. P., Hanson, W. B., & Flay, B. R. (1990). Relative effectiveness of comprehensive community programming for drug abuse prevention with high-risk and low-risk adolescents. *Journal of Consulting and Clinical Psychology, 58,* 447–456.

Johnson, K., Bryant, D., Strader, T., Bucholtz, G., Berbaum, M., Collins, D., and Noe, T. (1996). Reducing alcohol and other drug use by strengthening community, family, and youth resiliency. *Journal of Adolescent Research, 11*(1), 36–67.

Johnson, R. (1972). *Aggression in man and animals.* Philadelphia, PA: Saunders.

Johnson, R. E. (1986). Family structure and delinquency: General patterns and gender differences. *Criminology, 24,* 65–80.

Johnston, L. D. (1996). *The rise in drug use among American teens continues in 1996.* Ann Arbor, MI: University of Michigan.

Johnston, L. D., O'Malley, P. M., & Bachman, J. G. (1991). *Drug use among American high school seniors, college students and young adults, 1975–1990.* Washington, DC: National Institute on Drug Abuse, U.S. Department of Health and Human Services publication ADM 91-1813, U.S. Government Printing Office.

Johnston, L. D., O'Malley, P. M., & Bachman, J. G. (1996). *National survey results on drug use from the monitoring the future study, 1975–1995.*

Washington, DC: NIDA publication 96-4139, U.S. Government Printing Office.

Johnston, L. D., O'Malley, P. M., & Bachman, J. G. (1997). *National survey results on drug use from the monitoring the future study. 1975–1997*. (NIDA Publication 98-4345). Washington, DC: U.S. Government Printing Office.

Johnston, M. I., & Hoth, D. F. (1993). Present status and future prospects for HIV therapies. *Science, 260*, 1286–1291.

Jones, A. (1973). Personality and value differences related to the use of LSD-25. International *Journal of the Addictions, 8*, 549–557.

Jones, H. (1949). Adolescence in our society. In *The family in a democratic society*. New York: Columbia University Press.

Jones, M. C. (1968). Personality correlates and antecedents in drinking patterns in males. *Journal of Clinical and Consulting Psychology, 32*, 2–12.

Jones, R. M. (1992). Ego identity and adolescent problem behavior. In G. R. Adams, T. P. Gullotta, & R. Montemayor (Eds.), *Identity formation during adolescence*. Newbury Park, CA: Sage.

Jones, R. T. (1980). Human effects: An overview. In R. C. Petersen (Ed.), *Research 31: Marijuana Research Findings*. Washington, DC: NIDA, DHHS publication ADM 80-1001, U.S. Government Printing Office.

Jones, R. T. (1987). The pharmacology of cocaine. In J. Grabowski (Ed.), *Cocaine: Pharmacology, effects, and treatment of abuse*. Washington, DC: U.S. Department of Health and Human Services publication ADM 87-1326, U.S. Government Printing Office.

Jones, R. T. (1990). The pharmacology of cocaine smoking in humans. In C. N. Chiang, & R. L. Hawks (Eds.), *Research findings on smoking abused substances*. Washington, DC: DHHS publication ADM 90-1690, U.S. Government Printing Office.

Jorgensen, S. R. (1993). Adolescent pregnancy and parenting. In T. P. Gullotta, G. R. Adams, & R. Montemayor (Eds.), *Adolescent sexuality*. Newbury Park, CA: Sage.

Jorgensen, S. R., King, S. L., & Torrey, R. A. (1980). Dyadic and social network influences on adolescent exposure to pregnancy risk. *Journal of Marriage and the Family, 42*(1), 141–155.

Josselson, R. (1982). Personality structure and identity status in women as viewed through early memories. *Journal of Youth and Adolescence, 11*, 293–299.

Joselson, R. (1987). *Finding herself: Pathways to identity development in women*. San Francisco: Jossey–Bass.

Journal American Medical Association (1998, Sept. 9). New herpes treatment approved.

Jurich, A., & Jurich, J. (1974). The effect of cognitive moral development upon the selection of premarital sexual standards. *Journal of Marriage and the Family, 36*, 736–741.

Kacergius, M. A., & Adams, G. R. (1980). Erikson stage resolution: The relationship between identity and intimacy. *Journal of Youth and Adolescence, 9*, 117–126.

Kagan, D. M., & Squires, R. L. (1984). Eating disorders among adolescents: Patterns and prevalence. *Adolescence, 19*, 15–29.

Kagan, J. S. (1969). Inadequate evidence and illogical conclusions. *Harvard Educational Review, 39*, 274–277.

Kahn, S., Zimmerman, G., Csikszentmihali, M. K., & Getzels, J. W. (1985). Relations between identity in young adulthood and intimacy at midlife. *Journal of Personality and Social Psychology, 49*, 1316–1322.

Kalafat, J. (1997). Prevention of youth suicide. In R. P. Weissberg, T. P. Gullotta, R. L. Hampton, B. A. Ryan, & G. R. Adams (Eds.), *Healthy children 2010: enhancing children's wellness* (pp. 175–213). Thousand Oaks, CA: Sage.

Kalafat, J., & Elias, M. J. (1995). Suicide prevention in an educational context: broad and narrow foci. *Suicide and Life-Threatening Behavior, 25*, 123–132.

Kalliopuska, M. (1982). Body-image disturbances in patients with anorexia nervosa. *Psychological Reports, 51*, 715–722.

Kalmuss, D., Namerow, P. B., and Bauer, U. (1992). Short-term consequences of parenting verus adoption among young unmarried women. *Journal of Marriage and the Family, 54*(1), 80–90.

Kalter, N. (1977). Children of divorce in an outpatient psychiatric population. *American Journal of Orthopsychiatry, 47*, 40–51.

Kandel, D. B. (1981a). Drug use by youth: An overview. In D. J. Lettieri & J. P. Lundford (Eds.), *Drug abuse and the American adolescent* (pp. 1–24). Washington, DC: NIDA Research Monograph No. 38, ADM 81-1166, U.S. Government Printing Office.

Kandel, D. B. (1981b, April). Peer influences in Adolescence. Paper presented at the meeting of the Society for Research in Child Development, Boston.

Kandel, D. B. (1990). Parenting styles, drug use, and children's adjustment in families of young adults. *Journal of Marriage and the Family, 52*, 183–196.

Kandel, D. B., & Davies, M. (1996). High school students who use crack and other drugs. *Archives of General Psychiatry, 53*, 71–80.

Kandel, D. B., & Faust, R. (1975). Sequence and stages in patterns of adolescent drug use. *Archives of General Psychiatry, 32*, 923–932.

Kandel, D. B., & Logan, J. A. (1984). Patterns of drug use from adolescence to young adulthood. I. Periods of risk for initiation, continued use, and discontinuation. *American Journal of Public Health, 74*, 660–666.

Kandel, D. B., & Wu, P. (1995). The contributions of mothers and fathers to the intergenerational transmission of cigarette smoking in adolescence. *Journal of Research on Adolescence, 5*(2), 225–252.

Kandel, D. B., Kessler, R., & Margulies, R. (1978). Adolescent initiation into stages of drug use: A developmental analysis. In D. B. Kandel (Ed.), *Longitudinal research on drug use: Empirical findings and methodological issues*. Washington, DC: Hemisphere–Wiley.

Kandel, D. B., Treiman, D., Faust, R., & Single, E. (1986). Adolescent involvement in legal and illegal drug use: A multiple classification analysis. *Social Forces, 55*, 438–458.

Kandel, D. B., & Yamaguchi, K., & Chen, K. (1992). Stages of progression in drug involvement from adolescence to adulthood: Further evidence for the gateway theory. *Journal of Studies on Alcohol, 53,* 447–457.

Kane, F. J., Moan, C. A., & Bolling, B. (1974). Motivational factors in pregnant adolescents. *Diseases of the Nervous System, 34*(3), 131–134.

Kanki, P. J., Alroy, J., & Essex, M. (1985). Isolation of T-lymphotropic retrovirus related to HTLV-III/LAV from wild-caught African green monkeys. *Science, 230,* 951–954.

Kanter, J. F., & Zelnick, M. (1972). Sexual experience of young unmarried women in the United States. *Family Planning Perspectives, 4,* 9–18.

Kanter, J. F., & Zelnick, M. (1973). Contraception and pregnancy: Experience of young unmarried women in the United States. *Family Planning Perspectives, 5,* 21–35.

Katz, D. L., & Pope, H. G. (1990). Anabolic-androgenic steroid-induced mental status changes. In G. C. Lin & L. Erinoff (Eds.), *Anabolic steroid abuse.* Washington, DC: U.S. Department of Health and Human Services publication ADM 91-1720, U.S. Government Printing Office.

Katz, M. B. (1973). *Education in American history.* New York: Praeger.

Katz, M. B. (1975). *Class, bureaucacy, and schools: The illusion of educational change in America.* New York: Praeger.

Kaufman, J. E., & Rosenbaum, J. E. (1992). The education and employment of low-income Black youth in White suburbs. *Educational Evaluation and Policy Analysis, 14,* 229–240.

Kazdin, A. E. (1987). Treatment of antisocial behavior in children: Current status and future directions. *Psychological Bulletin, 102,* 187–203.

Kazdin, A.E. (1992). Child and adolescent dysfunction and paths toward maladjustment: targets for intervention. *Clinical Psychology Review, 12,* 795–817.

Keating, C. F. (1985). Gender and the physiognomy of dominance and attractiveness. *Social Psychology Quarterly, 48,* 61–70.

Keating, D. (1990). Adolescent thinking. In S. S. Feldman & G. R. Elliott (Eds.), *At the threshold: The developing adolescent.* Cambridge, MA: Harvard University Press.

Keating, D. P. (1980). Thinking processes in adolescence. In J. Adelson (Ed.), *Handbook of adolescent psychology.* New York: Wiley.

Keating, D., & Sasse, D. K. (1996). Cognitive socialization in adolescence: critical period for a critical habit of mind. In G. R. Adams, R. Montemayor, & T. P. Gullotta (Eds.), *Psychosocial development during adolescence: progress in developmental contextualism.* Thousand Oaks, CA: Sage.

Keel, P. K., Fulkerson, J. A., & Leon, G. R. (1997). Disordered eating precursors in pre- and early adolescent girls and boys. *Journal of Youth and Adolescence, 26,* 203–216.

Keith, S. J., & Matthews, S. M. (1993). Introduction. *Psychopharmacology Bulletin, 29*(4), 427–430.

Keniston, K. (1970). *Youth and dissent.* New York: Harcourt Brace Jovanovich.

Keniston, K. (1975). Prologue: Youth as a stage of life. In R. J. Havighurst & P. H. Dreyer (Eds.), *Youth.* Chicago, IL: University of Chicago Press.

Keniston, K. (1977). *All our children.* New York: Harcourt, Brace, Jovanovich.

Kerfoot, M. (1980). The family context of adolescent suicidal behavior. *Journal of Adolescence, 3,* 335–346.

Kessler, M., & Albee, G. W. (1977). An overview of the literature of primary prevention. In G. W. Albee & J. M. Jaffe (Eds.), *Primary prevention of psychopathology: The issues* (Vol. 1). Hanover, NH: University Press of New England.

Kett, J. F. (1977). *Rites of passage: Adolescence in America 1790 to the present.* New York: Basic Books.

Kim, J. (1996). AOL plan overshadows earnings. *USA Today,* May 9, 3B.

Kincheloe, J. L., Steinberg, S. R., & Gresson, A. D. (1996). *Measured lies: The bell curve examined.* New York: St. Martin's Press.

King, P. (1988). Heavy metal music and drug abuse in adolescence. *Postgraduate Medicine, 83,* 295–301, 304.

Kinsey, A., Pomeroy, W., & Martin, C. (1948). *Sexual behavior of the human male.* Philadelphia, PA: Saunders.

Kinsey, A., Pomeroy, W., Martin, C., & Gebhard, P. (1953). *Sexual behavior of the human female.* Philadelphia, PA: Saunders.

Kishton, J. M., & Dixon, A. C. (1995). Self-perception changes among sports camp participants. *Journal of Sports Psychology, 2,* 135–141.

Kleck, R. E. (1975). Issues in social effectiveness: The case of the mentally retarded. In M. J. Begab & S. A. Richardson (Eds.), *The mentally retarded and society.* Baltimore: University Park Press.

Kleiber, D., & Kirshnit, F. (1991). Sport involvement and identity formation. In L. Diamant (Ed.) *Mind–body maturity: Psychological approaches to sports, exercise, and fitness* (pp. 193–211). New York: Hemisphere.

Klein, K., Forehand, R., Armistead, L., & Long, P. (1997). Delinquency during the transition to early adulthood: Family and parenting predictors from early adolescence. *Adolescence, 32,* 61–80.

Klein, D. C., & Goldston, S. E. (Eds.) (1977). *Primary prevention: An idea whose time has come National Institute of Mental Health.* Washington, DC: DHEW publication ADM 77-447, U.S. Government Printing Office.

Klein, S., Petersilia, J., & Turner, S. (1990). Race and imprisonment decisions in California. *Science, 247,* 812–816.

Klitzner, M., & Blasinsky, M. (1990). Substance abuse and suicide. In M. J. Rotherham-Borus, J. Bradley, & N. Obolensky (Eds.), *Planning to live.* Tulsa, OK: National Resource Center for Youth Services.

Kloep, M. (1995). Concurrent and predictive correlates of girls' depression and antisocial behavior under conditions of economic crisis and value change: The case of Albania. *Journal of Adolescence, 18*(4), 445–458.

Knox, D., & Wilson, K. (1981). Dating behaviors of university students. *Family Relations, 30,* 255–258.

Kochakian, C. D. (1990). History of anabolic steroids. In G. C. Lin & L. Erinoff (Eds.), *Anabolic steroid abuse*. Washington, DC: U.S. Department of Health and Human Services publication ADM 91-1720, U.S. Government Printing Office.

Koester, A. W., & May, J. K. (1985). Profiles of adolescents' clothing practices: Purchase, daily selection, and care. *Adolescence, 20*(77), 97–113.

Koff, E., Rierdan, J., & Jacobson, S. (1981). The personal and interpersonal significance of menarche. *Journal of the American Academy of Child Psychiatry, 20*, 148–158.

Koff, E., Rierdan, J., & Silverstone, E. (1978). Changes in representation of body image as a function of menarcheal status. *Developmental Psychology, 14*, 635–642.

Kohlberg, L. (1969). Stage and sequence: The cognitive-developmental approach to socialization. In D. A. Goslin (Ed.), *Handbook of socialization theory and research*. Chicago: Rand–McNally.

Kolata, G. (1987). Clinical trials planned for new AIDS drug. *Science, 235*, 1138–1139.

Koop, C. E. (1987). Surgeon general's report on acquired immune deficiency syndrome. *Public Health Reports, 102*, 1–2.

Kozel, N. J., & Adams, E. H. (1986). Epidemiology of drug abuse: An overview. *Science, 234*, 970–974.

Kramer, L. R. (1991). The social construction of ability perceptions: An ethnographic study of gifted adolescent girls. *Journal of Early Adolescence, 11*, 340–362.

Kreipe, R. E. (1986). Inpatient management of anorexia nervosa and bulimia. *Seminars in Adolescent Medicine, 2*, 27–36.

Kroger, J. (1985). Separation-individuation and ego-identity status in New Zealand University students. *Journal of Youth and Adolescence, 14*, 133–147.

Kroger, J. (1989). *Identity in adolescence*. London: Routledge.

Kroger, J. (1995). The differentiation of "firm" and "developmental" foreclosure identity statuses: A longitudinal study.

Journal of Adolescent Research, 10, 317–337.

Kroger, J., & Green, K. (1996). Events associated with identity status change. *Journal of Adolescence, 19*, 477–490.

Kroger, J., & Haslett, S. J. (1988). Separation-individual and ego identity status in late adolescence: A two-year longitudinal study. *Journal of Youth and Adolescence, 17*, 59–80.

Kronenberg, J., Nachshoni, T., Neumann, M., and Gaoni, B. (1994). The treatment of anorexia in a general hospital: A case vignette of a multidisciplinary general hospital-based approach. *Journal of Adolescence, 17*(2), 163–171.

Kronholm, W. (1986, May 22). Funds sought to combat venereal disease. *The Day*, A9.

Kuhn, D. (1976a). Relation of two Piagetian stage transitions to IQ. *Developmental Psychology, 12*, 157–161.

Kuhn, D. (1976b). Short-term longitudinal evidence for the sequentiality of Kohlberg's early stages of moral judgment. *Developmental Psychology, 12*, 162–166.

Kurdek, L. A., & Siesky, A. E. (1980). Effects of divorce on children: The relationship between parent and child perspectives. *Journal of Divorce, 4*, 85–90.

Kurdek, L. A., Blisk, D., & Siesky, A. E. (1981). Correlates of children's long-term adjustment to their parent's divorce. *Developmental Psychology, 17*, 565–579.

Kurtines, W., Hogan, R., & Weiss, D. (1975). Personality dynamics of heroin use. *Journal of Abnormal Psychology, 84*, 87–89.

Kurtz, P. D., Kurtz, G. L., & Jarvis, S. V. (1991). Problems of maltreated runaway youth. *Adolescence, 26*, 543–556.

Kuther, T. L., & Fisher, C. B. (1998). Victimization by community violence in young adolescents from a suburban city. *Journal of Early Adolescence, 18*, 53–76.

Lab, S. P. (1984). Patterns in juvenile misbehavior. *Crime and Delinquency, 30*, 293–308.

LaBarre, M. (1968). Pregnancy experiences among married adolescents. *American Journal of Orthopsychiatry, 38*, 47–55.

Laenaars, A. A., & Lester, D. (1995). The changing suicide pattern in Canadian adolescents and youth compared to their American counterparts. *Adolescence, 30*, 539–547.

LaFromboise, T. D., & Bigfoot, D. S. (1988). Cultural and cognitive considerations in the prevention of American Indian adolescent suicide. *Journal of Adolescence, 11*, 139–153.

LaFromboise, T. D., & Low, K. G. (1989). American Indian children and adolescents. In J. T. Gibbs & L. N. Huang (Eds.), *Children of color*. San Francisco: Jossey–Bass.

Lamanna, M. A., & Reidmann, A. (1991). *Marriages and families: Making choices and facing change* (4th ed.). Belmont, CA: Wadsworth.

Lamb, R., & Zusman, J. (1979). Drs. Lamb and Zusman reply. *American Journal of Psychiatry, 136*, 1949.

Lamke, L. K. (1982). The impact of sex-role orientation on self-esteem in early adolescence. *Child Development, 53*, 1530–1535.

Lamke, L. K., & Abraham, K. G. (1984, October). Adolescent identity formation and sex-role development: Critical linkages. Paper presented at the annual meeting of the National Council on Family Relations, San Francisco.

Landers, S. (1993). Family leave ushers in new era. *NASW News, 3*, 1, 8.

Langan, P. A. (1991). America's soaring prison population. *Science, 251*, 1568–1573.

Langer, L. M., Zimmerman, R. S., & Katz, J. A. (1995). Virgins' expectations and nonvirgins' reports: How adolescents feel about themselves. *Journal of Adolescent Research, 10*(2), 291–306.

Laperriere, A., Compere, L., D'Khissy, M., Dolce, R., & Fleurant, N. (1994). Mutual perceptions and interethnic strategies among French, Italian, and Haitian adolescents of a multiethnic school in Montreal. *Journal of Adolescent Research, 9*, 193–217.

Larson, R. W., Richards, M. H., Moneta, G., Holmbeck, G., & Duckett, E. (1996). Changes in adolescents' daily interactions with their families from ages 10 to 18: Disengagement and transformation. *Developmental Psychology, 32,* 744–754.

Laub, J. H. (1983). Urbanism, race, and crime. *Journal of Research in Crime and Delinquency, 20,* 183–198.

Lausen, E., & Rickle, A. (1998). Treating the juvenile offender in correctional settings. In T. P. Gullotta, G. R. Adams, & R. Montemayor (Eds.), *Delinquent violent youth.* (pp. 230–255). Thousand Oaks, CA: Sage.

LaVoie, J. C. (1976). Ego identity formation in middle adolescence. *Journal of Youth and Adolescence, 5,* 371–385.

LaVoie, J. C., & Collins, B. R. (1975). Effect of youth culture music on high school students' academic performance. *Journal of Youth and Adolescence, 4,* 57–65.

Lawrence, F. C., Tasker, G. E., Daly, C. T., Orthiel, A. L., & Wozniak, P. H. (1986). Adolescents' time spent viewing television. *Adolescence, 21,* 431–436.

Lazear, D. (1991). *Seven ways of knowing: Understanding multiple intelligences.* Palatine, IL: Skylight.

Leadbeater, B. J., & Dionne, J. (1981). The adolescent's use of formal operational thinking in solving problems related to identity resolution. *Adolescence, 16,* 111–121.

Lech, S., Gary, D., & Ury, H. (1975). Characteristics of heavy users of outpatient prescription drugs. *Clinical Toxology, 8,* 599–610.

Lee, V. E., Burkam, D. T., Zimiles, H., & Ladewski, B. (1994). Family structure and its effects on behavioral and emotional problems in young adolescents. *Journal of Research on Adolescence, 4,* 405–437.

Lehman, A. K., & Rodin, J. (1989). Styles of self-nurturance and disordered eating. *Journal of Consulting and Clinical Psychology, 57,* 117–122.

Lehnert, K. L., Overholser, J. C., & Spirito, A. (1994). Internalized and externalized anger in adolescent suicide attempters. *Journal of Adolescent Research, 9*(1), 105–119.

Leibert, R. M., & Sprafkin, J. (1988). *The early window effect of television on children and youth.* (3rd ed.) New York: Pergamon.

Leigh, G. K. (1986). Adolescent involvement in family systems. In G. K. Leigh & G. W. Peterson (Eds.), *Adolescents in families.* Cincinnati: South-Western.

Lenard, L. (1982, November). The battle to wipe out herpes. *Science Digest,* 36–38.

Lennon, S. J. (1986). Adolescent attitudes toward designer jeans: Further evidence. *Adolescence, 21,* 475–482.

Lerner, R. M. (1995). *America's youth in crisis: Challenges and choices for programs and policies.* Thousand Oaks, CA: Sage

Lerner, R. M., & Lerner, J. V. (1977). Effects of age, sex, and physical attractiveness on child-peer relations, academic performance, and elementary school adjustment. *Developmental Psychology, 13,* 585–590.

Leshner, A. (1997). Addiction is a brain disease, and it matters. *Science, 278,* 45–46.

Lester, D. (1991). Social correlates of youth suicide rates in the United States. *Adolescence, 26,* 55–58.

Letvin, N. L. (1998). Progress in the development of an HIV-1 vaccine. *Science, 280,* 1875–1880.

Leukefeld, C. G. (1997). Juvenile delinquency. In T. P. Gullotta, G. R. Adams, and R. Montemayor (Eds.), *Delinquent violent youth.* Thousand Oaks, CA: Sage.

Leukefeld, C. G., & Fimbres, M. (1987). *Responding to AIDS.* Silver Spring, MD: National Association of Social Workers.

Leukenfeld, C. G., & Haverkos, H. W. (1993). Sexually transmitted diseases. In T. P. Gullotta, G. R. Adams, & R. Montemayor (Eds.), *Adolescent sexuality.* Newbury Park, CA: Sage.

Leukefeld, C. G., Logan, T. K., Clayton, R. R., Martin, C., Zimmerman, R., Cattarello, A., Milich, R., & Lynam, D. (1998). Adolescent drug use, delinquency, and other behaviors. In T. P. Gullotta, G. R. Adams, & R. Montemayor (Eds.), *Delinquent violent youth* (pp. 98–128). Thousand Oaks, CA: Sage.

LeVay, S. (1991). A difference in hypothalamic structure between heterosexual and homosexual men. *Science, 254,* 1034–1037.

Levine, M., & Levine, A. (1992). *Helping children: A social history.* New York: Oxford.

Levy, J. E., & Kunitz, S. J. (1987). A suicide prevention program for Hopi youth. *Social Science and Medicine, 25,* 931–940.

Lewis, D. O., Balla, D. A., & Shanok, S. S. (1979). Some evidence of race bias in the diagnosis and treatment of the juvenile offender. *American Journal of Orthopsychiatry, 49,* 53–61.

Lewis, D. C., Duncan, D. F., & Clifford, P. R. (1997). Analyzing drug policy. *Journal of Primary Prevention, 17,* 351–361.

Lightman, A. (1983, May). Nothing but the truth. *Science, 83,* 24–26.

Lin, G. C., & Glennon, R. A. (1994). *Hallucinogens: An update.* Washington, DC: NIDA Research Monograph 146, U.S. Government Printing Office.

Lips, H. M., & Colwill, N. L. (1978). *The psychology of sex differences.* Englewood Cliffs, NJ: Prentice-Hall.

Lipton, D.S. (1996). Prison-based therapeutic communities. *National Institute of Justice Journal, 230,* 12–20.

Littrell, M. A., Damhorst, M. L., & Littrell, J. M. (1990). Clothing interests, body satisfaction, and eating behavior of adolescent females: Related or independent dimensions? *Adolescence, 25,* 77–96.

Loeber, R. (1982). The stability of antisocial and delinquent child behavior: A review. *Child Development, 53,* 1431–1446.

Logan, D. D. (1980). The menarche experience in twenty-three foreign countries. *Adolescence, 15,* 247–256.

Logan, D. D., Calder, J. A., & Cohen, B. L. (1980). Toward a contemporary tradition for menarche. *Journal of Youth and Adolescence, 9,* 263–269.

Logan, R. D. (1978). Identity diffusion and psychosocial defense mechanisms. *Adolescence, 13,* 503–508.

Lombardo, J. A. (1990). Anabolic-androgenic studies. In G. C. Lin & L. Erinoff (Eds.), *Anabolic steroid abuse.* Washington, DC: U.S. Department of Health and Human Services publication ADM 91-1720, U.S. Government Printing Office.

Long, N., Forehand, R., Fauber, R., & Brody, G. H. (1987). Self-perceived and independently observed competence of young adolescents as a function of parental marital conflict and recent divorce. *Journal of Abnormal Child Psychology, 15,* 15–27.

Lorenzi, M. E., Klerman, L. V., & Jekel, J. F. (1972). School-age parents: How permanent a relationship? *Adolescence, 12,* 13–22.

Lowe, C. S., & Radius, S. M. (1987). Young adults' contraceptive practices: An investigation of influences. *Adolescence, 22,* 291–304.

Lucas, A. R. (1986). Anorexia nervosa: Historical background and biopsychosocial determinants. *Seminars in Adolescent Medicine, 2,* 1–9.

Lui, K., Darrow, W. W., & Rutherford, G. W. (1988). A model-based estimate of the mean incubation period for AIDS in homosexual men. *Science, 240,* 1333–1335.

Lum, D. (1996). *Social work practice & people of color* (3rd ed.). Pacific Grove, CA: Brooks/Cole.

Lumiere, R., & Cook, S. (1983). *Healthy sex.* New York: Simon & Schuster.

Lumpkin, A., Stoll, S., & Beller, J. (1994). *Sport ethics: Applications for fair play.* St. Louis, MO: Mosby.

Lundman, R. J. (1984). *Prevention and control of juvenile delinquency.* New York: Oxford University Press.

Luster, T., & Small, S. A. (1994). Factors associated with sexual risk-taking behaviors among adolescents. *Journal of Marriage and the Family, 56,* 622–632.

Luthar, S. A., & Zigler, E. (1991). Vulnerability and competence: A review of research on resilience in childhood. *American Journal of Orthopsychiatry, 61,* 6–22.

Lyman, H. M., Fenger, C., Jones, H. W., & Belfield, W. T. (1887). *The practical home physician.* Albany, NY: Shelleck, Ross.

Maccoby, E., & Jacklin, C. N. (1974). *The psychology of sex differences.* Stanford, CA: Stanford University Press.

Maccoby, E. E. (1990). Gender and relationships: A developmental account. *American Psychologist, 45,* 513–520.

Macdonald, D. I. (1987). *Suicide among youth* (ages 15–24). Washington, DC: ADAMHA Update (mimeograph), U.S. Government Alcohol, Drug Abuse, and Mental Health Administration.

MacDonald, W. L., & DeMars, A. (1995). Remarriage, stepchildren, and marital conflict: Challenges to the incomplete institutionalization hypothesis. *Journal of Marriage and the Family, 57,* 387–398.

Maguire, K., & Pastore, A. L. (1995). *Bureau of justice statistics: Sourcebook.* Washington, DC: Department of Justice, NCJ-154591, U.S. Government Printing Office.

Maguire, K., & Pastore, A. L. (1996). *Bureau of justice statistics sourcebook of criminal justice statistics—1996.* Washington, DC: NCJ-165361, U.S. Government Printing Office.

Maharaj, S. I., & Connolly, J. A. (1994). Peer network composition of acculturated and ethnoculturally-affiliated adolescents in a multicultural setting. *Journal of Adolescent Research, 9,* 218–240.

Mann, B. J., & Bourduin, C. M. (1991). A critical review of psychotherapy outcome studies with adolescents: 1978–1988. *Adolescence, 26,* 505–541.

Mann, C. C. (1994). Behavioral genetics in transition. *Science, 264*(5166), 1686–1689.

Mannarino, A. P., & Marsh, M. E. (1978). The relationship between sex role identification and juvenile delinquency in adolescent girls. *Adolescence, 13,* 643–651.

Marcia, J. (1966). Development and validation of ego-identity status. *Journal of Personality and Social Psychology, 3,* 551–558.

Marcia, J. (1976). Identity six years after: A follow-up study. *Journal of Youth and Adolescence, 5,* 145–160.

Marcia, J. E. (1980). Identity in adolescence. In J. Adelson (Ed.), *Handbook of adolescent psychology.* New York: Wiley.

Marcia, J. E., Waterman, A. S., Matteson, D. R., Archer, S. L., & Orlofsky, J. L. (1993). Ego identity: A handbook for psychosocial research. New York: Springer-Verlag.

Marcotte, D. (1997). Treating depression in adolescence: a review of the effectiveness of cognitive-behavioral treatments. *Journal of Youth and Adolescence, 26,* 273–283.

Marcus, R. F. (1996). The friendships of delinquents. *Adolescence, 31*(121), 145–158.

Marelich, W. D., & Rotheram-Borus, M. J. (1999). From individual to social change: Current and future directions of health interventions. In T. P. Gullotta, G. R. Adams, R. Hampton, B. Ryan, & R. Weissberg (Eds.), *Child health care: Issues for the year 2000 and beyond.* Thousand Oaks, CA: Sage.

Maresh, C. M. (1992). Parents' behavior disgraces school sports events. *Hartford Courant,* January 19, C3.

Mark, V. H., Sweet, W. H., & Ervin, F. R. (1967). The role of brain disease in riots and urban violence. *Journal of the American Medical Association, 201,* 895.

Markos, A. R., Wade, A. A. H., & Walzman, M. (1994). The adolescent male prostitute and sexually transmitted diseases, HIV and AIDS. *Journal of Adolescence, 17*(2), 123–130.

Markstrom, C. A., Sabino, V. M., Turner, B. J., & Berman, R. C. (1997). The psychosocial inventory of ego strengths: Development and validation of a new Eriksonian measure. *Journal of Youth and Adolescence, 26,* 705–732.

Markstrom-Adams, C., & Spencer, M. B. (1994). A model for identity intervention with minority adolescents. In S. L. Archer (Ed.), *Interventions for adolescent identity development* (pp. 84–102). Thousand Oaks, CA: Sage.

Markus, H., & Kunda, Z. (1986). Stability and malleability of the self-concept. *Journal of Personality and Social Psychology, 51,* 858–866.

Marshall, E. (1995). NIH's gay gene study questioned. *Science, 268*(5219), 1841.

Marshall, W. A., & Tanner, J. M. (1969). Variations in the pattern of pubertal changes in girls. *Archive of Disease in Childhood, 44,* 130.

Marshall, W. A., & Tanner, J. M. (1970). Variations in the pattern of pubertal changes in boys. *Archive of Disease in Childhood, 45*, 13.

Marta, E. (1997). Parent-adolescent interactions and psychosocial risks in adolescents: An analysis of communication, support, and gender. *Journal of Adolescence, 20*, 473–487.

Martin, C. L., & Halverson, C. F. (1981). A schematic processing model of sex typing and stereotyping in children. *Child Development, 52*, 1119–1134.

Martinez, V., Thomas, K., & Kemerer, F. R. (1994). Who chooses and why: A look at five school choice plans. *Phi Delta Kappan, 75*, 678–681.

Marx, J. L. (1986). The slow, insidious nature of the HTLV's. *Science, 231*, 450–451.

Marx, J. L. (1989). Do sperm spread the AIDS virus? *Science, 245*, 30.

Marx, J. L. (1994). Obesity gene discovery may help solve weighty problem. *Science, 266*(5190), 1477–1478.

Marziali, E., & Alexander, L. (1991). The power of the therapeutic relationship. *American Journal of Orthopsychiatry, 61*, 383–391.

Masters, W. H., & Johnson, V. E. (1966). *Human sexual response.* New York: HarperCollins.

Masters, W. H., Johnson, V. E., & Kolodny, R. C. (1994). *Heterosexuality*, New York: HarperCollins.

Mathews, D. (1996). *Is there a public for public schools?* Dayton, OH: Kettering Foundation Press.

Matteson, D. R. (1977). Exploration and commitment: Sex differences and methodological problems in the use of identity status categories. *Journal of Youth and Adolescence, 6*, 353–374.

McCabe, M. P., & Collins, J. K. (1984). Measurement of depth of desired and experienced sexual involvement at different stages of dating. *Journal of Sex Research, 20*, 377–390.

McCall, R. B., Appelbaum, M. J., & Hogarty, P. S. (1973). Developmental changes in mental performance. *Monographs of the Society for Research in Child Development, 38*(3, Serial No. 150), 60–93

McCammon, S., Knox, D., & Schacht, C. (1993). *Choices in sexuality.* St. Paul, MN: West.

McCandless, B. R. (1970). *Adolescents: Behavior and development.* Hinsdale, IL: Dryden Press.

McCarthy, B. R., & Smith, B. L. (1986). The conceptualization of discrimination in the juvenile justice process: The impact of administrative factors and screening decisions on juvenile court dispositions. *Criminology, 24*, 41–64.

McCarthy, F. B. (1977). Should juvenile delinquency be abolished? Crime and Delinquency, *23*, 196–203.

McCaul, M. E., Srikis, D. S., Turkkan, J. S., Bigelow, G. E., & Cromwell, C. C. (1990). Degree of familial alcoholism: Effects on substance use by college males. In L. S. Harris (Ed.), *Problems of drug dependence: 1989.* Washington, DC: U.S. Department of Health and Human Services publication ADM 90-1663. U.S. Government Printing Office.

McClure, G. M., Timimi, S., & Westman, A. (1995). Anorexia nervosa in early adolescence following illness—the importance of the sick role. *Journal of Adolescence, 18*(3), 359–369.

McConaghy, T. (1994). Downsizing: Changing Canada's educational landscape. *Phi Delta Kappan,, 76*(2), 172–173.

McConaghy, T. (1995). Multicultural policy under attack. *Phi Delta Kappan, 76*(6), 498–499.

McCord, J. (1978). A thirty-year follow-up of treatment effects. *American Psychologist, 33*, 284–289.

McCord, J., & McCord, W. (1964). The effects of parental role model on criminality. In R. Cavan (Ed.), *Readings in juvenile delinquency.* Philadelphia, PA: Lippincott.

McCord, W., & Sanchez, J. (1982). Curing criminal negligence. *Psychology Today, 16*, 79–82.

McCreary, M. L., Maffuid, J., & Stepter, T. A. (1998). Bridges to effective treatment: Family therapy and family psychoeducational interventions with maltreating and substance abusing fam-

ilies. In R. L. Hampton, V. Senatore, & T. P. Gullotta (Eds.), *Substance abuse, family violence, and child welfare* (pp. 220–248). Thousand Oaks, CA: Sage.

McCullough, M., & Scherman, A. (1991). Adolescent pregnancy: Contributing factors and strategies for prevention. *Adolescence, 26*, 809–816.

McDermott, D. (1984). The relationship of parental drug use and parents' attitudes concerning adolescent drug use to adolescent drug use. *Adolescence, 19*(73), 89–97.

McKenry, P. C., Tishler, C. L., & Christman, K. L. (1980). Adolescent suicide and the classroom teacher. *Journal of School Health, 50*, 130–132.

McKenry, P. C., Walters, L. H., & Johnson, C. (1979). Adolescent pregnancy: A review of the literature. *Family Coordinator, 28*, 16–28.

McNamara, V., King, L. A., & Green, M. F. (1979). Adolescent perspectives on sexuality, contraception, and pregnancy. *Journal of MAG, 68*, 811–814.

Mead, M. (1928). *Coming of age in Samoa.* New York: Morrow.

Mead, M. (1949). *Male and female.* New York: Morrow.

Mead, M. (1970). *Culture and commitment: A study of generation gap.* Garden city, NY: Natural History Press.

Mecklenburger, J. A. (1993). The braking of the "break-the-mold" express. *Phi Delta Kappan, 74*, 280–289.

Medrow, K. (1995). *Street terms: Drugs and the drug trade.* Washington, DC: Office of National Drug Control Policy, NCJ-151622, U.S. Government Printing Office.

Medway, F. J., & Smircic, J. M. (1992). Willingness to use corporal punishment among school administrators in South Carolina. *Psychological Reports, 71*, 65–66.

Meilman, P. W. (1979). Cross-sectional age changes in ego identity status during adolescence. *Developmental Psychology, 15*, 230–231.

Meltzer, F. (1987). Editor's introduction: Partitive plays, pipe dreams. *Critical Inquiry, 13*, 215–221.

Mennel, R. (1973). *Thorns and thistles: Juvenile delinquency in the United States.* Hanover, NH: University of New England Press.

Menninger, K. A. (1938). *Man against himself.* New York: Harcourt, Brace, Jovanovich.

Menninger, K. A. (1965). *The human mind.* New York: Knopf.

Merton, R. K. (1937). Social structure and anomie. *American Sociological Review, 3,* 672–682.

Meyer, A. (1995). Primary prevention approaches to reducing substance misuse. In T. P. Gullotta, G. R. Adams, & R. Montemayor (Eds.), *Adolescent substance misuse.* Newbury Park, CA: Sage.

Meyer, V. F. (1991). A critique of adolescent pregnancy prevention research. The invisible white male. *Adolescence, 26,* 217–222.

Mikulecky, L. (1990). National adult literacy and lifelong learning goals. *Phi Delta Kappan, 72,* 304–309.

Miller, A. (1949/1983). *Death of a salesman.* New York: Penguin.

Miller, A. T., Eggertson-Tacon, C., & Quigg, B. (1990). Patterns of runaway behavior within a larger systems context: The road to empowerment. *Adolescence, 25,* 271–290.

Miller, B. C., Christensen, R., & Olson, T. D. (1987). Self-esteem in relation to adolescent sexual attitudes and behavior. *Youth and Society, 18,* 16–32.

Miller, B. C., Christopherson, C. R., & King, P. K. (1993). Sexual behavior in adolescence. In T. P. Gullotta, G. R. Adams, & R. Montemayor (Eds.), *Adolescent sexuality.* Newbury Park, CA: Sage.

Miller, B. C., & Fox, G. L. (1987). Theories of adolescent heterosexual behavior. *Journal of Adolescent Research, 2,* 269–282.

Miller, B. C., & Heaton, T. B. (1991). Age at first sexual intercourse and the timing of marriage and childbirth. *Journal of Marriage and the Family, 53,* 719–732.

Miller, B. C., McCoy, J. K., & Olson, T. D. (1986). Dating age and stage as correlates of adolescent sexual attitudes and behavior. *Journal of Adolescent Research, 1,* 361–371.

Miller, B. C., McCoy, J. K., Olson, T. D., & Wallace, C. M. (1986). Parental discipline and control attempts in relation to adolescent sexual attitudes and behavior. *Journal of Marriage and the Family, 48,* 503–512.

Miller, B. C., & Moore, K. A. (1990). Adolescent sexual behavior, pregnancy, and parenting: Research through the 1980s. *Journal of Marriage and the Family, 52,* 1025–1044.

Miller, B. C., Norton, M. C., Fan, X., & Christopherson, C. R. (1998). Pubertal development, parental communication, and sexual values in relation to adolescent sexual behavior. *Journal of Early Adolescence, 18,* 27–52.

Miller, J. B. (1976). *Toward a new psychology of women.* Boston, MA: Beacon Press.

Miller, J. B., & Stiver, I. P. (1997). *The healing connection: How women form relationships in therapy and in life.* Boston, MA: Beacon Press.

Miller, P., & Simon, W. (1974). Adolescent sexual behavior: Context and change. *Social Problems, 22,* 58–75.

Miller, R. L. (1989). Desegregation experiences of minority students: Adolescent coping strategies in five Connecticut high schools. *Journal of Adolescent Research, 4,* 173–189.

Miller, R. L. (1990). Beyond contact theory: The impact of community affluence of integration efforts in five suburban high schools. *Youth & Society, 22,* 12–34.

Mills, C. J. (1981). Sex roles, personality, and intellectual abilities in adolescents. *Journal of Youth and Adolescence, 10,* 85–112.

Mintz, J. (1997, January 13). Getting a financial high from rope. *Washington Post Weekly Edition,* 18.

Mischel, W. (1973). Toward a cognitive social learning reconceptualization of personality. *Psychological Review, 80,* 252–283.

Mischel, W. (1979). On the interface of cognition and personality: Beyond the person-situation debate. *American Psychologist, 34,* 740–754.

Mitchell, J. E. (1976). Adolescent intimacy. *Adolescence, 11,* 275–280.

Mitchell, J. E., Hatsukami, D., Eckert, E. D., & Pyle, R. L. (1985). Characteristics of 275 patients with bulimia. *American Journal of Psychiatry, 142,* 482–485.

Moffitt, T. E., Gabrielli, W. F., Mednick, S. A., & Schulsinger, F. (1981). Socioeconomic status, IQ, and delinquency. *Journal of Abnormal Psychology, 90,* 152–156.

Molin, R. S. (1986). Covert suicide and families of adolescents. *Adolescence, 21*(81), 177–184.

Money, J. (1994). The concept of gender identity disorder in childhood and adolescence after 39 years. *Journal of Sex & Marital Therapy, 20,* 163–177.

Monroe, P. (1940). *Founding of the American public school system.* New York: Macmillan.

Montemayor, R. (1981, April). Correlates of parent-adolescent conflict. Paper presented at the meeting of the Utah Council on Family Relations, Provo, UT.

Montemayor, R. (1990). Continuity and change in the behavior of nonhuman primates during the transition of adolescence. In R. Montemayor, G. R. Adams, & T. P. Gullotta (Eds.), *From childhood to adolescence: A transitional period?* Newbury Park, CA: Sage.

Montemayor, R. (1994). *Parent-adolescent relations. Vision 2010: Families and Adolescents* (pp. 2–3). Minneapolis: National Council on Family Relations.

Montemayor, R., Adams, G. R. & Gullotta, T. P. (1994). *Personal relationships during adolescence.* Thousand Oaks, CA: Sage.

Montemayor, R., & Flannery, D. J. (1991). Making the transition from childhood to early adolescence. In R. Montemayor, G. R. Adams, and T. P. Gullotta (Eds.), *From childhood to adolescence: A transitional period?* Thousand Oaks, CA: Sage.

Montemayor, R., & Gregg, V. R. (1994). Current theory and research on personal relationships during adolescence. In R. Montemayor, G. R. Adams, & T. P. Gullotta (Eds.), *Personal relationships during adolescence* (pp. 236–245). Thousand Oaks, CA: Sage.

Montemayor, R., & Hanson, E. (1985). A naturalistic view of conflict between adolescents and their parents and siblings. *Journal of Early Adolescence, 5*(1), 23–30.

Montemayor, R., & Van Komen, R. (1980). Age segregation of adolescents in and out of school. *Journal of Youth and Adolescence, 9*, 371–381.

Moodley, K. A. (1995). Multicultural education in Canada: Historical development and current status. In J. A. Banks, & C. A. M. Banks (Eds.), *Handbook of research on multicultural education* (pp. 801–820). New York: Simon & Shuster/Macmillan.

Moore, S., & Rosenthal, D. (1991). Adolescent invulnerability and perceptions of AIDS risk. *Journal of Adolescence* Research, *6*, 164–180.

Moran, P. B., & Eckenrode, J. (1991). Gender differences in the costs and benefits of peer relationships during adolescence. *Journal of Adolescent Research, 6*, 396–409.

Morell, V. (1993). Enzyme may blunt cocaine's action. *Science, 259*, 1828.

Moreno, A. B., & Thelen, M. H. (1995). Eating behavior in junior high school females. *Adolescence, 30*(117), 171–174.

Morgan, C., Chapar, G. N., & Fisher, M. (1995). Psychosocial variables associated with teenage pregnancy. *Adolescence, 30*(118), 277–289.

Morrison, D. R., & Cherlin, A. J. (1995). The divorce process and young children's well-being: A prospective analysis. *Journal of Marriage and the Family, 57*, 800–812.

Mortimer, J. T., Finch, M., Shanahan, M., & Rhu, S. (1992). Work experience, mental health, and behavioral adjustment in adolescence. *Journal of Research on Adolescence, 2*, 25–57.

Morton, R. (1720). *Phthisiologia: Or a treatise of consumptions, wherein the differences, nature, causes, signs, and cure of all sorts of consumptions are explained.* London: Sam, Smith, & Beny.

Moscicki, E. K. (1995). Epidemiology of suicide behavior. *Suicide and Life-Threatening Behavior, 25*, 22–33.

Mosher, D. L., & Tomkins, S. S. (1987). Scripting the macho man: Hypermasculine socialization and enculturation. *The Journal of Sex Research, 26*, 60–84.

Mosteller, F. (1995). The Tennessee study of class size in the early school grades. *The Future of Children, 5*(2), 113–127.

Mosteller, F., & Moynihan, D. P. (1972). *On equality of educational opportunity.* New York: Vintage.

Mrazek, P. J., & Haggerty, R. J. (1994). *Reducing risks for mental disorders.* Washington, DC: National Academy Press.

Mullis, R. L., & McKinley, K. (1989). Gender-role orientation of adolescent females: Effects on self-esteem and locus of control. *Journal of Adolescent Research, 4*, 506–516.

Mulvey, E. P., & LaRosa, J. F. (1986). Delinquency cessation and adolescent development: Preliminary data. *American Journal of Orthopsychiatry, 56*, 212–224.

Munro, G., & Adams, G. R. (1977b). Ego-identity formation in college students and working youth. *Developmental Psychology, 13*, 523–524.

Munoz, R. F. (1997). The San Francisco depression prevention research project. In G. W. Albee & T. P. Gullotta (Eds.), *Primary prevention works.* (pp. 380–400) Thousand Oaks, CA: Sage.

Murphy, N. T., & Price, C. J. (1988). The influence of self-esteem, parental smoking, and living in a tobacco production region on adolescent smoking behaviors. *Journal of School Health, 58*, 401–404.

Murray, J. P. (1980). *Television and youth: 25 years of research and controversy.* Boys Town, NE: Boys Town Center for the Study of Youth Development.

Murstein, B. I., & Mercy, T. (1994). Sex, drugs, relationships, contraception, and fears of disease on a college campus over 17 years. *Adolescence, 29*(114), 303–322.

Musgrove, F. (1964). *Youth and the social order.* Bloomington, IN: Indiana University Press.

Muuss, R. E. (1985). Adolescent eating disorder: Anorexia nervosa. *Adolescence, 20*, 525–536.

Muuss, R. E. (1986). Adolescent eating disorder: Bulimia. *Adolescence, 21*, 257–267.

Muuss, R. E. (1996). *Theories of adolescence* (6th ed.). New York: McGraw–Hill.

Nabokov, V. (1955/1989). *Lolita.* New York: Vintage.

Nadelman, E. A. (1989). Drug prohibition in the United States: Costs, consequences, and alternatives. *Science, 245*, 939–947.

Nadelson, C. C., Notman, M. T., & Gillon, J. W. (1980). Sexual knowledge and attitudes of adolescents: Relationship to contraceptive use. *Obstetrics and Gynecology, 55*, 340–345.

Nagata, D. K. (1989). Japanese American children and adolescents. In J. T. Gibbs & L. N. Huang (Eds.), *Children of color.* San Francisco: Jossey–Bass.

Nasaw, D. (1979). *Schooled to order: A social history of public schooling in the United States.* New York: Oxford University Press.

National Advisory Mental Health Council (1990). *National plan for research on child and adolescent mental disorders.* Washington, DC: National Institute of Mental Health.

National Commission on Children (1991). *Speaking of kids.* Washington, DC: Author.

National Council on Crime and Delinquency (1984). *Rethinking juvenile justice: National statistical trends.* Minneapolis, MN: University of Minnesota Press.

National Institute of Alcohol Abuse and Alcoholism (1984). *Alcohol and health* Washington, DC: DHHS publication ADM 84-1291, U.S. Government Printing Office.

National Institute of Alcohol Abuse and Alcoholism (1997). Patient-treatment matching. *Alcohol Alert, 36*, 3–6.

National Institute of Alcohol Abuse and Alcoholism (1997a). Youth drinking: Risk factors and consequences. *Alcohol Alert, 37*, 1–6.

National Institute of Alcohol Abuse and Alcoholism (1997b). Alcohol, violence, and aggression. *Alcohol Alert, 38*, 1–6.

National Institute of Alcohol Abuse and Alcoholism (1998). Alcohol and tobacco. *Alcohol Alert, 39,* 1–6.

National Institute on Drug Abuse (1978a). *Inhalants.* Washington, DC: DHHS publication ADM 79-742, U.S. Government Printing Office.

National Institute on Drug Abuse (1982). *Marijuana and youth: Clinical Observations on motivation and learning.* Washington, DC: DHHS publication ADM 82-1186, U.S. Government Printing Office.

National Institute on Drug Abuse (1987a). *Cocaine/crack.* Washington, DC: DHHS publication ADM 87-1427, U.S. Government Printing Office.

National Institute on Drug Abuse (1987b). *Drug abuse and drug abuse research: The second triennial report to Congress.* Washington, DC: DHHS publication ADM 87-1486. U.S. Government Printing Office.

National Institute of Drug Abuse (1995). *Inhalant abuse.* Washington, DC: NIDA Capsule 44, U.S. Government Printing Office.

National Institute of Drug Abuse (1995). *LSD* (Lysergic Acid Diethylamide). Washington, DC: NIDA Capsule 39, U.S. Government Printing Office.

National Institute of Mental Health (1977). *Trends in mental health: Self-destructive behavior among younger age groups.* Washington, DC: DHEW publication ADM 77-365, U.S. Government Printing Office.

National Research Council (1993). *Losing generations: Adolescents in high-risk settings.* Washington, DC: National Academy Press.

Needle, R. H., Su, S. S., & Doherty, W. J. (1990). Divorce, remarriage, and adolescent substance use: A prospective longitudinal study. *Journal of Marriage and the Family, 52,* 157–169.

Neher, L. S., & Short, J. L. (1998). Risk and protective factors for children's substance use and antisocial behavior following a parental divorce. *American Journal of Orthopsychiatry, 68,* 154–161.

Neider, C. (Ed.) (1959). *The Autobiography of Mark Twain.* New York: Harper.

Nelson, M. B. (1995). *The stronger women get, the more men love football: Sexism and the American culture of sports.* New York: Harcourt, Brace, Jovanovich.

Nettina, S. L. (1990). Syphilis. *American Journal of Nursing, 43,* 68–70.

Newcomb, M. D. (1984). Sexual behavior, responsiveness, and attitudes among women: A test of two theories. *Journal of Sex and Marital Therapy, 10,* 272–286.

Newcomb, M. D., & Bentler, P. M. (1986). Substance use and ethnicity: Differential impact of peer and adult models. The *Journal of Psychology, 120,* 83–95.

Newcomb, M. D., Huba, G. J., & Bentler, P. M. (1983). Mothers' influence on the drug use of their children: Confirmatory tests of direct modeling and mediational theories. *Developmental Psychology, 19,* 714–726.

Newcomb, M. D., Huba, G. J., & Bentler, P. M. (1986). Determinants of sexual and dating behaviors among adolescents. *Journal of Personality and Social Psychology, 50,* 428–438.

Newcomb, M. D., Maddahian, E., Skager, R., & Bentler, P. M. (1987). Substance abuse and psychosocial risk factors among teenagers: Associations with sex, age, ethnicity, and type of school. *American Journal of Drug and Alcohol Abuse, 13,* 413–433.

Newman, B. M. (1976). The study of interpersonal behavior in adolescence. *Adolescence, 11,* 127–142.

Newman, P. R., & Newman, B. M. (1976). Early adolescence and its conflict: Group identity versus alienation. *Adolescence, 11,* 261–274.

Newton, M. (1995). *Adolescence.* New York: Norton.

Newton-Ruddy, L., & Handelsman, M. M. (1986). Jungian feminine psychology and adolescent prostitutes. *Adolescence, 21,* 815–825.

New York Times (1993). Repotted, March 7, 1, 9.

New York Times News Service (1990). AIDS discovered in tissue from 1959.

Nicholson, T. (1992). The primary prevention of illicit drug problems: An argument for decriminalization and legalization. *Journal of Primary Prevention, 12,* 275–288.

Nicholson, T. (1995). Social policy and adolescent drug consumption: The legalization option. In T. P. Gullotta, G. R. Adams, & R. Montemayor (Eds.), *Adolescent substance misuse.* Newbury Park, CA: Sage.

Nielson, A., & Gerber, D. (1979). Psychosocial aspects of truancy in early adolescence. *Adolescence, 14,* 313–326.

Niles, F. S. (1981). The youth culture controversy: An evaluation. *Journal of Early Adolescence, 1*(3), 265–271.

Nisbet, P. A. (1996). Protective factors for suicidal black females. *Suicide and Life-Threatening Behavior, 26,* 325–329.

Nitz, K., Ketterlinus, R. D., and Brandt, L. J. (1995). The role of stress, social support, and family environment in adolescent mothers' parenting. *Journal of Adolescent Research, 10*(2), 358–382.

Novas, H. (1994). *Everything you need to know about latino history.* New York: Penguin.

Nowak, R. (1994). Nicotine scrutinized as FDA seeks to regulate cigarettes. *Science, 263*(5153), 1555–1556.

Nyamathi, A., & Vasquez, R. (1995). Impact of poverty, homelessness, and drugs on Hispanic women at risk for HIV infection. In A. M. Padilla (Ed.), *Hispanic psychology: Critical issues in theory and research* (pp. 213–227). Thousand Oaks, CA: Sage.

Nye, I. F. (1957). Child adjustment in broken and in unhappy broken homes. *Marriage & Family Living, 19,* 356–361.

Nye, I. F. (1958). *Family relationships and delinquent behavior.* New York: Wiley.

Nye, I. F., & Lamberts, M. B. (1980). *School-age parenthood.* Pullman: Washington State University Cooperative Extension.

Obot, I. S. (1996). Problem drinking, chronic disease, and recent live events. In H. W. Neighbors & J. S. Jackson (Eds.), *Mental health in Black America* (pp. 45–61). Thousand Oaks, CA: Sage.

O'Brien, C. P. (1997). A range of research-based pharmacotherapies for addiction. *Science, 278,* 66–69.

Oetting, E. R., & Beauvais, F. (1982). *Drug use among American youth: Summary of findings* (1975–1981). Fort Collins, CO: Western Behavioral Studies.

Oetting, E. R., Beauvais, F., & Edwards, R. (1988). Alcohol and Indian youth: Social and psychological correlates and prevention. *The Journal of Drug Issues, 18*, 87–101.

Offer, D., Marohn, R., & Ostrov, E. (1979). *The psychological world of the juvenile delinquent*. New York: Basic Books.

Office of Technology Assessment (1991). *Adolescent health* (Vol. II, No. OTA-H-466). Washington, DC: U.S. Government Printing Office.

Ogbu, J. U. (1987). Variability in minority school performance: A problem in search of an explanation. *Anthropology & Education Quarterly, 18*, 312–334.

Ogbu, J. U. (1997). Understanding the school performance of urban Blacks: Some essential background knowledge. In H. J. Walberg, O. Reyes, & R. P. Weissberg (Eds.) *Children and Youth* (pp. 190–222). Thousand Oaks, CA: Sage.

Ohlrich, E. S., & Stephenson, J. N. (1986). Pitfalls in the care of patients with anorexia nervosa & bulimia. *Seminars in Adolescent Medicine, 2*, 81–88.

Olson, D. H., Russell, C. S., & Sprenkle, D. H. (1980). Marital and family therapy: A decade review. *Journal of Marriage and the Family, 42*, 973–994.

O'Neill, B. (1994, March 6). The history of a hoax. *New York Times Magazine*, pp. 46–49.

O'Neill, E. (1955/1984). *Long day's journey into night*. New Haven, CT: Yale University Press.

Opinion Research Corporation (1976). *National statistical survey on runaway youth* (Part 1). Princeton, NJ: Author.

Orbach, I., Gross, Y., & Glaubman, H. (1981). Some common characteristics of latency-age suicidal children: A tentative model based on case study analysis. *Suicide and Life-Threatening Behavior, 11*(3), 180–190.

Orcutt, H. K., & Cooper, M. L. (1997). The effects of pregnancy experience on contraceptive practice. *Journal of Youth and Adolescence, 26*, 763–778.

Orentlicher, D. (1992). Corporal punishment in schools. *Journal of the American Medical Association, 267*(23), 3205–3208.

Orlofsky, J., & Frank, M. (1986). Personality structure as viewed through early memories and identity status in college men and women. *Journal of Personality and Social Psychology, 50*, 580–586.

Orlofsky, J., Marcia, J., & Lesser, I. (1973). Ego identity status and the intimacy vs. isolation crisis in young adulthood. *Journal of Personality and Social Psychology, 27*, 211–219.

Orlofsky, J. L. (1978). Identity formation, achievement, and fear of success in college men and women. *Journal of Youth and Adolescence, 7*, 49–62.

Orthner, D. K. (1990). Parental work and early adolescence. *Journal of Early Adolescence, 10*, 246–259.

Osvold, L. L., & Sodowsky, G. R. (1993). Eating disorders of white American, racial and ethnic minority American, and international women. *Journal of Multicultural Counseling and Development, 21*, 143–154.

Osvold, L. L., & Sodowsky, G. R. (in press). Eating attitudes of Native American and African American women: Differences by ethnicity/race and acculturation. *Explorations in Ethnic Studies*.

Pabon, E., Rodriguez, O., & Gurin, G. (1992). Clarifying peer relations and delinquency. *Youth and Society, 24*, 149–165.

Pace, N. A. (1981). Driving on pot. In L. H. Gross (Ed.), *The parent's guide to teenagers*. New York: Macmillan.

Paglia, A., & Room, R. (1999). Preventing substance use problems among youth: A literature review and recommendations. *Journal of Primary Prevention, 20*.

Paikoff, R. L., & Brooks-Gunn, J. (1991). Do parent–child relationships change during puberty? *Psychological Bulletin, 110*, 47–66.

Paikoff, R. L., Brooks-Gunn, J., & Warren, M. P. (1991). Effects of girls' hormonal status on affective expression over the course of one year. *Journal of Youth and Adolescence, 20*, 191–214.

Palca, J. (1991). HIV risk higher for infants born twins. *Science, 254*, 1729.

Palca, J. (1992). Human SIV infections suspected. *Science, 257*, 606.

Palmer, R. B., & Liddle, H. A. (1996). Adolescent drug abuse: Contemporary perspectives on etiology and treatment. In G. Blau & T. P. Gullotta (Eds.), *Adolescent dysfunctional behavior* (pp. 114–138). Thousand Oaks, CA: Sage.

Palladino, G. (1996). *Teenagers: An American history*. New York: Basic Books.

Pallas, A. M., & Alexander, K. L. (1983). Sex differences in quantitative SAT performance: New evidence on the differential coursework hypothesis. *American Educational Research Journal, 20*, 165–182.

Paluszny, M., Davenport, C., & Kim, W. J. (1991). Suicide attempts and ideation: Adolescents evaluated on a pediatric ward. *Adolescence, 26*, 208–215.

Parish, T. S. (1987). Family and environment. In V. B. Van Hasselt & M. Hersen (Eds.), *The handbook of adolescent psychology*. New York: Pergamon Press.

Parish, T., & Taylor, J. (1979). The impact of divorce and subsequent father absence on children's and adolescents' self-concepts. Journal of Youth and Adolescence, 8, 427–432.

Parloff, M. B. (1977). *Shopping for the right therapy*. Washington, DC: National Institute of Mental Health, DHEW publication ADM 77-426, U.S. Government Printing Office.

Parsons, T. (1959). The school class as a social system. *Harvard Educational Review, 29*, 297–318.

Pascale, R., Hurd, M., & Primavera, L. H. (1980). The effects of chronic marijuana use. *Journal of Social Psychology, 110*, 273–283.

Pate-Bain, H., Achilles, C. M., Boyd-Zaharias, T., & McKenna, B. (1992). Class size does make a difference. *Phi Delta Kappan, 74*, 253–256.

Patton, W., & Nolles, P. (1991). The family and the unemployed adolescent. *Journal of Adolescence, 14*, 343–362.

Paulson, J. E., Koman, J. J., & Hill, J. P. (1990). Maternal employment and parent-child relations in families of seventh graders. *Journal of Early Adolescence, 10*, 279–295.

Pauwels, L. & Bergier, J. (1988). *The morning of the magicians.* New York: Dorset Press.

Paykel, E. S. (1989). Stress and life events. In *Report of the secretary's task force on youth suicide: Risk factors for youth suicide* (Vol. 2), Washington, DC: U.S. Department of Health and Human Services publication ADM 89-1622, U.S. Government Printing Office.

Paxton, S. J, (1993). A prevention program for disturbed eating and body dissatisfaction in adolescent girls: A one year follow-up. *Health Education Research, 8*, 43–51.

Peck, D. L. (1987). Social-psychological correlates of adolescent and youthful suicide. *Adolescence, 22*, 863–878.

Peele, S. (1986). The implications and limitations of genetic models of alcoholism and other addictions. *Journal of Studies on Alcohol, 47*(1), 63–73.

Peiser, N. C., & Heaven, C. L. (1996). Family influences on self-reported delinquency among high school students. *Journal of Adolescence, 19*, 557–568.

Perkins, D. (1995). *Outsmarting IQ: the emerging science of learnable intelligence.* New York: Free Press.

Perrin, L., & Telenti, A. (1998). HIV treatment failure: Testing for HIV resistance in clinical practice. *Science, 280*, 1871–1873.

Perry, C. L., & Murray, D. M. (1985). The prevention of adolescent drug abuse: Implications from etiological, developmental, behavioral, and environmental models. *Journal of Primary Prevention, 6*(1), 31–52.

Pestrak, V. A., & Martin, P. (1985). Cognitive development and aspects of adolescent sexuality. *Adolescence, 20*, 981–987.

Petersen, A. C. (1979, March). The psychological significance of pubertal changes to adolescent girls. Paper presented at the meeting of the Society for Research in Child Development, San Francisco.

Petersen, A. C., & Taylor, B. (1980). The biological approach to adolescence. In J. Adelson (Ed.), *The handbook of adolescent psychology.* New York: Wiley.

Petersen, A. C., Leffert, N., & Graham, B. L. (1995). Adolescent development and the emergence of sexuality. *Suicide and Life-Threatening Behaviors, 25*, 4–17.

Peterson, P. L., Hawkins, J. D., Abbott, R. D., & Catalano, R. F. (1994). Disentangling the effects of parental drinking, family management, and parental alcohol norms on current drinking by black and white adolescents. *Journal of Research on Adolescence, 4*(2), 203–227.

Pettinatti, H. M., & Wade, J. H. (1986). Hypnosis in the treatment of anorexia and bulimia patients. *Seminars in Adolescent Medicine, 2*, 75–80.

Pfeffer, C. R. (1981a). The family system of suicidal children. *American Journal of Psychotherapy, 35*(3), 330–341.

Pfeffer, C. R. (1981b). Suicidal behavior of children: A review in the implications for research and practice. *American Journal of Psychiatry, 138*(2), 154–159.

Pfeffer, C. R. (1989). Family characteristics and support systems as risk factors for youth suicide behavior. In ADAMHA. *Report of the secretary's task force on youth suicide: Risk factors for youth suicide.* (Vol. 2), Washington, DC: U.S. Department of Health and Human Services publication ADM 89-1622, U.S. Government Printing Office.

Pfeffer, C. R., Klerman, G. L., Hurt, S. W., Lessor, M., Peskin, J. R., & Siefker, C. A. (1991). Suicidal children grow up: Demographic and clinical risk factors for adolescent suicide attempts. *Journal American Academy of Child Adolescent Psychiatry, 30*, 609–616.

Pfeffer, C. R., Plutchik, R., & Mizruchi, M. S. (1983). Suicidal and assaultive behavior in children: Classification, measurement, and interrelations. *American Journal of Psychiatry, 140*(2), 154–157.

Philips, S., McMillen, C., Sparks, J., & Ueberle, M. (1995). Concrete strategies for sensitizing youth-serving agencies to the needs of gay, lesbian, and other sexually minority youths. *Child Welfare, 76*, 393–409.

Phillips, D. P., & Carstensen, L. L. (1988). The effect of suicide stories on various demographic groups 1968–1985. *Suicide and Life-Threatening Behaviors, 18*, 100–114.

Phinney, J. S. (1989). Stages of ethnic identity development in minority group adolescents. *Journal of Early Adolescence, 9*, 34–49.

Phinney, J. S. (1992). The multigroup ethnic identity measure: A new scale for use with diverse groups. *Journal of Adolesent Research, 7*, 156–176.

Phinney, J. S. (1995). Ethnic identity and self-esteem. In A. M. Padilla (Ed.), *Hispanic psychology: Critical issues in theory and research* (pp. 57–70). Thousand Oaks, CA: Sage.

Phinney, J. S., & Chavira, V. (1992). Ethnic identity and self-esteem: An exploratory longitudinal study. *Journal of Adolescence, 15*, 271–281.

Phinney, J. S., Chavira, V., & Williamson, L. (1992). Acculturation attitudes and self-esteem among high school and college students. *Youth & Society, 23*, 299–312.

Phipps-Yonas, S. (1980). Teenage pregnancy and motherhood. *American Journal of Orthopsychiatry, 50*, 403–441.

Photiadis, J. D. (1985). *Community and family change in rural Appalachia.* Morgantown, WV: West Virginia University.

Pierce, R. V. (1895). *The People's Common Sense Medical Advisor.* Buffalo, NY: World's Dispensary Printing Office and Bindery.

Piot, P., Plummer, F. A., Nhalu, F. S., Lamboray, J., Chin, J., & Mann, J. M. (1988). AIDS: An international perspective. *Science, 239*, 573–579.

Pipho, C. (1998). Living with zero tolerance. *Phi Delta Kappan, 79*, 725–726.

Piran, N. (2000). Eating disorders: A trial of prevention in a high risk school setting. *Journal of Primary Prevention, 20*, in press.

Plant, R. (1999). The future of psychotherapy in a changing health care system. In T. P. Gullotta, G. R. Adams, R. Hampton, B. Ryan, & R. Weissberg (Eds.) *Child health care: Issues for the Year 2000 and beyond* (in press). Thousand Oaks, CA: Sage.

Plath, S. (1963). *The bell jar.* New York: Harper and Row.

Pleck, J. H. (1979). Men's family work: Three perspectives and some new data. *Family Coordinator, 28*, 481–495.

Pleck, J. H. (1983). The theory of male sex role identity: Its rise and fall, 1936–present. *In M. Lewin* (Ed.), *In the shadow of the past: Psychology portrays the sexes.* New York: Columbia University Press.

Pleck, J. H., Sonenstein, F. L., & Ku, L. C. (1991). Adolescent males' condom use: Relationships between perceived cost-benefits and consistency. *Journal of Marriage and the Family, 53*, 733–745.

Pleck, J. H., Sonenstein, F. L., & Ku, L. C. (1993). Masculinity ideology: its impact on adolescent males' heterosexual relationships. *Journal of Social Issues, 49*(3), 11–29.

Pleck, J. H., Sonenstein, F. L., & Ku, L. C. (1994). Problem behaviors and masculinity ideology in adolescent males. In R. D. Ketterlinus & M. E. Lamb (Eds.), *Adolescent problem behaviors: Issues and research* (pp. 165–186). Hillsdale, NJ: Erlbaum.

Plomin, R. (1990). The role of inheritance in behavior. *Science, 248*, 183–188.

Plomin, R. (1990). *Nature and nurture.* Pacific Grove, CA: Brooks/Cole.

Plomin, R. (1994). *Genetics and experience.* Thousand Oaks, CA: Sage.

Plomin, R., Owen, M. J., & McGuffin, P. (1994). The genetic basis of complex human behavior. *Science, 264*(5166). 1733–1739.

Plotnick, R. D., & Butler, S. S. (1991). Attitudes and adolescent nonmarital childbearing. *Journal of Adolescent Research, 6*, 470–492.

Podd, M. H. (1972). Ego identity status and morality: The relationship between two developmental constructs. *Developmental Psychology, 6*, 499–507.

Polk, V. (1984). Juvenile diversion: A look at the record. *Crime and Delinquency, 30*, 648–659.

Pollock, G. H. (1997). Fallen from grace. *Readings, 12*, 12–16.

Pong, S. (1997). Family structure, school context, and eight-grade math and reading achievement. *Journal of Marriage and the Family, 59*, 734–746.

Poppen, P. J. (1994). Adolescent contraceptive use and communication: Changes over a decade. *Adolescence, 29*(115), 503–514.

Porter, M. R., Vieira, T. A., Kaplan, G. J., Heesch, J. R., & Colyar, A. B. (1973). Drug use in Anchorage, Alaska: A survey of 15,634 students in grades 6 through 12–1971. *Journal of the American Medical Association, 223*, 657–664.

Portes, P. R., Dunham, R. M., & Williams, S. (1986). Assessing child-rearing style in ecological settings: Its relation to culture, social class, early age intervention, and scholastic achievement. *Adolescence, 21*, 723–735.

Poulin, J. E. (1991). Racial differences in the use of drugs and alcohol among low income youth and young adults. *Journal of Sociology & Social Welfare, 20*, 159–166.

Potter, L. B., Powell, K. E., & Kachur, S. P. (1995). Suicide prevention from a public health perspective. *Suicide and Life-Threatening Behavior, 25*, 82–91.

Powell, A. G. (1985). Being unspecial in the shopping mall high school. *Phi Delta Kappan, 67*, 255–261.

Prager, K. J. (1982). Identity development and self-esteem in young women. *Journal of Genetic Psychology, 141*, 177–182.

Prager, K. J. (1983). Identity status, sex-role orientations, and self-esteem in late adolescent females. *Journal of Genetic Psychology, 143*, 159–167.

Prause, J., & Dooley, D. (1997). Effect of under-employment on school-leavers' self-esteem. *Journal of Adolescence, 20*, 243–260.

President Carter's Address to the U.S. Congress on Drug Use (1977, September/October). *Drug Survival News, 6.*

Pressley, J. S., & Whitley, R. L. (1996). Let's hear it for the "Dumb Jock": What athletics contribute to the academic program. *NASSP Bulletin, 80*, 74–83.

Price, R., Cowen, E., Lorion, R., & Ramos-McKay, J. (Eds.) (1988). *14 ounces of prevention: A casebook for practitioners.* Washington, DC: American Psychological Association.

Price, R. W., Bres, B., Sidtis, J., Rosenblum, M., Scheck, A. C., & Cleary, P. (1988). The brain in AIDS: Central nervous system HIV-1 infection and AIDS dementia complex. *Science, 239*, 586–592.

Price, W. H., Whatmore, P. B., & McClemont, W. F. (1966). Criminal patients with XYY sex chromosome complement. *Lancet, 1*, 565–566.

Proctor, C. D., & Groze, V. K. (1994). Risk factors for suicide among gay, lesbian, and bisexual youths. *Social Work, 39*, 504–513.

Protinsky, H., & Wilkerson, J. (1986). Ego identity, egocentrism, and formal operations. *Adolescence, 21*, 461–466.

Protter, B. S. (1973). Ego identity status: Construct validity and temporal orientation. Unpublished doctoral dissertation, Purdue University.

Radford, J. L., King, A. J. C., & Warren, W. K. (1989). *Street youth and AIDS.* Ottawa, Ontario: Human Resource Development, Canada.

Rahav, G. (1977). Juvenile delinquency as minority crime. *Adolescence, 12*, 471–475.

Rains, P. (1971). *Becoming an unwed mother.* Chicago, IL: Aldine–Atherton.

Ralph. J., Keller, D., & Crouse, J. (1994). How effective are American schools. *Phi Delta Kappan, 76*(2), 144–150.

Ramirez, O. (1989). Mexican American children and adolescents. In J. T. Gibbs & L. N. Hung (Eds.), *Children of color: Psychological intervention with minority youth.* San Francisco: Jossey–Bass.

Ramsey, C. E. (1967). *Problems of youth.* Belmont, CA: Dickinson.

Ramsey, G. (1943). The sexual development of boys. *American Journal of Psychiatry, 56*, 217–234.

Range, L. M., Goggin, W. C., & Steede, K. K. (1988). Perception of behavioral contagion of adolescent suicide. *Suicide and Life-Threatening Behavior, 18*, 334–341.

Rangell, L. (1988). The decision to terminate one's life: Psychoanalytic thoughts on suicide. *Suicide and Life-Threatening Behavior, 18*, 28–36.

Rappaport, H., Enrich, K., & Wilson, A. (1985). Relation between ego identity and temporal perspective. *Journal of Personality and Social Psychology, 48*, 1609–1630.

Rasmussen, J. E. (1964). Relationship of ego identity to psychosocial effectiveness. *Psychological Reports*, *15*, 815–825.

Ravert, A. A., and Martin, J. (1997). Family stress, perception of pregnancy, and age of first menarche among pregnant adolescents. *Adolescence*, *32*, 261–269.

Read, D., Adams, G. R., & Dobson, W. R. (1984). Ego-identity status, personality, and social influence style. *Journal of Personality and Social Psychology*, *46*, 169–177.

Redmond, M. A. (1985). Attitudes of adolescent males toward adolescent pregnancy and fatherhood. *Family Relations*, *34*, 337–342.

Reed, M. K. (1994). Social skills training to reduce depression in adolescence. *Adolescence*, *29*(114), 293–302.

Reinhard, D. W. (1977). The reaction of adolescent boys and girls to the divorce of their parents. *Journal of Clinical Child Psychology*, *6*(2), 21–23.

Reisman, J. M. (1985). Friendship and its implications for mental health or social competence. *Journal of Early Adolescence*, *5*(3), 383–391.

Reiss, A. J. (1952). Social correlates of psychological types of delinquency. *American Sociological Review*, *17*, 710–718.

Reiss, I. (1967). *The social context of premarital sexual permissiveness*. New York: Holt, Rinehart & Winston.

Reiss, I. L., & Reiss, H. M. (1997). *Solving America's sexual crisis*. Amherst, NY: Prometheus Books.

Reiss, I. L., Banwart, A., & Foreman, H. (1975). Premarital contraceptive usage: A study and some theoretical explorations. *Journal of Marriage and the Family*, *37*, 619–630.

Reiss, A. J., & Roth, J. A. (Eds.) (1993). *Understanding and preventing violence*. Washington, DC: National Science Academy Press.

Remafedi, G. (1987). Adolescent homosexuality: Psychosocial and medical implications. *Pediatrics*, *79*, 331–339.

Remafedi, G., Farrow, J. A., & Deisher, R. W. (1991). Risk factors for attempted suicide in gay and bisexual youth. *Pediatrics*, *87*, 869–875.

Remez, L. (1996). One in ten adolescents had recurrent sexually transmitted disease. *Family Planning Perspective*, *28*, 239–240.

Reppucci, J. D., Revenson, T. A., Aber, M., & Reppucci, N. D. (1991). Unrealistic optimism among adolescent smokers and non-smokers. *Journal of Primary Prevention*, *11*, 227–236.

Resnick, H. (Ed.) (1990). *Youth and drugs: Society's mixed messages* (ADM 90-1689). Washington, DC: Public Health Service.

Resnick, M. D., Bearinger, L. H., Stark, P., & Blum, R. W. (1994). Patterns of Communication among adolescent minors obtaining an abortion. *American Journal of Orthopsychiatry*, *64*, 310–316.

Reynolds, A. J., & Gill, S. (1994). The role of parental perspectives in the school adjustment of inner-city Black children. *Journal of Youth and Adolescence*, *23*, 671–694.

Rice, K. G., & Mulkeen, P. (1995). Relationships with parents and peers: A longitudinal study of adolescent intimacy. *Journal of Adolescent Research*, *10*(3), 338–357.

Rich, C. L., Sherman, M., & Fowler, R. C. (1990). San Diego suicide study: The adolescents. *Adolescence*, *25*, 855–865.

Richardson, R. A., Barbour, N. E., & Bubenzer, D. L. (1995). Peer relationships as a source of support for adolescent mothers. *Journal of Adolescent Research*, *10*(2), 278–290.

Richardson, R. L., & Gerlach, S. C. (1980). Black dropouts. *Urban Education*, *14*, 489–494.

Rickel, A. U., & Hendren, M. C. (1993). Aberrant sexual experiences in adolescence. In T. P. Gullotta, G. R. Adams, & R. Montemayor (Eds.), *Adolescent sexuality*. Newbury Park, CA: Sage.

Rierdan, J., & Koff, E. (1997). Weight, weight-related aspects of body image, and depression in early adolescent girls. *Adolescence*, *32*, 615–624.

Riggs, D. S., O'Leary, K. D., & Breslin, F. C. (1990). Multiple correlates of physical aggression in dating couples. *Journal of Interpersonal Violence*, *5*, 61–73.

Riley, W. T., Barenie, J. T., Mabe, P. A., & Myers, D. R. (1990). Smokeless tobacco use in adolescent females: Prevalence and psychosocial factors among racial/ethnic groups. *Journal of Behavioral Medicine*, *13*, 207–220.

Rist, R. (1970). Student social class and teacher expectations: The self-fulfilling prophecy in ghetto education. *Harvard Educational Review*, *40*, 411–451.

Rist, R. C. (1982). Playing on the margin. *Society*, *19*(6), 15–18.

Rivera, V. R., & Kutash, K. (1994). *Components of a system of care: What does the research say?* Tampa, FL: Florida Mental Health Institute.

Roberts, G. (1993). Motivation in sport: Understanding and enhancing the motivation and achievement of children. In R. Singer, M. Murphey, & L. K. Tennant (Eds.), *Handbook of research on sport psychology* (pp. 405–420). New York: Macmillan.

Robins, L. N. (1989). Suicide attempts in teen-aged medical patients. In *Report of the secretary's task force on youth suicide: Strategies for the prevention of youth suicide* (Vol. 4). Washington, DC: U.S. Department of Health and Human Services publication ADM 89-1622, U.S. Government Printing Office.

Robinson, I., Ziss, K., Ganza, B., Katz, S., & Robinson, E. (1991). Twenty years of the sexual revolution, 1965–1985: An update. *Journal of Marriage and the Family*, *53*, 216–220.

Robinson, P. A. (1978). Parents of beyond control adolescents. *Adolescence*, *13*, 109–118.

Robinson, W. J. (1939). *Sexual disorders in men and women*. New York: Eugenics.

Rockwell, J. (1990). Kingmen of 'Lovie Louie' Fame get royalties for rock classic. New York Times, April 20.

Rodriguez-Andrew, S. (1985). Inhalant abuse. *Children Today*, *14*, 23–25.

Rodriguez, J. F. (1980). Youth employment: A needs assessment. In *A review of youth employment problems, programs, and policies: The vice-president's task force on youth employment* (Vol. 1). Washington, DC: U.S. Government Printing Office.

Rogers, C. R. (1965). The therapeutic relationship: Recent theory and research. *Australian Journal of Psychology, 17,* 95–108.

Ronfeldt, H. M., Kimerling, R., & Arias, I. (1998). Satisfaction with relationship power and the perpetration of dating violence. *Journal of Marriage and the Family, 60,* 70–78.

Rosen, L. (1985). Family and delinquency: Structure or function? *Criminology, 23,* 553–573.

Rosen, L. W., Shafer, C. L., Dummer, G. M., Cross, L. K., Deuman, G. W., & Malmberg, S. R. (1988). Prevalence of pathogenic weight-control behaviors among Native American women and girls. *International Journal of Eating Disorders, 7,* 807–811.

Rosenbaum, C. P., & Beebe, J. E. (1975). *Psychiatric treatment.* New York: McGraw–Hill.

Rosenberg, M. (1979). *Conceiving the self.* New York: Basic Books.

Rosenberg, M. (1985). Self-concept and psychological well-being in adolescence. In R. L. Leaky (Ed.), *The development of the self* (pp. 205–242). New York: Academic Press.

Rosenberg, M., & Kaplan, H. B. (Eds.). (1982). *Social psychology of the self-concept.* Arlington Heights, IL: Harlan Davidson.

Rosenberg, P. S. (1995). Scope of the AIDS epidemic in the United States. *Science, 270*(5240), 1372–1375.

Rosenkrantz, A. L. (1978). A note on adolescent suicide: Incidence, dynamics, and some suggestions for treatment. *Adolescence, 13,* 209–213.

Rosenthal, R., & Jacobson, L. (1968). *Pygmalion in the classroom.* New York: Holt, Rinehart & Winston.

Rothberg, I. C. (1990). I never promised you first place. *Phi Delta Kappan, 72,* 296–303.

Rothberg, I. C. (1995). Myths about test score comparisons. *Science, 270*(5241), 1446–1447.

Rothbaum, F. (1977). Developmental and gender differences in the sex stereotyping of nurturance and dominance. *Developmental Psychology, 13,* 531–532.

Rotheram, M. J. (1987). Evaluation of imminent danger for suicide among youth. *American Journal of Orthopsychiatry, 57*(1), 102–110.

Rotheram-Borus, M. J. (1990). Adolescents' reference-group choices self-esteem, and adjustment. *Journal of Personality and Social Psychology, 59,* 1075–1081.

Rotheram-Borus, M. J., & Fernandez, M. I. (1995). Sexual orientation and developmental challenges experienced by gay and lesbian youths. *Suicide and Life-Threatening Behavior, 25,* 26–34.

Rotheram-Borus, M. J. (1997). Mental health services for children and adolescents. In R. P. Weissberg, T. P. Gullotta, G. R. Adams, R. L. Hampton, & B. A. Ryan (Eds.), *Establishing preventing service.* Thousand Oaks, CA: Sage.

Rothman, E. K. (1987). *Hands and hearts: A social history of courtship in America.* Cambridge, MA: Harvard University Press.

Rouse, R. A. (1995). *Substance abuse and mental health statistics sourcebook.* Washington, DC: DHHS publication SMA 95-3064, U.S. Government Printing Office.

Roush, W. (1995). Conflict marks crime conference. *Science, 269,* 1808–1809.

Rousseau J. J. (1762/1966). *Emile* (B. Foxley, translation). New York: Dutton.

Rowe, I., & Marcia, J. E. (1980). Ego identity status, formal operations, and moral development. *Journal of Youth and Adolescence, 9,* 87–100.

Rowley, S. (1987). Psychological effects of intensive training in young athletes. *Journal of Child Psychology and Psychiatry, 28,* 371–377.

Roy, A. (1989). Genetics and suicidal behavior. In ADAMHA. *Report of the secretary's task force on youth suicide: Risk factors for youth suicide* (Vol. 2), Washington, DC: U.S. Department of Health and Human Services publication ADM 89-1622, U.S. Government Printing Office.

Royce, J. E. (1981). *Alcohol problems and alcoholism.* New York: Free Press.

Rua, J. (1990). *Treatment works.* Washington, DC: U.S. Government Printing Office.

Rubenstein, J. L., Heeren, T., Housman, D., Rubin, C., & Stechler, G. (1989). Suicidal behavior in "normal" adolescents. *American Journal of Orthopsychiatry, 59,* 59–71.

Ruble, D. N., & Brooks-Gunn, J. (1982). The experience of menarche. *Child Development, 53,* 1557–1566.

Runck, B. (1986). *Coping with AIDS.* Washington, DC: DHHS Publication No. ADM 85-1432, U.S. Government Printing Office.

Russ-Eft, S., Sprenger, M., & Beever, A. (1979). Antecedents of adolescent parenthood and consequences at age 30. *Family Coordinator, 18,* 173–178.

Ryan, B. A., & Adams, G. R. (1995). The family-school relationships Model. In B. A. Ryan, G. R. Adams, T. P. Gullotta, R. P. Weissberg, & R. L. Hampton (Eds.), *The family-school connection: Theory, research and practice.* Thousand Oaks, CA: Sage.

Ryan, B. A., Adams, G. R., Gullotta, T. P., Weissberg, R. P., & Hampton, R. L. (Eds.) (1995). *The family-school connection: Theory, research and practice.* Thousand Oaks, CA: Sage.

Sabbath, J. C. (1969). The suicidal adolescent: The expendable child. *Journal of the American Academy of Child Psychiatry, 8,* 272–289.

Sabo, D. F., & Runfola, R. (Eds.) (1980). *Jock: Sports and the male identity.* Englewood Cliffs, NJ: Prentice–Hall.

Sagrestano, L. M., & Paikoff, R. L. (1997). Preventing high-risk sexual behavior, sexually transmitted diseases, and pregnancy among adolescents. In R. P. Weissberg, T. P. Gullotta, R. L. Hampton, B. A. Ryan, & G. R. Adams (Eds.), *Enhancing children's wellness* (pp. 76–104). Thousand Oaks, CA: Sage.

Salinger, J. D. (1951). *Catcher in the rye.* Boston, MA: Little, Brown.

Salokun, S. O. (1994). Positive change in self-concept as a function of improvement performance in sports. *Perceptual and Motor Skills, 78,* 752–754.

Samuels, V. J., Stockdale, D. F., & Crase, S. J. (1994). Adolescent mothers' adjustment to parenting. *Journal of Adolescence, 17*(5), 427–443.

Santrock, J. W. (1987). The effects of divorce on adolescents: Needed research perspectives. *Family Therapy, 14,* 47–157.

Sarason, S. B. (1997). The public schools: America's achilles hell. *American Journal of Community Psychology, 25,* 771–786.

Sato, N., & McLaughlin, M. W. (1992). Context matters: Teaching in Japan and in the U.S. *Phi Delta Kappan, 73,* 359–366.

Savin-Williams, R. C. (1979). Dominance hierarchies in groups of early adolescents. *Child Development, 50,* 923–935.

Savin-Williams, R. C., & Rodriguez, R. G. (1993). A developmental, clinical perspective on lesbian, gay male, and bisexual youths. In T. P. Gullotta, G. R. Adams, & R. Montemayor (Eds.), *Adolescent sexuality.* Newbury Park, CA: Sage.

Savin-Williams, R. C. (1994). Dating those you can't love and loving those who can't date. In R. Montemayor, G. R. Adams, & T. P. Gullotta (Eds.), *Personal relationships during adolescence* (pp. 196–215). Thousand Oaks, CA: Sage.

Savin-Williams, R. C. (1998). The disclosure to families of same-sex attractions by lesbian, gay, and bisexual youths. *Journal of Research on Adolescence, 8,* 49–68.

Scarr, S., & Weinberg, R. A. (1976). IQ test performance of Black children adopted by white families. *American Psychologist, 31,* 726–730.

Scarr, S., Weinberg, R. A., & Levine, A. (1986). *Understanding development.* New York: Harcourt, Brace, Jovanovich.

Schaefer, E. S. (1959). A circumplex model for maternal behavior. *Journal of Abnormal and Social Psychology, 59,* 226–235.

Scheier, L. M., & Botvin, G. J. (1998). Relations of social skills, personal competence, and adolescent alcohol use: A developmental exploratory story. *Journal of Early Adolescence, 18,* 77–114.

Schelling, T. C. (1992). Addictive drugs: The cigarette experience. *Science, 255,* 430–433.

Schenkel, S. (1975). Relationship among ego identity status, field-independence, and traditional femininity. *Journal of Youth and Adolescence, 4,* 73–82.

Schiedel, D. G., & Marcia, J. E. (1985). Ego identity, intimacy, sex role orientation, and gender. *Developmental Psychology, 21,* 149–160.

Schinke, S. P., McAlister, A. L., Orlandi, M. A., & Botvin, G. J. (1990). The social environmental constructs of social competency. In T. P. Gullotta, G. R. Adams, & R. Montemayor (Eds.), *Developing social competency in adolescence.* Newbury Park, CA: Sage.

Schinke, S. P., Moncher, M. S., Palleja, J., Zayas, L. H., Schilling, R. F. (1988). Hispanic youth, substance abuse, and stress: Implications for prevention research. *The International Journal of the Addictions, 23,* 809–826.

Schlegel, A., & Barry, H. (1991). *Adolescence: An anthropological inquiry.* New York: Free Press.

Schlesier-Carter, B., Hamilton, S. A., O'Neil, P. M., Lydiard, R. B., & Malcolm, R. (1989). Depression and bulimia: The link between depression and bulimic cognitions. *Journal of Abnormal Psychology, 98,* 322–325.

Schneider, B., & Lee, Y. (1990). A model for academic success: The school and home environment of East Asian students. *Anthropology & Education Quarterly, 21,* 358–377.

Schneider, S. (1982). Helping adolescents deal with pregnancy: A psychiatric approach. *Adolescence, 17*(66), 285–292.

Schrut, A. (1968). Some typical patterns in the behavior and background of adolescent girls who attempt suicide. *American Journal of Psychiatry, 125,* 69–74.

Schuckit, M. A., & Schuckit, J. J. (1989). Substance use and abuse: A risk factor in youth suicide. In ADAMHA. *Report of the secretary's task force on youth suicide: Risk factors for youth suicide* (Vol. 2). Washington, DC: U.S. Department of Health and Human Services publication ADM 89-1622, U.S. Government Printing Office.

Schutte, N. S., Malouff, J. M., Post-Gorden, J. C., & Rodasta, A. L. (1988). Effects of playing video games on children's aggressive and other behaviors. *Journal of Applied Psychology, 18,* 454–460.

Schwartz, D. M., & Thompson, M. G. (1981). Do anorectics get well? Current research and future needs. *American Journal of Psychiatry, 138,* 319–323.

Schwartz, D. M., Thompson, M. G., & Johnson, C. L. (1985). Anorexia nervosa and bulimia: The sociocultural context. In S. W. Emmett (Ed.), *Theory and treatment of anorexia nervosa and bulimia.* New York: Brunner/Mazel.

Schwartz, I. M., Steketee, M. W., & Schneider, V. W. (1990). Federal juvenile justice policy and the incarceration of girls. Unpublished manuscript.

Science (1989). AIDS tests fail. *Science, 246,* 1564.

Science (1991a). Children who want to bear children. *Science, 254,* 1215.

Science (1991b). Tracking the AIDS drugs. *Science, 254,* 1113.

Sears, R. R., Maccoby, E., & Levin, H. (1957). *Patterns of child rearing.* New York: Harper & Row.

Sebald, H. (1989). Adolescent peer orientation: Changes in the support system during the last three decades. *Adolescence, 24,* 937–945.

Secretary of Health and Human Services (1994). *Eighth special report to the U.S. Congress on alcohol and health* (NIH publication 94-3699). Washington, DC: U.S. Government Printing Office.

Seffrin, J. R., & Seehafer, R. W. (1976). Multiple drug use patterns among a group of high school students: Regular users vs. nonusers of specific drug types. *Journal of School Health, 46,* 413–416.

Sege, R. (1998). The media and violence. In T. P. Gullotta, G. R. Adams, & R. Montemayor (Eds.), *Delinquent violent youth.* Thousand Oaks, CA: Sage.

Segest, E., Mygind, O., Harris, C. N., & Bay, H. (1991). The correlation between general disease prevention and prevention of HIV-contagion among adolescents. *Journal of Adolescence, 14,* 389–396.

Select Committee on Children, Youth, and Families (1992, December 22). *A decade of denial: Teens and AIDS in America.* Washington, DC: U.S. Government Printing Office.

Seligman, P. (1986). A brief family intervention with an adolescent referred for drug taking. *Journal of Adolescence, 9*(3), 123–133.

Sellers, R. M., Kupermine, G. P., & Dumas, A. (1997). The college life experiences of African-American women athletes. *American Journal of Community Psychology, 25*, 699–720.

Selnow, G. W., & Crano, W. D. (1986). Formal vs. informal group affiliations: Implications for alcohol and drug use among adolescents. *Journal of Studies on Alcohol, 47*(1), 48–52.

Selva, P. C. D., & Dusek, J. B. (1984). Sex-role orientation and resolution of Eriksonian crisis during the late adolescent years. *Journal of Personality and Social Psychology, 47*, 204–212.

Sessa, F. M., & Steinberg, L. (1991). Family structure and the development of autonomy during adolescence. *Journal of Early Adolescence, 11*, 38–55.

Seydlitz, R., & Jenkins, P. (1998). The influence of family, community, and peers on deviant behavior. In T. P. Gullotta, G. R. Adams, & R. Montemayor (Eds.), *Delinquent violent youth* (pp. 53–97) Thousand Oaks, CA: Sage.

Shaffer, D., Pettigrew, A., Wolkind, S., & Zajicek, E. (1978). Psychiatric aspects of pregnancy in school girls: A review. *Psychological Medicine, 8*, 119–130.

Shafii, M. (1985). Psychological autopsy of completed suicide in children and adolescents. *American Journal of Psychiatry, 142*, 1061.

Shakespeare, W. (1623/1969). *William Shakespeare: The complete works.* Balitmore, Md: Penguin.

Shanahan, J. (1995). Television viewing and adolescent authoritarianism. *Journal of Adolescence, 18*, 271–288.

Shapiro, I. (1990, May). Guns and dolls. *Newsweek*, 56–65.

Sharp, C. W., Beauvais, F., & Spence, R. (1992). *Inhalant abuse: A volatile research agenda* (NIDA Research Monograph 129). Washington, DC: U.S. Government Printing Office.

Sharpton, A. (1996). *Go and tell the pharaoh.* New York: Doubleday.

Shatin, L. (1981). Psychopathogenic abuses of music in hospitals. *Interaction, 4*, 61–68.

Shaw, G. B. (1957). *Pygmalion.* New York: Dodd, Mead.

Shaw, J. S. (1982). Psychology, androgyny and stressful life events. *Journal of Personality and Social Psychology, 43*, 145–153.

Sher, K. J., Gershuny, B. S., Peterson, L., & Raskin, G. (1997). The role of childhood stressors in the intergenerational transmission of alcohol use disorders. *Journal of Studies on Alcohol, 58*, 414–427.

Sherry, M. (1993). Searching for new American schools. *Phi Delta Kappan, 74*, 299–302.

Shestowsky, B. J. (1983). Ego identity development and obesity in adolescent girls. *Adolescence, 18*, 551–559.

Shields, D., & Bredemeier, B. (1995). *Character development and physical activity.* Champaign, IL: Human Kinetics.

Shimahara, N. K. (1985). Japanese education and its implications for U.S. education. *Phi Delta Kappan, 67*, 418–421.

Shipman, G. (1968). The psychodynamics of sex education. *Family Coordinator, 17*, 3–12.

Shisslak, C. M., Crago, M., Neal, M. E., & Swain, B. (1987). Primary prevention of eating disorders. *Journal of Consulting and Clinical Psychology, 55*, 660–667.

Shneidman, E. S. (Ed.) (1976). *Suicidology: Contemporary developments.* New York: Grune & Stratton.

Shorter, E. (1975). *The making of the modern family.* New York: Basic Books.

Shumer, R. (1994). Community-based learning: Humanizing education. *Journal of Adolescence, 17*(4), 357–367.

Shucksmith, J., Hendry, L. B., & Glendinning, A. (1995). Models of parenting: Implications for adolescent well-being within different types of family contexts. *Journal of Adolescence, 18*, 253–270.

Sickmund, M. (1990). *Runaways in juvenile courts.* (NCJ 124881). Washington, DC: U.S. Department of Justice No. U.S. Government Printing Office.

Siegel, L. S. (1995). Does the IQ god exist? *Alberta Journal of Educational Research, 41*, 283–288.

Siegel, R. K. (1987). Changing patterns of cocaine use: Longitudinal observations, consequences, and treatment. In J. Grabowski (Ed.), *Cocaine: Pharmacology, effects, and treatment of abuse* Washington, DC: U.S. Department of Health and Human Services publication ADM 87-1326, U.S. Government Printing Office.

Simmons, D. D. (1970). Development of an objective measure of identity achievement status. *Journal of Projective Techniques and Personality Assessment, 34*, 241–244.

Simmons, R. G., Blyth, D. G., & McKinney, K. L. (1983). The social and psychological effects of puberty on white females. In J. Brooks-Gunn & A. C. Peterson (Eds.), *Girls in puberty: Biological and psychosocial perspectives* (pp. 229–272). New York: Plenum.

Simmons, R. G., Blyth, D. A., Van Cleave, E. F., & Bush, D. M. (1979). Entry into early adolescence: The impact of school structure, puberty, and early dating on self-esteem. *American Sociological Review, 44*, 948–967.

Simon, P. M., Morse, E. V., Osofsky, H. J., and Balson, P. M. (1994). HIV and young male street prostitutes: A brief report. *Journal of Adolescence, 17*(2), 193–197.

Sizer, T. R. (1983, June). High school reform: The need for engineering. *Phi Delta Kappan, 65*, 679–683.

Slade, J. (1989). The tobacco epidemic: Lessons from history. *Journal of Psychoactive Drugs, 21*, 281–291.

Slap, G. B., Khalid, N., Paikoff, R. L., Brooks-Gunn, J., & Warren, M. P. (1994). Evolving self-image, pubertal manifestations, and pubertal hormones: Preliminary findings in young adolescent girls. *Journal of Adolescent Health, 15*, 327–335.

Sloman, L. (1979). *The history of marijuana in America: Reefer madness.* New York: Bobbs–Merrill.

Slugoski, B. R., Marcia, J. E., & Koopman, R. J. (1984). Cognitive and social interactional characteristics of ego identity statuses in college males. *Journal of Personality and Social Psychology, 47,* 646–661.

Smart, R., & Jones, D. (1970). Illicit LSD users: Their personality characteristics and psychotherapy. *Journal of Abnormal Psychology, 75,* 286–292.

Smead, V. S. (1983). Anorexia nervosa, buliminarexia, and bulimia: Labeled pathology and the western female. *Women and Therapy, 2,* 19–35.

Smetana, J. G., Yau, J., & Hanson, S. (1991). Conflict resolution in families with adolescents. *Journal of Research on Adolescence, 1,* 189–206.

Smith, A., Goodwin, R., Gullotta, C. F., & Gullotta, T. P. (1979). Community mental health and the arts: The experiences of a small New England community. *Children Today, 8*(1), 17–20.

Smith, E. A., & Udry, J. R. (1985). Coital and non-coital sexual behavior of White and Black adolescents. *American Journal of Public Health, 75,* 1200–1203.

Smith, J. E., Hillard, M. C., & Roll, S. (1991). Rorschach evaluation of adolescent bulimics. *Adolescence, 26,* 687–696.

Smith, P. B., Munford, D. M., & Hammer, E. (1979). Childrearing attitudes of single teenage mothers. *American Journal of Nursing, 79,* 2115–2116.

Smith, T. E. (1976). Push versus pull: Intrafamily versus peer-group variables on possible determinants of adolescent orientations toward parents. *Youth and Society, 8,* 5–26.

Smolak, L., & Levine, M. P. (1996). Eating smart, eating for me: A pilot test of an elementary school eating curriculum. *The Renfrew Perspective, 2,* 9–10.

Smollar, J., & Ooms, T. (1987). *Young unwed fathers.* Rockville, MD: Shared Resource Center.

Snyder, E. E. (1969). Socioeconomic variations, values, and social participation among high school students. In D. Rogers (Ed.), *Issues in adolescent psychology.* New York: Appleton-Century-Crofts.

Snyder, H. N., & Sickmund, M. (1995). *Juvenile offenders and victims: A national report.* Washington, DC: Department of Justice, NCJ-153569, U.S. Government Printing Office.

Snyder, M., Tanke, E. D., & Berscheid, E. (1977). Social perception and interpersonal behavior: On the self-fulfilling nature of social stereotypes. *Journal of Personality and Social Psychology, 35,* 656–666.

Solomon, M. R. (1986, April). Dress for effect. *Psychology Today,* 20–26.

Sommer, B., & Nagel, S. (1991). Ecological and typological characteristics in early adolescent truancy. *Journal of Early Adolescence, 11,* 379–392.

Sonenstein, F. L., Pleck, J. H., and Ku, L. C. (1991). Levels of sexual activity among adolescent males in the United States. *Family Planning Perspectives, 23,* 162–167.

Sorensen, R. (1973). *Adolescent sexuality in contemporary America.* New York: World.

South, S. J. (1996). Mate availability and the transition to unwed motherhood: A paradox of population structure. *Journal of Marriage and the Family, 58,* 265–279.

Sowell, T. (1981). Historical data show Black/White IQ gap neither unique nor related to segregation. *Phi Delta Kappan, 62,* 753.

Sowell, T. (1986). *Education: Assumptions versus history.* Stanford, CA: Hoover Institution Press.

Spence, J. T., & Helmreich, R. L. (1979). Comparison of masculine and feminine personality attributes and sex-role attitudes across age groups. *Developmental Psychology, 15,* 583–590.

Spencer, A. F. (1996). Ethics in physical and sport education. *Journal of Physical and Sport Education, 67,* 37–39.

Spergel, I. A., & Chance, R. L. (1991). National youth gang suppression and intervention program. *National Institute of Justice Reports, 224,* 21–24.

Sperling, M. (1967). School-phobia classification, dyamics, and treatment. *Psychoanalytic Study of the Child, 22,* 375–401.

St. Lawrence, J. S., Brasfield, T. L., Jefferson, K. W., Allyene, E., and Shirley, A. (1994). Social support as a factor in African-American adolescents' sexual risk behavior. *Journal of Adolescent Research, 9*(3), 292–310.

Stack, S. (1988). Suicide: Media impacts in war and peace, 1910–1920. *Suicide and Life-Threatening Behavior, 18,* 342–357.

Stack, S., Gundlach, J., & Reeves, J. L. (1994). The heavy metal subculture and suicide. *Suicide and Life Threatening Behavior, 24*(1), 15–23.

Stanley, E. J., & Barter, J. T. (1970). Adolescent suicidal behavior. *American Journal of Orthopsychiatry, 40,* 87–96.

Stanton, C., & Meyer, A. (1998). A comprehensive review of community-based approaches for the treatment of juvenile offenders. In T. P. Gullotta, G.R. Adams, & R. Montemayor (Eds.), *Delinquent violent youth,* (pp. 205–229). Thousand Oaks, CA: Sage.

Staub, E. (1996). Cultural-societal roots of violence: The examples of genocidal violence and of contemporary youth violence in the United States. *American Psychologist, 51,* 117–132.

Steffensmeier, D. J., & Steffensmeier, R. H. (1980). Trends in female delinquency. *Criminology, 18,* 62–85.

Stein, J. A., Newcomb, M. D., & Bentler, P. M. (1987). An 8-year study of multiple influences on drug use and drug use consequences. *Journal of Personality and Social Psychology, 53,* 1094–1105.

Steinberg, L., & Steinberg, W. (1994). *Crossing paths: how your child's adolescence triggers you own crisis.* New York: Simon and Schuster.

Steinberg, L. D. (1979, March). Changes in family relations at puberty. Paper presented at the meeting of the Society for Research in Child Development, San Francisco.

Steinberg, L. D., & Hill, J. P. (1978). Patterns of family interaction as a function of age, the onset of puberty, and formal thinking. *Developmental Psychology, 14,* 683–684.

Steinkamp, M., & Maehr, M. (1984). Gender differences in motivational orientations toward achievement in school science: A quantitative synthesis. *American Educational Research Journal, 21,* 39–59.

Steinhausen, H. (1977). Psychoendocrinological studies of dwarfism in childhood and adolescence. *Zeitschrift fur Kinder-und Jugendpsychiatrie, 5,* 346–359.

Stekel, W. (1967). [Untitled comments.] In P. Friedman (Ed.), *On suicide: With particular reference to suicide among young students.* New York: International Universities Press.

Sternberg, R. (1977). *Intelligence, information processing, and analogical reasoning: The componential analysis of human abilities.* Hillsdale, NJ: Erlbaum.

Sternberg, R. J. (1988). *The triangle of love.* New York: Basic Books.

Sternberg, R. J., & Powell, J. S. (1983). The development of intelligence. In J. H. Flavell & E. M. Markman (Eds.), *Handbook of child psychology: Cognitive development* (Vol. 1). New York: Wiley.

Sternberg, R. J., Torff, B., & Grigorenko, E. (1998). Teaching for successful intelligence raises school achievement. *Phi Delta Kappan, 79,* 667–669.

Sternberg, R. J., & Wagner, R. K. (Eds.) (1994). *Mind in context.* Cambridge: Cambridge University Press.

Stevenson, J. F., McMillan, B., Mitchell, R. E., & Blanco, M. (1998). Project HOPE: Altering risk and protective factors among high risk Hispanic youth and their families. *Journal of Primary Prevention, 18,* 287–318.

Stice, E., & Gonzales, N. (1998). Adolescent temperament moderates the relation of parenting to antisocial behavior and substance use. *Journal of Adolescent Research, 13,* 5–31.

Strang, S. P., & Orlofsky, J. L. (1990). Factors underlying suicidal ideation among college students: A test of Teicher and Jacobs' model. *Journal of Adolescence, 13,* 39–52.

Strasburger, V. C. (1983). Children, Adolescents, and the media: Five crucial issues. *Adolescent medicine, 4,* 479–493.

Strasburger, V. C. (1995). *Adolescents and the media.* Thousand Oaks, CA: Sage.

Straus, M. A., & Kanter, G. K. (1994). Corporal punishment of adolescents by parents: A risk factor in the epidemiology of depression, suicide, alcohol abuse, child abuse, and wife beating. *Adolescence, 29*(115), 543–561.

Streitmatter, J. L. (1989). Identity development and academic achievement in early adolescence. *Journal of Early Adolescence, 9,* 99–111.

Streitmatter, J. L., & Pate, G. S. (1989). Identity status development and cognitive prejudice in early adolescents. *Journal of Early Adolescence, 9,* 142–152.

Strober, M., & Humphrey, L. L. (1987). Familial contributions to the etiology and course of anorexia nervosa and bulimia. *Journal of Consulting and Clinical Psychology, 55,* 654–659.

Strother, D. B. (1986). Dropping out. *Phi Delta Kappan, 68,* 325–328.

Strouse, J. S., Buerkel-Rothfuss, N., and Long, E. C. J. (1995). Gender and family as moderators of the relationship between music video exposure and adolescent sexual permissiveness. *Adolescence, 30*(119), 505–521.

Substance Abuse and Mental Health Administration (SAMHSA) (1996). *The relationship between family structure and adolescent substance abuse* (BDK206). Washington, DC: U.S. Government Printing Office.

Substance Abuse and Mental Health Administration (SAMHSA) (1997). *Heroin Abuse in the United States* (RPO919). Washington, DC: U.S. Government Printing Office.

Suitor, J. J., & Reavis, R. (1995). Football, fast cars, and cheerleading: Adolescent gender norms, 1978–1989. *Adolescence, 30*(118), 265–272.

Sulloway, F. J. (1983). *Freud: Biologist of the mind.* New York: Basic Books.

Sun, S. W., & Lull, J. (1986). The adolescent audience for music videos and why they watch. *Journal of Communications, 36,* 115–125.

Susman, E. J., Inoff-Germain, G., Nottelmann, E. D., Loriaux, D. L., & Cutler, G. B. (1987). Hormones, emotional dispositions, and aggressive attributes in early adolescence. *Child Development, 58,* 1114–1134.

Sutherland, M., Hale, C. D., & Harris, G. J. (1995). Community health promotion: The church as partners. *Journal of Primary Prevention, 16*(2), 201–216.

Swaim, R. C., Oetting, E. R., Edwards, R. W., & Beauvais, F. (1989). Links from emotional distress to adolescent drug abuse: A path model. *Journal of Consulting and Clinical Psychology, 57,* 227–231.

Sweet, R. W. (1990). *Missing children: Found facts.* Washington, DC: U.S. Department of Justice, No. NCJ 130916. U.S. Government Printing Office.

Swinton, D. H. (1980). Towards defining the universe of need for youth employment policy. In *A review of youth employment problems, programs, and policies: The Vice President's Task Force on Youth Employment* (Vol. 1). Washington, DC: U.S. Department of Labor.

Tanda, G., Pontieri, F. E., and Di Chiara, G. (1997). Cannabinoid and heroin activation of mesolimbic dopamine transmission by a common opioid receptor mechanism. *Science, 276,* 2048–2050.

Tanner, J. M. (1962). *Growth at adolescence.* Springfield, IL: Charles C. Thomas.

Tanner, J. M. (1975). Growth and endocrinology of the adolescent. In L. I. Gardner (Ed.), *Endocrine and genetic diseases of childhood* (2nd ed.). Philadelphia, PA: Saunders.

Taris, T. W., & Semin, G. R. (1997). Parent-child interaction during adolescence, and the adolescent's sexual experience: Control, closeness, and conflict. *Journal of Youth and Adolescence, 26,* 373–398.

Tasker, F. L., & Richards, M. (1994). Adolescents' attitudes toward marriage and marital prospects after parental divorce: A review. *Journal of Adolescent Research, 9,* 340–362.

Taub, D. E., & Blinde, E. M. (1994). Disordered eating and weight control among adolescent female athletes and performance squad members. *Journal of Adolescence Research, 9*(4), 483–497.

Tubes, G. (1994). Will new dopamine receptors offer a key to schizophrenia? *Science, 256*(5175), 1034–1035.

Taubes, G. (1998). As obesity rates rise, experts struggle to explain why. *Science, 280,* 1367–1368.

Taylor, R. D. (1996). Adolescents' perceptions of kinship support and family management practices: Association with adolescent adjustment in African American families. *Developmental Psychology, 32,* 687–695.

Taylor, R. J. (1986). Receipt of support from family among Black Americans: Demographic and familial differences. *Journal of Marriage and the Family, 48,* 67–77.

Taylor, R. J., Hardison, C. B., & Chatters, L. M. (1996). Kin and non-kin as sources of informal assistance. In H. W. Neighbors & J. S. Jackson (Eds.), *Mental health in Black American* (pp. 130–145). Thousand Oaks, CA: Sage.

Taylor, R. L. (1994). Black youth in crisis. In R. Staples (Ed.), *Black families: Essays and studies* (5th ed., pp. 214–229). Belmont, CA: Wadsworth.

Teicher, J. D., & Jacobs, J. (1966). Adolescents who attempt suicide: Preliminary findings. *American Journal of Psychiatry, 122,* 1248–1257.

Telfer, M. A., Baker, D., Clark, F. R., & Richardson, C. E. (1968). Incidence of gross chromosomal errors among tall criminal American males. *Science, 185,* 1249–1250.

TenHouten, W. D. (1989). Application of dual brain theory to cross-cultural studies of cognitive development and education. *Sociological Perspectives, 32,* 153–167.

Tennant, F., Black, D. L., & Voy, R. O. (1988). Anabolic steroid dependence with opioid-type features. *New England Journal of Medicine, 84,* 578.

Terre, L., & Burkhart, B. R. (1996). Problem sexual behavior in adolescence. In G. M. Blau & T. P. Gullotta (Eds.), *Adolescent dysfunctional behavior* (pp. 139–166). Thousand Oaks, CA: Sage.

Tesch, S. A., & Whitbourne, S. K. (1982, September). Intimacy status, identity status, and sex-role orientation in adulthood. Paper presented at the meeting of the American Psychological Association, Montreal.

Thomas, D. L., & Carver, C. (1990). Religion and adolescent social competence. In T. P. Gullotta, G. R. Adams, & R. Montemayor (Eds.), *Developing social competency in adolescence*. Newbury Park, CA: Sage.

Thompson, C. (1996). Can some infants beat HIV? *Science, 271*(5248), 441.

Thompson, K. P. (1993). Media, music, and adolescents. In R. M. Lerner (Ed.), *Early adolescents: Perspectives on research, policy, and intervention*. Hillsdale, NJ: Erlbaum.

Thornberry, T. P., Moore, M., & Christenson, R. L. (1985). The effect of dropping out of high school on subsequent criminal behavior. *Criminology, 23,* 3–18.

Thornberry, T. P., Smith, C. A., & Howard, G. J. (1997). Risk factors for teenage fatherhood. *Journal of Marriage and the Family, 59,* 505–522.

Thornberry, T. P., Tolnay, S. E., Flanagan, T. J., & Glynn, P. (1991). *Children in custody*. Washington, DC: U.S. Department of Justice No. NCJ 127675, U.S. Government Printing Office.

Thornburg, H. D. (1981). The amount of sex information learning obtained during early adolescence. *Journal of Early Adolescence, 1,* 171–183.

Thornton, A. (1990). The courtship process of adolescent sexuality. *Journal of Family Issues, 11,* 239–273.

Thornton, A., & Camburn, D. (1989). Religious participation and adolescent sexual behavior and attitudes. *Journal of Marriage and the Family, 51,* 641–653.

Thornton, A. D., & Camburn, D. (1987). The influence of the family on premarital sexual attitudes and behavior. *Demography, 24,* 323–340.

Thornton, A., Alwin, D. E., & Camburn, D. (1983). Causes and consequences of sex-role attitudes and attitude change. *American Sociological Review, 48,* 211–227.

Tims, F. M., Deleon, G., & Jainchill, N. (1994). *Therapeutic community: Advances in research and application* (NIDA Research Monograph 144). Washington, DC: U.S. Government Printing Office.

Timms, D. (1996). Teenage mothers and the adult mental health of their sons: Evidence from a Stockholm cohort. *Journal of Adolescence, 19,* 545–556.

Tishler, C. L., & McKenry, P. C. (1982). Parental negative self and adolescent suicide attempts. *Journal of American Academy of Child Psychiatry, 21*(4), 404–408.

Tishler, C. L., McKenry, P. C., & Morgan, K. C. (1981). Adolescent suicide attempt: Some significant factors. *Suicide and Life-Threatening Behavior, 11*(2), 86–92.

Tobin-Richards, M. H., Boxer, A. M., & Petersen, A. C. (1983). The psychological significance of pubertal change: Sex differences in perceptions of self during early adolescence. In J. Brooks-Gunn & A. C. Petersen (Eds.), *Girls at puberty*. New York: Plenum.

Tobler, N. S. & Stratton, H. H. (1997). Effectiveness of school-based drug prevention programs: A meta-analysis of the research. *Journal of Primary Prevention, 18,* 71–128.

Toder, N., & Marcia, J. (1973). Ego identity status and response to conformity pressure in college women. *Journal of Personality and Social Psychology, 26,* 287–294.

Tolson, J. M., & Urberg, K. A. (1993). Similarity between adolescent best friends. *Journal of Adolescent Research, 8,* 274–288.

Tolstoy, L. (1872/1952). War and peace. Chicago, IL: Encyclopaedia Brittanica.

Tooley, K. M. (1980). The remembrance of things past. *American Journal of Orthopsychiatry, 48*(1), 174–182.

Took, K. J., & Weiss, D. S. (1994). The relationship between heavy metal and rap music and adolescent turmoil: Real or artifact. *Adolescence, 29*(115), 613–621.

Torres, J. B. (1998). Masculinity and gender roles among Puerto Rican men: Machismo on the U.S. mainland. *American Journal of Orthopsychiatry, 68,* 16–26.

Townsend, J. K., & Worobey, J. (1987). Mother and daughter perception of their relationship: The influence of adolescent pregnancy status. *Adolescence, 22,* 487–496.

Trautman, P. D. (1989). Specific treatment modalities for adolescent attempters. In *Report of the Secretary's task force on youth suicide Vol. 3: Prevention and interventions in youth* suicide (Vol. 3).

Washington, DC: U.S. Department of Health and Human Services publication ADM 89-1622, U.S. Government Printing Office.

Trent, K. (1994). Family context and adolescents' fertility expectations. *Youth and Society, 26*, 118–137.

Trueba, H. T. (1988). Culturally based explanations of minority students' academic achievement. *Anthropology & Education Quarterly, 19*, 270–287.

Tucker, L. A. (1986). The relationship of television viewing to physical fitness and obesity. *Adolescence, 21*(84), 797–806.

Turner, R., Shehab, Z., Osborne, K., & Hendley, J. O. (1982). Shedding and survival of herpes simplex virus from "fever blisters." *Pediatrics, 70*(4), 547–549.

Turner, S. (1995). Family variables related to adolescent misuse: Risk and resiliency factors. In T. P. Gullotta, G. R. Adams, & R. Montemayor (Eds.). *Substance misuse in adolescence.* Thousand Oaks, CA: Sage.

Turner, S. L., Hamilton, H., Jacobs, M., Angood, L. M., & Dwyer, D. H. (1997). The influence of fashion magazines on the body image satisfaction of college women: An exploratory analysis. *Adolescence, 32*, 603–614.

Umpierre, S. A., Hill, J. A., & Anderson, D. J. (1985). Effect of "Coke" on sperm motility. *New England Journal of Medicine, 313*, 1351.

Urberg, K. A. (1979). Sex role conceptualizations in adolescents and adults. *Developmental Psychology, 15*, 90–92.

USA Today (1993). Elders in "Quotes," 12/10/93.

U.S. Advisory Board on Child Abuse and Neglect (1991). *Creating caring communities.* Washington, DC: (U.S. Department of Health and Human Services 017-092-00104-5), U.S. Government Printing Office.

U.S. Bureau of the Census (1991). Does education really pay off? In *Census and You* (Vol. 26, pp. 8–9). Washington, DC: U.S. Government Printing Office.

U.S. Bureau of the Census (1991). The economics of family disruption. In *Census and You* (Vol. 26, p. 5). Washington, DC: U.S. Government Printing Office.

U.S. Bureau of the Census (1992). *Statistical Abstract of the United States: 1992* (112th ed.). Washington, DC: U.S. Government Printing Office.

U.S. Bureau of the Census (1993). Nation's population projected to grow by 50 percent over next 50 years. In *Census and You* (Vol. 28, p. 1). Washington, DC: U.S. Government Printing Office.

U.S. Bureau of the Census (1996). *Statistical abstract of the United States: 1996* (116th ed.). Washington, DC: U.S. Government Printing Office.

U.S. Bureau of the Census (1996). Detailed age estimates. In *Census and You* (Vol. 31(7), 9).

U.S. Bureau of the Census (1997). *Statistical Abstract of the United States: 1997* (117th ed.). Washington, DC: U.S. Government Printing Office.

U.S. Bureau of the Census (1997). Kids first and foremost. *Census and You, 32*(8), 1.

U.S. Bureau of the Census (1997). More obstacles for children living with single parents who's never been married. *Census and You, 32*(1), 6.

U.S. Bureau of Justice Statistics (1995). *Drugs and crime facts, 1994.* Washington, DC: Department of Justice, NIJ-154043, U.S. Government Printing Office.

U.S. Department of Education (1989). *An international assessment of mathematics and science.* Washington, DC: U.S. Government Printing Office.

U.S. Department of Health and Human Services (1985). *Vital statistics in the U.S. 1980: Mortality* (Vol. 2, Part A). Washington, DC: U.S. Government Printing Office.

U.S. Department of Health and Human Services (1991a). *Facts and information resources: Underage drinking. Healthy Difference Program.* Washington, DC: U.S. Government Printing Office.

U.S. Department of Health and Human Services (1991b). *Drug abuse and drug abuse research.* Washington, DC: DHHS publication ADM 91-1704.

Valenstein, E. (1986). Great and desperate cures. New York: Basic Books.

Vandenplas-Holper, C., & Campos, B. P. (Eds.). (1990). *Interpersonal and identity development: New directons.* Louvain-LaNeuve, Belgium: Academia.

Vanek, J. (1980). Work, leisure, and family roles on U.S. farms. *Journal of Family History, 5*, 422–431.

Van Roosmalen, E., & Krahn, H. (1996). Boundaries of youth. *Youth & Society, 28*, 3–39.

Vener, A., & Stewart, C. (1974). Adolescent sexual behavior in Middle America revisited: 1970–1973. *Journal of Marriage and the Family, 36*, 728–735.

Vener, A., Stewart, C., & Hager, D. (1972). The sexual behavior of adolescents in Middle America: Generational and American–British comparison. *Journal of Marriage and the Family, 34*, 696–705.

Vicary, J. R., & Lerner, J. V. (1986). Parental attributes and adolescent drug use. *Journal of Adolescence, 9*(2), 115–122.

Vicary, J. R., Klingaman, L. R., & Harkness, W. L. (1995). Risk factors associated with date rape and sexual assault of adolescent girls. *Journal of Adolescence, 18*(3), 289–306.

Villanueva, H. F., James, J. R., & Rosecrans, J. A. (1990). Evidence of pharmacological tolerance to nicotine. In L. S. Harris (Ed.), *Problems of drug dependence: 1989.* Washington, DC: U.S. Department of Health and Human Services publication ADM 90-1663, U.S. Government Printing Office.

Vincent, R. C., Davis, D. K., & Bronszkowski, L. A. (1987). Sexism in MTV: The portrayal of women in rock videos. *Journalism Quarterly, 64*, 750–755, 941.

Vinovskis, M. A. (1981). An "epidemic" of adolescent pregnancy? Some historical considerations. *Journal of Family History, 6*(2), 205–230.

Violent schools–safe schools: The Safe School Study report to the Congress—Executive Summary. (1979). In R. Rubel (Ed.), *Crime and disruption in schools* (Stock No. 027-000-0863-3). Washington, DC: U.S. Government Printing Office.

Viscarello, R. R. (1990). Human immunodeficiency virus infection and pregnancy. *Resident and Staff Physician, 37*, 35–42.

Visher, E. B., & Visher, J. S. (1978). Common problems of stepparents and their spouses. *American Journal of Orthopsychiatry, 48*, 252–262.

Visher, E. B., & Visher, J. S. (1983). Stepparenting: Blending families. In H. I. McCubbin & C. R. Figley (Eds.), *Stress and the family: Coping with normative transitions* (Vol. 1). New York: Brunner/Mazel.

Vitaliano, P. P., Boyer, D., & James J. (1981). Perceptions of juvenile experience: Females involved in prostitution versus property offenses. *Criminal Justice and Behavior, 8*(3), 325–342.

Vogel, G. (1998). Northern Europe tops in high school. *Science, 279*, 1297.

Wadsworth, B. J. (1971). *Piaget's theory of cognitive development.* New York: McKay.

Wagenaar, A. C., & and Perry, C. L. (1994). Community strategies for the reduction of youth drinking: Theory and application. *Journal of Research on Adolescence, 4*(2), 319–345.

Wagner, B. M., Cohen, P., & Brook, J. S. (1996). Parent/adolescent relationships moderators of the effects of stressful life events. *Journal of Adolescent Research, 11*, 347–374.

Waite, B., Foster, H., & Hillbrand, M. (1992). Reduction of aggressive behavior after removal of music television. *Hospital and Community Psychiatry, 43*, 173–175.

Walker, B. A., & Mehr, M. (1983). Adolescent suicide—A family crisis: A model for addictive intervention by family therapists. *Adolescence, 28*(70), 285–292.

Walker, T. R., & Ehrenberg, M. F. (1998). An exploratory study of young persons' attachment styles and perceived reasons for parental divorce. *Journal of Adolescent Research, 13*, 320–342.

Wall, J. A., Power, T. G., & Arbona, C. (1993). Susceptibility to antisocial peer pressure and its relation to acculturation in Mexican-American adolescents. *Journal of Adolescent Research, 8*, 403–418.

Wallace, J. M., & Bachman, J. G. (1991). Explaining racial/ethnic differences in adolescent drug use: The impact of background and lifestyle. *Social Problems, 38*, 333–357.

Wallerstein, J. S. (1983). Children of divorce: The psychological tasks of the child. *American Journal of Orthopsychiatry, 53*, 230–243.

Wallerstein, J. S. (1985). Children of divorce: Preliminary reports of a 10-year follow-up of older children and adolescents. *Journal of American Academy of Child Psychiatry, 24*, 545–553.

Wallerstein, J. S. (1987). Children of divorce: Report of a ten-year follow up of early latency-age children. *American Journal of Orthopsychiatry, 57*(2), 199–211.

Wallerstein, J. S. (1989, January 22). Children after divorce: Wounds that don't heal. *New York Times Magazine*, 19–21, 41–44.

Wallerstein, J. S., & Blakeslee, S. (1989). *Second chance: Men, women, and children a decade after divorce.* New York: Tricknor & Fields.

Wallston, B. (1973). The effects of maternal employment on children. *Journal of Child Psychology and Psychiatrist, 14*, 81–95.

Walsh, B. T., & Devlin, M. J. (1998). Eating disorders: Progress and problems. *Science, 280*, 1387–1390.

Walters, J., & Walters, L.H. (1980). Trends affecting adolescent views of sexuality, employment, marriage, and child rearing. *Family Relations, 29*, 191–198.

Walters, J., McKenry, P. C., & Walters, L. H. (1979). Adolescents' knowledge of child bearing. *Family Coordinator, 28*, 163–171.

Wanamaker, C. E., & Reznikoff, M. (1989). Effects of aggressive and nonaggressive rock songs on projective and structured tests. *The Journal of Psychology, 123*, 561–570.

Wang, M. C., Haertel, G. D., & Walberg, H. J. (1993). Toward a knowledge base for school learning. *Review of Educational Research, 63*, 249–294.

Warren, M. P. (1983). Physical and biological aspects of puberty. In J. Brooks-Gunn & A. C. Petersen (Eds.), *Girls at puberty.* New York: Plenum.

Washington Social Legislation Bulletin (1998). Office of juvenile justice reports decline in juvenile violence arrests 1994–1996. Published by the *Social Legislation Information Service, 35*, 1–8.

Waterman, A. S. (1982). Identity development from adolescence to adulthood: An extension of theory and a review of research. *Development Psychology, 18*, 341–358.

Waterman, A. S. (1984). *The psychology of individualism.* New York: Praeger.

Waterman, A. S. (1986). A rejoinder to Berzonsky: Identity formation, metaphors, and values. *Journal of Early Adolescence, 6*, 119–121.

Waterman, A. S. (1992). Identity as an aspect of Optimal Psychological Functioning. In G. R. Adams, T. P. Gullotta, & R. Montemayor (Eds.), *Identity formation during adolescence.* Newbury Park, CA: Sage.

Waterman, A. S., & Goldman, J. A. (1976). A longitudinal study of ego identity development at a liberal arts college. *Journal of Youth and Adolescence, 5*, 361–370.

Waterman, A. S., & Waterman, C. K. (1970). The relationship between ego identity status and satisfaction with college. *Journal of Educational Research, 64*, 165–168.

Waterman, C. K., & Waterman, A. S. (1974). Ego identity status and decision styles. *Journal of Youth and Adolescence, 3*, 1–6.

Waterman, C. K., Beubel, M. E., & Waterman, A. S. (1970). Relationship between resolution of the identity crisis and outcomes of previous psychosocial crises. *Proceedings of the 78th annual convention of the American Psychological Association, 5*, 467–468. [Summary]

Watson, J. B., (1914). Behavior: *An introduction to comparative psychology.* New York: Holt, Rinehart & Winston.

Wattenberg, B. J. (1987). *The birth dearth.* New York: Pharos Books.

Waugh, I. (1977). Labeling theory. In *Preventing delinquency* (Vol. 1) (LEAA Publication No. 0-241-090/26). Washington, DC: U.S. Government Printing Office.

Wechsler, D. (1955). *Manual of the Wechsler Adult Intelligence Scale.* New York: Psychological Corp.

Weinstein, R. J. (1996). Eating disorders. In G. Blau & T. P. Gullotta (Eds.),

Adolescent dysfunctional behavior. Thousand Oaks, CA: Sage.

Weissberg, R. P., Caplan, M., & Harwood, R. L. (1991). Promoting competent young people in competence-enhancing environments: A systems-based perspective on primary prevention. *Journal of Consulting and Clinical Psychology, 59,* 830–841.

Weissberg, R. P., Barton, H. A., & Shriver, T. (1997). The social-competence promotion program for young adolescents. In G. W. Albee & T. P. Gullotta (Eds.), *Primary prevention works* (pp. 268–290). Thousand Oaks, CA: Sage.

Weisz, J. R., Weiss, B., Alicke, M. D., & Klotz, M. L. (1987). Effectiveness of psychotherapy with children and adolescents: A meta-analysis for clinicians. *Journal of Consulting and Clinical Psychology, 55,* 542–549.

Weiss, R. A. (1993). How does HIV cause AIDS. *Science, 260*(5112), 1273–1278.

Weller, R. A., & Halikas, J. A. (1985). Marijuana use and psychiatric illness: A follow-up study. *American Journal of Psychiatry, 142,* 848–850.

Wellesley College Center for Research on Women (1992). *How schools shortchange girls.* Washington, DC: National Education Association.

Wells, K. (1980). Gender-role identity and psychological adjustment in adolescence. *Journal of Youth and Adolescence, 9,* 59–74.

Welpton, D. (1968). Psychodynamics of chronic lysergic acid diethylamide use. *Journal of Nervous and Mental Diseases, 147,* 377–385.

Welsh, R. S. (1978). Delinquency, corporal punishment, and the schools. *Crime and Delinquency, 24,* 336–354.

Welte, J. W., & Barnes, G. M. (1987). Alcohol use among adolescent minority groups. *Journal of Studies on Alcohol, 48,* 329–336.

Wentzel, K. R., Feldman, S. S., & Weinberger, D. A. (1991). Parental child rearing and academic achievement in boys. *Journal of Early Adolescence, 11,* 321–339.

Wesson, D. R., & Smith, D. E. (1979). Treatment of the polydrug abuser. In R. Dupont, A. Goldstein, & J. O'Donnell (Eds.), *Handbook on drug abuse.* Washington, DC: U.S. Government Printing Office.

Wesson, D. R., & Smith, D. E. (1985). Cocaine: Treatment perspectives. In N. J. Kozel & E. H. Adams (Eds.), *Cocaine use in America: Epidemiological and clinical perspectives.* Washington, DC: NIDA research monograph 61, ADM 85-1414, U.S. Government Printing Office.

West, L. J. (1989). Persuasive techniques in contemporary cults: A public health approach. In M. Galanter (Ed.), *Cults and new religious movements* (pp. 165–192). Washington, DC: American Psychiatric Association.

West, S. (1983). One step behind a killer. *Science, 4*(2), 36–45.

Westermeyer, J. (1974). "The drunken Indian": Myths and realities. *Psychiatric Annals, 4,* 29–36.

Westney, O. E., Cole, O. J., & Mumford, T. L. (1986). Adolescent unwed prospective fathers: Readiness for fatherhood and behavior toward the mother and the expected infant. *Adolescence, 21,* 901–911.

Whaley, A. L. (1998). Racism in the provision of mental health services: A social-cognitive analysis. *American Journal of Orthopsychiatry, 68,* 47–57.

Wheeler, L., Reis, H., & Nezlek, J. (1983). Loneliness, social interaction, and sex roles. *Journal of Personality and Social Psychology, 45,* 943–953.

Whitaker, C. J., & Bastian, L. D. (1991). *Teenage victims.* Washington, DC: U.S. Department of Justice, NCJ-128129, U.S. Government Printing Office.

Whitbeck, L. B., Simons, R. L., Conger, R. D., & Lorenz, F. O. (1989). Value socialization and peer group affiliation among early adolescents. *Journal of Early Adolescence, 9,* 436–453.

Whitbourne, S. K., & Tesch, S. A. (1985). A comparison of identity and intimacy statuses in college students and alumni. *Developmental Psychology, 21,* 1039–1044.

White, M. (1987). *The Japanese educational challenge.* New York: Free Press.

Whittaker, S., & Bry, B. H. (1991). Overt and covert parental conflict and adolescent problems: Observed marital interaction in clinic and nonclinic families. *Adolescence, 26,* 865–877.

Whybrow, P. C. (1997). *A mood apart.* New York: Basic Books.

Wickelgren, I. (1998). Obesity—How big a problem? *Science, 280,* 1364–1367.

Wichstrom, L., Skogen, K., and Oia, T. (1994). Social and cultural factors related to eating problems among adolescents in Norway. *Journal of Adolescence, 17*(5), 471–482.

Widom, C. S. (1989). The cycle of violence. *Science, 244,* 160–166.

Widom, C. S. (1996, February). *The cycle of violence revisited* (pp. 1–4). NIJ Research Preview, U.S. Department of Justice, NIJ-153272.

William T. Grant Foundation Commission on Work, Family and Citizenship (1988). *The forgotten half: Pathways to success for America's youth and young families.* Washington, DC: William T. Grant Foundation.

Williams, C. L., & Berry, J. W. (1991). Primary prevention of acculturative stress among refugees. *American Psychologist, 46,* 632–641.

Williamson, D. A., Kelley, M. L., Davis, C. J., Ruggiero, L., & Blouin, D. C. (1985). Psychopathology of eating disorders: A controlled comparison of bulimia, obese, and normal subjects. *Journal of Consulting and Clinical Psychology, 53,* 161–166.

Williamson, S., Gossop, M., Powis, B., Griffiths, P., Fountain, J., & Strang, J. (1997). Adverse effects of stimulant drugs in a community sample of drug users. *Drug and Alcohol Dependence, 44,* 87–94.

Wilson, E. O. (1975). *Sociobiology: The new synthesis.* Cambridge, MA: Harvard University Press.

Wilson, J. Q. (1990). Against the legalization of drugs. *Commentary, 89,* 21–28.

Wilson, J. Q., & Hernstein, R. J. (1985). *Crime and human nature.* New York: Simon & Schuster.

Wilson, P. M., & Wilson, J. R. (1992). Environmental influences on adolescent educational aspirations: A logistic transform model. *Youth & Society, 24,* 52–70.

Wilson, W. J. (1978). *The declining significance of race: Blacks and changing American institutions.* Chicago, IL: University of Chicago Press.

Wise, R. A. (1987). Neural mechanisms of the reinforcing action of cocaine. In J. Grabowski (Ed.), *Cocaine: Pharmacology, effects, and treatment of abuse.* Washington, DC: U.S. Department of Health and Human Services publication ADM 87-1326, U.S. Government Printing Office.

Wise, S., & Grossman, F. K. (1980). Adolescent mothers and their infants: Psychological factors in early attachment and interaction. *American Journal of Orthopsychiatry, 50*(3), 454–468.

Wonderlich, S. A., & Swift, W. J. (1990). Perceptions of parental relationships in the eating disorders: The relevance of depressed mood. *Journal of Abnormal Psychology, 99,* 353–360.

Woodring, P. (1989). A new approach to the dropout problem. *Phi Delta Kappan, 70,* 468–469.

Woody, G. E., & Blaine, J. (1979). Depression in narcotics addicts. In R. Dupont, A. Goldstein, & J. O'Donnell (Eds.), *Handbook on drug abuse.* Washington, DC: U.S. Government Printing Office.

Wooley, S., & Wooley, O. (1979). Obesity and women: A closer look at the facts. *Women's Studies International, 2,* 69–79.

Work, W. C., Cowen, E. L., Parker, G. R., & Wyman, P. A. (1990). Stress resilient children in an urban setting. *Journal of Primary Prevention, 11,* 3–17.

Worland, J., Weeks, D. G., & Janes, C. L. (1987). Predicting mental health in children at risk. In E. J. Anthony & B. J. Cohler (Eds.), *The invulnerable child* (pp. 185–210). New York: Guilford.

Wyatt, G. E. (1990). Changing influences on adolescent sexuality over the past forty years. In J. Bancroft & J. M. Reinisch (Eds.), *Adolescence and puberty.* New York: Oxford University Press.

Yablonsky, L. (1970). *The violent gang.* Baltimore, MD: Penguin.

Yaffe, E. (1982). High school athletics: A Colorado study. *Phi Delta Kappan, 64,* 177–181.

Yager, J. (1982). Family issues in the pathogenesis of anorexia nervosa. *Psychosomatic Medicine, 44,* 43–60.

Yamaguchi, K., & Kandel, D. (1984). Patterns of drug use from adolescence to young adulthood. III. Predictors of progression. *American Journal of Public Health, 74,* 673–681.

Yeh, H. S., Chen, Y. S., & Sim, C. B. (1995). Analysis of drug abuse among adolescent psychiatric inpatients at veterans general hospital—Taipei. *Chung Hua I Hsueh Tsa Chih, 56,* 325–330.

Yep, G. A. (1995). Communicating the HIV/AIDS risk to Hispanic populations. In A. M. Padilla (Ed.), *Hispanic psychology: Critical issues in theory and research* (pp. 196–212). Thousand Oaks, CA: Sage.

Yesalis, C. E., Anderson, W. A., Buckley, W. E., & Wright, J. E. (1990). Incidence of the nonmedical use of anabolic-androgenic steroids. In G. C. Lin & L. Erinoff (Eds.), *Anabolic steroid abuse.* Washington, DC: U.S. Department of Health and Human Services, U.S. Government Printing Office.

Young, E., & Parish, T. (1977). Impact of father absence during childhood on the psychological adjustment of college females. *Sex Roles, 3,* 217–227.

Youniss, J., McLellan, J. A., & Strouse, D. (1994). "We're popular, but we're not snobs": Adolescents describe their crowds. In R. Montemayor, G. R. Adams, T. P. Gullotta (Eds.), *Personal relationships during adolescence.* (pp. 101–122). Thousand Oaks, CA: Sage.

Youniss, J. U., & Smollar, J. (1985). *Adolescent relations with mothers, fathers, and friends.* Chicago, IL: University of Chicago Press.

Zacks, R. (1994). *History laid bare.* New York: HarperCollins.

Zakin, D. F., Blyth, D. A., & Simmons, R. G. (1984). Physical attractiveness as a mediator of the impact of early pubertal changes for girls. *Journal of Youth and Adolescence, 13,* 439–450.

Zawitz, M. W. (July 1995). *Guns used in crime. Selected Findings* (pp. 1–8). Washington, DC: U.S. Department of Justice, NCJ-148201.

Zayas, L. H., Schinke, S. P., & Casareno, D. (1987). Hispanic adolescent fathers: At risk and under researched. *Children and Youth Services Review, 9,* 235–248.

Zellman, G., Johnson, P. B., Giarrusso, R., & Goodchilds, J. D. (1979, September). Adolescent expectations for dating relationships: Consensus and conflict between the sexes. Paper presented at the meeting of the American Psychological Association, New York.

Zelnick, M. (1979). Sex education and knowledge of pregnancy risk among U.S. teenage women. *Family Planning Perspectives, 11,* 355–357.

Zelnick, M., & Kantner, J. F. (1980). Sexual activity, contraceptive use and pregnancy among metropolitan-area teenagers: 1971–1979. *Family Planning Perspectives, 12,* 230–237.

Ziegler, C., & Dusek, J. B. (1985). Perceptions of child rearing and adolescent sex role development. *Journal of Early Adolescence, 5,* 215–227.

Ziegler, C. B., Dusek, J. B., & Carter, D. B. (1984). Self-concept and sex-role orientation: An investigation of multidimensional aspects of personality development in adolescence. *Journal of Early Adolescence, 4,* 25–39.

Zill, N., & Schoenborn, C.A. (1990). *Developmental, learning, and emotional problems: health of our nation's children, United States 1988.* Advance Data: National Center for Health Statistics, No. 190.

Zimmer, L., & Morgan, J.P. (1997). *Marijuana myths, marijuana fact.* New York, Lindesmith Center.

Zimmerman, M. A., Salem, D. A., & Maton, K.I. (1995). Family structure and psychosocial correlates among urban African-American adolescent males. *Child Development, 66,* 1598–1613.

Zimmerman, R. S., Sprecher, S., Langer, L. M., & Holloway, C. D. (1995). Adolescents' perceived ability to say "no" to unwanted sex. *Journal of Adolescent Research, 10,* 383–399.

Zimring, F. E. (1982). *The changing legal world of adolescence.* New York: Free Press.

Zinberg, N. E. (1979). Nonaddictive opiate use. In R. Dupont, A. Goldstein, & J. O'Donnell (Eds.), *Handbook on drug abuse*. Washington, DC: U.S. Government Printing Office.

Zukin, S. R., & Javitt, D. C. (1990). Mechanisms of phencyclidine (PCP)-N-methyl-D-aspartate (NMDA) receptor interaction: Implications for drug abuse research. In L. S. Harris (Ed.), *Problems of drug dependence: 1989*. Washington, DC: U.S. Department of Health and Human Services publication ADM 90-1663, U.S. Government Printing Office.

CHAPTER 1

3, Images Ⓡ copyright 1999 PhotoDisk, Inc. **10,** Images Ⓡ copyright 1999 PhotoDisk, Inc. **15,** Ⓒ Rob Gage/FPG International LLC. **18,** Images Ⓡ copyright 1999 PhotoDisk, Inc.

CHAPTER 2

21, 36, Ⓒ Dennie Cody/FPG International LLC. **23,** Corbis/Austrian Archives Ⓒ. **24,** Corbis Ⓒ. **26,** Corbis/Ted Streshinsky Ⓒ. **29,** Corbis Ⓒ. **32,** Images Ⓡ copyright 1999 PhotoDisk, Inc.

CHAPTER 3

47, Ⓒ Rob Gage/FPG International LLC. **49,** Images Ⓡ copyright 1999 PhotoDisk, Inc. **57,** Corbis/Farrell Grehan Ⓒ. **62,** Images Ⓡ copyright 1999 PhotoDisk, Inc. **69,** ⒸTSM/John Henley, 1995.

CHAPTER 4

73, 82, Images Ⓡ copyright 1999 PhotoDisk, Inc. **78,** Images Ⓡ copyright 1999 PhotoDisk, Inc. **85,** Images Ⓡ copyright 1999 PhotoDisk, Inc. **87,** Images Ⓡ copyright 1999 PhotoDisk, Inc. **93,** Images Ⓡ copyright 1999 PhotoDisk, Inc.

CHAPTER 5

101, Images Ⓡ copyright 1999 PhotoDisk, Inc. **103,** Corbis Ⓒ. **114,** Ⓒ Bob Penn, 1986/Motion Picture & Television Photo Archive.

CHAPTER 6

125, 130, Ⓒ TSM/C/B Productions, Inc., 1996. **134,** (top) Ⓒ Michael Keller/FPG International LLC; (left) Ⓒ James Levin/FPG International LLC; (right) Ⓒ Mark Scott/FPG International LLC. **138,**

ⓒ TSM/Tom and DeeAnn McCarthy, 1996. **143,** ⓒ TSM/C.B.P. Photoproductions, 1997. **148,** ⓒ TSM/ROB & SAS, 1995. **152,** Images Ⓡ copyright 1999 PhotoDisk, Inc.

CHAPTER 7

163, Images Ⓡ copyright 1999 PhotoDisk, Inc. **165,** ⓒ Michael Krasowitz/FPG International LLC. **167,** ⓒ Dick Luria/FPG International LLC. **171,** Corbis/Jennie Woodcock; Reflections Photolibrary ⓒ. **175,** ⓒ VCG/FPG International LLC. **179,** ⓒ VCG/FPG International LLC. **186,** Corbis/Laura Dwight ⓒ.

CHAPTER 8

193, 196, Images Ⓡ copyright 1999 PhotoDisk, Inc. **209,** Corbis/Henry Diltz ⓒ. **214,** Images Ⓡ copyright 1999 PhotoDisk, Inc. **217,** Images Ⓡ copyright 1999 PhotoDisk, Inc. **220,** Corbis/Owen Franken ⓒ.

CHAPTER 9

225, 248, Images Ⓡ copyright 1999 PhotoDisk, Inc. **232,** (top) Images Ⓡ copyright 1999 PhotoDisk, Inc.; (bottom) ⓒ Richard Gaul/FPG International LLC. **239,** Images Ⓡ copyright 1999 PhotoDisk, Inc. **256,** Images Ⓡ copyright 1999 PhotoDisk, Inc. **271,** Images Ⓡ copyright 1999 PhotoDisk, Inc. **273,** Images Ⓡ copyright 1999 PhotoDisk, Inc.

CHAPTER 10

279, ⓒ VCG/FPG International LLC. **282,** ⓒ Ron Chapple/FPG International LLC. **291,** ⓒ Ron Chapple/FPG International LLC. **297,** Images Ⓡ copyright 1999 PhotoDisk, Inc. **299,** ⓒ Barbara Peacock/FPG International LLC.

CHAPTER 11

305, 320, Images Ⓡ copyright 1999 PhotoDisk, Inc. **308,** ⓒ TSM/Mug Shots, 1992. **312,** Images Ⓡ copyright 1999 PhotoDisk, Inc. **330,** Images Ⓡ copyright 1999 PhotoDisk, Inc. **338,** ⓒ Gary Buss/FPG International LLC.

CHAPTER 12

343, 365, Images Ⓡ copyright 1999 PhotoDisk, Inc. **347,** ⓒ TSM/Tom and DeeAnn McCarthy, 1996. **362,** Images Ⓡ copyright 1999 PhotoDisk, Inc. **373,** Images Ⓡ copyright 1999 PhotoDisk, Inc. **377,** Images Ⓡ copyright 1999 PhotoDisk, Inc.

CHAPTER 13

393, 416, Images Ⓡ copyright 1999 PhotoDisk, Inc. **400,** Images Ⓡ copyright 1999 PhotoDisk, Inc. **401,** ⓒ VCG/FPG International LLC. **405,** Images Ⓡ copyright 1999 PhotoDisk, Inc. **423,** Corbis/Charles Harris; Pittsburgh Courier ⓒ. **426,** Images Ⓡ copyright 1999 PhotoDisk, Inc. **434,** Images Ⓡ copyright 1999 PhotoDisk, Inc.

CHAPTER 14

439, Images Ⓡ copyright 1999 PhotoDisk, Inc. **442,** ⓒ Ken Ross/FPG International LLC. **445,** Images Ⓡ copyright 1999 PhotoDisk, Inc. **453,** ⓒ 1995 SPL/Custom Medical Stock photo.

CHAPTER 15

457, 472, © Arthur Tilley/FPG International LLC. **460,** Arthur Tilley/FPC International LLC. **464,** © VCG/FPG International LLC. **467,** © David McGlynn/FPG International LLC. **477,** © VCG/FPG International LLC. **484,** © Ron Chapple/FPG International LLC.

CHAPTER 16

493, 495, Corbis ©. **497,** Images ® copyright 1999 PhotoDisk, Inc. **500,** Images ® copyright 1999 PhotoDisk, Inc. **504,** Images ® copyright 1999 PhotoDisk, Inc.